P9-DHB-884

FUNDAMENTALS
OF CLINICAL SUPERVISION

THIRD EDITION

JANINE M. BERNARD

Syracuse University

RODNEY K. GOODYEAR

University of Southern California

PEARSON

Boston   New York   San Francisco
Mexico City   Montreal   Toronto   London   Madrid   Munich   Paris
Hong Kong   Singapore   Tokyo   Cape Town   Sydney

Executive Editor: Virginia Lanigan
Editorial Assistant: Robert Champagne
Marketing Manager: Tara Whorf
Editorial Production Service: Whitney Acres Editorial
Manufacturing Buyer: Andrew Turso
Cover Administrator: Kristina Mose-Libon
Electronic Composition: Omegatype Typography, Inc.

For related titles and support materials, visit our online catalog at
www.ablongman.com.

Copyright © 2004, 1998, 1992 by Pearson Education, Inc.

All rights reserved. No part of the material protected by this copyright notice may be
reproduced or utilized in any form or by any means, electronic or mechanical, including
photocopying, recording, or by any information storage and retrieval system, without
written permission from the copyright owner.

To obtain permission(s) to use material from this work, please submit a written request
to Allyn and Bacon, Permissions Department, 75 Arlington Street, Boston, MA 02116
or fax your request to 617-848-7320.

Between the time Website information is gathered and then published, some sites may have
closed. Also, the transcription of URLs can result in typographical errors. The publisher would
appreciate being notified of any problems so that they may be corrected in subsequent editions.

Library of Congress Cataloging-in-Publication Data

Bernard, Janine M.
    Fundamentals of clinical supervision / Janine M. Bernard.—3rd ed.
      p. ; cm.
    Includes bibliographical references and index.
    ISBN 0-205-38873-6 (Casebound)
      1. Psychotherapists—Supervision of. 2. Counselors—Supervision of. 3. Clinical
psychologists—Supervision of. I. Title.
      [DNLM: 1. Health Personnel—organization & administration. 2. Mental Health
Services—organization & administration. 3. Clinical Competence. 4. Health Facility
Administrators—education. 5. Interprofessional Relations. 6. Models, Organizational. 7.
Personnel Management—methods. WM 21 B519f 2004]

  RC480.5.B455   2004
  362.2'0425'0683—dc22

                                2003058177

Printed in the United States of America
10 9 8 7 6   08 07

CONTENTS

Preface   xiv

CHAPTER 1   **INTRODUCTION TO CLINICAL SUPERVISION**   **1**

Context and Importance of Supervision   1
Professional Self-regulation Affects Supervision Amount and Type   *2*
Most Mental Health Professionals Eventually Supervise   *3*
Clinical Supervision in the Preparation of Mental Health Professionals   4
Supervision: Essential to Experiential Learning   *4*
Necessary Preparation to Supervise   *5*
Defining Supervision   7
Supervision Is a Distinct Intervention   *8*
Teaching versus Supervision   *8*
Counseling versus Supervision   *9*
Consultation versus Supervision   *10*
Member of Same Profession   *10*
Supervision Is Evaluative   *11*
Supervision Extends over Time   *12*
Purposes of Supervision   *12*
Enhancing Professional Functioning   *13*
Monitoring Client Care   *13*
Person-specific Understandings of Supervision   *14*
Family Metaphors   *15*
A Conceptual Model of Supervision   *17*
Supervision Parameters   *17*
Supervisee Developmental Level   *17*
Supervisor Tasks   *18*
Using the Model   *18*
Conclusion   18

CHAPTER 2   **EVALUATION**   **19**

Criteria for Evaluation   21
Favorable Conditions for Evaluation   23
The Process of Evaluation   26
The Supervision–Evaluation Contract   *27*
Choosing Supervision Methods for Evaluation   *27*

Choosing Evaluation Instruments   28
Communicating Formative Feedback   30
Encouraging Self-assessment   33
Communicating Summative Evaluations   35
Impairment and Incompetence   39
Additional Evaluation Issues   43
The Subjective Element   43
   Similarity   43
   Familiarity   44
   Priorities   44
   Rating Idiosyncracies   45
Consequences of Evaluation   47
Chronic Issues with Evaluation   47
Conclusion   48

CHAPTER 3   ETHICAL AND LEGAL CONSIDERATIONS   49

Major Ethical Issues for Clinical Supervisors   50
Due Process   50
Informed Consent   52
   Informed Consent with Clients   52
   Informed Consent Regarding Supervision   53
   Informed Consent with Trainees   54
Dual Relationships   55
   Dual Relationships between Supervisees and Clients   56
   Preventing Supervisee Ethical Transgressions   57
   Dual Relationships between Supervisor and Supervisee   57
Competence   62
   Monitoring Supervisee Competence   63
   Competence in the Practice of Supervision   63
   Remaining Competent   64
Confidentiality   64
Marketplace Issues   66
Legal Ramifications for Clinical Supervisors   67
Malpractice   67
   The Duty to Warn   68
Direct Liability and Vicarious Liability   69
Preventing Claims of Malpractice   70
Ethical Decision Making   71
Conclusion   72

CHAPTER 4   SUPERVISION MODELS   73

Theory in Clinical Supervision   73
   Qualities of Therapy and
   Supervision Theory   73
      Theories and Models
      in Supervision   74
Supervision Models Grounded in
Psychotherapy Theory   76
   Psychodynamic Supervision   76
      Psychodynamic Concepts
      and Practices   77
   Person-centered Supervision   78
   Cognitive–Behavioral Supervision   80
   Systemic Supervision   81
   Constructivist Approaches   83
      Narrative Approaches
      to Supervision   83
      Solution-focused Supervision   84
Developmental Approaches to Supervision   85
   The Integrated Developmental Model   87
   The Rønnestad and Skovholt Model   87
      Themes and Concluding Comments   90
   The Loganbill, Hardy, and
   Delworth Model   90
      The Three Stages   90
      Eight Basic Supervisee Issues   92
      Interventions   93
   Conclusions about Developmental Models   93
Social Role Models   94
   The Discrimination Model   95
   The Hawkins and Shohet Model   98
   The Holloway Systems Model   99
Conclusion   100

CHAPTER 5   THE SUPERVISORY RELATIONSHIP:
THE INFLUENCE OF INDIVIDUAL
AND DEVELOPMENTAL
DIFFERENCES   101

The Uniqueness of Two Persons
in Relationship   101
Cognitive Style, Cognitive Complexity, Theoretical
Orientation, Cognitive Development, and Level of
Experience of the Supervisee   102
   Cognitive or Learning Styles   102

*The Myers–Briggs Type Indicator
and Supervision   102*
*Systemic Cognitive–Developmental
Supervision   104*
*Theoretical Orientation and
Cognitive Style   107*
*Cognitive Complexity, Cognitive Development,
and Level of Experience   108*
    *Cognitive Complexity and Cognitive
    Development   108*
    *Experience as an Indicator of
    Developmental Level   109*
    *Experience Level and
    Moderating Variables   111*
    Supervision Environment   112
Developmental Constructs: Pulling It
All Together   113
Cultural Differences   116
    *Political Nature of the
    Helping Professions   118*
    The Psychotherapy Culture   119
    *Racial and Ethnic Issues within
    Multicultural Supervision   119*
        Empirical Results   122
    *Gender Issues within
    Multicultural Supervision   125*
        Different Voices   126
        Gender Role Conflict   127
        *Differences between Male
        and Female Supervisors   127*
        Empirical Results   128
        Feminist Supervision   130
    *Lesbian, Gay, and Bisexual Issues within
    Multicultural Supervision   131*
Multicultural Constructs: Pulling It
All Together   133
Conclusion   135

CHAPTER 6   **THE SUPERVISORY RELATIONSHIP:
PROCESSES AND ISSUES OF
THE SUPERVISORY TRIAD
AND DYAD   136**

Supervision as a Triadic System   136
    Parallel Processes and Isomorphism   137
        Parallel Process   138
        Implication for Supervisors   139

Research Concerning
Parallel Processes   *140*
Concluding Comments about
Parallel Processes   *140*
Isomorphism   *141*
Interpersonal Triangles   *142*
Interpersonal Triangles
in Supervision   *143*
The Supervisory Dyad   144
Shared Goals   *145*
Antecedents and Consequences
of Effective Supervisory Alliances   *146*
Alliance Antecedents:
Supervisor Behavior   *148*
Alliance Antecedents:
Supervision Processes   *150*
Supervisory Alliance Outcomes   *152*
The Supervisory Alliance as
a Dynamic Process   *154*
Conflicts Arising from Miscommunications
or Mismatched Expectations   *155*
Normative Conflicts   *156*
Conflicts Arising from Participants'
Interpersonal Dynamics   *157*
Conclusion   157

CHAPTER 7   **THE SUPERVISORY RELATIONSHIP:**
SUPERVISEE AND SUPERVISOR
CONTRIBUTING FACTORS   158

The Supervisee in the Relationship   158
Supervisee Resistance   *158*
Manifestations of
Supervisee Resistance   *159*
Circumstances That Elicit
Supervisee Resistance   *160*
Interventions   *161*
Summary Comments about
Supervisee Resistance   *161*
Supervisee Attachment   *162*
The Role of Supervisee Shame
in Supervision   *163*
Supervisor Responses   *164*
Supervisee Anxiety   *164*
Effects of Anxiety on the Supervisee   *165*
Supervisor Management of Supervisee
Anxiety   *168*

Supervisees' Need to Feel and
Appear Competent   169
Supervisee Transference   170
    Implications for Supervisors   171
The Supervisor in the Relationship   171
Supervisor Attachment   172
Interpersonal Power   172
    Social Influence Theory   173
    An Interpersonal Perspective   174
    Implications for Supervisors   176
Supervisor Countertransference   176
Conclusion   179

**CHAPTER 8   ORGANIZING THE SUPERVISION
EXPERIENCE   180**

Importance of Competence in
Organizing Supervision   182
The Role of Institutional Culture   184
The Essential Ingredient: A Supervision Plan   186
Context for Supervision: Two
Different Worlds   187
*Graduate Program as Context
for Supervision   187*
The Field Site as Context for Supervision   188
    Goals   188
    Communication   190
Foundational Tasks for
Organizing Supervision   190
*Advising Trainees for
Clinical Instruction   190*
Selecting Sites   191
*Initial Communication between Graduate
Program and Site   192*
The Interview   194
Orientation   195
Role Induction   195
The Supervision Contract   196
Professional Disclosure Statements   198
Ongoing Organizational Tasks   198
*Communication, Communication,
Communication   198*
    Communication and Evaluation   200
    Supervisor as Agency Representative   200
Managing Time   201
    Time Management and Burnout   202

Time Management and Choosing
Supervision Methods 202
Record Keeping 202
Planning for the Exceptions 205
Evaluation and Debriefing 207
Some Final Thoughts 207
Get Support 207
Know Yourself 207
Gather Data 208
Get Feedback 208
Be Intentional 208
Conclusion 208

CHAPTER 9 **SUPERVISION INTERVENTIONS:**
INDIVIDUAL SUPERVISION **209**

Initial Criteria for Choosing
Supervision Interventions 209
Structured versus Unstructured Interventions 211
Methods, Forms, and Techniques
of Supervision 211
Self-report 211
Process Notes and Case Notes 213
Audiotape 213
Planning Supervision 214
Written Critique of Audiotapes 216
Transcripts 216
Videotape 217
Interpersonal Process Recall 220
The Reflective Process 223
Live Observation 225
Technology and Supervision 226
Timing of Supervision 228
Supervision Formats: Frequency
of Use 229
Supervisor Use of Data 229
Putting It All Together 231
Conclusion 233

CHAPTER 10 **SUPERVISION INTERVENTIONS:**
GROUP SUPERVISION **234**

Group Supervision: Definition
and Conceptualization 234
Types of Supervision Groups 235
The Utility of Group Supervision 236

x   CONTENTS

Advantages of Group Supervision   *236*
Limitations of Group Supervision   *238*
Supervisor Roles, Tasks, and Strategies:
General   239
Maximizing Helpful Phenomena
and Minimizing Those That
are Hindering   *240*
Supervisor Roles, Tasks, and Strategies: Specific
to Group Stage   241
Stages of Group Supervision   *241*
Pregroup   *241*
Screening Group Members   *241*
Meeting Place(s)   *243*
Forming Stage   *243*
Frequency of Meetings   *244*
Attendance   *244*
Manner of Case Presentation   *244*
Storming   *245*
Norming   *247*
Performing Stage   *247*
Final Observations about the Performing Stage   249
Adjourning Stage   *250*
The Time-limited Group   *250*
The Ongoing Supervision Group   *251*
A Procedure for Supervisee Assessment
and Feedback   *251*
Evaluation and Feedback of
the Supervisor   *253*
Group Supervision Variants   253
Balint Groups   *253*
Peer Group Supervision   *253*
The Process of Peer
Supervision Groups   *255*
Advantages and Disadvantages of Peer
Supervision Groups   *255*
Conclusion   256

CHAPTER 11   SUPERVISION INTERVENTIONS:
LIVE SUPERVISION   257

Methods of Live Supervision   258
Bug-in-the-Ear   *258*
Monitoring   *258*
In Vivo   *259*
The Walk-in   *259*
Phone-ins and Consultation Breaks   *259*

*Using Computers and Interactive Television
for Live Supervision*   *259*
The Live Supervision Intervention   260
Bug-in-the-Ear Interventions   *261*
Telephone Interventions   *261*
Consultation Break Interventions   *262*
Presession Planning and
Postsession Debriefing   263
Implementing Live Supervision   264
Advantages and Disadvantages   266
Advantages   *266*
Disadvantages   *267*
Team Supervision   268
The Reflecting Team   *269*
Other Novel Forms of Team Supervision   *270*
Team Dynamics   *271*
In-session (Midsession) Dynamics   *272*
Pre- and Postsession Dynamics   *272*
*Advantages and Disadvantages of Team
Supervision*   *273*
Advantages   *273*
Disadvantages   *274*
Research Results and Questions   274
Live Supervision in Different Contexts   277
Conclusion   278

CHAPTER 12   **TEACHING AND
RESEARCHING SUPERVISION**   **279**

Becoming Supervisors: Developmental and
Teaching Processes   279
Supervisor Development Models   *279*
Alonso's Model   *280*
Hess's Model   *281*
Rodenhauser's Model   *281*
The IDM Model   *281*
Watkins's Model   *282*
*Conclusions Regarding Supervisory
Development Models*   *283*
Training and Supervising Supervisors   *283*
Minimum Qualifications for SITs   *284*
*SIT Assessment: The First Step
in Training*   *285*
*The Didactic Component of
Supervisor Training*   *286*
Laboratory Skills Training for SITs   *287*

Supervision-of-Supervision   *288*
Research on Supervision
Training Outcomes   *291*
Conclusions   *291*
Supervision Process and Outcome Research   292
Research Strategies for a Science
of Supervision   *293*
Stage 1: Descriptive Research   *293*
Stages 2 and 3: Hypothesis and
Theory Building   *295*
Criteria and Measures in
Supervision Research   *299*
Choice of Variables and Criteria   *300*
Conclusion   302

THE SUPERVISOR'S TOOLBOX   **303**
Supervision Toolbox Contents   303
Documents for Use in Supervision   *303*
Sample Counseling
Supervision Contract   *305*
Professional Disclosure Statement   *308*
Supervisee's Bill of Rights   *310*
Supervision Agreement Based on the
Supervisee's Bill of Rights   *313*
Measures for Supervision Research
and Practice   *303*
Supervision Questionnaire   316
Group Supervision Scale   317
Supervisee Levels Questionnaire,
Revised   318
Supervisee Perceptions
of Supervision   320
Evaluation Process within
Supervision Inventory   322
Supervisory Working Alliance—
Supervisor Form   324
Supervisory Working Alliance—
Trainee Form   326
Working Alliance Inventory—
Supervisor Form   328
Working Alliance Inventory—
Supervisee Form   330
Supervisory Styles Inventory   332
Counselor Supervisor
Self-efficacy Scale   333

Multicultural Supervision
Competencies Questionnaire   336
Supervision Ethics Codes   340
The Approved Clinical Supervisor Code
of Ethics   340
Ethical Guidelines for Counseling
Supervisors, Association for Counselor
Education and Supervision   342

REFERENCES   347

NAME INDEX   396

SUBJECT INDEX   406

PREFACE

This third edition of *Fundamentals of Clinical Supervision* has benefited from a professional literature that has become increasingly sophisticated and discriminating. Our hope is that this text reflects this development. There is more to choose from when discussing each facet of clinical supervision than there was a decade ago (though admittedly some topics still call for far more investigation). As a result, our task was altered from covering "what was out there" to choosing those contributions that best exemplify the seminal works from the past and those that best describe where clinical supervision is today and give us some indication of where it is going.

We have remained true to two goals that have informed both former editions: We continued to resist writing a text that promotes any one approach to clinical supervision; second, we attempted to write a review of the clinical supervision field that will be useful to both the student of supervision and to the supervision practitioner as a professional resource. That is, we intended the book to be both scholarly (accomplished through a comprehensive review of the literature) and pragmatic (accomplished through our choice of topics and manner of writing). To this latter end, the book reflects the content required in courses and training for the Approved Clinical Supervisor credential (Center for Credentialing and Education, 2001), a credential available to all licensed or certified mental health practitioners (see www.nbcc.org).

While some things are the same, there have been significant changes as well. First and foremost, the topics covered in the text have been rearranged to reflect our bias regarding those aspects of supervision that are foundational and those that represent supervision tasks or functions (see Figure 1.2). Therefore, the topics of evaluation and ethical and legal considerations have moved from the back of the text to the front. Consequently, supervision modalities appear in the last half of the book. Despite our understanding that those conducting supervision often are drawn to the "how to" initially, we hope that the organization of the text will communicate the peril involved in the practice of supervision without ample attention to supervision parameters.

Chapter 1 defines supervision and differentiates it from other related professional activities, including training. It is intended to establish a foundation for the chapters that follow. To assist in this goal, Chapter 1 introduces a conceptual model for supervision that addresses parameters of supervision, supervisor functions, and the developmental level of the supervisee as interacting factors.

Chapter 2 asks the reader to consider the important (and foundational) task of evaluation. Included in the chapter are criteria for evaluation, favorable conditions for evaluation, the process of conducting evaluation, and addressing supervisee impairment. Chapter 3 also addresses professional responsibilities of the supervisor by covering ethical and legal parameters for supervision. Throughout this chapter, counseling dimensions that the supervisor must oversee and ethical and legal issues that are endemic to supervision are differentiated. Both are reviewed in detail, along with leading expert opinion that determines accepted practice today.

Chapter 4 presents the principal models that inform clinical supervision at this time. Following an overview of the entire conceptual field, models are presented within the following categories: models grounded in psychotherapy theory, developmental models, and social role models. These first four chapters offer ample contextual background to allow the reader to consider the last parameter of supervision, the supervision relationship.

What constituted two chapters in the second edition has grown to three chapters in this edition. This reflects the attention given to the supervision relationship in the professional literature over the past six years. It also reflects the centrality of the supervisory relationship to clinical supervision. We consider the supervisory relationship through several lenses. Chapter 5 addresses the role of individual differences as supervisor and supervisee form a working relationship. The chapter includes a discussion of learning styles, cognitive development, cultural differences, and experience levels and how each of these, separately and in combination, must be addressed in forming a supervision environment.

Chapter 6 focuses on the supervisory triad and dyad specifically and covers such topics as parallel processes, interpersonal triangles, supervisory alliances, and supervisory conflicts. Chapter 7 returns to the domain of individual contributions to relationship, but addresses more intrapersonal topics, such as resistance, anxiety, attachment, transference, and countertransference, and how these play out within supervision.

Having introduced topics that represent supervision parameters, the text now turns its attention to supervision tasks or functions. Chapter 8 takes a serious look at the organizational skills that are required to conduct exemplary supervision. While this chapter bypasses essential qualities such as sensitivity to the relationship and clinical skill, we take the position that these qualities are not adequate if supervision is disorganized, untimely, or poorly documented. Therefore, Chapter 8 covers topics such as supervisor-friendly organizational characteristics, supervision contracts, professional disclosure statements, and record keeping.

Chapters 9, 10, and 11 cover the primary supervision interventions. Chapter 9 is a comprehensive review of the methods used for the individual supervision session, ranging from self-report and the use of case notes to videotape usage and live observation. In addition, this edition introduces sections on the reflective process and on technology and supervision. Chapter 10 focuses on group supervision and offers the reader a rationale for the use of group supervision, a review of the dynamics that determine the success of the group, and different models for use in supervision groups. Finally, Chapter 11 is devoted to live supervision, a method of supervision that continues to be popular in training programs and, having its own unique advantages and challenges, does not fit within either individual or group supervision.

Chapter 12 builds on the previous eleven chapters. It focuses both on the teaching and supervision of supervision and on issues in the conduct of supervision research.

While the above represents the content of the text, we are happy to introduce Clinical *Supervision: A Handbook for Practitioners,* co-authored by Marijane Fall and Jack Sutton, that accompanies the third edition. This handbook is intended to be used in conjunction with the text and contains vignettes of supervision sessions, activities to help the student of supervision assimilate material, discussion questions, and suggestions for workshop activities. It is our hope that the addition of the handbook will help us significantly in meeting our goal of offering our readers a resource for both academic and practitioner use.

Finally, with this edition of *Fundamentals,* we are introducing a website that can be used by our readers to stay current with ideas, developments, and resources in clinical supervision as they become available to us. The URL is www.ablongman.com/bernard3e.

As we complete this edition, we want to thank colleagues both at our institutions and elsewhere for the many discussions that we have engaged in with them on this topic. We thank the reviewers of our book who helped to guide us as we wrote the third edition: Karla D. Carmichael, University of Alabama; Madonna G. Constantine, Teachers College, Columbia University; Stephen S. Feit, Idaho State University; and Mary Lee Nelson, University of Washington. We also want to extend our appreciation to present and former students. They allow the literature to come alive on a regular basis.

CHAPTER 1

INTRODUCTION TO CLINICAL SUPERVISION

Most mental health professionals eventually will supervise. This book is intended to provide technical and conceptual tools necessary for that work. We believe it will be useful to both graduate students and postdegree professionals.

We recognize that virtually anyone reading this book will do so with some previously developed attitudes, beliefs, and expectations about supervision. This will have occurred through experiences as supervisees and, for many, as supervisors. Such foreknowledge can make the reading more relevant and personally meaningful. But it also can invite critical responses to material that they find dissonant. In such cases, we hope that we have written in a sufficiently objective manner that readers can evaluate the dissonance-producing content dispassionately.

Two important premises guide our writing:

- *Clinical supervision is an intervention in its own right.* It is possible, therefore, to isolate and describe issues, theory, and technique that are unique to it. Just as with any other psychological intervention, its practice demands specific preparation.
- *The several mental health professions are more alike than different in their practice of supervision.* Regardless of professional discipline, supervision can be described in terms of core skills and common processes. Therefore, there exists a corpus of knowledge about clinical supervision that is broader than what is found in the literature of any one of these professions (e.g., psychology, counseling, social work, family therapy, psychiatry, psychiatric nursing). Because of this assumption, we have

drawn from an interdisciplinary literature to address the breadth of issues and content that seems to characterize clinical supervision in mental health practice.

Our purpose for this chapter is to establish a foundation for those that follow. In it, we address the historical context, importance, and prevalence of supervision. We then consider definitions, both formal and more personal. We conclude by presenting the conceptual model that both informs our understanding about supervision and guides the organization of this book.

CONTEXT AND IMPORTANCE OF SUPERVISION

Like Goodyear and Guzzardo (2000), we begin by anchoring our consideration of supervision to the tasks and responsibilities of the professions. The first step in doing this is to differentiate professions from other occupations. Most prominent among the differences between the two are that professionals

- have substantially more autonomy than those in other occupations;
- need to make judgments under conditions of uncertainty (Sechrest et al., 1982); and
- rely on a knowledge base that is sufficiently unique and specialized that the average person would have difficulty grasping it and its implications.

Because of these attributes, there is a general assumption that lay people are incapable of regulating the professions. They lack the requisite knowledge. Therefore, society maintains what might be understood as an implicit contract with the professions: They are permitted to self-regulate in return for the assurance that they will place the welfare of society and of their clients above their own self-interests (see, e.g., Schein, 1973; Schön, 1983).

In self-regulating, the professions control who is admitted to practice, set standards for members' behavior, and discipline incompetent or unethical members. Supervision is central to these purposes. It provides a means to impart necessary skills, socialize novices into the profession's values and ethics, protect clients, and, finally, monitor readiness of supervisees to be admitted to the profession. In short, "supervision plays a critical role in maintaining the standards of the profession" (Holloway & Neufeldt, 1995, p. 207).

Supervision's role in professional regulation is at least as old as medicine, the longest standing profession. Moreover, educators and supervisors have been held in high esteem, as the first few lines of the famous Hippocratic oath suggest:

> I SWEAR by Apollo the physician, and Aesculapius, and Health, and All-heal, and all the gods and goddesses, that, according to my ability and judgment, I will keep this Oath and this stipulation—*to reckon him who taught me this Art equally dear to me as my parents, to share my substance with him, and relieve his necessities if required; to look upon his offspring in the same footing as my own brothers....* (Hippocrates, ca. 400 BC; italics added for emphasis)

Professional Self-regulation Affects Supervision Amount and Type

Three primary mechanisms through which the mental health professions self-regulate are state regulatory boards, professional credentialing groups, and accreditation. Perhaps the most important of these is the state regulatory boards. They have underscored the importance of supervision by treating it as a regulated activity and therefore codifying its practice. They stipulate the

- amounts of supervision that licensure candidates are to accrue;

- conditions under which this supervision is to occur (e.g., the ratio of supervision to hours of professional service; what proportion of the supervision can be in a group format; who can do the supervising); and
- qualifications of those who supervise.

In addition to statutory boards, there are independent groups that credential mental health professionals (e.g., the Academy of Certified Social Workers, the American Board of Professional Psychology, the National Board for Certified Counselors, and the American Association for Marriage and Family Therapists). The credentials that these groups award usually are for advanced practitioners and certify competence above the minimal level necessary for public protection. Like the regulatory boards, these credentialing groups also stipulate amounts and conditions of supervision. Box 1.1 provides Internet addresses for sites that provide access to information about licensure, credentialing, and accreditation for key mental health professions.

Whereas licensure and credentialing affect the individual professional, accrediting bodies govern the training programs that prepare them. The guidelines used by these groups address supervision with varying degrees of specificity. For example, the American Psychological Association (APA, 1996) leaves it to the individual training program to establish that supervised training has been sufficient. But other groups are very specific about supervision requirements. For example, any graduate of an AAMFT accredited program is to have received at least 100 hours of face-to-face supervision and this should have been in a ratio of at least 1 hour of supervision for every 5 hours of direct client contact (American Association for Marriage and Family Therapists, 2002). The Council for the Accreditation of Counseling and Related Educational Programs (CACREP, 2001) requires that a student receive a minimum of 1 hour per week individual and 1.5 hours of group supervision during practicum and internship.

But a person's supervised training does not end with the receipt of a professional degree. State licensure boards almost invariably stipulate a par-

Box 1.1_____

Web-based Sources of Information about Licensure, Credentialing, and Accreditation Supervision Requirements

LICENSURE

The Council on Licensure, Enforcement and Regulation (CLEAR) has a Web site with links to licensure boards for most professions and in all the states and Canadian provinces: *http://www.clearhq.org/boards.htm*

CREDENTIALING

AAMFT Approved Supervisor Credential: *http://www.aamft.org/membership/ASRequirements.htm*

American Board of Examiners in Social Work: Board Certified Diplomate in Clinical Social Work: *http://www.abecsw.org/applicants/bcd/a_sub_the_bcd.shtml*

The American Board of Professional Psychology (ABPP): *http://www.abpp.org/aboutus.htm*

National Board of Certified Counselors: The National Certified School Counselor and Certified Clinical Mental Health Counselor Credentials: *http://www.nbcc.org/depts/certmain.htm*

British Association for Counselling and Psychotherapy: Accredited Supervisor (in this case, accreditation is equivalent to credential): *http://www.bac.co.uk/members_visitors/members_login/registration/members_registration_supacc.htm*

ACCREDITATION

American Psychological Association Guidelines and Principles for Accreditation of Programs in Professional Psychology: *http://www.apa.org/ed/G&P2.pdf*

Council for Accreditation of Counseling and Related Educational Programs (CACREP): The 2001 Standards: *http://www.counseling.org/cacrep/2001standards700.htm*

Commission on Accreditation for Marriage and Family Therapy Education: Standards of Accreditation 10.1: *http://www.aamft.org/about/COAMFTE/standards_of_accreditation.htm*

Approved Clinical Supervisor: *http://www.cce-global.org/acs.htm*

---

ticular amount of supervised clinical experience that must be acquired postdegree. As well, many agencies require newly hired professionals to be supervised as a way of ensuring quality of care for their clients. In fact, this is expected in Britain and some other countries, as evident in the statement from the British Association for Counselling and Psychotherapy's Ethics Code (see our Supervisor's Toolbox for a Web link) that "There is an obligation to use regular and on-going supervision to enhance the quality of the services provided and to commit to updating practice by continuing professional development." Moreover, many—perhaps most—postgraduate, credentialed practitioners *want* and do continue some level and type of supervision (see, e.g., Borders & Usher, 1992; McCarthy, Kulakowski, & Kenfield, 1994; Wiley, 1994). This is good for them. But it also is good

for their clients. Slater (2003) stated, "I remember a patient once asking me, 'who do you talk about me with?' He wasn't asking out of fear, but hope. What suffering person doesn't want many minds thinking about how to help?"

Most Mental Health Professionals Eventually Supervise

Because supervision is such an essential aspect of professional training and because so much of it is required, it should not be surprising that so many people provide it. Supervision is one of the more frequent activities of mental health professionals. More than 25 years ago, Garfield and Kurtz (1976) found that supervision was fifth in a list of activities in which clinical psychologists engaged, ranking ahead of such activities as group therapy and research. More recently, Norcross, Prochaska, and Farber (1993), found that clinical supervision was the second most frequently reported activity among members of APA's Division of Psychotherapy (barely edging out diagnosis and assessment). Similar results have been obtained in studies of counseling psychologists (e.g., Fitzgerald & Osipow, 1986; Watkins, Lopez, Campbell, & Himmell, 1986).

These trends exist internationally as well. In a study of 2,380 psychotherapists from more than a dozen countries, Rønnestad, Orlinsky, Parks, and Davis (1997) confirmed what most of us might expect: there is a relationship between the amount of one's professional experience and the likelihood that he or she will have become a supervisor. In their study, the percentage of therapists who supervised increased from less than 1% in the first 6 months of practice to between 85% and 90% for those who have more than 15 years of practice.

Acknowledging the prevalence and importance of supervision, both the NBCC and AAMFT have developed separate credentials for clinical supervisors. As well, the 2002 APPIC Competencies Conference treated supervision as one of eight core competencies. In fact, the supervision work group at that conference included in their report (Falender et al., in press) the assertion that "There is consensus that supervision should be considered a core competence in the practice of psychology." This stance was preceded by the educational model of the National Council of Schools and Programs of Professional Psychology (Peterson, Peterson, Abrams, & Stricker, 1997), which identifies "management and supervision" as one of five core competencies.

CLINICAL SUPERVISION IN THE PREPARATION OF MENTAL HEALTH PROFESSIONALS

The foregoing has provided a larger societal context for understanding the importance and therefore ubiquity of supervision. Yet supervisees and their clients experience the most immediate and tangible effects of supervision. The following section addresses the processes that result in these effects.

Supervision: Essential to Experiential Learning

Because the professions rely on specialized bodies of knowledge, training for them is lengthy. At its most basic level, professional preparation centers on two general realms of knowledge (Schön, 1983).

1. Formal theories and observations that have been confirmed, or are confirmable, by research
2. The knowledge and accompanying skills that have accrued through the professional experiences of practitioners

These realms, which often are talked about, respectively, as "science" and "art," are both essential bases of knowledge for any profession. Each should complement and inform the other. In fact, this assumed complementarity is at the heart of the scientist–practitioner model in which most psychologists and many other mental health professionals are trained (Baker & Benjamin, 2000). Yet the two knowledge realms are differentially valued, and therefore it often is difficult to reach an optimal balance between the two. Within universities the first realm too often is regarded as that of *real* knowledge, whereas the latter is either ignored or even regarded with some disdain. The reverse prejudice too often is true among practitioners.

These prejudices are one barrier to students being able to appropriately integrate the two knowledge domains. Another is that students typically are exposed to these domains sequentially. That is, they first learn formal theory and research in the classroom. They gain the practitioner-driven knowledge later when they actually begin to participate in the delivery of human services and to solicit the wisdom of other service providers.

Clinical supervision provides the crucible in which supervisees can blend these two knowledge types and begin to incorporate them as their own working knowledge. It is teaching that occurs in the context of practice and that provides a bridge between campus and clinic (Williams, 1995), the bridge by which supervisees begin to span the "large theory–practice gulf" to which Rønnestad and Skovholt (1993, p. 396) allude.

In fact, a necessary condition for supervisees to develop their professional competence is that they practice their skills in laboratory and clinical settings. Fortunately, most supervisees are excited about this aspect of their training and therefore are committed to it. To practice these professional activities was why they entered the field in the first place!

In discussing the development of competence, Peterson (2002) told the joke about the New York City tourist who, lost, stopped a cabbie to ask, "How can I get to Carnegie Hall?" The cabbie's response was "practice, practice, practice." Peterson noted that this joke's punch line is significant in that the cabbie did not say "read, read, read." *Practice* is the essential factor for skill development.

But practice alone is an insufficient means to attain competence. Beutler (1988) argued that the "germ theory" of psychotherapy education has been too prevalent in the past. That is, students and supervisees were expected to acquire—or "catch"—skills through exposure to practice. But unless practice is accompanied by the systematic feedback and reflection that supervision provides, supervisees may gain no more than the illusion that they are developing professional expertise.

Dawes (1994) asserted that

Two conditions are important for experiential learning: one, a clear understanding of what constitutes an incorrect response or error in judgment, and two, immediate, unambiguous and consistent feedback when such errors are made. In the mental health professions, neither of these conditions is satisfied. (p. 111)

Dawes's assertions about the two conditions necessary for experiential learning are compelling. But we believe his assertion that *neither* condition is met in the mental health professions is overstated. We predicated our writing of this book on the assumption that supervision can satisfy these and other necessary conditions for learning.

It is true that it may not be necessary to have a "supervisor" (by whatever name) to attain many motor and performance skills. In these domains, simply to perform the task may provide sufficient feedback for skill mastery. Learning to type is one example. Learning to drive an automobile is another (Dawes, 1994). When driving, the person who turns the steering wheel too abruptly receives immediate feedback from the vehicle; the same is true if the driver is too slow applying the brakes when approaching another vehicle. In these and other ways, experience behind the wheel gives the person an opportunity to obtain immediate and unambiguous feedback. Driving skills are therefore likely to develop and improve simply with the experience of driving.

But psychological practice skills are of a different type. In this domain, experience alone rarely provides either of the two conditions that Dawes stipulated as necessary for experiential learning to occur. The practitioner's skills cannot be shaped by simple experience in the same automatic manner that occurs with the development of driving skills. She or he must receive intentional, clear feedback such as is available in supervision. Research data confirm that unsupervised counseling experience does *not* accelerate the clinical progress of trainees (Hill, Charles, & Reed, 1981; Wiley & Ray, 1986).

Confidence in one's abilities can exist independently of actual competence. It is, however, still a desired training goal. Therefore, Bradley and Olson's (1980) findings concerning clinical psychology students' felt competence as psychotherapists are significant. Of all the variables examined as possible correlates of felt competence (e.g., total number of hours of therapy conducted; amount of therapy coursework), only two were related to it: (1) the number of hours of formal supervision in which the students had participated and (2) the number of supervisors they had.

In short, supervision must accompany practice if students in the mental health professions are to acquire the necessary practice skills and conceptual ability. As Brashears (1995) noted, "arguments have been made about how long supervision should last and how much supervision is needed, but not over its necessity'" (p. 692).

Necessary Preparation to Supervise

We began this chapter by stating our assumption that supervision is a distinct intervention. We go further at this point to assert that the practice of supervision requires specific preparation. In fact, this seems an ethical imperative.

We have observed among mental health practitioners two prevailing assumptions that have kept mental health professionals from seeking training for the role of supervisor. The less frequent of these assumptions is that having been a supervisee is sufficient preparation to be a supervisor. This, though, is analogous to someone believing that he or she could be a therapist simply on the basis of having been a client.

The much more frequent assumption is that to be an effective therapist is a sufficient prerequisite to being a good supervisor. Yet to assume that therapy skills translate automatically to supervisory skills is analogous to assuming that a good athlete inevitably will make a good coach (or, perhaps, a good sports announcer). We all can find an instance in which that has not been the case. The great players tend not to become the great coaches, and vice versa. But, at the same time, most great coaches have "played the game," and some have played well. Carroll (1996), though, said, "It sounds a terrible choice, but given the option between a good counsellor who was a poor educator, or a poor counsellor who was a good educator, I would choose the latter as a supervisor" (p. 27).

It is the close, but imperfect, relationship between therapy and supervision that perpetuates the belief by some that supervision training is unnecessary. In fact, supervisors may lack specific training in supervision, but they find themselves doing it—and typically believe they are pretty good at it. But self-assessments of competence and actual competence are often independent of one another. Professionals who have assumed supervisory roles in this manner are more inclined to believe that, if they have learned it without formal preparation, their students and supervisees can as easily do so. These faculty and field supervisors serve as role models to supervisees, who then receive mixed messages about the actual importance of supervision training. In this way, then, they hinder more general acceptance that training in supervision is necessary.

Although earlier studies (Hess & Hess, 1983; McColley & Baker, 1982) found supervision training to be a relatively infrequent activity, it is our impression that the situation has improved. Certainly, the professional climate has changed, so training for supervision has become expected. Accrediting bodies now stipulate that students receive this training. Both CACREP- and AAMFT-accredited doctoral programs now are required to offer a supervision course, and the accreditation guidelines for APA stipulate supervision as a competence area; the Association for Counselor Education and Supervision (ACES) has endorsed Standards for Counseling Supervisors, and the American Association for Marriage and Family Therapy has a supervisor membership category that requires specified training.

Thus, whereas Ross and Goh (1993) found that only 11.2% of school psychologists reported supervision coursework or training during their graduate programs in school psychology, this likely will change as the new accreditation guidelines are followed. At the very least, there seems a growing sensitivity that, wherever supervision is learned, it initially should be supervised. In a study of Canadian psychology supervisors, Johnson and Stewart (2000) found that only a very few reported having received training in supervision while in graduate school. Yet two of their findings were encouraging: (1) those who had received supervision training reported themselves to feel more ready to supervise than those who had not, and (2) more than half (55.1%) reported that their initial supervision experience was itself supervised.

Scott, Ingram, Vitanza, and Smith (2000) surveyed APA-accredited (1) internships and (2) training programs. They found interesting specialty and setting differences in the emphasis given to supervision training. For example, among counseling psychology programs, 85% had a didactic course in supervision and 79% had a supervision practicum; those percentages for clinical psychology programs were 34% and 43% respectively. Compared to other types of internships, those in university counseling centers were more likely to offer a supervision seminar (73% vs. 27%) or to offer the opportunity to supervise (89% vs. 44%).

State licensure boards also are beginning to require that mental health professionals who provide supervision receive at least some training in supervision. For example, beginning in 2003, California-licensed psychologists who want to supervise must participate in one 6-hour supervision workshop during every 2-year licensure cycle. Sutton (2000) reported that 18% of counselor licensure boards require a course or its equivalent for persons providing supervision and another 12% require training in supervision, but do not specify the type or amount. Presently, three of these boards have a specialty license for supervisors.

DEFINING SUPERVISION

Many supervisors must entertain the fantasy of having "super vision." In fact, it is possible for a supervisor to gain a clarity of perspective about counseling or therapy processes precisely because she or he is not one of the involved parties. The supervisor works from a vantage point that is not afforded the therapist, who is actually involved in the process.

Levenson (1984) spoke to this when he observed that, in the ordinary course of his work as a therapist, he spent a considerable time perplexed, confused, bored, and "at sea." But "when I supervise, all is clear to me!" (p. 153). He reported finding that theoretical and technical difficulties were surprisingly clear to him. Moreover, he maintained that people whom he supervised and who seemed confused most of the time that they were supervisees reported that they attained a similar clarity when they were supervising. He speculated that this is "an odd, seductive aspect of the phenomenology of the supervisory process itself" (p. 154) that occurs at a different level of abstraction than therapy. Perhaps this is the perspective of the "Monday morning quarterback."

Despite this, though, the etymological definition of supervision is simply *to oversee* (Webster's, 1966). This is what supervisors in virtually any profession do. This definition, though, does not speak to the teaching and learning that occur during clinical supervision. It is important, therefore, to have a more precise and specific definition.

Definitions that various authors have offered differ considerably as a function of such factors

as the author's discipline and training focus. Our intent in this book is to offer a definition that is specific enough to be helpful, but at the same time broad enough to encompass the multiple roles, disciplines, and settings associated with supervision. Before offering this definition, it is useful to consider two that have been offered.

Loganbill, Hardy, and Delworth (1982) defined supervision as "an intensive, interpersonally focused one-to-one relationship in which one person is designated to facilitate the development of therapeutic competence in the other person" (p. 4). In contrast to the definition of supervision as "to oversee," which was too broad and inclusive to be helpful, this definition suggested a too narrow and restrictive focus. For example, in their consideration of supervision as something that occurs only in the context of a one-to-one relationship, Loganbill et al. (1982) overlook group supervision, a modality clinical supervisors frequently employ (Goodyear & Nelson, 1997).

Also, in declaring their goal to be the development of the supervisee's therapeutic competence, Loganbill et al. left no room for supervising such other psychological services as psychoeducation or career counseling. Although the larger portion of this book will focus on the supervision of psychotherapy, we believe that many of the essential issues and processes remain the same in the supervision of other psychological interventions. Finally, the Loganbill et al. definition did not acknowledge explicitly the client-protective function of supervision.

Hart (1982) defined supervision as "an ongoing educational process in which one person in the role of supervisor helps another person in the role of the supervisee acquire appropriate professional behavior through an examination of the trainee's professional activities" (p. 12). This definition more closely approximates that which we intend to consider, though it, too, seems to suggest a one-to-one focus.

For this book, we are offering the working definition of supervision provided in Box 1.2. Because this definition is succinct, it merits further explication. For such explication, it would be

Box 1.2

Supervision Defined

Supervision is an intervention provided by a more senior member of a profession to a more junior member or members of that same profession. This relationship is

- evaluative,
- extends over time, and
- has the simultaneous purposes of enhancing the professional functioning of the more junior person(s), monitoring the quality of professional services offered to the clients that she, he, or they see, and serving as a gatekeeper for those who are to enter the particular profession.

useful to break it into its component parts and then engage in a more extended consideration of each component. Prior to doing this, however, we wish to offer a brief discussion of the terms we will use in this book.

We will use *counseling, therapy,* and *psychotherapy* interchangeably. Distinctions among these terms are artificial and serve little function (cf. Patterson, 1986). Also, we will follow the convention suggested by Rogers (1951) of referring to the recipient of therapeutic services as a client.

We distinguish between supervision and training. Stone (1997) made the point that the definition of supervision "occasionally suffers from cycles of inflation and deflation" (p. 265), depending on whether authors are confusing supervision with training. Both are essential components in the imparting of therapeutic skills, and they often are treated together in reviews of literature (e.g., Matarazzo & Patterson, 1986). Training differs from supervision, however, in its more limited scope, its following of prescribed protocols, and its focus on specific skills (e.g., how to offer restatements of client affect and content). Also, such training often takes place in laboratory courses, rather than with real clients.

Paralleling this training versus supervision distinction is the one that we make between *trainee* and *supervisee.* We believe that *supervisee* is the more inclusive term. *Trainee* connotes a supervisee who is still enrolled in a formal training program; it seems less appropriate for postgraduate

professionals who seek supervision. Therefore, in most cases we will use *supervisee.* Occasionally, when a more delimited term seems necessary, we will use either *trainee* or *therapist* (to designate either predegree or postdegree supervisees) as appropriate.

We turn now to a more complete explication of our working definition of supervision. Each of the following sections will address a specific element of this definition.

Supervision Is a Distinct Intervention

Supervision is an intervention, just as are teaching, psychotherapy, and mental health consultation. There are substantial ways in which supervision overlaps with these other interventions (see Box 1.3). In fact, in later chapters we will discuss how good supervisors will draw from each of these roles. But, despite these overlaps, supervision is a unique intervention.

Teaching versus Supervision.   One goal of supervision is to teach, and the supervisee does have the role of learner (cf. the title of the classic Ekstein and Wallerstein book, *The Teaching and Learning of Psychotherapy* 1972). Moreover, teaching and supervision are alike in that there is an evaluative aspect to the intervention. Relatedly, each ultimately serves a gatekeeping function, regulating who is legitimized to enter the world of work in their chosen area.

Box 1.3

Supervision versus Teaching, Counseling, and Consultation

	SIMILARITIES	DIFFERENCES
Teaching	• Both have the purpose of imparting new skills and knowledge • Both have evaluative and gatekeeping functions	• Whereas teaching is driven by a set curriculum or protocol, supervision is driven by the needs of the particular supervisee and his or her clients
Counseling or therapy	• Both can address recipients' problematic behaviors, thoughts, or feelings	• Any therapeutic work with a supervisee must be only to increase their effectiveness with clients • Supervision is evaluative, whereas counseling is not • Clients often have greater choice of therapists than supervisees have of supervisors
Consultation	• Both are concerned with helping the recipient work more effectively professionally; for more advanced trainees, the two functions may become indistinguishable	• Consultation is a relationship between equals, whereas supervision is hierarchical • Consultation can be a one-time event, whereas supervision occurs across time • Consultation is more usually freely sought by recipients than is supervision • Supervision is evaluative, whereas consultation is not

Teaching, however, typically relies on an explicit curriculum with goals that are imposed uniformly on everyone. But even though the focus of supervision at its broadest level might seem to speak to common goals (e.g., to prepare competent practitioners), the actual intervention is tailored to the needs of the individual supervisee and the supervisee's clients.

Counseling versus Supervision. There are elements, too, of counseling or therapy in supervision. That is, supervisors often help supervisees to examine aspects of their behavior, thoughts, or feelings that are stimulated by a client, particularly as these may act as barriers to their work with the client. As Frawley-O'Dea and Sarnat (2001) observe, to have "a rigidly impenetrable boundary

between teaching and 'treating' in supervision is neither desirable nor truly achievable" (p. 137). But still there should be boundaries. Therapeutic interventions with supervisees should be made only in the service of helping them become more effective with clients: To provide therapy that has broader goals is ethical misconduct (see, e.g., Ladany, Lehrman-Waterman, Molinaro, & Wolgast, 1999; Neufeldt & Nelson, 1999).

There are other differences, too. For example, clients generally are free to enter therapy or not; when they do, they usually have a voice in choosing their therapists. On the other hand, supervision is not a voluntary experience for supervisees. Moreover, they often have no voice in who their supervisor is to be. Given this circumstance, it is salient to note that Webb and Wheeler (1998) found in their study that supervisees who had chosen their own supervisors reported being able to disclose to their supervisors more information of a sensitive nature about themselves, their clients, and the supervisory process than supervisees who had been assigned a supervisor.

The single most important difference between therapy and supervision may reside in the evaluative responsibilities of the supervisor. Although few would maintain that counseling or therapy is or could be entirely value free, most therapists actively resist imposing their values on clients or otherwise making explicit evaluations of them. On the other hand, supervisees are evaluated against criteria that are imposed on them by others.

Consultation versus Supervision.   Mental health consultation is yet another intervention that overlaps with supervision. In fact, for more senior professionals, supervision often evolves into consultation. That is, the experienced therapist might meet informally on an occasional basis with a colleague to get ideas about how to handle a particularly difficult client or to regain needed objectivity. We all encounter blind spots in ourselves, and it is to our benefit to obtain help in this manner.

But, despite the similarities, there are distinctions between consultation and supervision. Caplan (1970), for example, suggested that the parties in the consultation relationship are often not of the same professional discipline (e.g., a social worker might consult with a teacher about a child's problem). Another distinction is that consultation is more likely than supervision to be a one-time-only event.

Two consultation–supervision distinctions echo distinctions already made between therapy and supervision. One is that supervision is more likely imposed, whereas consultation typically is freely sought. More significantly, there is no evaluative role for the consultant (e.g., Caplan maintained that the relationship was between two equals), whereas evaluation is one of the defining attributes of supervision.

In summary, then, specific aspects of such related interventions as teaching, therapy, and consultation are also present as components of supervision. But, although there are common skills across these several interventions, the manner in which they are arrayed is unique in each. Martin (1990) made some useful observations about skills that have implications for thinking about supervision and its relationship to the related interventions of counseling, education, and consultation:

> *The word* skill *has a specific meaning. It is an ability that can be perfected by training and exercise of the ability itself, usually without much regard to the particular context in which it may be put to use. Thus, dribbling a basketball is a skill; so too is typing or enunciation of words and phrases in oral speech. Of course, matters are complicated somewhat by the fact that any skill typically can be subdivided into various subskills. Skills also can be combined with other skills, at a similar level and category, to comprise more inclusive skills. Nonetheless, there is much more to playing basketball, writing meaningful prose, or effective public speaking than dribbling, typing or enunciating.* (p. 403)

To put this into a context relevant to this book, then, supervision should be thought of as an intervention comprised of multiple skills, many of which are common to other forms of intervention. Yet their configuration is such as to make supervision unique among psychological interventions. Moreover, there is at least one phenomenon, that of parallel or reciprocal processes (e.g., Doehrman, 1976; Searles, 1955), that is unique to supervision and distinguishes it from other interventions (parallel processes are discussed in Chapter 6).

Member of Same Profession

The widely acknowledged purpose of supervision is to facilitate supervisees' development of therapeutic and case management skills. Certainly, this is essential. Moreover, it is possible to accomplish this purpose when the supervisory dyad is comprised of members of two different disciplines (e.g., a marital and family therapist might supervise the work of a counselor). But, though this arrangement results in technical competence, it overlooks the socialization function that supervision serves. Supervisees are developing a sense of professional identity, and this is best acquired through association with more senior members of the supervisees' own professional discipline.

Ekstein and Wallerstein (1972) spoke to this when they noted that it would be possible for a training program to prepare its supervisees with all the basic psychotherapeutic skills, but still to fall short. Skill acquisition is not enough: "What would still be missing is a specific quality in the psychotherapist that makes him [or her] into a truly professional person, a quality we wish to refer to as his [or her] professional identity" (p. 65).

To socialize supervisees into a profession must be accomplished by supervisors serving as role models. It follows, then, that most supervisors with whom a supervisee works should be of the profession of which the supervisee intends to be a member. Social work students should receive supervision from social workers, psychology students should receive supervision from psychologists, and so on. Each of these professions is in some ways distinct, with its own history and philosophy; each also has functions more typical of it than for the others. Most state laws that govern the licensure of mental health professions stipulate that the licensure applicant have a certain portion of his or her supervised clinical hours from supervisors of a like profession. Ekstein and Wallerstein (1972) observed that this is normative. The major exception occurs with multidisciplinary training institutes that offer postgraduate preparation in a specific approach (e.g., psychoanalytic, Jungian, rational emotive, strategic, and so on).

In a cautionary tale of the adverse consequences of using members of one profession to supervise neophyte members of another profession, Albee (1970) invoked the metaphor of the cuckoo: The cuckoo is a bird that lays its eggs in the nests of other birds, who then raise the offspring as their own. His case in point was clinical psychology, which had used the Veterans Administration system as a primary base of training in the decades following World War II. From Albee's perspective, this was unfortunate, for the clinical psychology fledglings were put in the care of psychiatrists, who then socialized them into their way of viewing the world. Albee asserted that a consequence of this pervasive practice was that clinical psychology lost some of what was unique to it as its members incorporated the perspectives of psychiatry.

Supervision Is Evaluative

We have already mentioned several times that evaluation stands as one of supervision's hallmarks, distinguishing it from both counseling or therapy and consultation. Evaluation is implicit in the supervisors' mandate to safeguard clients, both those currently being seen by the supervisee and those who would be seen in the future by the trainee if the trainee were to finish the professional program.

That supervisors have an evaluative function provides them with a tool, giving them an important source of interpersonal influence. For example, although most supervisees have a very high degree of intrinsic motivation to learn and to use feedback to self-correct, evaluation can provide supervisees with an additional, extrinsic motivation to change or evolve.

But, despite its importance as a component of supervision, both supervisor and supervisee can experience evaluation with discomfort. Supervisors, for example, were trained first in the more nonevaluative role of counselor or therapist. Indeed, they may well have been attracted to the field because of this feature of counseling. The role of evaluator therefore can be not only new, but uncomfortable as well.

The role of evaluator also affects the trainee's perception of the supervisor. Students are not only taught psychotherapy by their supervisors, they are also evaluated by them. The criteria for evaluating students' performances tend to be subjective and ambiguous, in large part because the skills being evaluated are highly complex, intensely personal, and difficult to measure. Students know that their psychological health, interpersonal skills, and therapeutic competence are being judged against unclear standards. . . . Supervisors are thus not only admired teachers but feared judges who have real power. (Doehrman, 1976, pp. 10–11)

That supervision is evaluative means that it is hierarchical. This has seemed problematic to some (e.g., Edwards & Chen, 1999; Porter & Vasquez, 1997), who have suggested the term *covision* as an alternative to supervision and to signal a more collaborative relationship. Yet hierarchy and evaluation are so intertwined with supervision that to remove them makes the intervention something other than supervision.

Evaluation, then, is an important, integral component of supervision. But it is one that often is the source of problems for supervisors and supervisees alike. Therefore, we have devoted an entire chapter of this book to the topic of evaluation. Although there is no way in which evaluation could (or should) be removed from supervision, there are ways to enhance its usefulness and to minimize problems attendant to it.

Supervision Extends over Time

A final element of our definition of supervision is that it is an intervention that extends over time. This distinguishes supervision from training, which might be brief, for example, in a brief workshop intended to impart a specific skill; it distinguishes supervision, too, from consultation, which might be very time limited as one professional seeks the help of another to gain or regain objectivity in his or her work with a client.

The fact that it is ongoing allows the supervisor–supervisee relationship to grow and develop. Indeed, many supervision theorists have focused particular importance of the developing nature of this relationship. In recognition of this, we devote two chapters of this book to the supervisory relationship, including ways that it evolves and changes across time.

Purposes of Supervision

In our definition, we suggest that supervision has two central purposes:

1. *To foster the supervisee's professional development* (a supportive and educational function)

2. *To ensure client welfare* (we regard supervisors' gatekeeping function as a variant of the monitoring of client welfare)

Each is an essential purpose. It is possible, however, for a supervisor to more heavily emphasize one than the other. For example, a student working at a field placement might have both a university-based and an on-site supervisor. In this situation, it is possible for the university-based supervisor to give relatively greater emphasis to the teaching–learning goals of supervision and the on-site supervisor to give relatively greater emphasis to the client-monitoring aspects. Feiner (1994) alluded to this dichotomy of goals when he suggested that

> *Some supervisors assume that their most important ethical responsibility is to the student's patient. This would impel them to make the student a conduit for their own expertise. Others make the assumption that their ultimate responsibility is to the development of the student. . . . Their concern is the possible lowering of the student's self-esteem when confronted by the supervisor and his rising fantasy that he should become a shoe salesman.*

It is important to acknowledge other possible purposes for supervision. For example, Proctor (quoted in Hawkins & Shohet, 1989) asserted that supervision serves three purposes that she labeled *formative* (equivalent to our teaching–learning purpose), *normative* (generally equivalent to ensuring client welfare), and then also *restorative*. This last purpose is to provide supervisees the opportunity to express and meet needs that will help them to avoid burnout.

Occasionally, too, supervision is mandated as a method to rehabilitate impaired professionals (see, e.g., Frick, McCartney, & Lazarus, 1995). This overlaps with both the training and client-protective purposes of supervision, but really should be considered an additional purpose. We will not specifically address this purpose of supervision in this book and refer interested readers to discussions of the topic by Cobia and Pipes (2002) and Walzer and Miltimore (1993).

Both the restorative and rehabilitative purposes of supervision are important in some supervision.

But they are not common to *all* supervision, as are the two purposes that are part of our definition of supervision. We address each in turn in the sections that follow.

Enhancing Professional Functioning. We state the teaching–learning goal simply as "to enhance professional functioning." This is a pragmatic definition that meets our need to provide a succinct and generally applicable definition of supervision. It is silent about any performance criteria that supervisees are to meet or even about the content of learning.

To enhance professional functioning, then, is a broad conceptual goal. In actual practice, supervision will have goals that vary both in their specificity and time orientation. That is, the supervisor should have some very precise and concrete goals to accomplish with the supervisee during their work together; in the best of circumstances, the supervisee will share these goals. Typically, these derive from some combination of the supervisor's own theory or model, the supervisee's particular developmental needs, and the supervisee's expressed wishes.

In addition, the supervisor almost certainly would want the supervisee to be developing skills and competencies necessary for eventual licensure or certification. This is a utilitarian goal that has the virtue of specificity. That is, supervisors generally know what competencies the supervisee will have to demonstrate for licensure, at least in his or her own state. Moreover, this is a logical target in that to attain licensure is the point at which the supervisee makes the transition to an autonomously functioning professional and is no longer legally mandated to be supervised.

Other long-term goals for supervisees are more abstract. One is to move the supervisee along a continuum of proficiency: She or he begins training as a novice, but gradually grows in expertise. This process, however, is an extended one. Fried (1991) offered the folk wisdom that it takes 10 years to become a really good psychotherapist. In fact, Hayes (1981) estimated that it requires about 10 years to become an expert in any skill domain;

Ericcson and Lehmann (1996) referred to this as "the ten year rule of necessary preparation." Yet, for many professionals, time alone will be insufficient to attain expert status. Supervisors, then, should consider expertise an aspirational goal.

Another aspirational goal is to help supervisees to attain clinical wisdom. Williams (1995), in particular, made a strong argument in favor of this as a training goal. Although this is a multifaceted construct, a succinct working definition might be "the ability of a professional to make clinical decisions under conditions of uncertainty." Yet wisdom has proved inordinately difficult to operationalize (cf. Sternberg, 1990).

Consider, for example, that wisdom traditionally has been regarded as an attribute of older people. Yet only *some* older people might be considered wise, and to obtain consensus about who among these are wise would be hard. Perhaps it should be no surprise, then, that Smith, Staudinger, and Baltes (1994) found no relationship between clinical psychologists' ages and their demonstrated wisdom. They did, however, find (as had Staudinger, Smith, & Baltes, 1992) that clinical psychologists scored higher on a measure of wisdom than did control samples.

Monitoring Client Care. The teaching and learning purposes of supervision receive particular attention in the literature. Nevertheless, it is important that supervisors not lose sight of the fact that monitoring client care is an essential supervision goal. In fact, Loganbill et al. (1982) correctly maintained that this is the supervisor's *paramount* responsibility. Blocher (1983) stated it bluntly when he observed that clients "are not expendable laboratory animals to be blithely sacrificed in the name of training" (p. 29). And should a sense of professional responsibility be insufficient motivation to keep the supervisor focused on monitoring quality of client care, self-interest should; as we will discuss in Chapter 3, the concept of vicarious liability is that the supervisor can be held liable for any harm done by the supervisee under supervision.

It is useful to remember that the original purpose of clinical supervision was to monitor client care. Supervision in the mental health disciplines almost certainly began with social work supervision, which "dates from the nineteenth century Charity Organization Societies in which paid social work agents supervised the moral treatment of the poor by friendly visitors" (Harkness & Poertner, 1989, p. 115). The focus of this supervision was on the client.

Eisenberg (1956) noted that the first known call for supervision to focus on the professional, rather than exclusively on the client, was expressed by Zilphia Smith in 1901. This supervisory focus did not become more prominent until "Psychotherapy supervision began in the 1920s when Max Eitington, a psychoanalyst in Berlin, proposed that psychoanalysts in training conduct supervised psychoanalysis sessions" (Hutto, 2001).

But, despite its importance, the need to ensure quality of client care is one job demand with particular potential for causing dissonance in the supervisor. Most of the time, supervisors are able to perceive themselves as allies of their supervisees. Yet they also must be prepared, should they see harm being done to clients, to risk bruising the egos of their supervisees or, in extreme cases, even to steer the supervisee from the profession. From the perspective of supervisees, especially those with autonomy conflicts, this aspect of supervision can lead to the perception that supervisors are conducting "snooper vision" (Kadushin, 1976).

PERSON-SPECIFIC UNDERSTANDINGS OF SUPERVISION

It is essential that a formal definition, such as we have just provided, guide supervisory practice. But it is inevitable that both supervisors and supervisees also will attach more idiosyncratic, personal definitions to their roles and to the supervision process based on their histories and expectations. These more individualized, and usually implicit, definitions often can affect supervision processes in important ways.

Bartlett (1932, 1958) is credited with suggesting the concept of schema (in the plural, schemata), which now is widely used among cognitive psychologists and mental health professionals. A

schema helps us to interpret our world by providing a mental framework for understanding and remembering information. More formally stated, it is a knowledge representation based on our past experiences and inferences that we use to interpret a present experience. In short, people have a tendency to understand one domain of experience in terms of another, that is, to think metaphorically. Mental health professionals, in fact, base much of their work on the assumption that a person's previous life experiences can and often do function metaphorically for current ones (i.e., the very notion of transference is based on this assumption).

In other words, then, particular life experiences and patterns serve us as something of a template: Our perceptions and responses to a new situation are organized and structured as they were in a previous similar situation. Because of their apparent similarities, we then respond to the new situation *as if* it were the earlier one. Moreover, the more ingrained the role, the more it is likely to intrude on later learned roles. The schema the people develop for supervision is shaped in this manner. Figure 1.1 shows, for example, that gender and ethnicity roles are among the most ingrained and therefore permeate much of our behavior, including supervision (see Chapter 5 for a discussion of these roles in supervision).

Professional roles are learned later and therefore are less an ingrained part of ourselves. But, even so, earlier learned professional roles (such as

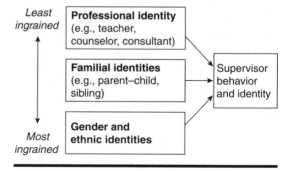

FIGURE 1.1 Life and Professional Roles That Affect Supervisory Role Behavior

that of counselor) are likely to affect later learned professional roles. For those taking on the later learned roles, it is natural, perhaps inevitable, to attempt to understand them in terms of things we do know: It is merely human to attempt to understand that which is the new in terms of that which is familiar.

It should be no surprise, then, that the roles of supervisor and supervisee are at least partially understood as metaphoric expressions of other life experiences. Proctor (1991), for example, commented,

> A number of my colleagues asked me what archetypes went into taking the trainer role; we immediately identified a number. There are the Guru, or Wise Woman, from whom wisdom is expected, and the Earth Mother—the all-provider, unconditional positive regarder. In contrast there is the Clown or Jester—enjoying performance, and cloaking his truth in riddles, without taking responsibility for how it is received. The Patriarch creates order and unselfconsciously wields power. The Actor/Director allocates roles and tasks and holds the Drama; the Bureaucrat demands compliance to the letter of the law. The Whore gives services for money, which can be indistinguishable from love, and re-engages with group after group. There is even the Warrior—valiant for truth; and of course the Judge—upholding standards and impartially assessing. The Shepherd/Sheep-dog gently and firmly rounds up and pens. (p. 65)

These are some possible metaphors for the supervisor. There also are metaphors that speak to the process or experience of supervision, independent of the roles. Therefore, a supervisee (or supervisor) might understand supervision as akin to a lighthouse beacon that provides one with bearings in often foggy situations. Participants in workshops that our colleague, Michael Ellis has run have described supervision as a shepherd and flock, as an oasis on the desert, and (more ominously) as going to the principal's office.

Page and Wosket (1994) employ the metaphor of bicycle riding to describe supervisory process. They suggest that the domain of counseling or therapy might be

> represented by bicycles. There are many different types of two-wheel cycles, some different because

> they are designed and made by different manufacturers who give priority to a particular quality in their product. . . . [W]e could liken counsellor supervision to the tandem—having two riders rather then the usual one . . . [and that they] offer a means whereby an experienced rider might coach an inexperienced one in the saddle. (pp. 3–4)

We believe that these metaphors exist at various levels of awareness. But they often are present and affect participants' expectations and behaviors. The following discussions of more frequently occurring metaphors are therefore in the service of making them available for consideration.

Family Metaphors

Family metaphors seem to be particularly common in supervision. And the most basic of these is that of the parent–child relationship. Lower (1972), for example, employed this metaphor in alluding to the unconscious parent—child fantasies that he believed are stimulated by the supervisory situation itself. In fact, Itzhaky and Sztern (1999) cautioned supervisors against allowing themselves to behave without awareness in what they termed a "pseudo-parental role" (p. 247).

Many theorists have, of course, employed this metaphor of parent–child relationship as a way to think about therapy. As it may apply to supervision, the metaphor simultaneously is both less and more appropriate than for therapy. It is *less* apt in that personal growth is not a primary goal of the intervention, as it is in therapy, but rather is an instrumental goal that works in the service of making the supervisee a better therapist. It is *more* apt, on the other hand, in that supervision is an evaluative relationship just as parenting is—and therapy presumably is not.

Just knowing that they are being evaluated is often sufficient to trigger in supervisees an expectation of a guilt–punishment sequence that recapitulates early parent–child interactions. Supervisors can, through their actions, intensify such transference responses among supervisees, triggering perceptions of them as a good or bad parent. We have heard, for example, of instances in which supervisors posted publicly in the staff lounge the names of supervisees who had too many client "no-shows." The atmosphere created in situations such as this can easily establish supervisory staff as "feared parents."

Still another parallel between parent–child and supervisor–supervisee relationships is that status, knowledge, maturity, and power differences between the participants eventually will begin to disappear. The parties who today are supervisor and supervisee can expect that one day they might relate to one another as peers and colleagues.

The parent–child metaphor is suggested, too, in the frequent use of developmental metaphors to describe supervision. And Hillerbrand's (1989) suggestion that supervisors begin to consider the theorizing of Vygotsky (1978) also suggested this. The following description of Vygotsky's thinking really derives at the most basic level from the manner in which parents teach life tasks to their children:

> [Vygotsky] *proposed that cognitive skills are acquired through social interaction. Unskilled persons learn cognitive skills by assuming more and more responsibility from experts during performance (what he called "expert scaffolding"). Novices first observe an expert's cognitive activity while the experts do most of the work. As novices begin to perform the skills, they receive feedback from the experts on their performance; as they learn to perform the skill correctly, they begin to assume more responsibility for the cognitive skill. Finally, novices assume the major responsibility for the cognitive skill, and experts become passive observers.* (Hillerbrand, 1989, p. 294)

A second family metaphor that can pertain in supervision is that of older and younger sibling. For many supervisory dyads, this probably is more apt than the parent–child metaphor. The supervisor is farther along on the same path being traveled by the supervisee. As such, she or he is in a position to show the way in a nurturing, mentoring relationship. But, as with siblings, issues of competence can sometimes trigger competition over who is more skilled or more brilliant in understanding the client.

The older–younger sibling metaphor is structurally similar to the relationship between master craftspersons and their apprentices. Such relationships have existed for thousands of years and are perpetuated in supervision. In these relationships, master craftspersons serve as mentors to the people who aspire to enter the occupation, showing them the skills, procedures, and culture of the occupation. In this manner, too, master craftspersons help to perpetuate the craft. Eventually, after what is usually a stipulated period of apprenticeship, the apprentices becomes peers of the craftspersons.

These metaphors, particularly those of parenting or sibling, occur at fundamental and often primitive levels. Because they influence in an immediate and felt way, they have special and probably ongoing influence on the supervisory relationship. Moreover, such metaphors probably operate outside the awareness of the supervisor.

If it is true that supervision is a unique intervention, then one might reasonably infer that there is a unique role characteristic of supervisors in general. In a broad sense, this is true, and we can identify at least two major components of this generic supervisory role. The first of these is the perspective from which the supervisor views his or her work; the second pertains to the commonly endorsed expectation that the supervisor will give feedback to the supervisee.

This topic of supervisor roles is one to which we will give greater attention in Chapter 4, as we discuss social role models of supervision. There are, though, aspects of it that are important to cover at this point.

Liddle (1988) discussed the transition from therapist to supervisor as a role-development process that involves several evolutionary steps. An essential early step is for the emerging supervisor to make a shift in focus. That is, the supervisor eventually must realize that the purpose of supervision is neither to treat the client indirectly through the supervisee nor to provide psychotherapy to the supervisee.

Borders (1992) discussed this same step in the supervisor-to-be's professional evolution. She maintained that the supervisor-to-be must make a cognitive shift as he or she switches from the role of counselor or therapist. To illustrate how difficult this often is for new supervisors, she gave the example of a neophyte supervisor who persisted for some time in referring to his supervisee as "my client." Until he was able to correctly label the trainee's role in relation to himself, his perceptual set remained that of a therapist.

This shift, then, requires the supervisor to give up doing what might be thought of as "therapy by proxy," "therapy by remote control," or what Fiscalini (1997) called therapy "by ventriloquism." We would note, however, that the pull to doing this may always remain present, even if unexpressed in practice. In part, this is reinforced by the supervisor's mandate always to function as a monitor of client care, vigilant about how the client is functioning. Similarly, the longer the person has functioned as a therapist, the harder it may be for the supervisor to make the necessary shift in perspective. It is interesting to note, for example, that Carl Rogers talked about having occasionally experienced the strong impulse to take over the therapy of a supervisee, likening himself to an old fire horse heeding the call (Hackney & Goodyear, 1984).

Borders (1989a), in fact, observed that untrained professionals do not necessarily make this shift on their own, simply as a result of experience as a supervisor. As a matter of fact, some "experienced" professionals seem to have more difficulty changing their thinking than do doctoral students and advanced master's students in supervision courses. This is consistent with what we depict in Figure 1.1: The more ingrained the role, the more it is pervasive and influencing of current behavior.

A CONCEPTUAL MODEL OF SUPERVISION

The conceptual model depicted in Figure 1.2, an adaptation of the competencies cube developed by Bent et al. (2002) is the framework that guides our thinking about supervision. It also has influenced our organization of this book. This is a three-dimensional model in which the three dimensions are what we have labeled *Supervisor Tasks, Parameters of Supervision,* and *Supervisee Developmental Level.*

Supervision Parameters

These are the features of supervision that undergird *all* that occurs in supervision, regardless of the particular supervisory function or the level of the supervisee. For example, the supervisor's model or theory is a factor at all times. So, too, is the supervisory relationship and each of the other of the parameters listed in the figure.

Supervisee Developmental Level

We assume that supervisees need different supervisory environments as they develop professionally. Although we discuss supervisee developmental levels specifically in only Chapters 5 and 6, concern with this issue pervades the entire book. The manner in which supervisors intervene differs according to supervisee level. As well, the expression of each parameter (e.g., relationship or evaluation) is affected by developmental level.

As we discuss later in the book, different supervision theorists each have suggested a different number of stages through which supervisees

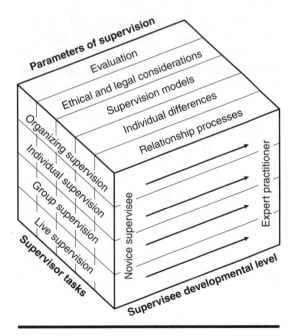

FIGURE 1.2 Conceptual Model of Supervision

progress. We have drawn Figure 1.2, though, in a way to suggest that we do not take a stand on exactly how many of these stages there actually are. We believe it is sufficient here simply to make clear that developmental processes affect all that we do as supervisors.

Supervisor Tasks

Supervisor tasks are the actual behaviors of the supervisors. In this book, we discuss the four depicted in Figure 1.2. It is possible, of course, to think of more. But we believe these four are the most frequently employed.

Using the Model

We assume that the three dimensions interact with one another. To illustrate, consider the supervisor who is using individual supervision: He or she will do so within the context of a relationship and that work will be guided by the supervisor's particular theory or model, attention to supervisee's individual differences (e.g., ethnicity or gender), and ethical and legal factors; the fact of evaluation will affect it as well. The developmental level of the supervisee, then, moderates each of these things.

We should note that we are not attempting in this model to capture *all* that occurs in supervision. This is especially true with respect to our discussion of supervisor tasks. We recognize, for example, that individual, group, and live supervision are not the only modalities. Kell and Burow (1970), for example, discussed the use of conjoint treatment as a supervision modality. But, although this is not a modality included in Figure 1.2, it is easy enough to see how conjoint treatment might be fit into the conceptual model.

The next ten chapters each address features of this model. We hope that with this conceptual framework the reader will more readily see how the particular topic being covered fits within the larger picture of supervision, as least as we envision that picture.

The book's final chapter does not speak specifically to the conceptual model. Instead, it address topics—the teaching of supervision and supervision research issues—that have the purpose of enhancing supervisory practice.

CONCLUSION

The purpose of this chapter was to lay the groundwork for the material that follows. We hope we have been effective in establishing the basis for and importance of supervision, by offering a formal definition of supervision and considering possible idiosyncratic definitions of supervision that occur at less manifest levels. We also hope our conceptual model will be useful in thinking about supervision and the ways its various aspects relate to one another.

We also address the historical context, importance, and prevalence of supervision. We then consider definitions, both formal and more personal. We conclude by presenting the conceptual model that both informs our understanding about supervision and guides the organization of this book.

We alluded early in the chapter to the two realms of knowledge (Schön, 1983) that are the basis of professional training: the theory and research that are the focus of university training and the knowledge derived from practitioners' experience. We asserted, too, that these actually are complementary knowledge domains (e.g., Holloway, 1995). Because of this conviction, material in this book is drawn from both realms of knowledge with the belief that each informs the other. That is, in the course of our work we draw both from theoretical and empirical literature and from literature that describes the insights and practices of supervisors themselves.

CHAPTER 2

EVALUATION

Evaluation could be viewed as the nucleus of clinical supervision. In fact, as we noted in Chapter 1, evaluation is a defining aspect of supervision. Supervisors direct and encourage, but also monitor, those who enter the helping professions. The ethical and legal issues surrounding supervision are primarily embedded in the evaluation function. Many of the more direct methods for conducting clinical supervision have developed, in part, as a response to a need to evaluate more accurately.

As central as it is to proper functioning of clinical supervision, most supervisors are troubled by evaluation, at least occasionally. Some view it as a necessary evil; a few see it as antithetical to the helping professions (Cohen, 1987). Part of the problem is that clinical supervisors were first trained as counselors–therapists, and their values often lie within that domain. Therapists are taught to accept their clients' limitations and to respect their clients' goals. Like good parents, good therapists learn to respect the boundary between clients' ambitions for themselves and therapists' ambitions for them. The good therapist is a facilitator of another's change and is not a decision maker about what change is necessary.

Many of the working conditions within supervision reflect those for therapy. Yet there is an essential, paradigmatic difference: The supervisor might want to use the supervisee's progress as the critical criterion for evaluation, but responsibility to the profession and to the supervisee's future clients would preclude this. The supervisor is charged to evaluate the supervisee based on some external set of criteria. These criteria must meet institutional standards, but also reflect national standards of practice (Robiner, Fuhrman, Ristvedt, Bobbitt, & Schirvar, 1994). An essential assumption underlying evaluation is that the criteria chosen or derived from professional standards reflect competent practice. Herein lies the first major obstacle in conducting sound evaluation.

Robiner, Fuhrman, and Ristvedt (1993) described clinical competence as a "moving target with an elusive criterion" (p. 5). Although the accrediting and state regulatory bodies of the helping professions prescribe knowledge and skill standards, the research continues to undermine the assumption that particular types of therapist knowledge, skill, or level of experience determine client outcome (Herman, 1993). Rather, reviews of the outcome literature have produced mixed results (e.g., Pinsof & Wynne, 1995; Shaw & Dobson, 1988), and some continue to support the notion that nonspecific factors such as the counselor's personal characteristics might be the more predictive of successful outcome with clients (Herman, 1993; Orlinsky, Grawe, & Parks, 1994; Shaw & Dobson, 1988). Because of this, helping professionals have not yet determined definitively the educational experiences that yield competent practitioners nor have they developed performance measures that reliably distinguish competent from incompetent practitioners (Robiner et al., 1993).

Of course, the confrontive conclusion that some or much of training may be irrelevant to producing a competent practitioner makes highly credentialed professionals defensive, including most clinical supervisors. Intuitively, most professionals believe, even in the absence of conclusive data, that training and experience matter and that there are specific knowledge and skill that professionals must possess. As a logical outgrowth of this belief, clinical supervisors assume that they are responsible for monitoring trainees' development of knowledge and skill. The helping professions continue to seek better research to indicate which aspects of training are especially important; in the meantime, it is safe to assume that supervisors will continue to evaluate supervisees based on their own knowledge of what is understood in their professional community to constitute acceptable standards of practice.

Given the consistent finding that personal characteristics of therapists are highly predictive of success (Herman, 1993; Sakinofsky, 1979), it may be of some comfort to clinical supervisors that the personal characteristics of trainees and supervisors alike have always been considered relevant to supervision, as is evidenced in this text by the amount of space given to issues like the supervision relationship, individual differences, and ethics as personal morality. On the other hand, these same personal characteristics often lead to some of the most difficult evaluation moments, as we will review later in this chapter (Forrest, Elman, Gizara, & Vacha-Haase, 1999). Finally, this is a time when the call for more rigorous evaluations has increased due to legal accountability and the escalating sophistication of therapy modalities (Glenn & Serovich; 1994; Hahn & Molnar, 1991). In summary, then, clinical supervisors must evaluate within professional guidelines (that may reflect the accumulated experience of the profession in the absence of clear outcome research), sensitive to the importance of trainees' personal characteristics (including cultural characteristics) that parallel training, but are not necessarily affected by it, and cognizant of an increasingly litigious society. They do this in the absence of any comprehensive understanding of what exactly contributed to their own competence, as either a counselor–practitioner or a supervisor.

These two factors, then, the incompatibility of evaluation with their professional identity as helping professionals and the inadequacy of relevant outcome studies to determine the salient ingredients of therapeutic competence, can combine to cause considerable dissonance when supervisors are required to evaluate. Supervisors have two choices for managing this dissonance: They can throw up their hands and minimize the function of evaluation in their supervision or they can work

to counteract both dissonance-causing factors by thoughtful planning, structuring, intervening, and communicating. The rest of this chapter can be viewed as an outline of topics for consideration by those who will face evaluation head on and complete its requirements to the best of their ability, even in light of imperfect or incomplete criteria, within a social context that exhibits greater demands for accountability.

The first step for the supervisor is to plan a clear distinction between *formative* and *summative* evaluation. Robiner et al. (1993) described formative assessment as the process of facilitating skill acquisition and professional growth through direct feedback. As such, they contended that formative evaluation causes little discomfort for clinical supervisors. Formative evaluation indeed represents the bulk of the supervisor's work with the supervisee and does not necessarily feel like evaluation, because it stresses the process and progress of professional competence, rather than outcome. Nevertheless, it is important to remember that there is an evaluative message in all supervision. When supervisors tell trainees that an intervention was successful, they are evaluating. When supervisors say nothing, trainees may either decide that their performance was exemplary or too awful to discuss. In other words, by virtue of the nature of the relationship, evaluation is a constant variable in supervision. Some of the supervisor's evaluative comments are deliberately sent (encoded) by the supervisor to the trainee; others are received (decoded) by the trainee and may or may not be an accurate understanding of the supervisor's assessments. Because we are always communicating, an evaluative message can always be inferred.

Summative evaluation, on the other hand, is what many of us mean when we discuss evaluation and causes far more stress for both supervisors and supervisees. This is the moment of truth when the supervisor steps back, takes stock, and decides how the supervisee measures up. To do this, supervisors must be clear about the criteria against which they are measuring supervisees. Furthermore, the supervisee should possess the same yardstick.

In truth, summative evaluations are often stressful because they are disconnected from what has come before in the supervision relationship. Either because of lack of organization or lack of a clear set of standards, the supervisor may conduct summative evaluation in a vague or biased way. A supervisor who is helpful and articulate during the formative contacts can appear rushed and insecure at a summative conference. Robiner et al. (1993) asserted that, because of the trepidation or ambivalence caused by summative assessment, a generalized disdain for evaluation may result "despite its central importance in the supervisory process" (p. 4). Because summative evaluations are those that influence major educational and administrative decisions, such disdain is highly problematic. The chief antidote to summative disdain is the amount of time and care invested in the formative evaluation process. But before any evaluation begins, the difficult task of identifying criteria must be addressed.

CRITERIA FOR EVALUATION

Choosing criteria for evaluation is a less than perfect process when the research regarding what is essential for supervisees to learn under supervision is generally wanting. Ironically, although the professions lack clear empirical direction about the necessary conditions for competence, the increasing fear of litigation has forced professionals to grapple with definitions of impairment (i.e., gross lack of competence). We will address the issue of impairment later in this chapter.

Overholser and Fine (1990) cited five areas of competence that should be established for any supervisee: factual knowledge, generic clinical skills, orientation-specific technical skills, clinical judgment, and interpersonal attributes. Each of the mental health professions tends to address similar areas of competence for trainees. For example, Perlesz, Stolk, and Firestone (1990) tracked criteria for competence in marriage and family therapy and used perceptual skills (ability to make pertinent and accurate observations), conceptual skills (the process of attributing meaning to ob-servations), and executive–intervention skills (ability to respond within sessions in a deliberate manner), as well as demonstrated personal development, as the targeted criteria. With the growing sensitivity to cultural variables in therapy, multicultural competence is increasingly identified as essential (Larson et al., 1992; Vasquez, 1999).

Interpersonal and intrapersonal skills are essential as well. Frame and Stevens-Smith (1995) have made a serious attempt to operationalize and categorize those skills. Based on a review of the literature, Frame and Stevens-Smith identified nine trainee functions that have been cited as essential for success as professional counselors: students being open, flexible, positive, and cooperative; willing to accept and use feedback; aware of one's impact on others; and able to deal with conflict, accept personal responsibility, and express feelings effectively and appropriately. Frame and Stevens-Smith suggested that these functions be published for student consumption and that students be evaluated on them on a regular basis.

Although there are frequent messages in the professional literature about the importance of theoretical consistency, published information about the formation of criteria refers to this criterion only in the most general way (e.g., Overholser & Fine, 1990). For training programs that insist on theoretical consistency, criteria must be developed that are also theoretically consistent. Because professional standards tend to be theory neutral, it is up to training programs and clinical sites to translate standards into adequately specific criteria. For example, if a supervisor is working with a supervisee who has declared cognitive behavioral theory as the theory of choice, the supervisor needs to measure the supervisee's progress based on criteria that reflect a cognitive behavioral approach to working with clients. If the supervisor uses, for example, Bernard's (1979, 1997) Discrimination Model, the supervisor must develop criteria that describe the interventions used in cognitive behavioral therapy, the ways to conceptualize a problem that reflect a cognitive behavioral approach, and the therapist's appropriate use of self when conducting cognitive behavioral therapy. Developing such criteria would in and of itself be a highly worthwhile supervision activity and could become part of the supervision contract (see Chapter 8). And, of course, if the supervisor feels uncomfortable, inadequate, or simply unwilling to supervise according to a particular model of treatment, that too would be negotiated as an aspect of the contract.

The point is that models of delivering therapeutic services and models of supervision are not independent from the task of establishing criteria. If criteria do not directly reflect these, they will be less helpful to the supervisee. If they contradict these, they become an obstruction to learning, rather than a guide.

Focusing on criteria for one aspect of clinical expertise (the ability to conduct a diagnostic interview), Rudolph, Craig, Leifer, and Rubin (1998) identified the following: structure the interview, forge a working alliance, facilitate interviewee participation and disclosure, collect data and pursue inquiry, and maintain professional conduct. Rudolph et al. asserted that trainees welcome clear communication of expectations. Therefore, they argued that the faculty time spent in developing and agreeing on criteria for each major clinical function was worthwhile.

Another approach to arriving at criteria is to conduct a systemic investigation of what supervisors tend to focus on during supervision sessions (e.g., Carey & Lanning, 1993; Lanning & Freeman, 1994). By tracking the behavior of supervisors, a list of criteria will eventually develop. Basically, this process adheres to a "trust what I do, not what I say" assumption.

Accrediting bodies have become central in defining criteria, though they tend to avoid any reference to personal characteristics except in terms of admissions and termination policy. All the mental health professions have accrediting bodies that establish standards for the education of persons entering the profession. These standards include core areas of knowledge and often specialized curricular areas (e.g., school counseling or mental health counseling), as well as stipulations for clinical training. These standards, then, become the criteria for evaluation, at least for predegree candidates. Bradley and Fiorini (1999) found that CACREP programs' translation of standards for criteria demonstrating clinical competence are fairly uniform.

Accreditation standards also tend to increase in number over time, whether because of the increased complexity of mental health delivery (Hahn & Molnar, 1991) or because it is human nature to add rather than subtract when it comes to criteria (Mohl, Sadler, & Miller, 1994). For better or worse, professional standards are used by training institutions and state regulatory bodies to assess persons entering specific mental health professions and are therefore legitimate compilations of criteria for evaluation. It should be noted, however, that even when criteria are specified, expected competency *levels* often remain illusive to both supervisees and supervisors (Magnuson, 1995).

Robiner et al. (1993) reported the result of APA's Joint Council on Professional Education in Psychology's (Stigall et al., 1990) attempt to delineate exit criteria for psychology doctoral internships. The eight areas of competence identified by the council are effective interpersonal functioning; ability to make sound professional judgments; ability to extend and expand basic assessment and intervention techniques to meet the needs of different settings, problems, and populations; ability to apply ethical and legal principles to practice; ability to assess and intervene appropriately with clients manifesting diverse characteristics; development of a primary professional identity as a psychologist; awareness of personal strengths and limitations and the need for continued supervision, consultation, and education; and preparedness to enter residency training and to choose appropriate advanced training. In addition to these, the Joint Council recommended that personal characteristics such as psychological health and awareness of self be considered as entry-level criteria for admission to professional training programs. Although generic in nature, these criteria most definitely offer a place to begin for outlining more specific behaviors for evaluation and can easily be translated to other mental health professions. The sentiment of attending to the psychological health of trainees was echoed by Johnson and Campbell (2002), who chastised the profession of psychology for not establishing character and fitness criteria for entrance into professional programs. Noting that the remediation efforts of impaired or incompetent practitioners have not been particularly promising, they asserted that criteria for entrance and retention in programs must be more rigorous.

Job analyses, or an investigation of the knowledge and skills used by persons in targeted mental health positions, are also used as a method for arriving at criteria for evaluation (e.g., Fitzgerald & Osipow, 1986; National Board for Certified Counselors, 1993). The limitation of job analyses, however, is that "they inform us *what is* rather than what *should* or *could be.* While this process is legally defensible (e.g., as a licensure exam), it does not move a profession forward. Forward movement occurs in the interplay among market forces, training programs, and accrediting bodies (Goodyear, Cortese, Guzzardo, Allison, Claiborn, & Packard, 2000).

In summary, establishing criteria for evaluation may be the most challenging and conceivably most labor-intensive aspect of the evaluation process. To meet this challenge, the supervisor will draw from accrediting body standards, program values, research, and general advice of professionals found in the mental health literature and in practice. The difficulty of establishing criteria for evaluation and the equally difficult task of measuring them is a professional reality. We do not presume to offer a definitive list of criteria. Rather, we stress that, regardless of what criteria the supervisor identifies, the formative and summative evaluations should relate directly to these same criteria. It is not unheard of for supervisors to find themselves hunting for an evaluation form at the end of the supervisory relationship as if the summative evaluation had no relationship to the formative sessions that had preceded it. On the contrary, whatever is to be used at the end of supervision to summarize the trainee's progress should be introduced early in supervision, should serve as teaching–learning objectives, and should be used

throughout supervision as the basis for intermittent feedback.

FAVORABLE CONDITIONS FOR EVALUATION

A major problem with evaluation in the helping professions is that it hits so close to home. Because counseling and therapy draw heavily on interpersonal and intuitive abilities, it can be difficult for trainees to draw a boundary between their performance as helping professionals and their worth as a person. For this reason and because of the vulnerability accompanying any evaluation process, it is important that supervisors do all that is possible to create favorable conditions when evaluating. Favorable conditions not only make evaluation more palatable, but directly influence the overall outcome of supervision. As Ekstein and Wallerstein (1972) noted, when the context of supervision is favorable, the trainee stops asking "How can I avoid criticism?" and starts asking "How can I make the most of this supervision time?"

Several authors have addressed the conditions that make evaluation a more positive experience. Several of these conditions also assure that the evaluation process is conducted in an ethical manner (see Chapter 3). They also draw on information presented elsewhere in this text. The following list of conditions draws from our own thoughts as well as the work of Borders et al. (1991); Coffey (2002); Ekstein and Wallerstein (1972); Forrest et al. (1999); Fox (1983); Fried, Tiegs, and Bellamy (1992); Kadushin (1992a); Ladany, Hill, Corbett, and Nutt (1996); Lopez (1997); Mathews (1986); and Olson and Stern (1990):

1. Supervisors must remember that supervision is an unequal relationship. No amount of empathy will erase the fact that supervisors' reactions to supervisees will have consequences for them, some of which may be negative. Being sensitive to the position of the supervisee will make supervisors more compassionate evaluators.

2. Clarity adds to a positive context. Supervisors need to state clearly their administrative as well as clinical roles. Who will be privy to the feedback that supervisors give supervisees? Will the supervisor be making decisions regarding the supervisee's continuation in a graduate program or job? If not, what is the supervisor's relationship to those persons who make these decisions? For example, most graduate programs conduct periodic student reviews. At these reviews the evaluation by the clinical supervisor is often weighed more heavily than other evaluations. Students should be aware, at the very least, that their performance in the clinical component of the program will be discussed by the total faculty at some point in the future. Clarity can also be communicated by structure. Supervisors must provide structure appropriate to the developmental level of the supervisee. Congenial supervisors who allow supervisees to flounder will eventually forfeit any goodwill that they initially may have earned.

3. Clarity of supervisee expectations and roles is essential as well. For example, Nelson and Friedlander (2001) found the unclear role expectations among supervisees was highly predictive of conflictual supervision.

4. Evaluation procedures should be spelled out in advance. Whatever process has been decided on, it should be known by the supervisee. Differences between formative and summative evaluation should be explained. Among the procedural topics that should be included are the projected length of the supervisory relationship, the preferred methods of supervision and how these will be used, any additional sources that will be used to determine the supervisee's progress, the frequency of supervision conferences, and how the evaluation will be conducted and used.

5. Supervisees' defensiveness should be addressed openly (Coffey, 2002; Costa, 1994). Supervision makes trainees feel naked, at least initially. It is natural, if not desirable, that they attempt to defend themselves. Trainees differ in their coping styles, some exhibiting behaviors that are far more productive than others. Some will deal with their feeling of defensiveness by "digging in deeper" and doing all that they can to get on the same page as the supervisor; others will defend by trying to outguess the supervisor; still others will

appear vulnerable and helpless. The truth is that all supervisees are vulnerable, and supervisors need to be sensitive to this fact and not hold their vulnerability against them.

Coffey (2002) suggested that supervisors take time at the outset of supervision to teach students how to receive corrective feedback. The source of defensive reactions and how they have served one in the past need to be understood by supervisees so that they can process these reactions in light of the present situation. Coffey proposed that the use of awareness-enhancing exercises is well worth the time spent so that supervisees can understand their defensive reactions and process them when they occur, so as to be in a better position to determine the usefulness of the supervisor's corrective feedback.

6. Along with defensiveness, individual differences should be addressed openly. Evaluation may well be affected by differences of background, gender, race, and so forth, particularly if these differences are not understood to be relevant to supervision. Furthermore, competence in therapy includes the ability to communicate in ways that are culturally flexible. The first cultural context to be addressed, therefore, is the supervision context.

7. Evaluation should be a mutual process and a continuous process. The supervisee should be actively involved in determining what is to be learned (Lehrman-Waterman & Ladany, 2001). In a sense, the supervisor is there to serve the trainee, and this contractual dimension should not get lost. Also, the formative aspect of evaluation should be the most active. Although both parties know that there must be a taking stock down the road, the process and evaluation of the learning should not feel static.

8. Evaluation must occur within a strong administrative structure. Whether in an educational or work setting, supervisors must know that their evaluations will stick. Nothing is as frustrating and damaging as when a supervisor risks the consequences of a negative evaluation only to have this overturned by an administrator in the organization. When this happens, more often than not, one of two things has happened. Either due process was not followed, or the supervisor did not have a clear sense of administrative support beforehand. In other words, the supervisor assumed that he or she would be backed up without bothering to check. Or the supervisor did not have the political savvy to inform his or her superiors prior to the evaluation, both to warn them and to make sure that the process would be supported. Whether the supervisor is correct in the evaluation can be a moot issue if the trainee's rights were not protected, or appeared not to be protected, during the evaluation process. It is as important that the system be trustworthy in the supervisee's eyes as from the supervisor's perspective. If the history of the system is that evaluation is arbitrary or capricious, supervisees will risk less and will be more defensive overall in their interactions with supervisors.

Finally, it is as important that the supervisee be cognizant of a supportive structure as it is for the supervisor. Supervisees must know that there is a place to go if they think an evaluation is unfair or incomplete. On university campuses, the grievance committee is usually the administrative body of choice once the head of the department has been consulted; in employment settings, the supervisor's immediate superior would be the appropriate person. If there is no such protective body or person, it is up to the supervisor to establish some sort of safeguard for the supervisee (e.g., through a Professional Disclosure Statement that provides pertinent information in this regard). Supervision objectives will be greatly handicapped if anyone in the system feels trapped. (Chapter 8 addresses administrative practices that assist the evaluation process.)

9. Premature evaluations of supervisees should be avoided. Whether a supervisor is working with one trainee or several, it is important to resist overreacting to the person who shows unusual potential or the person who seems to be faltering. We are not implying that one should withhold feedback or be dishonest. Rather, we believe that supervisors often react too quickly and, by evaluating too quickly, can do serious disservice to talented supervisees, as well as to those who need more grounding to begin their better work. If supervision occurs in a group, morale is hurt when it becomes obvious that early distinctions have been made among trainees. On the contrary, when the group is challenged to ensure that everyone achieve competence, the atmosphere is energetic, supportive, and competitive in the best sense.

Some trainees will enter supervision expecting to be recognized and treated as stars. It is the supervisor, however, who makes such a designation happen by relying on initial impressions and forgetting that some counseling or therapy skills can only be assessed accurately over the long term. Whether a trainee wears well will be terribly important to the trainee's future colleagues, supervisors, and clients. This cannot be determined in a few weeks, regardless of the strength of the supervisee's entry behavior or the intuitive abilities of the supervisor.

10. Supervisees need to witness the professional development of their supervisors. As a supervisor, the best way to do this is to invite feedback and use it. Supervisees feel empowered if they sense that they have something valuable to offer their supervisors. Additionally, a supervisor's involvement and sharing of continuing education activities models the need for development across the life-span of one's career. For supervisors to present new ideas that they have recently been exposed to gives a much more accurate picture of the profession than for them to play the part of the all-knowing guru. Also, presenting some tentativeness in thinking will remind the supervisor to be tentative about the work of trainees. Supervisors must constantly remind themselves that they do not deal in a profession of facts, but of concepts.

11. Supervisors must always keep an eye to the relationship, which interacts with all aspects of supervision. Evaluation becomes especially difficult when the relationship has become too close or too distant. In fact, it is the reality of evaluation that behooves the supervisor to maintain both a positive and supportive relationship with the supervisee— yet one that is professional, not personal. If relationships are strained for whatever reason, supervisors must ask themselves if they can evaluate objectively enough. (No evaluation is totally objective; the goal is to keep objective standards in mind while considering subjective impressions.) This point was underscored by Ladany et al. (1996), who found that negative reactions to the supervisor, personal issues, clinical mistakes, and evaluation concerns were the top four categories of supervisee nondisclosures in supervision. A weak relationship between supervisor and supervisee, then, can cause the supervisee to withhold essential supervision information.

Some personalities clash, and the best intentions do not make the initial dislike for the trainee or supervisor disappear. The supervisee should not bear the brunt of this kind of situation. Whenever supervision is conducted, some thought should be given to the possibility of strong incompatibility, and at least a sketchy plan should be in place for how to resolve such a problem. In short, it is the supervisee's right to trust the supervisor. A relationship without trust will be one of avoidance and mixed messages, which is poor material to culminate in an accurate evaluation.

12. No one who does not enjoy supervising should supervise. For this final condition, we go back to the point we made at the beginning of this chapter: Evaluation is difficult, even for those supervisors who love the challenge of supervision. For the supervisor who is supervising for any lesser reason, evaluation may feel like too great a burden. When this is the case, the supervisor will shortchange the trainee and give perfunctory evaluations or avoid the task, especially if the evaluation could be confrontive. Supervisors always have many other responsibilities to use as rationalizations for keeping a trainee at arm's length. It is not difficult to find a helping professional who can attest to the frustration of getting little or no constructive feedback from a supervisor (Magnuson, Wilcoxon, & Norem, 2000). Whenever a trainee is denied appropriate supervision and evaluation, the professional community is diminished.

Although the conditions listed above will not compensate for weak criteria or a poor process, they assure a sensitivity to the supervisee's rights and a realization of the seriousness of the contract between supervisor and supervisee. Seriousness, however, is an attribute that Sanville (1989) en-couraged supervisors to keep in check and is a point we will close with. Viewing play as a primary source of creative curiosity, imagination, and openness to surprise, Sanville advanced playfulness in supervision as a favorable condition. She described effective playfulness as including (1) an awareness that the activity is voluntary, (2) an appreciation that supervision is separate from real life, thus allowing the supervisee to recollect feelings from therapy sessions in a less charged manner than might be the case otherwise, (3) a realization that confusion is normative and the ability to tolerate "not knowing" is a prerequisite to arriving at new insights, (4) a feeling that supervision is a safe place where failures do not lead to catastrophic consequences, and (5) permission to challenge even the most sacrosanct methods and assumptions of the profession.

THE PROCESS OF EVALUATION

We have discussed the important task of choosing criteria and have made brief reference to using some sort of evaluation instrument to communicate a final assessment regarding the supervisee's level of competence. These, respectively, comprise the beginning and the end of evaluation. *Process* defines how supervisors conduct their business between these two markers and how they incorporate the issue of evaluation from the beginning of supervision to its completion. In other words, the process of evaluation is not separate from the process of clinical supervision, but is embedded within it. The evaluation process also includes the means by which supervisors obtain the data that they use to make their assessments, a topic more completely addressed in Chapters 9, 10, and 11. For our discussion here, the process of evaluation will be considered as having six elements, most of which interact throughout the supervision experience: negotiating a supervision–evaluation contract, choosing evaluation methods and supervision interventions, choosing evaluation instrument(s), communicating formative feedback, encouraging self-assessment, and conducting formal summative evaluation sessions.

The Supervision–Evaluation Contract

When students register for a course, they receive a syllabus identifying requirements, course objectives, an outline of activities or topics to be discussed, and the instructor's plan for evaluation. Whether or not clinical experience is gained within a course structure, each supervisee should be provided with a plan that parallels a syllabus. Unlike most course syllabi, however, the supervision contract should include components that are individualized. Described as goal-directed supervision, Talen and Schindler (1993) asserted that supervisee-initiated goals set the stage for a collaborative relationship with the supervisor. Similarly, Lehrman-Waterman and Ladany (2001) found that goal setting with supervisees was highly correlated with a supervisory working alliance and to overall supervisee satisfaction with supervision. Mead (1990) suggested that ample time be given during this process to considering discrepancies between the trainee's goals and those set for the trainee by the supervisor. Mead advised that some goals identified by the trainee may be a residue from past experiences in supervision and may need thorough discussion and modification. A conference regarding a supervision contract serves a purpose for new trainees also in that it helps them to understand the difference between clinical supervision and other learning experiences. Although plans can vary, all supervision contracts should establish training goals, describe criteria for evaluation, establish supervision methods that will be used, describe the length and frequency of supervision contacts, and establish how a summative evaluation will be achieved. The relationship of formative feedback to summative feedback should also be explained to the supervisee. (A more thorough discussion of the makeup of a supervision contract is included in Chapter 8.)

To proceed in a manner that is consistent with goal-directed supervision, each supervisory conference can and perhaps should end with a plan of action for goal attainment and a time frame for completion of the plan. In the same way, each conference should begin with an update on progress toward the goals set at the beginning of the su-pervisory relationship. Middleman and Rhodes (1985) suggested that formative evaluation occur often enough for changes to be suggested with time to implement them before the summative evaluation. In other words, evaluation should be dynamic and relevant throughout the supervision experience, not just at the beginning and end.

A final note about the supervision contract, and one that was confirmed by Talen and Schindler (1993), is the compatibility between this activity and the developmental needs of relatively inexperienced supervisees (Stoltenberg, McNeill, & Delworth, 1998). The structure offered through the process of establishing learning goals supplies the supervisee with a concrete anchor to help weather the onslaught of clinical sessions with all their unknowns.

Choosing Supervision Methods for Evaluation

Each method of supervision—process notes, self-report, audio- or videotapes of therapy sessions, or live supervision—influences evaluation differently. Some supervisors rely heavily on group supervision and may even encourage some form of peer evaluation among supervisees. This approach provides markedly different information than that gathered from, for example, self-report. When the ultimate responsibility to evaluate is paramount in the supervisor's awareness, however, the supervisor will seek supplemental data if they are needed to arrive at a balanced evaluation.

Supervisees can be at a disadvantage when the form of supervision changes from one setting to the next. For example, Collins and Bogo (1986) have observed that early training experiences (on campus) tend to use a good amount of technology, whereas field supervision is more likely to be based on self-report and case notes. Therefore, they found that supervision in the field was far more reflective in nature than that on campus, which focused more on skills. Perhaps supervisors need not only to inform their students about the forms of supervision that they use, but also to educate them about the forms that they do not use.

Of paramount importance is that supervisors realize that supervision interventions have both instructional and evaluation consequences. A supervisor may favor one form of gathering supervision material (e.g., audiotape), but the supervisor must realize that each method is a lens through which to view the work of the supervisee. Some lenses provide the sharper image of one aspect of the supervisee's work, but a wide angle may be desirable on occasion to allow the supervisor a different perspective from which to evaluate. Therefore, multiple methods are the surest way to get an accurate picture of the supervisee's strengths and weaknesses (Harris, 1994).

Choosing Evaluation Instruments

There are nearly as many evaluation instruments as there are training programs in the helping professions. Supervisors tend to develop and use Likert-type measures for summative conferences. Depending on how well a measure reflects criteria that already have been selected and communicated by the supervisor (or negotiated between supervisor and supervisee), the measure may help supervisees to appreciate their progress toward predetermined goals. When evaluation measures have not been integrated into the supervision experience, their use can be superficial or frustrating from the standpoint of the supervisee.

A scientist–practitioner model would call for evaluation measures that are more than communication tools. And yet, to date, most evaluation measures are homegrown and have not weathered psychometric scrutiny. Therefore, they continue to be used primarily as a way to organize feedback for the supervisee and little more.

The most common evaluation instrument continues to be a homegrown, Likert scale, perhaps with some open-ended questions as well. Because of the subsequent quantification of evaluations, supervisees may need some assistance in translating the feedback received. For example, the supervisor must decide what is adequate (numerically speaking) for the supervisee to be assured that this is a positive evaluation. Additionally, it should be clear what level of performance is below standards and what level would be considered as meeting the

highest standards. If a trainee comes into supervision with superior ability in several areas, the Likert-scale ratings should reflect this. Some supervisors use scales differently, deciding that no supervisee should receive a score higher than a certain number (e.g., 5 out of a possible 7) until the supervisory experience is at least half complete. If this is the supervisor's policy, it is important that the supervisee know this. When the supervisor uses a scale in this way, however, the supervisor bypasses the issue of level of accomplishment.

There has been an increasing interest in the development of anchored rubrics (Hahn & Molnar, 1991; Hanna & Smith, 1998). Hahn and Molnar supported their 7-point scale with adequate descriptions at each level in the supervision process (see Table 2.1), especially for summative evaluation. Hanna and Smith developed a similar scale using a 5-point anchored model. Because rubrics describe behaviors expected at different levels of competence, Hanna and Smith argued that they give supervisees a more accurate picture of the level at which they are performing, thus communicating the essential message that clinical competence is a developmental process more than an outcome. Hanna and Smith offered an example of how they use their scale with the skill of establishing a counseling relationship. For Level 5, they suggested that "at least 97% of the time, [the trainee] makes a conscious effort to use the core conditions of counseling: empathy, unconditional positive regard, genuineness, and concreteness/intentionality" (p. 276). A Level 3 is defined as doing so at least 85% of the time "or may have problems with any one core condition on a more frequent basis" (p. 276). A Level 1 is defined as having significant difficulty showing either knowledge or use of these same conditions. Levels 2 and 4 are simply defined as being between a lower and higher level.

Hanna and Smith acknowledged that developing rubrics for clinical assessment is a time-consuming process. It also requires consensus building among all those responsible for the supervision and training of individual trainees. To aid those serious about developing rubrics for as-

TABLE 2.1   Intern Rating Scale

Rate intern using the following 7-point scale:

Level 1   Performs inadequately for an intern in this area. Requires frequent and close supervision and monitoring of basic and advanced tasks in this area.

Level 2   Requires supervision and monitoring in carrying out routine tasks in this area and requires significant supervision and close monitoring in carrying out advanced tasks in this area.

Level 3   Requires some supervision and monitoring in carrying out routine tasks in this area. Requires guidance, training, education, and ongoing supervision for developing advanced skills in this area.

Level 4   Displays mastery of routine tasks in this area. Requires ongoing supervision for performance of advanced skills in this area. The intern occasionally, spontaneously demonstrates advanced skills in this area.

Level 5   Displays mastery of routine tasks in this area. Requires periodic supervision for refinement of advanced skills in this area.

Level 6   Displays mastery of routine tasks in this area. Could continue to benefit from some supervision on advanced and/or nonroutine tasks in this area.

Level 7   Performs at the independent practice level in this area and is capable of teaching others in this area. Performs without the general need of supervision, but consults when appropriate.

From K. Hahn and S. Molnar (1991). *The Counseling Psychologist, 19,* 414–430. Copyright © by the Division of Counseling Psychology. Reprinted by permission of Sage Publications, Inc.

sessment purposes, the authors suggested a 15-step process that begins and ends by seeking consultation from others and includes identifying standards to be evaluated, operationalizing goals, revising on a regular basis, including specific goals for individual trainees, and encouraging self-evaluation for supervisees.

Supervisees also can be encouraged to use Likert-type formats to communicate with their supervisors. Marek, Sandifer, Beach, Coward, and Protinsky (1994) suggested asking supervisees to scale themselves from 1 to 10 on three different issues: satisfaction with therapy, level of confidence in achieving their goals, and level of willingness to do so. By having supervisees make such judgments, communication between supervisor and supervisee is enhanced around these key aspects of supervisee development. In addition to challenging supervisees to reflect about their therapy sessions, Marek et al. suggested using scaling to encourage open communication about the supervision process itself.

The supervisor can also utilize these questions in connection to other issues brought forth by the supervisee and/or to assess how the supervisee's needs are being met in the present context. For example, "Where are you on the scale right now in terms of the case related issues you brought in to supervision today?" "What happened to allow you to move from a seven (7) to an eight (8)?" "What would it look like if you were at an eight and a half (8½)?" "What would you be doing differently?" (p. 62)

Ranging from the most simple measure to a comprehensive rubric, most evaluation tools continue to be paper and pencil instruments that reflect a traditional view of assessment. However, some research activity in the development of new evaluation tools (e.g., Lambert & Meier, 1992) takes advantage of computer technology and may offer ways to standardize supervisee evaluation. Modern advancement notwithstanding, the traditional evaluation tool continues to be almost universal.

Finally, and congruent with a scientist–practitioner posture, supervisors may seek client input or client outcome data for the sake of formative or summative evaluation of supervisees (Galassi & Brooks, 1992). The Session Evaluation Questionnaire developed by Stiles and Snow (1984), for example, is a brief evaluation tool that can be used after each therapy session to obtain impressions from both supervisees and clients regarding session depth (i.e., felt power and value) and smoothness (i.e., comfort and pleasantness) using pairs of bipolar adjective scales. These quantitative scales can be supplemented with open-ended sentence stems such as "I believe the *most* helpful things that happened in today's counseling session were . . . ," "I believe that the *least* helpful things that happened in today's counseling session were . . . ," and "In my next counseling session I would like. . . ." With the high level of control available in many training programs, various types of data, including that derived from single-case designs, can become part of the evaluation strategy (Galassi & Brooks, 1992; White, Rosenthal, & Fleuridas, 1993).

As well, repeated measures of client outcome (i.e., data obtained at each session) can be plotted to provide important trainee feedback. Lambert, Whipple, Smart, Vermeersch, Nielsen, and Hawkins (2001), for example, demonstrated that such feedback to therapists increases levels of eventual gains. To that end, a number of university counseling centers now are using the Outcome Questionnaire-45 (Lambert, Hansen, Umpress, Lunnen, Okiishi, & Burlingame, 1998).

Increasingly, there are more and better choices for clinical supervisors when selecting evaluation instruments. What each supervisor must determine is whether a particular instrument is consistent with the supervisor's criteria, when and how to introduce the instrument to the supervisee, and how to use the instrument as an evaluation *intervention,* rather than being simply a completed form to be filed and forgotten.

Communicating Formative Feedback

When supervisees reflect on their supervision, what comes to mind most often is the quality and quantity of the feedback that they received. Giving feedback is a central activity of clinical supervision and the core of evaluation (Hahn & Molnar, 1991). In a review of the literature describing effective feedback, Lehrman-Waterman and Ladany (2001) reported that feedback should be consistent and objective, ideally based on behaviorally defined standards, free from bias, timely, and clearly understood and specific. Curiously, researchers have given little specific attention to feedback within supervision. The study of Friedlander, Siegel, and Brenock (1989) is a notable exception. It described feedback as a process in which the supervisor verbally shares thoughts and assessment of the supervisee's progress. The evaluation can be either explicit or implicit. For their study, they did not include questions or nonevaluative observations as feedback. Three raters were trained to high levels of agreement (median interjudge agreement rate of 0.92) about the presence or absence of feedback in a particular supervisor speaking turn. These raters then examined each speaking turn of one supervisor across nine supervision sessions (ranging from 45 to 60 minutes in length) with one supervisee. They identified only 14 speaking turns as containing feedback. Eight speaking turns occurred in the last two sessions; sessions 3, 4, and 6 had no feedback whatsoever.

The Friedlander et al. (1989) study was an intensive case study. Therefore, the results might be idiosyncratic to the particular dyad studied and may not apply to supervision in general. Yet supervisees who responded in Kadushin's (1992b) national survey also reported receiving far too little direct feedback in supervision, especially feedback that was critical. Therefore, it seems reasonable to ask the question of how frequently constructive feedback, as most supervisors understand it, actually is provided in supervision. This question is especially important to ask in light of the findings Magnuson et al. (2000) that former supervisee's listed not receiving adequate feedback as one definition of "lousy supervision." Similarly, Lehrman-Waterman and Ladany (2001) found receiving feedback to be highly related to satisfaction with supervision. In fact, these authors recommended that supervisors engage in increased goal setting and feedback if they feel they have a troubled relationship with a supervisee. Feedback, then, is viewed by these researchers as a corrective measure to put the supervisory relationship back on good footing.

The feedback described thus far relies primarily on a linear model, originating from the supervisor to the supervisee. Another view of feedback is the interactional (e.g., see Claiborn & Lichtenberg, 1989), which allows us to think of feedback as ongoing and constant between the supervisor and the supervisee. Two premises are basic to understanding the interactional perspective. The first is that you cannot *not* communicate. This premise has been suggested as an axiom of communication by Watzlawick, Beavin, and Jackson (1967). It means, for example, that even the act of ignoring another person is feedback to that person, communicating a message such as "Leave me alone" or, perhaps, "You are not important enough for me to talk with."

The second premise essential to understanding the interactional perspective is that any communication to another person contains both a message about the relationship between the two parties and a message about some particular content (Watzlawick et al., 1967). For example, within the context of supervision, the content may be about a particular, difficult moment in the supervisee's session with a client; the message about the relationship, however, might be "I enjoy working with you" or "This relationship is very tenuous." If the feedback about the relationship is negative or more pronounced than the content, it will be more difficult for the supervisee to hear the content in the way that the supervisor would like. For this reason, the relationship between supervisor and supervisees receives much attention in the professional literature (see Chapters 5, 6, and 7). Finally, it is imperative to remember that the supervisor is not only delivering both levels of feedback, but receiving both levels and reacting to these. The idea of supervisor feedback, therefore, is deceptively simple when compared to the actual interactive process.

There are instances when supervisor and supervisee do not see eye to eye. Ratliff, Wampler, and Morris (2000) studied communication styles using a qualitative design when there was a lack of consensus between supervisor and supervisee. Their findings suggested that supervisors tend to be subtle more often than not in attempting to direct supervisees toward their own position. At the same time, Ratliff et al. found that supervisors engaged in a progression of supervision strategies, from low confrontation (e.g., asking leading questions) to high confrontation (e.g., giving explicit direction), when lack of consensus about the direction of therapy emerged. In their discussion, these authors raised the issue of increased autonomy (i.e., accurate self-evaluation) among supervisees as an important goal of supervision. They suggested that supervisors consider the negative consequences when consensus is the goal, especially if they rely on confrontational strategies to accomplish consensus, potentially leading to heightened supervisee dependency in the process.

Despite an acknowledgment that supervision includes give and take, convergence of thinking and occasional divergence, most supervisors conceptualize feedback per se as communicating to the supervisee an evaluation of particular behaviors as either on target or off, as either progressing toward competence or diverging in a different direction. The clarity of supervisors' communications is of paramount importance. Each message will affirm, encourage, challenge, discourage, confuse, or anger a supervisee. If the meta-message is different from the stated message, the result will be an unclear communication. The most serious communication problem is when the message is dishonest, either intentionally or unintentionally. This typically happens when the supervisor does not want to deal with the fact that the trainee is not meeting expectations. As a result, the supervisor is not prepared to address the critical issues (Magnuson et al., 2000).

The interaction of supervisor discomfort and lack of communication clarity is why evaluation is often considered one of the supervisor's weaker areas (Bernard, 1981). Borders and Leddick (1987) suggested that feedback to trainees focus on specific behavior and delineate alternative behavior. They also addressed the importance of the supervisor's willingness to confront and pointed out that confrontations challenge strengths rather than weaknesses. But, as Munson (2002) asserted, there will be times when the supervisor must criticize the trainee. Borrowing from the work of Weisinger and Lobsenz (1981), Munson outlined 20 suggestions for supervisors to consider when delivering criticism. Among these, Munson urged supervisors to criticize only in ways that promote personal growth and that allows the trainees to use the criticism to their own advantage and benefit; to focus only on behaviors that can be changed and to be specific in their criticism; to offer criticism as opinion, not fact; to work to separate personal feelings about the supervisee from the need to criticize; and to steer away from accusatory comments or ultimatums. Abbott and Lyter (1998) further suggested that supervisors model self-critique, that critical appraisal be supported by professional literature, and that criticism be followed by brainstorming through which both supervisor and supervisee are involved in identifying methods and means for removing deficiencies and achieving competencies.

Hawkins and Shohet (1989) have suggested that supervisors use a particular mnemonic to help remember how to give their supervisees good feedback. That mnemonic is CORBS, which stands for *Clear, Owned, Regular, Balanced,* and *Specific.*

> **Clear**   *Try to be clear about what the feedback is that you want to give. Being vague and faltering will increase anxiety in the receiver and not be understood.*
>
> **Owned**   *The feedback you give is your own perception and not an ultimate truth. It therefore says as much about you as it does about the person who receives it. It helps the receiver if this is stated or implied in the feedback, e.g., "I find you . . ." rather than "You are. . . ."*
>
> **Regular**   *If the feedback is given regularly it is more likely to be useful. If this does not happen, there is a danger that grievances are saved until they are delivered in one large package. Try to give the feedback as close to the event as possible and early enough for the person to do something about it, i.e., do not wait until someone is leaving to tell them how they could have done the job better.*

> **Balance**   *It is good to balance negative and positive feedback and, if you find that the feedback you give to any individual is always either positive or negative, this probably means that your view is distorted in some way. This does not mean that each piece of critical feedback must always be accompanied by something positive, but rather a balance should be created over time.*
>
> **Specific**   *Generalized feedback is hard to learn from. Phrases like "You are irritating" can only lead to hurt and anger. "It irritates me when you forget to record the telephone message" gives the receiver some information which he or she can choose to use or ignore.* (pp. 83–84)

Poertner (1986) suggested that supervisor feedback be clear enough either to automatically reinforce trainees or give them direction for improvement. Directionality, therefore, is an important concept and one that the supervisor should attend to. It might be a good idea for the supervisor to ask herself before each supervision conference, "Do I like the direction things are going? If not, how do I help the supervisee change direction?"

Returning to the issue of clarity, there can be many reasons for unclear or inaccurate communications. The supervisor can be uncomfortable with the power that comes with the role of evaluator; the supervisor may be unprepared for the conference; the supervisor might be intimidated by the supervisee, professionally or personally; or the supervisor might have too little experience in giving negative feedback, for example, to do so kindly and clearly. Regardless of the reasons, the consequences for the trainee are the same: incomplete or inaccurate information, leaving the trainee ill-equipped to alter the course of his or her efforts (Ladany & Melincoff, 1999; Lehrman-Waterman & Ladany, 2001).

Example: Dana has been supervising Nicole for 2 months. Until now she has attempted to focus on Nicole's strengths while gently suggesting other strategies for Nicole to consider. Nicole has found supervision to be a very positive experience thus far. Unfortunately, in Dana's opinion, Nicole has not picked up on Dana's suggestions and therefore has not progressed at all in her counseling. Of particular concern is Nicole's work with one client, Shirley.

During the sessions that Dana has observed, Shirley regularly brings up her difficulties with her husband. Shirley is upset with his relationship with his ex-wife; the husband thinks that she is overly jealous. Nicole seems to keep the entire issue at arm's length and usually finds another topic to focus on.

DANA: I wanted to spend some time talking about Shirley's issues with her husband. These seem to keep coming up. What do you think is going on there?

NICOLE: I think Shirley's self-esteem is low and so she is insecure about her husband and his ex-wife. She doesn't like it that he has to deal with her around his kids. His behavior certainly seems reasonable to me.

DANA: I don't think there's any question that Shirley's self-esteem is low. I agree with you. But she keeps bringing up her husband and I don't see you doing much with that in the session. Is there a reason you avoid addressing that issue?

NICOLE: I just didn't see it as the real problem. Besides, Dr. M said that we can't deal with a marital issue if only one spouse is in the room.

DANA: OK. So you've been avoiding it because of Dr. M's advice. Is there any way you can view the problem that would allow you to focus on Shirley and not the interaction between her and her husband?

NICOLE: And still deal with her jealousy about her husband?

DANA: Right.

NICOLE: I could ask her how she feels about her husband, but I already know that.

DANA: Yes, I think you do. What about her thought processes?

NICOLE: I'm not sure what you mean.

DANA: Well, I've noticed that you pretty much focus on the client's feelings in all of your counseling. I think you're doing well there, but I don't think it's a complete enough approach. You need to figure out some way to address the client's thoughts if you're going to help Shirley any more than you have. And remember, addressing her thoughts will lead you to more of her internal life, including more of her feelings.

NICOLE: So, you don't think I'm helping Shirley?

DANA: I think you've gone about as far as you can go with the approach you've taken. But the issue is bigger than your work with Shirley. In order for you to become a better counselor, I think you

need to start looking at how you address cognitive issues. I'd like to focus on that for a while.

NICOLE: OK.

From the perspective of formative evaluation, we might ask how successful was this segment between Dana and Nicole? Was Dana's intent clear? Did she hear all of Nicole's messages? Did she react adequately to Nicole's feedback? What was the content of Dana's communication? The message about the relationship? What was the content of Nicole's communication? The message about the relationship? In the past, Nicole has not picked up on Dana's suggestions. Has Dana done anything to ensure that Nicole has heard her this time? Finally, Talen and Schindler's (1993) study found that an attitude of trust and positive regard from the supervisor, validating supervisees' strengths and accepting them at their present skill level, were considered to be the most important supervision strategies from the perspective of supervisees. With this in mind, has this session compromised the supervision relationship between Dana and Nicole? How might the session have been conducted differently?

Encouraging Self-assessment

Assisting supervisees to evaluate their own work has been identified as an important aspect of supervision (Bernstein & Lecomte, 1979; Borders et al., 1991; Falender et al., in press; Munson, 2002; Perlesz et al., 1990). In fact, Rønnestad and Skovholt (2003) have found that a commitment to ongoing self-reflection is a skill that characterized therapists at all points across the professional life span. It is our opinion that self-assessment is overused by supervisors and underused by beginning counselors–therapists; therefore, we will focus on the latter in this section. Blodgett, Schmidt, and Scudder (1987) noted that little is being done to help clinicians and supervisors to learn to self-evaluate. Assuming that their criticism is at least partially justified, the error in training is emphasized by the work of Dowling (1984), who found evidence that graduate student trainees were both accurate self-evaluators and good peer evaluators, a finding consistent with Hillerbrand's (1989) observations. Therefore, it would seem wise, if not an ethical imperative, for clinical supervisors to focus on supervisee self-evaluation and to be aware of conditions that aid in self-assessment and those that impede this skill.

From the vantage point of the clinical supervisor, one goal of supervision is to incorporate self-assessment into the larger framework of evaluation. Kadushin (1992a) argued that supervisory evaluation, in and of itself, makes learning conspicuous to the trainee and helps to set a pattern of self-evaluation. Ekstein and Wallerstein (1972) were more cautious, reminding the supervisor that asking trainees to self-evaluate will stimulate all their past experiences of being selected, rejected, praised, and so on. We challenge this caution in that self-evaluation, we believe, takes some of the parental-like authority away from the supervisor, rather than adding to it. If negative feelings are going to be experienced as a result of evaluation, these will be there regardless of whether the trainee is given an opportunity to contribute to the assessment.

The above notwithstanding, recent research has established that supervisors can affect supervisee self-assessment or self-efficacy, the latter defined as counselors knowing what to do and having judgments about their capabilities to effectively respond to upcoming counseling situations (Steward, Breland, & Neil, 2001). Furthermore, the influence of supervisors can be either positive or negative. In a study that initially appeared to be counterintuitive, Steward et al. found that accurate self-evaluation on the part of supervisees was negatively associated with supervisor attractiveness. In other words, the more friendly, flexible, supportive, open, positive, and warm the supervisor, the less accurate the novice supervisee's self-evaluation. These authors noted that, in general, supervisees tend to underestimate their abilities and supervisor attractiveness evidently reinforces this tendency. Finding one's supervisor as less attractive may stimulate the supervisee's own determination to approve of one's own work, thus resulting in making more accurate self-assessments. Steward et al. did not suggest that supervisors aspire to be unattractive to their supervisees. They did, however, state that

their study may underscore the importance of supervisors engaging in both supportive and challenging interventions. Steward et al. speculated that consistently supportive supervisors may not expect their supervisees to move beyond their comfort zones. This may, in turn, have negative implications for training, resulting in supervisees whose self-confidence, self-efficacy, and sense of accomplishment are compromised.

In a seemingly contradictory study, Daniels and Larson (2001) found that performance feedback from the supervisor influenced supervisee self-efficacy and anxiety in the directions expected (i.e., positive feedback increased self-efficacy and lowered anxiety, while negative feedback had the opposite effect). Unlike the Steward et al. study, Daniels and Larson used bogus feedback to manipulate supervisee reactions. They cautioned that their negative feedback in particular may have been too extreme. At the same time, the authors noted that the degree of anxiety that a supervisee presents in supervision should modify a supervisor's behavior. In other words, the balance between support and challenge needs to be tailored for each supervisee to arrive at optimal results. (We discuss the ramifications of supervisee anxiety in Chapter 7.)

As yet another consideration regarding supervisee self-efficacy, Steward (1998) raised the issue of the relationship between supervisee self-efficacy and supervisor self-efficacy. He cautioned training programs in particular to consider the degree to which they have integrated and monitored field supervisors who may be unaware of program expectations and/or may be inadequately trained as supervisors. Prior to assessing counselor self-efficacy and competence, Steward advised that training programs seek to provide trainees with uniform supervisory experiences.

Finally, Yogev (1982) raised an important interpersonal issue of the supervisor's reaction to the trainee's self-assessment. She warned the supervisor not to put trainees in a no-win situation by asking for their evaluation and then holding it against them. For example, if a trainee admits feeling overwhelmed and intimidated by the training experience, the supervisor should not later criticize the trainee for being weak and dependent. Therefore, if supervisors ask for candid disclosure as part of a self-assessment, they must be ready to handle respectfully what transpires.

There are several highly productive ways that the supervisee can be involved in self-assessment while in the context of supervision. The most obvious is for the supervisor to communicate an expectation that the supervisee will do some sort of self-assessment prior to each supervision session. It has been our experience that unless the supervisor follows through on this expectation most trainees will falter in their intentions to self-assess.

A useful self-evaluating activity is to ask the supervisee to periodically review a segment of a counseling session in greater depth for response patterns (Collins & Bogo, 1986). If the supervisee can identify nonproductive patterns, this exercise can be instrumental in breaking nontherapeutic habits.

Involving the supervisee in self-assessment throughout supervision has an added benefit of preparing the supervisee to be involved in the summative evaluation process. It is a sign of the distinct success of supervision when supervisees can end the supervisory relationship with a relatively accurate assessment of their strengths and weakness and articulate their goals for further professional development.

The rationale for emphasizing self-assessment, however, is that it ultimately has utility beyond the formal training context. In other words, part of the responsibility of clinical supervisors is to assist supervisees in establishing a habit of self-scrutiny that will follow them into their professional careers. Although supervision is always warranted in the early years of practice, it is not always forthcoming, at least not always at an optimal level. Skill in self-assessment, therefore, can be crucial for practice (e.g., see Elks & Kirkhart, 1993).

Sound self-assessment skills also contribute to a related activity, that of peer supervision. Like self-assessment, peer supervision tends to be underused as a complement to more traditional supervision. When peers are asked to work together for each other's benefit, the skill-level differences within the group become background as group cohesiveness is established. We have found that peers can be invaluable reviewers for each other, and it is consistently both humbling and inspiring when peers make observations that are absolutely correct and have been overlooked by the supervisor. But it is important to structure peer feedback. Often feedback is given verbally in group supervision, but we have found that the type of feedback that comes spontaneously, although valuable, is generally inferior to the type of feedback that is given more formally when a peer is asked to review an audio- or videotape between supervision sessions. When, in addition, the peer's critique is evaluated by the supervisor, thoughtful and highly useful reviews are most often the result. It has been our experience that the more supervisors share the responsibility for trainee development with the trainee group, the better the students perform and the more positive the overall experience.

Communicating Summative Evaluations

Although the word summative might imply a single final evaluation, summative evaluations usually occur at least twice during a typical supervisory relationship. In academic settings, there is usually a midsemester and a final summative evaluation. For off-campus externships, internships and work settings, the summative evaluations are given at the halfway mark and at the end or as annual reviews, respectively. If all has gone well within supervision, a final summative review should contain no surprises for the supervisee. In other words, the summative review should be the culmination of evaluation, not the beginning of it. The initial summative review is perhaps the more important because it is at this point that the supervisor will learn if the supervisee has understood the implications of formative assessments. If so, the summative evaluation will provide an opportunity to take stock and to plan a productive sequel to the supervision that has transpired to this point—a second supervision contract, so to speak. If formative assessment has been resisted by the supervisee, the first summative evaluation must be specific regarding the progress that is required for the supervisee to remain in good standing and must be conducted early enough for the supervisee to have a reasonable opportunity to achieve success. In all cases, summative evaluations should be conducted face to face and should also be put in writing (Belar et al., 1993).

Even when a correct process has been established for summative evaluations, their ultimate success depends on the communication skill of the supervisor. Unfortunately, supervisor training often gives short shrift to the process of conducting summative evaluation sessions. What follows are two segments taken from actual summative evaluation conferences conducted by supervisors-in-training with counselors-in-training. Both supervisor and counselor are female in each case. In the first segment, the pair begins by reviewing the Evaluation of Counselor Behaviors-Revised form (Bernard, 1997) that the supervisor completed prior to the session. The person referred to as Dr. P. is the counselor's faculty instructor.

S: Uh, I would put this more here, I think, and more here. Now you have to do another one of these? (*Referring to evaluation form on self*)
C: Are you asking me or telling me?
S: I'm asking.
C: I don't know.
S: Well then, you must not have to if you don't know (*laughs*).
C: I've not . . .
S: Have you not heard the news? (*laughs*)
C: I haven't seen it in my mailbox or anything. Of course, that doesn't mean that when I make contact with Dr. P., that he won't say that it has to be done.
S: And I think, you know, again, I did this here. I may go back and circle . . . if you see anything that you don't agree with, just go ahead and question it. I think you know how I look at it. I see you just having started to work.
C: Oh, I . . .
S: You know, you may not like that. I just think since that one big leap, when you started to consciously try to do things differently . . .
C: I can't even visualize 10 years down the line having you say that everything is excellent. I don't know. To me, you're asking for close to perfection.
S: It would be hard for me to get there (*laughs*). I wouldn't want to be evaluated.

C: So much that comes to me comes through experience.
S: Yeah. I suppose, you know, maybe it's the teacher part of me . . . whenever I see the word "always" (*referring again to the evaluation form*), I just can't . . . we're in trouble.
C: Yeah.
S: Even for me (*laughs*).
C: I understand. You know, as I look at this, it looks like a positive evaluation because of what you've said so far.
S: Um, well, you have a lot of 2's and 1's, but "good" to me is good. Letter grade wise, I don't know. I can't tell you. Part of me says, because of what has gone on the whole semester, you know, and part of me says, "Okay. What are you doing now?" So, you know, I don't assign grades. It won't be an A. I'm not too sure. I'd say probably a C+ to B− in that area.
C: But there are no pluses or minuses in the grading schedule.
S: That's right.
C: To me, a C is a failure and I'm assuming that you are not . . .
S: I don't think I look at it as a failure. I think that maybe, you know, when you do course work and things like that, maybe you could look at it that way. But I don't look at it as a failure because failure is an F.
C: Um hum.
S: If I were to have to assess a grade by skill level, it probably would be close to a C/D. But in looking from the beginning, you know, you've come a long way. But that isn't for me to assess. That's for Dr. P. to assess and I don't know how he will do it. I definitely think that there has been a lot of improvement.
C: And to me, it seems like it's been such a short time.
S: Yes, a very short time.

It is not difficult to see that there are several communication problems in this example. Actually, four things contribute to the ambiguity presented here: (1) the supervisor's personal style of communication is clouded. She does not finish many of her statements. She is not crisp. She would do well to practice the delivery of her feedback for clarity. (2) The process is ambiguous. Either Dr. P. has not been clear regarding procedures or neither supervisor nor counselor has attended to these details. The result is that the supervisor does not seem to know her role in the evaluation process. Another possibility is that, because of her discomfort, she is playing down her role and referring the counselor to Dr. P. for the difficult task of final evaluation. From the conversation as it stands, we cannot know which of these is the case. (3) Criteria for evaluation also seem to be ambiguous to the supervisor. She vacillates from references to skill level and references to progress. It is obvious that she is not clear about how Dr. P. will weigh each of these two factors. (4) The supervisor seems to be uncomfortable with the responsibility of evaluation, especially in this case where the practicum seems to be ending on a down note. We do not know if the supervisor has not prepared adequately for this conference or whether any amount of preparation would have countered her personal discomfort. The result is a series of mixed messages:

1. "You're not a very good counselor."/" 'C' isn't a bad grade."
2. "You've come a long way."/"You still aren't very good."
3. "I'm trying to be fair."/"I wouldn't want to be in your shoes."
4. "I'm recommending between a C+ and a B."/"I don't assign grades."

In our second summative session, the supervisor and counselor have had a better working relationship and the results are more positive.

S: I came up with some agenda items, things I thought we needed to touch base on. You can add to this agenda if you'd like. The concern that you expressed previously about the deadlines, wrapping up, dealing with your clients, and then talking about termination–continuation issues. Kind of finishing up, so that it concludes not only your client situations, but practicum. Again, the other issue I have down is evaluation. I am not sure how he (Dr. P.) . . . did he mention that in class today? How he's

going to handle that? Do you have a conference with him?

C: There will be the conference next Monday with the three of us and then it seems to me that the other was kind of nebulous as to if we had another conference with him about you. Is that what you mean?

S: No, no. I meant about you. See, I was not aware that we were meeting on Monday (*laughs*).

C: Yes, yes.

S: O.K. (*laughs*). What time did he say?

C: We had to choose a time and I chose 2:00 next Monday afternoon.

S: Oh, O.K. I wondered.

C: He sent around a piece of paper so that we could sign up for Monday or Tuesday.

S: Well, that's nice to be aware of. Surprise!

C: Yeah.

S: (*Laughs*)

C: So it will be the three of us for evaluation.

S: So I thought, depending on if you had any concern about that, that maybe we can discuss that ahead of time. I don't know if we need to here today or not or whatever, but that was something that I had as a possibility at least.

C: There are other things that are more urgent.

S: Yes (*laughs*).

C: That's next week.

S: Uh huh.

(*Supervisor and counselor then talk about a particularly difficult case. The following occurs later in the same session.*)

C: You've been very supportive. I really appreciate your feedback that you give me. A lot of good supportive feedback. It's not all the positive. There's been good constructive criticism you give too. I appreciate that.

S: You perceive that there has been enough of a balance?

C: Um, you've been heavier on the positive, but maybe it's just because I've done such a good job (*laughs*).

S: (*Laughs*) I'm laughing because you're laughing.

C: You very nicely have couched the constructive criticism, preceding it with a lot of positive. "I like the way you did this, and then when you said this, it was very good, and then this was good and now you, probably if you had said this, perhaps you would have. . . ." You preceded criticism with about two or three positive things, which helps, helps the ego. I've appreciated that a lot.

S: Good.

C: Um, you know, I just, I think that we have learned a lot just being in the sessions, all the counselors, that we have learned from mistakes, and that there are times when we just haven't seen our mistakes. I think it's good to have them pointed out and I think you have done it very nicely. I appreciate that.

S: Kind of while we are on the subject, is there something that you can pinpoint at all that you feel that you've learned the most from practicum? Not necessarily from your clients, just anything in general. Is there something that sticks out in your mind that you have learned a lot from?

C: Um, well, with my two clients who were the most difficult, I feel that with both of them, I needed to be more forceful, and so, that's a lesson learned, that I'm not doing people a favor by letting them ramble on and on. That oftentimes I would do people a favor by stopping them and saying, "Now let's back up a little. Let's focus a little bit more." I haven't been quite assertive enough and I think I've learned that about myself. (*counselor continues*)

S: I've seen you do continually more intervening and trying different things, being aware of this and trying to do things about it. Do you feel like, as you go away from here, you'll be able to take away something so that you can do that when you get into situations like this again?

C: Yeah, I've really learned that, and I do feel that I am doing it more.

S: Oh, yes, I think so.

The most dramatic difference between this pair and the previous pair is the quality of the relationship. Apparently, this has been a positive experience for both supervisor and counselor. There may or may not be some lack of comfort for the supervisor with evaluation in that what might have been a summative conference became a preconference by their mutual choice. But the important characteristic of their interaction, as it appears here, is that they seem to be current with each other. Evidently, there has been enough formative communication along the way that each person appears to know where she stands. Notice, however, that the same administrative problem that appeared in the first example appears here, too. Again, we see that communication between the instructor and the supervisor has not occurred and this leaves the supervisor at a disadvantage in the conference. Because both of these sessions transpired in the same training program, we could come to the conclusion that the doctoral supervisors need more support from the faculty in the form of clearer guidelines about their role in the evaluation process and clearer communication down the administrative hierarchy.

Thus far we have discussed summative evaluations as they relate to the instructional needs of the supervisee. The process of arriving at the summative evaluation can also be a valuable learning experience for the supervisor. Too often this is an activity done alone. There is great value, however, in the use of additional evaluators to arrive at summative assessments. The following evaluation format was used in a counseling center where doctoral students served as the individual supervisors for master's-level counselors: One doctoral student was assigned to three master's-level students. Most semesters, there were 12 counselors and 4 supervisors. In addition to working closely with the supervisees, each doctoral student was required to observe (usually through a two-way mirror) three other counselors at least twice during the semester. The doctoral students did not have to share their observations with the counselors; their charge was simply to have some knowledge of the counselor's ability. Additionally, weekly supervision-of-supervision conferences were held, which included listening to taped supervision sessions between the doctoral supervisors and their three supervisees. When it was time to evaluate the counselors, the faculty instructors for both groups (supervisors and counselors), the center coordinator (who read all counselors' intake and termination reports), and the group of doctoral supervisors met together. Therefore, the work of each counselor was known by at least four people, and all were encouraged to voice their opinion.

These evaluation meetings provided both a learning experience for supervisors and the opportunity to arrive at consensus evaluations of the counselors. One of the most obvious dynamics in these meetings was the investment that each supervisor had in the three supervisees that they had mentored. At times the supervisor would get noticeably defensive if the supervisor's counselors were seen as weaker than some others. Such reactions were always processed, and awareness was increased that the supervisory relationship can be a powerful one and can cloud a supervisor's ability to be objective.

A secondary issue was whether the supervisor felt responsible for the counselor's level of performance. Sometimes it was thought that the supervisor might have been partially responsible for a counselor's modest improvement over the semester, but usually this was not the case. The most important lesson, however, was appreciating that different views could be held about the same supervisee, even when seemingly objective criteria were in place.

IMPAIRMENT AND INCOMPETENCE

Virtually all training programs in the helping professions admit students with the intention of graduating and ultimately endorsing them. Similarly, mental health agencies hire professionals with only optimistic expectations. The unpleasant idea of dismissal of students or employees is something most supervisors attempt to repress. And yet evaluation of mental health professionals must include the possibility that the person being evaluated may fail to meet minimal criteria. Though supervisors typically exhibit a high commitment to their supervisees, they must be ever cognizant that "duty to the public and the profession takes precedence" (Pearson & Piazza, 1997, p. 93).

Impairment has been defined in two ways. Muratori (2001), in her discussion of supervisor impairment, focused on the situation in which a formerly competent professional exhibits diminished functioning. This can result from a variety of sources, including emotional and physical depletion or burnout. Manifestations of impairment can include substance abuse, boundary violations, misuse of power, and diminished clinical judgment (Muratori, 2001).

A broader definition of impairment includes not only a reversal of previously adequate functioning, but incompetence or the inability to attain minimal performance standards. For example, impairment for psychologists has been defined as a serious deficit in the areas of knowledge and application of professional standards, to include ethics, relevant mental health law, and professional behavior; competency in areas such as conceptualization, diagnosis and assessment, and appropriate interventions; and personal functioning, to include awareness of self, the use of supervision, and management of personal stress (Lamb, Cochran, & Jackson, 1991; Lamb et al., 1987). In a more recent review of trainee impairment, Forrest, Elman, Gizarra, and Vacha-Haase (1999) found that incompetence and impairment were often both included under the term *impairment* in the professional literature.

While clinical supervisors may indeed observe a reversal of performance level in their supervisees, the more vexing problem, it seems to us, is when supervisees fail to attain a level of competence that allows supervisors to endorse them for entry-level professional practice. While impairment raises the issue of remediation, incompetence raises the issue of dismissal, a seemingly harsher alternative.

We should add that impairment is often used by training programs as a term to describe what are considered nonacademic traits that interfere significantly with trainee performance. Forrest et al. (1999) found that studies of trainee impairment identified clinical deficiencies, interpersonal problems, problems in supervision, and personality disorders as the four most common forms of impairment. While this use of impairment might assist supervisors in identifying issues that do not surface in a traditional classroom setting, we will include them in our definition of incompetence as long as the supervisee has never demonstrated minimal ability in one of these target areas.

Chapter 3 addresses informed consent and due process as ethical issues for supervision. However, because the identification of incompetence is ultimately an evaluation issue, we will include these ethical mandates around this assessment here. As an informed-consent safeguard, Lamb et al. (1987) suggested that information given to new supervisees include agency and/or training program expectations; agency and/or program responsibilities in assisting supervisees to meet expectations; and evaluation procedures, including time frame, content of evaluations, use of verbal and written feedback, evaluation forms, and opportunities for supervisee feedback. Describing it as a "gatekeeping model," Lumadue and Duffey (1999) outlined the six informed consent goals that faculty of one counselor training program agreed on:

1. To identify the qualities and behaviors expected of students
2. To reach faculty consensus on the expectations for student fitness and performance
3. To devise a rating form listing these qualities and behavior
4. To standardize evaluation procedures within the department by using these forms
5. To communicate these expectations to all students in each class
6. To include these expectations in the admissions packets issued to interested students (p. 106)

The rating form developed by the program was published later (Kerl, Garcia, McCullough, & Maxwell, 2002) and included five areas of evaluation: counseling skills and abilities, professional responsibility, competence, maturity, and integrity. Students are assessed as not meeting, meeting minimally, or not meeting each criterion. All criteria except those listed under counseling skills and abilities are shown in Table 2.2.

In addition to informed consent that alerts trainees about expectations and procedures, due process needs to be addressed when supervisors judge that a supervisee is incompetent or impaired. Traditionally, faculties have been concerned about their legal standing if they should attempt to dismiss a student based on what they consider "nonacademic" grounds. Lumadue and Duffey (1999) and Kerl et al. (2002) have performed a significant service to educators and supervisors by reviewing court cases that have addressed this issue. Their conclusion is that courts have consistently viewed personal attitudes or behaviors that are necessary for adequate performance within a profession to be included as an academic issue. Therefore, characteristics such as low impulse control, limited empathy for clients, and cultural insensitivity could be defended as part of an academic dismissal. This is important because, legally, academic dismissals are the purview of the faculty, while disciplinary dismissals require additional documentation and a formal hearing. The due process obligation for the faculty when the issue is an academic one is met simply by notifying the supervisee prior to dismissal regarding his or her failure or impending failure to meet program standards (Kerl et al.).

Legal requirements notwithstanding, most clinical training programs offer students–supervisees a more elaborate due process procedure when they are in danger of being dismissed. Lamb et al. (1991) outlined four important due process steps for interns that ensure both supervisee protection and institutional credibility:

1. *Reconnaissance and identification.* This phase encompasses that period of time when the supervisee is seeing clients under supervision and the areas of strength or vulnerability are observed. Lamb et al. suggested that supervisors meet regularly to consult with each other as these evaluations are occurring. Forrest et al. (1999) further recommended that behaviors that cause concern be matched to evaluation criteria.
2. *Discussion and consultation.* Once an intern has been identified as displaying the possibil-

TABLE 2.2   Items Included in the Professional Counseling Performance Evaluation

Professional Responsibility
- Conducts self in an ethical manner so as to promote confidence in the counseling profession
- Relates to peers, professors, and others in a manner consistent with stated professional standards
- Demonstrates sensitivity to real and ascribed differences in power between themselves and others, and does not exploit or mislead other people during or after professional relationships
- Demonstrates application of legal requirements relevant to counseling training and practice

Competence
- Recognizes the boundaries of her or his particular competencies and the limitations of her or his expertise
- Takes responsibility for compensating for her or his deficiencies
- Takes responsibility for assuring client welfare when encountering the boundaries of her or his expertise
- Demonstrates basic cognitive, affective, sensory, and motor capacities to respond therapeutically to clients
- Provides only those services and applies only those techniques for which she or he is qualified by education, training, and experience

Maturity
- Demonstrates appropriate self-control (such as anger control, impulse control) in interpersonal relationships with faculty, peers, and clients
- Demonstrates honesty, fairness, and respect for others
- Demonstrates an awareness of his or her own belief systems, values, needs, and limitations and the effect of these on his or her work
- Demonstrates the ability to receive, integrate, and utilize feedback from peers, teachers, and supervisors
- Exhibits appropriate levels of self-assurance, confidence, and trust in own ability
- Follows professionally recognized conflict-resolution processes, seeking to informally address the issue first with the individual(s) with whom the conflict exists

Integrity
- Refrains from making statements that are false, misleading, or deceptive
- Avoids improper and potentially harmful dual relationships
- Respects the fundamental rights, dignity, and worth of all people
- Respects the rights of individuals to privacy, confidentiality, and choices regarding self-determination and autonomy
- Respects cultural, individual, and role differences, including those due to age, gender, race, ethnicity, national origin, religion, sexual orientation, disability, language, and socioeconomic status

Adapted from S. B. Kerl, J. L. Garcia, S. McCullough, and M. E. Maxwell (2002). Systemic evaluation of professional performance: Legally supported procedure and process. *Counselor Education and Supervision, 41*, 321–334.

ity of incompetence, Lamb et al. suggested that extreme care be taken to protect both the intern and the staff through extensive discussion among all relevant personnel. Furthermore, all former impressions and interventions should be reviewed. Finally, supervisors need to make a qualitative decision about the seriousness of the situation and review their documentation of the process up to this point.

3. *Implementation and review.* If more serious action is called for, this is the point at which it will occur. Probation or even termination may

be the decision of the staff. (It is also possible that, after careful scrutiny of their own behavior and consultation, the staff will find a less dramatic intervention that is appropriate.) If probation is the avenue of choice, Lamb et al. suggested that a letter be sent to the intern that should include the following:

a. Identify the specific behaviors or areas of professional functioning that are of concern.

b. Directly relate these behaviors to the written evaluations (e.g., not showing up for counseling sessions as an example of inadequate professional functioning). Provide several specific ways that these deficiencies can be remediated (e.g., from additional training to personal therapy).

c. Identify a specific probation period after which the performance of the intern will be reviewed (long enough for reasonable changes, but not so long that further action cannot be taken).

d. Stipulate, if appropriate, how the intern's functioning in the agency will change during the probation period (e.g., additional time in supervision).

e. Reiterate the due process procedures available to challenge the decision (Lamb et al., 1991, p. 293).

Lamb et al. advised that a probation period be an active time of ongoing feedback to the intern and frequent consultation and documentation among staff. Finally, Lamb et al. are equally compendious if the decision is to terminate, advising that all implications be reviewed before action is taken, that the intern receive a letter reiterating the probation conditions and the reasons for dismissal, and that the intern be provided with an opportunity to appeal. Only then should the dismissal occur.

4. *Anticipating and responding to organizational reaction.* Lamb et al. (1991) wisely concluded that removing an impaired or incompetent intern is not only an action that will call for support of that intern, but a systemic intervention as well. All levels of the system should be considered, including clients of the intern, super-

visors who were pivotal in the decision, administration, and other staff and interns. Although the intern's rights to privacy must be protected, all persons who will be aware of the decision will have a reaction, and there should be some mechanism for their reactions to be addressed.

As a potential antidote to the above, Meyer (1980) expressed concern about evaluation procedures that were overly fastidious, especially is they were employed with all students, but with the impaired or incompetent student in mind. Miller and Rickard (1983) offered a middle of the road posture regarding procedures, warning that too elaborate a process can be burdensome and time consuming and can build inflexibility into the system, which they believed can work against trainees as often as it works for them. They favored having a simple, but precise, evaluation process for all students (not just those who are in trouble) and refraining from trying to articulate a procedure for problems that are unlikely to arise. Miller and Rickard referred to J. L. Bernard's (1975) four evaluation steps, which they used with clinical psychology students and which attend to both informed consent and due process:

> *Incoming students should be presented with written material fully describing conditions under which a student may be terminated, including personal unsuitability for the profession. All students should be routinely evaluated at least once a year, and this evaluation should include a section on personal functioning. If inadequacies are identified, the student is so advised, a remediation plan with a time line should be put in place, and the student should be made aware of the consequences of failure to remedy. If sufficient remediation is not accomplished in the time designated, the student should be given time to prepare a case; then this should be presented to the faculty and the faculty then make a decision. If the student is terminated, all of the above should be summarized in writing to the student.* (Miller & Rickard, 1983, p. 832)

In summary, there is no more dreaded evaluation situation than the possible assessment of a supervisee as unable or unfit to practice in the profession that he or she has chosen. At the same time, this task is representative of the gatekeeping function required of all clinical supervisors. Historically, when supervisors avoided this responsibility, they have done so using the nebulousness of the professions as their argument. More recently, the serious implications of failing to serve as gatekeepers has balanced this posture.

ADDITIONAL EVALUATION ISSUES

At the beginning of this chapter, we mentioned that evaluation is a difficult task because of the personal nature of the skills being evaluated. Relatively clear criteria, good evaluation instruments, and a credible process go far to diminish the difficulty of evaluation. But the therapeutic process is not sterile and neither is the evaluation process. What is called for when supervisors evaluate is a judgment based on as much objective data as possible. But the judgment will still include a subjective element.

The Subjective Element

Clinical supervisors all work hard to be fair and reasonable in their evaluations. Without some awareness of the pitfalls to objective evaluation, however, supervisors are at a disadvantage for attaining this goal. But supervisors must also be continually aware that the subjective element cannot and should not be totally eliminated. There is something intrinsically intuitive about psychotherapy, and this is equally true for clinical supervision. Supervisors are in a position to supervise because they have had more fine tuning of their intuitions. Evaluation is a delicate blend of subjective judgment and objective criteria. Yet sometimes our *personal subjectivity* contaminates our *professional subjectivity,* and evaluation becomes less intuitive and more biased (Robiner, Saltzman, Hoberman, Semrud-Clikeman, & Schirvar, 1997). No clinical supervisor is above this dilemma. Being aware of the possibility, however, may help the supervisor to draft a checklist of personal vulnerabilities and potential blind spots to review when evaluating.

Each clinical supervisor will have a separate list of subjective obstacles to navigate when facing the task of evaluation. Our list is only a partial delineation of some of the more common problems, ones that we have experienced or that have received attention in the professional literature.

Similarity. An assumption that has spawned a good deal of empirical investigation is that attraction (which includes the concept of similarity) influences the therapeutic process and, likewise, the supervision process (Turban & Jones, 1988). Kaplan (1983), however, reported that findings were mixed when personality characteristics and value systems of supervisors and supervisees were the focus of research efforts. Royal and Golden (1981), on the other hand, found that attitude similarity between supervisor and employee had a significant influence on the evaluation of the employee's intelligence, personal adjustment, competence, quality of work, quantity of work, and motivation, among other things.

Similarity with one's supervisor is probably more of an advantage than a disadvantage, but there are times when this is not so. If the supervisor is suffering from a poor self-image, this may spill over to the supervisee. From another vantage point, dissimilarity is an advantage for the supervisee if the lack of similarity gives the trainee additional influence in the relationship. For example, if the supervisor is young and relatively inexperienced and the supervisee is older and has more life experience, such dissimilarity might translate to a better evaluation than if the supervisor were the same age as the supervisee. There is evidence also that females rate males higher in competence; therefore, a female supervisor might rate a male supervisee higher than a male supervisor would (Goodyear, 1990). (Goodyear cited several such studies, but in his own study found no evidence of gender bias in trainee evaluations.)

There is a situation-specific form of similarity that the supervisor should consider. When life has dealt two people the same hand, or at least some of the same cards, this tends to create a bond between them. Both supervisor and supervisee might have recently been through a divorce, have children of the same age, or have an alcoholic sibling. Depending on each person's comfort level about these life situations, such similarity can be an advantage or a disadvantage. Regardless, they must be considered.

Ultimately, the issue seems to be one of liking, rather than similarity only. Turban, Jones, and Rozelle (1990) found that liked supervisees received more psychological support during supervision than disliked supervisees, supervisors extended more effort in working with liked supervisees, and supervisors evaluated liked supervisees more favorably than disliked supervisees. It is difficult to determine whether liking leads to inflated performance evaluation or if better performing supervisees are more liked; perhaps both are true. The fact that liking affects the interactions between supervisor and supervisee long before summative evaluation, however, makes this a variable to which supervisors should be alerted.

Familiarity. "He's difficult to get to know, but he wears well." How many of us have had negative first impressions of people who we now hold in high esteem? Not all of a person's qualities are apparent in the short run, and sometimes it takes a significant amount of time (in graduate training terms) to arrive at what later would look like a balanced view of the trainee's strengths and weaknesses. In conjunction with this, when affection for someone has grown over time, it can become more and more difficult to evaluate objectively (Robiner et al., 1997). In fact, one can come to like Charlie so much that one might have to ask "How would I react if Marco did that instead of Charlie?" to have any hope of arriving at a fair judgment.

Some empirical evidence supports the case that familiarity affects evaluation. Fried, Tiegs, and Bellamy (1992) established that supervisors are reluctant to evaluate at all unless a supervisee has been under supervision for a certain amount of time (which is subjectively determined). Blodgett, Schmidt, and Scudder (1987) found that supervisors rated the same trainees differently depending on how long they knew the trainees. If a supervi-

sor had had the trainee in a class prior to the supervision experience, the supervisor was more likely to evaluate the trainee more positively. Blodgett et al. noted that the trainees who had received their undergraduate and graduate training at the same institution had a distinct advantage in this particular study. The authors warned that it would be unwise, however, to assume that familiarity always works to the trainee's advantage. Our experience would support this admonition. Just as some trainees wear well, others do not.

A corollary to the issue of familiarity is the perseverance of first impressions (Sternitzke, Dixon, & Ponterotto, 1988). Although we have already stated that our first impressions are not always our last, it is important to mention that first impressions can be long-lasting. If supervisors attribute dispositional characteristics to their trainees early in their relationship, it may require an inordinate amount of evidence for the trainee to reverse the supervisor's opinion. In this case, the trainee may be familiar to the supervisor, but the trainee might be far from known.

Priorities. Each supervisor has an individual set of priorities when judging the skill of a trainee. Most often, supervisors are not cognizant that their priorities are partially subjective and that an equally qualified supervisor might have a somewhat different list of priorities. All perception is selective, and we process more quickly what is familiar to us (Atwood, 1986) or what we value more.

We have some evidence (Bernard, 1982) that, when viewing the same therapy session, supervisors rate the trainee differently on the same criteria, depending on the value attributed to each criterion by each supervisor. During a pilot investigation, supervisors were first analyzed using the Discrimination Model (Bernard, 1979, 1997) to discern if they had a primary focus; that is, did they tend to approach supervision from an intervention, conceptual, or personal skill perspective regardless of the therapy session that they observed? In a majority of cases, a primary focus was identified. During the second stage of this investigation, the supervisors were asked to view two videotapes and to evaluate each trainee using a Likert scale for 15 items equally divided among the three focus areas. Again, a sizable number (although not statistically significant) of supervisors rated each trainee lower on their primary focus than on the other two categories. For example, when observing trainee A, supervisor A with an intervention focus rated trainee A lower on intervention skills than on conceptual skills and personalization skills, while supervisor B with a conceptual focus rated trainee A lower on conceptual skills than on intervention skills and personalization skills. (See Chapter 4 for a description of the Discrimination Model.) This formula was substantiated for all three focus possibilities. In other words, the trainee was rated relative to the supervisor's bias and independently of a more objective set of criteria. Yet all supervisors thought that they were being objective and, in several cases, were not aware of having a focus bias or priority. These results are supported by attribution theory as explained by Sternitzke et al. (1988). Building on the work of Ross (1977), they identified egocentric bias as a common problem for supervisors when observing trainee behavior and explained the nature of the bias as follows:

> One's estimate of deviance and normalcy are egocentrically biased in accord with one's own behavioral choices, because observers tend to think about what they would have done in a similar situation and then compare their hypothesized behavior with the actor's actual behavior. If the observers believe they would have acted differently, then there is an increased tendency for them to view the actor's [behavior] as deviant. If the observers believe they would have acted in a similar fashion, then their tendencies are to view the actor's behavior as normal. (p. 9)

Evidence of an egocentric bias is more reason to share the responsibility of evaluation whenever possible, rather than keep it as a private activity.

Rating Idiosyncracies.   Robiner et al. (1993) addressed idiosyncratic tendencies for individual supervisors to demonstrate a leniency bias, a strictness bias, or a central-tendency bias. In a subsequent study of 62 supervisors, Robiner et al. (1997) found that an acknowledgment of evalua-

tion bias was commonplace (59%), with only 10% of supervisors believing that their evaluations were free from bias and 31% being unsure. Of those who admitted bias, 40% of supervisors felt that they leaned toward leniency in their ratings of interns; 45% felt that they leaned toward central tendency; only 7% felt that they exhibited a strictness bias.

According to Robiner et al. (1993), a leniency bias, that is, the tendency to evaluate more favorably than objective data might warrant, may result from any of four sources: (1) measurement issues, such as a lack of clear criteria; (2) legal and administrative issues, such as a concern about a grievance procedure; (3) interpersonal issues, such as experiencing the anguish about damaging a supervisee's career; or (4) supervisor issues, such as having limited supervision experience. In all, Robiner et al. listed 23 potential bases for a lenient evaluation (see Table 2.3).

Strictness bias is the tendency to rate supervisees more severely than warranted. This kind of bias would seem to be the most difficult for the supervisee. Ward, Friedlander, Schoen, and Klein (1985) suggested that such ratings can lead to excessive defensiveness on the part of the supervisee or attempts to manipulate the supervisor to gain more positive ratings. Robiner et al. (1993) proposed that critical ratings could lead to assumptions about training programs (e.g., weaker applicants being admitted), but are more likely to suggest problems within the supervisor (e.g., unrealistic standards or displaced personal frustration).

The central-tendency bias is the tendency to rate supervisees uniformly average. When this is the supervisor's bias, supervisees are denied feedback that would allow them to address deficits seriously or to appreciate that their performance was well above average. According to Robiner et al. (1993), "Central-tendency bias potentially is more misinformative than leniency bias or strictness bias, insofar as training directors cannot correct [supervisors'] neutral rating for positive slant or negative slant" (p. 8).

Although several different types of subjective variables can influence evaluation, a single action may serve to counter their effect: consultation.

TABLE 2.3 Factors Contributing to Leniency or Inflation in Faculty Evaluations of Interns

Definition and Measurement Issues
1. Lack of clear criteria and objective measures of competence or incompetence in psychology
2. Lack of clear criteria and objective measures of impairment or distress in psychology
3. Supervisor awareness of subjectivity inherent in evaluation
4. Apprehension about defending evaluations due to lack of clear criteria and objective measures

Legal and Administrative Issues
5. Concern that negative evaluations may result in administrative inquiry, audit, grievance, or litigation
6. Lack of awareness of internship or institutional policies and procedures involved in negative evaluations
7. Social and political dynamics: feared or perceived lack of support from institutions, directors of training, and colleagues for providing negative evaluations
8. Concern that failing to "pass" an intern may result in loss of future training funds or training slots or the need to find additional funds to extend the intern's training
9. Concern that failing to "pass" an intern may result in adverse publicity that could affect institutional reputation and the number of internship applicants

Interpersonal Issues
10. Fear of diminishing rapport or provoking hostility from supervisees
11. Fear of eliciting backlash from current or future trainees
12. Anguish about damaging a supervisee's career or complicating or terminating his or her graduate training

Supervisor Issues
13. Supervisors' wish to avoid scrutiny of their own behavior, competence, ethics, expectations, or judgment of their clinical and supervisory practices
14. Limited supervisory experiences with impaired or incompetent trainees
15. Inability to impart negative evaluations (e.g., deficit in assertive communication skills)
16. Indifference to personal responsibility for upholding the standards of the profession
17. Discomfort with gatekeeper role
18. Identification with supervisee's problems
19. Inadequate attention to supervisee's performance or problems
20. Supervisors' presumption of supervisee competence (e.g., overreliance on selection procedures)
21. Minimization of incompetence or impairment in supervisees
22. Inappropriate optimism that problems will resolve without intervention
23. Preference to avoid the substantial energy and time commitment necessary to address or remediate deficient trainees

From W. Robiner, M. Fuhrman, and S. Ristvedt (1993). Evaluation difficulties in supervising psychology interns, *The Clinical Psychologist, 46*(1), 3–13. Copyright © (1993) by the Division of Clinical Psychology, Division 12 of the American Psychological Association. Reprinted by permission.

Supervision will be less vulnerable to subjective confounding when others are brought into the process. Supervisors are more likely to involve other opinions when there is a supervision crisis, especially if it has ethical or legal implications. The wise supervisor, though, involves others in the evaluation process when things are seemingly at their smoothest. Not only is this good practice, it affords the supervisor ongoing professional development that will assist the supervisor in becoming a better evaluator.

Consequences of Evaluation

Like most activities of any importance, the process of evaluation contains some risks. There have been false positives and false negatives in the evaluation experience of most clinical supervisors. Possibly because supervisors all know that they have evaluated incorrectly in the past, the consequences of their evaluations can loom before them like an unforgiving superego. Supervisors know that a positive evaluation may mean that a supervisee will be competitive in the job market or an employee will be promoted, while a negative evaluation may result in a student's being dropped from a training program or an employee's being the first to go. Because of supervisors' awareness of the consequences of evaluation, they find themselves doing extra soul searching over the evaluations of the strongest and weakest supervisees.

But even for the average evaluation, there are consequences. Levy (1983) referred to the "costs" of evaluation as the inordinate time it requires of the supervisor, the anxiety it causes the trainee, and the stress it puts on the supervisory relationship. Burke, Goodyear, & Guzzard (1998) found that evaluation interventions that resulted in breaches in the supervision working alliance left the supervision relationship vulnerable. Levy noted that, if the individual supervisee were all that was at stake, the costs might be inordinately high. But when the larger picture is considered, including the integrity of the program or organization and the welfare of future clients, then the costs are in line with the benefits.

In a highly pragmatic discussion, Kadushin (1992a) mentioned the administrative consequences for the supervisor when a negative evaluation is necessary. If in a work environment an employee is let go because of an evaluation, the supervisor will often be the person to feel the brunt of the extra workload until a replacement can be found. Even in a training program, a negative evaluation will typically mean more extensive documentation, the possibility of an appeal process, or, at the very least, a lengthy interview with the trainee involved. Robiner et al. (1997) established that, indeed, legal and administrative issues played a role in supervisor leniency bias. It is understandable, although not acceptable, that some supervisors shy away from negative evaluations in their work in order to avoid unattractive consequences. Such shortsightedness, however, does not acknowledge the much more significant consequences when evaluations are not done properly.

Chronic Issues with Evaluation

We hope that this chapter has aided the supervisor in defining parameters for evaluation and in clarifying some of the issues involved in the task of evaluation. Some problems, however, are chronic and cannot be eliminated through adherence to a model, use of an evaluation tool, or communicating in a certain way. As we conclude this chapter, we pose some of the issues that we believe still enter the awareness of the conscientious clinical supervisor and are only partially resolved by some of the guidelines that we have proposed to this point.

1. Should the same people be involved in administrative decisions and clinical supervision? Is it duplicitous to imply that clinical supervisors are ever free from administrative responsibility? Cohen (1987) included the role of "advocate" as an appropriate responsibility of the clinical supervisor, especially when a talented clinician is in some political trouble within the agency. Does adopting the role of advocate compromise the evaluative role?

2. Should peer evaluation ever be used for administrative purposes? If it is, what are the practical and ethical consequences of such a practice?

3. How do we determine how much of a trainee's development is the result of supervision? How does this affect evaluation?

4. Have supervisors trained their supervisees in all the skills that they later evaluate? Have they articulated adequately (to themselves) their overall goals for their trainees? Have they communicated these goals to their trainees?

5. Are supervisee evaluations based primarily on the competence of the supervisee or do they reflect more accurately the working relationship between the supervisor and the supervisee (Borders & Fong, 1991)? Lazar and Mosek (1993) found that the latter was more predictive of evaluation scores than the former.

6. To what extent are training programs supervising and evaluating in a manner that fits external reality, including client needs and certification and licensure requirements? In other words, does training reflect the employment demands that trainees will eventually face? Also, are supervisors sensitive to the fact that their trainees may or may not be eligible for a variety of professional certifications or licenses, and are they training and evaluating appropriately?

This is only a partial list of the issues related to evaluation that make the process more complicated. They must, however, be addressed, at least as limitations to the evaluation process, if clinical supervisors are to approximate fairness in their evaluations.

CONCLUSION

Evaluation poses the most extreme paradox for the clinical supervisor. It is at the same time the most disconcerting responsibility, the most challenging, and the most important. There are, however, conceptual and structural aids to help supervisors in this process that can increase confidence and competence and contribute to a productive evaluation process experience for the supervisee. Fall and Sutton (2004) offer additional assistance in the important task of evaluation.

CHAPTER 3

ETHICAL AND LEGAL CONSIDERATIONS

It is perhaps a sign of the times that ethics is an increasingly visible topic in the literature of the mental health professions. The passage of the first code of ethics specific to clinical supervision in the United States (Supervision Interest Network, 1993) advanced an awareness of the responsibilities and expectations of the supervisory role distinct from other professional roles. Other codes have followed suit (e.g., Approved Clinical Supervisor Code of Ethics, (1998); Center for Credentialing and Education, 2001; National Board for Certified Counselors, 1998). The mental health disciplines continue to search for answers to troubling ethical dilemmas and to identify the appropriate posture supervisors must take in a variety of situations. In more recent years, increased attention has been paid to precursors of unethical behavior. In this chapter, we will present the areas most critical and relevant to the ethical practice of clinical supervision.

In addition to their increased attention to ethics, the mental health professions have also become highly reactive to legal matters. This plight is not unique to the mental health professions, for litigiousness has become a characteristic of United States society. Furthermore, counseling and psychotherapy are sought by a wider range of consumers than in generations past, thus making it a more public enterprise. With increased exposure has come increased accountability. If the practice of psychotherapy was ever tranquil, it is no longer. One result is that, although suits against mental health professionals are still relatively rare, the fear of litigation has been a factor affecting how much of practice now is operationalized.

Even if ethics and legal matters are often related, each has a distinct purpose. Ethical codes are conceptually broad in nature, few in number, and open to interpretation by the practitioner (in most cases). Although they are sometimes perceived as safeguards to avoid professional liability, they are devised for a loftier purpose, that is, as a call to ethical excellence. Ethical standards are a statement from a particular profession to the general public regarding what they stand for.

The law, on the other hand, is specific in nature and is introduced when a particular act (or series of acts) has been perceived to have endangered or harmed those whom the profession serves. Furthermore, the law is not concerned with the highest standards of professional practice when judging someone, but only in minimally acceptable behavior. For a professional to be considered liable, therefore, it is generally accepted that the professional must have acted outside the bounds of accepted practice (Ogloff & Olley, 1998; Remley & Herlihy, 2001). As Guest and Dooley (1999) pointed out, the emergence of standards and ethical codes for supervisors has made those persons working outside these parameters more vulnerable to being held liable. At the same time, the presence of these standards and codes protects those who follow them.

The reader could assume that, because ethical codes are more stringent, to avoid litigation in one's supervision practice is simply a matter of behaving ethically. Unfortunately, it is not that simple. A moral act can at times subject one to retaliatory litigation. The opposite tendency seems to be the more prevalent, however, of an overly exclusive focus on legal tenets to the detriment of ethical deliberations. As Pope and Vasquez (1991) admonished, this tendency "can discourage ethical awareness and sensitivity. It is crucial to realize that ethical behavior is more than simply avoiding violation of legal standards and that one's ethical and legal duties may, in certain instances, be in conflict" (p. 48). At the same time, Meyer, Landis, and Hays (1988) advised that ethical standards can become legally binding for two reasons: (1) they may be used by the courts to determine professional duty, and (2) they are indirectly influential because they guide the thinking of others in the field who may be asked to testify.

It seems then that ethical standards and legal matters have a symbiotic rather than a perfectly symmetrical relationship. In this chapter, we will discuss first ethical issues and then legal ramifications.

MAJOR ETHICAL ISSUES FOR CLINICAL SUPERVISORS

The following are the major ethical themes of which clinical supervisors should be cognizant. We will present the implications of these themes for the practice of supervision based on our understanding and a review of the literature. We will limit our discussion to issues that have distinct and additional responsibilities for clinical supervisors and therefore will not discuss topics such as research. At the same time, several ethical issues have implications for both the supervisory relationship and the therapy relationship that the supervisor oversees. We will address each dimension separately.

Due Process

Due process is a legal term for a procedure that ensures that notice and hearing must be given before an important right can be removed (Disney & Stephens, 1994). As with other concepts that have legal precedents, due process has been adopted as an ethical mandate as well. In the human services, due process has surfaced as an issue mostly around the proper route to take if a client needs to be committed to a mental health hospital (Ponterotto, 1987; Schutz, 1982). Most hospitals are aware of their due process duties, and professionals who work with volatile populations also are aware of correct procedures.

Supervisees have due process rights too and, until recently, these were more likely to be over-

looked. Forrest, Elman, Gizara, and Vacha-Haase (1999) described the distinction between *substantive* due process and *procedural* due process. Substantive due process means that "the criteria and procedures that govern a training program must be applied consistently and fairly" (p. 656). Procedural due process has to do with the rights of the individual to be notified. This is understood to mean that the supervisee–student should be apprised of the academic and performance requirements and program regulations, receive notice of any deficiencies, be evaluated regularly, and have an opportunity to be heard if their deficiencies have led to a change in status (e.g., dismissed from a program). Most of the supervision literature that addresses due process focuses on procedural due process.

The ethical codes of the mental health professions and divisions within professions give some attention to supervision (e.g., ACA, AMHCA), but their primary purpose is still in detailing ethical behavior for the provider of counseling and therapy (cf. American Association for Marriage and Family Therapy, 1991; American Counseling Association, 1995; American Psychological Association, 1992; National Association of Social Workers, 1990). It is not surprising, therefore, that ethical guidelines developed specifically for the practice of supervision (Center for Credentialing and Education, 2001; Supervision Interest Network, 1993) address the issue of due process concerning supervisees most directly (see Supervisor's Toolbox). For example, the Ethical Guidelines for Counseling Supervisors (Supervision Interest Network, 1993) states that:

> *Supervisors should incorporate the principles of informed consent and participation; clarity of requirements, expectations, roles and rules; and due process and appeal into the establishment of policies and procedures of their institution, program, courses, and individual supervisory relationships. Mechanisms for due process appeal of individual supervisory actions should be established and made available to all supervisees.* (section 2.14)

The most blatant violation of Guideline 2.14 occurs when a supervisee is given a negative final evaluation or dismissed from a training program or job without having had either prior warning that his or her performance was inadequate or a reasonable amount of time to improve (a procedural due process issue). Ladany, Hill, Corbett, and Nutt (1996) found that being denied adequate performance evaluation was the most frequently cited supervisor violation reported by supervisees in their study. This ethical dilemma seems to originate, at least in part, from an avoidance of evaluation by supervisors in training programs and clinical sites. Perhaps, as a consequence, they tend to take a reactive posture to the issues of supervisee inadequacy or impairment. They place their emphasis on screening for admission (Bradey & Post, 1991) with the unrealistic expectation that accepted students will uniformly complete training successfully. A national study of APA internship sites found that, by and large, supervisors appeared to be "waiting for the ax to fall" regarding impaired interns (Boxley, Drew, & Rangel, 1986). As a result, these sites also "appear not to have established formal guidelines in dealing with impaired trainees and, as a result, student due process procedures are missing in many of [the] internship experiences" (p. 52). Another study surveying social work training programs found similar results, leading the authors to comment that the gatekeeping assumption of training programs is at odds with the absence of policies for nonacademic termination of students (Koerin & Miller, 1995).

When a full due process procedure is followed (see the process suggested by Lamb, Cochran, & Jackson, 1991), the supervisee in question is guaranteed a respectful review of a situation and the expert opinions of professionals, in addition to that of the person initiating the complaint. By following such a procedure, the institution is equally protected from the accusation that its action was capricious or arbitrary, a due process violation.

Although most supervisees do not challenge violations of due process rights, several authors have documented those cases for which litigation followed such violations (e.g., Disney & Stephens, 1994; Forrest et al., 1999; Knoff & Prout, 1985; Meyer, 1980). As we stated in Chapter 2, when due

process procedures have been followed, the courts have shown great deference to faculty evaluations (Forrest et al., 1999). Disney and Stephens (1994) advised that, strictly speaking, due process (legal) rights are only protected within public institutions. Therefore, private institutions of higher learning and/or mental health sites that do not receive significant public funding would not be held legally accountable regarding due process procedures unless they were stipulated in the institution's official published materials. Because of the variability of due process protections legally, the ethical mandate to employ due process is especially important for supervisors.

Frame and Stevens-Smith (1995) and Forrest et al. (1999) proposed the development of a policy statement to emphasize the importance of personal characteristics and to use for ongoing evaluation of students during their training program. Students' due process rights are protected by the publication of the policy statement and the availability of the evaluations done for each student. When students are found to be in jeopardy, Frame and Stevens-Smith utilized a procedure very similar to that described by Lamb et al. (1991).

> ***Example:*** Hannah is in a master's program in mental health counseling. She has completed 10 courses in the program and is currently in practicum. Hannah has received a great deal of formative feedback throughout the practicum indicating that she had many areas that needed improvement. At the conclusion of the practicum, Hannah's instructor assigns Hannah a grade of F for the course. At this time, Hannah is informed that a failing grade in the practicum is grounds for dismissal from the program. Hannah is told that she may retake the practicum one time, but that the faculty are not optimistic that she will improve enough to receive a B or better, a condition for her continuing in the program. Although Hannah knew that she was not doing as well in the practicum as some others, she had no awareness that she was in danger of being terminated from the program until the final evaluation.

It is likely that Hannah will take the advice of the faculty and will discontinue the training program at this time. However, have her due process rights been protected? How vulnerable is her practicum instructor and the program if she should decide to challenge their decision? Even if Hannah does not appeal, what are the potential systemic implications of such a process? Even though there is no ill will evident in the action of the faculty and no indication that their decision was capricious or arbitrary, did the process that they followed adequately protect the student and was it legally defensible?

Informed Consent

The concept of informed consent has been handed down to us from the medical profession. Within this context, informed consent requires physicians to inform patients about medical procedures that could be potentially harmful to them. Patients should also be apprised of any risks of a recommended treatment and of the alternative treatments available. The failure of physicians to inform their patients constitutes malpractice and leaves the physician vulnerable to liability should injuries occur as a result of treatment. The doctrine of informed consent has been extended to other health service providers, including those in the mental health fields (Disney & Stephens, 1994).

There is perhaps no ethical standard as far reaching as that of informed consent for the practice of psychotherapy. This is underscored by Woody and associates (1984), who asserted that informed consent is the best defense against a charge of malpractice for the practitioner. For the supervisor, there are really three levels of responsibility: (1) The supervisor must determine that clients have been informed by the supervisee regarding the parameters of therapy, (2) the supervisor must also be sure that clients are aware of the parameters of supervision that will affect them, and (3) the supervisor must provide the supervisee with the opportunity for informed consent. We will discuss each of these separately.

Informed Consent with Clients. It is essential that clients understand and agree to the procedures of therapy prior to its beginning. This is not to imply that there will be no ambiguity in therapy or even that the therapist should be able to predict everything that will happen during the course of therapy. But it does imply that some assessment must occur that will be shared with clients, that goals will be determined, and that the general course of therapy will be outlined for the clients' approval. If it is determined later that a redirection of therapy would be beneficial, this process should be repeated.

Partly because of theoretical orientation, some therapists have resisted this process. But even less directive forms of therapy can and should be explained to clients prior to their commitment to the process. As Woody and associates (1984) stated,

> *[T]he professional should be the last person to object to a requirement of informed consent. If anything, the professional should reach to the maximum allowed by public policy to ensure that the service recipient does, in fact, understand and consent to the treatment. To do otherwise is to court a disciplinary action for unethical conduct and/or a legal suit for malpractice.* (p. 376)

According to Haas (1991), there are seven categories of information that, if revealed, would constitute necessary and sufficient informed consent. The first four apply to the therapeutic relationship. Haas began with the information most directly related to the medical precedent, that of the risks and benefits of treatment. In both cases, only what is reasonable needs to be covered. The risks may be mild, such as embarrassment if others should learn that one is receiving counseling (Disney & Stephens, 1994), or they may be serious, such as the risk of terminating a marriage if one begins to address chronic relationship issues. Likewise, the potential benefits of therapy (Haas's second category) should be discussed.

Haas's (1991) third category encompassed the logistics of treatment, including the length of sessions, cost, opportunity for telephone consultations, and the like. With the growing emphasis on managed care in the mental health service area, the limits of treatment in terms of numbers of sessions is a new critical area that must be covered by the supervisee (Haas & Cummings, 1991). Acuff et al. (1999) expressed overall concern about ethical practice within the requirements and limits of managed care and identified informed consent as one of four vulnerable areas. Finally, if the supervisee is a student assigned to a site for a limited amount of time (say, one semester), this information is important to convey for purposes of informed consent.

The fourth category described by Haas (1991) includes information about the type of counseling or therapy that clients will be offered. If one is behaviorally oriented and will require homework, if the supervisee is in training as a marriage and family therapist and will require additional family members to be present, if one's approach to working with particular issues includes the use of group work, such stipulations should be explained at the outset of therapy. Disney and Stephens (1994) suggested that preferred alternatives to the type of treatment being suggested, as well as the risks of receiving no treatment at all, should be explained at this time as well.

> *Example:* Julian is a trainee in a mental health agency. He has been seeing Ellen for four months in individual counseling. It has become apparent that Ellen and her husband need marriage counseling. Julian has been trained in marriage and family therapy. He very much wants to follow this case to its conclusion. Without discussing alternatives, he suggests that Ellen bring her husband to the next session. Ellen says that she is relieved that he is willing to work with them. She was afraid that Julian would refer them to another therapist. Having Julian work with both her and her husband is exactly what she was hoping for.

In this example (in addition to the therapeutic error of risking triangulation), we must ask if Ellen has been given the opportunity of informed consent. Has her husband? Is there information about the therapy process that Julian should have offered to help both Ellen and her husband make the best decision for their present situation? At the very least, Julian has erred in not discussing alternatives. Julian's supervisor must now help Julian backtrack. If the supervisor had any inkling that

marital therapy might be indicated, the supervisor was negligent for not coaching Julian regarding the client's informed consent rights, as well as her husband's.

Informed Consent Regarding Supervision. The client must not only be aware of therapeutic procedures, but also of supervision procedures. Whether sessions will be taped or observed, who will be involved in supervision (one person or a team of persons), how intrusive will be the supervision, all these need to be communicated to the client.

Haas's (1991) final three categories regarding informed consent are related to supervision. The fifth area of information for which clients should be apprised are emergency procedures that are in place. Because the supervisor should always be involved in an emergency situation, we have placed this category here. Clients should know if direct access to the therapist is available in case of emergency. Will the supervisor be available to the client? This leads to the next category of confidentiality. Most supervisees are apprised of their obligation to inform clients when confidentiality will be breached for reasons other than supervision, for example, if there was an indication that the client might do harm to another. However, the issue of confidentiality is equally relevant to the supervisory relationship. According to Disney and Stephens (1994), "supervisees place themselves in a position to be sued for invasion of privacy and breach of confidentiality if they do not inform their clients that they will be discussing sessions with their supervisor" (p. 50). Most training programs use written forms to alert clients of the conditions of supervision. It may be wise for the supervisor to meet with clients personally before the outset of therapy for a number of reasons: (1) By meeting the supervisor directly, the client usually is more comfortable with the prospect of supervision, (2) it gives the supervisor an opportunity to model for trainees the kind of direct, open communication that is needed to ensure informed consent, and (3) by not going through the trainee to communicate with clients, it is one less way that the supervisor could be vicariously responsible should the trainee not be clear or thorough.

The last area of information to be given to clients has to do with the qualifications of the provider (Haas, 1991). As several authors have noted (e.g., Disney & Stephens, 1994; Harrar, VandeCreek, & Knapp, 1990; Knapp & VandeCreek, 1997; Pope & Vasquez, 1991; Worthington, Tan, & Poulin, 2002), it is vitally important for ethical and legal reasons that clients understand when they are in therapy with a supervisee who is in training. Any attempt to obscure the status of a supervisee may expose both supervisee and supervisor to civil suits alleging fraud, misrepresentation, deceit, and lack of informed consent.

Even when clients are aware that their therapist is under supervision, informed consent can be compromised when trainees downplay the parameters of supervision. Situations occur when supervisees use ambiguous language like, "If it's all right with you, I'll be audiotaping our session," when what they mean is, "I am required to audiotape our sessions if I am to work with you." This leaves the trainee in the awkward position of setting an unwise precedent or of having to backpedal to explain the true conditions of therapy and supervision.

Example: Beth is a social worker who counsels battered women. She is well trained to do initial interviews with women in crisis, and her supervisor is confident in Beth's abilities to carry out these interviews without taping them. Additionally, there is the obvious concern that the use of audiotape would be insensitive to women who are frightened and vulnerable during the interview. The conditions of supervision, however, require Beth to audiotape all subsequent sessions.

Janell was one of Beth's interviewees. After the initial session, Janell decided that she was ready to receive counseling regarding her abusive marriage. She explained to Beth that she was afraid of her husband's reaction to counseling, so she made her first appointment for a day when she knew he would be out of town. When Janell arrived for counseling, Beth discussed the conditions of counseling, including the requirement that she audiotape sessions for supervision. Janell became quite upset and told Beth that she never would have agreed to counseling if she had

known that the sessions would not be held in strictest confidence. Beth attempted to explain that would still be the case, but Janell left and did not return.

How do you react to Beth's method of handling this situation? Were Janell's informed consent rights violated? What alternatives did Beth have that would protect both her and her client?

Informed Consent with Trainees. It is as important that trainees be as well informed as clients. In addition to being informed about the personal and interpersonal strengths required of them for retention in a training program (Forrest et al., 1999), trainees should enter the supervisory experience knowing the conditions that dictate their success or advancement. It also should be clear to them what their responsibilities are and what the supervisor's are. Consider the following examples:

1. Ronald, a student in a professional counseling master's program, makes an appointment to see his academic advisor to discuss his internship now that he is near the end of his training program. He plans to do his internship in a local mental health agency. His advisor tells Ronald that the faculty recently evaluated students and that he was viewed as not having the capacity to be successful in clinical work. It was suggested that he pursue an internship in a "softer" area such as career counseling. Ronald states that he has no interest in career counseling. Ronald's advisor states that such an internship site is the only type that will be approved for him.

2. Ruth has been assigned to a local mental health hospital for her field placement to work with patients who are preparing to be discharged. It is her first day at the site and she is meeting with her site supervisor. He gives her a form to fill out, which asks for information regarding her student malpractice insurance. When Ruth tells her supervisor that she does not carry such insurance, he advises her that it is their policy not to accept any student who does not have insurance. The supervisor also expresses some surprise, because this has always been the hospital's policy and Ruth is not the first student to be assigned to them from her training program.

3. Latoya is in her predoctoral internship, working with very difficult clients. In supervision she shares that one client in particular has been "getting to her," most likely because some of the client's situation is so similar to Latoya's past. Latoya's supervisor immediately suggests that Latoya receive counseling regarding this issue. When Latoya says that she believes her past therapy was sufficient and that she would prefer to view the situation as a supervision one, her supervisor states that she will only continue to work with Latoya if she commits to counseling.

4. Pauline is in her first month of employment at a residential center for troubled youth. Most of her assignments have been what she considers "babysitting," rather than any serious work with her charges. When she talks to her supervisor about this, she is informed that she will not be assigned a case load for the first 6 months and only then if she is perceived as "ready." This is news to Pauline. She is frustrated because she turned down another job where she could have begun to work with kids immediately. Pauline is upset further because her husband has been notified by his firm that he will be transferred in 9 months to another location. Had Pauline known the conditions of her present position, she would not have accepted the job.

In each situation, how egregious is the violation of the supervisee's right to informed consent? To what extent do institutional materials cover issues of consent? How might each situation have been handled to better address the rights of the supervisee?

Whiston and Emerson (1989) addressed the informed consent violation if supervisors refer their trainees for therapy as a condition for continuing in a training program when their trainees were not aware of this possibility from the outset of training. In other words, if there is a possibility that personal counseling will be recommended for any trainees in a given program, all trainees should be cognizant of this practice upon entering the program (e.g., Standard 7.02 in APA's Ethical Principles of Psychologists and Code of Conduct, 2002, is very explicit about this). Similarly, Patrick (1989) warned against allowing trainees in a program to volunteer to be clients for a laboratory course if these trainees are not aware that exposing some types of personal information might lead to a change of status in that program.

These are only a few of the many types of information that trainees should be alerted to by their supervisors before they encounter any consequences. Others include the choice of supervisor, the form of supervision, the time that will be allotted for supervision, the expectations of the supervisor, the theoretical orientation of the supervisor, and the type of documentation required for supervision (Cohen, 1987; McCarthy et al., 1995; Pope & Vasquez, 1991). Simply put, the surprises in store for the trainee should be due to the learning process itself and the complexity of human problems, not to oversights on the part of the supervisor.

As a final comment about informed consent, we refer to Stout's (1987) injunction that supervisors and supervisors-in-training also be forewarned about the parameters of supervision. "Supervisors, as such, should be allowed the prerogative of informed consent, that is, they need to be fully aware of the heavy responsibility, accountability, and even culpability involved in [providing] supervision" (p. 96).

Dual Relationships

Ethical standards of all mental health disciplines strongly advise that dual relationships, or engaging in relationships in addition to the professional relationship, between therapists and clients be avoided. Probably the most flagrant type of dual relationships are sexual relationships between therapists and clients, which are condemned. In most states, sexual exploitation of a client is grounds for the automatic revocation of licensure or certification. It is the responsibility of the supervisor to be certain that supervisees understand the definition of a dual relationship and avoid all such relationships with clients.

Dual relationships between supervisors and supervisees have proved to be a much more difficult issue to resolve and have been a topic of significant discourse in the professional literature. Problematic dual relationships with supervisees can include intimate relationships, therapeutic relationships, work relationships, and social relationships. Most authors concede that supervisors often have more than one professional relationship with a supervisee (e.g., supervisee and research assistant); these typically have been viewed as unavoidable. Borders (2001) cautioned that it is because of the frequency of dual relationships between supervisors and supervisees that supervisors need to be vigilant regarding boundary violations. As a result, the focus of much of the supervision professional literature has been in clarifying when a dual relationship is problematic. Simply put, what makes a dual relationship unethical is (1) the likelihood that it will impair the supervisor's judgment and (2) the risk to the supervisee of exploitation (Hall, 1988b).

Pearson and Piazza (1997) criticized much of the literature for treating dual relationships as static rather than dynamic. Pearson and Piazza also asserted that most professionals are well meaning and attempt to behave ethically. However, they "are probably unaware or minimally aware of situations that may lead to the development of relationships with serious ethical implications" (pp. 91–92). Pearson and Piazza offered five categories of dual relationships in an attempt to reflect some of the fluidity of human relationships in general: (1) *Circumstantial multiple roles* or dual relationships that happen by coincidence (e.g., a supervisor's adult son begins dating a young woman who turns out to be a student in his mother's practicum class). (2) *Structured multiple professional roles,* when supervisor and supervisee have more than one professional role. This is what is usually being referred to when authors note that dual relationships are ubiquitous to doctoral training programs. (3) *Shifts in professional roles* (e.g., when a doctoral student who was formally a classmate in a course with a master's student becomes that student's practicum supervisor). (4) *Personal and professional role conflicts,* a category that includes preexisting professional relationships that are followed by a personal relationship or a personal relationship that is followed by the professional one. (5) *The predatory professional,* a category for those who deliberately seduce or exploit others for their personal gain. We will refer to Pearson and Piazza's categories as we discuss dual relationships.

Dual Relationships between Supervisees and Clients. The literature attending to therapist misconduct (though not necessarily trainee misconduct) with clients is vast and cannot be fully addressed here. A few authors, however, have attended to dual relationships as a supervision issue, that is, grappling with the importance of both monitoring relationships between supervisees and clients and assisting supervisees in ways that will reduce the likelihood of their involvement in exploitative relationships in the future. Hamilton and Spruill (1999) speculated that trainee vulnerability to boundary violations included loneliness, prior paraprofessional or friendship "counseling" experiences in which levels of intimacy were higher than the professional norm, and failure to recognize ethical conflicts. They criticized supervisors for not addressing sexual attraction to clients or trainees as normative and for stereotyping the problem in a sexist manner.

Research conducted by Fly, van Bark, Weinman, Kitchener, and Lang (1997) confirmed that boundary transgressions (sexual and nonsexual) were indeed among the most common ethical transgression among psychology trainees, second only to violations of confidentiality. Furthermore, these two categories of ethical transgressions combined accounted for 45% of the total reported by training directors. In another study that surveyed ethical violations reported to state counselor licensure boards, the most frequent violation involved nonsexual dual relationships with clients (24%), followed by incompetence in the facilitation of a counseling relationship (17%). Sexual dual relationship accounted for 7% of complaints reported (Neukrug, Milliken, & Walden, 2001). Maki and Bernard (2002) stated that, because it is not uncommon for persons attracted to mental health fields to have unresolved personal issues, supervisors should not be surprised that trainees may need assistance with boundary negotiation.

In more recent years, there has been increased interest in precursors to ethical transgressions, especially those that involve sexual misconduct with clients. Jackson and Nuttall (2001) found that three out of five mental health practitioners in their sample who reported a history of severe childhood sexual abuse reported sexual boundary violations with clients. As a corollary to this finding, Somer and Saadon (1999) found that clients in these situations were also more likely to be victims of childhood sexual abuse. As a result, these authors suggested that therapists do routine childhood trauma screenings for all clients. This advice is well taken for trainees who need to know when they are working with clients who might be more sensitive to what the trainee might consider innocuous boundary relaxation.

Celenza (1998) found problems with self-esteem and unresolved anger toward authority figures included among precursors to therapist sexual misconduct. These data suggest that supervisors should conduct an assessment of their trainees in order to assist them to avoid such transgressions.

Preventing Supervisee Ethical Transgressions. Although there is no foolproof way to assure the ethical behavior of supervisees, several authors have encouraged a proactive supervisor posture. To date, virtually all the professional literature addressing trainee transgressions have focused on sexual intimacies with clients. Among the most common strategies recommended are preventive education (Samuel & Gorton, 1998) and honest discussion between supervisors and trainees about the possibility, if not the probability, of occasional sexual attraction to clients, supervisees, or supervisors (Bridges & Wohlberg, 1999; Hamilton & Spruill, 1999; Ladany et al., 1997; Ladany & Melincoff, 1999). Furthermore, as with other sensitive issues, it is imperative that the supervisor accept responsibility for raising the topic. Ladany et al. found that, otherwise, only about half of trainees who experience sexual attraction to clients will share this with their supervisors. Bridges (1999) further emphasized the importance of supervisor openness and candor in assisting trainees to manage intense feelings. "Ethical supervision is embedded in a clearly articulated supervisor–student relationship that monitors misuse of power and boundary crossings, yet is capable of deeply personal discourse" (Bridges, 1999, p. 218).

Hamilton and Spruill seemed to agree with Pearson and Piazza (1997) that well-intended trainees may find themselves blindly approaching ethical slippery slopes. They suggested that all trainees receive instruction in the following areas *prior* to seeing clients: (1) the powerful effects on attraction of familiarity, similarity, self-disclosure, and physical closeness; (2) testimonials from well-respected clinicians about their encounters with sexual attraction in therapy; (3) specific actions to take when feelings of attraction arise, with emphasis on the importance of supervision; (4) suspected risk factors for and signs of client–therapist intimacy; (5) consequences of therapist sexual misconduct on the client; (6) social skills training to increase skill and decrease anxiety related to enacting ethical behavior; and (7) a clear explanation of program policy regarding ethical transgressions, with emphasis on a clear distinction between feelings that are to be expected and actions that are unacceptable (p. 320).

Finally, the use of professional disclosure statements for both supervision (Blackwell, Strohmer, Belcas, & Burton, 2002; Cobia & Boes, 2000) and counseling or therapy are well advised as deterrents to boundary violations. A professional disclosure statement (PDS), which includes details about one's training and experience, as well as about issues such as confidentiality, has the potential of alerting both trainee and client to the professional nature of the relationship. It also typically includes contact information for an outside authority should there be some concern about what has transpired in the relationship. This alone, it would seem, communicates a high regard for professionalism and integrity. (See the Supervisor's Toolbox and Fall and Sutton, 2004, for examples of a PDS.)

Dual Relationships between Supervisor and Supervisee. As with the literature regarding trainees, by far the dual relationship within supervision that has received the most attention is sexual involvement between supervisor and supervisee. Prior to reviewing all types of dual relationships between supervisors and supervisees, we will review briefly a number of studies that have attempted to grasp how widespread this particular issue is. An early study (Pope, Levenson, & Schover, 1979) found that 10% of psychologists admitted to having sexual contact, as students, with their educators, and 13% reported having had a sexual relationship with their students now that they were educators. As might be expected, more female trainees reported having had sexual contact with their educators than male trainees. Furthermore, for those women who had graduated closer to the time of the study, the incidence was much higher (25%) compared to women who had graduated 20 years earlier (5%). Two other studies involving clinical psychologists (Glaser & Thorpe, 1986; Robinson & Reid, 1985) found similar results.

Bartell and Rubin (1990), in a follow-up to Pope et al., found that of those women who had sexual relationships as students, a striking 23% had similar relationships as educators. By contrast, only 6% of those educators who had not had such relationships as students had sexual relationships as educators. Bartell and Rubin, therefore, believed that there is an important modeling effect that may contribute to the perpetuation of unethical behavior in supervision.

A more recent study (Lamb & Catanzaro, 1998), however, found that having been involved in a sexual boundary transgression as a trainee did not increase one's likelihood to be a transgressor as a professional. Their study also found a lower rate (8%) of sexual boundary violations by professional psychologists. Of these, 6% represented violations with clients. The authors speculated that these newer findings may reflect better documentation from the profession regarding the negative outcomes of such transgressions for clients, as well as clearer messages about the negative consequences, both legal and professional, for transgressors. One disturbing finding, however, was that, over time, sexual transgressions with supervisees and/or students were not viewed as negatively by the transgressors as those with clients. It is impossible to know whether these relationships fell into Pearson and Piazza's (1997) personal and professional role conflicts category or the preda-

tory professional category. Lamb and Catanzaro also found that professionals who engaged in sexual boundary violations were also more likely to engage in nonsexual boundary violations.

A study using a similar definition of sexual contact as studies done in psychology found a similar rate (6%) of sexual intimacy between counselor educators and their students (Miller & Larrabee, 1995). Thoreson, Shaughnessy, Heppner, and Cook (1993) surveyed male counselors and found that 16.9% admitted having sexual contact within professional relationships, with the majority occurring after the professional relationship had ended, a rate more similar to earlier studies involving psychologists. Additionally, Glaser and Thorpe (1986) investigated the issue of coercion. Of those individuals who reported sexual contact, the majority felt that they had not been coerced (72%). However, 51% saw some degree of coercion in retrospect. When asked their current opinion of sexual contact between educators and students, 95% considered it to be unethical and harmful, thus reflecting the wisdom of hindsight. Finally, Tabachnick, Keith-Spiegel, and Pope (1991) conducted a survey to poll psychology educators and found that 11% of a national sample reported having sexual intimacies with students. Whether 6% or 16%, these statistics alert the mental health professions that dual relationships must be viewed as a significant issue for both therapy and supervisory relationships.

All relevant ethical codes for the mental health professions make some reference to dual relationships between supervisors and supervisees. Sonne (1994) criticized the previous APA Code of Ethics (American Psychological Association, 1992) for neither defining a multiple relationship nor describing the conditions by which a dual relationship becomes unethical. It seems that this criticism could be directed at other codes as well. Those codes directly related to clinical supervision (see the Supervisor's Toolbox) are clearest in their admonishments against sexual dual relationships. Sexual issues between supervisors and supervisees have been addressed in several ways in the professional literature and will be separated here for discussion.

Sexual Attraction. Sexual attraction does not necessarily mean that a dual relationship will develop. And yet, it is the wisdom of the profession, that, if not handled professionally, there is more of a chance that it will. In one study (Rodolfa, Rowen, Steier, Nicassio, & Gordon, 1994), one quarter of interns in postdoctoral internship sites reported feeling sexually attracted to their clinical supervisors. Ellis and Douce (1994) identified sexual attraction as one of eight recurring issues in supervision. Ladany, Hill, et al. (1996) found that both counselor–client attraction issues and supervisee–supervisor attraction issues were among the topics that trainees were unwilling to disclose in supervision (9% of study participants for each category). In a later study, Ladany and Melincoff (1999) found that 10% of supervisors also chose to be nondisclosive about their own attraction to their supervisees. Several authors (e.g., Ellis & Douce, 1994; Pope & Vasquez, 1991; Vasquez, 1988) have criticized training programs for not teaching trainees how to handle sexual attraction openly and ethically and to view it as a relatively normative part of both supervision and therapy dynamics. It seems that supervisors need to be trained similarly. Ellis and Douce further admonished that acting on sexual attraction in supervision results in "calamity."

Sexual Harassment. Unlike sexual attraction, sexual harassment is an aberration of the supervision process and is never acceptable. Sexual harassment clearly falls into Pearson and Piazza's (1997) category of the predatory professional. Those supervisors who expect or request sexual favors or who take sexual liberties with their trainees are clearly in violation of all ethical codes for the helping professions. They have abused the power afforded them due to their professional status and serve as poor role models for future therapists (Corey, Corey, & Callanan, 1993). It is never acceptable for supervisors to put their own needs and wants in the foreground to the detriment of the professional development needs of the supervisee (Peterson, 1993). Sexual harassment can be insidious and subtle, leaving the victims doubting themselves (Anonymous, 1991) and/or manipulated into the role of caretaker (Peterson, 1993).

DeMayo (2000) investigated the issue of sexual harassment from a different source. He looked at how supervisors reacted when supervisees reported sexual harassment by a client. In his study, 45% of experienced supervisors recalled at least one incident in which a supervisee had been harassed. A range of supervisor reactions followed such reports. Most supervisors discussed the incident in supervision, helped the supervisee to clarify events, and assisted the supervisee in establishing firm boundaries with the client. At other times, supervisors needed to be more directive, including having a joint session with the client, transferring the client to another therapist, or, in extreme cases, ensuring the safety of the supervisee. DeMayo suggested that all trainees should have a conceptual framework for understanding harassment in therapy, ranging from understanding that sexualized feelings are commonplace to trusting their "gut" feelings of harassment. DeMayo also reiterated the suggestion of others that supervisors who are candid and self-disclose with their supervisees are more likely to hear about these important incidents from their supervisees.

Consensual (but Hidden) Sexual Relationships. Results of national studies indicate that the majority of sexual relationships between supervisor and supervisees fall in this category. It is also assumed that the large majority of such relationships do not predate the supervision relationship. Therefore, they fall into Pearson and Piazza's role conflict category. By necessity, the word consensual is used broadly. As reported earlier, in retrospect, many persons believe that there was more coercion involved in a sexual relationship than they thought at the time. Furthermore, as Brodsky (1980) cautioned, when "one person in a relationship has a position of power over the other, there is no true consent for the acceptance of a personal relationship" (p. 516). The frequency of these relationships, however, would indicate adequate levels of consensus at the time, even if in retrospect the situation could also be described as sexual coercion; furthermore, we have evidence that supervisors feel less badly about such relationships in hindsight than they do about a sexual relationship with a client (Lamb & Catanzaro, 1998). The bulk of literature that depicts sexual dual relationships as inherently unethical seems to be directed at these liaisons (e.g., Bonosky, 1995; Bowman, Hatley, & Bowman, 1995; Larrabee & Miller, 1993; Miller & Larrabee, 1995; Slimp & Burian, 1994). In the most measured of commentary, Bartell and Rubin (1990) advised that "[s]exual involvement may further a human relationship, but it does so at the expense of the professional relationship" (p. 446).

Intimate Romantic Relationships. There is virtually no distinction in the majority of the professional literature between those dual relationships that occur within supervision and those that *begin* there but far outlive the supervisory relationship. By contrast, Lazarus (1995) asserted that the American Psychiatric Association, although discouraging all sexual involvement between supervisors and trainees, "realized that romantic relationships often develop in professional settings and that it in no way intended to stifle them" (p. 66). Sexual relationships that grow from positive, caring feelings on the part of both participants are more troublesome to label as clearly inappropriate. In fact, most of us know at least one dual-career couple whose relationship began while one or both was in training. When adults are working closely together in the intense context of clinical work, it is understandable that intimate relationships might emerge. The question, therefore, is not how to prevent such relationships from occurring, but how to assure that such a relationship poses no ethical compromise for the supervisor or trainee and no negative consequence for the trainee's clients.

An obvious characteristic of a healthy relationship is the fact that it is centered in respect and concern for all involved. Therefore, when intimate relationships evolve within supervision, parties should begin a process of ending the supervisory relationship. Usually, another supervisor is easily available to take over the supervisory responsibil-

ities. Consultation with the original supervisor may be needed during a time of transition. If there are no other options, technology offers possibilities for using a supervisor off-location that may not have been available in the past. There is no reason for a professional couple to hide an important relationship or to feel unethical because their feelings for one another began while one was supervisor and one was supervisee. It also is very important that those in administrative roles honor the attempt of the couple to *be* ethical and not treat the situation as an a priori ethical violation.

Nonsexual Dual Relationships. Goodyear and Sinnett (1984) argued that it is inevitable that supervisors and their supervisees will have dual relationships, an opinion shared by others (Aponte, 1994; Clarkson, 1994; Cornell, 1994; Magnuson, Norem, & Wilcoxon, 2000; Ryder & Hepworth, 1990). Unlike therapy relationships, persons who work together will share other experiences with each other. In addition, the same person who serves as a trainee's therapy supervisor could be a member of the same trainee's doctoral research committee, an instructor for another course, or the supervisor for an assistantship. In an agency or school, it sometimes happens that someone under supervision is the same person that the supervisor learned to count on in a crisis or is someone with a personal style that allows the supervisor to be more candid than he or she is with other professional peers. Some of these structured multiple professional relationships (Pearson & Piazza, 1997) are very gratifying, and we would not choose to avoid them. It seems to us, therefore, that we should approach this matter, as Aponte (1994) suggested, by attempting to differentiate between dual relationships that abuse power, exploit supervisees, or harm the supervisee and those that occur within the positive context of a maturing professional relationship.

Lloyd (1992) charged that some professional writings have created "dual relationship phobia" while attempting to caution supervisors about unethical relationships. He was critical of those who have elevated their hypervigilance to the status of ethical standards, rather than charging educators and supervisors to exercise their responsibility as decision makers and resolvers of conflict. Lloyd's comments seemed particularly salient when considering social contact and/or additional professional roles with supervisees. Taking a somewhat more conservative position, Burian and Slimp (2000) cautioned supervisors of doctoral student interns about the potential risks involved when social dual relationships emerge. These authors offered a decision-making model to help supervisors to make responsible decisions that includes an assessment of the intern's ability to leave the social relationship without repercussions, the probable impact on other interns, and the probable impact on other staff members.

One area of dual relationships for which there is particular agreement in the field, however, is the inappropriateness of doing therapy with one's supervisee. Because supervision can stimulate personal issues in the supervisee, it is quite likely that a supervisor will be faced with the challenge of determining where supervision ends and therapy begins (Whiston & Emerson, 1989; Wise, Lowery, & Silvergrade, 1989). In spite of some confusion, most authors (e.g., Bridges, 1999; Burns & Holloway, 1989; Green & Hansen, 1986; Kitchener, 1988; Patrick, 1989; Stout, 1987; Whiston & Emerson, 1989; Wise et al., 1989) recommend that supervisors be clear from the outset of supervision that personal issues might be activated in supervision and, if these issues are found to be substantial, that the supervisee will be asked to work through them with another professional. Furthermore, it is important to stress that this ethical question is not a novel one for supervisors. The collective wisdom of those authors who have grappled with this issue has been that supervisors have the responsibility to help supervisees to identify their issues, especially as they interfere with their work as counselors and therapists, but "after the supervisor identified the personal issues, the trainees must then be given the responsibility for resolving those issues" (Whiston & Emerson, 1989, p. 322).

Dual relationships appear to exist on a behavioral continuum (Dickey, Housley, & Guest, 1993) from extremely inappropriate and unethical behavior, that is, those included in Pearson and Piazza's (1997) predatory professional category, to behavior that could easily be construed as part of the mentoring process, such as taking a few students to a social occasion at a professional meeting. Neither end of the continuum causes much confusion among clinical supervisors. However, many situations in the middle represent "the murky pool of ambiguity" (Peterson, 1993, p. 1). Peterson cautioned that dual relationship challenges abound in supervisory relationships and cannot be regulated out of existence. At the same time, Erwin (2000) found that supervisors displayed less "moral sensitivity" when things indeed were murky. Therefore, it is important to have a plan for situation analysis. We will consider the parameters of ethical decision making at the end of this chapter.

Example: Vanessa has been a marriage and family therapist at an agency for 6 months. Gary, one of the other three therapists in the agency and the only other single therapist, is her clinical supervisor. It will take Vanessa 2 years under supervision to accrue the experience she needs to be eligible to sit for the state licensing examination for her LMFT. One evening Gary calls Vanessa to inquire whether she would like to go to a day-long workshop with him. The speaker for the workshop specializes in a kind of therapy in which Vanessa has expressed interest. Vanessa accepts and the workshop turns out to be an excellent professional experience. On the way home, Vanessa and Gary stop for dinner. Vanessa picks up the tab to thank Gary for including her.

The following day Vanessa is sharing some of the experiences of the workshop with Camille, another therapist at the agency. When Camille asks, "Isn't Gary your supervisor?" Vanessa feels defensive and misunderstood. Later that day, Vanessa decides to go to her agency director and ask his opinion of the situation. He tells her not to be concerned about it and that Camille "worries about everything." During her next supervision session, Vanessa chooses not to mention either conversation to Gary.

Is Gary in danger of violating the principle of avoiding dual relationships? Has he already violated this principle? Was Camille's reaction appropriate? The agency director's? How do you evaluate Vanessa's choice to talk to her agency director? To not apprise Gary of the conversations with Camille and the agency director?

Example: Derek is a professor of clinical psychology. He is a gay male whose research is in the area of developmental issues for gay youth. When a candidate for admission lists a gay support group as a counseling activity in which he'd engaged, Derek insists that he be interviewed, although his academic record was not as strong as some other candidates. Louis is interviewed and Derek is his sole supporter. Although the admissions committee is a bit uncomfortable with their decision, they decide to admit Louis and they assign him to Derek for advising. Derek calls Louis immediately to suggest that he be involved in Derek's research. Louis, who informs Derek that he is gay, is ecstatic.

Does this situation describe the early stages of a dual relationship or a legitimate example of professional mentoring? Would the situation have been different if Louis had applied to this academic program for the distinct purpose of working with Derek? Are there other ethical issues that the faculty should be considering? What would have been your opinion if you were on the admissions committee? Would you feel differently if the faculty member in question was the sole woman on the faculty and the student was one of the few female applicants for the year?

Example: Sharon is a good therapist. In her work with Jeanne, her supervisor, she has been very open and unguarded. Sharon had a very troubled past and she has struggled hard to get where she is. A couple of times Sharon has shared some of her personal pain with Jeanne during intense supervision sessions. Sharon and Jeanne feel very close to each other. In the past couple of weeks, Sharon has not looked well. She's jumpy and short with Jeanne. When Jeanne pursues this change in behavior, Sharon begins to cry and tells Jeanne that she has recently returned to an old cocaine habit. She begs Jeanne not to share her secret, promising that she will discontinue using the drug. She also asks that she be allowed to continue seeing clients.

How is power being negotiated in this example? How does each person stand to be damaged by this dual relationship? Has Jeanne been inappropriate up to this point? What should Jeanne do at this point to be ethical?

Example: Margaret is a school counselor who has been assigned a trainee from the local university for the academic year. As she observes Noah work with elementary school children, she is increasingly impressed with his skills. She asks him to work with Peter, a 9-year-old, who has not adjusted well to his parents' recent divorce. Again, she is impressed with Noah's skill, his warmth and understanding, and, ultimately, with the success he has in working with Peter. Margaret is a single parent who is concerned about her 9-year-old son. She decides to ask Noah to see him. Noah is complimented by her confidence in him. Margaret's son attends a different school, but she arranges to have Noah see him after school hours.

How is Noah vulnerable in this example? How is Margaret's son vulnerable? If Noah had had second thoughts about this situation, what are his recourses for resolution?

Competence

We all remember the feelings we had when we saw our first client. We might have doubted the sanity of our supervisor to trust an incompetent with someone who had a problem. And if we were observed for that session, it was even worse. (One of us recalls a nightmare in which I am electrocuted by my audio recorder as I try to record my first counseling session!) For most of us, those feelings waned with time, helped by encouraging feedback from our supervisors and the accumulation of experience. The feelings also lessened as we grew to appreciate that counseling and therapy are at least part art and probably a combination of many things, only some of which we control. Finally, the feelings diminished through the authenticity of the relationships that we shared with our clients and the positive results of those relationships. The issue of our own competence became less and less bothersome to us. Eventually, we felt good enough about our own abilities that we agreed to supervise the work of another. Now we are involved in the developmental process at two levels: We are overseers of the initial steps taken by our supervisees while we continue to develop ourselves and, at times, we can appreciate how far we have come by observing the tentative work of those under our charge.

There is something very self-assuring about having some experience and being able to see from where one has come. There also is something seductive, and even dangerous, about being in such a position: Supervisors can forget to question their own competence. This is not to imply that it is admirable to remain professionally insecure, but that it is vital for supervisors to remember that the issue of competence is one of the most central questions in the process of clinical supervision. Supervisors must remain competent not only as therapists, but also as judges of another's abilities, while being competent in many facets of supervision itself. In fact, the whole issue of competence, both for supervisors and supervisees, is central to the most pressing ethical responsibility of all, that of monitoring client welfare (Sherry, 1991).

Monitoring Supervisee Competence. By definition, the supervisee is not yet competent to practice independently. But if supervisees are to improve as practitioners, they must be challenged. Attending to the best interests of both client and supervisee *simultaneously* is the greatest clinical and ethical challenge of supervision (Sherry, 1991). Furthermore, monitoring supervisee competence begins with the assumption that the supervisor is a knowledgeable clinician.

The first of 11 core areas promulgated by ACES in the *Standards for Counseling Supervisors* (Supervision Interest Network, 1990) requires that the supervisor be an effective counselor. The supervisor must be more advanced than the trainee in all areas that the trainee is practicing. This relates not only to the generic practice of psychotherapy, but to specific clinical problems as well. Most supervisors realize that they cannot be all things to all people. Yet they are tempted to ignore this bit of wisdom when a trainee wants to gain some experience in an area in which the supervisor is unfamiliar. The helping professions, for better or for worse, have become fields with many specialties. At times it can be a difficult decision whether the supervisor's skills are sufficient to supervise in a

particular area. Supervisors would be wise to have a clear sense of the kinds of cases that they would either not supervise or would supervise only under certain conditions (e.g., for a limited number of sessions, for the purposes of referral, or, as suggested by Hall, 1988a, and Sherry, 1991, with the aid of a consultant). Examples of specialties that some supervisors might choose to shy away from include substance abuse, sexual or physical abuse, eating disorders, or certain personality disorders.

As the field has become more aware of the importance of cultural factors in therapy, experts in ethical issues have included competence in cultural matters as a significant area to be monitored by supervisors (Lopez, 1997; Sherry, 1991; Vasquez, 1992). Again, such competence must first be acquired by the supervisor in order for the supervisor to assist the supervisee to work with persons representing diverse groups, as well as for the supervisor to be successful on this dimension in supervisory relationships. We will discuss this issue in greater detail in Chapter 5.

Finally, Vasquez (1992) noted that part of the responsibility of the supervisor is to help the supervisee become a self-evaluator. In other words, if one of the ethical mandates of all helping professions is to practice only within one's competence, supervisees must become able to make such determinations for themselves. The relevance of this admonition was confirmed by research conducted by Neukrug et al. (2001) in which incompetence was found to be the second most frequent complaint made to counseling licensure boards.

Competence in the Practice of Supervision. As the knowledge and skill base for clinical supervision has increased, it has become more compulsory that supervisors be competent in the practice of supervision *above and beyond their competence as a therapist.* Although there are examples of professions already demanding such competence for clinical supervisors (e.g., AAMFT), this expectation is not yet uniform. At the same time, the expectation that clinical supervisors have training in supervision is growing. Borders and Cashwell (1992) surveyed legislation regarding supervisor criteria and conduct of supervision for counselor licensure applicants and found that few state boards recognized the need for specialized training in supervision. Several years later, however, Sutton, Nielson, and Essex (1998) found that 17 boards obligated supervisors to be trained in supervision, with other boards considering this requirement.

If, as Rinas and Clyne-Jackson (1988) charged, training program faculty are too academic in their approach to supervision, it is sometimes the case that field supervisors are too caught up in their immediate context and do not stay abreast of changes in national standards for practice. Navin, Beamish, and Johanson (1995) studied the ethics practice of field supervisors and compared them to the ACES *Ethical Guidelines for Counseling Supervisors* (Supervision Interest Network, 1993). Whether the problem was standards that are too lofty or field settings that lack adequate regulation, these authors found a good bit of disparity between standards and practice, at least for the supervision of practitioners at the master's level. Disney and Stephens (1994) noted that national standards (such as those for counseling supervisors) may represent the ideal and that liability is more likely to be determined using state standards. However, the court may refer to such standards as a guide. It would be an error, therefore, to assume that national standards are irrelevant for local practice (Guest & Dooley, 1999).

Remaining Competent.   Many seasoned professionals become complacent with their degree of competence and wean themselves from the professional literature and/or attendance at professional meetings or workshops (Campbell, 1994). When licenses or certifications do not require continuing education, this separation from the evolution of mental health practice can be complete (Overholser & Fine, 1990). Although most professionals would probably agree with the necessity of continuing education for all practitioners, and for supervisors in particular, the task itself can be daunting. Not only should supervisors be current in their own professional specialties, but they should also be aware of the substantial developments that are being made in the area of clinical supervision. Some would add that supervisors should be at least minimally aware of specialties that coincide with

their own. And, as has already been stated, awareness of current developments to assist an understanding of the impact of cultural phenomena in both therapy and supervision is also required.

In addition to continuing education, a liberal use of consultation with professional peers is important to prevent the kind of isolation that diminishes competence (Sherry, 1991). Supervision is a serious activity and one with unforeseen challenges. It is important that a supervisor have a network of colleagues, a place to go, for consultation so that the demands of supervision can be met adequately.

Being able to consult with a colleague seems especially important when trying to balance the client's therapy needs with the supervisee's training needs (Upchurch, 1985). There can be a rather narrow band of case complexity that will challenge the trainee without jeopardizing the client. Furthermore, interactions with another supervisor can increase a supervisor's skills in ways that may not have been predicted.

> ***Example:*** Dwayne has been a licensed psychologist in private practice for over 20 years. His therapeutic approach is primarily psychodynamic. Dwayne receives a call from a small group practice consisting of mental health counselors and marriage and family therapists. They are looking for a psychologist who wants to contract with them for supervision. Their interest is mostly that the psychologist be able to evaluate certain clients for possible referral to a psychologist or a psychiatrist. Dwayne has never supervised anyone and is ready for a new challenge. He makes an appointment to meet with the staff of the practice group.

What are the competency issues imbedded in this example? If Dwayne decides to take this group on, what does he need to consider to be ethically sound? What conditions for supervision are advisable? As you understand it, is this arrangement legally defensible?

Confidentiality

Confidentiality is the ethical principle given the most attention in most training programs. In addition to liability concerns, we believe this is so because confidentiality represents the essence of counseling and therapy (a safe place where secrets and hidden fears can be exposed) and because much of our professional status comes from being the bearer of such secrets. We earn our clients' respect and the respect of others by the posture we take toward confidentiality. There was a time when confidentiality was a sacred obligation. In recent years, however, confidentiality has become the step-sibling to safety and judicial judgment. As a result, the issues surrounding confidentiality have become more complicated. Pope and Vetter (1992) surveyed over 1,300 psychologists about incidents that they found ethically troubling. Of the 703 incidents reported, the greatest number (128) fell into the category of confidentiality. Similarly, Fly et al. (1997) found that the most frequent trainee ethical violation concerned confidentiality. Therefore, it seems that the most sacred trust in mental health practice is also the most vulnerable to insult. And as with all therapeutic components, the implications for supervision are more complex still.

Before we consider the legal realities regarding confidentiality, we would like to outline those dimensions that the supervisor must safeguard. First, the supervisor must be sure that the trainee keeps confidential all client information except for the purposes of supervision. Because supervision allows for a third-party discussion of the therapy situation, the trainee must be reminded that this type of discourse cannot be repeated elsewhere. In group supervision, the supervisor must reiterate this point and take the extra precaution of having cases presented using first names only and with as few demographic details as possible (Strein & Hershenson, 1991). When videotape or live supervision is employed with additional trainees present, the only recourse for the supervisor is to emphasize and reemphasize the importance of confidentiality. When students are asked to tape their sessions, they must be reminded that they have in their possession confidential documents. Notes on clients should use code numbers rather than names and be guarded with great care.

In addition to having some assurance that trainees are meeting the requirement of confidentiality, the supervisor must be sure that trainees view the information received in supervision as confidential and not as akin to something read in a text of case studies. There is a certain discipline required to view someone else's clients as one's own as far as privacy is concerned.

Finally, there is the trainee's right to privacy and the supervisor's responsibility to keep information confidential. It is inevitable that supervision will be an opportunity for the supervisor to hear something about the trainee that would not be discovered in a less personal learning situation. For example, the trainee might share some painful aspect of childhood as it relates to a client. The divulging of such information might come from the trainee's concern that personal history should not detract from therapy and with the request that the supervisor monitor the case more closely. We can all imagine several situations in which such an encounter could take place; the topics could range from family secrets and sexual orientation to prejudicial attitudes that the trainee believes must be divulged. Prior to such an occurrence, the supervisee should understand the circumstances for revealing information obtained in supervision. Knowing that evaluative information from supervision may be passed along to faculty and that any particular issue that troubles the supervisor may be discussed with faculty colleagues allows the supervisee to make an informed decision about what to reveal in supervision (Sherry, 1991).

There is still some occasional confusion in the helping professions regarding the distinctions between confidentiality, privacy, and privileged communication. Confidentiality is defined by Siegel (1979) as follows: "Confidentiality involves professional ethics rather than any legalism and indicates an explicit promise or contract to reveal nothing about an individual except under conditions agreed to by the source or subject" (p. 251). Privacy is the other side of confidentiality. It is the client's right not to have private information divulged without informed consent, including the information gained in therapy. Privileged communication, on the other hand, is a legal concept and is the result of state statute. It refers to the right of clients not to have their confidential communications used in open court without their consent. Therefore, "although all privileged communications are confidential communications, some confidential communications may not be privileged" (Disney & Stephens, 1994, p. 26).

Although these three terms are vital in therapy and supervision, they are not absolute. In fact, knowing the limits of each is as serious a responsibility for the clinician as honoring their intent. It is ultimately an individual decision as to when the therapist or supervisor will decide to overturn the client's (or supervisee's) right of privacy and break confidentiality. However, in a number of cases either legal precedent, state law, or a value of a higher order dictates such a direction. Those typically included as exceptions to privilege are reported by Falvey (2002) as follows:

- When a client gives informed consent to disclosure
- When a therapist is acting in a court-appointed capacity
- When there is a suicidal risk or some other life-threatening emergency
- When a client initiates litigation against the therapist
- When a client's mental health is introduced as part of a civil action
- When a child under the age of 16 is the victim of a crime
- When a client requires psychiatric hospitalization
- When a client expresses intent to commit a crime that will endanger society or another person (duty to warn)
- When a client is deemed to be dangerous to himself or herself
- When required for third-party billing authorized by the client
- When required for properly utilized fee collection services (p. 93)

Because privileged communication is a legal matter, it is always wise to receive legal counsel when confidential information is demanded. Outside court proceedings, many situations fall into gray areas.

The trend in the helping professions seems to be toward a less robust view of confidentiality. This professional obligation seems to be increasingly vulnerable to legal interpretation (Falvey,

2002). It is considered wise, therefore, to make a discussion of confidentiality and its limits a common practice in therapy and supervision.

Marketplace Issues

As more states pass legislation to regulate all the mental health professions, the need for clinical supervisors to supervise postacademic professionals is increasing (Magnuson, Norem, & Wilcoxon, 2000). At the same time, changes in mental health delivery systems require that supervisors stay informed so as to keep supervisees informed and to avoid any business arrangements that would prove to be unethical and/or illegal.

A common practice of the past involved the supervisor "signing off" for supervisees, often not because supervision was taking place but because the supervisor's credentials allowed for third-party payment, whereas the supervisee's did not. This practice is, of course, unethical and illegal. But other marketplace issues are more ambiguous ethically. For example, should a supervisor accept payment from a supervisee for supervision that will lead to certification or licensure? Under what conditions might this be acceptable? If one is a supervisor for someone outside one's place of employment, what kinds of protections are necessary for the clients of the supervisee? The supervisee? The supervisor? (Wheeler & King, 2000). With the introduction of managed care, new duties regarding informed consent are likely, as well as a careful selection of appropriate providers of care (Acuff et al., 1999; Appelbaum, 1993). What is the implication of providing (or supervising) counseling services offered over the Internet for supervisors (Kanz, 2001; Maheu & Gordon, 2000)? In short, the marketplace is changing dramatically as a result of legislation, changes in health care systems, and advances in technology. It is the ethical and legal responsibility of clinical supervisors to stay abreast of relevant developments and to assure that supervisees' practice is consistent with ethical mandates and the law.

The Supervisee's Perspective

Most of the data we have regarding ethical issues come from therapists or supervisors. Furthermore, the ethical issues addressed are those that can manifest in either therapy or supervision (e.g., boundary violations). In contrast, Worthington, Tan, and Poulin (2002) conducted an exploratory investigation on supervisee ethical behavior that focused specifically on supervision issues. In their distinctive study, they conceptualized supervisee transgressions to include themes such as intentional nondisclosure of important information (to supervisors), mismanagement of case records, actively operating at an inappropriate level of autonomy, failure to address (in supervision) personal biases that impact counseling, inappropriate methods of managing conflict with supervisors, and failure to engage in necessary professional development activities. The authors identified 31 questionable behaviors and asked over 300 supervisors and supervisees (combined) to judge each item on its ethicality. Twenty-eight of their items were viewed as more unethical than ethical and there was relatively high agreement between supervisors and supervisees about these behaviors. The behaviors ranged from forging a supervisor's signature on case material (viewed as most unethical) to gossiping about a conflict with her/his supervisor without discussing the issue in supervision (considered mildly unethical). As a second function of the study, supervisees were asked to report how frequently they had engaged in each behavior. As might be expected, supervisees engaged in behaviors considered less unethical more often than the most egregious behaviors. Finally, supervisees were asked to identify reasons for engaging in ethically questionable conduct. Six reasons surfaced as most prevalent: (1) It is an indirect way of coping with or expressing my feelings toward my supervisor; (2) My personal problems sometimes affect my judgment; (3) I feel that I should be given more professional autonomy; (4) My relationship with my supervisor feels unsafe; (5) Sometimes I feel like I know more than my supervisor does; and (6) My workload is too heavy (pp. 342–343).

While the Worthington et al. (2002) study was descriptive in nature and based on self-report, it offers a unique glimpse into the many aspects of supervision that have ethical implications. The authors rightly conclude that their data contain implications for training as well as for monitoring supervisees. Future research in this area would be fruitful.

LEGAL RAMIFICATIONS FOR CLINICAL SUPERVISORS

Malpractice

An ethical violation becomes a legal issue when the aggrieved party makes such a claim (Maki & Bernard, 2002). In other words, the difference between a claim of an ethical violation and a claim of malpractice is not determined by the egregiousness of the behavior committed by the supervisee, counselor–therapist, or supervisor. Rather, it is determined by whether the aggrieved choose to bring their complaints to a regulatory body or to civil court. In fact, it is not uncommon for the same claim to be brought to both a regulatory body and to court as a malpractice lawsuit (Montgomery, Cupit, & Wimberley, 1999). That being said, it is safe to assume that there are far more complaints made to regulatory bodies than there are lawsuits. There are at least two reasons for this: (1) the cost of litigation is a deterrent; (2) whereas a regulatory body (peer review board) would investigate whether the professional breached relevant professional ethics, civil court is quite different. Briefly, a legal complaint is restricted by tort law; therefore, the defendant must be able to prove that the negligence claimed resulted in harm. Many complaints cannot meet such a level of proof.

There are two types of torts (i.e., civil wrongs other than breach of contract), intentional and unintentional (Swenson, 1997). It is highly unlikely that the therapist or supervisor would be sued for an intentional tort. For this to be the case, the *intention* of the supervisor or therapist would be to cause harm. As an example, a supervisor and therapist may decide to suggest to a client behavior that they believe will cause her to lose her job (thinking, perhaps, that she needs to experience such a crisis to face some intrapsychic issues). Such a case could be argued under intentional tort. Similarly, a supervisor could decide to be overly critical with a supervisee in order to force the supervisee out of a training program. Again, this kind of Machiavellian behavior would fall under intentional tort law.

Virtually all malpractice cases in the mental health professions, however, are unintentional torts, or negligence cases (Swenson, 1997). Malpractice is defined as "harm to another individual due to negligence consisting of the breach of a professional duty or standard of care. If, for example, a mental health professional fails to follow acceptable standards of practice and harm to clients results, the professional is liable for the harm caused" (Disney & Stephens, 1994, p. 7). Four elements must be proved for a plaintiff to succeed in a malpractice claim (Ogloff & Olley, 1998): (1) A fuduciary relationship with the therapist (or supervisor) must have been established. Within supervision, this means that the supervisor is working in the best interests of the supervisee and the supervisee's clients and not in his or her own interests (Remley & Herlihy, 2001); (2) the therapist's (or supervisor's) conduct must have been improper or negligent and have fallen below the acceptable standard of care; (3) the client (or supervisee) must have suffered harm or injury, which must be demonstrated; and (4) a causal relationship must be established between the injury and the negligence or improper conduct. We are not aware of any suits brought against supervisors by trainees for inadequate supervision. It is more likely that supervisors would be involved in legal action as a codefendant in a malpractice suit (Snider, 1985) based on the alleged inadequate performance of the supervisee.

Therapists' (and supervisors') vulnerability is directly linked to their assumption of professional roles. When they take on the role of therapist or supervisor, they are expected to know and follow the law, as well as the profession's practice and ethical standards. Additionally, though it is not uncommon to hear professionals bemoan the increasing litigiousness of society, at least part of the problem seems to lie with faulty self-regulation within the mental health professions. Research seems to support that helping professionals have great difficulty in judging peers' or sometimes even supervisees' competence (Forrest et al., 1999; Haas, Malouf, & Mayerson, 1986) and are reluctant to report known ethical violations of peers or supervisees (Bernard & Jara, 1986; King & Wheeler, 1999) or peers or supervisees who are impaired (Forrest et al.; Wood, Klein, Cross, Lammers, & Elliot, 1985).

Sociological factors also contribute to the increase in lawsuits against helping professionals. Cohen's (1979) claim seems even more relevant today that the three primary factors for the increase are (1) a general decline in the respect afforded helping professionals by clients and society at large, (2) increased awareness of consumer rights in general, and (3) highly publicized malpractice suits for which settlements were enormous, leading to the conclusion that a lawsuit may be a means to obtain easy money. All these factors increase the likelihood of potential lawsuits (however spurious) against the practitioner (however ethical). As M. H. Williams (2000) noted, there is little that therapists or supervisors can do to totally protect themselves from persons who attempt to use the court for disturbed or vengeful reasons. At the same time, there are some precautions that professionals can take, and these will be covered later in this section.

Although failure to warn accounts for a very small number of legal claims (Meyer, Landis, & Hays, 1988), the Tarasoff case has made this issue highly visible. The Tarasoff case also involved a clinical supervisor and thus introduces the concept of vicarious liability or *respondeat superior* (literally, "let the master answer"). Following the discussion regarding the duty to warn, therefore, will be a review of salient direct and vicarious liability issues.

The Duty to Warn.   The duty to warn is a prime example of a legal precedent becoming a direct influence on ethical codes. The duty to warn stems from the famous Tarasoff case (*Tarasoff* v. *Regents of the University of California,* 1976). In the landmark case, a university therapist believed that his client (Poddar) was dangerous and might do harm to a woman who had rejected Poddar's romantic advances (Tatiana Tarasoff). Because Poddar refused voluntary hospitalization, the therapist notified police to have him taken to a state hospital for involuntary hospitalization. The police spoke to Poddar and decided that he was not dangerous. *On the advice of his supervisor, who feared a lawsuit for breach of confidence* (Lee & Gillam, 2000), the therapist did not pursue the matter further. Poddar did not return to therapy. Two months later Poddar killed Tarasoff. Although most mental health professionals believe that the Tarasoffs won this case based on the duty to warn, actually the court only determined that they could file a suit on these grounds. Rather, the case was settled out of court (Meyer et al., 1988). Furthermore, the Supreme Court of the State of California actually heard the Tarasoff case twice and articulated the *duty to protect* at this second hearing (Chaimowitz, Glancy, & Blackburn, 2000). Chaimowitz et al. argued that the duty to warn, therefore, must be assessed as it relates to the duty to protect. They further asserted that warning an intended victim may be insufficient to meeting the duty to protect, although there may be times that it could exacerbate a tenuous situation. In short, these authors suggested that more than a knee-jerk decision to warn is called for, but rather a reasoned strategy that holds the duty to protect at its center.

In spite of the ambiguous outcome of the original case, the duty to warn and protect has become a legal standard for all mental health professionals and has become the law in several states. It remains an important case for supervisors as well as therapists, because the supervisor was implicated in the case.

It is imperative, then, for supervisors to inform supervisees of conditions under which it would be appropriate to implement the duty to inform for the protection of intended victims(s). Two issues are embedded in the duty to warn and protect: assessing the level of dangerousness of the client and the identifiability of potential victims (Ahia & Martin, 1993; Lee & Gillam, 2000). The practitioner and supervisor are not expected to see the unforeseeable. There is no foolproof way to predict all human behavior. Rather, there is an expectation

that sound judgment is used and reasonable or due care is taken regarding the determination of dangerousness. For this reason, most authorities on such legal matters strongly advise that consultation with others and documentation of all decisions are vital in any questionable case.

In other situations, there is some indication that the client might be dangerous, but no potential victim has been named. In fact, there might not be a particular person in danger, but rather the client's hostility might be nonspecific. At present, ethical standards and legal experts seem to lean in favor of client privilege unless there is clear evidence that the client is immediately dangerous and there is an identifiable (or highly likely) victim (Ahia & Martin, 1993; Fulero, 1988; Lee & Gillam, 2000; Schutz, 1982; Woody and associates, 1984). In other words, therapists and supervisors are not expected to, nor should they, read between the lines when working with clients. Many clients make idle threats when they are frustrated. It is the job of mental health practitioners to make a reasonable evaluation of these threats. In fact, in the eyes of the law, it is more important that reasonable evaluation be made than that the prediction be accurate.

Direct Liability and Vicarious Liability

Direct liability would be argued when the actions of the supervisor were themselves the cause of harm. For example, if the supervisor did not perform supervision adequate for a novice counselor or if the supervisor suggested (and documented) an intervention that was determined to be the cause of harm (e.g., suggesting that a client use "tough love" strategies with a child that ended in physical harm to the child). Results reported by Montgomery, Cupit, and Wimberley (1999) suggested that direct liability is still rare for supervisors, though two reported malpractice suits involved supervision (evaluation of a supervisee and a billing issue). Potentially, all supervision practice standards, if violated, could lead to a supervisor being found to be directly liable. These include issues such as violation of informed consent, breach of confidentiality, inability to work with cultural differences, or an inappropriate dual relationship (Maki & Bernard, 2002).

Vicarious liability, on the other hand, represents possibly the worst nightmare for the clinical supervisor, that is, being held liable for the actions of the supervisee when these were not suggested or perhaps even known by the supervisor. In such cases, the supervisor becomes liable by virtue of the relationship with the supervisee. Therefore, the supervisor generally is only held liable "for the negligent acts of supervisees if these acts are performed in the course and scope of the supervisory relationship" (Disney & Stephens, 1994, p. 15). Falvey (2002) outlined three conditions that must be met for vicarious liability to be established:

1. Supervisees must voluntarily agree to work under the direction and control of the supervisor and act in ways that benefit the supervisor.
2. Supervisees must be acting within the defined scope of tasks permitted by the supervisor.
3. The supervisor must have the power to control and direct the supervisee's work. (pp. 17–18)

Disney and Stephens (1994) reported additional factors that might be used to establish whether an action fell within the scope of the supervisory relationship. These included the time, place, and purpose of the act (e.g., was it done during counseling or away from the place of counseling?); the motivation of the supervisee (e.g., was the supervisee attempting to be helpful?); and whether the supervisor could have reasonably expected the supervisee to commit the act (p. 16). Disney and Stephens (1994) observed that, should the supervisor be found guilty based on vicarious responsibility, then the supervisor, if found not to be negligent in subsequent court proceedings, could recover damages from the supervisee.

Remley and Herlihy (2001) cautioned that each legal case is unique; therefore, generalizability from one situation to another may be limited. They stressed the importance of establishing the amount of control a supervisor had over a supervisee in order to arrive at a judgment of vicarious liability. Because of this, they indicated that supervisors at the clinical site are more likely to be held account-able for a therapist's negligence than off-site (e.g., university) supervisors. Falvey (2002) speculated that supervisors who received part of a fee paid to a supervisee were more likely to be found vicariously liable, because such a situation clearly benefits the supervisor, meeting one of the conditions for vicarious liability.

Preventing Claims of Malpractice

Snider (1985) offered four guidelines to supervisors to reduce the likelihood of being named as a codefendant in a malpractice suit that continue to be relevant today. First, maintain a trusting relationship with supervisees. Within a context of mutual trust and respect, supervisees will be far more likely to voice their concerns about their clients, themselves, and each other. Second, keep up to date regarding legal issues that affect mental health settings and the professional in general. Additionally, supervisors need to have a healthy respect for the complexity of the law and recognize the need for competent legal aid. Third, if the supervisor is the administrative head of an agency, it is essential that the supervisor retain the services of an attorney who specializes in malpractice litigation. If this is not the supervisor's decision, the supervisor should be sure that the organization has appropriate legal support. Fourth, supervisors should have adequate liability insurance and should be sure that their supervisees also carry liability insurance. Although this final precaution does not reduce the chances of being sued, it does, obviously, minimize the damage that could accrue from such an unfortunate experience.

In addition to these admonitions, supervisors are advised to stay current with professional standards of practice and to seek consultation with trusted colleagues when necessary (Ogloff & Olley, 1998). Another important risk-management strategy is record keeping (Falvey, Caldwell, & Cohen, 2002; Woodworth, 2000). Methods of documenting supervision will be covered in Chapter 8. Finally, Woodworth (2000) also recommended that helping professionals (including supervisors) attend to their emotional and physical well-being.

Being professionally or personally overextended is too often a precursor to making foolish errors.

Regrettably, there is little comfort to offer the timid supervisor who is afraid of the tremendous responsibility and potential legal liability inherent in supervision. Short of refusing to supervise, we believe protection for the supervisor lies in the same concepts of reasonable care and sound judgment that protect counselors and therapists. This includes an awareness of and command of the concepts and skills presented in this book. It also includes a commitment to investing the time and energy to supervise adequately and to document all supervisory contacts. Ultimately, the most fruitful approach to practice "involves a unique blend of professional wisdom and human wisdom. In addition to some distinct knowledge, skill, and good work habits, healthy, respectful relationships and keen, unencumbered self-knowledge add significant protection to the clinical supervisor. In short, insight, integrity, and goodwill are enormous barriers to professional difficulty" (Maki & Bernard, 2002, p. 402).

ETHICAL DECISION MAKING

As we already have conveyed, the relationship between ethics and the law is generally perceived to be very close. This is not only true for the human services, but also for society at large. The great danger of this perception is the pairing of what is "right" with "what I can get away with," leaving only "what I can't get away with" as "wrong." Knowing full well that most unethical behavior is not confronted, the practitioner becomes more likely to lose sight of the moral constants. The potential consequence is that the helping professions become another example of the law dictating professional ethics or, at worst, professional behavior dictated by self-interest.

The only reasonable alternative to this approach is putting ethics in the foreground, in both training and practice, for therapists and clinical supervisors. Thinking regarding ethical issues should be proactive and not reactive. Waiting for ethical issues to emerge in supervision seems to set

up the conditions for crisis training, not ethics training. The point is that ethical practice is a way of professional existence, not a command of a body of knowledge. Anything short of this is an inadequate posture for the clinical supervisor.

One aid to ethical development is for training programs to use experiential learning and/or case analysis (cf. Storm & Haug, 1997). Many ethical mishaps result from acts of omission, not intentional malice (Bernard, 1981). Such omissions are more likely if professionals have not had an opportunity to experience the ins and outs of a similar situation. The use of simulation and behavioral rehearsal is an excellent way to safely allow both trainees and supervisors to face difficult situations, try alternative resolutions, and evaluate their outcomes.

Hansen and Goldberg (1999) outlined a seven-category matrix of considerations that could be used to assess ethical and legal dilemmas, both in training and in actual situations. They rightly argued that a linear model of ethical decision making, one that begins by identifying an ethical dilemma and ends with a decision to act, belies the complexity of most situations with ethical and legal overtones. By considering multiple influencing variables as interfaced with a linear process, the mental health professional is more likely to arrive at a sound course of action.

Hansen and Goldberg reiterated the work of others (e.g., Kitchener, 1984) that moral principles are of primary importance when evaluating a difficult situation. The principles that Kitchener advocated are *autonomy* (both being responsible for one's behavior and having freedom of choice), *beneficence* (contributing to the well-being of others), *nonmaleficence* ("above all, do no harm"), *justice* (fairness in dealings with all people), and *fidelity* (the promotion of honesty and fulfilling commitments and contracts). Tarvydas (1995) noted that much of our influence on supervisees may lie in our ability to model these principles. In addition to these, Hansen and Goldberg (1999) asserted that professionals are influenced by personal (e.g., political or religious) values. Training in ethical decision making that does not acknowledge the importance of personal values does trainees an injustice.

Hansen and Goldberg's second consideration involved clinical and cultural factors. For example, as stated earlier in our discussion about the duty to warn, the therapist and supervisor must make an assessment of a client's level of risk in order to make an informed decision about a course of action. What may be ethical in one situation may violate a client's rights in another. In addition to clinical assessment, cultural assessments must be made. Hansen and Goldberg noted, for example, that the boundaries of confidentiality can take on different meaning when viewed with cultural sensitivity.

Hansen and Goldberg's next four considerations are less fluid and include professional codes of ethics; agency or employer policies; federal, state, and local statutes; and rules and regulations that elaborate statutes. All these call for a certain amount of vigilance from the professional to stay informed about changes in professional and regulatory pronouncements. At the same time, it must be said that codes, statutes, rules, and regulations are not sufficient for all (even most) difficult situations. In fact, Pope and Bajt (1988, as referenced in Hansen and Goldberg) found that 75% of a sample of senior psychologists, all of whom were known for ethics expertise, believed that formal codes and statutes should sometimes be violated to ensure client welfare or because of personal values.

Finally, Hansen and Goldberg identified case law as an important consideration when making an ethical decision. Because case law calls for interpretation regarding its relevance for a particular ethical or legal dilemma, it could be viewed as more fluid than statutes and codes of ethics. Additionally, case law represents the history of our most dramatic struggles as mental health professionals, thus providing a rich context for deliberation.

Betan and Stanton (1999) added another dimension to ethical decision making that goes beyond personal beliefs and values. They studied the effect of concerns and emotions on willingness to implement ethical knowledge and found that anxiety or guilt interfered with action, whereas compassion (i.e., concern, empathy, and loyalty) and confidence that a situation can change (i.e., optimism) enhanced action. These findings need to be addressed adequately in training for ethical decision making. Betan and Stanton concluded that awareness of how one's emotions may be influencing ethical decision making can lead to appropriate management of these emotions.

Finally, once we have carefully attended to the multiple factors already noted, we must eventually return to a process that will end in some form of resolution. This includes consideration of alternative courses of action (often weighing one aspect of the situation against another), an attempt to predict the consequences of each potential course (both short term and long term and for each of the parties involved), and making a decision on which course of action to take that includes a willingness to take responsibility for the consequences of the selected action (Hadjistavropoulos & Malloy, 2000).

CONCLUSION

As gatekeepers of the profession, clinical supervisors will continue to be heavily involved with ethical standards for practice. The most instrumental approach to this responsibility is to be well informed and personally and professionally sanguine. Both are accomplished by continually putting ethics in the foreground of discussion, contemplation, and practice. In this case, perhaps more than any other, supervisors' primary responsibility is to model what they aspire to teach. For practice in addressing a variety of ethical dilemmas, see Fall and Sutton (2004).

CHAPTER 4

SUPERVISION MODELS

For practitioners and researchers alike, "there is nothing so practical as a good theory" (Kurt Lewin as quoted by Marrow, 1969). Theories enable us to make sense of and organize what otherwise might be overwhelming amounts of information. As Schermer (2001) noted, "The facts never just speak for themselves. They must be interpreted through the colored lenses of ideas: percepts need concepts" (p. 38). For practitioners, theory has the added benefit of guiding their interventions.

We began Chapter 1 by noting that one characteristic of professionals is that they make decisions under conditions of uncertainty. It is *theory* that enables them to do so.

A study by Strupp and Hadley (1979) illustrates just how essential theory is to practitioners. In that study, college professors working as paraprofessional therapists obtained similar treatment outcomes to experienced clinical psychologists against whom they were being compared. Given this context, it is interesting that one professor tended to explain his male clients' problems in terms of "girl troubles." This is theory of the most rudimentary sort, yet it apparently provided a necessary cognitive map for this professor–therapist.

The Strupp and Hadley example suggests another important reality: theories need not actually be "true" to be useful. Eye Movement Desensitization and Reprocessing (EMDR; Shapiro, 2001) perhaps also illustrates this point, for it is a model with at least some demonstrated effectiveness, but that relies on an unlikely theory. And to offer a third example, Levenson (1984) discussed how people in the Middle Ages were convinced that to avoid malaria they should build their houses on high land, make sure there was no stagnant water in or around the house, and close the windows at night. This is a generally effective strategy. The *theory* behind it, though, concerned avoiding evil effects from the humors and the night air, whereas the more contemporary theory is that anopheles mosquitoes serve as disease-carrying agents.

THEORY IN CLINICAL SUPERVISION

Clinical supervisors first were therapists and therefore bring to their supervisory role an existing appreciation for theories of practice. This chapter introduces models that they might use in supervision. As Hart (1982) noted, "One can imitate an outstanding supervisor, but without theory or a conceptual model one does not really understand the process of supervision" (p. 27).

Qualities of Therapy and Supervision Theory

Before we discuss the actual models of supervision, we want to offer some criteria by which to evaluate theory. To keep these criteria in mind can be helpful in evaluating the overall merits of the particular models available to supervisors.

Patterson (1986) suggested five criteria to evaluate theory. These are *preciseness and clarity* (a theory should be understandable, free from ambiguities, and internally consistent); *parsimony or simplicity* (also known as Occam's razor after the 14th-century English epistemologist, William of Occam; a theory should employ only the minimum number of assumptions and interrelationships among them necessary to explain the domain that is the focus of the theory); *operationality* (it should be possible to specify a theory's hypotheses and concepts in clear and measurable terms); *practicality* (even if it is not actually "true," as in our example of the night humors and malaria, a theory should be useful to practitioners); and *comprehensiveness* (a theory should make use of the known data in the particular domain of interest).

This last criterion, comprehensiveness, remains largely aspirational. There is a classic Indian story of six blind men who, encountering an elephant for the first time, attempted to understand it. Each, having touched a different part of the elephant, made his own inferences about its nature. For example, the one who touched its side likened the elephant to a wall, the one who touched its tusk likened it to a spear, the one who touched its knee likened it to a tree, and so on (Saxe, 1865).

It is not difficult to see this parable's relevance to therapy or supervision theory. Therapy and supervision are complex interventions, and the models for them are developed by individuals who are necessarily limited in what they are able to perceive and describe.

To the five criteria Patterson (1986) suggested, we would add a sixth. This is Popper's (1935/1959) criterion of *falsifiability*. It is impossible to "prove" that any theory is correct or true. But the theory should be formulated in such a manner that its propositions can be *disproved*. By this criterion, some therapeutic theories have fallen short. This is especially true of psychoanalysis, for some of its propositions have been set up so that they are virtually impossible to disprove (see, e.g., Popper, 1968).

Theories and Models in Supervision. Patterson's six criteria apply to scientific theories. Theories used by psychological practitioners, however, tend to be less formal and precise and therefore are more likely to fall short when assessed against one or more of these criteria. In a strict sense, therefore, most theories of therapy and supervision more accurately should be described as *models,* which meet fewer of these six criteria, especially that of comprehensiveness. As a practical matter, it probably does not make a great deal of difference which

term is used. Although, we will use both terms, our use of model will predominate.

Another important point to make concerns a bias in the literature that will affect our emphasis here. That is, most theorists and researchers have focused on supervision as an intervention that occurs in the context of a one-to-one relationship. As a result, most supervision theory has evolved independently of the advancements made in group and/or team supervision. As a consequence, we discuss group and team forms of supervision only tangentially in this chapter and more fully later in Chapters 10 and 11.

In the remainder of this chapter we selectively review supervision models. Unfortunately, the limited space we have affects both the number of models that we cover and the comprehensiveness with which we do it.

The organization we employ, depicted in Figure 4.1, recognizes three broad categories of supervision models: the first is comprised of models based on psychotherapy theories; the other two were developed specifically for supervision. Our organization reflects Holloway's (1992) suggestion that models developed specifically for supervision generally can be typed as being either developmental or social role. Figure 4.1 also serves as something of an advance organizer for the chapter in that it depicts the order in which we will discuss the specific models.

We note here that, whereas Kagan's Interpersonal Process Recall (IPR; Kagan, 1976, 1980; Kagan & Kratwohl, 1967; Kagan, Kratwohl, & Farquahar, 1965; Kagan, Kratwohl, & Miller, 1963; H. Kagan & Kagan, 1997) often is treated as a model, we have come to treat it instead simply as an intervention. We cover IPR in Chapter 9.

Before beginning our discussions, we want to note that entire books are devoted to some of these models. Yet we are limited to such an extent that we are able to cover each at only a relatively general level. But even this limited coverage is important for several reasons. One is that the development of many of these models is intertwined with the development of supervision itself and so is important to better understanding the field. An-

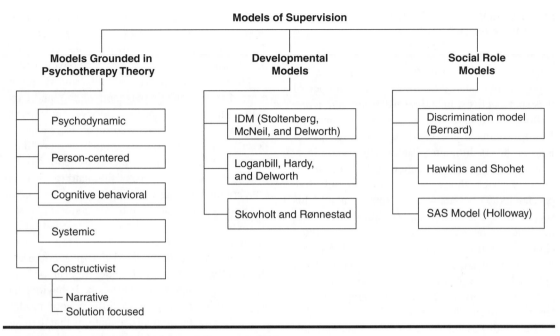

FIGURE 4.1   Models of Supervision: A Conceptual Map

other is that our coverage of these models establishes a context for discussing material in the following chapters. We will not necessarily link supervisor interventions to models in these discussions. But as the Friedlander and Ward model in Figure 4.2 shows, these interventions are affected by theoretical orientation. It is important, therefore, that the reader have at least some exposure to the more prominent supervision models.

In the model in Figure 4.2, *assumptive world* refers to the person's past professional and life experience, training, values, and general outlook on life. It influences the person's choice of *theoretical orientation* (e.g., behavioral, psychoanalytic, or eclectic), which in turn influences his or her choice of *style* or *role*. Style or role determines *strategy–focus* which in turn influences choice of *format* (or *method;* e.g., live supervision or group supervision), which in turn influences choice of strategy. In short, then, the model assumes the following path of causal influence: assumptive world → theoretical orientation → style–role → strategy–focus → format → technique.

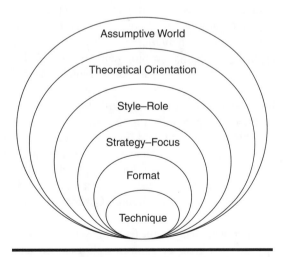

FIGURE 4.2   Successively Higher Ordered Determinants of Supervisor Behavior

From "Development and Validation of the Supervisory Styles Inventory," by M. L. Friedlander and L. G. Ward, 1984. *Journal of Counseling Psychology, 31,* 541–557. Reprinted with permission.

SUPERVISION MODELS GROUNDED IN PSYCHOTHERAPY THEORY

By many estimates, there are several hundred theories, or at least aspiring theories, of therapy. Supervision has been described from a number of these perspectives, including Adlerian (e.g., Kopp & Robles, 1989), reality (e.g., Smadi & Landreth, 1988), Gestalt (Hoyt & Goulding, 1989; Resnick & Estrup, 2000), Jungian (Kugler, 1995), and integrative therapies (e.g., Tennen, 1988). In the interest of space, though, we will cover only five psychotherapy-based models of supervision. In this section we will describe supervision derived from the widely endorsed models of the psychoanalytic, client-centered, and cognitive–behavioral. As well, we address systemic models and then constructivist approaches. The former addresses the work of supervisors of marriage and family therapy; the latter is less specific to modality.

Before discussing these models, it is important first to contextualize this discussion, beginning with the inevitable continuity in how supervisors conceptualize their work as therapists versus work as supervisors. As Shoben (1962) and others have argued, therapists work from an implicit theory of human nature that also must influence how they construe reality, including interpersonal behavior, normal personality development (or family development), and abnormal or dysfunctional development. This is another way of asserting that a therapist's assumptive world will affect theory, as depicted in Figure 4.2. It is reasonable to assume that this assumptive world is constant across situations, affecting professionals' work as both therapist *and* supervisor (see, for example, data from Friedlander & Ward, 1984; Goodyear, Abadie, & Efros, 1984; Holloway, Freund, Gardner, Nelson, & Walker, 1989).

Moreover, many of the techniques used in therapy are used in supervision as well. Lambert and Arnold (1987), in fact, made the strong assertion that research on the effects of supervision "will not progress faster than knowledge about the effective ingredients of psychotherapy" (p. 222).

In their survey of 84 psychology interns from 32 sites, Putney, Worthington, and McCulloughy (1992) documented the extent to which theories of therapy affected supervisors' focus and behavior. They found that supervisees perceived cognitive–behavioral supervisors to employ a consultant role and to focus on supervisees' skills and strategies more than humanistic, psychodynamic, and existential supervisors (see, also, Goodyear & Robyak, 1982). Supervisees perceived supervisors who adhered to these latter models, though, as more likely to use the relationship, to employ something of the therapist role during supervision, and to focus on conceptualization of client problems. Findings of the Putney et al. study can be understood in terms of Figure 4.2, whereby theoretical orientation determines style or role.

That study demonstrated that psychotherapy theory affects supervisor functioning. But because supervisees adopt their supervisors' behaviors and ways of thinking, supervisors' therapeutic models *also* affect the theoretical orientations that their supervisees adopt (Guest & Beutler, 1988).

It is inevitable, then, that supervisors will use their particular models of therapy as one of the lenses through which they view supervision. But supervisors who rely on this as their exclusive lens will miss important information about their supervisee's and about the range and impact of interventions they might use to help those supervisees. Often, this single lens also can lead supervisors to think in "therapeutic" rather than educational ways about their supervisees.

There are important differences between supervisors who make their own, direct extrapolations to supervision from their theories of therapy and those who look to the *supervision concepts and models* that have evolved from these theories of therapy. This is a nontrivial distinction.

Psychodynamic Supervision

Psychoanalytic conceptions of supervision have a long history. Arguably, these conceptions have affected supervision theory and practice more than those of any other model. For example, the two psychodynamically derived concepts of *working alliance* and *parallel processes,* both of which are discussed in Chapter 6, are dominant supervision concepts that have informed the work of supervisors of all orientations.

Freud seems to deserve credit not only for developing the "talking cure," but also for being the first psychotherapy supervisor. Social work supervision had began at roughly the same time, with "the nineteenth century Charity Organization Societies in which paid social work agents supervised the moral treatment of the poor by friendly visitors" (Harkness & Poertner, 1989, p. 115). But Freud supervised actual therapeutic practice. He reported that supervision began in 1902 with "a number of young doctors gathered around me with the express intention of learning, practicing, and spreading the knowledge of psychoanalysis" (Freud, 1986, p. 82).

Jacobs, David, and Meyer (1995) argued that the first *recorded* psychoanalytic supervision occurred in the treatment of 5-year-old Herbert Graf ("Little Hans"; Freud, 1909). The boy had developed a fear that one of the large horses he saw pulling wagons might bite him and that one would fall down. In this case, Freud began working through the boy's father. "In an attempt to help his son, Max Graf began to interview him and to report his sessions to Freud in detail" (p. 15). Freud began seeing in Little Hans's situation an example of the Oedipal complex that he previously had described theoretically. "Freud . . . demonstrated that the source of Herbert's phobia lay in his repressed erotic longings for his mother and his competitive and death wishes toward his father, whom he also loved. The little boy was trying to deal with these unacceptable wishes by erecting barriers of disgust, shame, and inhibition and by developing a phobia" (pp. 15–16).

Jacobs et al. report that this

is the first detailed account we have of a psychodynamically oriented supervision. Freud seemed unaware of how tangled and intrusive an educational experience it was for everyone involved. At times, it is not clear who is treating Herbert—Freud or the boy's father. For the most part, Freud relied on suggestion and didactic instruction in his supervision of the treatment. But through this educational process,

flawed as it may have been, the patient got better, the therapist developed a deeper understanding of his patient's dynamics, and the supervisor further developed and elaborated his own ideas. (p. 16)

Frawley-O'Dea and Sarnat (2001) noted that

Freud was the first supervisor and thus represents the archetypal supervisor to whom we all maintain a transference of some kind. In his model of supervision, he combined a positivistic stance analogous to his model of treatment with a personal insistence on maintaining a position as the ultimate arbiter of truth, knowledge, and power. (p. 17)

Psychodynamic Concepts and Practices. Supervision soon became an institutionalized aspect of the psychoanalytic enterprise. Frayn (1991) suggested that formal psychotherapy supervision was first instituted in the early 1920s by Max Eitingon at the Berlin Institute of Psychoanalysis. And Caligor (1984) noted that, in 1922, to standardize training, the International Psychoanalytic Society adopted formalized standards that stipulated formal coursework and the treatment of several patients under supervision.

During the 1930s, two competing views developed concerning the place of "control analysis," which was the psychoanalytic term for supervision. One group (the Budapest School) maintained that it should be a continuation of the supervisee's personal analysis (with the same analyst in each case) and focus on transference in the candidate's therapy and countertransference in his or her supervision. The other group (the Viennese School) maintained that the transference and countertransference issues should be addressed in the candidate's personal analysis, whereas supervision itself should emphasize didactic teaching.

Ekstein and Wallerstein (1972) were the first to articulate a model of supervision that most psychodynamic (and many other) supervisors accepted. They portrayed supervision as a teaching and learning process that gives particular emphasis to the relationships between and among patient, therapist, and supervisor and the processes that interplay among them. Its purpose is not to provide therapy, but to teach, and the reason for working closely with the trainee is to have him or her learn how to understand the dynamics of resolving relational conflicts between supervisor and trainee (cf. Bordin, 1983; Mueller & Kell, 1972) for the benefit of future work with clients.

Because of the diversity within the psychoanalytic perspective and the richness of its conceptualizations, it has continued to provide ideas and concepts that have been infused throughout supervision. Psychoanalytic writers have been prolific contributors to the supervision literature. This continues, as illustrated by their many recent books, including those by Gill (2001), Frawley-O'Dea and Sarnat (2001), Jacobs et al. (1995), and Rock (1997).

Among these recent authors, the work of Frawley-O'Dea and Sarnat (2001) is sufficiently novel and well articulated to warrant specific mention. Although grounded in psychodynamic theory, theirs is a supervision model in its own right.

To set the stage for their model, Frawley-O'Dea and Sarnat reviewed the development of psychodynamic supervision. They observed, for example, that the earliest supervision was "patient centered," focusing on the client's dynamics and employing a didactic role. Later psychodynamic supervisors, beginning with Ekstein and Wallerstein (1972), began to conduct "supervisee centered" supervision, giving greater attention to the supervisee's dynamics.

Both types of supervision place the supervisor in the role of an "uninvolved expert" on theory and technique. In contrast, the relational model that Frawley-O'Dea and Sarnat advocate allows the supervisor to focus either on the therapeutic *or* the supervisory dyad. The supervisor's authority stems less from his or her role as expert on theory and practice and more from his or her role "as an embedded participant in a mutually influencing supervisory process" (p. 41).

The framework Frawley-O'Dea and Sarnat propose for describing supervisory models provides a useful conceptual map for all supervision. Its three dimensions are the following:

Dimension 1: The nature of the supervisor's authority in relationship to the supervisee. Supervisors' authority can be understood as existing somewhere on a continuum between two poles. On one end is authority that derives from the knowledge that the supervisor brings to supervision. His or her stance is that of the objective and uninvolved expert who helps the supervisee know "what is 'true' about the patient's mind and what is 'correct' technique" (p. 26). On the other end is authority that derives from the supervisor's involved participation. He or she certainly has more expertise than the supervisee, but makes no absolute knowledge claims. His or her authority resides in supervisor–supervisee relational processes.

Dimension 2: The supervisor's focus. This concerns the relevant data on which supervision is based. Specifically, the supervisor can focus attention on (a) the client, (b) the supervisee, or (c) the relationship between supervisor and supervisee.

Dimension 3: The supervisor's primary mode of participation. Despite its label, this is not actually a dimension. It concerns roles and styles that supervisors might adopt. Among those that the authors describe are didactic teacher, Socratic "asker of questions," a container of supervisee affects, and so on.

In summary, it is safe to assert that psychoanalytic or psychodynamic models have influenced supervision as have no other. They certainly have historical importance. But, as well, they have served as a rich source of observations and as a springboard for various conceptions of supervision.

Person-centered Supervision

Supervision was a central and long-standing concern of Carl Rogers, as it was for those who later identified with the person-centered model. Rogers (1942; and also Covner, 1942a, 1942b) was among the very first to report using electronically recorded interviews and transcripts for supervision purposes. Until then, supervision had been based entirely on self-reports of supervisees, as it still often is in psychoanalytically oriented supervision.

Rogers (1942) concluded from listening to these early recordings of therapy interviews that mere didactic training in what then was called nondirective methods was insufficient. Only when students had direct access to the content of their interviews could they identify their natural tendencies to provide advice or otherwise control their sessions. This is consistent with Patterson's (1964) contention two decades later that client-centered supervision was an influencing process that incorporated elements of teaching and therapy, though it was neither.

Rogers's own conception of supervision seemed to lean more toward therapy. In an interview with Goodyear, he stated, "I think my major goal is to help the therapist to grow in self-confidence and to grow in understanding of himself or herself, and to grow in understanding the therapeutic process. And to that end, I find it very fruitful to explore any difficulties the therapist may feel he or she is having working with the client. Supervision for me becomes a modified form of the therapeutic interview" (Hackney & Goodyear, 1984, p. 283).

Later, when he was asked how he differentiated supervision from therapy, Rogers answered:

I think there is no clean way. I think it does exist on a continuum. Sometimes therapists starting in to discuss some of the problems they're having with a client will look deeply into themselves and it's straight therapy. Sometimes it is more concerned with problems of the relationship and that is clearly supervision. But in that sense, too, I will follow the lead, in this case, the lead of the therapist. The one difference is I might feel more free to express how I might have done it than I would if I were dealing with a client. (p. 285)

It is clear from Rogers's words that his counseling theory informed his supervision in a relatively direct way. He believed the facilitative conditions (i.e., genuineness, empathy, warmth) were necessary for trainees and clients alike. Rice (1980) described person-centered supervision as relying on a theory of *process* in the context of *relationship*. The successful person-centered supervisor must have a profound trust that the trainee has within himself or herself the ability and motivation to grow and explore both the therapy situation and the self. This is the same type of trust that the therapist must have (Rice, 1980). Patterson (1983), too, emphasized the similarity between the conditions and processes of therapy and those that occur during supervision.

Patterson and Rice both outlined the attitudes toward human nature and change and the attitude toward self that the supervisor must model for the trainee. First and foremost is the belief in the growth motivation and in the person's ability to differentiate and move toward self-actualization. The trainee who is unable to accept this as true will be unable to offer the kind of psychological environment necessary for clients to change. Other blocks to successful use of this theory are a strong belief in the dynamic unconscious and/or a basic need to control and be directive. Finally, the therapist and supervisor must accept themselves and be able to "prize" each other and the clients with whom they work.

In preparing this chapter, we conducted an electronic literature search using PsychInfo. Using the terms "person-centered," "client-centered," and "supervision," we located only two publications since the 1980s, an article by Freeman (1993), and Patterson's (1997) chapter describing a client-centered perspective on supervision. That virtually no new literature is being generated on this topic seems to corroborate Gelso and Carter's (1985) assessment that the Rogerian perspective has reached its upper limits in what it can offer counselors and practitioners.

But even if they are correct, this does not diminish the profound and enduring influence the Rogerian perspective has had on supervision and, especially, training. Most counseling and psychology programs now train students in basic interviewing skills using procedures that have a direct lineage to Rogers. Rogers and his associates (e.g., Rogers, Gendlin, Kiesler, & Truax, 1967) developed rating scales to assess the level at which therapists' demonstrated use of Rogers's (1957) relationship variables. To operationalize these relationship attitudes or conditions then enabled two of Rogers's research associates, Robert Carkhuff and Charles Truax, to propose procedures to teach these relationship attitudes as specific *skills* (e.g., Carkhuff & Truax, 1965). This skill-building approach and its variants are now in nearly universal use.

Cognitive–Behavioral Supervision

Behavioral therapy and the rational and the cognitive therapies initially evolved independently of each other. The former has had a focus on observable behaviors and a reliance on conditioning (classical and operant) models of learning. The latter was concerned with modifying clients' cognitions, especially those that were manifest as "self-talk" (e.g., Beck, Rush, Shaw, & Emery, 1979; Ellis, 1974; Mahoney, 1974, 1977; Meichenbaum, 1977). As the models have become more blended (see, e.g., most of the chapters in Barlow, 2001), the convention has become one of grouping them into the broader category of *cognitive–behavioral* models. Moreover, as Rosenbaum and Ronen (1998) noted, "CBT is continuously developing and expanding on both the theoretical and applied fronts" (p. 221).

CBT therapists operate on the assumption that both adaptive and maladaptive behaviors are learned and maintained through their consequences. It is probably no surprise that behavioral supervisors have been more specific and more systematic than supervisors of other orientations in their presentation of the goals and processes of supervision. Rosenbaum and Ronen (1998) noted, for example, that the CBT supervisor will negotiate with the supervisee an agreed-upon agenda at the beginning of each session. As well, the supervisor will continuously assess and monitor the supervisee's progress.

Leddick and Bernard (1980) reported that Wolpe, Knopp, and Garfield (1966) were among the first to outline procedures for behavioral supervision. During the past 30 years, a number of authors have discussed their particular perspectives on CBT supervision (e.g., Boyd, 1978; Delaney, 1972; Friedberg & Taylor, 1994; Jakubowski-Spector, Dustin, & George, 1971; Levine & Tilker, 1974; Linehan, 1980; Perris, 1994; Rosenbaum & Ronen, 1998; Safran & Muran, 2001; Schmidt, 1979) and the closely related Rational Emotive supervision (e.g., Ellis, 1989; Wessler & Ellis, 1983; Woods & Ellis, 1996). Common to most of these is an endorsement of some variation on the following four propositions Boyd (1978) had proposed:

1. *Proficient therapist performance is more a function of learned skills than a "personality fit." The purpose of supervision is to teach appropriate therapist behaviors and extinguish inappropriate behavior.*
2. *The therapist's professional role consists of identifiable tasks, each one requiring specific skills. Training and supervision should assist the trainee in developing these skills, applying and refining them.*
3. *Therapy skills are behaviorally definable and are responsive to learning theory, just as are other behaviors.*
4. *Supervision should employ the principles of learning theory within its procedures.* (p. 89)

The supervisory methods typically described by behavioral supervisors include establishing a trusting relationship, skill analysis and assessment, setting goals for the trainee, construction and implementation of strategies to accomplish goals, and follow-up evaluation and generalization of learning (Bradley, 1989). Rosenbaum and Ronen (1998) discuss the importance of behavioral practice by the supervisee, both during the counseling sessions that they conduct and in the supervision sessions using such means as imagery exercises, behavioral rehearsals, and role playing. In fact, Milne and James (2000) found these interventions to be associated with positive supervision outcomes, as were careful assessment and close monitoring.

Assessment and close monitoring also are associated with the use of treatment manuals. Although CBT therapists are not alone in using manuals, they dominate the list of empirically validated treatments (see, e.g., Chambliss et al., 1998), all of which employ treatment manuals. Moreover, CBT manuals tend to be much more specific and detailed than those of other models (cf. Barlow, 2001). For adherents of treatment manuals, treatment fidelity (i.e., whether the therapist is adhering to what the manual dictates) is an important matter. Assessment and monitoring become even more central to supervision.

Rosenbaum and Ronen (1998) noted that the CBT supervisor will rely heavily on Socratic questioning. Liese and Beck (1997) noted that they also employ the cognitive therapy approach of challenging supervisee cognitions and misperceptions, just as do Ellis and his associates when conducting supervision (e.g., Ellis, 1989; Wessler & Ellis, 1983; Woods & Ellis, 1996).

Finally, it is important to acknowledge some recent attempts to integrate other approaches into cognitive therapy. Among the most important of these is the work of Safran and Muran (2000), who have incorporated relational concepts into cognitive therapy. In particular, they have discussed the importance of addressing ruptures and repairs in the alliance (their work informs our discussion in Chapter 6 of the rupture–repair process). They also have extended this integrative model to supervision in an article that is rich, both conceptually and practically.

In summary, behavioral supervisors define the potential of the trainee as the potential to learn. Supervisors take at least part of the responsibility for learning to occur, for they are the experts who can guide the trainee into the correct learning environment. Perhaps more than most supervisors, they are concerned about the extent to which trainees demonstrate technical mastery and that their work has fidelity with the particular mode of treatment being taught.

Systemic Supervision

Systemic supervision is characterized by attention to the interlocking family and supervisory systems. It is, then, virtually synonymous with family therapy supervision, which has a literature dating back at least to the late 1960s (Liddle, Becker, & Diamond, 1997). Liddle et al. reviewed the key publications and trends that have affected the development of this specialty, making clear that this has occurred independently of psychotherapy supervision:

> *Family therapy supervision and psychotherapy supervision, paralleling the parent fields of family therapy and psychotherapy, have not interacted much throughout their respective histories. Like proverbial ships passing in the night, these kindred areas of thinking, research, and practice do not interrelate. For that matter, each barely acknowledges the existence of the other and they remain intellectual strangers.* (p. 400)

One of the unique theoretical contributions of systemic supervision has been that of isomorphism, that is, the replication of family dynamics within the supervisory relationship. We discuss isomorphism and its implications in Chapter 6 and therefore simply note it here. Similarly, live supervision, which—though not unique to family therapy supervision, strongly characterizes it—is discussed in Chapter 11.

McDaniel, Weber, and McKeever (1983) reviewed the structural, strategic, Bowenian, and experiential schools of systemic family therapy and argued that supervision in these schools should be theoretically consistent. Therefore, if the goal of the therapy was to maintain a clear boundary between therapist and family (and between parents in the family and the children), then there should be a clear boundary between the supervisor and the therapist. And like family therapy itself, family therapy supervision is "active, directive, and collaborative" (Liddle et al., 1997, p. 413).

Furthermore, if therapy focused on family of origin issues, the therapist must be encouraged to relate training to his or her own family of origin issues. In fact, Montgomery, Hendricks, and Bradley (2001) elaborated on that point, noting that

> *The activation of family-of-origin dynamics is a supervision issue because they affect the degree of objectivity and emotional reactivity that counselors have with their clients and hence their therapeutic capabilities. . . . Therefore, supervision should provide trainees with opportunities to attain higher levels of differentiation and emotional maturity.* (p. 310)

In discussing the function of systemic supervision, Papadopoulos (2001) noted that

> *One of the main principles of systemic thinking, as applied to psychotherapeutic work, has been the distinction between information and data. . . . not everything a therapist hears in a session or learns from the referring network matters or is helpful to the therapeutic process. . . . one of the main functions of supervision is precisely to develop the therapists' skills to discriminate between information and data and to increase their effectiveness in eliciting appropriate information.* (pp. 406–407)

There has been some discussion regarding the appropriateness of theory-based supervision when the therapy on which supervision is based is non-egalitarian, if not overtly manipulative. Strategic family therapy supervision has become a case in point. Many strategic directives are paradoxical in nature or, at the very least, do not rely on the insight of the recipient. Strategic supervisors have asked themselves, therefore, if strategic interventions are appropriate for trainees.

To date, at least as reflected in the scant literature on the topic, the answer seems to be yes. Storm and Heath (1982) reported that their supervisees expected their supervisors to use strategic interventions with them. But when supervisors were caught using such an approach, the supervisees' reactions were negative. In other words, supervisees were comfortable with the notion that they might need to be manipulated in order to learn, but they expected the manipulation to be very clever and subtle. This begs the question about what to do as supervisees gained in their own clinical skill.

Protinsky and Preli (1987) offered at least a partial solution to this dilemma. In their discussion of strategic supervision, they proposed that interventions (though admittedly manipulative) follow the development of the trainee. Therefore, as the trainee gained in therapeutic skill, the supervisor would create a situation in which the trainee would enter more of an egalitarian relationship with the supervisor. Protinsky and Preli mirrored Storm and Heath's (1982) issue of supervisee awareness, stating that "the best strategic supervisory interventions seem to be those that remain out of the awareness of the supervisee. This out-of-awareness prevents self-reflexive thinking and is useful in producing behavior change in the supervisee" (p. 23). They went on to suggest, however, that once a supervisee had made the breakthrough that the intervention called for, it was appropriate, if not desirable, for the supervisor to initiate a discussion aimed at supervisee insight.

Protinsky and Preli offered seven examples of strategic supervisory interventions ranging from the use of paradox to "graduating to equality" (p. 22). The following example was described as the use of an aversive reframe. The therapist in the example has been working with a family made up of an acting-out adolescent, a meek and submissive mother, and an arrogant and abrasive father. The therapist repeatedly has gotten caught in struggles with the father. The supervisor has attempted to explain the situation systemically, pointing out the circular nature of the sequence (i.e., adolescent acts out, mother acts overwhelmed, father acts abrasive, therapist reacts to father); however, there has been no progress to this point.

In a postsession meeting the supervisor suddenly changed her position and framed the therapist's protection of the mother as positive. Who wouldn't protect a woman from such an abrasive man! She then left without discussing the case further. The trainee was a social worker who had previously stated that she prided herself on her objectivity. Therefore, the reframe was aversive and succeeded in angering her.

The therapist at first complained how mistaken the supervisor was to the other trainees. She did not like to be perceived as protecting the mother and stated that she would never knowingly do such a thing. At the next session, however, she modified her behavior so that she could prove that she was objective. By reacting more positively toward the father and refraining from protecting the mother, the therapist was then able to use effective strategic interventions.

Constructivist Approaches

A significant development in the human sciences has been the emergence of a world view that has been characterized as postmodern, postpostivist, or constructivist. The terms are not completely synonymous, but do have in common the position that reality and truth are contextual and exist as creations of the observer. For humans, truth is a construction grounded in their social interactions and informed by their verbal behavior.

Mahoney (1991) pointed out that the term constructivism originates from the Latin *construere,* which "means 'to interpret' or 'to analyze,' with emphasis on a person's active 'construing' of a particular meaning or significance" (p. 96). Constructivism has been adopted as an approach to science. But it also increasingly has begun to inform thinking about psychotherapy. George Kelly generally is credited as having developed (e.g., 1955) the most formal expression of constructivism in psychotherapy. But more recently a number of other models have been developed that are informed by a constructivist perspective.

"What joins constructivists is their commitment to a common epistemology, or theory of knowledge. . . . [C]onstructivists believe that 'reality' . . . lies beyond the reach of our most ambitious theories, whether personal or scientific, forever denying us as human beings the security of justifying our beliefs, faiths, and ideologies by simple recourse to 'objective circumstances' outside ourselves. . . . [P]sychotherapy can be viewed as a kind of collaboration in the construction and reconstruction of meaning" (Neimeyer, 1995, p. 3).

Constructivist approaches to therapy share some similarities with person-centered and other humanistic models. For example, constructivists are less concerned with objective representations of the real world than with the individual person's subjective experience. And, like the humanistic theorists, the constructivists assume that people are not simply reactive to their environments, but agentic.

Constructivist approaches differ though in at least a couple of respects. One is in their assumption that there are multiple truths that are understood in a contextual way. Another is the strong emphasis that constructivists give to the use of language. They understand it to be the means by which we construct our realities.

Constructivism is a broad umbrella under which there is a family of therapies that might include, for example, feminist approaches. As these therapies have developed, there has been a corresponding attention to the nature and process of supervision. What seems common among these approaches to supervision is a heavy reliance on a consultive role for the supervisor, an attempt to maintain relative equality between participants (i.e., a downplaying of hierarchy), and a focus on supervisee strengths. Both narrative and solution-focused authors have addressed supervision. In the sections that follow, we will briefly summarize these perspectives.

Narrative Approaches to Supervision. The narrative model (Bob, 1999; Parry & Doan, 1994; Polkinghorne, 1988) constitutes one constructivist approach. Therapists who work from this perspective assume that people inherently are "story tellers" who develop a story about themselves that serves as a template both to organize past experience and to influence future behavior. This story is populated with characters who are chosen for, or who are influenced to perform, certain roles in the story.

The narrative approach seems an intellectual heir of Adler's ideas about life-style (Ansbacher & Ansbacher, 1956) and Berne's ideas about life scripts (1972), but with the postmodern perspective concerning the relativism of truth. Family therapists (e.g., Hardy, 1993; Parry, 1991) have been especially, although not exclusively, interested in this approach (see, e.g., Gonccalves, 1994; Vogel, 1994).

Parry and Doan (1994) have developed what may be the most fully articulated version of the narrative approach. Clients come to therapy with a story about themselves that they have developed over a lifetime. The therapist's role is to help the person to tell his or her story, while being careful not to "be violent" with the client by insisting that she or he accept a particular point of view. The therapist serves as a story "editor." In this role, the therapist is careful to ask questions in the subjunctive ("as if") rather than the indicative ("this is the way it is") mode.

Whereas the client has a generally developed story of self that he or she is seeking to modify, the trainee is just beginning to develop his or her own story of self-as-professional. The supervisors' role, then, is both to assist the trainee in the editing of the client's story and also to help the trainee to develop his or her own professional story. Supervision, from the perspective of these authors, is a process of revising stories that trainees (1) tell about their clients (i.e., a *metastory*), (2) tell about themselves, and (3) tell about other therapists.

The role of the supervisor, then, is to serve as an editor or catalyst to help trainees to write and revise the scripts that define who they are as therapists and what they do in that role (Clifton, Doan, & Mitchell, 1990). They contrast the stance of *knowing* (which is manifest as straightforward declarations of fact) versus the stance of *curiosity* (which is expressed in a questioning or wondering way). For example, "At that moment with the client, you seemed to be feeling overwhelmed" (knowing) versus "I am wondering what you were feeling at that moment with the client" (curiosity). In this way, the technique is similar to that of Kagan (e.g., 1980). That is, by expressing interventions as questions or implied questions rather than statements, the trainee is invited to participate actively as an editor of the constantly evolving script of who she or he is as a therapist.

We also should note that the live supervision technique of reflection teams (e.g., Landis & Young, 1994; Prest, Darden, & Keller, 1990) has been embraced as a modality of narrative therapists, even though it is not exclusive to this model. We discuss reflection teams in Chapter 11.

Solution-focused Supervision.   Developed by de Shazer and colleagues (e.g., Molnar & de Shazer, 1987), solution-focused therapy focuses on enabling clients to get what they want, rather than on what is wrong with them. It is grounded in the assumptions that clients know what is best for them; that there is no single, correct way to view things; that it is important to focus on what is possible and changeable; and that curiosity is essential. One of the best known features of the model is what its adherents call the "miracle question," which has this basic form: "Imagine that a miracle has occurred: the problems for which you are seeking treatment magically disappear. What, *specifically,* will you notice that will tell you that this has occurred? What else (and so on)." Not only does this question have a goal-setting intent, but it also focuses on the positive.

An increasing number of authors have begun to discuss solution-focused supervision (see, e.g., Rita, 1998; Triantafillou, 1997). Juhnke (1996), Presbury, Echterling, and McKee (1999), and Thomas (1996) have provided some basic assumptions to guide the work of the solution-focused supervisor. These include (1) rather than being didactic, the supervisor should help the supervisee to draw on his or her own resources, learn to behave independently, and make changes; (2) resistance is understood to reside in the supervisory relationship itself; the way to avoid or circumvent it is to establish a collaborative relationship; (3) focus on supervisees' strengths and successes rather than faults; (4) supervisors should take advantage of the snowball effect and work toward small changes, rather than only the large ones; (5) rather than attempting dramatic or radical changes, supervisors work to achieve what is possible; and, (6) accept that there is no one correct way to understand or intervene.

To be true to this model, the supervisor not only will attend to the positive in the client, but also to that in the supervisee (i.e., to positive changes rather than faults). As with the narrative approach, the supervisor employs a consultant role (e.g., using questions to guide interactions) and gives particular attention to language usage. Presbury et al. (1999) distinguished between subjunctive and presuppositional language. The former supposes a possibility (e.g., "Can you think of a time when you were able to be assertive with your client?"), whereas the latter supposes an actuality (e.g., "Tell me about a time when you were able to be assertive with your client"). Supervisees are less likely to dismiss the latter. As well, in their use of presuppositional language, supervisors convey an assumption of the supervisee's competency.

Presbury et al. (1999) provided some possible examples of questions that a solution-focused supervisor might ask a supervisee. For example, in an effort to direct discussion toward supervisee achievements and competencies, he might ask, "What aspect of your counseling have you noticed getting better since we last met?" or "Tell me the best thing you did with your client this week" (p. 151).

Should the supervisee focus too heavily on problems that she or he is experiencing with the client, the supervisor might ask, "As you begin to get better at dealing with this situation, how will you know that you have become good enough at it so that you can take it on your own?" and then, later, "What will you be doing differently" or "When you get to the point at which you won't need to deal with this issue in supervision any more, how will you know?" (p. 151). They further note

If the counselor-in-training persists in framing his or her own behavior as a problem, the use of a scale can set expectations of success. The supervisor may say, "On a scale of 1 to 10, with 1 being that the problem is at its absolute worst, and 10 being that the problem is completely solved, where would you say you are today?" After the counselor offers an estimate, the supervisor replies, "When you are on your way to a (the next highest number to the one named), how will you know?" The supervisor may follow this invitation by explicitly asking, "What, in particular, will be different about the way you handle that situation?" or "How will you have changed as a counselor?" By answering these questions, instead of exploring more minutia and facets of the problem, the supervisee is beginning to envision

more clearly the strategies that may succeed in achieving a solution. (pp. 151–152)

In short, the constructivist models of therapy (at least as expressed in the narrative and solution-focused models) are fostering promising supervision ideas. Even for the therapist who does not ascribe to a constructivist approach, many of the techniques of these models could be useful.

DEVELOPMENTAL APPROACHES TO SUPERVISION

The remainder of this chapter will focus on models developed specifically for supervision, independent of particular models of psychotherapy. This particular section focuses on what typically are described as developmental models. Their primary focus is on how supervisees change as they gain training and supervised experience. Although they all have implications for how supervisors might then work with the developing supervisee, they vary in the extent to which they are both thorough and specific.

Chagnon and Russell (1995) pointed out that developmental conceptions of supervision are based on two basic assumptions. The first is that, in the process of moving toward competence, supervisees move through a series of stages that are qualitatively different from one another. The second is that the supervisee stages each require a qualitatively different supervisory environment if optimal supervisee satisfaction and growth are to occur.

Several key developmental models of supervision were published during the 1950s (Fleming, 1953), 1960s (Hogan, 1964), and 1970s (Littrell, Lee-Bordin, & Lorenz, 1979). But interest in the topic virtually exploded during the 1980s. By 1987, Holloway was able to comment "developmental models of supervision have become the Zeitgeist of supervision thinking and research" (p. 209). That same year, Worthington (1987) reviewed the literature and found 16 models of counselor trainee development; in a later expansion of this review, Watkins (1995d) identified 6 more (one of which was his own). But it now looks as though attention to the topic has slowed considerably. In their *Handbook of Counseling Psychology* review of supervision, Goodyear and Guzzardo (2000) found that little new theory or research had been reported since the previous *Handbook* chapter on supervision (Holloway, 1992). Nevertheless, these models remain an essential feature of supervision. In fact, knowledge of how trainees develop was identified as a core competency for supervisors by the Supervision Workgroup at the 2002 APPIC Competencies Conference (see Falender et al., in press).

In the meantime, one recent review reached less sanguine conclusions about the developmental literature than had previous reviewers such as Holloway (1992) and Stoltenberg, McNeill, and Crethar (1994). Ellis and Ladany (1997) characterized the results of their rigorous review of the developmental literature as a "disheartening experience." In particular, they found that methodological problems and failures to eliminate rival hypotheses have so characterized this area of research that "data from these studies are largely uninterpretable . . . [and] little viable information about supervisee development has been gained" (p. 483). Whether the conclusions of Ellis and Ladany are accepted or not, they do provide researchers with useful guidelines for conducting future research on this topic. More important, they remain invaluable for supervision practitioners.

The catalyst for the huge surge in interest in developmental conceptions that dominated supervision literature for more than a decade was the work of a small cadre of workers at the University of Iowa. Cal Stoltenberg (1981), who conceived his developmental model when he still was a doctoral student there, was influenced by Ursula Delworth. The following year, Delworth herself coauthored a developmental model with two other University of Iowa Counseling Center staff members (Loganbill, Hardy, & Delworth, 1982). These articles, along with several other contemporary ones (e.g., Blocher, 1983; Littrell et al., 1979) struck a resonant chord in the supervision community.

Various authors have differed in their conclusions about the developmental literature and the

ways to organize it. Borders (1986) divided developmental models into three categories: (1) those that focus on the role of the supervisor (e.g., Littrell et al., 1979); (2) those that focus on the dynamics of the trainee (e.g., Loganbill et al., 1982); and (3) those that focus on the learning environment of supervision (e.g., Stoltenberg, 1981).

Russell, Crimmings, and Lent (1984) divided developmental models into two categories: (1) those in the Eriksonian tradition that offer definitive linear stages of development (e.g., Hogan, 1964; Littrell et al., 1979; Stoltenberg, 1981) and (2) those that propose a step-by-step process for conflict resolution or skill mastery, a process that will be repeated as the trainee faces more complicated issues (e.g., Ekstein & Wallerstein, 1972; Loganbill et al., 1982; Mueller & Kell, 1972).

Holloway (1987) divided them into (1) those that have linked their origins to psychosocial developmental theory (Blocher, 1983; Loganbill et al., 1982; Stoltenberg, 1981) and (2) those that have not (Hogan, 1964; Littrell et al., 1979).

Finally, in his comprehensive review of developmental models and the empirical studies spawned by these models, Worthington (1987) divided the literature into (1) models and studies that have addressed supervision of the developing counselor (e.g., Hill, Charles, & Reed, 1981; Loganbill et al., 1982; Stoltenberg, 1981) and (2) those that have taken the complementary tack of addressing supervision by the developing supervisor (e.g., Alonso, 1983; Hess, 1986).

In the next section, we review several developmental models. We chose these particular models to illustrate both some of the apparent between-model commonalities, as well as some of their differences. Also, whereas the first four are based on clinical observation, the latter two evolved from research findings.

There are a number that warrant attention, including, for example, those of Friedman and Kaslow (1986), Hill et al., (1981), Littrell et al. (1979) and others that we already have cited. For reasons of space we are limiting our coverage to three models that we chose for meeting at least some of the multiple criteria of (1) having historical importance, (2) having utility for supervision practitioners, and (3) representing diverse types of developmental conceptions.

The Integrated Developmental Model

Stoltenberg (1981) defined four stages or levels in his (cognitive) Complexity Model. This model was an integration of Hogan's (1964) suggestions about stages through which trainees progress and Harvey, Hunt, and Schroeder's (1961) work on conceptual level (CL). CL is a construct concerning how people at different cognitive development levels will think, reason, and understand their environment.

Stoltenberg's (1981) model struck an immediate, resonant chord among both practitioners and researchers, stimulating a number of studies. However, he since has continued to develop and refine the model, adding a new collabator with each iteration (Stoltenberg & Delworth, 1987; Stoltenberg, McNeill, & Delworth, 1998). This, the Integrated Developmental Model, now has become the best known and most widely used counseling development model (see, e.g., Maki & Delworth, 1995). It has the virtue of being both *descriptive* of trainee processes and *prescriptive* with respect to supervisor interventions.

There had been some disagreement (Holloway, 1987; Stoltenberg & Delworth, 1988) about the applicability of the conceptual-level model to trainee development, which was a basis for Stoltenberg's (1981) model. Perhaps as a consequence, CL was dropped in the Stoltenberg et al. (1998) version of the model. The model still had a cognitive basis, but this was less prominent and relied instead on Anderson's (1996) work on the development of expertise, as well as on others who have conceptualized the development of schemas.

The Integrated Development Model (IDM) describes counselor development as occurring through four stages. Each of these levels is characterized by changes on "three overriding structures that provide markers in assessing professional growth" (Stoltenberg et al., 1998, p. 16). These three structures are:

- *Self-other awareness* ("where the person is in terms of self-preoccupation, awareness of the client's world, and enlightened self-awareness," p. 16)
- *Motivation* ("reflects the supervisee's interest, investment, and efforted expended in clinical training and practice," p. 16)
- *Autonomy* (this reflects the degree of independence that the supervisee is manifesting)

Box 4.1 summarizes manner in which these three structures are reflected for the four supervisee developmental levels. Supervisors interested in assessing their supervisees' levels of functioning on these three structures have available to them the Supervisee Levels Questionnaire, Revised (McNeill, Stoltenberg, & Romans, 1992). It is available in the Supervisor's Toolbox at the end of this book.

Stoltenberg et al. (1984) also specify eight domains of professional functioning in which the supervisee will develop. These are *intervention skills competence* (confidence and ability to carry our therapeutic interventions); *assessment techniques* (confidence and ability to conduct psychological assessments); *interpersonal assessment* (this extends beyond the formal assessment period and includes the use of self in conceptualizing client problems; its nature will vary according to theoretical orientation); *client conceptualization* (diagnosis, but also pertains to the therapist's understanding of how the client's circumstances, history, and characteristics affect his or her functioning); *individual differences* (an understanding of ethnic, racial, and cultural influences on individuals); *theoretical orientation* (this pertains to the level of complexity and sophistication of the therapist's understanding of theory); *treatment plans and goals* (how the therapist plans to organize his or her efforts in working with clients); and *professional ethics* (how professional ethics intertwine with personal ethics).

The Rønnestad and Skovholt Model

Most models of counselor development focus primarily on the period of graduate and internship

BOX 4.1_____

Supervisee Characteristics and Supervisor Behavior for Each of the Four IDM-specified Supervisee Developmental Levels

Level 1. These supervisees have limited training, or at least limited experience in the specific domain in which they are being supervised.

Motivation: Both motivation and anxiety are high; focused on acquiring skills. Want to know "the correct" or "best" approach with clients.

Autonomy: Dependent on supervisor. Needs structure, positive feedback, and little direct confrontation.

Awareness: High self-focus, but with limited self-awareness; apprehensive about evaluation.

Level 2. Supervisees at this level are "making the transition from being highly dependent, imitative, and unaware in responding to a highly structured, supportive, and largely instructional supervisory environment" (p. 64). Usually after two to three semesters of practicum.

Motivation: Fluctuating as the supervisee vacillates between being very confident to unconfident and confused.

Autonomy: Although functioning more independently, he or she experiences conflict between autonomy and dependency, much as an adolescent. This can manifest as pronounced resistance to the supervisor.

Awareness: Greater ability to focus on and empathize with client. However, balance still is an issue. In this case, the problem can be veering into confusion and enmeshment with the client.

Stoltenberg et al. notes that this can be a turbulent stage and "supervision of the Level 2 therapist . . . [requires] considerable skill, flexibility, and perhaps a sense of humor" (p. 87).

Level 3. Supervisees at this level are focusing more on a personalized approach to practice and on using and understanding of "self" in therapy.

Motivation: Consistent; occasional doubts about one's effectiveness will occur, but without being immobilizing.

Autonomy: A solid belief in one's own professional judgment has developed as the supervisee moves into independent practice. Supervision tends to be collegial as differences between supervisor and supervisee expertise diminish.

Awareness: The supervisees return to being self-aware, but with a very different quality than at Level 1. Supervisees at this level are able to remained focused on the client while also stepping back to attend to their own personal reactions to the client and then to use this in decision making about the client.

Level 3i (Integrated). This level occurs as the supervisee reaches Level 3 across multiple domains (e.g., treatment, assessment, conceptualization). The supervisee's task is one of integrating across domains. It is characterized by a personalized approach to professional practice across domains and the ability to move easily across them. This supervisee has strong awareness of his or her strengths and weaknesses.

---

training. Yet professional development no more stops at graduation than does our personal development. The work of Rønnestad and Skovholt (1993, 2003; Skovholt & Rønnestad, 1992) is therefore important for its articulation of the ways that therapists continue to develop across the life-span. It is not the only one to have originated inductively from data (see, e.g., Hill et al., 1981). It is, though, the first to derive from a qualitative study.

This model is based on interviews with 100 counselors and therapists who ranged in experience from the first year of graduate school to 40 years beyond graduate school. In their initial analyses of the data, they identified eight stages of therapist development, each of which might be characterized along a number of dimensions (e.g., predominant affect, predominant sources of influence, role and working style, style of learning, and determinants of effectiveness and satisfaction). As well, they identified 20 themes that were not specifically stage related, but that characterized therapist development across time.

They (Rønnestad & Skovholt, 2003) recently have offered a more refined and parsimonious model, based on reinterviews with some therapists, feedback obtained over the past decade, and their own reanalyses of the data. They have collapsed the model so that there now are only six phases (a term that they now believe is more technically accurate than stages) of development and 14 themes. Because of the importance of this model, we will summarize these phases and then the themes. It is useful to note that the early phases correspond well to stages that Stoltenberg et al. (1998) described.

Phase 1: The Lay Helper Phase. Novices already will have had the experience of helping others (e.g., as a friend, parent, or colleague). "The lay helper typically identifies the problem quickly, provides strong emotional support, and gives advice based on one's own experience." (Rønnestad & Skovholt, 2003, p. 10). Lay helpers are prone to boundary problems, tend to become overly involved, and express sympathy rather than empathy.

Phase 2: The Beginning Student Phase. Although this is an exciting time for students, they often feel dependent, vulnerable, and anxious and have fragile self-confidence. Therefore, they especially value their supervisors' encouragement and support. Perceived criticism from either their supervisors or their clients can have a severe effect on their self-confidence and morale. They actively search for "the right way" to function, looking for models and expert practitioners to emulate.

Phase 3: The Advanced Student Phase. These students, usually at the advanced practica or internship stage, have the central task of functioning at a basic established, professional level. They feel pressure to "do it right" and therefore have a conservative, cautious, and thorough style (versus one that is relaxed, risk-taking, or spontaneous).

Students at this level recognize that they have profited from training and are feeling more comfortable, yet they still can feel insecure and vulnerable. The support and confirmation of supervision become increasingly important. As well, the opportunity to provide supervision to beginning students "can be a powerful source of influence for the advanced student" (Rønnestad & Skovholt, 2003, p. 15), who are able to see how much they have learned. Moreover, the provision of supervision helps them to consolidate learning.

Phase 4: The Novice Professional Phase. The years immediately postgraduation can be a heady time, for the person now is free of the demands of graduate school and the constraints of supervision. Still, many find that they are not as well prepared as they had imagined.

The new therapist increasingly integrates his or her own personality in treatment. As this occurs, the therapist becomes more at ease. He or she also uses this period to seek compatible work roles and environments.

Phase 5: The Experienced Professional Phase. Counselors and therapists with some years and types of experience have the core developmental task of finding a way to be authentic, specifically, developing a working style that is highly congruent with their own values, interests, and personality. Virtually all have come to understand ways in which the therapeutic relationship is crucial for client change. Techniques that they employ are used in flexible, personalized ways. As well, they have come to understand that it frequently is impossible to have clear answers for the situations that they encounter.

One characteristic of this phase is the ability to calibrate levels of involvement with clients so that they can be fully engaged when with the clients, but then can let go afterward.

Clients are a valuable source of learning, as is the mentoring many therapists do with more junior professionals. Often they also begin looking outside the profession to areas such as religion or poetry or even theater or cinema to expand their knowledge of people.

Phase 6: The Senior Professional Phase. These professionals, usually with more than 20 years of experience, typically have developed very individualized and authentic approaches. Despite their felt-competence, they generally have become more modest about their own impacts on clients. They also tend to have become skeptical that anything really new will be added to the field. Loss is a prominent theme in this phase. This is both anticipatory, as they look toward their own retirements, and current, for "their own professional elders are no longer alive and same age colleagues are generally no longer a strong source of influence" (Rønnestad & Skovholt, 2003, p. 26).

Themes and Concluding Comments. The 14 themes are summarized in Box 4.2. When the label is not sufficient to fully express its meaning, we have added explanatory text. Together with the six phases, these themes provide supervisors with an important cognitive map. Like the other models, this suggests the importance to beginning students of having clear, direct models for practice and perhaps greater attention to a didactic approach early on. But it also adds support for providing a supervision course during graduate training (i.e., as a source of development for the supervisor-in-training) and makes clear how the mentoring of newer professionals is a source of professional development to therapists at Phases 5 and 6.

In short, this is a unique and important model. Its applications to supervision, though, are not as direct as is true with some other models—or as likely will be true with continued development of this model. This model was developed through a research study of therapist development and therefore still is more descriptive than prescriptive.

The 14 themes vary in their level of implication for supervisors. For example, whereas theme 3 concerning self-reflection has very important, direct implications for supervisors (who then can design interventions to foster the self-reflective process), other themes are more distantly related to supervision. As a final note, it is our impression that the themes could be collapsed in the interest of simplifying. Goodyear, Wertheimer, Cypers, and Rosemond (2003) demonstrated, for example, that it is possible to cluster these 14 themes into 6.

The Loganbill, Hardy, and Delworth Model

Holloway (1987) observed that Loganbill et al. (1982) probably were the first to publish a comprehensive model of counselor development. Of the three developmental models featured in this chapter, however, it is the least current in terms of updates. Yet it is both sufficiently unique (especially in its cyclical conception of development) and important to warrant coverage.

Their model involves three stages and eight supervisory issues that can manifest during these stages. They proposed five supervisor interventions to help supervisees to move through these stages and issues.

The Three Stages. Loganbill et al. (1982) suggested that the supervisor's role is to assess each trainee according to his or her standing on each issue and to attempt to move the trainee to the next stage of development. This is a complex model, requiring the supervisor to track the trainee's progress through 24 different positions with respect to the model (8 issues times 3 stages).

Each of the three stages depicted in Figure 4.3 is typified by characteristic attitudes toward (1) the world, (2) the self, and (3) the supervisor. In contrast to other developmental models, which assume a linear progression across stages, this model assumes that the counselor will cycle and recycle through the stages, increasing their levels of integration at each cycle. To explain, Loganbill et al. used the metaphor of changing a tire: "One tight-

BOX 4.2

Rønnestad and Skovholt's 14 Themes
of Therapist–Counselor Development

1. *Professional development involves an increasing higher-order integration of the professional self and the personal self.* Across time, a professional's theoretical perspective and professional roles become increasingly consistent with his or her values, beliefs, and personal life experiences.

2. *The focus of functioning shifts dramatically over time, from internal to external to internal.* During formal training, a person drops an earlier ("lay helper") reliance on an internal, personal epistemology for helping in order to rely on the professionally based knowledge and skills that guide practice. Later, during postdegree experience, professionals gradually regain an internal focus and, with it, a more flexible and confident style.

3. *Continuous reflection is a prerequisite for optimal learning and professional development at all levels of experience.* A straightforward observation, but its implications for supervision are substantial. It implies, for example, that supervisees should be taught self-reflection and self-supervision (cf. Dennin & Ellis, 2003).

4. *An intense commitment to learn propels the developmental process.* Importantly, Rønnestad and Skovholt found that, for most of their respondents, enthusiasm for professional growth tended not to diminish with time.

5. *The cognitive map changes: Beginning practitioners rely on external expertise, seasoned practitioners rely on internal expertise.* Early on, supervisees seek "received knowledge" of experts and therefore prefer a didactic approach to supervision. They later shift increasingly to developing "constructed knowledge" that is based on their own experiences and self-reflections.

6. *Professional development is a long, slow, continuous process that can also be erratic.*

7. *Professional development is a lifelong process.*

8. *Many beginning practitioners experience much anxiety in their professional work. Over time, anxiety is mastered by most.*

9. *Clients serve as a major source of influence and serve as primary teachers.*

10. *Personal life influences professional functioning and development throughout the professional life span.* "Family interactional patterns, sibling and peer relationships, one's own parenting experiences, disability in family members, other crises in the family, personal trauma and so on influenced current practice and more long term development in both positive and adverse ways" (Rønnestad & Skovholt, 2003, p. 34).

11. *Interpersonal sources of influence propel professional development more than "impersonal" sources of influence.* Growth occurs through contact with clients, supervisors, therapists, family and friends, and (later) younger colleagues. Rønnestad and Skovholt have found that, when asked to rank the impact of various influences on their professional development, therapists ranked clients first, supervisors second, their own therapists third, and the people in their personal lives fourth.

12. *New members of the field view professional elders and graduate training with strong affective reactions.* It is likely that the power differences magnify these responses, which can range from strongly idealizing to strongly devaluing teachers and supervisors.

13. *Extensive experience with suffering contributes to heightened recognition, acceptance, and appreciation of human variability.* Through this process, therapists develop wisdom and integrity.

14. *For the practitioner there is realignment from Self as hero to Client as hero.* Over time the client's contributions to the process are better understood and appreciated, and therapists adopt a more realistic and humble appreciation of what they actually contribute to the change process. "If these 'blows to the ego' are processed and integrated into the therapists' self-experience, they may contribute to the paradox of increased sense of confidence and competence while also feeling more humble and less powerful as a therapist" (Rønnestad & Skovholt, 2003, p. 38).

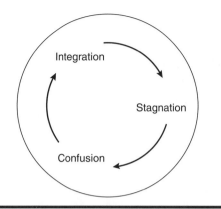

FIGURE 4.3   The Three Loganbill et al. (repeating) Stages of Development

ens the bolts, one after another, just enough so that the wheel is in place; then the process is repeated. Each bolt is tightened in turn until the wheel is entirely secure. In a similar way, stages of the process can be gone through again and again with each issue receiving increasing thoroughness" (p. 17).

Stagnation.   For more novice trainees, this stage is characterized by unawareness of deficiencies or difficulties. The more experienced trainee, though, is more likely to experience it either as stagnation (or "stuckness") or as a blind spot concerning his or her functioning in a particular area. The supervisee at this stage is likely to engage in cognitively simple, black and white thinking and to lack insight into his or her impact on the supervisor or client. He or she also may experience counseling as uninteresting or dull.

Supervisees at this stage may exhibit one of two patterns during supervision. In one, the supervisee will be especially dependent on the supervisor and idealize him or her. Alternatively, the supervisee may view the supervisor as somewhat irrelevant, at least with respect to the issue with which the supervisee is dealing. The tone, though, more likely is one of neutrality or unawareness.

Confusion.   The onset of this stage can be either gradual or abrupt. Its key characteristics are "instability, disorganization, erratic fluctuations, disturbance, confusion, and conflict" (p. 18). It is a

stage in which the supervisee "becomes liberated from a rigid belief system and from traditional ways of viewing the self and behaving toward others" (p. 18). This can be troubling, for the supervisee realizes that something is wrong, but does not yet see how it will be resolved.

In this stage, the supervisee recognizes that the answer will not come from the supervisor. The dependency that characterized the earlier stage is replaced by anger or frustration toward the supervisor, who either is withholding or incompetent, depending on the supervisee's particular perception.

Integration.   This stage, the "calm after the storm," is characterized by "a new cognitive understanding, flexibility, personal security based on awareness of insecurity and an ongoing continual monitoring of the important issues of supervision" (p. 19). At this stage, the supervisee sees the supervisor in realistic terms, as a person with strengths and weaknesses. The supervisee takes responsibility for what occurs during supervision sessions and has learned to make the best use of the supervisor's time and expertise. His or her expectations are consistent with what is possible from supervision.

Eight Basic Supervisee Issues.   Loganbill et al. (1982) suggested that there are at eight basic developmental issues with which supervisees typically grapple. These issues were adapted from Chickering's (1969) model of college student development. They did not suggest a sequence in which supervisees address the issues, though Sansbury (1982) did in his reaction to the model. In a naturalistic study, Ellis (1991) later tested Sansbury's assertions by examining critical incidents reported by supervisors and supervisees and then coding them (note that he expanded the model by including two additional issues). He concluded that there was modest support for Sansbury's proposed hierarchy. The issues are listed in Table 4.1, along with Sansbury's ordering of them and Ellis's findings.

Loganbill et al. (1982) suggested that having an awareness of these issues can help the supervisor to more quickly identify assess areas in which the

TABLE 4.1 Supervisee Developmental Issues Proposed by Loganbill et al.

ISSUES OF:	SANSBURY: PROPOSED RANK	ELLIS: OBSERVED RANK
Supervisory relationship[a]	—	1
Competence	1	2
Emotional awareness	4	3
Purpose and direction	2	4
Autonomy	6	5
Personal (e.g., blind spots)[a]	—	6
Respect for individual differences	5	7
Professional ethics	7	8
Motivation	8	9
Identity	3	10

[a]These two were not in the original Loganbill et al. article, but were added by Ellis, based on work by Rabinowitz, Heppner, and Roehlke (1986). Note, also, that the Ellis data reported here are the combined data from both the supervisors and supervisees.

supervisee is experiencing conflict. Moreover, this understanding can "help the supervisor anticipate or even encourage the emergence of certain themes that need to be addressed from a developmental perspective" (p. 20). The work of Sansbury (1982) and Ellis (1991) is additive in that it helps to anticipate, at least at a general level, the relative sequence in which supervisee issues will emerge.

Interventions. Loganbill et al. (1982) suggested five types of supervisor interventions. Although these interventions vary in their level of specificity, practicing counselors or therapists either already will have most skills or can easily extrapolate from their current skill repertoire for their work as supervisors. (See Chapter 9.)

Conclusions about Developmental Models

A developmental approach to supervision is intuitively appealing, for most of us believe that we become better with experience and training. We therefore are able to validated the general approach in a very personal way. This perspective also is hopeful.

Yet these attributes, which make this approach attractive, may then blind their advocates to competing explanations of what goes on in supervision. Most empirical investigations of developmental

models of supervision report "partial" or "some" support (e.g., Krause & Allen, 1988; Miars, Tracey, Roy, Cornfield, O'Farrell, et al., 1983; Reising & Daniels, 1983). A smaller number of studies (e.g., Fisher, 1989; Moy & Goodman, 1984) found no support for developmental theory. Perhaps the assumptions of developmental models are, as yet, only partially salient. In other words, perhaps there is a developmental process that we experience intuitively, but are still only in the beginnings stages of operationalizing.

Russell et al. (1984) criticized most developmental models as being too simplistic. They implied that the development of the professional helper involves a great deal more than these models would suggest. Holloway (1987) articulated a similar view and suggested that supervision is only one event going on in the trainee's professional and personal life, perhaps not the most important. Empirically, therefore, Holloway proposed that it is too early to assume a predictable development paradigm:

Although researchers are interpreting their results as tentatively supporting a developmental model, lack of developmental-specific methodology, confinement to the supervisory experience as a source of information, predominant use of structured self-report questionnaires, and lack of evidence of distinct, sequential stages in trainee's growth reflect the prematurity of such claims. (p. 215)

In subsequent publications (Holloway, 1988; Stoltenberg & Delworth, 1988), a dialogue has been established that will further our understanding of the cognitive constructs and behavioral and affective components of different levels of therapeutic competence, as well as the training prerequisites at each level.

In his excellent review of empirical studies based on developmental models, Worthington (1987) reached the following conclusions about developmental supervision:

- There is some support for general developmental models.
- For the most part, perceptions of supervisors and trainees have been broadly consistent with developmental theories.
- The behavior of supervisors changes as trainees gain experience.
- The supervision relationship changes as counselors gain experience.
- Supervisors do not become more competent as they gain experience.

In their review of the research that has been published since the Worthington (1987) review, Stoltenberg et al. (1994) concluded that "evidence appears solid for developmental changes across training levels" (p. 419). They also noted that, whereas experience alone is a relatively crude measure of "development," it has been used in most studies. For this reason and given that most of this research had focused on a restricted range of experience (e.g., first practicum versus second practicum versus internship), Stoltenberg et al. found that "it is remarkable that so many differences have been found among trainees based on this categorization" (p. 419).

SOCIAL ROLE MODELS

In Chapter 1 we discussed some root metaphors that might influence expectations and behaviors of supervisors and supervisees. These are metaphors based on enduring, ingrained role behaviors such occur in parent–child, sibling, and mentor–apprenticeship relationships. Because these relationships are so very basic and indelible,

they may affect supervision in ways that remain outside our awareness.

Another class of metaphors consists of the professional roles that supervisors already have mastered in their professional work. It is logical, then, that these would become metaphors or templates for their work as supervisors. Ekstein and Wallerstein (1972) addressed this point in stating that "The one confronted with something new will try at first to reduce the new to the familiar. The psychotherapist who becomes a teacher of psychotherapy will frequently be tempted to fall back on skills that represent prior acquisitions. He will thus try to convert the teaching relationship into a therapeutic relationship" (pp. 254–255).

This tendency of supervisors to draw on what already has been learned is complemented by the fact that it is possible to consider supervision a higher-order role that encompasses other professional roles. For example, we have heard colleagues state that supervision is more than teaching and less than therapy. Though this is only superficially accurate, it does suggest the point we intend to make. Perhaps Douce (1989) stated this even better when she pointed out that "supervision is a separate skill similar to teaching—but different; similar to counseling—but different; and similar to consulting—but different" (p. 5). This reflects the point suggested in the title of Ekstein's (1964) article, "Supervision of Psychotherapy: Is It Teaching? Is It Administration? Or Is It Therapy?"

But there are a number of determinants of the role or roles that a supervisor will employ at any given point. It therefore is useful to consider the model Friedlander and Ward (1984) developed, which is depicted in Figure 4.2. Each of its concentric circles is successively less broad and encompassing; at the same time, each influences the level "below" it. Too, this model makes clear in a visual way that terms such as *role, theory, focus,* and *technique* are *not* interchangeable. Not all authors have been clear about these distinctions. Figure 4.2, to which we alluded earlier in this chapter, is very useful in clarifying these relationships.

There are, though, only a relatively few roles that supervisors employ. This is illustrated in Table 4.2, which depicts the supervisory roles suggested

TABLE 4.2 Supervisor Roles as Suggested by a Sample of Theorists

BERNARD (1979)	EKSTEIN (1964)	WILLIAMS (1995)	HESS (1980)	HOLLOWAY[a] (1995)	CARROLL[a] (1996)
			Lecturer		
				Relating	
Teacher	Teacher	Teacher	Teacher	Instructing and advising	Teaching
				Modeling	
Counselor	Therapist	Facilitator	Therapist	Supporting and sharing	Counseling
Consultant		Consultant	Consultant	Consulting	Consulting
		Evaluator	Monitor and evaluator	Monitoring and evaluating	Monitoring Evaluating
			Case reviewer and master therapist		
	Administrator				Administrating

[a]Holloway (1995) suggested making the transformation from nouns (roles) to verbs (functions); Carroll (1996) followed that same convention.

by several authors (Bernard, 1979; Carroll, 1996; Ekstein, 1964; Hess, 1980; Holloway, 1995; Williams, 1995). This selection of authors is not inclusive, but includes those who have been most influential. Moreover, these models are sufficient to convey the range of supervisor roles. It is clear from this table that the two roles of counselor–therapist and teacher were suggested by all these authors; also, all but one suggested the role of consultant. The next most frequently suggested role is that of evaluator or monitor. Holloway (1992) characterized the supervision models that have given particular focus to these roles as social role models. In the following sections, we will briefly summarize three of them. As will be clear, whereas the focus on roles is in each case foundational to the model, this is but one aspect of that model.

The Discrimination Model

Bernard (1997) recently reported that she developed what she called the Discrimination Model in the mid-1970s as a teaching tool. She was assigned to teach a supervision course and "having recently received my doctorate, I was close enough to the experience of assuming the role of supervisor for the first time to understand my students' need for an aid to organize their initial supervision activities" (p. 310). The result of her efforts was "the simplest of maps to direct their teaching efforts" (p. 310). It is an eclectic model that claims the virtues both of parsimony and versatility.

The Discrimination Model (Bernard, 1979) attends to three separate foci for supervision as well as three supervisor roles:

Foci: Supervisors might focus on trainee's *intervention* skills (what the trainee is doing in the session that is observable by the supervisor); the trainee's *conceptualization* skills (how the trainee understands what is occurring in the session, identifies patterns, or chooses interventions, all covert processes); and the trainee's *personalization* skills (how the trainee interfaces a personal style with therapy at the same time that he or she attempts to keep therapy uncontaminated by personal issues and countertransference responses).

Roles: Once supervisors have made a judgment about their trainee's abilities within each focus area, they must choose a role to accomplish their supervision goals. The available roles are those of *teacher, counselor,* or *consultant.*

As a consequence, the supervisor might be responding at any given moment in one of nine different ways (i.e., three roles by three foci). Table 4.3 illustrates how the model might operate in practice.

The model is situation specific. In fact, it is called the Discrimination Model precisely because

TABLE 4.3   The Discrimination Model

FOCUS OF SUPERVISION	SUPERVISOR ROLE		
	Teacher	*Counselor*	*Consultant*
Intervention	Se would like to use systematic desensitization with a client but has never learned the technique	Se is able to use a variety of intervention skills, but with one client uses question asking as his primary style	Se finds her clients reacting well to her use of metaphor and would like to know more ways to use metaphor in counseling
	Sr teaches the Se relaxation techniques, successive approximation, hierarchy building, and the desensitization process	Sr attempts to help Se determine the effect of this client on him, which limits his use of skills in therapy sessions	Sr works with Se to identify different uses of metaphor in counseling and to practice these
Conceptualization	Se is unable to recognize themes and patterns of client thought either during or following therapy sessions	Se is unable to set realistic goals for her client, who requests assertion training	Se would like to use a different model for case conceptualization
	Sr uses session transcripts to teach Se to identify thematic client statements (e.g., blaming, dependence)	Sr helps Se relate her cognitive blocks to her own inability to be assertive in several relationships	Sr discusses several models for Se to consider
Personalization	Se is unaware that her preference for a close seating arrangement reflects her own cultural background and intimidates the client	Se is unaware that his female client is attracted to him sexually	Se would like to feel more comfortable working with older clients
	Sr assigns the reading of literature summarizing proximity studies	Sr attempts to help the Se confront his own sexuality and his resistance to recognizing sexual cues from women	Sr and Se discuss developmental concerns of older people

Sr, supervisor; Se, supervisee.

Adapted from "Supervisor Training: A Discrimination Model," by J. M. Bernard, 1979. *Counselor Education and Supervision, 19,* 60–69.

it implies that supervisors will tailor their responses to the particular supervisee's needs. This means that the supervisor's roles and foci should change not only across sessions, but also *within* session.

Supervisors should employ each focus as appropriate. The problems arise either when the supervisor attends to one focus at the expense of the supervisee's more salient needs or, relatedly, when the supervisor is rigid in a preference for one particular focus. There are many reasons to choose a role, but the worst reason is habit or personal preference independent of the trainee's needs.

Theory and research concerning developmental approaches suggest that supervisors are more likely to employ the teaching role with novice supervisees and the consultant role with those who are more advanced. Also, supervisors of beginning trainees might expect to focus predominantly on intervention skills, whereas supervisors of more advanced students might expect to offer more balance across foci.

But these are general tendencies. Bernard (1979, 1997) would argue that the effective supervisor will be prepared to employ all roles and address all foci for supervisees at any level.

Our own professional experience as has been that the Discrimination Model is useful in training and supervising supervisors. Nevertheless, it merits some specific critical examination.

1. Because it suggests both roles and foci, this model is more inclusive than are most social role models. In fact, the discrimination model is rooted in a technical eclecticism. It frees the user to be broadly flexible in responding to the supervisee.

The fact is, though, that supervisors never can or will divorce themselves totally from the influence of their theoretical beliefs. Moreover, they often will invoke theory as a rationalization for what actually is personal idiosyncrasy. But whether theory or rationalization, the net result is to block the supervisor's flexibility demanded to fully use the discrimination model.

2. The discrimination model is concerned specifically with interactions within the supervision session as these relate to immediate learning needs of the supervisee. Therefore, it does not speak to the role of evaluator or monitor, which is important as a means to ensure quality of client care. But, though that role is not spoken to in the model, its presence is assumed.

3. Russell et al. (1984) correctly noted that very little research has tested models of supervision that suggest supervisor roles. One strength of the Discrimination Model is that it is among the most researched of these models. During the 1980s, a number of studies either explicitly tested the Discrimination Model or employed it as a way to frame research questions (e.g., Ellis & Dell, 1986; Ellis, Dell, & Good, 1988; Glidden & Tracey, 1989; Goodyear, Abadie, & Efros, 1984; Goodyear & Robyak, 1982; Stenack & Dye, 1982; Yager, Wilson, Brewer, & Kinnetz, 1989). The model seems generally to have been supported in the various findings of these studies.

Interestingly, the role of consultant has remained somewhat elusive in these studies. For example, Goodyear et al. (1984) found that a sample of experienced supervisors was able to differentiate among the supervision sessions of four major psychotherapy theorists according to their use of the teacher and counselor roles, but not the consultant role. Similarly, the counselor and teacher roles were validated, but the consultant role was not, in a factor analytic study by Stenack and Dye (1982). In multidimensional scaling studies by Ellis and Dell (1986) and Glidden and Tracey (1989), the teaching and counseling roles were found to anchor opposite ends of a single dimension; the consultant role did not clearly emerge from their data.

This is curious, because the idea of the consultant role for supervisors is intuitively appealing, especially in work with more advanced supervisees (e.g., Gurk & Wicas, 1979). One possible explanation is that the consultant role is "fuzzier" than the others. Though it is frequently endorsed, there is not the common understanding of it that is true of the counselor and teacher roles.

Finally, we would note that Friedlander and Ward (1984; see Figure 4.2) did not differentiate between *styles* and *roles.* In fact, their Supervisory Styles Inventory (SSI; in the Supervisor's Toolbox at the end of this book) measures three styles that correspond roughly to Bernard's three roles (i.e., teacher = task oriented; consultant = attractive; and counselor = interpersonally sensitive). The fairly substantial literature on the SSI therefore reasonably can be understood to bear on the Discrimination Model as well.

The Hawkins and Shohet Model

U.S. researchers and theorists have developed virtually all the models we have covered. But supervision is receiving attention worldwide. British (e.g., Carroll, 1996; Hawkins & Shohet, 1989) and Australian (Williams, 1995) theorists have been especially prominent in this domain. In this section, we will cover the Hawkins and Shohet (1989; 2000) model.

The orienting metaphor for their work is that of the "good enough" supervisor. The supervisor is there not only to offer support and reassurance,

but also to contain the otherwise-overwhelming affective responses the trainee might have. Theirs is a social role model in that the supervisor is expected to employ different roles or styles. However, Hawkins and Shohet maintain that the particular style is driven by the focus the supervisor employs. They therefore devote relatively more attention to focus than to roles or style.

Hawkins and Shohet (2000) have suggested that supervisors might focus on seven different phenomena and therefore have developed what they describe colorfully as the "six-eyed model of supervision." Their model (depicted in Figure 4.4) recognizes that two interlocking systems occur in supervision: (1) the *therapy system* and (2) the *supervisory system*. These are the main categories of supervisor attention. These two systems exist "within a wider context which impinges upon and colours the processes within it (p. 71). The various "modes of focus" (p. 71) are:

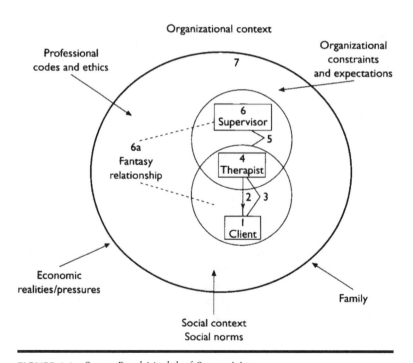

FIGURE 4.4   Seven-Eyed Model of Supervision

From Hawkins, P. & Shohet, R. (2000). *Supervision in the Helping Professions, Second edition.* Buckingham, UK: Open University Press. Copyright © (2000) by Open University Press. Reprinted by permission.

Mode 1: *the content of the therapy session:* the supervisee's narrative about the phenomena of the therapy session, including clients' verbal and nonverbal behaviors; examining how material from one session is related to that of other sessions.

Mode 2: *strategies and interventions:* attention to the supervisee's interventions with clients.

Mode 3: *the therapy relationship:* attention to the system the supervisee and client create together (rather than on either as an individual).

Mode 4: *the therapist's process:* attention to the internal processes of the supervisee, especially countertransference, and their effects on the counseling.

Mode 5: *the supervisory relationship:* attention to parallel processes (which are discussed in Chapter 6).

Mode 6: *the supervisor's own process:* attention to the supervisor's own countertransference reactions to the supervisee.

Mode 6a: *the supervisor-client relationship:* attention to fantasies the supervisor and client have about one another.

Mode 7: *the wider context:* attention to the professional community of which the supervisor and supervisee are members. This includes the organization in which they work as well as their profession.

In an unpublished manuscript, Michael Ellis suggested that in making the decision about where to focus, supervisors should employ the following continuum: supervisor chooses focus → supervisor offers option of focus → supervisor helps supervisee review options → supervisee chooses focus. Ellis also suggested that that the determinants of focus should include such matters as: the contract with the supervisee; the developmental stage of the supervisee; the supervisees' theoretical orientation; identified learning needs from previous session/s; if the supervisee is a student, any tie-in to current course learning; the stage of the supervisee's work with the client; time constraints; the mood of the moment.

Attention to focus is central to the Hawkins and Shohet model. It is not, though, the only feature of that model. We do not have the space here to cover the five factors of their full model, but would note here that these are (1) the style or role of the supervisor; (2) the stage of development of the supervisee; (3) the counseling orientation of both the supervisor and trainee; (4) the supervisor–supervisee contract; (5) the setting, or what we would call modality (individual; group; etc.).

The Holloway Systems Model

It is clear from the number of times and the contexts that we cite throughout this book that Holloway has been among the most prolific and influential supervision researchers and theorists. Hers (Holloway, 1995) is perhaps the most comprehensive of the available models. It takes into account a *number* of factors, including the supervisory relationship itself (including phase, contract, and structure); characteristics of the supervisor; characteristics of the institution in which the supervision occurs; characteristics of the client; and characteristics of the trainee.

The model certainly warrants greater coverage than we are able to provide here. To link it to the social role models, we will summarize here only the aspects of the model that concern functions and tasks. These are, respectively, the *what* and *how* of supervision.

> *Tasks:* monitoring–evaluating, instructing–advising, modeling, consulting, supporting–sharing
> *Functions:* counseling skill, case conceptualization, professional role, emotional awareness, self-evaluation

The consequence is a 5 (task) by 5 (function) matrix, with 25 resulting task–function combinations. A supervisor might, for example, engage in monitoring–evaluating (the how) of the trainee's counseling skill (the what) or in consulting concerning the trainee's emotional awareness, and so on.

Holloway (1997) noted that "hypothetically a supervisor may engage in any [task] with any [function, but] . . . realistically there probably are some task and function matches that are more likely to occur in supervision" (p. 258). So that readers can more easily see the relationship between Holloway's model and others such as Bernard (1979, 1997), they should understand that her functions correspond to what others have called foci; that her tasks are the verb form of what others have used to describe supervisor roles.

CONCLUSION

Supervisors traditionally have employed their theories of therapy to inform their work with supervisees. Because of supervision's close relationship to therapy, it is inevitable that this will occur. But it is a mark of the vitality of supervision as an area of practice and inquiry that increasingly models have been developed specifically for supervision. Although our coverage of these models was necessarily scant, we hope it will help to orient aspiring supervisors to literature that they can explore in more detail.

In presenting these models, we also are aware that most supervisors are likely to behave as eclectics or integrationists. Because of the confusion and diversity around the terms, we will offer Norcross and Napolitano's (1986) culinary metaphor to suggest the nuances between them. They asserted that, whereas "the eclectic selects among several dishes to constitute a meal, the integrationist creates new dishes by combining different ingredients" (p. 253).

Most supervisors eventually develop their own, unique integrationist perspectives. Indeed, one central finding of Skovholt and Rønnestadt's (1992a, 1992b) model was that developing such an individualized perspective was a hallmark of the advanced practitioner; Stoltenberg et al. (1998) made a similar assertion.

Norcross and Halgin (1997) suggested that in developing an integrationist perspective supervisors should attend to what they called *cardinal principles of integrative supervision.* Among these were to customize supervision to the individual student; conduct a needs assessment; construct explicit contracts; blend supervision methods; address with trainees their "relationships of choice"; operate from a coherent framework; match supervision to trainee variables; consider the therapy approach (in general, "the 'how' of supervision [method] should parallel the 'what' of supervision [content]," p. 15), the developmental level of the trainee, the cognitive style of the trainee, and the trainee's personal idiom; assess the trainee' therapeutic skills; and evaluate the outcomes.

In short, we believe that to develop an integrationist perspective probably is inevitable. Perhaps the above mentioned suggestions of Norcross and Halgin (1997) will help this process.

CHAPTER 5

THE SUPERVISORY RELATIONSHIP
THE INFLUENCE OF INDIVIDUAL AND DEVELOPMENTAL DIFFERENCES

Striking similarities exist between the processes of counseling and of clinical supervision. Perhaps the most pronounced of these are the centrality and role of the interpersonal relationship. Just as a positive and productive relationship is critical to successful counseling, so too is a positive and productive relationship critical to successful supervision (Rønnestad & Skovholt, 1993; Worthen & McNeill, 1996). Understanding relationship variables that affect the supervisory relationship and having the skill to establish a productive supervisory relationship have been cited as requisite for supervision preparation and practice (Borders et al., 1991; Supervision Interest Network, 1990). In fact, when supervision participants are asked to identify critical incidents in supervision, the most frequently cited incidents cluster around the supervisory relationship (Ellis, 1991a; Nelson & Friedlander, 2001).

This chapter will examine the effect that individual, cultural, and developmental differences can have on the supervisory relationship. More specifically, we will discuss how these unique characteristics of the supervisee require the supervisor to behave in certain ways, often referred to as the *supervision environment*. Individual differences refer to those unique personal qualities that are often referred to as one's personality. Although the influence of most aspects of personality on either counseling or supervision represents unchartered waters, there is a small amount of literature that considers cognitive style and supervision. Cultural differences include cultural identities and the meanings attached to these identities. The supervision literature addressing cultural identity has

grown significantly in recent years. Finally, developmental differences refer to one's placement along the continuum of counseling skill acquisition. For example, many behaviors and perceptions of the first-year student will be different when the student is in the second or third year of training.

Whereas Chapters 6 and 7 will focus more directly on the *interpersonal processes* and issues that may occur between supervisors and supervisees, this chapter focuses primarily on characteristics descriptive of the individual and how these have been found to affect supervision. Our goal, then, is to consider the following topics and how they should inform the supervisory process (environment): cognitive–learning style, cognitive complexity, cognitive development, experience level, and multiple cultural identities. We have depicted the interaction of these factors in Figure 5.1.

THE UNIQUENESS OF TWO PERSONS IN RELATIONSHIP

The supervisory relationship is a product of the uniqueness of two individuals, embedded within the process of supervision and modified by the demands of the various contexts within which supervision occurs. Knowing some of the personal variables that have been considered in the professional literature will arm supervisors with additional tools to assist the supervisee in achieving competence. Furthermore, because we have some evidence that personal compatibility between supervisor and supervisee will affect evaluation (see Chapter 2), it is essential that the supervisor be

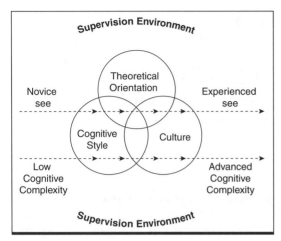

FIGURE 5.1 Supervisee Charactertistics Calling for the Appropriate Supervision Environment

aware of personal and interpersonal style variables to avoid biased reviews.

Personal (or individual) variables include relatively stable attributes, such as cognitive–learning style, and attributes that change over time, including cognitive development and experience in the field. In addition, individual variables include the various ways that an individual identifies herself or himself culturally. The first half of this chapter addresses cognitive–learning style, cognitive complexity, cognitive development, and experience and how these call for different supervision responses. The second half of the chapter addresses the complex topic of cultural differences.

COGNITIVE STYLE, COGNITIVE COMPLEXITY, THEORETICAL ORIENTATION, COGNITIVE DEVELOPMENT, AND LEVEL OF EXPERIENCE OF THE SUPERVISEE

Cognitive style and cognitive complexity have not received the same level of attention in the supervision literature as have developmental differences, including the developmental differences based on level of experience. Furthermore, unlike the literature on developmental differences, cognitive style and cognitive complexity research and model development seem to be more disparate. These limits aside, we begin with a consideration of *cognitive–learning styles* and *cognitive complexity*. We also briefly consider the *theoretical orientation* of the supervisee as a subset of cognitive style.

Cognitive or Learning Styles

Cognitive or learning styles concern a person's particular ways of processing information and different preferences in learning. Specifically, they represent ways in which individuals receive, interpret, store, and retrieve information (Rigazio-DiGilio, 1998). These do not indicate differential ability. And, unlike cognitive complexity, cognitive or learning styles are assumed to be nonhierarchical. Rigazio-DiGilio (1998) has noted that, although there are many classification systems for cognitive processing, few have been considered for their utility in clinical supervision. We will use the two different lenses to consider this topic that has surfaced in the literature: (1) the work using the Myers–Briggs Type Indicator (Myers, 1962; Myers & McCaulley, 1985) to differentiate trainees and (2) the contributions of Rigazio-DiGilio and her colleagues (e.g., Rigazio-DiGilio & Anderson, 1994; Rigazio-DiGilio, Daniels, & Ivey, 1997) in applying the work of Ivey (1986) to formulate systemic cognitive–developmental supervision. Taken together, these authors offer a relatively rich discussion of the importance of cognitive or learning style in establishing and monitoring the supervisory relationship. We will begin by considering the implication of MBTI.

The Myers–Briggs Type Indicator (MBTT) and Supervision. The MBTI produces a profile that addresses the following differences:

- Focus of interest (*Extroversion,* E), focusing on the outer world of people and things, versus *Introversion* (I), directed toward the inner world of ideas
- Information gathering (*Sensing,* S), relying on facts and data, versus *Intuiting* (N), relying on intuition to understand meaning

- Involvement with information (*Feeling,* F), focusing on subjective experience, versus *Thinking* (T), looking to objective analysis
- Information management (*Judging,* J), attempting to regulate and control, versus *Perceiving* (P), looking to experience life and adapt to it

Although the study focused on communication disorders, Craig and Sleight (1990) found significant differences between supervisors and trainees. Supervisors were far more likely to have a psychological type profile of ENTJ, INTJ, or ESTJ. Not surprisingly, these same profiles have been found to be common among those drawn to college teaching. The most dramatic differences between supervisors and supervisees had to do with the T–F scale and the J–P scale.

Craig and Sleight (1990) addressed some of the implications of these findings. For example, a Thinking–Judging supervisor (i.e., the most common profile among supervisors in academic settings) will find a trainee who makes decisions based on subjective data to be frustrating. Similarly, the well-organized supervisor (J) may be critical of the supervisee whose paper work or general approach to learning seems too random. At the same time, FP trainees may in fact be more capable of achieving empathy with clients than their supervisors.

Another area of distinction is the N–S scale. Because the preference represented by this scale has to do with gathering of information, it can affect supervision in a number of ways. A Sensing trainee will be attempting to understand through a collection of facts; therefore, an intuitive insight from an N supervisor may only confuse and frustrate the supervisee who cannot track the origin of the suggestion (Craig & Sleight, 1990). Furthermore, students who are Intuitive rather than Sensing have been found to receive far more regard from supervisors and were evaluated as significantly more competent than Sensing trainees (Handley, 1982). (Despite these findings, Handley also reported that the cognitive style of the su-

pervisor did not affect trainees' ratings of their relationship with their supervisors or their satisfaction with supervision.) Carey and Williams (1986) attempted a partial replication of the Handley study and found no significant relationship between trainees' cognitive style and supervisors evaluations of them. At the same time, their findings were consistent with others that supervisors were more likely to score higher on the NT scales, whereas counseling students were more likely to demonstrate SF preferences. As a result of their literature review, Goodyear and Guzzard (2000) concluded that the best assessment at this point is that the relationship between S–N and supervisee evaluations is inconclusive.

Swanson and O'Saben (1993) also found the MBTI to be relevant to supervision: Supervisees with a Thinking–Perceiving profile expressed a greater need for supervisors who were willing to struggle and argue with them, as well as to confront them about more personal aspects of behavior; supervisees who were Intuitive expressed a need for gentle confrontation and direct supervision of counseling sessions and less need for supervision that provided tangible intervention in crises or supervision that excluded personal issues; and Introvert trainees expressed a greater need for gentle confrontation and lesser need for direct supervision of sessions. Although individual scales correlated with particular perceptions of the supervisory environment, a complete profile was not significant for any of the analyses. This finding makes interpretation of individual scales suspect (Goodyear & Guzzard, 2000).

Finally, Lochner and Melchert (1997) reasserted the importance of cognitive style by examining whether supervisees' cognitive style determined the type of supervision these supervisees preferred. The authors hypothesized that supervisees with high scores on the Intuiting, Feeling, and Perceiving scales (and low scores on Sensing, Thinking, and Judging) would prefer relationship-oriented supervision, whereas those scoring high on Sensing, Thinking, and Judging would prefer task-oriented supervision. The results of their research supported these hypotheses. As we will discuss later, Lochner and Melchert used these results to challenge some of the assumptions of the developmental models of supervision.

In summary, psychological type seems to be a factor in supervision, though it must be viewed as only one factor of many that can affect the supervisory relationship. Kitzrow (2001) has outlined strengths and weaknesses of supervisory styles based on each scale of the MBTI (see Table 5.1). Although the psychometric adequacy of the MBTI occasionally has been challenged, the most recent meta-analytic data (Capraro & Capraro, 2002) are reassuring. With some appreciation of the strengths and deficits of their profiles, supervisors may be more effective with supervisees who have different psychological types.

Systemic Cognitive–Developmental Supervision (SCDS). Rigazio-DiGilio and her colleagues have extended the earlier work of Ivey (1986) to develop a model that encourages supervisors to track and intervene with supervisees based on the cognitive style of the supervisee (Rigazio-DiGilio, 1997; Rigazio-DiGilio & Anderson, 1994; Rigazio-DiGilio, Daniels, & Ivey, 1997). Although it is referred to as a developmental model using Piagetian terms to describe different types of learners (supervisees), there is no assumption within the model that one type of learner is superior to another. Rather, each of the four world views has its advantages and disadvantages for conducting therapy. The task of the supervisor is to identify the primary orientation(s) of each supervisee and to assist each supervisee to become more flexible and to see the world from additional orientations to the one(s) that comes naturally. When supervisees can access all four world views, they can shift gears when necessary during therapy, thus enabling them to offer assistance that is more likely to be on target. What follows is a description of each cognitive orientation as described by Rigazio-DiGilio (1995). The descriptions reflect both the competencies and the constraints of each orientation when it is dominant.

The first type of orientation described by Rigazio-DiGilio et al. (1997) is the *sensorimotor.* These supervisees are affected emotionally, if not viscerally, by their experiences. They can identify feelings easily and process them, permitting them to work through issues of transference and countertransference (Rigazio-DiGilio, 1995). If constrained by this world view, supervisees can be overstimulated by their emotions and this can interfere with their conceptual skills. They may also rely on "what feels right" as the basis for interventions, rather than solid treatment planning. Rigazio-DiGilio suggested that the supervisor working with the sensorimotor supervisee use a directive style that provides the supervisee with a safe environment to explore sensory data. The goal is to help the supervisee translate an abundance of sensorimotor data into a viable framework for conducting therapy.

The second cognitive style is *concrete,* and these supervisees see the world (and their clients) through a linear, cause–effect lens. The concrete learner can describe the events described by the client, often in the same order as the client presented them. Because of their if–then reasoning ability, concrete thinkers can anticipate patterned behavior of their clients. At the same time, supervisees with a concrete orientation can foreclose regarding their understanding of the client and can have difficulty seeing alternative perspectives. They also have difficulty moving from the specific to the more comprehensive in understanding the direction of counseling or therapy.

Rigazio-DiGilio's (1995) third orientation is the *formal.* These supervisees can analyze situations from multiple perspectives and are naturally reflective. They can easily modify their treatment plans based on supervisory feedback. They have no difficulty linking a specific session to the overall direction of therapy. If the formal orientation is too strong, supervisees will have difficulty translating their understanding of client themes to actual practice. They can also underestimate the role of feelings and behavior in counseling. Because they see their analytical abilities as their strength, they may have difficulty challenging these.

TABLE 5.1 Supervisory Style Based on Psychological Type

The Extraverted Supervisor

Natural Strengths and Characteristics
Active approach
Helps students explore a broad range of interests and issues
Open, expressive, and energetic
Processes information and solves problems externally through interaction and discussion

Supervision Skills to Work on
Help students to explore issues and cases in depth
Slow down and allow time for reflection and processing
Talk less and listen more

The Introverted Supervisor

Natural Strengths and Characteristics
Allows students time to process information internally
Helps students explore issues and cases in depth
Reflective approach
Skilled at one-to-one communication

Supervision Skills to Work on
Help students focus on action as well as reflection
Talk more and make an effort to be more open and expressive

The Sensing Supervisor

Natural Strengths and Characteristics
Focuses on dealing with present issues and concerns
Good at details and facts
Helps students come up with practical, step-by-step action plans
Practical and realistic

Supervision Skills to Work on
Be open to a variety of approaches rather than just traditional, tried and true methods
Encourage students to use and value intuition and imagination, as well as facts
Step back to consider the big picture, patterns, and new possibilities

The Intuitive Supervisor

Natural Strengths and Characteristics
Encourages students to use and trust intuition and imagination
Enjoys abstract thinking, theory, and identifying patterns and meanings
Focuses on dealing with potential issues and concerns that may arise in the future
Skilled at helping students see the big picture and possibilities

Supervision Skills to Work on
Be more attentive to facts, details, and issues that need attention now
Integrate theory with practical applications

The Thinking Supervisor

Natural Strengths and Characteristics
Good at solving complex problems
Intellectually challenging
Logical
Objective, analytical approach

(continued)

TABLE 5.1 Continued

The Thinking Supervisor (continued)

Supervision Skills to Work on
Balance theory with practical approaches and concrete examples
Be more subjective; take feelings and values, as well as logic and analysis, into consideration
Moderate the tendency to be overly challenging and critical
Remember to give positive feedback

The Feeling Supervisor

Natural Strengths and Characteristics
Empathetic, supportive, collaborative
Good at facilitating growth and development in others
Seeks harmony, avoids conflict
Subjective, interpersonal appraoch

Supervision Skills to Work on
Address conflicts and problems that may arise in the supervisory relationship, and help students address
    these issues with clients
Be more objective; take analysis and logic, as well as feelings and values, into consideration
Provide challenge as well as support

The Judging Supervisor

Natural Strengths and Characteristics
Attends to details, schedules, and deadlines
Helps students plan and implement therapeutic goals in a structured manner
Structured and organized; dislikes disruption in routine or last minute changes

Supervision Skills to Work on
Be more flexible, spontaneous, and open to innovative approaches
Focus on process, not just on goals or deadlines
Remember to give positive feedback

The Perceiving Supervisor

Natural Strengths and Characteristics
May overlook schedules and deadlines
Open to new and innovative approaches; encourages students to try new approaches
Spontaneous, flexible, and tolerant; adapts to last-minute change or crisis well
Tends to procrastinate and put off tasks and decisions

Supervision Skills to Work on
Be aware of tendency to procrastinate and inattention to deadlines, details, and requirements of supervision,
    i.e., routine paperwork, viewing tapes, reading case notes
Conduct supervisory sessions in a more punctual and structured manner
Help students develop goals and structured treatment plans

From M. A. Kitzrow (2001). "A model of supervisory style based on psychological type." *The Clinical Supervisor, 20*(2), 133–146. Copyright © (2001) by Haworth Press, Inc. Reprinted by permission.

Finally, Rigazio-DiGilio (1995) described the *dialectic* orientation as one in which supervisees challenge their own assumptions that inform their case conceptualization. In other words, these supervisees are drawn to think about how they think. Because of their tendencies to conceptualize broadly, dialectic thinkers are more likely to consider the broader environment, including historical and cultural contexts. The supervisee with a strong dialectic orientation can become overwhelmed by multiple perspectives, unable to commit to one because other competing perspectives appear equally valid (or invalid). Clients may have a difficult time integrating the complex thinking of a dialectic therapist.

In discussing supervision environments, Rigazio-Digilio and Anderson (1994) suggested that there are advantages to *both* matched and unmatched supervisory interventions. That is, supervisors often will choose to assist the supervisee to access the most positive characteristics within a particular orientation; at other times, the supervisor will attempt to mismatch the environment in order to challenge the supervisee to acquire some of the skills of another orientation. As might be expected, it is most feasible for a supervisee to understand an orientation that is only one orientation removed from the supervisee's orientation of choice.

The SCDS model, MBTI, and other learning-style models can probably offer all supervisors some additional understanding of their supervisees. (For example, it is not too difficult to figure out a supervisee's Myers–Briggs type and, with a little practice, whether the supervisee is concrete or dialectic in her orientation.) At the same time, a superficial application of these models may be a disservice to supervisees, leading to cognitive stereotyping, rather than a more sophisticated appreciation of what cognitive-style models can offer and what they cannot. Although the profession waits for additional empirical data regarding their utility, these models at the very least remind us that individual differences include how we process information, more specifically how we process the information received during the helping process and during supervision. Because of this, supervisors may need to operate from other than their preferred style of thinking and acting if they intend to be of service to a variety of supervisees. The consideration of cognitive and learning style especially underscores the educational nature of supervision.

Theoretical Orientation and Cognitive Style

There is a great deal of speculation and some evidence (e.g., Kennard, Stewart, & Gluck, 1987) that similarity of theoretical orientation between supervisor and supervisee is consequential for the relationship. Guest and Beutler (1988) presented data to suggest that several years after training early supervisory experiences can still exert an effect on the supervisee's theoretical position. Even so, when compared to other relationship factors, such as respect for the supervisee, theoretical orientation has been found to be the lesser influence (e.g., Schacht, Howe, & Berman, 1989; Wetchler, 1989). Putney, Worthington, and McCullough (1992) have shed some light on this issue.

As others (e.g., Holloway, Freund, Gardner, Nelson, & Walker, 1989) have observed, Putney et al. (1992) found that the supervisor's theory is much more likely to drive supervision than is the supervisee's. In other words, most supervisors direct supervisees based on their vision of psychotherapy and do not attend to the differences between their vision and the supervisee's. In light of this finding, it is understandable that theoretical compatibility would benefit the supervisee. These authors concluded, however, that *perceived* similarity was more important than *actual* similarity. Furthermore, for pairs who shared theoretical assumptions, weak adherence to theory by the supervisor led to increased trainee autonomy.

As the heading of this section implies, however, we think that theoretical orientation is best placed within the realm of cognitive style. Andrews's (1989) thoughtful and provocative work is highly relevant here. Andrews proposed that standard theoretical orientations reflect the personal visions of the authors who formulated them. The theories of psychotherapy that are taught in most training programs, then, are just a handful of "personal visions" that resonate with enough consumers to keep them alive. Part of their attractiveness, of course, is their high degree of cohesiveness and better than average insight into the human condition. Yet, Andrews's point remains that these theories emerged from the vision of one person or several persons of "like mind." Andrews argued that psychotherapists needed to strive for total theoretical integration (so that they may be tooled to react to the various visions presented by clients). Although Andrews does not mention supervision, his position begs the question of acknowledging individual vision in supervision as well as therapy. The important point here, however, is that theoretical orientation may be more a matter of individual difference than an academic construct handed down from supervisor to supervisee.

Research conducted by Lochner and Melchert (1997) partially supports Andrews's premise. These authors found that theoretical orientation operated similarly to cognitive style (Myers–Briggs type) in predicting a preference for a particular supervisory style. It seems then that orientation to theory may be as idiosyncratic as whether one is a Perceiving type or a Judging type (perhaps similar to Friedlander and Ward's, 1984, "assumptive world" as depicted in Figure 4.2). Supervisors may need to view alternative theoretical biases as true individual differences. This would put the findings of Putney et al. (1992) in a different light. The fact that supervisors *chose* the theoretical orientation within which supervision would occur could be viewed similarly to the supervisor who ignores learning style or cultural variables. Rather than offering their supervisees theoretical consistency, these supervisors could be accused of requiring theoretical foreclosure (Bernard, 1992). Although we need additional empirical evidence regarding the rightful place of theoretical orientation in training and supervision, Andrews's seminal work may offer the most practical posture for practicing supervisors.

Cognitive Complexity, Cognitive Development, and Level of Experience

We have ample evidence that trainees with high cognitive complexity are more capable of several

of the tasks of counseling, such as increased empathy and less prejudice (Stoppard & Miller, 1985), more sophisticated descriptions of client characteristics (Borders, 1989), more parsimonious conceptualization of specific counseling situations (Martin, Slemon, Hiebert, Hallberg, & Cummings, 1989), and more ability to stay focused on counseling and less on themselves (Birk & Mahalik, 1996). Because of this, the mental health professions have been invested in determining (or confirming) how cognitive development transpires so that supervisees will attain the desired level of conceptual competence by the end of their formal training and be poised for additional development after training.

Simultaneously, the supervision literature has been dominated by developmental assumptions about training and supervision, most of which assume that experience under supervision and cognitive development enjoy a symbiotic relationship. The professional literature does not neatly divide into these three topics; rather, most research addresses at least two of the three. In the following pages, we will attempt to review pertinent literature in order to answer the following questions: How and to what extent are cognitive complexity and cognitive development related? To what extent does cognitive development occur during training programs? How does it occur? Is supervised experience the most potent training variable for assuring or accelerating cognitive development?

Although it is impossible to isolate these three variables entirely, we will begin this section by a brief discussion of the relationship between cognitive complexity and cognitive development and follow this with a more elaborate discussion of the role of experience in supervisee development. We conclude with a discussion of cognitive development that does not revolve around experience as the assumed primary cause.

Cognitive Complexity and Cognitive Development.   As is stated above, cognitive complexity has been found to be correlated with competencies that are important to successful counseling. The assumption of the mental health professions has been that training and supervision stimulate cognitive development among trainees that culminates in cognitive complexity by the end of training. In recent years, empirical scrutiny has found that, whereas development does indeed seem to occur as a result of training (e.g., Duys & Hedstrom, 2000), it could not be described as uniformly robust, nor does it cover all aspects of cognitive complexity (Fong, Borders, Ethington, & Pitts, 1997; Granello, 2002; Lovell, 1999; Stein & Lambert, 1995). In fact, to date, there is little to challenge the work of Skovholt and Rønnestad (1992a), which concluded that the majority of cognitive development in the mental health fields occurred after formal training.

What is unknown at this point is the relationship between baseline cognitive complexity and cognitive development through training. In other words, although there is an assumption that baseline cognitive complexity is an advantage, little is known about its lasting advantage throughout training and beyond. Stoltenberg, McNeill, and Delworth (1998) asserted that, whereas all trainees begin at level 1 of their developmental model, the speed of transitions depends to some extent on the cognitive growth that they have attained in their individual lives.

As Stoltenberg (1981) had implied in his earlier work, Granello (2002) speculated that persons of higher cognitive complexity must "re-progress" (p. 292) through earlier stages of development as they conceptualize the intricacies of counseling (a possibility that Holloway, 1987, had challenged), but that the learning for trainees of high cognitive complexity may be more accelerated. Although these assumptions make intuitive sense, Lovell (1999) found that the amount of supervised clinical experience accounted for more cognitive development than individual cognitive complexity, although the latter also contributed significantly. Similarly, Granello (2002) found that the bulk of cognitive development occurred between the midpoint and end of training, that is, when the trainee is under supervision. This finding is consistent with the study conducted by Fong et al. (1997).

In summary, it would seem that high cognitive complexity has a substantial role to play in cognitive development. At the same time, develop-

ment as a counselor is multifaceted and integrative. Evidently, the role of supervised experience is key to assisting trainees to attain the level of cognitive complexity that will allow them to assimilate and analyze counseling information in a productive manner (Granello, 2002).

Experience as an Indicator of Developmental Level. The supervisee's level of experience has been one of the more broadly researched areas of counselor development. Although there are a few exceptions (e.g., Friedlander & Snyder, 1983), the great majority of empirical studies have suggested that supervisees have different characteristics and different abilities based on the amount of supervised experience that they have accrued (e.g., Borders, 1990; Burke, Goodyear, & Guzzard, 1998; Cummings, Hallberg, Martin, Slemon, & Hiebert, 1990; Granello, 2002; Ladany, Marotta, & Muse-Burke, 2001; Lovell, 1999; Mallinckrodt & Nelson, 1991; McNeill, Stoltenberg, & Pierce, 1985; McNeill, Stoltenberg, & Romans, 1992; Olk & Friedlander, 1992; Shechtman & Wirzberger, 1999; Swanson & O'Saben, 1993; Tracey, Ellickson, & Sherry, 1989; Tracey, Hays, Malone, & Herman, 1988; Wiley & Ray, 1986; Williams, Judge, Hill, & Hoffman, 1997; Winter & Holloway, 1991). Other reviewers of the empirical literature (Goodyear & Guzzard, 2000; Holloway, 1992, 1995; Stoltenberg, McNeill, & Crethar, 1994) also identified experience level as an important point of departure for understanding the developmental needs of the supervisee.

Several authors (Ellis & Ladany, 1997; Fong et al., 1997; Granello, 2002) have echoed Holloway's (1992) earlier caution, however, that there are multiple problems in interpreting the results of most developmental studies, one of these being the lack of longitudinal studies. In other words, without tracking the same supervisees over time, it is very difficult to discern whether the significant results of various studies depict true *development* or cohort effects. But even without this and other issues fully resolved, there is still ample empirical evidence to support an examination of the supervisee's experience level as one indicator of developmental level. Because of the variability of operational definitions across studies, we will be careful to stipulate the levels of experience used by the particular researchers discussed.

Researchers have examined the relationship between amount of training and supervisee behavior. Looking at the beginning practicum student, Borders (1990) found significant change in supervisee self-reports for self-awareness, dependency–autonomy, and theory–skills acquisition over one semester. McNeill, Stoltenberg, and Pierce (1985) obtained similar results when they compared beginning trainees to intermediate trainees. Examining prepracticum student growth over a period of one semester, Williams et al. (1997) found that trainees at the end of the semester decreased in anxiety and were better at managing their own transference and countertransference reaction.

Studies that considered larger experience differences have reported inconsistent and more complex results. Cummings et al. (1990) and Martin, Slemon, Hiebert, Hallberg, and Cummings (1989) found that experienced counselors were more efficient in their conceptualization, employing well-established cognitive schemata to conceptualize clients, although novice counselors seemed to require much more specific information about the clients to conceptualize the problem; they were more random in their information seeking, and their ultimate conceptualizations were less sophisticated.

Hillerbrand and Claiborn (1990) arrived at somewhat different conclusions. They found no differences in cognitive processes used by experienced and novice counselors when asked to diagnose client cases of different complexity. What they did find was that confidence and clarity in presenting cases were greater for the more experienced counselors. Hillerbrand and Claiborn's findings might be explained by the fact that they defined novice as doctoral students with one to three semesters of practicum; experts were defined as professionals with at least 5 years of postdoctoral experience.

Other researchers have also looked at a broader continuum of experience. Tracey et al. (1988) studied counselor responses across three experience levels: beginning counselors (0 to 1 year of practicum), advanced counselors (graduate students with more than 1 year of practicum), and doctoral counselors (at least 2 years of postdoctoral experience). When supervisee interventions (i.e., dominance, approach–avoidance, focus on affect, immediacy, breadth versus specificity, meeting client demands, verbosity and confrontation) were compared across groups, doctoral-level counselors were less dominant (yet confronted more), were less verbose, and yielded less to client demands than non-doctoral-level counselors (Tracey et al., 1988).

Burke, Goodyear, and Guzzard (1998) investigated the working alliance of 10 supervisor–supervisee dyads in terms of events that "weakened" and interventions that "repaired" the alliance. Even though all their supervisees had a master's degree in a mental health discipline, experience effects were found in the types of issues that were raised in supervision, as well as in the supervisee's approach to supervision. Less experienced supervisees (i.e., 1 year or less of postdegree experience) raised issues that revolved around the development of professional skills (e.g., definitions of diagnostic terms or the delivery of particular techniques). Less experienced supervisees also devoted considerable time to a single case and often did not meet previously established supervision goals. On the other hand, more experienced supervisees were more active in prioritizing the supervision agenda. They also tended to treat their supervisors more as consultants. When issues emerged, they tended to be around differences in theoretical orientation, presentation style, and treatment planning. The Burke et al. results, therefore, support several assumptions of developmental models of supervision.

Finally, an investigation conducted by Ladany et al. (2001) involved supervisees who were seeking a master's degree in counseling and supervisees seeking a doctoral degree in a mental health discipline. Ladany et al. sought to determine if general experience (i.e., length of time engaged in the practice of counseling) was related to cognitive complexity or if number of clients seen was a better predictor. Results indicated that experience alone accounted for cognitive complexity around diagnostic and treatment conceptualization. Seeing a greater number of clients over a shorter time span did not show similar gains in cognitive development. The authors hypothesized that too many clients may discourage the supervisee from reflective activity or may mean that supervision will be less intensive for any particular case, either of which might account for the diminished returns.

A final comment regarding experience is in order before we proceed. Most studies that demonstrate supervisee development over time have confounded experience with training. We have very little evidence that experience alone leads to developmental gains. Yet the changes observed within supervisees under supervision are promising. An inference one can draw is that experience obtained under close scrutiny and with specific feedback is necessary for learning to occur. The more direct methods of supervision that have been espoused in recent years, therefore, may account for some of the differences that have been observed among supervisees at different experience levels.

Experience Level and Moderating Variables. We have already indicated that cognitive complexity interacts with experience; that is, the trainee who has attained high conceptual ability will advance more quickly. Cultural factors may also enhance or interfere with the expected gains of supervised experience, and these are addressed in the second half of this chapter. We have examples of research that found experience level to be secondary to other individual characteristics in its effect on development. Although our examples are few, they raise the possibility that there may be other, perhaps many, variables that compromise or negate the effects of experience on professional development.

Winter and Holloway (1991) found that less experienced trainees were more likely to focus on conceptualization of the client, whereas more advanced trainees were more likely to focus on personal growth. Trainees with higher conceptual levels were more likely to request a focus on the development of counseling skills and to request feedback, thus indicating less concern about evaluation. Both level of experience and conceptual

level (cognitive complexity), therefore, produced significant results in this study.

Borders, Fong, and Neimeyer (1986) found neither experience nor ego development relate to perceptions of clients for trainees at three different levels within a master's program. Despite the nonsignificant findings, the authors noted that students at the higher ego levels "seemed to have a greater awareness of the interactive nature of the counselor–client relationship, perhaps thinking of their clients more often in terms of this process than did students at low ego levels" (p. 46). A later study by Fong et al. (1997) again found no measurable differences in ego development for master's-level trainees over the course of their program of study, thus prompting the authors to suggest that educators and supervisors need to more deliberately attend to the cognitive development of trainees.

Swanson and O'Saben (1993) reported that trainees' Myers–Briggs Type Indicator (MBTI) profile, amount of practicum experience (ranging from prepracticum to 15 completed semesters of practicum), and type of program (counseling psychology, clinical psychology, or counselor education) all produced significant differences in terms of supervisee needs and expectations for supervision. Program membership was the least dramatic predictor of differences, and level of experience produced the greatest differences. Level of experience differences produced results similar to other experience studies, indicating that supervisees with less experience expected more supervisor involvement, direction, and support.

Finally, whereas Granello (2002) found evidence of cognitive development with experience, she also found that program concentration was a moderating variable. Granello used an instrument that taps Perry's (1970) model of cognitive development. As expected, beginning counselors-in-training demonstrated dualistic thinking, whereas more advanced trainees demonstrated multiplistic thinking. (As in Perry's, 1981, research, relativistic thinking was not demonstrated.) However, in contrast to students majoring in mental health counseling, rehabilitation counseling, or marriage and family therapy, students majoring in school counseling became more dualistic in their thinking over the course of their training, not less. Granello also found that experience in human services prior to the training program, age, or GPA accounted for no differences in cognitive complexity.

Supervision Environment

Much research interest has been shown in the relative importance of matching supervisee developmental level with the appropriate supervisory conditions, typically referred to as the *supervision environment.* The assumptions regarding the appropriate environment have been based primarily on the work of early counselor development theorists, especially Stoltenberg and his colleagues (Stoltenberg, 1981; Stoltenberg & Delworth, 1987; Stoltenberg, McNeill, & Delworth, 1998). As described in Chapter 4, the model asserts that during the initial stages of supervision the supervisee should be offered significant structure, direction, and support to assure movement in a positive direction. As supervisees gain some experience, expertise, and confidence, they are ready to have some of the structure diminished, to be challenged with alternative conceptualizations of the cases that they have been assigned, to be given technical guidance as needed, and to begin to look at personal issues that affect their work. In short, to accommodate the different developmental needs of supervisees, supervisors alter their interventions or the supervision environment.

By and large, research has supported, or partially supported, the supervision environment premises of counselor developmental models (Bear & Kivlighan, 1994; Borders & Usher, 1992; Dodenhoff, 1981; Fisher, 1989; Glidden & Tracey, 1992; Guest & Beutler, 1988; Heppner & Handley, 1982; Heppner & Roehlke, 1984; Holloway & Wampold, 1983; Krause & Allen, 1988; Lazar & Eisikovits, 1997; Miars et al., 1983; Murray, Portman, & Maki, 2003; Rabinowitz, Heppner, & Roehlke, 1986; Reisling & Daniels, 1983; Stoltenberg, Pierce, & McNeill, 1987; Usher & Borders, 1993; Wetchler, 1989; Wiley & Ray, 1986; Williams, Judge, Hill, & Hoffman, 1997;

Winter & Holloway, 1991; Worthington & Stern, 1985). The questions that have driven this body of research include these: Has the matching of environment to development level of supervisee significantly enhanced supervisee learning, and do supervisees prefer a supervision environment that is developmentally appropriate?

These questions have received some support, although there certainly have been mixed results when the literature is examined closely. A recent study conducted by Ladany, Walker, and Melincoff (2001) produced results that challenged developmental models. As part of their research, Ladany et al. hypothesized that a relatively low level of cognitive complexity, limited experience, and unfamiliarity with a particular type of client would lead supervisees to seek supervision that was more task focused. Instead they found that all supervisees wanted supervisors to be moderately high on all supervision environments. Ladany et al. concluded that "the theoretical assumption that beginning trainees need more structure is an overgeneralization or a misguided view based more on clinical lore than on research, which specifically attends to changes in trainees' conceptual understanding of clients" (p. 215). Sumerel and Borders (1996) obtained similar findings and concluded that it may not be the supervision environment (intervention) per se that matters, but the style of delivery. Although inexperienced supervisees are expected to find a focus on personal issues to be less helpful, Sumerel and Borders suggested that, when this is done in a manner that is warm, supportive, and instructional, supervisees can benefit.

It seems, then, that moderating variables operate to change the needs of supervisees, making them occasionally inconsistent with the assumptions of developmental models. A case in point is an interesting study conducted by Tracey, Ellickson, and Sherry (1989). Tracey et al. considered the interaction of level of experience (beginning or advanced counseling psychology doctoral students), reactance potential (an individual's need to resist or comply with imposed structure), supervision structure (low structure or high structure), and content of supervision, (crisis or noncrisis), using Brehm's (1966) concept of reactance potential. The authors found that advanced trainees with high reactance (i.e., high need to resist structure) preferred supervision with less structure than did advanced trainees with low reactance. In noncrisis situations (i.e., when all things were equal), beginning trainees preferred structured supervision, whereas more experienced trainees preferred less structure. However, in crisis situations, *all* trainees preferred structured supervision regardless of their level of experience or reactance.

This last finding is reinforced by Zarski, Sand-Pringle, Pannell, and Lindon (1995), who noted that supervision must be modified based on the severity of individual cases. For supervisees working with difficult or volatile situations (e.g., family violence), more structure may be needed for advanced trainees until they have attained a necessary level of comfort and competence. Similarly, when Wetchler and Vaughn (1992) surveyed marriage and family therapists at multiple levels, supervisor directiveness was the most frequently identified supervisor skill that therapists thought enhanced their development. This result may indicate that more advanced supervisees take more difficult cases to supervision, thus requiring more direction from the supervisor around these identified cases.

In summary, although supervisors seem to offer different environments when supervisees' developmental differences are pronounced, empirical findings do not as yet support some of the finer distinctions made by developmental theorists. It is difficult to determine if the problem is in the design of particular studies or with the developmental models themselves (Ellis & Ladany, 1997). It is important to recall, however, that development is multifaceted, and the ability to address different levels of competence at any one point in the supervision process is difficult indeed. Additionally, we do not know what stage of development might take precedence at any measuring point. It is likely that supervisees master particular aspects of the therapeutic process, thus reflecting more advanced developmental characteristics around these, while still faltering with other aspects of skill develop-

ment. One group of supervisees, therefore, may represent several levels of development when measured on one variable; at the same time, if multiple variables are considered, each supervisee may offer a developmental profile in which the supervisee is more advanced on some variables than on others. If differing developmental levels require different supervision interventions, each supervisee may need a variety of interventions offered in a discriminating fashion. In short, it is probably best if the supervisor consider both development and environment to be dynamic and fluid, requiring astute observation and flexibility during all levels of training and for posttraining supervision as well.

DEVELOPMENTAL CONSTRUCTS: PULLING IT ALL TOGETHER

By now it is clear to the reader that "individual differences" covers a lot of territory. As supervisors approach a supervisory relationship, how do they weigh the different developmental contingencies we have addressed thus far? Some empirical findings are conflicting, yet some themes definitely warrant serious attention. Before we embark on what we know about cultural characteristics, we offer the following as guidelines to consider regarding the various constructs relevant to development.

• *Cognitive complexity matters.* High cognitive complexity (or conceptual level) is an important predictor of key counseling tasks, such as offering increased empathy (Stoppard & Miller, 1985) and developing accurate conceptualizations of client situations (Martin et al., 1989). Supervisees with low cognitive complexity will need assistance in forming cognitive maps that can be used to assess client issues and in goal setting and strategy selection. Supervision interventions that challenge this supervisee to conceptualize in highly abstract ways will be counterproductive.

Supervisees with high cognitive complexity appear more confident and ask for more feedback to improve counseling skills and thus seemingly are less concerned about evaluation. It is likely that

the process of counseling is more exciting to supervisees with high cognitive complexity because
they are able to produce and weigh more options
and choose the most appropriate intervention
(Gordon, 1990; Holloway & Wampold, 1986).

• *Cognitive style matters.* Although conceptual
level–cognitive complexity connotes a hierarchy
of ability, cognitive style represents the way we
think naturally (as opposed to how well we think!).
Though the evidence is still modest, we have
growing evidence that cognitive style affects how
supervisees organize data about clients, how they
present these data to their supervisors, and how
they interact with both clients and supervisors,
Lochner & Melchert, 1997; Rigazio-DiGilio,
Daniels, & Ivey, 1997; Swanson & O'Saben, 1993.

• *Supervisors also exhibit cognitive styles.* As a
key player in the supervisory relationship, the supervisor cannot be excluded in an assessment of
cognitive styles. Supervisors who understand the
importance of the supervisee's manner of making
sense of the world will certainly understand that
their cognitive style is equally relevant. If outside
of one's awareness, differences in cognitive styles
may serve to frustrate the supervision process
(Craig & Sleight, 1990), whereas compatibility in
cognitive style may lead to enhanced evaluation
(Handley, 1982), but also potentially limited
growth for the supervisee.

• *Theoretical orientation is intrinsically tied to
individual differences.* Although the mental health
professions have certainly appreciated that theory
represents a "world view," they have been slow to
view theoretical orientation as something that relates to cognitive style, if not cultural contexts (e.g.,
feminist theory). We have evidence that perceived
theoretical compatibility enhances clinical supervision (Putney, Worthington, & McCullough, 1992),
but the supervision literature has been relatively
quiet about theoretical orientation, except to say that
declarations of one's orientation should be made in
places like the supervision contract. The discourse
around theory may evolve quite differently if it were
appreciated as an aspect of cognitive style.

• *Experience under supervision matters.* Because of the field-specific nature of conceptual

level, Stoltenberg (1981) and Blocher (1983) were
among those who initially suggested that, at least
for novices, experience and conceptual level are
highly correlated. Indeed, they suggested that it is
possible to predict conceptual level from experience. It is not surprising, then, that much of the
development of clinical supervision practice has
been informed by this assumption.

Although we have a substantial body of research that supports the claim that supervised experience results in developmental advances for
trainees, the research has its critics (e.g., Ellis &
Ladany, 1997). As we reviewed earlier in this
chapter, the discourse regarding the relative
strength of experience to increase the supervisee's
competence has become more complicated and
more interesting.

• *Experience may be trumped by cognitive style.*
Although experience is a good predictor of
supervision needs, cognitive style can be a powerful moderating variable. With a group of supervisees all at the same experience level, Lochner
and Melchert (1997) found that Myers–Briggs
Type Indicator predicted the type of supervision
that supervisees preferred.

We should note that all supervision environments will appeal to some supervisees based on
cognitive style. This could inadvertently contribute to mixed results when attempting to conduct developmental supervision research.

• *Experience may be trumped by circumstances.* As we presented, despite the fact that
research consistently suggests that the more advanced supervisee will want or require less structure in supervision, several variables can change
this prediction, including a crisis situation (Tracey
et al., 1989) or a particularly difficult client population (Zarski et al., 1995). It is important to
remember, therefore, that in most instances supervision of an advanced supervisee is more idiosyncratic than supervision of a novice supervisee.
In other words, the novice supervisee will most
likely need some structure across his or her client
load, whereas the advanced supervisee may benefit from more autonomy with some clients, more
structure with others, support with difficult clients,

and challenge with those clients that may push the supervisee's personal buttons.

• *Experience level is typically paired with certain developmental characteristics. Supervisors should know these.* With experience, the supervisee should exhibit an increase of (1) self-awareness of behavior and motivation within counseling sessions, (2) consistency in the execution of counseling interventions, and (3) autonomy (Borders, 1990; McNeill, Stoltenberg, & Romans, 1992). If these are not forthcoming, supervisors need to ask what might be blocking learning (e.g., cognitive complexity, personality, or cultural issues) and to consider this more carefully.

With experience, it is expected that supervisees will develop more sophisticated ways to conceptualize the counseling process and the issues that their clients present and be less distracted by random specific information (Cummings, Hellberg, Martin, Slemon, & Hiebert, 1990). Novice supervisees will be more rigid and less discriminating in their delivery of therapeutic interventions. An "exaggerated forcefulness" (Tracey et al., 1988) in the delivery of an intervention may indicate that the supervisee is at the front end of a learning curve regarding this intervention. A hallmark of more advanced supervisees is that they are more flexible and less dominant when delivering interventions such as confrontation.

• *Supervision environment matters.* Supervisee characteristics and developmental agendas must be met with appropriate supervisor interventions in order for growth to occur. Although there are a plethora of supervision techniques to consider, these need to be used in ways that are appropriate to the developmental stage of the supervisee. To date, the research would support using experience level as a determinant for supervision environment, at least initially.

• *Supervision environment should be informed by awareness of cognitive complexity and cognitive style, not only by experience level of supervisee.* Even though experience level is an appropriate place to begin in establishing the supervision environment, it is overly simplistic as the sole variable to take into consideration. Because other supervisee characteristics can trump experience, the supervision environment must follow the predominant characteristic in order to be maximally successful.

• *Development only begins during formal training.* In their seminal longitudinal study of professional development, Skovholt and Rønnestad (1992a) established that development for the mental health professional was a long road with many intriguing complexities along the way. They also established that most of the development for serious professionals occurred after formal training. More recently, Fong et al. (1997) and Granello (2002) found that counselor (cognitive) development occurred only in the latter half of training programs. All this underscores the importance of clinical supervision beyond training and the early years in the field.

• *Developmental concepts are* **important,** *but not* **sufficient.** We have noted the inconsistencies in the research about the relative predictive power of development versus more stable individual characteristics such as cognitive style. In the second half of this chapter, we address cultural variables that must also inform supervision. In short, although we find developmental assumptions to be compelling, we advise clinical supervisors to expand beyond them in their practice.

• *Development of the trainee must be an intentional process.* Finally, we concur with others (e.g., Fong et al., 1997; Granello, 2002; Peace & Sprinthall, 1998) that, although some cognitive development occurs as a result of supervised experience, we may not be as intentional in promoting development as we could be. Fong et al. noted that skills development receives much more consistent attention than cognitive development in many training programs. Similarly, it is not uncommon for personal growth (intrapersonal and interpersonal) to serve as a hallmark of a training program. Overall cognitive development, however, has been a sidebar.

Granello (2000) suggested the application of Bloom's Taxonomy (Bloom, Englehart, Furst, Hill, & Krothwohl, 1956) as offering supervisors a tool to assist supervisees in their cognitive development. Bloom's work is a familiar classification of cognitive operations to educators and includes six competencies that increase in cognitive complexity: knowledge (which Granello reframed as "recall"), comprehension, application, analysis, synthesis, and evaluation. Granello has translated the concepts to be used in clinical supervision and suggested that Bloom's work lends itself as a tool for assessing the supervisee's cognitive level around any particular issue. She also proposed that whenever a supervisee is floundering the supervisor can use the taxonomy to propose questions to form interventions that will be helpful to the supervisee developmentally. Granello's application of Bloom's Taxonomy to counselor supervision is shown in Table 5.2.

CULTURAL DIFFERENCES

When two people meet in supervision or counseling, there is a negotiation that always happens. First, similarities are assessed, then dissimilarities. Color might be one . . . being from the same region might be another . . . having parents with similar emphases on education might be yet another. We then look to see how many of those dissimilarities can be bridged. The greater the effectiveness we have in bridging those dissimilarities the greater the multicultural competence we have in supervision or counseling. (Hird, Cavalieri, Dulko, Felice, & Ho, 2001, p. 117)

The influence of cultural phenomena on the helping process has received increasing attention in recent years. Pedersen (1991) postulated that virtually all counseling is multicultural, because culture incorporates the influences of race, ethnicity, gender, sexual orientation, religion, class, and so on, on our thoughts, assumptions, and behaviors. In discussing supervisory interactions, Killian (2001) reiterated Pedersen's sentiment by asserting, "Since we all inhabit various social locations on ecosystemic axes of race, gender, class, and culture, to name but a few, and these locations intersect in unique and sometimes contradictory ways, we are all multicultural, and our interactions with others must necessarily be so as well" (p. 63). Any dis-

cussion of individual differences, therefore, must include a serious discussion of cultural differences.

We wish to emphasize that the separation of these many developmental, cognitive-style, and cultural characteristics in this chapter is done for the purpose of exploring the contribution each makes to the process of supervision. In reality, however, cultural context, development, theoretical orientation, and cognitive style all interact in a dynamic and continuous fashion (Hird et al., 2001). Said differently, culture influences and shapes what we think of as individual characteristics, such as personality (Daniels, D'Andrea, & Kim, 1999), and may significantly affect cognitive style and developmental trajectories. It is with some dissonance, therefore, that we separate out the cultural influences on supervision (and further separate culture into even more discrete topics). By looking through these more discrete lenses, however, we hope to add clarity to the reader's understanding of each of these important constructs. The real challenge for the reader (and for all supervisors) is to remain flexible (able to switch lenses) and integrative (able to consider the impact of multiple lenses simultaneously).

Virtually all the professional literature concerned with multicultural issues continues to revolve around what could be described as disenfranchised groups, that is, cultural groups that experience diminished power and privilege in the United States. Although individual contributions to the literature typically concern one such group, we have made great strides in understanding that cultural phenomena involve all people in their interpersonal interactions.

There is still work to be done to assist members of the dominant culture to understand that they are cultural beings (cf. Preli & Bernard, 1993), but, for the most part, the days of a true "us–them" mentality regarding culture are behind us in the mental health professions. Although we assert this basic tenet, we also acknowledge tremendous gaps in knowledge and sensitivities and the stubborn stereotypes that continue to diminish the effectiveness of psychotherapy and clinical supervision. A necessary first step for supervisors is to become

TABLE 5.2 Application of Bloom's Taxonomy to Counseling Supervision

COMPETENCY	SAMPLE SKILLS	QUESTION STEMS	SAMPLE QUESTIONS
Knowledge	Recall of information related to client or case. Knowledge of core classroom-based information.	What When Name List Define	When did the client enter treatment? What is the diagnosis? What are the stages of group? What does Adlerian theory say about family constellation?
Comprehension	Summarize facts related to cases. Predict consequences of interventions. Show comprehension of importance of data collection.	Summarize Describe Why Paraphrase Interpret	Summarize the client's history with the legal system. How do clinicians make a diagnosis? What is the reason clinicians order assessments? What does the research say about the prognosis for personality disorders?
Application	Use research to make clinical decisions and decide on interventions. Apply theories to current cases. Problem solve difficult client issues.	Apply Demonstrate Construct Interpret Practice	What stage of group is your trauma recovery group in? How could you use cognitive interventions with this client? What evidence exists for the diagnosis that you made? How can you use what you know about assertiveness training to work with this client?
Analysis	Identify patterns of behavior in clients. Identify parts of client history that are relevant to presenting problem. Compare and contrast similar interventions with different clients.	Analyze Classify Compare Contrast Experiment	What secondary gains are there for this client? Analyze the relationship between the client's substance abuse and his anger. What components of the client's problem support this intervention? Compare and contrast the client's role in her family of origin versus the role that she is assuming in her family of procreation.
Synthesis	Combine information from different academic courses to apply to real-world problems. Conceptualize cases, bringing together all relevant information. Design an intervention that uses all the client's resources.	Create Combine Integrate Design Generalize Hypothesize Construct Summarize	Taking into account what you know about the effects of racism and what you have learned about the client's trauma, how can you design an assessment program that accurately captures his current intellectual functioning? Could you predict the outcome if you used a cognitive–behavioral intervention? Construct a treatment plan based on the goals that you have developed.
Evaluation	Articulate a rationale for interventions. Assess the value or significance of a particular theory or intervention. Make choices based on reasoned arguments.	Appraise Assess Defend Evaluate Recommend Critique	Assess the effectiveness of your interventions with this client. What would you recommend to a counselor who might be taking over this case? Evaluate the client's progress to date. Which intervention has a better chance of success with this client?

From "Encouraging the Cognitive Development of Supervisees: Using Bloom's Taxonomy in Supervision." by D. H. Granello, 2000. *Counselor Education and Supervision, 40,* 31–46. Copyright © ACA. Reprinted with permission. No further reproduction authorized without written permission of the American Counseling Association.

aware of the power of their own cultural assumptions to influence their thinking and their interactions with others. This leads our discussion to the necessity of multicultural training prior to the onset of supervision.

Several authors have asserted that entry-level training in multicultural issues must precede supervision if the latter is to be productive (e.g., Bernard, 1994a; Constantine, 1997; Fong & Lease, 1997; Priest, 1994). Constantine (1997) found that 70% of the supervisees that she surveyed had received training in multicultural issues, whereas 70% of the supervisors in her study had received no such academic training. This represents a serious gap in supervisor competence and clearly supports the call for systematic training of clinical supervisors in the many dimensions of multicultural interactions.

Constantine (2001) found that providing multicultural supervision to trainees was associated with higher levels of multicultural counseling self-efficacy. Because of the importance of self-efficacy for the professional development of counselors, Constantine suggested that supervisors may, by offering multicultural supervision, serve as catalysts for increased attention to multicultural dimensions in the counseling offered by their supervisees. The fact that Gatmon et al. (2001) found a low frequency of supervisory conversations to concern culture may support Constantine's research, which determined that supervisors are inadequately prepared for this aspect of supervision. Ford and Britton (2002) found greater discourse about cultural matters in supervision than did Gatmon et al.; however, supervisees reported that these discussions only concerned clients, rather than supervisor-supervisee interactions. This finding reflects an incomplete approach to culture in supervision that is also consistent with Constantine's (2001) findings of inadequate training among supervisors.

In recent years, the multicultural supervision literature has grown moderately and unevenly (i.e., focusing far more on race and gender than on other cultural characteristics, such as class or disability, to name just two). The earlier years were characterized primarily by nonempirical contributions, but recently there has been growth in the research that will begin to balance the insights of experts in the field. The thrust of the available literature continues to reflect the accurate assumption that more supervisors represent White, middle-class cultural perspectives than do their supervisees or their supervisees' clients. Although this is changing slowly, our professional knowledge to date reflects the limits of where we are in the evolution of our understanding of culture and the implications of culture on both therapy and supervision. Prior to attending to the literatures that consider separate cultural characteristics, we want to address briefly the political nature of the helping professions and the culture of psychotherapy itself.

Political Nature of the Helping Professions

Another important notion to consider as part of our professional context is that the helping professions are sociopolitical in nature (Katz, 1985). By ignoring cultural differences, the dominant culture has been able to ignore much injustice done to nondominant cultures. Supervision is as vulnerable to reflecting the "theoretical myth of sameness" (Hardy, 1989) by ignoring the enormous and evasive effects of power and privilege as they influence interactions across cultural groups. Katz described this insensitivity as an "invisible veil" that affects our interactions with others, often outside our awareness. This blind spot leaves supervisees and clients unacceptably vulnerable when diagnostic or evaluative conclusions are made that are culturally uninformed.

In this context, all supervision is not only cultural, but also political. Because supervisors have position power, they, by definition, weigh in on one side or the other of the many cultural struggles that define one's place in society, whether the person affected is the supervisee or the client or both. Killian (2001) asserted that "it is important for us to anchor or locate supervisors in terms of their own privilege and power ecosystemically so that they can more fully understand how that social location informs what happens in supervision" (p. 85). Porter (1994) stated that the final stage of multicultural supervision must be social action for clients, supervisees, supervisors, and institutions. To have a lesser vision significantly compromises the ability of supervisors to have influence that might actually make a positive difference around the values espoused by the psychotherapy culture.

The Psychotherapy Culture

Not only does counseling and psychotherapy continue to reflect the dominant culture in the United States, but it also makes up a culture in and of itself, "with its own belief systems, language, customs, governance, and norms" (Holiman & Lauver, 1987, p. 184). Holiman and Lauver made the excellent point that client-centered practice is perhaps far more difficult to achieve than is commonly assumed because of the counselor's enmeshment with the therapy culture. "To the extent that practitioners are acculturated within the counseling culture, their relationships with clients from outside of this culture are subject to barriers of cross-cultural understanding" (p. 185).

If the supervisee has been successfully acculturated into the psychotherapy culture (and thus socialized into a particular helping profession), this may provide a bridge between supervisor and supervisee that might enhance the relationship. In fact, O'Byrne and Rosenberg (1998) noted that supervision is indeed a central force in socializing the supervisee into the profession's culture. One danger of having a cultural characteristic in common is the consequent denial of other cultural influences (Killian, 2001). Widening the cultural circle, then, is the key multicultural task of the clinical supervisor. In the following sections, we consider some discrete aspects of cultural identity as they have been considered in the literature. We begin each section with a review of evolving critical thought and follow with a discussion of the modest amount of empirical work to date.

Racial and Ethnic Issues within Multicultural Supervision

In his seminal work, Bradshaw (1982) addressed the implications of race in the supervisory relationship, asserting that race is a highly charged cat-alyst in our society, one that is bound to emerge, even if not addressed, in supervision. Helms and Piper (1994) magnified this assumption when they claimed that racial identity has evolved to occupy the greatest percentage of self-concept. Killian (2001) cited Carter and Qureshi (1995) as asserting that race is considered the most significant difference between people because racial characteristics tend to be more enduring, whereas other cultural characteristics are often more fluid and flexible. In short, we continue to be a society within which we are often defined, and divided, by the social construction of race.

Bradshaw focused on situations in which Blacks and Whites interact, a theme that has remained dominant in the supervision literature that addresses race (cf. Leong & Wagner, 1994). He noted that a Black client seeing a White therapist who is supervised by a White supervisor is presently the most common multicultural occurrence in mental health practice. At the time of his writing, Bradshaw was visionary in alerting supervisors to be cautious that the White supervisor–White therapy dyad not ignore culture-based phenomena presented by Black clients. In more recent years, the supervision literature has moved forward (1) to recognize that supervisors who ignore culture within the supervisory relationship are far less likely to be prepared to successfully monitor therapy that is multicultural and (2) to begin to collect data on cross-racial supervision, including dyads in which the supervisor, not the supervisee, is identified as a member of an ethnic minority group.

Fong and Lease (1997) provided a comprehensive overview of the issues salient to the White supervisor attempting to provide culturally sensitive supervision to persons of a different race. They asserted that most of the challenges facing the White supervisor can be categorized by one of the following: (1) unintentional racism, (2) power dynamics, (3) trust and the supervisory alliance, and (4) communication issues. Basic to both unintentional racism and power dynamics, it seems to us, is the power and privilege of the supervisor to address the topic of race. In fact, we now have evidence that if supervisors do not initiate discussions about cultural issues in supervision, very few discussions will occur (Duan & Roehlke, 2001; Gatmon et al., 2001).

Kleintjes and Swartz (1996) interviewed a group of Black clinical psychology trainees in a predominately White university in South Africa and found that, when race was not addressed by supervisors, trainees were reluctant to bring up the topic for any of six reasons: (1) they experienced the university as a "colorless zone" where, due to their strong antiapartheid stance, faculty deny any acknowledgment of race; (2) they feared being seen as using their Blackness as an excuse for poor performance; (3) they feared being seen to be using their Blackness as a defense against other issues; (4) they feared being seen as pathologically occupied with the issue of color and discrimination; (5) they were uncertain whether these issues were best shared or dealt with personally; and (6) they acknowledged their own personal insecurities as the reasons for not bringing up the issue of race. This list, which could just as easily have been composed in the United States, reflects the lack of power felt by the supervisees interviewed.

Cook (1994) addressed power in two ways: the power inherent in the role of the supervisor and the power of being a member of the dominant culture in a sociopolitical context that is overtly and covertly racist. The latter is central to the concern of unintentional racism. Though inexcusable at this point in the evolution of the mental health professions, it is sadly conceivable that supervisors may remain ignorant of their racism due to their own limited racial identity development (Cook, 1994; Fong & Lease, 1997). Helms and Cook (1999) provided an outline adapted from Helm's (1994) racial identity development model of potential supervisor dynamics for both Whites and persons from visible racial and ethnic groups (see Table 5.3). As Fong and Lease stated, supervisors are ill equipped to conduct multicultural supervision if they are below the immersion–emersion stages of development. Additionally, Cook addressed the development of the supervisor relative to the supervisee, describing progressive supervision as occurring when the supervisor's racial identity development is beyond the supervisee and

regressive supervision when the supervisor's development lags behind. Because of the power inherent in the role of supervisor, it is that person's sophistication regarding cross-racial interactions that will drive supervision. Therefore, the helping professions can only begin to claim that multicultural supervision is normative when reaching this minimum stage of racial identity development becomes a prerequisite for assuming the role of supervisor (Bernard, 1994a). In our discussion of key empirical work, we review the work of Ladany, Brittan-Powell, and Pannu (1997) on racial identity development.

In a discussion about the Black supervisor working with a White supervisee, Priest (1994) alluded to both trust and communication issues as hampering supervision, a point reiterated by Williams and Halgin (1995). Priest assumed that White supervisees would have negative outcome expectations when working with a Black supervisor and that ignorance of different communication styles between the racial groups would lead to harmful miscommunication. Remington and Da-Costa (1989) also focused on the Black supervisor–White supervisee combination and particularly difficult moments that can occur in supervision, such as the supervisee counseling a racist client. Because of the trust and communication issues that can arise, Remington and DaCosta warned supervisors that they do not have time to wait for ethnocultural issues to "come up." They were among the first to admonish that it is the supervisor's responsibility to attend to such concerns, thus setting the stage for a context in which all four of Fong and Lease's (1997) issues can be addressed. Remington and DaCosta also acknowledged the difficulty of supervising persons of a different race and suggested that supervisors not work in isolation, but in conjunction with other supervisors, a suggestion we would underscore.

Other authors have attempted to both highlight potential racial–ethnic areas of concern and offer plausible remedies. Zuniga (1987) reported a pilot project with Mexican American supervisees in which supervision focused on ethnic identity, family history, acculturation, and racism experiences.

TABLE 5.3 Statuses and Potential Approaches to Racial Issues (PARI)

CONFORMITY (VREG)	CONTACT (WHITE)

PARI: Ignores race of client, supervisee, and supervisor. Assumes theoretical approach generalizes to all individuals; focuses only on "common humanity."

DISSONANCE (VREG)	DISINTEGRATION (WHITE)

PARI: Acknowledges client's race as demographic or descriptive characteristic; lacks awareness of assumptions being made about the client based on race. Ignores supervisee's and supervisor's race.

IMMERSION–EMERSION (VREG)	REINTEGRATION (WHITE)

PARI: Recognizes own race as standard for "normal" behavior of client and "effective" performance of partner. Recognizes other-race clients, but cultural differences are seen as deficits or forms of "resistance." Holds biases toward theoretical approaches that represent own cultural perspective.

	PSEUDO-INDEPENDENCE (WHITE)

PARI: Discusses racial differences only if interacting with POC. Discusses cultural differences based on generalized assumptions about various racial groups. Recognizes cultural biases of theories; lacks working knowledge of how to adapt theories to VREG.

	IMMERSION–EMERSION (WHITE)

PARI: Acknowledges race of client, supervisee, and supervisor and their respective cultural assumptions and racial attitudes. Considers sociopolitical implications of race in therapy and supervision.

INTERNALIZATION (VREG)	AUTONOMY (WHITE)

PARI: Integrates personal cultural values and therapeutic and supervision values. Acknowledges race of client, supervisee, and supervisor and the cultural and sociopolitical influences on the therapeutic and supervisory relationships. Names cultural conflicts in supervision interactions without internalizing racial prejudices of other-race supervision partner.

INTEGRATIVE AWARENESS (VREG)	

PARI: Recognizes races as an aspect of each person's identity and potential variability in racial identity attitudes. Acknowledges cultural assumptions of supervision partners and negotiates culturally sensitive approaches to supervision and therapy. Serves as advocate for oppressed groups in interactions with agencies and training program.

From *"Using Race and Culture in Counseling and Psychotherapy: Theory and Process,"* by Janet E. Helms and Donelda A. Cook, 1999. Published by Allyn and Bacon, Boston, MA. Copyright © 1999 by Pearson Education. Reprinted by permission of the publisher.

When trainees vacillated between feelings of competence and inadequacy, these were processed within a cultural context. "As they talked about painful school experiences, they could compre- hend how they had introjected the negative expectations of former teachers and school peers who assumed they would perform poorly because they were Mexican American" (p. 18). These insights were used not only for the interns' own growth but also as a vehicle for them to work with Mexican American clients. As a corollary to these discussions, supervision also focused on the strong survival attributes of these interns to negotiate their former hostile environments.

Although most discussions about cross-racial supervision are centered around persons who share the complicated racial history of the United States, Killian (2001) collected interviews with supervisors who had supervised international students as well. One White male supervisor had this to say about his experience supervising a female student from Japan:

> *Looking back . . . I don't think I was able to speak her "language." I did broach the subject of culture, and we did discuss some cultural concepts explicitly, and we were comfortable. But I did not take into account her own background in terms of education system and how that might influence her expectations of the training she would receive from me as a . . . supervisor. And so, I was . . . trying to be collaborative and non-hierarchical and just "getting together to talk about some clinical scenarios." And now, I think that's not at all what she was expecting. These differences had an impact on our relationship, but, unfortunately, they were not always processed or made explicit during supervision. For example, I think that now we would be much more likely to talk about our respective values around indirect communication, saving face, training style, and power.* (p. 75)

One Russian male supervisee explained his experience as a cross-ethnic international supervisee in the United States:

> *I felt like sometimes they didn't know what to do with me, like they didn't know how to approach me. They were very cautious. It felt like they had to go an extra mile and I felt like a burden. I could see that they were having to make an extra effort. I couldn't help thinking that they would prefer to have an American student as a supervisee because it makes life easier.* (pp. 74–75)

This last example underscores the complexities that are included in the terms *multicultural* or *diversity*. Killian (2001) quoted a Jewish female supervisor who stated, "As trainers, we want to be

sensitive to gender, ethnicity, race, culture, class, but we tend to see one of these more clearly than the others, possibly because it's been experienced as crucial to our own sense of being, possibly because we tend to look at only one thing at a time" (p. 78). This supervisor addresses the difficulty of sustaining the complexity of multicultural supervision because we "tend to privilege or resonate with a particular ecosystemic axis of power more than others" (Killian, 2001, p. 78).

Empirical Results.   VanderKolk (1974) apparently conducted the earliest study regarding race and supervision, investigating the relationship variables of personality, values, and race as these affected the anticipation of supervision with a White supervisor. No differences were found for personality or values. Black students, however, were more likely to anticipate that their supervisors would lack empathy, respect, and congruence than were White students. This study did not include an investigation of the actual relationships that ensued; its contribution was to help to establish the salience of race as a key variable as relationships between supervisors and supervisees were being established.

Cook and Helms (1988) studied 225 Asian, Black, Hispanic, or Native American supervisees to examine their satisfaction with cross-cultural supervision. Of the variables that they considered, perceived supervisor liking and perceived conditional interest were found to contribute to greater satisfaction, with the perception that the supervisor liked them being the strongest factor by far. Regarding the second variable, the authors hypothesized that

> *supervisees may value conditional supervisory relationships as long as they perceive that the conditions occur in an atmosphere of caring. Perhaps in such a context supervisees are able to use the information communicated by the supervisor's conditions to help them figure out what is expected of them in this particular cross-cultural environment.* (p. 273)

Overall, the supervisees tended to report a guarded relationship with their supervisors; additionally, Native American and African American supervisees were least satisfied with cross-cultural supervision and Asian Americans were most satisfied. As Leong and Wagner (1994) later suggested, however, the lack of a White sample of supervisees makes these results difficult to interpret.

Duan and Roehlke (2001) also found that perception of the relationship was significant in cross-racial supervision. Duan and Roehlke surveyed 60 supervision dyads, all of which were cross-racial. Interestingly, results revealed similar patterns whether supervisors were White or a racial minority. Findings were that supervisees were more sensitive to cultural and racial issues than were supervisors, supervisors reported making greater efforts to engage in multicultural supervision than supervisees perceived, and satisfaction with supervision was related to supervisees' self-disclosure and both members of the dyad perceiving positive attitudes toward each other. These results seem to support the concern stated by others that supervisors are not carrying their weight in the process of multicultural supervision (Constantine, 1997; Ford & Britton, 2002).

In a provocative examination of field instructors' and supervisees' working relationships within a cross-racial context, McRoy, Freeman, Logan, and Blackmon (1986) found that actual problems were few, but that both supervisors and supervisees expected more problems than benefits in such relationships. Several Black supervisors reported that White supervisees had questioned their competence and resisted their supervision. Hispanic supervisors also noted experiences that were related to a lack of acceptance of their authority by supervisees. Together, these supervisors (12 in number) represented 28% of the total sample. When problems did occur, those supervisees who addressed the problem with their supervisors were satisfied with the outcome. Of the seven students (16%) who had experienced difficulty, however, only two chose to approach their supervisors about it. The others felt it was too threatening to do so because of the power differential in supervision. This study points to the vital issue of supervisor and supervisee expectations that influence cross-racial encounters. It also reinforces the

assertions by others (e.g., Cook, 1994; Gatmon et al., 2001; Vargas, 1989) that it is up to the supervisor to initiate cultural issues and to nurture a supervisory context in which it is sufficiently safe to explore difference.

Hilton, Russell, and Salmi (1995) investigated the effects of supervisor support and race on counselor anxiety, perceived performance, satisfaction, and perceptions of the supervisory relationship. All supervisees were White; supervisors were either White or African American. Whereas supervisor support emerged as a main effect, supervisor race did not. Similarly, Chung, Marshall, and Gordon (2001) found no main effect for race in studying bias in evaluation and feedback. These kinds of discrimination studies, which weigh the effect of race against other relationship variables, are sorely needed in the supervision literature.

In a pilot study, Fukuyama (1994) elicited critical incidents from racial–ethnic minorities who had completed an APA internship. They were asked to offer positive and negative incidents and to describe organizational or environmental conditions that contributed to their professional development. Positive incidents fell into three categories: *openness and support* (e.g., not being stereotyped, supervisors demonstrating belief in their abilities), *culturally relevant supervision* (i.e., receiving supervision that addressed cultural implications both for the supervisee and for the clients seen), and *opportunity to work in multicultural activities* (i.e., positively validating opportunities to contribute in ways that included cultural expertise).

Although very few trainees offered negative incidents, these were divided into two categories: *lack of supervisor cultural awareness* (e.g., interpreting culturally consistent behavior as a countertransference issue or using expressions that were offensive to the supervisee) and *questioning supervisee abilities* (e.g., not trusting the supervisee's interpretation of a client's behavior as culturally relevant when supervisee and client shared the same heritage). Suggestions offered by subjects to sensitize internship settings included providing more multicultural training, encouraging more discourse within supervision about cultural factors, and, conversely, cautioning supervisors not to overestimate cultural diversity issues in an attempt to be "politically correct," an admonition emphasized by McNeill, Hom, and Perez (1995).

Gatmon et al. (2001) explored the effect of discourse around the cultural variables of gender, ethnicity, and sexual orientation on the supervisory working alliance and satisfaction with supervision. Furthermore, only the discussion of differences and similarities regarding ethnicity significantly enhanced the supervisory working alliance, though not satisfaction with supervision. Interestingly, matching supervisor and supervisee for all variables studied did not improve working alliance or satisfaction. It should also be emphasized that the incidence of discussion of cultural variables was low overall, leading the authors to reiterate the concerns of Constantine (1997) and Kleintjes and Swartz (1996). At the same time, the authors found that *difference* on cultural variables stimulated more discussion than similarity. This last finding may indicate that we are making progress on multicultural supervision when differences are visible or known, but that we still have work to do to assist all supervisory dyads to acknowledge the importance of discourse about their cultural identities.

Perhaps the most promising research around cross-race supervision is the work of Ladany and his colleagues on racial identity development. Ladany, Brittan-Powell, and Pannu (1997) found that, whereas racial matching between supervisor and supervisee did not affect the supervisory working alliance in a positive manner, racial identity similarity were predictive in some instances. Specifically, those dyads who shared higher racial identity attitudes (parallel–high interactions) had the strongest supervisory working alliance; they also were found to have positive feelings of liking and trust for each other. Progressive interactions (i.e., a supervisor with higher racial identity development than the supervisee) had the next most positive interactions. The authors speculated that, in these relationships, the supervisor was able to provide both a safe and challenging context for supervisees that benefited the relationship. Regressive interactions (for which the supervisee's racial identity development is higher than the supervisor's) predicted the weakest supervisory alliance. Finally, both parallel–high interactions and progressive interactions were correlated with supervisee perception of supervisor influence on multicultural development.

Ladany, Inman, Constantine, and Hofheinz (1997) shed additional light on the topic of racial identity development and supervision. This study found that for both White supervisees and supervisees of color, racial identity development was related to self-reported multicultural competence. Specifically, White students at the pseudo-independence stage and ethnic minority supervisees at the dissonance and awareness stages (see Table 5.3) reported higher levels of multicultural competence. In light of the definitions of both dissonance and pseudo-independence, the pairing of these levels of racial identity with perceived multicultural competence is not particularly comforting. Additionally, Ladany et al. found that perceived competence was not correlated with multicultural case conceptualization ability. Although the authors noted important limitations of their study, it seems that racial identity development will continue to be fruitful as one important indicator of what is occurring (and what needs to occur) in multicultural supervision.

Finally, in a relatively rare cross-ethnic study, Haj-Yahia and Roer-Strier (1999) reported results from two samples of Arab supervisees working with Jewish supervisors in Israel. This would seem to be a poignant example of what Killian (2001) referred to as politics encroaching on the supervisory process. Results having to do with the supervisory relationship revealed that, similar to studies done in the United States with cross-racial populations, supervisees in this study were far more likely to be attuned to cultural differences than were supervisors. Only 15% of the supervisors felt that relationship difficulties were attributable to supervising students "from a different cultural background in a complicated sociopolitical environment" (p. 27). By contrast, all Arab students could recall at least one cultural misunderstanding between them and their supervisors. Difficulties included different expectations about the supervision process, supervisor's lack of familiarity with the Arab students' cultural norms and values, differences in perception regarding clients' problems, and different styles of communication (e.g., supervisors noted that students would not "speak up"). By far the most frequent issues raised by supervisees revolved around cultural difference. Surprisingly, however, the authors reported that "supervisors hardly related to this aspect and only one of them expressed her interest in learning more about norms in Arab culture." Finally, and despite the difficulties this study brought to light, the vast majority of Arab supervisees preferred Jewish supervisors whom they described as "more open and liberal, better at expressing emotions and more professional" (p. 31). This study, it seems to us, is an excellent example of the competing and complex variables that contribute to the supervisory relationship, not the least of which is cultural difference.

A review of the sparse literature would seem to indicate that, although racial diversity plays a role in supervision, other supervisor attributes are equally, if not more, important. The willingness of the supervisor to open the cultural door and walk through it with the supervisee is perhaps the single most powerful intervention for multicultural supervision. Whether one is a therapist or a supervisor, multicultural competence is not easily attained in a society that is phobic about race (Bernard, 1994a; Porter, 1994). The will to attain such competence and the trust that can be engendered by such a commitment may be the most powerful operative variable within the supervisory relationship to move both supervisor and supervisee toward increased cultural competence.

Gender Issues within Multicultural Supervision

The status of women in our society has been a tenacious problem that has affected them economically and psychologically. Men have appeared to enjoy the benefits of gender bias, but more discriminating research has shown that gender bias is problematic for both men and women (cf. Good & Mintz, 1990; Wester & Vogel, 2002). Whereas racial and ethnic differences are more likely to be viewed as multicultural issues, gender may be resisted as such. Yet, as Gilbert and Rossman (1992) reminded us, gender is a pervasive organizer in our culture, as can be supported by the proportion of men and women in various occupational areas. Furthermore, Gilbert and Rossman asserted that gender is a process, leading to "beliefs and stereotypes, and their concomitant behavioral expectations, [that] appear to influence individuals' behavior in response to certain situational cues" (p. 234). Because these differences are more culturally determined than biologically determined, gender is legitimately included as a multicultural concern.

Turner (1993) stated that power shifts that are taking place in society will affect men and women in supervision, causing confusion and frustration. Rigazio-DiGilio, Anderson, and Kunkler (1995), on the other hand, contended that gender-sensitive supervision was at a developmental impasse, relying on a limited set of theoretical orientations. Both of these viewpoints can probably be supported at one time or another in every setting where supervision occurs. In this section we will attempt to navigate the supervision literature for its relevance to gender issues.

Like racial and ethnic issues, it is important that both supervisees and supervisors enter the supervision relationship having spent some time and energy addressing their own gender identities and assumptions and having been sensitized to the many ways that gender affects them in relationships, including relationships with clients (Stevens-Smith, 1995). Training should include a serious consideration of androgyny and the data that support the correlation of androgynous attitudes with successful interpersonal interactions (e.g., Fong, Borders, & Neimeyer, 1986). Ault-Riche (1988) and Nelson (1991) specifically advised supervisors to remain vigilant regarding their own gender biases prior to engaging in supervision. Especially if, for example, a supervisor works mostly with female supervisees, issues of power, sensitivity to feedback, communication style, resolving conflict, and boundary issues are apt to emerge *for both supervisee and supervisor* when the supervisor switches to a male supervisee. This will be different, of course, depending on whether the supervisor is male or female. If any issues related to these themes occur without the supervisor's having addressed these possibilities prior to the onset of supervision, the process is bound to be ragged. Each relationship will be unique and will include unique challenges; however, the supervisor must be prepared to address cultural issues as they emerge, including those that involve gender. Recent research indicates that clinical supervisors have a long way to go to achieve this goal.

Some types of dilemmas involving gender are fairly predictable:

- A female supervisee does not think her male supervisor takes her seriously.
- A male supervisee states that he expected his female supervisor to be more supportive.
- A male supervisor finds it easier to evaluate the strengths of his males supervisees than his female supervisees.
- A female supervisor gives her male supervisee feedback that he is treating his female client in a sexist manner. The supervisee feels ganged up on.

These are only a few of the complications around the issue of gender in the supervision process. The themes that seem to emerge with consistency, both in practice and in the supervision literature, have to do with the different voices of female versus male supervisors and supervisees, the different ways that power is awarded and used depending on the supervisor's or supervisee's gender, and the implications of matching gender in supervision or not. To the extent possible, these themes will be addressed separately. Whereas gender identity development may prove to be as fruitful as racial identity development for informing supervision, studies using identity development rather than gender have not yet emerged (Barnes & Bernard, 2003).

We will attempt to look at gender from several different angles, but we will not pay particular attention to the ethical issues that are covered in Chapter 3, specifically overt sexism, sexual harassment, and sexual exploitation. Such abuses of power are quite different from legitimate (if uninformed) cultural differences based on gender and represent a perversion of the supervision process (Bernard, 1994a).

Different Voices.   Carol Gilligan (1982) is usually credited with the "voice" metaphor, suggesting that women and men are socialized to approach interpersonal relationships differently; women take on the voice of care, which focuses on "loving and being loved, listening and being listened to, responding and being responded to" (Brown & Gilligan, 1990, p. 8), and men take on the voice of justice, which focuses on "a vision of equality, reciprocity, and fairness between persons" (Brown & Gilligan, 1990, p. 8). Twohey and Volker (1993) argued that, because the supervisory role has more often been held by men, the voice of justice has been the predominant voice in supervision, emphasizing objective and scientific perspectives.

Twohey and Volker (1993) asserted that the Western tradition of splitting intellectual and emotional events has been perpetuated by diminishing the care voice in supervision, a less than adequate model for supervision. By contrast, when the voice of care is included, some of the most pertinent issues in the supervision relationship can be addressed openly and in the context of support. The balance encouraged by Twohey and Volker is one for which gender differences are appreciated through a supervisory style that is androgynous, regardless of the gender of the supervisor. They implied, however, that supervisees should experience supervision from both men and women in order to assure well-rounded supervision.

Bernstein (1993) and Ellis and Robbins (1993) stressed the error in assuming that male supervisors (and supervisees) consistently speak from the voice of justice and that female supervisors (and supervisees) represent primarily the voice of care. They noted that this assumption is not supported empirically, a position ardently emphasized by Osterberg (1996). Furthermore, Ellis and Robbins addressed both the gains and disadvantages of matching the supervisee's voice. In other words, although Twohey and Volker seemed to indicate that the care voice is unrepresented in supervision and should be attended to more consistently, Ellis and Robbins took a more strategic approach and suggested that the supervisor choose the voice that will either challenge or support the supervisee, depending on the supervision goal at the time. All the authors in this discourse, however, emphasize that supervisors must appreciate that both voices represent conceptual frameworks for understanding the supervisory relationship and, therefore, must both be within the supervisor's repertoire.

Although Bernstein (1993) and Ellis and Robbins (1993) put forth a convincing argument for androgynous supervision, current gender stereotypes may confound the outcome. Ault-Riche (1988), for example, noted that capable female supervisors are often misinterpreted despite which voice they deliver. "Those supervisors who present as primarily nurturant are devalued for not being clear thinkers; those who present as primarily task-focused are experienced as dangerous" (p. 188). Ault-Riche's discussion implies that it would be naive for supervisors of either gender to think that their supervisees are not influenced by gender stereotypes. These stereotypes are, after all, the product of lifelong socialization. Whereas they can be modified by training and supervision, such modifications may occur only by increments.

Gender Role Conflict. Whereas much of the supervision literature on gender has focused on the issues of female socialization, Wester and Vogel (2002) have alerted us to the training and supervision issues for male supervisees based on the extent to which they reflect traditional male socialization. Male gender role conflict (GRC) occurs when the current situation calls for behaviors that confront previously held assumptions about appropriate male norms. Drawing on the work of O'Neil and his colleagues (O'Neil, 1981; O'Neil, Good, & Holmes, 1995; O'Neil, Halmas, Gable,

David, & Wrightsman, 1986), Wester and Vogel suggested that the learning required to become a good therapist could exacerbate GRC for some supervisees. As one example, these authors noted that the male pattern of excelling through competition is incompatible with the important skill of seeking feedback about skill deficits. Similarly, the emotional restrictiveness demanded of traditional norms, especially for men in their relationships with other men, would be confronted in many counseling and supervisory contexts. Wester (2002) found that male psychology interns reported more restrictive emotionality (RE) than practicing counselors (though less than males in the general population). He also found that higher levels of RE were correlated with lower self-efficacy as a counselor. Wester and Vogel admonished supervisors to use the skills endemic to all multicultural supervision in their work with GRC males.

Although it may be reasonable to assume that males who self-select to be helping professionals are not prone to GRC, recent research indicates that this is not the case. A review conducted by Heesacker et al. (1999) of six studies found that counselors consistently viewed men as "hypoemotional," that is, emotionally restrictive. It would seem, then, that the concerns communicated by Wester and Vogel have merit.

Differences between Male and Female Supervisors. The supervision literature regarding differences between male and female supervisors, as well as distinguishable reactions to supervisors because of their gender, draws both from conjecture and scientific investigation. Watson (1993), for example, warned that female supervisors might be more prone to find themselves in therapy-like dual relationships with their supervisees as an extension of their inclination or desire to be nurturant. Male supervisors might arrive at their perceptions more quickly, but may be employing less data to do so. Female supervisors might also take feedback from supervisees more to heart (Reid, McDaniel, Donaldson, & Tollers, 1987) than would their male counterparts.

Granello (1996) suggested that, because supervision is largely a conversational process, findings regarding the different conversational styles of men and women are relevant. As examples, Granello surveyed authors and researchers who have noted that males are not socialized to be listeners (Hotelling & Forrest, 1985); that males have been found to respond differently in conversations when they are in positions of power, whereas women do not (Sagrestano, 1992); and that males have been found to execute 75% of all conversational interruptions (Kollock, Blumstein, & Schwartz, 1985). Certainly, if unchecked, these gendered behaviors would interfere with a supervisory conference.

Empirical Results.   Empirical support for gender differences related specifically to supervision is growing and, in recent years, has expanded into several aspects of supervision, including the supervisory relationship, evaluation, the use of power in supervision, and interaction styles. What follows is a discussion of this research.

Sells, Goodyear, Lichtenberg, and Polkinghorne (1997) studied gender-related differences for both supervisors and supervisees. These authors found that female supervisors had a greater relational focus than did male supervisors, spending more time in supervision focused on the trainee. Male supervisors, on the other hand, spent a significantly greater amount of time focused on the trainee's client. When male supervisors worked with male trainees, these trainees rated their technical skills higher; when female supervisors worked with female trainees, the latter rated their personal awareness higher. Perhaps the most important finding of the Sells et al. study (from the perspective of the supervisee) was that gender was not related to an evaluation of the impact of supervision by either supervisor or supervisee, nor was it related to the supervisor's evaluation of the supervisee. Warburton, Newberry, and Alexander (1989) also reported that male and female supervisees were found to be equally effective with clients. Goodyear (1990) found no differences on how male and female supervisees were evaluated according to (a) skills, (b) conceptualization, and (c) personhood variables.

Research conducted by Chung, Marshall, and Gordon (2001) unfortunately did not support the gender-free conclusions of Sells et al. (1997) in terms of evaluation. Chung et al. found that male participants in their study (all of whom had served as clinical supervisors) rated hypothetical supervisees more negatively when the supervisee was depicted as being female than when the supervisee was male. Their rating difference approached one standard deviation. Female respondents, however, did not show this same kind of gender bias. Still, while each study may potentially shed some light on the gender maze, the fact is that the research on gender and evaluation is mixed.

The Chung et al. (2001) study might shed some light on a finding reported by Anderson, Schlossberg, and Rigazio-DiGilio (2000). Anderson et al. asked marriage and family therapists to recollect "best" and "worst" supervision experiences. Although "best" supervision was conducted by both male and female supervisors somewhat evenly, almost two-thirds of "worst" experiences were when the supervisor was male. Because most respondents were female, it is possible that their reactions might have reflected the critical evaluations of their male supervisors during their supervision.

Looking at evaluation from the supervisee's perspective, Warburton et al. (1989) reported that female supervisees tended to underestimate their accomplishments, whereas male supervisees overestimated them. It would seem, then, that attention to gender during the evaluation process is warranted. Our understanding of gender dynamics that inform evaluation may be enhanced by an understanding of how interpersonal power is manipulated in supervision.

Use of Power within Supervision.   Social or interpersonal power is a critical factor in supervision; power, or the capacity to influence the behavior of another person, is also endemic to gender relations. This combination makes it a consequential variable to be acknowledged within the supervision relationship (Turner, 1993; Watson, 1993).

Robyak, Goodyear, and Prange (1987) considered the topic of power and whether male and female supervisors were different in their use of power as it had been conceptualized by French and Raven (1959). They categorized power as either *expert* (the display of such resources as specialized knowledge and skills, confidence, and rationality), *referent* (derived from interpersonal attraction and based on trainees perceiving that they hold in common with supervisors relevant values, attitudes, opinions, and experiences), or *legitimate* (a consequence of perceived trustworthiness because the supervisor is a socially sanctioned provider of services who is not motivated by personal gain). Contrary to what one might expect, male supervisors reported greater preference for referent power than did female supervisors.

In a similar study that focused on supervisee behavior (Goodyear, 1990), both supervisees and their supervisors perceived female supervisees as more likely to employ a personal–dependent influence style in a conflict situation with their supervisors. This was the only significant finding of the study, which examined eight different influence strategies for supervisees of both genders interacting with supervisors of both genders. It is interesting to note that both male and female supervisors perceived the female supervisees similarly.

Nelson and Holloway (1990) provided an intriguing look at messages and interaction patterns within supervision for the manipulation of power by gender. Using all gender and role combinations possible, Nelson and Holloway found that both male and female supervisors were less likely to encourage the assumption of power in female trainees than in male trainees; furthermore, female trainees deferred to the power of the supervisor significantly more often than did male trainees. As explained by the authors,

It appears that individuals in the expert role, regardless of gender, may assume more power in interaction with their female subordinates than with their male subordinates, either by withholding support for the female subordinates' attempts at exerting power or by simply exerting stronger influence with female subordinates. In the supervisory relationship the female trainee may respond to this stance on the part of her supervisor by declining opportunities to assert herself as an expert. (p. 479)

Granello, Beamish, and Davis (1997) reported findings similar to those of Nelson and Holloway (1990) in a study with counselors in training. On average, male supervisees were asked for their opinion in supervision more than twice as often as female supervisees. Female supervisees were more often told what to do. This was the case whether the supervisor was male or female. Furthermore, these patterns remained constant over time. Granello et al. noted that the supervision given to male supervisees, therefore, reflected developmental models, whereas that for females did not. "With less external direction given over time, the male supervisees were encouraged to develop healthy internal supervisors by making more decision on their own . . . the experiences provided the female supervisee did not allow for their natural development to occur" (p. 313).

In a follow-up study (Granello, 2003), male supervisees were asked their opinions more often and offered more suggestions than female supervisees, regardless of the gender of the supervisor. An unanticipated finding of this study, however, was that the ideas of female supervisees were more often accepted and built on by supervisors. It may be that, intuitively, supervisors began to experience male supervisees as being able to "take care of themselves," while female supervisees need more encouragement. Granello also studied the interactional effects of age and gender. While the gender differences held (i.e., both older and younger males were asked their opinions more often and made suggestions more often than older and younger females), age seemed to exacerbate the situation. That is, the greatest differences were found between older male supervisees and older female supervisees. We need to reiterate that these differences are not only displayed by the supervisees themselves but reinforced by supervisors of both genders. Granello's results call for serious deliberation among supervisors regarding their reactions to both the gender and age of the supervisee.

In yet another similar study, Sells et al. (1997) reported that when the supervisor was male the influence over the structure of supervision was attributed to the supervisor; and when the supervisor was female, the structure of the supervision session was more often attributed to the trainee. These results were replicated by Lichtenberg and Goodyear (2000).

Finally, two studies that considered the postures that supervisors took with supervisees add to our discussion of power. In a study with marriage and family therapy supervisees, Moorhouse and Carr (2002) found that the supervisors' collaborative behavior (i.e., consultative rather than directive) was highest when males were supervising males and lowest when males were supervising females. Although the authors found these results to be surprising, because they expected males to be more directive with other males, the results point to the differential (preferred) status given to male supervisees.

Clearly, supervision is a relationship that includes a power dynamic that is endemic. Given the complexity of gender relationships, it is not surprising that power is manipulated differently in supervision for men and women. Holloway and Wolleat (1994) appealed to supervisors to make the supervisory relationship a context for the female supervisee to discover her own professional power. Similarly, Hipp and Munson (1995) advocated for feminist models of supervision to empower all supervisees. To date, these prescriptions seem to be more than justified.

Same-gender and Cross-gender Pairs in Supervision. There is some evidence that, when given a choice, supervisees prefer to work with a supervisor of the same gender (McCarthy, Kulakowski, & Kenfield, 1994). Behling, Curtis, and Foster (1988) found that matched gender (specifically, female–female pairings) resulted in the greatest satisfaction with supervision, and the most negative combination for supervision in the field occurred when a female supervisee was supervised by a male supervisor. Worthington and Stern (1985) found, on the other hand, that the closest rela-

tionships occurred in male–male pairings. Thyer, Sower-Hoag, and Love (1988) similarly found that same-gender pairs produced the most favorable ratings of supervision, but the authors made the point that gender accounted for only 5% of the variance. Therefore, the argument for matching supervisee and supervisor by gender may be tenuous. This conclusion is reinforced by research that found little additional advantage for female supervisees in being supervised by another female.

Although it is important that women, in particular, have an opportunity to work with female role models (Bruce, 1995), androgenous supervisors of both genders will be more advantageous to the supervisee than working exclusively with a person of one's own gender. In support of this assumption, Putney et al. (1992) found that cross-gender pairs resulted in increased autonomy for the supervisee. Developmentally, such an outcome might be critical for positive professional growth. In short, the ways in which gender affect supervision appear to be complex and call for both additional research and supervision practices that attend specifically to gender (Barnes & Bernard, 2003; Nelson, 1991).

Feminist Supervision. Following the lead of feminist family therapy, the concept of feminist supervision has begun to take hold (Prouty, 2001; Prouty, Thomas, Johnson, & Long, 2001). Prouty et al. conducted extensive interviews with clinical supervisors who considered themselves to be informed by feminist ideology. Their findings indicated that supervisors were intentional about their feminism throughout the supervision experience. For example, supervision contracts were approached in a manner that attempted to give maximum voice to the supervisee. Supervisee-identified goals were of paramount importance. This emphasis on the supervisee's voice continued in the methods chosen by the supervisors. For the most part, they preferred collaborative methods and providing options for supervisees, rather than directives. Even though subjects in the Prouty et al. study indicated that there were times when collaboration was not appropriate, they remained highly concerned about the use of "expert power" in supervision, returning as soon as possible to a more egalitarian posture.

Reporting on the same data, Prouty (2001) emphasized that the relationship was central to feminist supervisors and served as the cornerstone of their activity. As indicative of their emphasis on relationship, supervisors identified commitment, availability, respect, and a willingness to talk about the relationship as central values driving their work. When supervisees needed to be challenged, feminist supervisors attempted to do this in a way that empowered them; they refrained from exerting supervisor power. "Challenging the therapist was reflective of a deeper ability to join with the therapist in order to help them push their limits" (p. 182).

Finally, Prouty's subjects emphasized the larger themes of socialization, gender, power, diversity, and addressing emotion as key to their supervision. Their world view focused on multicultural issues, not on women's issues exclusively. We would note that the approach described by Prouty's subjects is wholly compatible with the suggestions proposed by Wester and Vogel (2002) for working with male supervisees who experience gender role conflict. For both, the importance of allowing the supervisee's voice to be heard and affirmed is essential. From the research we have to date, it seems that male supervisors in particular would be well served by attempting to adopt a feminist model of supervision.

Lesbian, Gay, and Bisexual Issues within Multicultural Supervision

As the mental health professions grapple with greater inclusion of cultural variables within supervision, they still lag behind in their attention to lesbian, gay, and bisexual (LGB) issues. The supervision literature available continues to be largely theoretical or anecdotal (e.g., Bruss, Brack, Brack, Glickauf-Hughes, & O'Leary, 1997; Buhrke, 1989; Buhrke & Douce, 1991; Gautney, 1994; Halpert & Pfaller, 2001; Russell & Greenhouse, 1997; Schrag, 1994; Woolley, 1991), though there is some empirical evidence that LGB

trainees have experienced discrimination during supervision (Pilkington & Cantor, 1996). A recent study by Murphy, Rawlings, and Howe (2002) found that 56% of clinical psychologists surveyed saw at least one LGB client. Of that group, 46% identified supervision as a place where training for working with LGB clients occurred, although only half found their supervisors to be knowledgeable about the concerns of LGB clients. Murphy et al. noted that this low percentage raises the issue of the quality of supervision and the likelihood of propagating poor practice.

Buhrke and Douce (1991) maintained that supervisees should enter supervision with at least initial skills in recognizing LGB identity development stages (including an ability to differentiate these from psychopathology), a readiness to assist clients in addressing intimacy issues within a gay or lesbian relationship, and a readiness to confront their own heterosexual assumptions. Although these prerequisites are sound, we doubt that all supervisees in the mental health professions meet them. Bruss et al. (1997), while reiterating Buhrke and Douce's assertion, also advised that supervisors be clear about their expectations with supervisees who are working with LGB clients. One expectation, then, could be that a supervisee "get educated" about sexual identity development and be prepared to discuss one's own affect and assumptions if knowledge and/or awareness were lacking in the supervisee. Bruss et al. also included supervisor self-awareness as the third "foundation" for supervision around LGB issues. They advised supervisors to share their own developmental struggles with supervisees, thus modeling what Gonzalez (1997) referred to as "supervisor-as-partial-learner" (pp. 367–370). Once the foundation is set, Bruss et al. used the Stoltenberg and Delworth (1987) model (see Chapter 4) to describe the goals for supervision as the supervisee moves toward autonomy as a practitioner. In short, supervisors use more structure and didactic interventions to assist the supervisee in Level 1, assist the supervisee in recognizing and confronting covert homophobia in Level 2 as the supervisee gains more independence, and, at Level 3, when the supervisee's sexual identity development has advanced, to help the supervisee find ways to use self as a catalyst for continued growth. Of course, these suggestions assume a nonhomophobic supervisor providing a safe learning environment.

Although Bruss et al. (1997) concerned themselves with the heterosexual counselor working with the LGB client, Buhrke (1989) addressed supervisory dynamics when any member of the supervisory triad was lesbian. Using broad strokes, Buhrke outlined four possibilities concerning lesbian-related issues within supervision. She divided them into nonconflictual and conflictual situations within the client–supervisee–supervisor triad. Of the nonconflictual situations, the most productive was when neither supervisor nor supervisee was homophobic. Under these circumstances, the following examples are possible: the lesbian supervisor can serve as a positive role model for her supervisees, the lesbian supervisor can openly discuss with the supervisee the appropriateness of coming out to a particular client, and mutual attraction between supervisor and supervisee (and the need to avoid a dual relationship) can be discussed openly and professionally.

Ironically, the second nonconflictual situation was described by Buhrke as "the worst of possible supervisory scenarios" (p. 200). In this case, both supervisor and supervisee are homophobic. Buhrke described mutual homophobia as blocking many productive interactions (including either supervisor or supervisee coming out). Because supervisor and supervisee will reinforce each other's biases, a lesbian client either will be underserved (i.e., references to lesbian life-style will be ignored) or will be badly served (e.g., her lesbianism will be viewed as pathological).

Buhrke (1989) similarly saw one conflict situation between supervisor and supervisee as potentially positive and one as highly problematic. When the supervisor is not homophobic, but the supervisee is, there is the potential for the supervisee to deal with her attitudes under the tutelage of the supervisor. Buhrke noted, however, that the supervisor must make a careful judgment call regarding the degree of homophobia (or the milder

form of homophobia, heterosexual bias) and the supervisee's ability to work productively with a lesbian client. When the supervisee is free from homophobia, but the supervisor is not, the power differential may make it difficult for the former to "challenge the supervisor's irrational beliefs about homosexuality" (p. 202). Furthermore, the lesbian supervisee might feel the necessity to conceal her life-style preference, a tragic outcome given the context in which it occurs. Russell and Greenhouse (1997) echoed our earlier statement regarding the political nature of the helping professions when they stated that "the intrusion of homophobia and heterosexism into the supervisory relationship represents the intersection of the personal and the political" (p. 27).

When the supervisor has a positive view of alternative life-styles, the supervisor can be an important role model for supervisees, gay and nongay alike (Schrag, 1994). Furthermore, when the supervisor takes such a posture, it is more likely that LGB supervisees will come out to the supervisor. As Schrag (1994) stated, "my openness models a method of moving from shame to self-empowerment, from abuse to compassion, and from secrecy to taking care of myself. These are pivotal for all therapists to acquire" (p. 7). Additionally, one lesbian supervisee who was "out" in supervision, but who never received supervision specific to her sexual orientation, now regrets the conspiracy of silence between her and her supervisor:

> The advice I am about to give is strictly from the perspective of a lesbian supervisee to supervisors: Bring it up. Talk about it. Whether your supervisee or her clients are heterosexual or homosexual, sexual orientation is a relevant issue that may be avoided unless you attend to it. Take the responsibility, because you probably have less to risk than your supervisees. And if your supervisee is gay or lesbian, believe me, they are already thinking about it. (Gautney, 1994, p. 7)

Both Buhrke and Douce (1991) and Russell and Greenhouse (1997) address some of the intrapsychic dimensions for multicultural supervision involving one or more persons with an LBG identity.

Buhrke and Douce considered transference and countertransference issues that might emerge when the supervisee counsels the same-gender coming-out client. Noting the strong emotions present throughout the coming-out process, it is quite likely that the client will experience attraction for the counselor, especially if that person is lesbian, gay, or bisexual. From the perspective of both gay and nongay supervisees, dealing with same-gender attraction is a topic that supervisors must be willing to address without disapproval. If supervisors shut down the supervisee by communicating distaste for the topic, the supervisee is far more vulnerable to handling the attraction inappropriately. Buhrke and Douce also noted that LGB supervisees working with LGB clients or supervisors are perhaps more vulnerable to dual relationships than nongay supervisees and supervisors because of the advocacy required in working with disenfranchised populations, as well as the reality of overlapping social circles common to the LGB community. Buhrke and Douce advised that a strict definition of dual relationships may not be appropriate in this situation; at the same time, the supervisee will need assistance in determining appropriate boundaries that allow the supervisee to practice ethically and productively.

Russell and Greenhouse (1997) focused on the discourse within supervision itself when the supervisor is a female heterosexual and the supervisee is lesbian. Among the most glaring errors the supervisor can make, according to Russell and Greenhouse, is assuming that sexual orientation is a nonissue for supervision. The authors addressed reasons for resistance to the topic from both supervisor and supervisee vantage points. Among the reasons for supervisor resistance, Russell and Greenhouse included the supervisor's discomfort in moving beyond the area within which she feels comfortable (competent), wanting to avoid the pain of truly understanding the experiences of an oppressed supervisee, and protecting herself against potential negative feedback from the supervisee. The therapist has her reasons for resisting the topic as well, including internalized homophobia, wanting to view her sexual orientation

as a "private matter," and wishing to avoid any additional vulnerability within supervision. Despite reasonable reluctance for either party, Russell and Greenhouse maintained that allowing these resistances to dictate the relationship represents an unfortunate collusion for ignoring an important cultural influence, one not only affecting their relationship, but those between the supervisee and her clients as well.

Division 44 of the American Psychological Association published *Guidelines for Psychotherapy with Lesbian, Gay, and Bisexual Clients* (2000). Included in these guidelines is the call for continued education and adequate supervision. The literature available to date indicates that supervisors themselves have much to learn to be competent in multicultural supervision in general and to supervise around sexual orientation issues in particular. At the very least, supervisors should strive to excel at all 16 guidelines advanced by Division 44. These are summarized in Table 5.4.

We have covered those cultural areas that have a "critical mass" of professional literature and research attesting to their role in the supervisory relationship. Other cultural categories may be as important to consider, but the professions have not evolved to the point of including them in their inquiry. For example, social class has not yet emerged in the supervision literature and spirituality and religion are barely represented (cf., Frame, 2001; Polanski, 2003). Therefore, we hope that the literature we have reported and our comments serve to inform discourse within supervision, but not to define it.

MULTICULTURAL CONTRUCTS: PULLING IT ALL TOGETHER

In many ways, we have only scratched the surface of culture and the ways that cultural differences play out in our interactions with others, including those interactions that transpire within supervision. Whereas our assumptions and fears often run unchecked, our knowledge is actually quite limited. What follows is an attempt to encapsulate

TABLE 5.4 Summary of Guidelines for Conducting Psychotherapy with LGB Clients

1. Understand that an LGB orientation is not indicative of mental illness.
2. Recognize that attitudes and knowledge about LGB issues may affect assessment and treatment of LGB clients. Seek consultation and referrals when indicated.
3. Strive to understand how prejudice, discrimination, and violence pose risks to the mental health of the LGB client.
4. Strive to understand how uninformed or prejudicial views of the LGB orientation may affect the client's presentation in treatment and the therapeutic process itself.
5. Strive to be knowledgeable and respectful of LGB relationships.
6. Strive to understand the unique challenges of LGB parents.
7. Recognize that families of LGB clients may include persons who are not legally or biologically related.
8. Strive to understand how a person's LGB identity may have an impact on that person's family of origin and the relationship to it.
9. Recognize that particular life issues may be related to multiple, sometimes conflicting, cultural norms for the LGB client.
10. Recognize the particular challenges of the bisexual client.
11. Strive to understand the special problems and risks for LGB youth.
12. Consider generational differences among persons, particularly when working with the older LGB client.
13. Recognize the particular challenges for the LGB client with disabilities.
14. Support the provision of professional education and training regarding LGB issues.
15. Seek continuing education, training, supervision, and consultation in LGB issues.
16. Make reasonable efforts to know relevant mental health, educational, and community resources for LGB clients.

Adapted from Guidelines for Psychotherapy with Lesbian, Gay, and Bisexual Clients, by Division 44/Committee on Lesbian, Gay, and Bisexual Concerns Joint Task Force on Guidelines for Psychotherapy with Lesbian, Gay, and Bisexual Clients, 2000. *American Psychologist, 55,* 1440–1451.

what we consider to be the most dominant guidelines that are justified by what we know:

• *All interactions are multicultural.* Multicultural supervision is not only about working with persons whom Helms and Cook (1999) refer to as VREGs (visible racial or ethnic groups). Instead, it is a constant and dynamic force in all supervisory interactions. If not defined broadly, we will forget to check out our assumptions too often and we will be awkward (if not incompetent) when cultural differences are significant.

• *Supervisors lag behind supervisees in multicultural awareness and knowledge.* We now have data (e.g., Constantine, 1997) to support our speculation that, by virtue of changes in training programs, supervisees come to supervision with training in multicultural concepts that their supervisors often lack. Supervisors must take in this discrepancy and do something about it. There are ample opportunities for continuing education and training. Cultural competence must be included in the supervisor's definition of supervisory efficacy.

• *Power and privilege are core to understanding multiculturalism.* It is not difference that matters. It is the power and privilege assigned to that difference. Ryde (2000) discussed the accumulated power of the supervisor who represents a powerful cultural group, has a strong personality, and is in the role of supervisor. Power has many sources, and these must be attended to in the supervisory relationship.

• *Identity development seems to be key.* It seems that, whether we are talking about race or gender or sexual orientation, our relative development in that area of identity may be more important in the long run than identification with a particular group. Referring to the research on race (Ladany et al., 1997), racial identity development of supervisor and supervisee appears to be a promising construct with more predictive power than race in cross-race supervision. Gender research also seems to be implying this distinction. We would speculate that, overall, cultural group membership will become a weak second to development within that identity as a factor affecting supervision. The potential for this kind of development is, of course, the basis for education and training in multiculturalism.

• *The supervisor is key.* Regardless of the cultural differences within the supervisory triad, it is the supervisor's cultural competence and openness that will dictate whether the experience will be positive. Although the research we have is limited, the evidence is clear that an uninformed or biased supervisor has instrumental power when cultural differences emerge within the supervision process. Furthermore, the supervisor must initiate the dialog around cultural matters. Position power dictates this (Ryde, 2000).

• *Gender as a "sleeper."* Although most concern and fear seem to revolve around cross-racial supervision, the limited research we have seems to indicate that gendered behaviors have been the most damaging within supervision. Our assumption is that our heightened sensitivity regarding race has made us more careful and potentially more responsible in those cross-cultural situations. Cross-gender supervision is more commonplace and gender assumptions perhaps more deeply ingrained. For whatever reason, whereas race typically is not found to be a significant factor in supervision, gender often is.

• *Avoiding stereotypes.* When it works, multicultural supervision allows us to respect a particular world view and to understand how it matters to the individual. Although the world view may be representative of others from a particular cultural group,

it may not. This is the hard part. But like other complex domains, the more sophisticated we become as multicultural supervisors, the more within-group distinctions we will discern. Stereotypes emerge when they more or less describe a sizable number of members of a particular cultural group. They often fail us when we attempt to build a relationship with an individual from that same group.

CONCLUSION

This chapter surveyed a variety of topics relevant to the formation of a supervisory relationship. The developmental status of the supervisee may be determined by level of experience or by other variables, but, though a reliable predictor of supervisee needs and expectations in many circumstances, developmental level can be secondary to cognitive and interpersonal style. Likewise, cultural variables are key to understanding each other within the supervision relationship. Fall and Sutton (2004) offer a variety of examples to stimulate discussion around these topics.

More than any other, the point of this chapter is that each supervisee brings to supervision a rich blend of experience, insight, and habit that will affect supervision with or without the supervisor's knowledge. In this respect, the topics covered in the chapter are only examples of the types of issues that might interest the supervisor in assessing where to begin with a supervisee. Broad themes of lifelong learning (developmental level), uniqueness (personal style, belief systems, and cultural identity), and oppression (disenfranchised groups) will affect how both the supervisor and the supervisee interact with the supervision process. Perhaps more than any other chapter, this discussion has underscored the part of supervision that is new with each supervisee, calling forth from the supervisor an openness to discovery in his or her work. In short, this chapter has attempted to explain what every supervisor knows: the experience with each supervisee is different.

CHAPTER 6

THE SUPERVISORY RELATIONSHIP
PROCESSES AND ISSUES OF THE SUPERVISORY TRIAD AND DYAD

In all aspects of our lives, relationships provide us with emotional nourishment as well as the contexts in which we learn. Feedback that we receive in the context of relationships is the mechanism by which we define ourselves (see especially the work of symbolic interactionists such as Mead, 1913, and Stryker & Statham, 1985).

These and other relationship processes permeate all of supervision. It is unsurprising, then, that entire books are devoted to supervisory relationships (e.g., Frawley-O'Dea & Sarnat, 2001; Gill, 2001). But whereas we address relationship processes in one way or another throughout this book, we are able to devote only this and the following chapter specifically to them. Because we must necessarily be selective in what we can cover, we will attempt to address the most salient relationship issues.

We begin by offering Gelso and Carter's (1985) definition of therapeutic relationships: "the feelings and attitudes that counseling participants have toward one another, and the manner in which these are expressed" (p. 159). This definition applies just as well to supervisory relationships.

As the Gelso and Carter (1985) definition implies, it would be misleading to consider "the relationship" as something uniform or static. Each supervisory dyad or triad has its own unique rhythm, sequences, and content. Many factors can affect a particular relationship. We discussed some of the individual differences variables (e.g., gender; race–ethnicity; developmental stage) in Chapter 5. But there are many others as well.

Supervisory relationship are multilayered and complex. To examine them is akin to scanning a forest through a telescope: Each focal range will reveal different aspects and details of the forest. Moreover, within each focal range there are any number of features that might be the object of attention. Fiscalini's (1997) term "supervisory ecology" (p. 43) suggests the complexity of the interactions among the focal ranges and possible features of interest.

In examining the figurative forest that is supervision, we will focus our telescope at three different ranges:

1. Supervision as a triadic system (the broadest focal range)
2. The supervisory dyad
3. Individual participants' contributions to the relationship (the most restricted range)

Chapter 7 will examine phenomena related to the most restricted of the focal ranges, that which considers the supervisee and supervisor contributions to the relationship. We consider the two broader focal ranges in this chapter, each in turn.

SUPERVISION AS A TRIADIC SYSTEM

In pyramid fashion, the supervisory relationship is a relationship about a relationship about other relationships.

(Fiscalini, 1997, p. 30)

It is important to be aware that the supervisory room is crowded with all sorts of "persons" who create anxieties for both the supervisor and the supervisee. It is often more crowded than the analytic one.

(Lesser, 1983, p. 126)

These two observations both underscore the complexity of the supervisory relationship system. Not only are the supervisor, supervisee, and client involved, but it is possible for other people in the client's life to have effects that reverberate throughout the system.

To keep our discussion manageable, however, we will limit it to only the three principals in the supervisory relationship: the client, therapist–supervisee, and supervisor. This triadic relationship is illustrated in Figure 6.1, which makes clear that the supervisee is the pivot point in this system (Frawley-O'Dea & Sarnat, 2001). This figure shows that there are two manifest relationships (client–supervisee and supervisee–supervisor) and that the person common to both is the supervisee. He or she serves as a conduit of both information and processes between the dyads.

At its least complicated level, this figure simply shows the transit route for material that clients generate and that supervisees bring to their supervisors. Consider, for example, Epstein's discussion of his supervisory focus (2001): "I place a great emphasis on working with the supervisee's countertransference reactions. This is especially important in supervising situations involving borderline and psychotic patients. I am referring to feelings of inadequacy, impotence, helplessness, stupidity, confusion, anger, hate [and so on]" . . . (p. 153).

In this assertion of his preferred supervisory focus, Epstein illustrated how particular client characteristics (diagnoses of psychosis or borderline personality disorder) might elicit supervisee reactions (feelings of inadequacy and so on) that in turn become the focus of supervision. This is a direct, linear transmission of processes, from client to supervisor.

This type of linear transmission is very common in supervision. But other, more complex processes

occur as well. The supervisory triad can be the basis, for example, for both parallel processes and isomorphic phenomena. It also is the basis for triangulations among the participants. These phenomena are discussed in the sections that follow.

Parallel Processes and Isomorphism

Friedlander, Siegel, and Brenock (1989) described parallel process as a phenomenon in which: "supervisees unconsciously present themselves to their supervisors as their clients have presented to them. The process reverses when the supervisee adopts attitudes and behaviors of the supervisor in relating to the client" (p. 149).

The concept of parallel process has its roots in psychodynamic supervision (Friedman, 1983; Grey & Fiscalini, 1987; Schneider, 1992). Searles (1955), who apparently was the first to employ this concept, referred to it as the "reflection process" between therapy and supervision. Others (e.g., Ekstein & Wallerstein, 1972; Mueller, 1982; Mueller & Kell, 1972) soon after began to employ the concept (using the term parallel process), which now has become perhaps the best known single phenomenon in supervision.

Structural and strategic family therapists have employed the related concept of isomorphism, which Haley (1976) has been credited for spearheading (Liddle & Saba, 1983). In choosing the term *isomorphism,* systemic supervisors have focused on the interrelational and structural similarities between therapy and supervision.

These concepts initially were described and promoted by adherents of specific models of treatment (i.e., parallel process by psychodynamic supervisors; isomorphism by family systems theorists). Yet parallel process and isomorphism are concepts that can be useful to *any* supervisor. They seem in many respects to be two sides of the same coin. Abroms (1977) came as close as anyone to blending the concepts of parallel process and isomorphism in his introduction of the term *metatransference:* "To think in terms of metatransference is to think in parallel structures at different levels of abstraction, that is, to recognize the

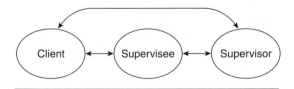

FIGURE 6.1 Supervisee as Relational Pivot Point in the Supervisory Triad

multilevel, isomorphic mirroring of interactional processes" (p. 93).

Nevertheless, these two phenomena are distinct enough to warrant separate treatment. Each will be covered in the following sections.

Parallel Process.   Russell, Crimmings, and Lent (1984) suggested two ways that parallel processes can be useful in supervision:

> *First, as the supervisee becomes aware of the parallels in the relationships with the client and the supervisor, understanding of the client's psychological maladjustment is increased. Second, the supervisee's understanding of the therapeutic process grows in that the supervisee learns how to respond therapeutically to the client just as the supervisor has responded to the supervisee." (p. 629)*

Initially, it was assumed that parallel process was a bottom-up phenomenon in which some characteristic of the client is displayed by the supervisee during supervision. Therefore, a supervisee working with a depressed client might present in supervision in an uncharacteristically depressed manner. Or the supervisee working with a particularly confused client might present in supervision in an uncharacteristically confused manner.

There have been various explanations for parallel processes. We have summarized some of these in Box 6.1. These all have in common that they focus on bottom-up processes and that:

- the parallel process is triggered either by the client or by some aspect of the client–supervisee relationship;
- it occurs outside awareness of the participants; and
- the supervisee is the conduit of the process from the client–therapist relationship to that of the supervisor–supervisee.

Ekstein and Wallerstein (1972) commented that parallel process is a "never-ending surprise," based on the "irrational expectation that the teaching and learning of psychotherapy should consist primarily of rational elements" (p. 177). The flavor of this comment, however, is that the supervisee expresses that irrationality. It reflects the bottom-up perspective to which we already have alluded, what Frawley-O'Dea & Sarnat (2001) characterized as the traditional view of parallel processes.

On the other hand, the contemporary view of parallel processes is that the supervisor is as likely

---

Box 6.1 _____

Some Explanations for the Occurrence of Parallel Processes

- Because of their identification with their clients, supervisees produce reactions in their supervisors that they themselves felt in response to their clients (Russell et al., 1984).
- The parallel the supervisee (unconsciously) chooses reflects the initial impasse formed between the client and the supervisee (Mueller & Kell, 1972).
- The supervisee selects part of the client's problem that parallels one that the supervisee shares (Mueller & Kell, 1972).
- The supervisee identifies unconsciously with some aspect of the client's psychological functioning. Because the supervisee is unaware of this identification, she or he "cannot verbally discuss

- this aspect of the patient in supervision but, rather, enacts the patient's dynamic with the supervisor" (Frawley-O'Dea & Sarnat, 2001, p. 171).
- Through lack of skill, the supervisee is prone to those aspects of the client's problem that parallel the supervisee's specific learning problems in supervision (Ekstein & Wallerstein, 1972).
- Parallel process has "similarities with the repetition compulsion, namely, that what is not understood is enacted" (Arkowitz, 2001, p. 53).
- When supervisor, therapist, and/or client represent different cultural backgrounds, some parallel processes are likely to reflect cross-cultural issues. (Vargas, 1989)

to initiate a dynamic that would then be played out in the supervisee's therapy as is the reverse. This expanded perspective began with Doehrman's (1976) dissertation research findings that parallel processes were bidirectional. For example, she observed that a supervisor–supervisee relationship impasse was mirrored by a supervisee–client impasse. When the supervisory relationship impasse was resolved, so too was that between supervisee and client.

Frawley-O'Dea and Sarnat (2001) discuss this bidirectional conception as "symmetrical parallel processes":

> *The central conceptualization of symmetrical parallel process is that a transference and countertransference configuration arises in either the supervised treatment or in the supervision. At this point, the relational pattern in play is out of the conscious awareness of the members of the dyad. It is not available for conscious elaboration, discussion, meaning making, or negotiation because it has not been linguistically formulated yet by either party to the dyad. The supervisee, however, the common member of both dyads, nonverbally exerts relational pressure on the member of the other dyad to enact a similar transference and countertransference matrix with the supervisee, in the often unconscious hope that someone can contain, enact, process, and put words to what is transpiring now in both dyads. The key to symmetrical parallel processes is that both the treatment and the supervisory dyads play out similar relational constellations.* (p. 182)

This makes clear that, regardless of direction, "the conduits for parallel processes are supervisees: they are members of both systems (though with different roles) and carry one system into the other" (Carroll, 1996, p. 107). This is what we have illustrated in Figure 6.1.

Mothersole (1999) alluded to a third phenomenon that might have the general appearance of a parallel process. This is the situation in which problematic issues from the supervisee are "'beaming out' in both directions and affecting the therapeutic and supervisory relationships" (p. 118). He noted, however, that whereas this might have the *appearance* of a parallel process

it is a false one that is a function of either unresolved problems or lack of skills in the supervisee.

Implications for Supervisors.   Virtually all theorists who discuss parallel processes now embrace the more contemporary, symmetrical view. Nevertheless, most discussions of possible interventions for the supervisor focus only on the traditional view in which the supervisee is transmitting client material to the supervisory dyad. Likely, this is because it is possible for the supervisor to observe this phenomenon. On the other hand, it would be much more difficult for the supervisor to observe phenomena that originate with him or her. Heidegger's observation that "Fish are the last ones to discover water" perhaps is apt in this situation.

Neufeldt, Iverson, and Juntunen (1995) pointed out that, whereas a supervisor might anticipate many interventions in advance, opportunities to address parallel processes typically will occur serendipitously. They also noted that, whereas psychodynamic supervisors are likely to point out or interpret parallel processes to more advanced supervisees as they observe them, this can be confusing to less advanced students. Moreover, for a supervisee simply to have awareness of a particular parallel process does not make it disappear (Carroll, 1996).

Neufeldt et al. (1995) recommended instead that the supervisor respond less directly and serve as a model for the supervisee about how to respond to the client issues that the supervisee is mirroring in the supervisory sessions. For more intractable situations, Carroll (1996) recommended that the supervisee role play the client in order to gain a clearer perspective.

McNeill and Worthen (1989) cautioned that too much focus on the *process* of supervision might become tiresome for supervisees and that, in general, more advanced supervisees are most likely to benefit from a discussion of transference and countertransference. Finally, Vargas (1989) noted that, when supervisor, therapist, and/or client represent different cultural backgrounds, parallel processes will reflect cross-cultural issues.

Research Concerning Parallel Processes. Research on parallel process has been hampered by two important factors. One is that the concept is sufficiently vague that it has been difficult to operationalize clearly. The other is that it is hard to predict when parallel processes will manifest themselves and therefore be available for study.

In response to these factors, the relatively few studies of parallel processes have employed primarily a case study design (e.g., Alpher, 1991; Doehrman, 1976; Friedlander et al., 1989), though these have varied in sophistication. McNeill and Worthen (1989) concluded from their review that, whereas empirical support for parallel process is sparse, there is some. Not much had changed a decade later when Mothersole (1999) concluded from his review that "parallel process is a concept with a long history and is widely used, yet there is very little empirical evidence for its existence" (p. 117). Nevertheless, he asserted that the concept itself is robust and has utility for supervisors.

Two recent studies have used designs other than case studies that provide data linking the functioning of the supervisory dyad with that of the therapy dyad. One was that of Patton and Kivlighan (1997), who found that the week-to-week fluctuations in the quality of the supervisor–supervisee working alliances predicted the week-to-week fluctuations in the supervisee–client working alliance. Williams (2000) used 44 supervisory triads, having clients complete a measure of their counselors' interpersonal style and supervisees complete that same measure with respect to their supervisors. She found that the greater the supervisors' affiliative interpersonal style, the less controlling or dominant the supervisees' style in work with clients.

Other studies have examined which supervisors attend to parallel processes and how they perceive its effects. Perhaps unsurprisingly, Raichelson, Herron, Primavera, and Ramirez (1997) confirmed that psychodynamic supervisors and supervisees were more likely than their rational–emotive or cognitive–behavioral counterparts to recognize the existence and importance of parallel processes. In a qualitative study, Ladany, Constantine, Miller, Erickson, and Muse-Burke (2000) found that supervisors (of unspecified theoretical orientations) frequently identified parallel processes as sources of countertransference reactions that they had experienced toward supervisees.

Concluding Comments about Parallel Processes. Parallel process often has seemed an almost mystical phenomenon. McWilliams (1994) acknowledged that this apparent mysticism can be particularly troublesome for someone with the hard-nosed skepticism that often characterizes the scientist–practitioner. She suggested, though, that parallel processes become more comprehensible when one realizes that in the earliest years of life most communication with others is both nonverbal and complex and that we then continue to employ this mode throughout life without necessarily understanding the extent to which we do so. "People relating to babies figure out what they need largely on the basis of intuitive, emotional reactions. Nonverbal communication can be remarkably powerful, as anyone who has ever taken care of a newborn or been moved to tears, or fallen inexplicably in love can testify" (McWilliams, 1994, p. 34).

McWilliams was arguing against a too skeptical perception of parallel processes. But the complementary issue is one of invoking it too frequently and uncritically without considering alternative explanations for what may be occurring within the supervisory system. Schimel (1984), for example, acknowledged that, although the concept of parallel processes can be quite useful in supervision, it can be invoked in an irresponsible and possibly trivial manner to frame in psychological terms a matter that actually is one of skill and competence.

The basic observation is a simple one. The patient wants something from the therapist that is not forthcoming. He or she is displeased. This troubles the therapist, who, in turn, looks to the supervisor for help that may or may not be forthcoming. The therapist is displeased with the supervisor, who, in his turn, may be troubled and displeased with the supervisee and himself. This is a common situation. One has reason to expect, however, that with the increasing skill of the supervisee and the accumulat-

ing experience of the supervisor that this kind of situation will be recognized early and dealt with by putting it into an appropriate perspective. (p. 239)

Feiner (1994) is another who urged caution in putting too much credence in the parallel process as a supervision phenomenon:

The supervisor is allegedly "put" (not deliberately) in the position of a proxy therapist with the supervisee playing the part of the patient. Although out-of-awareness, the enactment is not taken by sophisticated supervisors as a simple, mechanistic repetition, but as more likely representing some sort of homology. It's as though the student were saying, "Do it with me and I'll know what to do with my patients." But . . . while the issues that belong to the patient may seem similar to the issues that the therapist-as-student brings into supervision . . . the similarity is more apparent than real. It's sort of like the descriptions of a spouse by a patient. The image of the described other cannot be taken as objective truth. (pp. 61–62)

Feiner pointed out that one risk of a too heavy reliance on parallel process thinking is that it may ignore, obscure, or even deny the supervisor's or the supervisee's own contributions to the interactions occurring between them.

Finally, we would point out that parallel processes can manifest in supervision-of-supervision as well (Ellis & Douce, 1994; see Chapter 12). In this case, the supervisory relationship system involves four people: client, supervisee, supervisor, and the supervisor's supervisor. Despite the added complexity of this situation, the material we have covered in this section should extrapolate readily to it.

Isomorphism

Isomorphism refers to the phenomenon whereby categories with different content, but similar form, can be mapped on each other in such a way that there are corresponding parts and processes within each structure. When this occurs, these parallel structures can be described as isomorphic, and each is an iso-morph of the other. Therefore, when the supervisory system is mapped onto the thera-peutic system, the roles of supervisor and supervisee correspond to those of the therapist and client, respectively.

(White & Russell, 1997, p. 317)

For systems therapists, isomorphism refers to the "recursive replication" (Liddle, Breunlin, Schwartz, & Constantine, 1984) that occurs between therapy and supervision. The focus is interrelational and not intrapsychic. As Liddle and Saba (1983) suggested, the two fields (therapy and supervision) constantly influence and are influenced by each other; both are interpersonal systems with properties of all systems, including boundaries, hierarchies, and subsystems, each with its own distinct characteristics. There is no linear reality in this construct, only reverberations. Content is important, but not nearly as important as repeating patterns.

Because supervision is viewed as the isomorph of therapy, Liddle et al. (1984) suggested that the same rules apply to both. These rules include the need to join with both clients and supervisees, the need for setting goals and thinking in stages, the importance of appreciating contextual sensitivity and the charge of challenging realities. "It suggests that trainers would do well to understand and intentionally utilize with their supervisees the same basic principles of change employed in therapy" (Liddle et al., p. 141).

The supervisor who is aware of this process will watch for dynamics in supervision that reflect the initial assessment that the supervisor has made about what is transpiring in therapy. In this way, the assessment is either verified or called into question. Because the client (family) is usually a group, and many systemic supervisors prefer team supervision (see Chapter 11), the interactions are easily replicated. For example, an overwhelmed parent will appeal to the supervisee for help (while other family members sit expectantly), which will be followed by an overwhelmed supervisee appealing to the supervisor for help (while other team members sit expectantly). When intervening into the therapeutic system (supervisee plus family), it is important that there be consistency down the hierarchy. For example, Haley (1987) recommended that if the goal is for the parents to be firm with their teenager the therapist must be firm with the parents. And to complete the isomorph, the supervisor must be firm with the therapist. In this way, content and process are matched and communicate the same message throughout the interconnected systems.

Liddle and Saba (1983) argued that live supervision, by requiring risk-taking and experiential behavior on the part of the therapist, parallels structural family therapy during which family members are actively put in direct contact with each other. Therefore, live supervision is an isomorphically correct form of supervision for structural family therapy.

White and Russell (1997) found that authors who had written about isomorphism had focused on four phenomena or "facets" related to it:

- **Facet 1:** *Identifying repetitive or similar patterns.* This refers to the replication of patterns across systems. Often this is the replication from another system (client–therapist system; family of origin for either the supervisor or supervisee; etc.) into the supervisory system. But it also can manifest as a replication of supervisor–supervisee pattern onto other systems, especially the therapist–client system. White and Russell (1997) note that the concept of parallel processes could just as well describe this facet of isomorphism.
- **Facet 2:** *Translation of therapeutic models and principles into supervision.* As we noted in Chapter 5, it is impossible for a person's therapeutic model not to affect his or her approach to supervision. To the extent that this occurs, this facet of isomorphism is operating.
- **Facet 3:** *The structure and process of therapy and supervision are identical.* Certainly, there are many structural similarities between supervision and therapy, at least with respect to individual therapy. For example, both typically involve two people isolating themselves in a room with a closed door to discuss sensitive material in private; in both, one person is to disclose material to another whose task is to examine and perhaps take action on some aspect of that material.
- **Facet 4:** *Isomorphism as an interventive stance.* The supervisor can alter the sequences in supervision with the purpose of influencing a corresponding alteration of sequences within therapy.

The following illustrates the first of these facets of isomorphism between therapy and supervision, the facet that is most difficult to differentiate from parallel process (White & Russell, 1997).

Ted is seeing the Doyles for marriage counseling. There is a supervision team observing the session. The Doyles, who have been married for 20 years, have no children. Mr. Doyle has fought depression through most of his adult life. Mrs. Doyle tells how hard it has been to help him, only to have her efforts go nowhere. She cries intermittently. It is obvious watching Ted that he is feeling this couple's plight. In the supervision room, there is virtually no movement. The team mirrors the sadness and despair of the couple. Half way through the session, Ted excuses himself to consult with the team. . . . As Ted is seated, Bill turns to him and says, "Boy, what do you do for them at this point?" Ted shrugs and looks around for help.

In addition to recognizing the isomorphic nature of what is transpiring, the supervisor must (1) determine how to approach the team, (2) predict Ted's role in the group, and (3) decide on an intervention that will not only help to stimulate Ted and the team, but will serve to initiate a direction for Ted to take with the Doyles.

On the face of it, isomorphic processes would seem easier to operationalize and study than parallel processes. Interestingly, this area seems to have no empirical research. Given the potential utility of the concept, it seems a fertile area to explore.

Interpersonal Triangles

It seems customary, at least in our culture, to think of the dyad as the basic social unit. However, Bowen (e.g., 1978) did a great deal to sensitize mental health professionals, especially family therapists, to the notion that the interpersonal triangle actually is the more fundamental unit of relationship. This conception certainly contains important implications for how supervisors and supervisees relate to one another and to the clients who are the focus of their work.

Conceptualizing relationships in terms of triangles is not new. Caplow (1968) noted that since at least the 1890s there have been theorists who maintained that triangles constitute a type of social geometry. Within any given triangle, two members will tend to be in a coalition, with the third either more peripheral or even perceived as antagonistic to them. Caplow (1968) maintained that the most distinctive feature of triadic social systems is "the transformation of strength into weakness and weakness into strength" (p. 3), according to the particular alignments occurring within the triangle.

Triangles occur in many ways in our day-to-day living. Psychoanalytic therapists have been concerned with the "Oedipal triangles" and family therapists have been concerned with the broader spectrum of possible triangles that can occur in a family system. Political scientists have been concerned with the triangles that occur within governments (e.g., with liberal, moderate, and conservative groups) and even among nations. We all can describe childhood (and current!) relationships in which, within a group of three friends, there were two who were particularly close. During times of tension between these two, however, the less involved third member was drawn into an alliance with one in that dyad; the other then becomes more peripheral.

One especially interesting characteristic of triangles is that they seem to have a catalytic effect on participants' behavior. That is, although coalitions can occur between two members of a triangle without the third member present, his or her presence almost always modifies the relationship of the other two. To illustrate, Caplow offered as an example the common playground situation in which the presence of a mutual antagonist enhances (1) the affection between two friends and (2) their felt hostility toward the antagonist. It is

not difficult to see how variants of this same scenario play out in the professional lives of adults as well.

One manifestation of a coalition (and therefore of triangulation) is the circumstance of two people secretly discussing a third. Most of us also have experienced this in our families and in work settings. But this occurs in counseling as well.

For example, triangulation is one reason it is so difficult for counselors to begin with an individual client and then later to include that person's spouse in the treatment. The initial client already will have discussed ("in secret") the spouse with the counselor, who almost inevitably will have adopted at least some of that person's perspective about the spouse. This situation has all the characteristics of the coalition of which Bowen spoke, making it very difficult for the spouse to enter a neutral situation.

Interpersonal Triangles in Supervision. In supervision the most obvious triangle is that of the client, counselor, and supervisor. This particular triangle does, however, have its own characteristics that constrain the possible coalitions. Two of these are (1) the way in which power is arrayed (the least powerful member of this group is the client; the most powerful, the supervisor) and (2) the fact that the supervisor and client rarely will have an ongoing face-to-face relationship with each other.

Within this triangle, the discussion between two people of the third person most often occurs between supervisee and supervisor. This, of course, suggests a counselor–supervisor coalition with the client as the third member. It is possible, though, for the counselor and client to discuss the supervisor. In this instance, it is possible to develop a coalition between counselor and client against the supervisor.

Strategically oriented family therapists sometimes employ this latter coalition possibility to their advantage, using the supervisory relationship for therapeutic purposes. The supervisor is deliberately set up in the "oppressor" role as a means both to catalyze the client–counselor bond and to steer the client toward a desired behavior. For example, the supervisor might direct the counselor to say something like this to the client: "My supervisor is convinced that your problem is _____ and that I should be doing _____ about it. Just between us, though, I think she's off base. In fact, I think she's pretty insensitive to the issues you are facing."

The goal of such a strategy is for the client to improve in order to prove the supervisor wrong. Supervision, of course, occurs in a larger context, and therefore not all the possible triangles of which the supervisor and supervisee might be a part of will necessarily involve the client. For example, the supervisee might "triangle in" another current or past supervisor by saying to his or her supervisor something like this: "I'm feeling confused: You are telling me this, but the supervisor I had last semester [or, the supervisor I have in my other setting] has been telling me something really different."

A statement such as this establishes a coalition between the supervisee and another supervisor who may not even realize that he or she has become a member of this particular triangle. Coalitions— even with a phantom member such as this— redistribute power. Whether or not the supervisee is doing this with deliberate intent, it has the effect of putting the current supervisor in the situation of being "odd person out."

In summary, interpersonal triangles are ubiquitous in human interactions. It is unsurprising, then, that they would occur between and among professionals. Our intent in this discussion was not to suggest that triangles are necessarily always to be avoided. We are convinced, though, that it is essential for supervisors to be aware of interpersonal triangles and their effects. With this knowledge, supervisors are better equipped to avoid problematic triangles and to manage others in a strategic manner.

THE SUPERVISORY DYAD

In the foregoing, we set our figurative telescope at a focal range that permitted the broadest view of the supervisory relationship: a three-person system that included the client, supervisee, and supervisor. In this next section, we restrict the range of that telescope to focus only on the supervisor and supervisee working together as a dyad.

Understandings of the supervisory dyad often have evolved as direct extensions of theory and research on the client–therapist relationship. For example, during the early 1970s, Carkhuff's (1969) extension of the Rogerian model became a dominant relationship paradigm, both for counseling and supervision. Carkhuff's (e.g., 1969) assertion that the level and quality of the supervisor's interpersonal skills may establish a ceiling for the supervisee's own skills for a time seemed to be the "received view" among many. This meant, for example, that the supervisee could be no more empathic, on average, with clients than the supervisee's supervisor was with him or her.

This hypothesis drove studies such as those of Pierce and Schauble (1970, 1971) and of Lambert (1974), which examined the extent to which supervisors' levels of empathy, regard, genuineness, and concreteness (i.e., facilitative conditions) influenced the development of these same conditions in their supervisees (for summaries of this and related research, see Lambert & Arnold, 1987; Lambert & Ogles, 1997; Matarazzo & Patterson, 1986). Based on their review, Lambert and Ogles concluded that "there exists little empirical evidence supporting the necessity of a therapeutic climate for the acquisition of interpersonal skills . . . and it appears that learning these skills can occur without high levels of empathy, genuineness, and unconditional positive regard, as long as the supervisee perceives the supervisor is indeed trying to be helpful" (p. 426). In short, although Rogerian-defined relationship dimensions are too important to ignore, they seem to have greater salience in the practice of therapy than in the practice of supervision.

But even in the domain of therapy, the Rogerian-based paradigm seems to have reached a ceiling in terms of what it can add to conceptualizations of the processes. In acknowledging this, Gelso and Carter

(1985) found promise in Bordin's (1979) working alliance model as a means to conceptualize therapeutic relationships. They anticipated what now has become a major focus of psychotherapy theorists and researchers, a trend substantially helped by the development of reliable and valid measures with which to assess it (Horvath & Luborsky, 1993).

Psychodynamic theorists had offered the initial conceptions of the working alliance. But through Bordin's work, the working alliance increasingly has been accepted as a concept that is independent of any particular theory. That is, it is pantheoretical.

Bordin suggested that the working alliance is a "collaboration to change" (p. 73). In his conception, the working alliance is composed of three elements: the extent to which the therapist and client agree on *goals,* the extent to which they agree on the *tasks* necessary to reach those goals, and the *bond* that develops between them (see Figure 6.2). Bordin (1983) asserted that relational bonds develop as a result either of working together on a common task to achieve shared goals or on the basis of shared emotional experiences. These bonds "will center around the feelings of liking, caring, and trusting that the participants share."

Although Bordin's initial work concerned therapeutic relationships, he later extended his working alliance model to include supervision (Bordin, 1983). In this, he had been foreshadowed by Fleming and Benedek (1966), who had introduced the term *learning alliance* to describe the supervisory relationship.

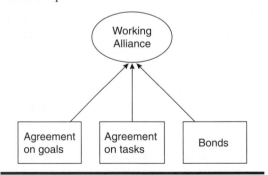

FIGURE 6.2 Model of the Working Alliance (Bordin, 1979)

As in the case of psychotherapy research, research on the supervisory alliance has been facilitated by the development of instruments to measure it. One strategy has been to modify the best known measure of the therapeutic alliance, the Working Alliance Inventory (Horvath & Greenberg, 1989), for use in supervision research (e.g., Bahrick, 1990; Baker, 1990). Another was that of Efstation, Patton, and Kardash (1990), who developed an alliance measure specific to supervision, the Supervisory Working Alliance Inventory (both the Baker and the Efstation et al. instruments are available in this text as part of the Supervisor's Toolbox).

Shared Goals. Of the three components, we want to elaborate here on shared goals. Although goals and expectations are not completely the same, they overlap sufficiently for us to treat them interchangeably in this section.

Bahrick, Russell, and Salmi (1991) and Olk and Friedlander (1992) addressed expectations in supervision; Ellis et al. (1994) made supervisor–supervisee expectations an explicit focus of their work. They define expectations as "a person's anticipatory beliefs about the nature (i.e., roles, behaviors, interactions, and tasks) or outcome of a particular event" (p. 3). Ellis et al. cited counseling and psychotherapy literature showing that *congruence* of expectations (i.e., shared goals) between or among people in a relationship is at least as important, and likely more important, than the expectations of any one person.

Sometimes supervisor and supervisee have differing expectations because the supervisee simply is uninformed about the appropriate role(s) that she or he is to assume as supervisee. To maximize the likelihood of supervisor–supervisee congruence in expectations for supervision, it is useful for the supervisor to ensure that initial negotiation or contracting between them occurs (see Chapter 8 for a description of supervision contracts). When the issue is that the supervisee simply does not know role options, as might be the case with a beginning supervisee, it is possible to educate him or her about expected behaviors and roles through, for example, discussions and audio- or videotape modeling.

Although little research has been done to investigate the effectiveness of this educational procedure, generally referred to as *role induction,* in supervision, its effectiveness with therapy clients has been demonstrated (see, e.g., Garfield, 1986; Kaul & Bednar, 1986). Bahrick et al. (1991) developed a 10-minute audiotaped summary of Bernard's (1979) supervision model and then administered it to 19 supervisees at one of several points in the semester. They found that after supervisees heard the tape they reported having a clearer conceptualization of supervision and being more willing to reveal concerns to their supervisors. This effect occurred regardless of when in the semester supervisees heard the tapes. In a more recent study, Ellis, Chapin, Dennin, and Anderson-Hanley (1996) found that a role induction that they conducted significantly decreased trainee anxiety compared to a control group.

Another potentially useful supervision strategy would be to assess participants' expectations. Tinsley and his associates (e.g., Tinsley, Workman, & Kass, 1980; Tinsley, Bowman, & Ray, 1988) have conducted programmatic research on client's expectations for counseling, and their instrument for assessing counselor–client expectations has been frequently employed in counseling research. But because supervision and counseling are different activities, it is important to be able to evaluate expectations for supervision. To that end, Ellis et al. (1994) did the field a service in developing parallel, 52-item scales (one for supervisees, another for supervisors) to examine expectations for supervision.

Finally, the importance of having mutually agreed upon goals suggests the importance of developing a supervision contract such as we address in Chapter 8. A useful example is the Supervision Agreement section of the Supervisee Bill of Rights (Giordano, Altekruse, & Kern, 2000), which is available both in our Supervisor's Toolbox and at http://www.coe.unt.edu/cdhe/Supervision.html.

Antecedent and Consequences of Effective Supervisory Alliances

We propose that a key task in early supervision is building a strong working alliance (Bordin, 1983) that can serve as a base from which future dilemmas in supervision can be managed. Ongoing maintenance of the alliance should be the supervisor's responsibility throughout the course of the relationship.

(Nelson, Gray, Friedlander, Ladany, & Walker, 2001, p. 408)

In this section and the next, we use the working alliance to organize our discussions of the supervisory dyad. In the section that follows this, we will consider the alliance as a process that fluctuates in quality and intensity. But, in this section, we conceive of the supervisory alliance as a phenomenon that has reasonable stability; although it changes in response to supervisee and supervisor behaviors and interactions, these changes occur in a generally predictable manner.

We begin this section with Figure 6.3, which both introduces a conceptual model for our discussion and visually depicts the results of the available studies. The notes on each arrow in the figure indicate which study or studies support that particular between-variable relationship (the key to these studies appears immediately below the figure). When the relationship between a particular variable and the supervisory alliance is negative (as is true, for example, with respect to the relationship between role conflict and ambiguity and alliance), this valence is provided in the figure (i.e., with the note, "negative relationship").

A few caveats about Figure 6.3 are in order.

- Some supervisee and supervisor attributes, especially attachment styles, predict the quality of the supervisory relationship. However, because these are addressed in Chapter 7, they are not included in this figure. In this sense, then, the figure is incomplete.
- The studies used to develop this figure were correlational and therefore do not permit strict

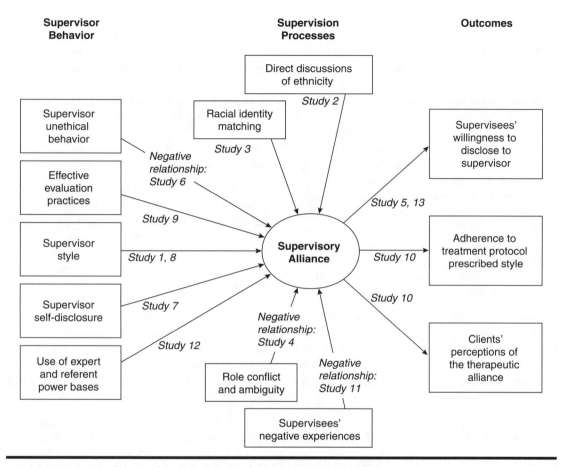

FIGURE 6.3   Antecedents and Consequences of Positive Supervisory Alliances

Studies Cited in Figure 6.3: 1. Chen & Bernstein (2000); 2. Gatmon, Jackson, & Koshkarian (2001); 3. Ladany, Brittan-Powell, & Pannu (1997); 4. Ladany & Friedlander (1995); 5. Ladany, Hill, Corbett, & Nutt (1996); 6. Ladany, Lehrman-Waterman, Molinaro, & Wolgast (1999); 7. Ladany & Lehrman-Waterman (1999); 8. Ladany, Walker, & Melincoff (2001); 9. Lehrman-Waterman & Ladany (2001); 10. Patton and Kivlighan (1997); 11. Ramos-Sánchez et al. (2002); 12. Schultz, Ososkie, Fried, Nelson, & Bardos (2002); 13. Webb & Wheeler (1998).

Note: All but one study used the perspective of the supervisee to measure alliance; study 8 used that of the supervisor.

causal inferences. It is possible, for example, that supervisee self-efficacy results in the supervisee's perception of a stronger alliance, rather than the opposite. The causal directionality that we imposed in this figure is based on what seemed theoretically justified (in virtually

all cases this was the causal direction that the authors themselves had assumed).

• There was no common measure of alliance across these studies. Some used either the Bahrick (1990) or Baker (1990) adaptation of the Working Alliance Inventory (Horvath &

Greenberg, 1989); others used the Efstation et al. (1990) measure.

- Working alliance measures have multiple sub-scales. In some cases, we indicate a relationship if not all subscales were statistically linked to the antecedent or outcome. For example, Ladany, Ellis, and Friedlander (1999) found that supervisee perceptions of bond predicted efficacy, but that shared tasks and bonds did not. But bond seems so central to the concept of alliance that we included this study in the figure.
- We address only studies that obtained significant results, and it is possible in some instances that similar studies did not obtain these results. One example is the Efstation et al. study, which found a relationship between alliance and supervisee self-efficacy, whereas Ladany, Ellis, et al. (1999) did not.

Despite these caveats, the figure provides important information about supervisory alliances. It also provides us with a means for organizing the following discussion. Our discussion begins with factors on the left side of the figure and then works toward its right side.

Alliance Antecedents: Supervisor Behavior

Supervisor's Ethical Behavior.   Ladany, Lehrman-Waterman, Molinaro and Wolgast (1999) examined the prevalence of 15 ethical behaviors that are particular to supervision. These included issues related, for example, to Performance Evaluation and Monitoring of Supervisee Activities, Confidentiality in Supervision, and Supervision Boundaries and Respectful Treatment. Some of the behaviors that they examined (e.g., "My supervisor allowed our sessions to be interrupted unnecessarily by people or events") would not rise to the level of ethical breaches that would warrant complaints to professional associations' ethics committees. The breadth of these authors' definition of ethical behavior is suggested by the fact that more than half the supervisees in the study reported that their current supervisors had not adhered to at least one of the ethical guidelines that Ladany et al. had developed.

Ladany et al. (1999) found that the greater the frequency with which supervisees reported unethical behaviors, the lower the supervisees rated supervisory bonds and agreement on tasks and goals. They also found that the greater the number of unethical behaviors, the less satisfied the supervisees were with supervision. To put in a more colloquial way, the more the supervisor had let down the supervisee, the less strong the supervisee's felt a connection to the supervisor.

Supervisor's Evaluative Practices.   The Ladany et al. (1999) study found that a third of the ethical violations that supervisees reported concerned the manner in which supervisors evaluated them. This strongly suggests that evaluative practices are an important area to which supervisors should attend.

Importantly, then, Lehrman-Waterman and Ladany (2001) reported the development of a measure to assess evaluation practices in clinical supervision, the Evaluation Process within Supervision Inventory (EPSI) (available in the Supervisor's Toolbox portion of this book). Two EPSI scales were used:

1. *Goal Setting*   Sample items: The goals my supervisor and I generated for my training seemed important. My supervisor and I created goals that were easy for me to understand.
2. *Feedback*   Sample items: My supervisor welcomed comments on his or her style as a supervisor. The feedback I received was directly related to the goals we established.

This was an instrument development study. But, as part of the validation process, Lehrman-Waterman and Ladany compared scores on the new measure with scores on measures that would be theoretically linked. Scores on both EPSI scales predicted supervisees' ratings of supervisory alliance (all three alliance elements: tasks, goals, bonds). As well, scores on these scales predicted satisfaction with supervision. It is logical to wonder about the extent to which the EPSI's Goal Setting scale and the Goal scale of the Working Alliance Inventory might actually be measuring the same construct, though (e.g., the correlation between the two was .78).

Reasonably, the clearer and fairer the evaluative process is perceived to be, the less supervisee anxiety and greater the level of trust. Both would have positive effects on the supervisory alliance.

Supervisor Style. Using the Supervisory Styles Inventory (SSI; Friedlander & Ward, 1984; see the Supervisor's Toolbox at the end of the book), Ladany, Walker, and Melincoff (2001) found that supervisory style predicted strength of supervisory alliance. The SSI's three styles (attractive, interpersonally sensitive, and task oriented) correspond generally to Bernard's (1997) three supervisory roles (consultant, counselor, and teacher).

It is interesting, therefore, to note that Ladany et al. (2001) found that use of an attractive supervision style (i.e., consultant role) predicted all three working alliance scales (bond, agreement on tasks, and agreement on goals), whereas use of either an interpersonally sensitive style (i.e., counselor role) or a task-oriented style (i.e., teacher role) predicted agreement on tasks only.

Providing additional support for the SSI was the finding that both the interpersonally sensitive and attractive styles predicted levels of supervisor self-disclosure. The task-oriented style did not.

Chen and Bernstein (2000) also found supervisory style to predict supervisory alliance. Using an intensive case study methodology, they studied attributes and processes of one supervisory dyad with a strong alliance and one with a weak alliance (these were chosen as the dyads with the best and worst working alliances from a sample of 10 dyads). Perhaps unsurprisingly, the two dyads differed in predicted ways on the SSI, regardless of whether the supervisor or the supervisee was rating supervisor style. In both cases, the attractive and interpersonally sensitive styles were more prominent in the dyad with the stronger alliance.

Supervisor Self-disclosure. In their review of the literature on self-disclosure in therapy, Hill and Knox (2002) noted that, although there were relatively few studies of the immediate outcomes of

self-disclosure in therapy, moderate levels of therapist self-disclosure tended to have a positive effect on the therapeutic relationship. Because supervisors are better known to their supervisees than counselors are to clients, and because they serve as role models, it stands to reason that supervisor self-disclosures would have at least as great an impact.

Whereas Ladany et al. (2001) focused on the link between supervisor style and self-disclosure, Ladany and Lehrman-Waterman (1999) were concerned with how supervisor self-disclosure predicted the strength of the supervisory alliance. They found that level of supervisory disclosures (which primarily concerned personal issues, neutral counseling experiences, and counseling struggles) predicted the strength of the supervisory alliance.

Supervisors' Use of Interpersonal Influence. Schultz, Ososkie, Fried, Nelson, and Bardos (2002) had rehabilitation counselors rate both the types of interpersonal influence that their supervisors used and the quality of their supervisory alliances with these supervisors. Social influence (or power) was defined in terms of French and Raven's (1959) taxonomy, wherein one person is assumed to exert influence over another to the extent that she or he uses one or more of five means of persuasion: reward power, coercive power, legitimate power, referent power, and expert power. Schultz et al. found that the greater the supervisor's use of the *expert* (i.e., the perception that the supervisor had knowledge and expertise) and *referent* power bases (i.e., the perception that the supervisor is similar to the supervisee on some dimensions important to the supervisee), the stronger the supervisory alliance. This seems consistent with the social influence research (e.g., Heppner & Claiborn, 1989), which shows that referent power (also referred to as "attractiveness") is related to the client's liking of the therapist.

One unique aspect of this study was that participants were agency-based rehabilitation counselors who had a range of training levels. Their relationships with their supervisors may not have been regular, and it is unclear to what extent the supervision was administrative versus clinical in nature.

Alliance Antecedents: Supervision Processes

Discussions of Ethnic Differences.   Using self-reports of a national sample of psychology interns, Gatmon, Jackson, and Koshkarian (2001) examined the extent to which frank discussions of differences in ethnicity, gender, and sexual orientations affected working alliance. Unsurprisingly, supervisors and supervisees were more likely to have discussed sexual orientation, gender, and ethnicity when between-participant differences existed.

Gatmon et al. (2001) found that supervisor–supervisee discussions of gender and sexual orientation did not predict working alliance. Importantly, though, discussions of similarities and differences in ethnicity predicted working alliance quality. Specifically, these discussions predicted higher levels on the bond subscale of the Working Alliance Inventory (Horvath & Greenburg, 1989). This does not resolve the question of who should initiate these discussions. It does, though, indicate that such discussions are important.

Racial Identity.   We addressed in Chapter 5 the impact of race and ethnicity on supervision. One study, however, warrants repetition here, that of Ladany, Brittan-Powell, and Pannu (1997). They obtained two important findings. One was that racial matching of supervisors and supervisees had no relationship to strength of working alliance. The other finding, though, was that racial identity (Helms, 1990) significantly predicted supervisory alliance. Specifically, supervisors and supervisees who shared high levels of racial identity had the highest agreement on goals and tasks. They also had the strongest emotional bonds.

Negative Supervisory Experiences.   It should be no surprise to anyone that the more negative the supervisory experience, the weaker the supervisory alliance. Ramos-Sánchez et al. (2002), though, confirmed this in their study. They asked a national sample of supervisees to provide both questionnaire data and free-response descriptions of negative experiences from their supervision. Descriptions from 27 (of 121) supervisees of negative supervisory events that they had encountered were coded into the following four categories: *interpersonal relationship and style* (e.g., differing attitudes and personal conflicts); *supervision tasks and responsibilities* (problems related to goals, expectations, activities, roles, and evaluation); *conceptual and theoretical orientation* (supervisor–supervisee conflict over client conceptualization, treatment, or diagnosis); and *ethical, legal, and multicultural issues.*

Ramos-Sánchez et al. (2002) compared participants who reported having experienced at least one negative event with those who had not. They found that the former group reported weaker alliances. Also, those who reported negative experiences reported (1) being less satisfied with supervision, (2) being at a lower developmental level as measured by the Supervisee Levels Questionnaire–Revised (SLQ–R; McNeill, Stoltenberg, & Romans, 1992; see the Supervisor's Toolbox), and (3) having less positive relationships with clients that they were seeing.

In some respects, this study is similar to that of Ladany et al. (1999) regarding supervisors' unethical behavior. In fact, one of the four categories in this study concerns that same phenomenon. But whereas the Ladany et al. study spoke specifically to supervisors' problematic behaviors, this one also included situations in which supervisor and supervisee misunderstood one another, disagreed in theoretical views, or differed in goals.

There are many ways, of course, for the supervisory experience to be made negative for the supervisee. Both Magnuson, Wilcoxon, and Norem (2000) and Nelson (2002) have cataloged ways for supervisors to provide what they termed "lousy" supervision. Box 6.2 lists the 22 ways Nelson found in her review of the literature. Regardless of how obvious items on this list might seem, to have this list in writing provides an important reminder to supervisors of behaviors to avoid.

Box 6.2_____

How to Be a Lousy Supervisor: Lessons from the Research

From Worthen and McNeill (1996)

1. Don't establish a strong supervisory alliance with your supervisee.
2. Don't reveal any of your own shortcomings to your supervisee.
3. Don't provide a sense of safety so that your supervisee can reveal his or her doubts and fears about competency.

From Kozlowska, Nunn, and Cousins (1997)

4. Place the importance of service delivery above your supervisee's educational needs.
5. Ignore your supervisee's need for emotional support in a new and challenging context.

From Wulf and Nelson (2000)

6. Involve your supervisee in the conflicted dynamics among professional staff in your setting.
7. Don't support your supervisee's strengths. Only point out weaknesses.
8. Don't take an interest in your supervisee's interests.
9. Talk mostly about your own cases in supervision.

From Nelson & Friedlander (2001)

10. Don't conduct a role induction process with your supervisee that involves being explicit about his or her and your own expectations about how supervision will proceed.

11. Allow yourself to feel threatened by your supervisee's competencies.
12. Retaliate against your supervisee for being more competent than you are in one or more areas or more mature than you are chronologically.
13. Insist that your supervisee work from the same theoretical orientation that you do.
14. Demand that your supervisee "act like a student rather than a colleague."
15. Criticize your supervisee in front of his or her peers.
16. Deny responsibility for interpersonal conflicts that arise between you and your supervisee.
17. If you sense the presence of conflict in the relationship, don't bring it up.
18. If your relationship with your supervisee becomes difficult, don't consult with someone else about it. It might reveal your lack of competence.
19. Treat your supervisee as a confidante. Use her or him as your counselor.
20. Be sexist, ageist, multiculturally incompetent, and the like.
21. Don't take your supervisee's expressed concerns about any of the above issues seriously.
22. Reveal intimate details about your own sexual experiences to your supervisee.

From M. L. Nelson (October, 2002). How to be a lousy supervisor: Lessons from the research. Paper presented at the convention of the Association for Counselor Education and Supervision, Park City, UT. Reprinted with permission.

Role Conflict and Ambiguity. Olk and Friedlander (1992) suggested that at various points the supervisee may be required to function in the roles of student, client, counselor, or colleague. Then, drawing from organizational psychology literature, they suggested *role ambiguity* or *role conflict* as two role-related problems that a supervisee might face.

Role ambiguity occurs when the supervisee is uncertain about the role expectations that the supervisor and/or agency has for him or her. Role conflict occurs either (1) when the supervisees are required to engage in two or more roles that

may require inconsistent behavior or (2) when the supervisees are required to engage in behavior that is incongruent with their personal judgment. Ladany and Friedlander (1995) provided illustrative examples of each. In the first case, supervisees may be required to reveal personal weaknesses and potential inadequacies while *also* needing to present themselves to the supervisor as competent so that they will pass the practicum. This might be understood as a conflict between the supervisee-as-client and supervisee-as-counselor. In the second case, the supervisor might give directives to behave in a manner that is inconsistent with the supervisee's ethical or theoretical beliefs. Here the conflict is between the roles of supervisee-as-student and supervisee-as-counselor.

To study these two types of supervisee role difficulties, Olk and Friedlander (1992) developed the Role Conflict and Role Ambiguity Inventory (RCRAI). Readers interested in using it in their own research or in monitoring supervisee role difficulties will find the RCRAI in the Supervisor's Toolbox at the end of this book.

Olk and Friedlander (1992) found that many supervisees did not report role difficulties. Those who did, however, were more likely to report work-related anxiety and dissatisfaction as well as dissatisfaction with supervision. They also found that supervisees reported less role ambiguity when they perceived themselves to have been offered clear statements from their supervisors about their expectations for supervision.

In a subsequent study in which they used both the RCRAI and a version of the Working Alliance Inventory (WAI; Horvath & Greenburg, 1989), Ladany and Friedlander (1995) obtained two findings of potential importance to supervisors. One was that the greater the strength of the supervisor–supervisee emotional bond, the less role conflict the supervisee experienced. This may suggest that the stronger their bond, the more likely that supervisor and supervisee will work together to resolve their conflicts. An alternative possibility is that the less role conflict in the first place, the greater the emotional bonds (e.g., with correlational data of this sort, it is possible only to know that these two variables—emotional bond and role conflict—negatively covary with each other).

Nelson and Friedlander (2001) did not specifically examine working alliances in their qualitative study of conflictual supervision that 13 trainees had experienced. However, their results do provide additional data to suggest that role conflict and ambiguity negatively affect the working alliance. In their study, all but one of the trainees scored substantially above the norm group means for both role conflict and role ambiguity. In addition, these trainees rated their supervisors substantially below norm group means for the Attractive and Interpersonally Sensitive scores on the SSI (Friedlander & Ward, 1984).

Supervisory Alliance Outcomes. Although there must be many other outcomes of a strong supervisory alliance, we found three that have been supported by the empirical literature. These are (1) supervisees' willingness to disclose material to their supervisors, (2) adherence to treatment protocols, and (3) quality of the therapeutic alliance between the supervisee and his or her clients.

Supervisees' Willingness to Disclose. Slavin (1994) posed this rhetorical question: "How often have we heard clinicians joke, privately and guiltily, about what they *don't* tell their supervisors?" (p. 256). In so doing, he highlighted a significant problem in supervision: supervisees vary in their willingness to reveal both what Sarnat and Frawley-O'Dea (2001) playfully call "crimes and misdemeanors" and more personal material.

Supervisees' failure to disclose relevant information to supervisors hinders their learning. It also puts the supervisor at risk legally, for the supervisor is liable if the supervisee is engaged in unethical or illegal activities.

For these reasons, we believe that the Ladany, Hill, Corbett, and Nutt (1996) study should rank as among the most important in the supervision literature. They examined what supervisees had failed to disclose to their supervisees and why. We have summarized their results in Box 6.3.

As these results indicate, supervisees report a number of reasons for having failed to disclose material. Although a poor alliance is only one of these, it was reported by half the supervisees. One indicator that these nondisclosures were not trivial is the fact that these supervisees report that 66% of what was not disclosed to supervisors was disclosed elsewhere.

Webb and Wheeler (1998) conducted a somewhat related study. Their focus was on psychodynamically oriented supervisees in Britain. They found that scores on the Rapport scale of the Supervisory Working Alliance Inventory (Efstation

BOX 6.3_____

What Supervisees Fail to Disclose and Why

In their sample of supervisees, Ladany et al. (1996) found the following:

WHAT THEY HAD FAILED TO DISCLOSE

- 90% failed to disclose negative feelings toward a supervisor
- 60% failed to disclose their own personal issues (e.g., thoughts about themselves; experiences; problems)
- 44% failed to disclose clinical mistakes
- 44% failed to disclose uneasiness or concerns about the supervisor's evaluations of them
- 43% failed to disclose general observations about the client (e.g., diagnosis; appearance; interventions; or counseling process)
- 36% failed to disclose negative (critical, disapproving, or unpleasant) reactions to the client

- 25% failed to disclose thoughts or feelings of attraction toward the client
- 23% failed to disclose positive feelings toward the supervisor
- 22% failed to disclose countertransference reactions to client

REASONS FOR NOT DISCLOSING

- 73%: perceived to be too personal
- 62%: perceived to be unimportant
- 51%: negative feelings such as shame, embarrassment, or discomfort
- 55%: feelings of deference (i.e., it was not his or her place to bring up material that would be uncomfortable to the supervisor)
- 50%: poor alliance with the supervisor
- 46%: impression management (i.e., to avoid being perceived negatively)

---

et al., 1990) predicted supervisees' willingness to report sensitive material to their supervisors.

Adherence to Treatment Protocols. Manualized treatments have been greeted with suspicion or even disdain by many mental health professionals who regard adherence to a protocol as an unnecessary constraint on their use of professional judgment and creativity. However, as Lambert and Arnold (1987) have pointed out, the use of treatment manuals is an excellent way for supervisees to learn a particular approach. Importantly, then, Holloway and Neufeldt (1995) suggested that the quality of the supervisory relationship should affect the level of trainees' adherence to a treatment manual.

Therefore, the results of Patton and Kivlighan's (1997) study are significant. In their examination of supervisees' adherence to a particular treatment model (Strupp and Binder's, 1984, time-limited psychodynamic therapy), they found that week-to-week fluctuations in the supervisory alliance accounted for a substantial portion of the week-

to-week fluctuations in adherence to general psychodynamic interviewing skills. The supervisory alliance did not, however, predict the use of specific manualized techniques.

Therapeutic Alliances. This same study by Patton and Kivlighan (1997) also provided evidence of one other important consequence of effective supervisory alliances. As we discussed earlier with respect to parallel processes, Patton and Kivlighan found that week-to-week fluctuations in the supervisory alliance predicted week-to-week fluctuations in the supervisee–client working alliance. This is an important finding, for it permits an inferential link between quality of supervision and client outcomes. That is, (1) client–therapist working alliances have been shown to predict therapeutic outcome (Horvath & Symonds, 1991; Orlinsky, Grawe, & Parks, 1994), (2) the Patton and Kivlighan study establishes a link between supervisory and therapeutic alliance, and (3) it is therefore possible to infer that supervisory alliances affect client outcomes.

The Supervisory Alliance
as a Dynamic Process

Sullivan's statement, "God keep me from a therapy that goes well!" can be extended to "Keep me from a supervisory relationship that goes well!" Going well may mean that there is more superficiality in the relationship, but less anxiety; a more comfortable atmosphere, but limited interpersonal engagement; a greater sense of certainty, but complexities are dissociated; more interpretations, but little structural change in the relatedness between the participants . . . disappointments and struggles have more likely been avoided, but the potential richness and joy of a significant relationship [are] lost.

(Lesser, 1983, p. 128)

In the preceding section, the implication was that the supervisory alliance is relatively stable: Its quality will be affected by factors such as those we discussed, but the changes occur in a relatively predictable way over time. It is equally valid, though, to employ a process view and consider the supervisory alliance as something that will fluctuate in quality and intensity. Lesser's (1983) quote immediately above effectively sets the stage for this discussion. We will employ this process perspective in this section.

Betcher and Zinberg (1988) asserted that supervisory and therapeutic relationships are similar in several important ways. One is that participants have the capacity to undo the human errors that they make, especially with one another. This is a particularly important aspect of the supervisory relationship. In fact, a central thesis of Mueller and Kell's (1972) now classic supervision book, *Coping with Conflict,* was that in any relationship, whether personal or professional, conflict inevitably will occur between or among the parties. This conflict can stem from conflicting goals that the two parties entertain, from a "mistake" that one party in the relationship has made, or through the repetition of a maladaptive interpersonal pattern. The manner in which the parties resolve, or fail to resolve, this conflict will dictate whether the relationship continues to grow and develop or

stagnates. This is similar to Bordin's (1983) assertion that (1) alliances undergo a continual "weakening and repair" (also referred to as "tear–repair," "rupture–repair," or "disruption–restoration") process and (2) this process constitutes a vehicle for therapeutic change.

It is likely that most supervisory relationship weakenings or conflicts are resolved within a single session. Some, however, last longer. In a relatively informal study of supervision with psychiatric residents, Nigam, Cameron, and Leverette (1997) examined supervisory "impasses" as stalemates that lasted at least three to four weeks. Interestingly, 40% of the respondents reported having experienced at least one such impasse as supervisees. The usefulness of this descriptive study was in its cataloging of types of interpersonal problems between the supervisor and supervisee that led to impasses including boundary violations; lack of acceptance of a trainee's sexual identity; inhibition of disclosure of pertinent information.

Finally, we should note that a few supervisor–supervisee conflicts never are resolved. When these are serious in nature, the supervisee can suffer lasting consequences (cf. Nelson & Friedlander, 2001). In these cases, clients, too, can be affected. Arkowitz (2001) noted that "A supervisee injured in supervision will act out these injuries with the patient, in confused attempts to repair them" (p. 59). Some support for this is provided by the finding of Ramos-Sánchez et al. (2002) that supervisees who had experienced problematic supervision experienced not only weaker supervisory alliances, but also less strong relationships with their clients.

Figure 6.4 visually models the weakening–repair process across just two conflict–resolution sequences in what actually is a series of such sequences that occur over the history of a supervisor–supervisee relationship. For the purposes of this figure, the sequences are punctuated to begin with a relationship conflict. If the relationship is then "repaired," it is strengthened and grows; if the relationship is *not* repaired, it suffers and is diminished. This sequence is repeated over time (the

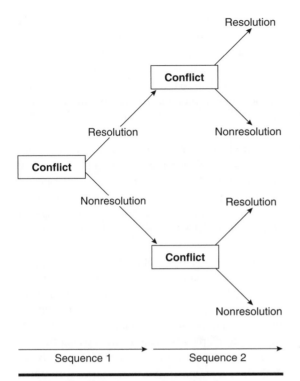

FIGURE 6.4 Conflictual Sequences and Relationship Trajectory

number and frequency of these sequences vary with the particular relationship). Each iteration is an opportunity for strengthening or weakening of the relationship.

This figure oversimplifies, of course, for it is unlikely that a supervisor–supervisee conflict will be either resolved or not in a dichotomous manner. In real life, the resolution can be understood as occurring in some degree. But this figure is useful in making the point that relationships have a history of a series of conflict–resolution sequences and that the overall course of a particular supervisory relationship will be affected by the successes in resolving these conflicts.

Supervisee–supervisor conflicts can arise from many sources, some of which are more problematic than others. It is useful to consider them as types that occur on a continuum from (1) those that occur as a function of either a supervisor

mistake or a miscommunication between the two, (2) those that occur because of normative processes, and (3) those that occur as a function of interpersonal dynamics and expectations of the supervisee. Each provides a learning opportunity. In the section that follows, each of these types is discussed in turn.

Conflicts Arising from Miscommunications or Mismatched Expectations. Evaluative feedback seems to make the supervisory relationship particularly vulnerable to conflict (Robiner, Fuhrman, & Risvedt, 1993). We already have noted that Ladany et al. (1999) found that a third of supervisee-reported ethical breaches were related to evaluation and that Lehrman-Waterman and Ladany (2001) found that the clearer the evaluation process, the less supervisee anxiety and the stronger the supervisory alliance.

These findings were confirmed in the only study yet to examine the weakening–repair process in supervisory alliances. In their observations of within-session tear–repair processes within 10 consecutive sessions of 10 supervisory dyads, Burke, Goodyear, and Guzzard (1998) found that the more affect-arousing and difficult to repair weakenings occurred as supervisors assumed evaluative roles. They also observed that the type of weakening events varied according to the experience level of the trainees. For example, alliance-weakening events with more advanced trainees were more likely to involve disagreements about theoretical or treatment-planning issues.

The February 2000 issue of the *Journal of Clinical Psychology: In Session: Psychotherapy in Practice* was devoted to the therapeutic alliance. Many of the alliance conflicts or ruptures that the several articles described were a function of either misunderstandings or disagreements on the goals or tasks of therapy (or, by extension, supervision). In their response to these articles, Safran and Muran (2000) discussed interventions that the therapist (or supervisor) could use in response to these misunderstandings or disagreements. Among them were these:

- **Direct intervention.** This involves (1) clarifying to the client (or supervisee) the rationale for the intervention and (2) addressing any misunderstandings that he or she might have.
- **Indirect intervention.** This involves giving particular attention to the tasks and goals that have relevance to the client (or supervisee), rather than trying to address the underlying conflict.

We already have noted that supervisees (and supervisors) are relatively less burdened by rigid or exaggerated personality styles than are clients. The quality and strength of their relationships are generally good. Therefore, direct intervention is likely the better option in most cases in which a supervisory conflict has arisen because of either a misunderstanding or incongruent expectations.

Normative Conflicts. Some supervisee–supervisor conflict is normative and occurs in response to the supervisee's developmental level. In particular, Rønnestad and Skovholt (1993) suggested that both supervisor–supervisee tension and dissatisfaction with supervision may be at its greatest with the more advanced student. Like most adolescents, supervisees at this level vacillate between feelings of confidence and insecurity. Rønnestad and Skovholt note that "The student has now actively assimilated information from many sources but still has not had enough time to accommodate and find her or his own way of behaving professionally" (p. 400). This is not, in itself, a matter for concern, particularly if the supervisor is able to understand and anticipate this particular developmental phenomenon.

Conflicts Arising from Participants' Interpersonal Dynamics. Probably the best known research program to focus on the resolution of therapeutic alliance ruptures is that of Safran and Muran (1996, 2000). Many of their observations apply as well to supervisory alliances, with one important caveat: In most cases, the maladaptive interpersonal cycle to which they refer is less prominent in supervision, for most supervisees will have less rigid or negative expectations about

others than will clients and therefore are less likely to elicit a complementary response from their supervisors. With this caveat, it is useful to consider Safran and Muran's observations. We will use their language and discuss client–therapist interactions. In most cases, though, it is reasonable to understand that these same observations apply as well to supervisee–supervisor interactions.

Safran and Muran note that there are two major subtypes of alliance ruptures, though they often work in some degree of combination with one another. In one, the *confrontation* rupture, the client will directly express unhappiness or even anger at some aspect of the therapy or the therapist. In *withdrawal* ruptures, the client disengages from the therapist or some aspect of the therapeutic process.

Therapists' initial attempts to resolve the ruptures often are complementary to the client's response, putting them into the role of perpetuating the "maladaptive interpersonal cycle" (Safran & Muran, 2000, p. 240). That is, therapists often respond to confrontation ruptures defensively or with their own anger and to withdrawal ruptures with their own controlling behavior. These responses generally replicate those of other people in the clients' lives.

To be effective, it is essential that the therapist be able to (1) be aware of his or her own reactions that the client has elicited and then (2) rather than participating further in the maladaptive interpersonal cycle, begin metacommunicating, that is, to communicate about their communications.

> *The process of extricating oneself from the dysfunctional dance that is being enacted is facilitated by inviting the client to take a step back and join with the therapist in a process of examining or metacommunicating about what is currently going on between them. The therapist's task is to identify his or her own feelings and to use these as a point of departure for collaborative exploration.* (p. 238)

The therapist's purpose is to help clients to learn that they can express their needs without endangering the therapeutic alliance. To do this, therapists have at least the following options in metacommunicating about an alliance rupture for tailoring their response to the specific client.

- Share his or her personal reactions and feelings by giving specific examples of client behaviors that might elicit them. "I feel dismissed or closed out by you, and I think it's because you don't seem to me to pause and reflect in a way that suggests you are really considering what I am saying" (Safran & Muran, 2000, p. 238). The therapist should then follow up with an inquiry such as "How does this match your perceptions?" to elicit the client's response.
- In response to the client's withdrawal or confrontation, offer an empathic statement as means both to convey understanding and to invite the client to explore the issue.
- Offer a more interpretive response, especially to clients who have limited access to their inner experience or who find it too anxiety provoking or chaotic to explore.

These seem useful strategies for the supervisor as well. Of the three, the last strategy is least likely to be of use in supervision to resolve impasses. That is, we can assume that most supervisees have reasonable access to their inner experience.

Mental health professionals generally acknowledge that therapists may not be expected to form an effective working relationship with every client that they see: Why should we have a different expectation for supervision? In the (fortunately rare) cases of intractable personality conflicts, the responsible supervisor will transfer the supervisee to another supervisor or otherwise work to protect the supervisee's interests. However, to be sensitive to the issues that we have raised here is likely to minimize the frequency with which such conflicts happen.

In summary, conflict occurs in any relationship, including that between supervisor and supervisee. The manner in which it is resolved affects the overall course and strength of the relationship and also provides useful learning opportunities for both supervisor and supervisee. In other sections of this book, we address the resolution of conflict. However, this section has given particular emphasis to the importance of the process.

CONCLUSION

More than any other, this chapter demonstrates just how complex the supervisory relationship is. It provides a compelling case for a supervisor to have good interpersonal skills, good clinical skills—and specific training in supervision.

CHAPTER 7

THE SUPERVISORY RELATIONSHIP
SUPERVISEE AND SUPERVISOR
CONTRIBUTING FACTORS

This is the second of two chapters in which we specifically address the supervisory relationship. We noted in Chapter 6 that to examine the supervisory relationship is akin to examining a forest through a telescope. Using that metaphor, we organized Chapter 6 to examine, in turn, two telescopic "focal ranges": that of the supervisory triad and then that of the dyad. In this chapter, we continue to use our figurative telescope, this time refocusing it to examine individual contributions of the supervisee and supervisor to the quality and effectiveness of the supervisory relationship.

Chapter 5 shares similarities with this chapter in that it focuses on individual differences and factors of supervisees and supervisors. Certainly, the variables addressed in that chapter affect the supervisory relationship. But, whereas Chapter 5 stresses between-supervisee and supervisor differences, our concern here is with more dynamic processes that affect the nature and the quality of the dyadic relationship.

The chapter has two sections. The first focuses on factors specific to the supervisee. The second focuses on factors specific to the supervisor. Because this book is intended to improve the work of supervisors, we discuss implications for supervisors in both sections. The supervisor and supervisee factors that we cover in this chapter are depicted in Figure 7.1.

THE SUPERVISEE IN THE RELATIONSHIP

Supervisee issues about attachment style, shame, anxiety, need for competence, and transference all affect the effectiveness and quality of the supervisor–supervisee relationship. As Figure 7.1 indicates, though, we are anchoring our discussions of these supervisee variables to the concept of resistance. It may seem in so doing that we are attending only to negative issues in the relationship. But, in fact, we understand supervisee behavior to exist on a continuum, with fully resistant behavior on one end and, on the other, an ideal relationship in which the supervisee feels and acts fully engaged.

Supervisee Resistance

The concept of client resistance in psychotherapy originated with psychoanalysis, but has found much broader application. In fact, a recent issue of the *Journal of Clinical Psychology: In Session: Psychotherapy in Practice* (February 2002) was comprised of articles that each offered a different theoretical perspective on client resistance. Beutler, Moleiro, and Talebi (2002a) wrote an integrative response to these various articles, beginning it with the assertion that

> *While they disagree with one another in many ways, the 400+ theories of psychotherapy that are practiced in contemporary society converge on the curious observation that some painfully distressed patients seeking assistance from expensive and highly trained professionals reject their therapists' best advice, fail to act in their own best interests, and do not respond to the most effective interventions that can be mustered on their behalf. . . . [but] While the descriptions offered of resistant behavior by dif-*

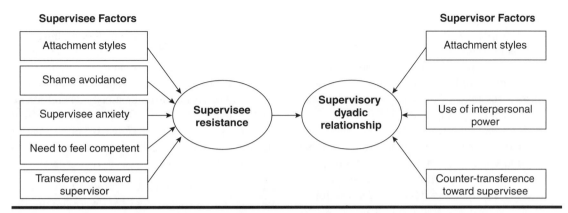

FIGURE 7.1 Supervisee and Supervisor Factors That Affect the Nature and Quality of the Supervisory Dyad

ferent theories are similar, they offer dramatically different explanations and intervention methods. (p. 207)

These observations concerned resistance in therapy. But they apply as well to supervision (cf. Bradley & Gould, 1994; Pearson, 2000), despite its educational rather than therapeutic purpose. Whether supervisors intentionally employ the concept of resistance, the phenomenon is there to be addressed. McColley and Baker (1982), for example, found that most novice supervisors that they surveyed identified their primary difficulty to be that of not knowing how to intervene effectively with trainee resistance.

Liddle (1986) suggested that supervisees' resistance should be understood as self-protective behavior that they employ in the face of some threat. It is likely that this conception accounts for many or even most instances of supervisee resistance. But supervisee resistance also can originate from other sources, including the supervisee's need to individuate from the supervisor (i.e., a developmental issue), supervisor–supervisee conflict, and disagreements about tasks and goals.

Before going farther, we want to assert that we introduce this discussion of supervisee resistance with some trepidation. In particular, we recognize how readily the language of resistance can result in blaming supervisees. Such blaming is wrong at

a conceptual level, because resistance can arise from a number of sources and often is a healthy response by the supervisee to a perceived threat. It also is wrong at a practical level, because it invites supervisor irritation or even anger toward the supervisee, which almost certainly will be counterproductive. Moreover, it also inappropriately absolves supervisors from interpersonal consequences of their own behaviors (see, e.g., Beutler et al., 2002b). Therefore, we hope the material in this chapter will be read with the understanding that supervisee resistance is a challenge to be addressed, but for which *blame* should not be invoked at all.

Manifestations of Supervisee Resistance. The term *resistance* implies that supervisees are resisting something. But both the target and style of supervisee resistance can vary substantially. The following four categories of resistance that we developed are imprecise and overlapping, but give some sense of the scope of supervisee resistance. Supervisees can:

1. *Resist the supervisor's influence* (e.g., by being nondisclosive about his or her behaviors or experiences; by deflecting discussions away from particular topics, or from a focus on some aspect of his or her behavior; by engaging in what the supervisor experiences as power struggles).

2. *Resist the supervisory experience itself* (which may be difficult to differentiate from the above). This is exemplified by Epstein's (2001) comment that "I operate on the assumption that persisting negative behaviors, such as lateness or missing sessions, are resistances signifying negative reactions to supervision" (p. 150).

3. *Be noncompliant with tasks related to the supervisory process.* A frequent example is that of supervisees' use of audio- or videotaping. Although we later will discuss the recent study by Ellis, Krengel, and Beck (2002), who found otherwise, we still find taping to raise supervisees' anxiety levels. Therefore, they often will resist doing so, sometimes overtly, sometimes through more indirect means such as projecting their fear on the client ("it will upset the client too much and therefore disrupt the therapy"), or by forgetting to bring equipment or tapes.

4. *Be noncompliant with mutually agreed upon plans with respect to clients.* This would apply, especially, to the implementation of particular interventions.

Circumstances That Elicit Supervisee Resistance. Many factors affect supervisee resistance. Those we discuss in the material immediately below all concern interpersonal processes. We follow that with a discussion of supervisee attributes.

Supervisee Trust. There is an old aphorism, "trust is efficient." That is, in interpersonal relationships, to trust means to relax vigilance, which consumes both energy and time. In general, the higher the supervisee's level of trust in the supervisor, the less he or she will need to exhibit the self-protective behavior that occurs as resistance; and, the less supervisee resistance, the more effective the supervisory relationship.

Trustworthiness, as discussed by Strong (1968), accrues to the counselor (or, here, the supervisor) as the client (or the supervisee) is able to believe that he or she is acting professionally and not in a way to exploit the relationship to meet his or her own needs. It creates an atmosphere of safety.

One characteristic of trust is that it always exists in some degree: It is not an all or nothing phenomenon. Another characteristic of trust is that it is earned over the course of many interactions and interpersonal risks taken together; it is not something that can occur instantaneously. Therefore, no single supervisor intervention or technique will earn a supervisee's trust. Trust is simply one of those broad goals that supervisors must work to achieve and maintain.

Client Issues Transmitted by Parallel Processes. Ekstein and Wallerstein (1972) were among the first authors to discuss supervisee resistance. They noted that it can arise by parallel processes, so that supervisee resistant behavior is a mirroring of the client's attitudes and behaviors, such as we discussed in Chapter 6.

Disagreement about Tasks and Goals. Supervisees are likely to become resistant when they do not agree with the tasks and goals of the supervisor. Resistance in this case can be understood as relationship rupture and is handled as we discussed in Chapter 6.

Supervisor Directiveness. Proctor and Inskipp (1988) made the useful distinction between *must* and *can* supervisory interventions. *Must* interventions are those that supervisors employ when they want to ensure that the supervisee will take some very specific action, for client welfare and other reasons. A *can* intervention, though, is one in which the supervisee has the choice about whether and when she or he might take a particular action.

Must interventions are more likely to arouse resistance. This is especially true when the supervisee does not understand or agree with the rationale for the intervention and therefore perceives the supervisor's intervention as an arbitrary directive. Brehm and Brehm (1981) discussed the concept of reactance as opposition that manifests itself when people perceive their freedom of choice and/or action being constrained: The less voice people (supervisees included) are given, the more oppositional they will behave. This concept is useful in understanding how it is that *must* interventions that are misunderstood or perceived as being arbitrary will elicit resistance.

Supervisee Trait Reactance. Brehm and Brehm (1981) conceptualized reactance as situation specific. However, Dowd (1989) and others later conceptualized reactance as a trait that each person possesses to a greater or lesser degree. A highly reactant person is hypersensitive to losses of freedom and is especially vigilant in the presence of people of authority.

Developmental Level. Various developmental models have shown supervisees to differ in their levels of resistance according to their levels of development (Rønnestad & Skovholt, 1993; Stoltenberg, McNeill, & Delworth, 1998). Much as an adolescent who needs to begin individuating, supervisees at particular levels will begin to assert themselves.

Interventions. Various interventions we discuss throughout this chapter are useful in addressing supervisee resistance. However, we want to highlight some selectively here.

Supervision Focus. Supervisory focus can affect supervisees' felt vulnerability, which in turn elicits reactance. Specifically, vulnerability is least when the supervisory focus is on the client (i.e., on case conceptualization issues), rather than on the supervisee's personhood or behavior. Therefore, case conceptualization might be given greater initial emphasis with supervisees whom the supervisor perceives to feel especially vulnerable.

In the following, Epstein (2001) is speaking as well to supervisor style:

> I favor, whenever possible, the use of what Spotznitz (1969) has termed "object-oriented questions" as contrasted with "ego-oriented questions." These questions direct the supervisee's attention to faults of the other, to myself, or to the patient rather than to his own faults. This technique might appear to further the supervisee's tendency to externalize responsibility for his own contribution to the failure of the supervision or of the treatment situation. Actually, it has the opposite effect. Object-oriented questions establish an atmosphere in which the supervisee becomes increasingly free, with a minimal sense of risk, to contact and directly communicate all of his feelings vis-á-vis both the supervision and his patient. (p. 298)

Supervisor Style. To the extent that the supervisee feels in control, his or her resistance will be minimized. This is especially true of those supervisees who are highly reactant. Beutler et al. (2002b) noted that it is useful for therapists to use one of the available scales to assess client reactance and then to calibrate their levels of directiveness accordingly. That is, the greater the client's reactance, the less directive and authoritative the therapist. In fact, with highly reactant clients, therapists might consider using defiance-based paradoxical techniques.

Although supervisees are unlikely to demonstrate the range of reactance that clients do, they will differ in their levels of it. Therefore, these guidelines reasonably can apply in supervision as well. Of the several supervisory styles or roles (Bernard, 1997), that of the consultant is probably least threatening and maximizes supervisees' sense of control. IPR (Kagan & Kagan, 1997) is a technique that is almost entirely consultive in style and therefore useful to use.

Supervisee Countertransference. Epstein (2001) noted that in some cases what may seem resistance to the supervision may actually reside elsewhere. For example, it could be that failure to carry through with agreed-upon interventions with the client stems from some particularly strong countertransference reaction to the client. In this case, the supervisor's intervention is one of helping the supervisee identify and express whatever those reactions might be.

Summary Comments about Supervisee Resistance. Supervisee resistance can be thought of as the supervisee applying the brakes when he or she perceives the vehicle that is supervision to be moving too fast, in the wrong direction, or on a too bumpy road. In most instances, the resistance will be akin to gently tapping the brakes. There are some instances, though, in which the supervisee will figuratively "lock-'em-up." For the supervisor to be effective, she or he should create a climate that minimizes supervisees' felt need to put on the brakes. As well, she or he must be alert to instances of resistance and then make informed decisions about the best response. In general, the best supervision will be that in which the least resistance occurs.

Patton, Kivlighan, and Multon (1997) report a pattern of resistance in counseling whereby the client initially displays low levels of resistance, then high levels, and then ends with low levels again. It is unclear how well this might apply to supervision. However, it would be useful for supervision process researchers to examine such possible patterns.

For the remainder of this portion of the chapter that concerns the supervisee, we will address specific *supervisee* factors that affect resistance and therefore the quality of the dyad relationship. We begin with attachment and then examine shame, anxiety, the need for competence, and finally transference.

Supervisee Attachment

From their review of the literature, Baumeister and Leary (1995) concluded that the evidence is strong in both that ''the need to belong is a powerful, fundamental, and extremely pervasive motivation'' (p. 497) and that difficulties maintaining attachments are associated with a variety of personal problems. In short, people are "hard wired" to be relational.

Attachment theory suggests ways in which a person expresses his or her need to belong. Bowlby (1977), attachment theory's primary developer, stated that "Briefly put, attachment behavior is conceived as any form of behavior that results in a person attaining or retaining proximity to some other differentiated and preferred individual, who is usually conceived as stronger and/or wiser" (p. 203).

Watkins (1995c; Pistole & Watkins, 1995) suggested that supervision is an attachment process

that involves the development and eventual loosening of an affectional bond. The supervisory relationship has many similarities to both parent–child relationships and many adult–adult relationships. Watkins argued, therefore, that attachment theory has useful implications for understanding supervisor–supervisee relationships.

Bowlby (1977, 1978) described two primary pathological attachment patterns or styles. One is *anxious attachment;* the other, *compulsive self-reliance.* A third, which is something of a variant on the second, is *compulsive caregiving.* Bowlby argued that a person's style (i.e., the way he or she approaches and maintains relationships) is learned during childhood, based on experiences with parents and other caregivers. The style then persists throughout life in relationships with important others, regardless of the style's current appropriateness. It endures across people and situations.

A supervisee with an anxious attachment style is likely to be very dependent and even "clingy," to call the supervisor constantly for help, to want to be the supervisor's favorite, and to resent the supervisor for not needing him or her in a reciprocal way. A supervisee who is a compulsive caregiver is likely to "rescue" clients, working to immediately lessen their concerns and problems (often at the expense of letting them fully grapple with and find resolution to their issues); this supervisee also is likely to be uncomfortable and even anxious in the supervisory context where she or he is the recipient of the supervisor's help and support. And a compulsively self-reliant supervisee is likely to refuse, resist, or even resent the supervisor's attempts to help.

Watkins (1995c) suggested that when supervisors encounter a supervisee with a pathological attachment style, they will feel caught up in something they may not initially understand. That is, they may be concerned about what they may have done to provoke the supervisee's responses, wonder about their competence, and feel quite exasperated. Watkins suggested that, for the relatively rare supervisee who actually does meet criterion for one of these three pathological attachment styles, psychotherapy is the appropriate intervention.

Watkins (1995c) noted that even though many supervisees may exhibit features of one or another of these three patterns, most have a sufficiently secure attachment style to allow supervision to occur in a satisfactory manner. Nevertheless, it is useful for supervisors to have these behavioral styles in mind as ways to conceptualize problematic bonding that is occurring between them and their supervisees.

We are aware of no studies of supervisee attachment as a predictor of supervisory alliance. Foster (2002), though, found that, compared to supervisees who rated themselves as having a secure attachment to their supervisors, those with fearful or preoccupied attachment were less interested in their work, less able to use self-referential perceptions to understand their clients, and less advanced in their overall development. None of these relationships was obtained, however, when the supervisor (as opposed to the supervisee) was rating supervisee attachment and level of supervisee development. This led Foster to conclude that supervisors and supervisees have differential perceptions of supervisees' attachment style and its relationship to supervisee development.

The Role of Supervisee Shame in Supervision

Although some people are especially shame prone (e.g., those who are narcissistic; Miller, 1996), it is an emotion we all experience. Moreover, it is one that supervision is especially likely to elicit in supervisees because of its evaluative components and the requirement that supervisees expose themselves and their work. Yet, as Hahn (2002) pointed out, only a little (e.g., Alonso & Rutan, 1988; Ladmilla, 1997) has been written about the role of supervisee shame in supervision. Because of its potentially detrimental effects on both the supervisee and the supervisory relationship, supervisee shame warrants more attention than it has so far received.

Shame, embarrassment, and guilt are self-conscious emotions. Of the three, guilt and shame seem the two that are most often confused. Lewis (1971) made what has become the generally ac-

cepted distinction between the two: That is, in shame, the focus of evaluation is the self (i.e., "I am flawed"), whereas in guilt, it is some thing (act, thought, etc.) that the person has performed ("I have done something wrong").

Tangney, Wagner, Fletcher, and Gramzow (1992) noted that "in guilt, behavior is evaluated somewhat apart from the self. There is remorse or regret over the "bad thing" that was done and a sense of tension that often serves to motivate reparative action. . . . Whereas guilt motivates a desire to repair, to confess, apologize, or make amends, shame motivates a desire to hide—to sink into the floor and disappear" (pp. 669–670).

Shame requires that the person experiencing it have a basic notion of the self and that she or he engage in some form of self-evaluation (Lewis, 2000). As well, shame has two other attributes that are particularly important to supervision. One is that it involves a sense of exposure or of being exposed; the other is that for it to occur there must be some level of bond between the person and the "observing other" (Retzinger, 1998).

Gilbert (1998) suggested that there are two basic categories of response to shame: submissive and aggressive. In his discussion of shame in supervision, Hahn (2002) drew from Nathanson (1992) to identify four common supervisee reactions to shame. The first two would fit Gilbert's passive category; the second two, the aggressive category. These are described next.

Withdrawal. Withdrawal can occur as a momentary response to shame (e.g., by pulling back, breaking eye contact). But, depending on the strength and pervasiveness of the shame reaction, supervisees can manifest withdrawal across time as forgetfulness, coming late to sessions, and even the adoption of a passive, noncurious style of interaction with the supervisor.

Avoidance. Whereas withdrawal is a more passive way to "minimize shame, avoidance reactions are relatively active efforts to prevent exposure and condemnation" (Hahn, 2002, p. 276). Among the many avoidance strategies that supervisees might employ are diverting the supervisor's attention away from their mistakes and failures and encouraging the supervisor to provide his or her own observations and wisdom about a particular case (versus exposing their own knowledge, feelings, or skills).

Attack on Others.   This externalizing behavior can vary in intensity from mild dismissiveness and devaluing of the supervisor (Yerushalmi, 1999) to more overt, hostile criticism. It is most likely to occur as a response to shame that is triggered by feeling devalued or in some way diminished by the supervisor (a feeling that can be based on an actual supervisor behavior or by some supervisee's unmet expectation of which the supervisor is unaware).

Attack on Self.   This internalizing behavior "also occurs on a continuum and may be manifested as deference on one end of the continuum to excessive self-criticism on the other" (Hahn, 2001, p. 280). Hahn notes that in supervision this defensive style can be used as a "preemptive strike": By criticizing himself or herself, the supervisor is deflected from doing so. A primary motivation for this strategy often is for the supervisee to maintain emotional connection with the supervisor.

Supervisor Responses.   The supervisor's role in addressing supervisee shame probably can be clustered into two types. The first is to create an environment that is minimally shame inducing. There is no single way to accomplish this. Among other things, it involves the supervisor creating a climate of trust and respect and employing a style and providing feedback in a way that is least likely to arouse shame (see, e.g., the Claiborn, Goodyear, & Horner, 2002, review of feedback in psychotherapy).

The second supervisor role is to recognize signs that the supervisee is or has been experiencing shame. For this second role, to be aware of these four major responses to supervisee shame provides supervisors with a conceptual tool to guide their responses.

Alonso and Rutan (1988) offered supervisory suggestions to enable the supervisee to examine

"secret failures that [he or she] was too horrified to admit" (p. 580). One is that the supervisor contribute to the supervisee's sense of dignity and security by offering consistent support and backing. Another is that supervisors take the risk of disclosing to supervisees embarrassing moments in their own work.

Bridges (1999) argued for creating a "shame free learning milieu." She suggested that this would have a couple of elements. One is to "normalize the trainee's shame, powerlessness, and self-consciousness about not knowing, being a trainee, and struggle with personal, painful feelings . . . helps create an interpersonal environment where self-exposure, risk taking, and clinical curiosity are possible" (p. 220). As one means to accomplish this normalization, she suggests that the supervisor be willing to share his or her own "mistakes, humiliating clinical moments, and examples of countertransference domination with attention to how to understand and manage these dilemmas" (p. 220).

Hemlick (1998) developed a measure of supervisee shame as her dissertation research. Perhaps with it and other such instruments, it will be possible to learn more about the role of shame in supervision—and then possible appropriate roles for supervisors.

Supervisee Anxiety

Supervisees experiences anxiety on *two* fronts: in their work with the client and in that with the supervisor. With respect to the latter front, there are many possible sources of anxiety, the most prominent of which is ambiguity—about expectations and roles and about the criteria and procedures of evaluation. Moreover, anxiety is related to experience level, with beginning students more vulnerable to it (cf. Chapin & Ellis, 2002).

One of the really striking findings in Skovholt and Rønnestad's (1992a, 1992b) qualitative study of therapists across the life-span was of the intense anxiety experienced by graduate students. Interestingly, though, they were less able to access this anxiety from their graduate student informants than they were from more senior practitioners who were reflecting back on their experiences in graduate school.

Whereas anxiety is a fact of life for the supervisee, there is no simple or uniform way to characterize it. This is so because a supervisee's anxiety may arise from a number of sources and is moderated by such factors as the supervisee's maturity, experience level, personality, and relationships with clients and the supervisor. In the material that follows, we will address, in turn, the (1) effects of supervisee anxiety, (2) sources, and (3) possible supervisor responses.

Effects of Anxiety on the Supervisee. In general, it is possible to think of three effects of supervisee anxiety (either the reaction to its actual presence or behaviors intended to forestall it occurring): (1) the supervisee's ability to learn, (2) how well she or he is able to demonstrate already present skills, and (3) his or her manner of responding to the supervisor. This is depicted visually in Figure 7.2. The first two are not necessarily related to the issue of resistance, which is the primary concept driving this section of the chapter, but are important and warrant attention.

Supervisee Learning. Although all learning processes begin with observation, a person's capacity to observe is reduced during states of high anxiety

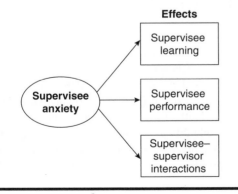

Effects

FIGURE 7.2 Consequence of Supervisee Anxiety

(Dombeck & Brody, 1995). For this reason, supervisee anxiety is a factor that can interfere with how much supervisees can profit from supervision.

This is not to suggest, though, that supervisee anxiety is always something to ward off. As counselors or therapists, we know that much of the time it is unhelpful to rush in with attempts to diminish a client's anxiety. The same rule pertains to supervisors' response to supervisee anxiety. Rioch (in Rioch, Coulter, & Weimberger, 1976) is among those who have observed that, within limits, the more anxiety counselors are able to allow themselves, the more they will learn. In part, this is because being able to "stay with" anxiety can be useful in identifying problem areas, either in what the client is presenting or in the supervisee's own history and characteristic ways of responding.

Supervisee Performance. Supervisee performance is concerned with what the supervisee actually has learned. When discussed in the context of anxiety, it certainly overlaps heavily with the process of supervisee learning. However, there is enough difference that we treat them distinctly here.

Friedlander, Keller, Peca-Baher, and Olk (1986) found that trainees' performance was inversely related to their anxiety levels. This is not to suggest, though, that supervisee anxiety always is to be minimized. Despite some conceptual and empirical questions about it (e.g., Matthews, Davies, & Lees, 1990; Neiss, 1988), Yerkes and Dodson's (1908) inverted-U hypothesis depicted visually in Figure 7.3, remains a useful way to think of anxiety. This is one of psychology's most famous hypotheses: that anxiety is an arousal state that, in moderate amounts, serves to motivate the individual and to facilitate task performance. Performance suffers, however, when the individual experiences either *too little* and *too much* anxiety: too little, and one lacks sufficient motivation to perform; too much, and one is debilitated.

If there is an optimal level of anxiety for supervisees to experience, then supervisors logically have the simultaneous goals of (1) helping to keep their supervisees from engaging in anxiety-avoidant behaviors and of (2) helping to keep

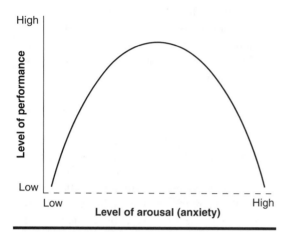

FIGURE 7.3 Depiction of the Yerkes–Dodson Inverted-U Hypothesis Regarding the Relationship between Level of Arousal and Level of Performance

supervisee anxiety in bounds so that it works in the service of performance. Kell and Burow (1970) noted, for example, that they worked "not only to facilitate . . . an awareness of the anxiety associated with the seriousness of learning, but also to leaven and help control the anxious experience" (p. 184).

One factor that affects supervisee anxiety, and therefore performance, is the fact that their work is observed and evaluated. To understand these effects on performance, it is useful to turn to social facilitation theory, which "focuses on changes in performance that occur when individuals perform in the presence of others versus alone" (Aiello & Douthitt, 2001, p. 163). Although this theory has a 100-year history, Aiello and Douthitt credit Zajonc (1965) for developing its contemporary version.

Zajonc distinguished between dominant responses (those it is easiest for the person to perform) and nondominant responses (those that are part of the person's skill repertoire, but are less likely to be performed). He noted that increases in arousal will facilitate performance of dominant responses, but impede performance of nondominant responses.

Athletics is a useful domain from which to draw to illustrate this effect. Olympic athletes have overlearned their particular athletic skill through thousands of hours of practice. Under conditions of competition and close scrutiny, their performance is enhanced and may attain record-breaking levels. In contrast, people who still are working to master their skills are much more prone to "clutching" when under conditions of observation.

Supervisees are akin to these beginning athletes in that they still are working to develop skills that have not yet become automatic (cf. Bargh & Chartrand, 1999). When observed or monitored by a supervisor, their performance is vulnerable to deterioration. That is, they are vulnerable to clutching.

But, despite consistent findings in support of this model in other domains, its applications to supervision are called into question by the results of studies by Ellis and his colleagues. From the Chapin and Ellis (2002), the Ellis et al. (2002), and several instrument development studies, Ellis (personal communication, October 15, 2002) has concluded that the role of supervisee anxiety may have been overstated in the supervision literature. He asserted that "It looks like less than 10 percent report even moderate anxiety in high anxiety supervision or training situations (e.g., first videotape review supervision in pre-practicum)." It appears, therefore, that more research is needed. In the meantime, it is useful for supervisors to be sensitive to the possible effects on the supervisee of observation.

Supervisee Interactions with Supervisor. Supervisee anxiety affects supervisor–supervisee interactions in a number of ways. One of the most obvious of these is what the supervisee reveals during supervision (see, e.g., Ladany, Hill, Corbelt, & Nutt, 1996). Rønnestad and Skovholt (1993) noted that "the anxious student may tend to discuss in supervision only clients who show good progress, choose themes in which he or she is functioning well, or choose a mode of presenting data that allows full control over what the supervisor learns" (p. 398). They suggested that the supervisor may therefore, in the beginning, allow the student to select or even distort data until some of that anxiety dissipates.

The wish to manage supervisors' impressions of them is motivated at least in part by supervisees' anxiety and certainly affects interactions. All of us are concerned about how others perceive us (e.g., Schlenker & Leary, 1982). That is, we want to convey a certain impression, but worry about how well we are accomplishing it. Supervisees, however, deal not only with these "ordinary" concerns about creating a desired social impression, but also with the added concern of creating the impressions necessary to earn them satisfactory evaluations from their supervisors.

Social psychologists have discussed the strategies that people use to cope with these concerns as *impression management* (or *strategic self-presentation*). This is the person's attempt to deliberately project a certain image. It is possible to use the perspective of the theater and think of *any* person's social behavior as being a performance given to create a desired effect on others.

A person's motivation to manage impressions can be influenced by a number of factors (Leary & Kowalski, 1990). One is the importance to the person of a particular goal (a supervisee, for example, is likely to want to present himself or herself as having the characteristics and skills that the supervisor believes necessary to be an effective mental health professional). Another motivator is the circumstance of being evaluated in some manner, a condition which *absolutely* applies to supervisees. Leary and Kowalski cited studies, for example, showing that a person is more likely to want to impression manage with teachers and employers than with friends.

Still another motivation to impression manage is the person's desire to resolve discrepancies between his or her desired versus current image. People will use impression management strategies to gain respect and admiration after their social image has been damaged. For example, when individuals believe that they have failed at an important task,

they tend to behave in a more self-enhancing manner in order to repair their image (Schlenker, 1980). They also are likely to become more self-enhancing about their task performance after they have received negative evaluations of their work.

Despite the clear relevance of the concept of impression management to supervision, only a couple of studies so far have examined directly supervisees' self-presentation motivations and impression construction strategies (Friedlander & Schwartz, 1985; Ward, Friedlander, Schoen, & Klein, 1985). It is important to note, however, that a number of supervision studies that have not been framed as ones in impression management actually have implications for that model of behavior. Ladany et al.'s (1996) study of what supervisees choose not to disclose to their supervisors is an excellent case in point. In summary, to understand behaviors that the supervisor otherwise might label "defensive" or even "manipulative" as impression management can open up new response possibilities for the supervisor.

Impression management is one supervisee response to anxiety. A complementary strategy is to engage in the psychological games that Berne (1964) first described and that Kadushin (1968) extended to supervision.

Although McWilliams (1994) was not using this framework, the following describes this type of psychological game: "Therapists in training who approach supervision in a flood of self-criticism are often using a masochistic strategy to hedge their bets: If my supervisor thinks I made a major error with my client, I've already shown that I'm aware of it and have been punished enough; if not, I get reassured and exonerated" (p. 263).

If the supervisor does respond to this "invitation" to behave in a sympathetic manner and therefore mutes the criticism that she or he otherwise would offer, this would seem to illustrate a classic interpersonal game (and one that is observed frequently in supervision). A game, then, is understood as a series of transactions that are to some extent stylized and that emanate from the interlocking or complementary roles that the participants adopt.

This assumes that each participant understands and accepts these roles with greater or lesser degrees of conscious awareness. One person may initiate the particular game, but it always requires the collusion of *both parties* to make it a game.

Although the concept of games can be useful, it easily can be understood as pejorative (as in the observation that someone is "gamy"). So we introduce it here, but invite those who might want to learn more to consult Kadushin (1968) or Bauman (1972).

Supervisor Management of Supervisee Anxiety. To the extent that supervisee anxiety is minimized, so too is supervisee resistant behavior. Therefore, it is useful to consider some possible strategies that supervisors might employ to minimize anxiety.

Optimizing Levels of Supervisor Challenge versus Support. All supervisees approach supervision expecting to be judged and, therefore, inevitably are anxious to some degree. The experience of positive supervision, however, is such that the supervisee's anxiety does not rise to such a level that the work of supervision is hindered. This occurs because the supervisor is able simultaneously to be supportive and encouraging, which seems to us to echo Blocher's (1983) argument that effective supervision demands an optimal balance between *support* (including structure) and *challenge* (reflected also in the findings of Worthington and Roehlke, 1979, whose factor analysis of supervisors' behaviors yielded two factors that they labeled *support* and *evaluation,* which certainly is a form of challenge).

Too much support robs the supervisee of initiative and the opportunity to try new behaviors. By the same token, the level of supervisor challenge needs to be optimized: too little and the supervisee will not have the external push to try new behaviors; too much and the supervisee may become overwhelmed and incapacitated.

We recognize that this mention of support versus challenge is abstract rather than concrete. We hope, however, that it will provide a useful conceptual frame to guide supervisors' thinking about their styles of interactions and their interventions with supervisees.

Supervision Structure. Theory (e.g., Stoltenberg & Delworth, 1987) and research (e.g., Tracey, Ellickson, & Sherry, 1989) suggest that trainees desire more structure in conditions of greater anxiety (e.g., when the context of counseling arouses anxiety, when the client presents "in crisis," when the trainee is relatively inexperienced). Freeman (1993) observed that supervisors can lessen trainee anxiety by providing structure, and she suggested, along with others (e.g., Friedlander & Ward, 1984; Sansbury, 1982; Usher & Borders, 1993), that the provision of structure is more important to the inexperienced counselor than to one who is more advanced.

Supervisees' experience levels moderate the amount of structure that they perceive themselves to need. That is, beginning supervisees perceive themselves as needing more structure than those who are more advanced (e.g., Heppner & Roehlke, 1984; McNeill, Stoltenberg, & Pierce, 1985; Reising & Daniels, 1983; Stoltenberg, Pierce, & McNeill, 1987; Tracey et al., 1989; Wiley & Ray, 1986). But across all levels of supervisee experience, ambiguity in the supervisory context apparently is a root cause of supervisee anxiety.

Interestingly, Lichtenberg, Goodyear, and McCormick (2000) found no relationship between supervisee anxiety and level of session structure. Perhaps the reason for this seemingly discrepant finding was the manner in which structure has been operationalized. Lichtenberg et al. defined it in terms of moment-to-moment verbal interaction patterns. Most others who have written about structure, though, have operationalized it in terms of supervisor directiveness and control of session content and process. Perhaps it would be useful for the field to develop a general understanding of this commonly used term.

Role Induction. Supervisees' uncertainty about roles and expectations is a common cause of their anxiety. Therefore, there is utility in specifically educating them about roles and expectations through, for example, discussions and audio- or videotape modeling. Generally referred to as *role induction,* this has had demonstrated effectiveness with counseling clients. In a recent meta-analysis of 28 studies, Monks (1996) found that for clients role induction had significant positive effects on (1) treatment outcome, (2) attendance, and (3) drop-out rates.

Less research has been done on role induction in supervision. However, what *has* been done has shown positive effects. For example, Bahrick, Russell, and Salmi (1991) developed a 10-minute audiotaped summary of Bernard's (1979) supervision model and administered it to 19 supervisees at one of several points in the semester. They found that after supervisees heard the tape they reported having a clearer conceptualization of supervision and being more willing to reveal concerns to their supervisors. This effect occurred regardless of when in the semester supervisees heard the tapes.

Ellis, Chapin, Dennin, and Anderson-Hanley (1996) found that a role induction that they conducted significantly decreased trainee anxiety compared to a control group. More recently, Chapin and Ellis (2002) again confirmed the utility of role induction. Moreover, they found in their multiple case study design that a role induction workshop interacted with supervisee level. That is, practicum students showed a decrease in anxiety following a role induction procedure, whereas interns either showed no difference or a brief *increase* in anxiety before it again decreased.

Supervisees' Need to Feel and Appear Competent

Whereas the need for felt competence is especially important at particular stages of childhood (e.g., White, 1959), it remains an important, lifelong need for all of us. Felt competence is similarly important to supervisees. And, just as is the case with children, its salience varies according to the supervisee's level of (professional) development. This is explicit in Loganbill, Hardy, and Del-

worth's (1982) developmental model. And Rabinowitz, Heppner, and Roehlke (1986) found that beginning practicum students, compared to intern-level supervisees, rated as significantly more important to them this issue: *Believing that I have sufficient skills as a counselor or psychotherapist to be competent in working with my clients.*

Bordin (1983) noted that, when he would contract with supervisees about goals that they wished to accomplish during supervision, he found that their overt request typically was for fairly limited and focused goals, such as "learning to deal more effectively with manipulative clients" or "becoming more aware of when my own need to nurture gets in my way of being therapeutic." Yet he found that his supervisees' unspoken agenda almost always seemed to be the wish for him to provide global feedback about their overall level of functioning.

> *At first, I thought that this goal would be satisfied by the feedback I was giving in connection with the more specifically stated ones. But I soon learned such feedback was not enough. Despite our reviews of what the therapist was doing or not doing and of its appropriateness and effectiveness, the supervisee seemed uncertain how I evaluated him or her. Only as I offered the remark that I saw him or her as typical of (or even above or below) those of his or her level of training and experience was that need satisfied.* (p. 39)

Stoltenberg (1981) hypothesized that supervisees at level 2 (of a four-level model in which level 4 is the most advanced) move from the strong dependency characteristic of beginning-level supervisees to a dependency–autonomy conflict. Correspondingly, "there is a constant oscillation between being overconfident in newly learned counseling skills and being overwhelmed by the increasing responsibility" (p. 62). This is very similar to the struggle that adolescents experience as they enter the middle ground between childhood and adulthood. Kell and Mueller (1966) vividly captured this struggle around adequacy by employing what they referred to as a topographic analogy. According to them, the supervisee's struggle can be characterized as

> *an effort to stay on a highway which is bordered on one side by the beautiful and inviting "Omnipotence Mountains" and on the other side by terrifying "Impotence Cliff." Clients can and often do tempt counselors to climb to the mountain tops. Sometimes the counselors own needs and dynamics can push him into mountain climbing. More often, the complex, subtle interaction of counselor and client dynamics together lead to counselor trips into the rarified mountain air. Yet the attainment of a mountain top may stir uneasy and uncomfortable feelings. From a mountain top, what direction is there to go except downward? The view to the bottom of the cliff below may be frightening and compelling. The trip down the mountain may well not stop at the highway. The momentum may carry our counselor on over the cliff where he or [she] will experience the crushing effects of inadequacy and immobilization. . . . It seems that either feeling state [omnipotence or impotence] carries the seeds of the other. . . . Rapid oscillation between the two kinds of feeling can occur in such a short time span as a five minute segment of an interview.* (pp. 124–125)

Another competence-related supervisee phenomenon is that of experiencing themselves as impostors (Harvey & Katz, 1985) who are vulnerable to being found out. This occurs when their level of actual competence exceeds that of their felt competence. Although they behave as therapists, they worry that they are acting a charade, that it will be only a matter of time before they are found out to be the impostors that they believe themselves to be. Significantly, then, Kell and Mueller (1966) contended that supervision is "a process of mobilizing [the supervisee's] adequacy" (p. 18). To the extent that they feel adequate or competent, supervisees will be less vulnerable to feeling like imposters.

Supervisee Transference

In a nontechnical sense, transference is a phenomenon in which a person transfers to someone in the present the responses and feelings that he or she has had to someone in the past. It is understood that clients develop transferences to their therapists. But, as well, supervisees develop transference-based responses to their supervisors (cf. Fiscalini, 1985). To illustrate, consider Lane's (1986) example of how supervisee transference can affect the supervisory process: "The supervisor becomes the father who died or who left them or the mother who was never there for them, and is accused of taking something from them. This gives them the right of refusal to take in anything from the supervisor parent" (p. 71).

Supervisee transference can take numerous forms. At the broadest level, these can be categorized as either negative or positive. To illustrate the former, the supervisee can develop a negative transference in which he or she perceives the supervisor to be more critical or punitive than actually is the case. Lewis (2001) suggested that one mechanism by which this occurs is the supervisee's projection of their own punitively self-critical evaluations of themselves onto the supervisor.

A frequently occurring positive transference is that in which supervisees idealize their supervisors (Allphin, 1987). To do so can fill an important need, especially at the very early stages of training. Specifically, it can be important for the neophyte to have a relationship with someone who seems more competent and therefore capable of guiding their learning and development, someone to serve as a model.

Sexual attractions can constitute a specific type of positive transference. Attractions toward the supervisor can have various origins, including such reality-based considerations as shared interests. Such feelings, however, often derive at least in part from supervisee transference (Frawley-O'Dea & Sarnat, 2001).

Frawley-O'Dea and Sarnat (2001) also asserted that at least some supervisee transference can originate in parallel processes. This speaks to the origin rather than the valence of the transference. The following example that they gave is one of negative transference, but positive ones are just as possible.

For example, a patient may experience his male ther-apist as a persecutory, demanding father who is never pleased. The therapist who is uncomfortable with the patient's transference may not become con-sciously aware of it and therefore ignores [it]. . . . Rather than consciously working with the patient's transference, the therapist resists awareness of it and instead begins to experience the supervisor as a persecutory figure who never can be satisfied. (p. 173)

Implications for Supervisors.   In therapy, trans-ference is most likely to occur when the therapist remains relatively anonymous to the client. In his discussion of transference in supervision, Lewis (2001) contrasted supervision with therapy, noting that in the former

you are not anonymous or abstinent. Here you are a real person. Here you show your warmth and openness and acceptance. Here you praise, support, encourage, and advise. Here you show empathy to the vulnerability of the learner. Here you share your own experiences, your own mistakes. Here you share your own doubts and anxieties as a learner. (pp. 76–77)

This is consistent with Carl Rogers's observa-tion that in supervision he shared more of his own thoughts and reactions than when he was in the role of therapist (Hackney & Goodyear, 1986). To the extent that the supervisor is known as a "real" person, supervisee transference is minimized.

Supervisee transference is yet another reason for supervisors to avoid providing therapy to their supervisees. To blur this "teach versus treat" dis-tinction not only is ethically problematic (Ladany, Lehrman-Waterman, Molinaro, & Wolgast, 1999; Neufeldt & Nelson, 1999), but also invites super-visee transference.

But even in an optimal supervisory environ-ment, supervisees still will develop transference reactions to their supervisors. How to handle them depends on the nature, intensity, and origin of the transference.

For example, with idealizing transference, the supervisor should steer a careful course. On the

one hand, it can be important to respect the su-pervisee's need to idealize the supervisor (e.g., it can be very important to the supervisee to be re-assured with the "knowledge" that the supervisor has it all under control). But the flip side is to not allow the idealization of the supervisor to cheat the supervisee of the chance to develop his or her own sense of competence. As an additional matter, the type and timing of supervisor interventions in the face of supervisee idealization should be moder-ated by the supervisee's developmental level (e.g., Stoltenberg et al., 1998).

Negative transference responses can be more difficult, both because of the greater difficulty in addressing them productively and because of their consequences to the supervisory relationship and to supervisee learning. To address them, as we dis-cussed in Chapter 6 concerning relationship rup-tures, can be one avenue.

THE SUPERVISOR IN THE RELATIONSHIP

So far in this chapter, we have been discussing su-pervisee factors and dynamics that affect the dyadic relationship. For the remainder we will focus on the supervisor. We will continue using Figure 7.1 to organize our discussion.

Before addressing the supervisor factors in Fig-ure 7.1, we want to acknowledge two other fac-tors that we addressed with respect to supervisees but that also have application to supervisors. For example, we discussed supervisee trust. But trust is important to the supervisor as well. Unless the supervisor can trust that supervisees are being honest and straightforward about material from their sessions, he or she will be especially vigilant because of liability and other issues. This can lead to attempts to constrain supervisee behaviors in a way that will affect not only their relationship but also the supervisee's learning.

We also discussed supervisee anxieties at some length. But the supervisor's anxieties also are a factor in supervision. Lesser (1983) discussed pos-sible sources of supervisor anxiety. Among these are the anxieties that arise in evaluation and the feelings of responsibility both to supervisees and to the public that they will serve if successful in training; criticism or praise, whether overt or covert, may elicit anxiety; anxiety can arise when a client is in crisis and the supervisor has some doubts, however small, about the supervisee's ability to handle it [that the supervisor is vicariously liable (see Chapter 3) certainly can amplify this feeling]; and anxieties can occur at times when the supervisor may feel no longer needed. The anxieties that supervisees express in response to these circumstances can affect the dyadic relationship.

Although we were not able to give more space to matters of supervisor trust and anxiety, we thought it important at least to acknowledge their importance. In the remainder of the chapter, we will address, in turn, supervisor attachment, power, and countertransference.

Supervisor Attachment

To date, attention to attachment style in supervision has been concerned primarily with that of the supervisee. Yet supervisors, too, have particular relational styles that they bring to supervision.

White and Queener (in press) used data from 67 supervisory dyads to examine the relationship of both supervisee and supervisor adult attachment styles to their ratings of the Supervisory Working Alliance Inventory (Efstation et al., 1990). Supervisees' attachment styles did not predict either supervisor or supervisee working alliance. Interestingly, however, *supervisors'* attachment styles predicted strength of alliance, as rated by both supervisor and supervisee. The authors noted that

> *Most models of supervision do not explicitly consider the individual characteristics of the supervisor and supervisee in understanding the dynamics of the supervisory relationship. This study suggests that supervisors' ability to make positive–affiliative attachments with others play[s] an important role in understanding the supervisory relationship.* (ms. p. 18)

This is a single study and maybe its results will stimulate more attention to supervisor attachment. Pending additional findings, we would note that

supervisors should have sufficient self-knowledge to know the effects of their relational styles on their supervisees. Presumably, they already will be applying this self-knowledge in their interactions with clients.

Interpersonal Power

Supervisory relationships are characterized by power inequality. Of course, this exists in psychotherapy, where several aspects of the therapeutic context contribute to it. For example, the person in a relationship who needs the other more (i.e., the client) typically has less power than the person who is needed; and the person who has permission to comment on the other's behavior also has the greater power. Not only are these factors similarly present in supervision, but so too is the supervisor's power of expertise and role, including that of evaluator.

But, though interpersonal power permeates their work, supervisors feel uncomfortable acknowledging it. In fact, it often is true in hierarchical relationships that the person with greater power is able to remain less consciously aware of it than is the person with less power. Holloway (1995) offered the following caution: "In the helping professions, power often has been viewed pejoratively because the concept of control and dominance has seemingly been antithetical to the tenets of mutuality and unconditional positive regard. This interpretation limits the ability of power in constructing a mutually empowering relationship" (p. 43).

Effective supervision requires that the supervisor recognize the sources, manifestations of, and ways to use the power that they have in the relationship. Eventually, supervisor–supervisee power discrepancies will dissipate, as Acker's (1992) observation suggests: "The supervisory relationship is a relationship between unequals, the objective of which is equalization. This would seem to be an inherent contradiction, a paradox, and is the challenge in supervision."

The "objective of equalization" does suggest that power and hierarchy differ in level according to supervisee developmental levels. But they remain nevertheless. This section deals with the challenge that Acker posed.

Two conceptions of interpersonal power have been especially important for supervisors and supervision researchers: social influence theory and the interactional perspective. We will address each in turn.

Social Influence Theory.   Power can be understood as the ability to influence others' behaviors and attitudes. Heppner and Claiborn (1989) asserted that literature applying social psychological concepts of interpersonal influence and attitude change to counseling and therapy probably began with the publication of Frank's (1961) *Persuasion and Healing.* Further articulation of that point of view occurred in such other works as those of Goldstein, Heller, and Sechrest (1966) and Strong (1968). In fact, Strong's article presenting a two-stage model of change probably was most directly instrumental in stimulating what now has become a substantial research literature.

In Strong's view, we individuals give interpersonal power (or the ability to influence) to those in our lives whom we perceive to have the resources necessary to meet our needs. This is consistent with social exchange theory, which posits that if A has what B wants, A has power over B. The extent of this power depends on the access that B has to alternative resources.

Strong (1968) adopted three of French and Raven's (1959) five types of interpersonal power to conceptualize counselors' influence. Strong asserted that a counselor will have interpersonal power or influence to the extent that the client perceives him or her to have *expertness, attractiveness* (i.e., perceived similarities in values, goals, etc.), and *trustworthiness.* This same model applies as well to supervision.

During the first of Strong's posited two stages, the supervisor's task is to establish himself or herself to the supervisee as a credible resource (i.e., a person who is perceived to possess the requisite expertness, attractiveness, and trustworthiness). Once the supervisor has established credibility, the

second stage is one in which he or she begins using these sources of power to influence the supervisee to make behavioral or attitudinal changes. This is the actual social influence process.

Appropriately, Strong (1968) had not employed in his model of counseling a fourth of French and Raven's types of interpersonal power, that of *coercion.* But, as we have noted repeatedly throughout this book, supervisors have an evaluative function. This suggests that supervisors have coercive power, even though counselors do not. Because supervisors were trained first as counselors or therapists, to have this type of power can be uncomfortable. Yet it is important for the supervisor to understand that this power, however latent it might be, is real to the supervisees.

Corrigan, Dell, Lewis, and Schmidt (1980) and Heppner and Dixon (1981) reviewed the first decade of research on this model. Heppner and Claiborn (1989) later reviewed the second decade of that work. In the meantime, a distinct body of literature had developed in which that model was employed in supervision research. Dixon and Claiborn (1987) reviewed that research. With a few exceptions, most research on this model has been analog in nature. The real-life applications that exist suggest that attractiveness (which we understand as relational bonding) probably is the greatest of the French and Raven power sources.

Petty and Cacioppo's (1986) elaboration likelihood model (ELM) is a more recent and complex model of attitude change and might be considered the "second-generation" social influence model. This model suggests that people can be influenced through two information processes routes: either *central* (involving an effortful elaboration of information) or *peripheral* (greater reliance on cues or on simple rules) for information processing. Influence that occurs through the central route is considered more enduring and has more effect on subsequent behaviors.

However, the route by which persuasion occurs depends on characteristics of the person who is the source of the information (e.g., credibility and attractiveness), message variables (i.e., the subjective strength of the arguments supporting a position), and recipient characteristics (e.g., degree of motivation to process the message). When people are motivated and able to consider messages that they perceive to have compelling arguments, they can then be influenced by a central route; otherwise, influence might occur through more peripheral means, such as the perceived expertness of the communicator. Both Claiborn, Etringer, and Hillerbrand (1995) and Stoltenberg, McNeill, and Crethar (1995) have discussed the promise of the ELM for research in supervision. Significantly, too, Stoltenberg et al. have attempted to incorporate what we already know about supervisee development into applications of the ELM.

The two models of social influence that we have reviewed both have a more formal and "scientific" language and structure than much of what we discuss in this book (see Blocher, 1987, and Martin, 1988, for discussions of distinctions between models to guide practice versus those to guide inquiry). But they are important models for supervisors to understand because they provide supervisors with valuable explanations of how power operates in their relationships with supervisees. Supervisors interested in learning more about their practice implications should consult articles such as those of Claiborn et al. (1995), Kerr, Claiborn, and Dixon (1982), and Stoltenberg et al. (1995).

An Interpersonal Perspective.   A second perspective on interpersonal power is more explicitly interactional. This perspective is concerned especially with the more dynamic give and take that occurs between people. It is grounded in the assumption that people always are negotiating their status (i.e., relative power) with respect to one another.

Gregory Bateson and Timothy Leary made two of the seminal contributions to this perspective. Bateson (1936/1958) proposed that status (which also has been referred to variously as dominance, control, or power) is a construct that influences all human relationships and communication. Timothy Leary (1957) later employed Sullivan's (1953) interpersonal theory of personality to develop a circumplex model in which behavior can be plotted according to its placement on a circle. One of the

two orthogonal dimensions in Leary's model is that of *power* (dominance versus submission). In this way, his model was similar to that of Bateson. But Leary's inclusion of *affiliation* as a second dimension (i.e., hostility versus nurturance) was a significant additive step. Leary's assumption that any given behavior can be described according to how it maps on these two dimensions has come to inform a great deal of current personality research. In fact, Tracey (in preparation) has shown that most people implicitly organize their perceptions of their interpersonal worlds along these two dimensions.

Issues of power always are being negotiated within any relationship. When two people are in a relationship, each person's behavior (both verbal and nonverbal) conveys information to the other about how he or she perceives himself or herself relative to the other with respect to status. Bateson (1936/1958) proposed that interpersonal interactions can be characterized as of two basic types:

> complementary (where there is an unequal amount of status) and symmetrical (where there is equal status). In a complementary interaction, each person is agreeing on the relative status positions (i.e., who determines what is to occur and who is to follow along). If the behaviors of the actors complement each other, there is a smooth interaction that is productive as the dyad agrees on what is to be done. In essence, one actor initiates and the other follows. However, if the behaviors of the two actors indicate equal status, resulting in a symmetrical interaction, there is more tension in the interaction and there is less accomplished. (Tracey, 2002, p. 268)

Tracey (2002) characterized the degree of complementarity in a relationship as one index of between-participant "harmony." It indicates that the two individuals are similarly defining their relative power within that relationship. Variants of Leary's circumplex model (e.g., Benjamin, 1974; Carson, 1969; Kiesler, 1983; Strong & Hills, 1986; Wiggins, 1985) have been used in studies of complementarity. For example, Figure 7.4 reproduces the Tracey, Sherry, and Albright (1999) variant. Using this figure, an example of complementarity would occur if a supervisor were to make a leading statement (e.g., "Would you turn on your tape so that we

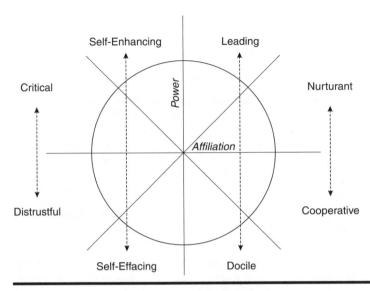

FIGURE 7.4 Interpersonal Stage Model of Complimentarity

From T. J. G. Tracey, P. Sherry, & J. M. Albright (1999). The interpersonal process of cognitive-behavioral therapy: An examination of complementarity over the course of treatment. *Journal of Counseling Psychology, 46,* 80–91. Copyright © 1999 by the American Psychological Association. Reprinted with permission.

can listen to some of what you have been describing?") to which the supervisee responds with a docile behavior (e.g., "Sure, let me pull out my tape recorder"). As the figure indicates, leading behaviors are high on dominance, whereas docile behaviors are low; both leading and docile behaviors are moderate in level of friendliness. The figure also indicates that nurturant behavior elicits cooperative behavior; self-enhancing behavior elicits self-effacing behavior; and critical behavior elicits distrustful behavior.

One variant of Leary's model that has been especially important to supervision researchers is that of Penman (1980). Although this model was not organized as a circumplex, it employed the same two dimensions of *power* and *involvement* to characterize interpersonal behaviors. At least four studies (Abadie, 1985; Holloway, Freund, Gardner, Nelson, & Walker, 1989; Martin, Goodyear, & Newton, 1987; and Nelson & Holloway, 1990) have employed Penman's system to analyze supervisory interactions. This model was useful, for example, in

the Nelson and Holloway (1990) finding that supervisors were more likely to reinforce high power statements by male supervisees than those by their female counterparts, thereby demonstrating that gender role affects how power is utilized in supervision. Holloway's (1995) model of supervision is grounded in this interplay between the dimensions of supervisor power and involvement.

Drawing from his and others' research, Tracey (1993) has proposed a three-stage model of counseling based on the notion of complementarity. In the initial phase, level of therapist and client complementarity is high; in the middle or working phase, it becomes lower as the relationship becomes more conflictual; and in the final stage the relationship returns to a situation of higher complementarity. But, although there seems generally solid support for this model in therapy, the one supervision study of this type (Tracey & Sherry, 1993) found no support for it. The authors speculated that their results might call into question the application of therapy models to supervision. It was, though, but a single study, so the question about whether Tracey's (1993) stage model of counseling applies to supervision is yet to be fully considered.

Implications for Supervisors.   Power often is thought to involve dominance or control by one person over the other. But to employ social psychological conceptions of power as the social influence by one person of another importantly broadens understandings of it. All behavior is communication, and communication is an act of influence (Watzlawick & Beavin, 1976). This perspective allows for *mutual* influence: that the supervisee also can influence the supervisor, even though the latter continues to have the greater possibility to influence the supervisee.

We recently heard a conference presenter assert that the person with greater power in a relationship is able to define reality for the other person. This does seem strong as an absolute statement. Yet, through the sorts of power that we have discussed in this section (e.g., expertness, attractiveness, and trustworthiness), the supervisor is able to persuade the supervisee to look through a particular theoretical lens to evaluate behavior and to adopt particular attitudes. In this sense, the supervisor is using interpersonal power to define (or at least shape) the supervisee's reality.

It is likely that the person with the less power in the relationship will be more conscious of this fact. Yet, precisely because of his or her greater power, the supervisor has a responsibility to be aware of it and to use it both effectively and nonabusively.

In short, the fact of the supervisor's greater power in the relationship is not in itself problematic. This power (in its multiple forms) is a tool that the supervisor uses in the service of both protecting the client and enhancing the learning of the supervisee. It can, though, invite supervisee resistance, depending on (1) how the supervisor uses the power and (2) the supervisee's response to it (either by virtue of developmental stage or level of reactance). It also can invite transference responses, either positive or negative. The challenge for the supervisor

is to be aware of the power that he or she has and to use in a way that maximizes effectiveness.

Supervisor Countertransference

[S]upervisor countertransference has been viewed as a complex and inevitable process that involves unconscious and exaggerated reactions stemming from a supervisory interaction customarily related to the supervisor's unresolved personal issues or internal conflicts.
(Ladany et al., 2000, p. 102)

Strean (2000) noted that mental health professionals generally recognize that therapist countertransference is as ubiquitous as client transference. He then suggested that, by analogy, supervisor countertransference is likely as ubiquitous as supervisee transference. Ekstein and Wallerstein (1972) noted that the mutual evaluation and reevaluation that occur in supervision do not occur at a strictly intellectual level. They will "be accompanied by interactions on every level, which would be described, were they to occur in a therapeutic context, as transference reactions of the one and countertransference reactions of the other" (p. 284).

Literature on this topic is relatively small. Ladany et al. (2000) note that Balint (1948) and Benedek (1954) apparently were among the earliest authors to acknowledge supervisor countertransference and its potentially harmful effects on supervisees. A number of authors have offered their observations about supervisor countertransference. For example, Lower (1972) observed that "the learning alliance . . . is threatened continuously by resistances that derive from immature, neurotic, conflict-laden elements of the personality" (p. 70). Teitelbaum (1990) suggested the term "supertransference" to characterize the reactions of the supervisor to the supervisee and to the supervisee's treatment.

But we know of only two studies of supervisor countertransference, one published (Ladany et al., 2000) and one unpublished (Walker & Gray, 2002). Each was a qualitative study designed to describe countertransference events. Both are quite recent.

Walker and Gray (2002) obtained 144 instances of supervisory countertransference during 70 post-supervision session interviews. In their preliminary clustering of these events, they identified four sources of supervisor countertransference: external stress from workload; disappointment that trainee is not taking work seriously; overidentification with what it is like to be a beginning counselor; and, wanting the trainee to be a better therapist.

An important aspect of this work was that the authors not only were interested in problematic countertransference reactions, but also in those that in one way or another facilitated the supervision. Other work has treated countertransference almost exclusively as problematic. For example, even positive countertransference is considered problematic when it has erotic overtones (e.g., Ladany et al., 2000).

Ladany et al. (2000) have conducted the single published investigation of supervisor countertransference. Their findings provide the most comprehensive knowledge to date about this phenomenon. Therefore, we devote more space than usual to summarizing this study's findings.

Theirs was a qualitative study of 11 supervisors at university counseling center internship sites. Raters coded the structured interviews with these participants, all of whom believed that this had affected the supervisory relationship in either positive or negative ways. Ladany et al. (2000) found that most supervisors reported the countertransference lasted more than 2 months. To deal with it, most reported having pursued one or both of two courses: (1) consulting with a colleague (coworker, the training director, a supervision group) and/or (2) discussing it with the supervisee as it was appropriate. A few reported using either personal therapy or developing increased awareness through self-reflection as a means to resolve it.

A particularly useful feature of the Ladany et al. (2000) study was their examination of cues that led the supervisor to become aware of his or her coun-

tertransference. There was no one type of cue that all 11 supervisors reported. However more than half reported each of the following types of cues:

- Having particularly strong positive or negative feelings when they interacted with the supervisee
- Experiencing feelings toward the supervisee that were uniquely different from those toward other supervisees with whom she or he had worked
- Experiencing a gradual change in feelings toward the supervisee or their sessions together
- Discussions with colleagues (especially their own supervisors)

Ladany et al. (2000) were able to identify six sources of supervisor countertransference. Two of these were reported by all respondents:

1. *Countertransference triggered by the interpersonal style of the supervisee.* In some cases, this was a defensiveness or guardedness; in others, an assertiveness; in others, passivity, shyness, or vulnerability; and finally, such positive qualities as warmth and being engaging (this last was especially true for erotic countertransference).

2. *Countertransference stemming from some aspect of the supervisor's own unresolved personal issues.* In some cases, this concerned personal and family issues; in others, concerns about his or her competency; his or her own interpersonal style (e.g., having unduly high self-expectations; strong need to be liked); or experiences in the past from work with other supervisees.

To have these two sources identified through an inductive, empirical technique is important. But because this literature still is small, we also will summarize next the four categories of supervisor countertransference that Lower (1972) had suggested some years ago.

1. Countertransference Stemming from General Personality Characteristics. This type of countertransference stems from the supervisor's own characterological defenses, which then affect the supervisory relationship.

2. Countertransference Stemming from Inner Conflicts Reactivated by the Supervisory Situation.   Lower's (1972) first category of supervisor countertransference focused on supervisors' characteristic ways of expressing themselves. The second category focused on supervisors' inner conflicts that are triggered by the supervision. Although some of the supervisor behaviors might resemble those of the first category, they have different origins.

The following list of other supervisor responses suggests the myriad ways that supervisors' own inner conflicts can be manifest in supervision. Lower (1972) suggested that they may

- Play favorites with the supervisees;
- Covertly encourage the supervisee to act out his or her own conflicts with other colleagues or encourage rebellion against the institution;
- Compete with other supervisors for supervisees' affection;
- Harbor exaggerated expectations of the supervisee that, when unmet or rejected by the supervisee, lead to frustration and perhaps even aggression;
- Have narcissistic needs to be admired that divert the supervisor from the appropriate tasks of supervision.

3. Reactions to the Individual Supervisee.   The types of supervisor countertransference discussed so far have been triggered by the supervisor's response to the supervisory situation. In addition to these, there may be aspects of the individual supervisee that stimulate conflicts in the supervisor, for example, if the supervisee seems brighter (or more socially successful, or financially better off, etc.) than the supervisor.

Sexual or romantic attraction is a specific instance of this type of supervisor countertransference (Frawley-O'Dea & Sarnat, 2001). Ellis and Douce (1994) have argued that issues of supervi-

sor attraction to supervisees has been too little emphasized during supervision training.

Another specific instance of this type of supervisor countertransference (i.e., reaction to the individual supervisee) is cultural countertransference. Vargas (1989) differentiated between this and prejudice: "Whereas prejudice refers to an opinion for or against someone or something without adequate basis, the sources and consequences of cultural countertransference are far more insidious and are often repressed by the therapist" (p. 3).

Vargas (1989) noted that cultural countertransference reactions can originate in either of two ways. The first, and more common instance, occurs when the supervisor has limited experience with members of the ethnic minority group to which the supervisee belongs. The second is the consequence of potent feelings associated with nonminority people in the supervisor's past with whom the current minority supervisee is associated.

Regardless of the source, however, these cultural countertransference reactions, like many social perceptions, occur at an automatic level, outside the observer's awareness (see, e.g., Bargh & Chartrand, 1999). Research such as that of Abreu (1999) illustrated how this applies in a mental health context. He showed that with subliminal priming (i.e., words flashed at 80 milliseconds, a speed that would preclude conscious recognition of them), using 16 words or stereotypes ascribed to African Americans (e.g., Negroes, Blacks, lazy, blues, rhythm, etc.), therapists would rate a client described in a vignette as more hostile. This was even though most indicated that they understood the client probably was White. This suggests the importance of ongoing attention to cultural sensitivity, even when at a conscious level the supervisor is not aware of stereotyping.

4. Countertransference to the Supervisee's Transference.   Perhaps the area in which supervisors are at the greatest risk of experiencing countertransference reactions to the supervisee is when the supervisee manifests transference responses to the supervisor. As a vivid illustration, Lower (1972) offered the following example.

A resident had been working in psychotherapy with a . . . young woman for about six months when a new supervisor questioned his formulations and treatment goals and suggested that they follow the patient in supervision over a period of time. The resident responded as though the supervisor were intruding on his relationship with the patient and became more and more vague in his presentation of material. In reaction, the supervisor became increasingly active in suggesting what the therapist should pursue with the patient and at last asked to see the patient together with the resident in order to make his own assessment. Only after the supervisor began the interview by asking the patient "Well how are you and Doctor what's his name here getting along" did he recognize the oedipal conflict within both himself and the resident that had interfered with the learning alliance. (p. 74)

CONCLUSION

Whereas Chapter 6 focused on triadic and dyadic supervision processes, this chapter was concerned more specifically with dynamic individual factors that affected the relationship. Certainly, each of the factors we addressed have implications for, or even direct influence on, the dyadic supervisory relationship. But to consider them at the level of the individual permits more prescriptive intervention (e.g., to minimize supervisee anxiety or transference or supervisors' countertransference). See Fall and Sutton (2004) for exercises that highlight relationship issues.

CHAPTER 8

ORGANIZING THE SUPERVISION EXPERIENCE

It is tempting to begin our supervisor tasks section of the book (see Figure 1.2) by delving into supervision interventions. Certainly, most supervisors envision themselves conducting individual, group, or live team supervision when they think of the actions of a clinical supervisor. Instead, we want to begin the section where we believe supervision must begin, with a process of assuring that supervision is organized with clear parameters and expectations. We will begin by looking at the available data that underscore the importance of organized or intentional supervision. We will then consider institutional characteristics that are supervision friendly. Mostly, we will discuss some of the activities and tools that add consistency and predictability to supervision. We see the content of this chapter as including many of the activities that often get neglected in supervision or are performed in a pro forma manner. While nothing in the chapter deals with the essence of clinical supervision (e.g., relationship issues, intervention selection, supervision models), the topics discussed here create the framework that makes it easier to attend to issues such as these. We refer to much in the chapter as the *organizational responsibilities* of the supervisor (which we sometimes refer to as managerial competence). We include what we consider essential for the process of mapping out the supervision experience before it begins and monitoring the experience for the duration of the relationship.

Traditionally, roles and responsibilities held by supervisors have been described as either administrative or clinical. Although there is almost always some overlap and, indeed, some supervisors fulfill both clinical and administrative duties for the same supervisees, these terms have helped to differentiate supervisory functions within an organization. The clinical supervisor has a dual investment in the quality of services offered to clients and the professional development of the trainee; the administrative supervisor, while obviously concerned about service delivery and staff development, must also focus on matters such as communication protocol, personnel concerns, and fiscal issues, to name just a few. The administrative supervisor will, by necessity, need to view supervision in the larger context of institutional expediency (Falvey, 1987); the clinical supervisor will view supervision and service delivery quite differently. In fact, the argument has been made that the tasks demanded of each role are divergent enough to make them essentially incompatible (Erera & Lazar, 1994).

Our position is that there is a strong and necessary component to clinical supervision that is managerial in nature, thus requiring organizational skills that are similar to those used by administrative supervisors. One would have a difficult time accepting the information presented in either the chapter on ethics and legal considerations or the chapter on evaluation without recognizing that these issues must be managed adequately within the supervisory relationship. Therefore, our goal in this chapter is to address some of the most essential managerial aspects of clinical supervision.

We have chosen the words *managerial* and *organizational* in order to avoid the word administrative. Borders et al. (1991) used the term *executive* to refer to the same set of behaviors and skills. All these terms imply some choreography within an institutional system to achieve clinical supervision goals.

At least three matters complicate a discussion of the organizational tasks of clinical supervision. The first is a bias among many mental health practitioners (clinical supervisors included) that such matters are tiresome, a necessary evil that detracts from, rather than enhances, one's clinical supervision. This bias is supported, in part, by Kadushin and Harkness (2002), who reported results from an earlier study conducted by Kadushin that the most highly ranked source of dissatisfaction reported by clinical supervisors was "dissatisfaction with administrative 'housekeeping'" (Kadushin & Harkness, 2002, p. 316). Additionally, Kadushin (1992, 1992b, 1992c) sampled a large number of social work supervisors and supervisees about supervisor strengths and shortcomings. Both supervisors and supervisees identified enacting managerial responsibilities as the major shortcoming of supervisors. Comments from both groups included the themes of communication, advocacy, time management, and planning. Although the supervisors were frank in delineating their shortcomings, it was the supervisees' comments that demonstrate the potential damage when managerial tasks are not attended to: "I never have his full attention," "My supervisor is wishy-washy . . . and doesn't support staff," "Morale is very low," "He shows a chronic inability to structure a conference so as to avoid interruptions," "There is a lack of periodic feedback. . . ." (Kadushin, 1992b, pp. 15–17). Kadushin (1992c) further reported that it was organizational failure that interfered with their work with clients that most distressed supervisees. Therefore, the organizational aspect of clinical supervision per se was viewed as distinct from other duties that required organizational skills. In short, the supervisees surveyed by Kadushin gave support to the notion that a lack of organizational skill can cancel out the supervisor's fine clinical skill. Supervisees can only benefit from knowledge and expertise that are transferred in a planned and consistent fashion.

From these two Kadushin studies, it would seem then that organizational tasks are avoided because they are stressful. We may surmise from this that supervisors are less prepared to accomplish these tasks than they are the clinical tasks of mentoring junior therapists.

A vicious cycle follows in which the clinical supervisor gives lower priority to those elements of clinical supervision that smack of management because these chores are inherently stressful, in part because the supervisor is not adequately prepared to succeed in their execution, thus leaving the supervisee frustrated with the supervisor around these issues, thus adding to the stress experienced by the supervisor when facing the supervisee's frustration, causing the supervisor to feel negatively about his or her role as a supervisor, and culminating in the avoidance of planning for (organizing) supervision in the future.

The second complicating matter is an assumption that clinical perceptiveness and organizational skill are rarely found in the same individual. This is similar to the assumption about absent-minded professors, that they can be brilliant in their field but have little ability to navigate the real world. Although there is some basis for most stereotypes, we believe that in many instances a lack of organization is the result of neglect, rather than a deficit of inherent individual ability. In other words, if the managerial aspects of clinical supervision are isolated for the purpose of strengthening these skills, such scrutiny will lead to increased managerial competence among clinical supervisors. On the other hand, if the myth is accepted that clinical skill and organizational skill are incompatible, little change will occur.

The third complicating factor to our discussion is the reality that in some organizations there is no distinction between clinical supervision and administrative supervision. Supervisors are asked to wear one blended hat without the luxury of a clear focus in either direction. Several authors have commented on the inherent challenges of blending administrative and clinical supervision (Erera & Lazar, 1994; Hardcastle, 1991; Henderson, 1994;

Kadushin, 1992a; Kadushin & Harkness, 2002; Rodway, 1991). We acknowledge this dilemma as a real one and hope that having some clarity on the types of managerial activities that directly affect clinical supervision will somehow help the blended supervisor with both sets of responsibilities to be more deliberate in all activities.

With these complications in mind, we begin by arguing for the importance of managerial–organizational competence for the delivery of clinical supervision. We then underscore the importance of understanding a particular institution's culture and how this can provide either a positive or negative context for clinical supervision. We follow with a consideration of the differences when supervision is offered within a graduate program (i.e., on campus) versus when supervision is conducted in the field. An examination of various tasks follows and a variety of tools to assist with those tasks are described. Finally, we suggest some ways to assist a clinical supervisor in achieving organizational competence.

IMPORTANCE OF COMPETENCE IN ORGANIZING SUPERVISION

Even though there are many references to the importance of being organized in one's delivery of clinical supervision, until recently very few direct data have supported the importance of organizational skills for clinical supervisors. Perhaps because the field has only recently begun to address and codify ineffective, conflictual, or "lousy" supervision, the importance of managing clinical supervision remained in the background. While the centrality of the supervision relationship to satisfactory supervision is clear (e.g., Magnuson, Wilcoxon, & Norem, 2000; Nelson & Friedlander, 2001; Worthen & McNeill, 1996), it is equally apparent that a significant amount of dissatisfaction can result from supervision that is poorly organized.

Nelson and Friedlander (2001) found that supervision had a negative impact when supervisees entered the relationship without a clear sense of what was expected of them or how supervision would proceed. They also found that unstable relationships between the site and home program had negative consequences. Kozlowska, Nunn, and Cousins (1997) surveyed psychiatric trainees and found that they were unsatisfied when their educational needs were neglected by their supervisors, pointing to supervision that is reactive, rather than organized and deliberate.

The most pointed results indicating the importance of organizational factors in supervision came from Magnuson, Wilcoxon, and Norem's (2000) qualitative study of "lousy" supervision. While the number of supervisees interviewed was small ($N = 11$), organizational–administrative issues emerged as one of three general spheres of lousy supervision (the other two being technical–cognitive and relational–affective). Specifically, subjects reported six areas in which organizational–administrative competence was lacking to their detriment: (1) failure to clarify expectations, (2) failure to provide standards for accountability, (3) failure to assess the supervisee's needs, (4) failure to be adequately prepared for supervision, (5) failure to provide purposeful continuity, and (6) failure to provide an equitable environment in group supervision.

It is not lost on us that the importance of organizational or management skills for the practice of clinical supervision becomes evident through a negative lens, rather than a more affirming lens. Our hypothesis is that well-organized supervision allows for other aspects of supervision to emerge; therefore, the organizational backdrop is likely to remain invisible. When a supervisee is given clear guidelines for supervision by a well-prepared supervisor, this is experienced as the norm. If, however, the supervisor confuses the supervisee, offers little or no structure for the experience, and seems unable to manage supervisory duties, the supervisee is more likely to become aware of the organizational skills requisite for good supervision.

Another body of literature that insinuates the importance of well-managed supervision is that of practitioner burnout (again, an appreciation of organizational skill through a negative lens). Several authors have asserted that practitioner burnout may indeed be related not only to service demands, but also to a poor administrative structure (Brashears, 1995; Kaslow & Rice, 1985; Malouf, Haas, & Farah, 1983; Murphy & Pardeck, 1986; Stoltenberg & Delworth, 1987). Murphy and Pardeck noted that either authoritarian or laissez-faire styles of management (supervision) adds to burnout and that burnout may be more organizational than psychological. They asserted the importance of appreciating that "a lack of planning is not understood to be the only method for encouraging individualism" (Murphy & Pardeck, 1986, p. 40). Brashears similarly noted that, when the administrative tasks of supervision are viewed as too distinct from service delivery, this false dichotomy contributed to job stress, burnout, and turnover. Brashears concurred with Karger (1989) that "[T]he values of advocacy, empowerment, and self-determination cannot be endorsed for clients and at the same time denied by the professionals who serve them" (Brashears, 1995, p. 697).

Finally, a study conducted by Russell, Lankford, and Grinnell (1983) suggested that the present situation in the helping professions is in great need of correction. When one large agency was surveyed, 21 of 44 clinical supervisors were perceived as exemplifying an "impoverished" management style, indicating a low concern for people and a low concern for production. Though this study is dated, we have no new data to challenge its relevance.

We wish to underscore the concept that burnout may be organizational as well as, if not rather than, psychological. From the supervisee's perspective, it makes intuitive sense to us that the best of supervisory relationships or the finest of clinical insights can be sabotaged by weak managerial skills (as was indicated by some of the near desperate comments made by supervisees in Kadushin's [1992b] study). This can be seen in training situations or in work situations when supervisees are no longer patient or tolerant of inconveniences or frustrations caused by the supervisor who cannot maintain some level of mastery of the supervisory plan. Supervisees often realize that a lack of organizational skill not only leaves them vulnerable but also leaves the client and agency vulnerable

as well. When messages are inconsistent, communication is erratic, procedures are unclear or not adhered to, and conferences are rushed, the entire experience of service delivery under supervision becomes compromised. Because of lack of experience, trainees or new employees are hard pressed to distinguish their feelings about service delivery from their feelings about supervision. Supervisors must realize, therefore, that signs of frustration or burnout may be feedback *to* the supervisor rather than *about* the supervisee.

As we have said, the focus on burnout or unsatisfactory supervision is a focus on the negative effects of managerial incompetence. Managerial competence, however, enhances positive experience or, as Lowy (1983) stated, "[T]he learning and teaching transactions in supervision require an organizational structure in order to become implementable" (p. 60). The educational literature is replete with studies confirming the need for structure in the learning process. Often, educational theory is ignored in the helping professions. Yet there is evidence that the process of acquiring clinical skill follows predictable developmental sequences. Sound educational advice, therefore, calls for a stable background (administrative structure) to ground the trainee who is being asked to take risks and meet challenges in the clinical arena.

Finally, we maintain the importance of managerial competence because certain supervisory functions are inextricably tied to such competence. Specifically, evaluation of supervisees and maintaining an operation that meets minimal ethical standards require organizational skill. Because a deficit in these areas can become threatening to supervisors and supervisees alike, we hope that the importance of organizational competence becomes self-evident. But with the minimal attention given to this topic in the clinical supervision literature, it is understandable that these skills remain underdeveloped.

Once the supervisor appreciates the importance of supervision that is thoughtful, organized, appropriate for the supervisee, and well executed, the supervisor will also appreciate the importance of a work environment that will support exemplary supervision. Even if the environment is one where supervision is expected to be an integral part, the institutional culture will play a part, often an enormous part, in either assisting or hampering the supervisor. It is important, then, to asses institutional culture as one task in managing clinical supervision.

THE ROLE OF INSTITUTIONAL CULTURE

Supervision is an integral and time-consuming aspect of the delivery of mental health services. When taken seriously and conducted properly, clinical supervision demands institutional support. It behooves supervisors to assess the culture of the organization to determine if it is supervision friendly. Otherwise, the most organized supervisor with the best laid plans will soon be frustrated by an institutional culture that works against supervision goals. Furthermore, because supervisors are persons of some authority, they have an opportunity and a responsibility to influence their organization's culture if it reflects characteristics that are anathema to clinical supervision. This is so whether their organization is a university program, a school or university setting, or a mental health agency. Therefore, we hope to provide some food for thought as supervisors assess their institutions and its underlying characteristics.

Osborn (in press) used the acronym STAMINA to describe a series of characteristics or behaviors that can assist counselors to thrive and remain fully engaged in the demanding contexts within which they find themselves. She encouraged mental health professionals to develop stamina, rather than "resisting burnout," seeing the latter as a reactive and less productive posture. Using Osborn's acronym, we will look at institutional culture and describe some of the essentials that must be in place if clinical supervision is to be managed optimally.

Selectivity.   Organizations cannot be all things to all constituents. Clinical supervision is often squeezed out because organizations are overburdened with heavy client loads, grant applications, new programs, and bureaucratic demands. There is probably no more essential characteristic for an organization to emulate than selectivity. For clinicians to become increasingly competent (and more valuable to the organization), clinical supervision must be selected *in,* not *out.* Institutions that deliberately *select* clinical supervision as a core activity understand that it will not occur (or will occur in a pro forma manner) if it is absent from a list of essential services. When given its rightful place in service delivery, supervision will thrive, and the voice of the supervisor will be more evident in the organization. As a result, selectivity as it relates to clinical supervision is imperative as an institutional characteristic.

Temporal Sensitivity.   Osborn described this characteristic as both a realistic understanding of the limits of time and a respect for the time that one is given. As is true for all aspects of stamina, temporal sensitivity will enhance the organization most dramatically if selectivity and other stamina traits are apparent as well. Organizations that value clinical supervision demonstrate this value by allocating the precious resource of time to it. There is no apology necessary in a supervision-friendly organization when adequate time is blocked out for supervision. Furthermore, this commitment to supervision is viewed as seriously as commitments to clients. Kadushin and Harkness (2002) reported a study of 885 supervisors and supervisees and found the time given to supervision to be a serious problem. Both supervisors and supervisees complained that there was too little time to conduct adequate supervision. Whether the problem was too little time to do too much or the status of supervision among competing duties is impossible to discern. The solution for such could be more clarity about priorities or improved time management, or both.

Just like individuals, organizations that are effective and efficient about time can accomplish more. These organizations are never frenetic, a characteristic more often associated with institutional cultures where time is perceived as the enemy and often managed poorly.

Accountability. Osborn was quick to state that she was not using the term accountability in its more reactive sense, that is, as a word to stifle creative practice. Rather, consistent with Osborn's definition, the organization that values accountability is *credible,* both within its boundaries and to outside units. Implicit in this kind of accountability is some ownership of the work that takes place within the organization and a desire to improve. Used in this way, clinical supervision is key to accountable counseling and therapy. Organizations that welcome accountability embrace the evaluative and developmental aspects of clinical supervision. Copeland (1998) stated that organizations that are instrumental in creating a context conducive to supervision expect more accountability from the supervisor. If framed in the way Osborn framed the term, this could only be a good thing.

Measurement and Management. As used by Osborn, measurement and management come closest to describing the kinds of activity necessary to organize effective supervision. While selectivity more broadly defines the mission of the organization, measurement and management reflect the day to day operations and the skills necessary to complete them effectively. An organization with this characteristic will be a resource to the clinical supervisor who intends to provide well-managed supervision. Many of the aspects of the organization (e.g., clarity regarding roles, good record-keeping practices) will automatically enhance the supervision function. It is a real advantage for the supervisor when clinical supervision is grounded in an efficient and effective organization.

Inquisitiveness. Osborn stated that the importance of a spirit of inquisitiveness for the long-term stamina of the individual counselor cannot be overstated. If one does not remain curious about one's work, stagnation can quickly set in. As an organizational trait, inquisitiveness is often translated as a respect for professional development and is viewed as essential for building and maintaining vibrant organizations (Frohman, 1998; Hawkins & Shohet, 2000). Clinical supervision is integral to professional development. Ongoing supervision can enhance the process of reflectivity (a form of inquisitiveness) that Skovholt and Rønnestad (1995) found was essential for professional development. Furthermore, the organization that reflects inquisitiveness will not allow the supervisor to function outside this value. Professional development at all levels of the organization will allow new ideas and new practices to inform supervision, as well as the activities supervised.

Negotiation. Osborn's inclusion of negotiation is essential for the supervisor-friendly organization. In this context, negotiation is defined as the ability to give and take without giving in. In other words, organizations that reflect the value of negotiation give their members voice. Others refer to the importance of collegiality within an organization (e.g., Frohman, 1998; Sparks & Loucks-Horsley, 1989). As Chapters 6 and 7 made clear, clinical supervision is highly sensitive to relationship. While a positive supervisory relationship can limp along within a caustic institutional context, it is unlikely that this could be sustained indefinitely. Organizations that value and nurture the kind of flexibility that collegiality requires are a great support to clinical supervisors.

Agency. Finally, Osborn suggested an appreciation of agency for the practicing counselor. By agency, Osborn was not referring to a place, but a quality, "an intangible, dynamic force." She viewed agency as coming close to the essence of stamina and including several empowering characteristics, such as having a sense of one's impact and being aware of one's resourcefulness. Translated to the institution, agency is a quality of those organizations that refuse to be dragged down by complications, unresponsive bureaucracies, or demanding client loads. These organizations are fed by their work, not depleted by it. They are the organizations that view clinical supervision as a building force, not a time drain. They communicate a confidence "in the possibility—indeed, inevitability—of positive, resilient resources, processes, and outcomes" (Osborn, in press). For such organizations, clinical supervision is key to agency.

Although these descriptions of organizational stamina may not include all that is necessary in an institution to support the functions of clinical supervision, they give the clinical supervisor one viable frame for such an assessment. Additionally, they can provide a handle for the supervisor in determining what feels wrong in an organization when attempting to meet supervisory responsibilities. For example, Congress (1992) noted that ethical decision making is controlled by agency culture, rather than individual input (perhaps reflecting the agency's view of accountability and management). The supervisor who has not attempted to evaluate organizational context may be unprepared for a discrepancy between a supervision goal and the culture within which supervision is occurring. Most likely, it is the supervision, not the culture, that will be compromised when there is such a discrepancy.

**THE ESSENTIAL INGREDIENT:
A SUPERVISION PLAN**

Before we look at the places where supervision occurs and the tasks that must be accomplished, we need to stress the importance of arriving at a general framework for supervision even before one meets the supervisee for the first time. In fact, it could be argued that the source of all sustained influence is planning and foresight (Covey, Merrill, & Merrill, 1994) and that these allow for other dimensions of supervision to emerge, such as the supervisory relationship. To some extent, planning includes methods for assuring accountability, and we will cover the importance of record keeping later in this chapter. But the driving force for the supervisor should be to plan an effective and efficient supervision experience that will culminate in the emergence of a capable and grounded practitioner, while safeguarding client welfare. This goal will be frustrated if supervision is random or repetitive. In other words, the antithesis of planning occurs when a supervisor accepts a super-

visee, sets weekly appointments with the supervisee, and lets things just happen, or when a university instructor places students in field sites and then conducts weekly group supervision sessions that are based on self-report and little else. In both of these instances, there is no evidence of an awareness of supervisees' developmental needs or of the desirability of some variety of learning modes. This is supervision as you go, not planned supervision.

Leddick and Dye (1987) reported that trainees often equate supervisor effectiveness with a comprehensive supervisory plan. "Trainees expect to learn from a variety of modalities including didactic presentations, feedback and evaluation, individual and group supervision, observing the supervisor as therapist, group discussion of cases and issues, and peer observation" (p. 149).

Focusing on supervision modalities, however, does not represent a complete plan. Hardcastle (1991) reviewed the four functions of agency supervision, all of which have implications for clinical supervision:

1. *Teaching, training, and consultation.* This is the aspect of clinical supervision that is most easily identifiable and usually most rewarding to supervisors. It includes case conferences where knowledge is transferred, the supervisee is tutored through either challenge or support, and clinical expertise is central.

2. *Monitoring and accountability.* Hardcastle found that this function was the most time consuming of the four. Such clinical supervision activities included observing the supervisee, monitoring supervisee development, overseeing written documentation of counseling, screening clients, and ensuring client welfare. This function may also include reporting the outcome of clinical services to others.

3. *Work design and coordination.* It is noteworthy that Hardcastle found this function to be one to which supervisors devoted the least amount of time. It is time spent here, however, that allows for a sophisticated supervision program to exist. Without taking the time to design supervision activities and to work out the logistics, supervision in busy settings can continue to resemble the tail wagging the dog. Beyond designing supervision from beginning to end, supervisors must also coordinate supervision with their other agency responsibilities and with the responsibilities of others. They should also be modeling these abilities for their supervisees.

4. *Communication and linkage within agency and with external resources.* Clinical supervisors may not perceive themselves as middle management, but they usually relate to feelings of being in the middle. Communication and linkage often become very time draining tasks. Supervisors become troubleshooters for their supervisees; conversely, they also serve as the voice of the organization (or program faculty) to supervisees. Furthermore, when client concerns translate to a need for referral or collaboration with external bodies, the supervisor inevitably is involved.

Hardcastle's (1991) descriptions of the different aspects of supervision can provide an outline for what must be included in the management of clinical supervision. A supervision plan, therefore, will address all areas delineated, allocating an appropriate amount of time to cover each. The driving force will be a vision of what must transpire for supervisees to achieve competence. From there, the clinical supervisor must create the context within which learning can occur. This context must be ideological and structural; that is, supervisors must not only understand how different activities support the supervisee's learning, but must organize the experience to make sure that the learning takes place. It is our impression that clinical supervisors to date have been much stronger in the ideological domain than the structural. With the ongoing emergence of a variety of supervision models and techniques, it is even more important that supervisors be organized and appreciative of the central role that foresight plays within supervision.

With a general idea of the importance of organizational skill, institutional culture, and a framework that defines clinical supervision broadly, we can now turn to more specific topics. We begin by looking at two different contexts within which supervision occurs.

CONTEXTS FOR SUPERVISION: TWO DIFFERENT WORLDS

Predominately, there are two different contexts for supervision: graduate programs and agencies (used generically to include schools, hospitals, mental health agencies, and the like). The fundamental difference between these two contexts, of course, is that one is organized around education and the other is organized around service delivery. Most students in graduate training programs will receive clinical supervision within the training context and in a field site (i.e., an agency) where they complete clinical hour requirements. Postdegree supervision is more contained (and therefore less complicated) within the agency. The challenges for postdegree supervision will be referenced later when we refer to field sites as the context for supervision. This section, however, will focus primarily on counselors and therapists-in-training and the contexts within which they will receive their clinical experiences.

Graduate Program as Context for Supervision

While navigating back and forth between the graduate training program and the field site is normative for most graduate students, some training programs run counseling centers or other service delivery training clinics on campus so that students receive clinical supervision and didactic education within the same context (Myers, 1994). Graduate programs often prefer such a setup for the very reasons that we will discuss in this chapter: It is much easier to negotiate one system than it is to react to two. Furthermore, because these training clinics are focused on training as their primary mission, supervision is central to their culture. As a result, neither faculty nor students need to spend time advocating for the importance of clinical supervision, leaving more time for the process itself.

Because of the educational advantages of program-based training clinics, these are usually viewed enviably by supervisors working in contexts with less of an emphasis on supervision. As was noted by Beavers (1986), training clinics are usually less hurried, supervisees can expect individual attention, facilities are usually more than adequate, and supervisors are typically well grounded theoretically. At the same time, the challenges for these training institutions have been noted by several authors and include the essential issue of balancing training responsibilities with the responsibilities of service delivery (Bernard, 1994b; Myers & Hutchinson, 1994); identifying, or perhaps recruiting, appropriate clients and matching clients with supervisees (Leddick, 1994; Scanlon & Gold, 1996); managing client expectations (Leddick, 1994), bridging the gap between the academic calendar and client needs (Scanlon & Gold, 1996); and clarifying roles of professional staff, especially when a tiered system exists, that is, master's-level students supervised by doctoral students who are themselves supervised by faculty supervisors (Dye, 1994; Scanlon & Gold, 1996; West, Bubenzer, & Delmonico, 1994).

As the above implies, there may be downsides to being supervised in a training facility. Beavers (1986) noted that, even though the staff may attempt to recruit a wide range of clients, it is most often the case that university settings offer a rather narrow and limited client population. Additionally, university supervisors may have less clinical experience than supervisors found in off-campus settings and are not as "street savvy." In other words, university settings may confront the supervisee with fewer dilemmas resulting from bureaucratic protocol, but this can be reframed as offering the supervisee fewer experiences in negotiating complex systems to achieve service delivery and professional development goals.

As we will see, as demanding as it is to keep both service delivery needs and training needs addressed within one context, the complexity of the task grows exponentially when more than one context is involved.

The Field Site as Context For Supervision

Often the supervisee in a graduate training program completes clinical experiences off campus and is supervised by a site supervisor. This, of course, is by design. Departments of social work and psychiatry were perhaps the first to realize the importance of field instruction to supplement academic instruction. Counseling, psychology, and marriage and family therapy, as well as a host of other clinical professions, also require the student to successfully complete a supervised field experience while still in a degree program. The site supervisor typically accepts the trainee because the supervisor enjoys the supervision process, including influencing trainees about real client issues and agency circumstances (Copeland, 1998; Holloway & Roehlke, 1987). Often the site supervisor would also like to influence the training program in terms of the preparation offered to trainees prior to field experience. Therefore, both contexts have an investment in one another that is both practical and educational. Yet the differences between these two types of organizations and their separate goals often are not acknowledged in a way that allows the principals to work them through. Additionally, adequate communication between the two is often wanting (Elman, Forrest, Vacha-Haase, & Gizara, 1999; Holtzman & Raskin, 1988; Igartua, 2000; Kahn, 1999; Olsen & Stern, 1990; Shapiro, 1988; Skolnik, 1988). We will address goals and communication separately.

Goals. Dodds's (1986) delineation of the major difference between the training institution and the service delivery agency as a difference in population to be served remains unchanged. As depicted in Figure 8.1, the training institution is invested in the education and training of its students, whereas the mental health agency is primarily invested in the delivery of quantity and quality services to a target population. Dodds warned, however, that to stereotype each system by these goals is to lose sight of each unit's investment in the other's mission. That notwithstanding, the basic goals

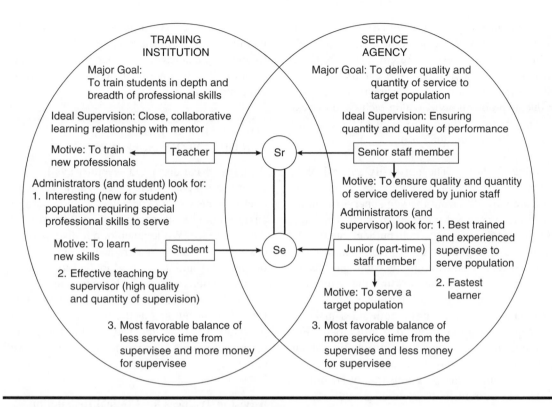

FIGURE 8.1 Overlapping Systems of a Training Institution and a Service Agency (Sr, supervisor; Se, supervisee)

From J. B. Dobbs (1986). Supervision of psychology trainees in field placements. *Professional Psychology: Research and Practice, 17,* 296–300. Copyright © 1986 by the American Psychological Association. Reprinted with permission.

of each system will determine the motives of the system's primary supervisor and the supervisor's managerial goals. As Figure 8.1 illustrates, the persons who have the responsibility for interfacing these two systems are the university and site supervisors involved. But if they default on this responsibility due to time constraints, disinterest, or the absence of managerial acumen, it is left to the supervisee to interface the two systems. When difficulties emerge, this leaves the least powerful individual (organizationally) to negotiate and attempt to find a resolution.

As an example of one of the many differences that grow out of each system's goals, Dodds

(1986) noted the "common source of stress [that] arises when the student participates simultaneously in two institutions with differing time rhythms" (p. 299). For instance, the trainee must perform the role of junior staff member on the agency's timetable, turning in reports and so on, regardless of whether the training institution is on semester break. Furthermore, the regularity of demand at the site will not be sensitive to pressure increases from the training institution, such as during midterm or final exams.

The first step in mastering the interface between the two systems is in understanding that there will be complications whenever two systems are simultaneously involved with a trainee because of each unit's systemic properties, including their different goals and even different calendars. Once this fact is accepted, supervisors can begin to predict issues that may arise. A primary strategy for reducing problems either within each system or especially between them is to increase the quantity and quality of communication.

Communication.   The university supervisor is often very clear about what kinds of communication are expected from the site supervisor; however, a reciprocity of information often is lacking. Shapiro (1988) reported a high burnout rate for site supervisors when there was a significant discrepancy between what was initially communicated to them regarding expectations and the actual demands of supervision, which superseded those expectations. Another error both sides make is to keep information too limited in its focus. For example, there can be ample information about placement expectations themselves from both sides. But university programs do not keep their field sites current with program growth or curriculum changes (Malouf, Haas, & Farah, 1983), and agencies do not let university programs know when administrative, fiscal, or programmatic changes are being planned or implemented. Programs do not always communicate clearly about the evaluation criteria that they adhere to (Elman et al., 1999). The result of such incomplete communication can be conflict that could have been avoided or two systems growing less and less relevant to each other without being aware of it. We will consider the types of communications that are desirable between graduate program and field site later in the chapter.

The remainder of this chapter will outline some of the tasks of supervision and some of the issues that can either enhance or detract from the goal of offering exemplary clinical supervision. We attempt to delineate which tasks are primarily the responsibility of the training program supervisor and which fall to the site supervisor. We also caution the reader that, in and of itself, well-organized supervision is not necessarily good supervision. But if clinical supervisors have addressed the tasks that follow, they can have some confidence that supervisory efforts will not be undermined by a crumbling structural base.

FOUNDATIONAL TASKS FOR ORGANIZING SUPERVISION

While we have discussed several ways in which supervisors prepare themselves to approach a productive supervision experience, we now turn our attention to tasks that involve the supervisor with the supervisee. While much of our discussion focuses on the trainee in a graduate program, many of the tasks outlined can be applied to all supervision relationships. As with many enterprises, it is also the case that most of the organizational activity is concentrated at the front end of the supervisory relationship. The reward for getting organized comes later when supervision is well underway.

Advising Trainees for Clinical Instruction

While all students in clinical training programs realize that there is a point at which they will begin seeing clients under supervision, students vary greatly in their awareness of the preparation process for this aspect of their education. For those graduate programs that use off-campus clinical sites, the first task is an advising one. Unless a training program has the luxury of a full-time (or even part-time) director of training or field placement coordinator, university supervisors must coordinate an advising system that will determine when students will be eligible to take either a practicum or internship and determine if there are ample supervisory resources to cover the number of requests in any given quarter or semester. In the absence of some system to manage the flow of clinical placements, some degree of chaos may reign. Among the consequences of random advising are rushed or inappropriate placements and rattled students. When matters are rushed, the field supervisor may think that the university program is slightly out of control and may feel less accountable to the program and the student as a result.

A key advising issue, then, is how much lead time a student should allow in finding an appropriate field placement. This will be determined by the following:

1. *The amount of local competition for field sites.* If there are other universities nearby or if other programs within the university are seeking the same sites, the student must start out earlier than if the market is wide open.
2. *The specificity of the student's interests.* If the student has a very specific interest not represented in a variety of sites (e.g., hospice work), then more lead time will be required.
3. *The policy of the specific agency.* Some agencies will only accept interns during a certain time period or may require a résumé and more than one interview, all of which are time consuming. To be assured enough time to find a site, the student should assume that there will be some hurdles to negotiate in the selection process.
4. *The relationship established between the university and a particular site.* Some sites not only want, but expect, students every semester. Because of their past dealings with the program, they require only minimal contact with the student prior to starting the field experience.

Selecting Sites

There is a good deal in the professional literature to assist doctoral students in selecting an appropriate practicum internship (e.g., Brill, Wolkin, & McKeel, 1987; Gloria & Robinson, 1994; Stewart & Stewart, 1996), with little attention given to this topic for the more common placement of premaster's-level mental health trainees. In some academic programs it is the training director or the faculty supervisor who makes the initial contact with a potential field site. In other programs it is the student who makes the first contact. In either case, the graduate program must assume a role in helping the student to determine the appropriateness of a particular site based on three categories of variables: program factors, student factors, and agency factors.

Program factors are those baseline conditions that must be met before a site can be accepted as meeting training goals. For example, the program may require that students not only see a variety of clients, but also have continuity in their work. Therefore, a crisis center that revolves around single-client contacts would not be an appropriate placement. Or the program may require that audiotaping be allowed for the purposes of campus supervision. This may be a nonnegotiable item for some sites and one that eliminates them.

Student factors can be introduced either by the student or observed by the supervisor. The student's career goals must be the most important variable in finding an appropriate site. Many other conditions can be survived if the site will increase the student's chances of pursuing a desired career path. Other student characteristics include whether the student is a self-starter or someone who needs a more structured atmosphere. The student's readiness for the demands of a particular site also must be of paramount importance. Developmentally, a desired site may not be appropriate for a particular student because of the difficulty of the clinical cases or the unavailability of close supervision that would ensure client protection. In addition to these, a variety of individual characteristics can be discussed to assist the student in identifying a site that will be both challenging and realistic for the student at this time.

Agency factors are the third consideration and include the atmosphere of the work environment (Stoltenberg & Delworth, 1987), the interest of the agency to work with students, the variety of opportunities within the agency, and the value placed on clinical supervision, to name a few. The agency factors may or may not be known by the campus supervisor or the student if the site has not been used before. Therefore, the student should be assisted in determining a list of things to look for when making contact with the site.

An early study (Raskin,1985) found that, for 12 accredited social work programs, student concerns ranked lowest in their impact on the placement decision. Instead, training program factors and environmental factors (e.g., availability of sites) ranked highest. This could be construed as the reality of the situation when many students compete for few good placements, and this, of course, is true in many geographical locations. It is also unlikely that conditions for site selection have improved significantly since the Raskin study was conducted. It is disheartening, however, to note that the educational needs of the student ranked 13 of 15 in importance when university field directors were seeking sites for their students. It would seem that this represents a breakdown in program goals. The solution might be a process that is more methodical in taking student factors into account as field placements are considered.

Table 8.1 adapts the work of Hamilton and Else (1983) to outline different agency dimensions that could be considered in making decisions regarding the appropriateness of a field placement site. It is doubtful that many sites will be optimal on all dimensions, but such an outline could serve to raise students' awareness of which items are most important to them.

Despite a program's best efforts to find a site that meets the student's and the program's expectations, it should also be noted that the advantage to the trainee of gaining clinical experience in the field is directly related to its untidiness (Beavers, 1986); in other words, mental health delivery systems are imperfect organizations, and the trainee who learns to navigate such organizations is better prepared to enter the job market. The challenge for graduate training programs is to weigh each organizational deficit with the opportunities afforded trainees. Is it better for the trainee to be provided with a steady flow of diverse clients or to have closely monitored supervision? Is it better for the trainee to work within one strong framework or to be challenged to work from a variety of perspectives? Is it more important to bow to accreditation

standards or to go with one's judgment of an exemplary experience? These kinds of questions must constantly be raised and resolved. It must be understood, however, that all but the most unique field placements represent some compromise for the training program.

Initial Communication between Graduate Program and Site

The reader will note that communication surfaces regularly in this chapter as a task for organizing supervision. While lip service is given to the importance of communication between all parties involved in a trainee's clinical supervision, a functional plan for communication is called for.

It is up to the university supervisor to communicate the program's expectations to the site supervisor, not the student's. Under the best of circumstances, this is done both in writing and in person. Personal contact allows the university supervisor to determine whether there is any resistance to meeting the program's requirements. It has been our experience that student trainees are typically not good judges of a site when the site is ambivalent about meeting program requirements. Perhaps they are too eager to find an appropriate site to be discriminating. Even when they do discern ambivalence, they are in a vulnerable position regarding the site and are uncertain about asserting themselves with potential site supervisors. Clearly, this is something the university supervisor can and should do. While we believe it is primarily the graduate program's responsibility to orient the site, Roberts, Morotti, Herrick, and Tilbury (2001) addressed the site's responsibility and urged site supervisors to seek full clarification of what is expected of them when they agree to take a supervisee.

Once a site has been chosen, it is important that the campus supervisor stay in touch with the site supervisor. A phone call or email a couple of weeks after the student has been placed is a good idea to be sure that things are going reasonably well. Additionally, there should be a plan for formal contacts in order to evaluate the student's

TABLE 8.1   Selecting an Appropriate Field Placement: Dimensions to Consider

Learning Opportunities
1. Administrative structure and location
   (a) Agency geared toward service delivery
   (b) Agency with high commitment to training
   (c) On-campus service delivery unit
2. Breadth of counseling issues represented
   (a) Primarily one problem area
   (b) Multiple problem areas
3. Theoretical orientation
   (a) Primarily one theoretical orientation
   (b) Two or more theoretical orientations
4. Methods of practice
   (a) One practice method
   (b) One primary, other secondary methods of practice
   (c) Multiple methods of practice (generalist orientation)
5. Interdisciplinary potential
   (a) One mental health discipline primary
   (b) Limited interdisciplinary exchange
   (c) Extensive interdisciplinary exchange
6. Primary service area
   (a) Rural
   (b) Small city
   (c) Inner city
   (d) Suburban
7. Diversity of population served
   (a) Services offered exclusively or primarily to one group (e.g., age, class, gender)
   (b) Services offered to persons representing diverse groups
8. Breadth of within-agency and across-agency experience
   (a) Experience in one program of one agency
   (b) Experience in several program units of one agency
   (c) Experience primarily in one agency with supplemental assignments to other agencies
9. Potential for student innovation
   (a) Work only with existing client groups using existing service delivery approaches
   (b) Potential for developing alternative service approaches and/or extending services to new client populations

Supervision Context
10. Sources of supervision
    (a) Single (exclusive) clinical supervisor
    (b) Primary supervisor plus supplemental supervisors
11. Number of students in field placement
    (a) One
    (b) Two to four
    (c) Over four
12. Supervision formats
    (a) Individual supervision
    (b) Group supervision
    (c) Live supervision
    (d) A mixture of two of the above

(continued)

TABLE 8.1   Continued

Field Placement Clinical Supervisor
13. Theoretical orientation
    (a) One theoretical perspective
    (b) One primary theoretical perspective with understandings and techniques from other perspectives integrated into practice
    (c) Several theoretical perspectives
    (d) Little emphasis on theoretical approach
14. Education of supervisor
    (a) Master's in same profession as supervisee
    (b) Master's in another helping profession
    (c) Postmaster's degree in same profession as supervisee
    (d) Postmaster's degree in another helping profession
15. Experience of supervisor as practitioner
    (a) Modest experience in area(s) of interest to supervisee
    (b) Extensive experience in area(s) of interest to supervisee
    (c) Modest experience in area(s) of interest to supervisee, but extensive experience in other areas of practice
16. Education and experience as a clinical supervisor
    (a) No formal training in supervision and limited experience as a supervisor
    (b) No formal training in supervision and extensive experience as a supervisor
    (c) Formal training in supervision and limited experience as a supervisor
    (d) Formal training in supervision and extensive experience as a supervisor
17. Supervisor's authority over supervision
    (a) Supervisor is responsible for supervision of supervisee
    (b) Supervisor reports to a superior regarding his or her supervision of supervisee
    (c) Supervisor is part of a team of persons who are responsible for supervision within agency
18. Time committed to supervision
    (a) Time is formally set aside for clinical supervision
    (b) Supervisor must adjust schedule to accommodate supervision demands

Adapted from *Designing Field Education: Philosophy, Structure, and Process,* by N. Hamilton and J. F. Else, 1983. Springfield, IL: Charles C Thomas.

progress. These can be done in person at the site or through written evaluations from the site. The site supervisor should know, however, when these will occur and what form they will take.

The Interview

The goal of the university training program is to place all students; the goal of the site supervisor is to make a judgment about the individual student's fit with the goals and work of the agency. Although background information is sometimes requested, the basis for the decision is usually the placement interview. It is essential that the site supervisor have a grasp of the attributes that are necessary for the student to take full advantage of the placement. If the site supervisor espouses a distinct model of therapy, this must be communicated clearly to the prospective supervisee (Olsen & Stern, 1990). It is equally essential that the site supervisor appreciate what a time-limited experience in the agency will be like and communicate this realistically to the candidate.

Trainees should receive feedback about this interview whether or not the site accepts them. Hearing the supervisor's perception of why one was seen as appropriate is a good beginning for a working relationship with the site supervisor. When the trainee is not accepted, it is important to know if the decision was made based on a negative evaluation of the student's competence or because of a perceived lack of fit. If the feedback is not given directly to the student, it should at least be given to the campus supervisor.

The interview may also serve as a metaphor for the agency. In other words, if the agency is unstructured and requires a great deal of creativity from staff, the interview should mirror this situation. If, on the other hand, the agency is highly structured with clear guidelines for each staff member's role, the interview should be handled similarly. This type of consistency serves two purposes: it becomes a first-level orientation for the student to the agency and its expectations, and it allows the site supervisor the opportunity to gain relevant data about the student on which to base a decision.

Orientation

Because of the relatively short duration of both practicum and of many internship situations, the trainee must be oriented to the organization and service delivery issues as efficiently as possible. There are some lessons that only a learn-as-you-go approach can accomplish. But many more things can be learned through an orientation. Unfortunately, many trainees feel that they are just getting a handle on procedures and policy issues as they wrap up their field experience. At least some of this can be attributed to an inadequate orientation process.

If an agency accepts trainees on a regular basis, the site supervisor would be wise to develop a trainee manual covering the major agency policies that must be mastered. (A good resource for such a manual is the trainees who are at the end of their field experience; they can usually be precise about what information would have made their adaptation easier.) If written orientation materials are not available, the site supervisor might schedule more intensive supervision the first week or so to cover orientation matters with the trainee. The supervi-

sor would be wise to use simulations of situations and ask the trainee to provide the correct procedure to be followed in order to determine if the policies are clear.

Role Induction

While the orientation helps the supervisee to navigate the nuts and bolts of practice within a specific agency, there is another potentially steep learning curve for which the student trainee needs assistance, and that is how to be a supervisee. Supervision relies on a different teaching process, one in which mistakes are expected and, alternatively, where several different approaches may be "correct." This paradigm shift from the vast majority of a supervisee's formal education can cause anxiety and frustration, especially for the more concrete learner. Supervision also shifts the balance of responsibility for learning to the supervisee, another condition that may be unfamiliar and/or uncomfortable to the supervisee. For these reasons, role induction has been suggested by some (e.g., Shanklin, 1994; Smith, 1994) as a potential remedy.

Role induction involves teaching about the role that one is about to adopt. Friedlander's (1980) early research on role induction for clients entering psychotherapy was promising and found role induction to be effective and long-lasting in enhancing clients' views toward the counseling process. In this study, role induction strongly emphasized client responsibility and role and minimized descriptions of counselor behaviors.

While some subsequent research on role induction for clients supported its effectiveness (e.g. Garfield, 1986; Kaul & Bednar, 1986), more recent studies have been less definitive (e.g., Strassle, 2001; Sutton, 1998). Despite these seeming contradictions, Monks's (1996) meta-analysis of 28 clinical studies found some support that role induction produced meaningful improvement.

Perhaps because of the intuitive attractiveness of role induction, the concept has also been examined for its utility in supervision. Again, results have been mixed. As we reported in Chapter 6, role induction has been found to increase disclosure among supervisees and can decrease supervisee anxiety (Bahrick, Russell, & Salmi, 1991; Chapin & Ellis, 2002; Ellis, Chapin, Dennin, & Anderson-Hanley, 1996). Yet, other studies found the utility of role induction to affect supervisees' readiness for a working alliance, for evaluation, for perception of supervision, as well as its effect on reducing supervisee anxiety, were inconclusive (Bahrick, 1989; Campione, 1993; Smith, 1994). While a deliberate effort to prepare supervisees for supervision seems only reasonable, exclusive reliance on role induction may not be warranted. Another intervention that should be considered for grounding supervisees and preparing them for the supervisory experience is the supervision contract.

The Supervision Contract

Supervision contracts or agreements of understanding have traditionally been good-faith documents between the training institution and the field site, stipulating the roles that would be played by the supervisee, the program supervisor, and the field site supervisor. Such agreements would also spell out the responsibilities for all parties and the opportunities that would be afforded to the supervisee for the duration of the contract. While such contracts are not binding in a legal sense, they serve the purpose of increasing accountability for those concerned.

More recently, emphasis has been placed on the supervision contract as a supervisory intervention. These more individualized supervision contracts should be created (usually with the supervisee) by the supervisor (either program or field) who will be the primary supervisor. While role induction is a one-time-only intervention, the supervision contract typically acts not only to orient the supervisee to supervision, but also as a roadmap for the entire experience. Hewson (1999) also hypothesized that contracts can have the positive effects of increasing mutuality of goals between supervisee and supervisor and minimizing covert agendas. Even so, supervision contracts can lean toward agency structure (i.e., how the supervisee must conform in order to be successful), toward reducing legal vulnera-

bility by outlining in detail ethical mandates and record-keeping imperatives (Falvey, 2002; Sutter, McPherson, & Geeseman, 2002), or toward the developmental learning goals of the supervisee (i.e., how supervision will be organized to maximize supervisee professional development).

Munson (2002) offered a supervision contract outline that reflects an emphasis on agency structure. Munson suggested that contracts include reference to the following:

1. *Timing element.* Frequency of supervision, length of session, and the duration of the supervision experience should be made clear.
2. *Learning structure.* Items that would fall under this heading have to do with approaches that the supervisor might use to enhance learning, including audiovisual techniques, cotherapy, assigned reading, and the like.
3. *Supervision structure.* Munson suggested that a contract include not only supervision modality (e.g., individual supervision, group supervision, or a combination), but also clear information about any change of supervisor, required rotation through different agency units, and explicit information about lines of authority.
4. *Agency conformity.* Items such as work hours, dress codes, agency rules regarding sharing phone numbers or emails, and record-keeping format would be covered in this section. Copeland (1998) also stressed the importance of transparency of agency parameters to protect both the supervisee and the supervisor.
5. *Special conditions.* Finally, Munson suggested that any requirements unique to a particular site should be delineated, as well as how the agency expects the supervisee to acquire the knowledge and skills listed. Among such requirements could include expertise in the DSM IV, familiarity with a particular assessment tool, or familiarity with medications.

Osborn and Davis (1996) developed contract guidelines that veer more toward the supervisee's professional development, while still covering necessary structural elements. Osborn and Davis argued that contracts not only help to clarify the supervision relationship, but can also be used to promote ethical practice by itemizing important ethical standards (e.g., informed consent) and their implementation within supervision. Osborn and Davis suggested that supervision contracts include the following:

1. *Purpose, goals, and objectives.* This category includes the obvious purpose of safeguarding clients, as well as promoting trainee development. Putting this in writing, however, is an important ritual for both supervisor and trainee. Additionally, the more immediate goal of, for example, completing the clinical requirements for a training program is listed as well.
2. *Context of services.* The contract must include where and when supervision will take place, what method of monitoring will be in place, and what supervision modalities will be used. We would add a description of the clientele to be served to this item.
3. *Method of evaluation.* Both formative and summative evaluation methods and schedules should be included. Any instrument that will be used for evaluation should be given to the trainee at this time.
4. *Duties and responsibilities of supervisor and supervisee.* In this section, both persons outline the behaviors that they are committed to in order that supervision evolve successfully. For the supervisor, this may include challenging the trainee to consider different treatment methods; for the trainee, this may include coming to each supervision session with a preset videotaped sample of one's use of a particular technique.
5. *Procedural considerations.* Part of the contract must address issues such as emergency procedures and the format for record keeping required by the agency. Osborn and Davis also advised that the contract include a procedure that is to be followed if either party feels that a conflict within supervision has not been resolved.
6. *Supervisor's scope of practice.* Finally, Osborn and Davis suggested that the supervisor's experience and clinical credentials be listed to "make explicit to themselves and their super-

visees their professional competence" (p. 130). A sample supervision contract adhering to Osborn and Davis guidelines is presented in the Supervisor's Toolbox.

While supervision contracts establish tasks and responsibilities for both supervisees and supervisors, a new nomenclature, that of the *supervisee bill of rights* (Giordano, Altekruse, & Kern, 2000; Munson, 2002), has emerged in the professional literature and clearly places the supervisee at the center of the contractual relationship. While such documents can include responsibilities of supervisees, they clearly emphasize the rights of supervisees to be the recipients of quality supervision. For example, Munson (2002) included five conditions as the bill of rights for the supervisee:

1. a supervisor who supervises consistently and at regular intervals;
2. growth-oriented supervision that respects personal privacy;
3. supervision that is technically sound and theoretically grounded;
4. be evaluated on criteria that are made clear in advance, and evaluations that are based on actual observation of performance; and
5. a supervisor who is adequately skilled in clinical practice and trained in supervision practice. (p. 43)

Giordano et al. (2000) have developed a comprehensive supervision document that outlines the nature of the supervisory relationship and clarifies expectations as part of the bill of rights. This is followed by a delineation of relevant ethical standards that regulate supervision. The authors subsequently offer a supervision contract template based on the bill of rights and an evaluation form to document the extent to which the supervisee experienced supervision as consistent with the bill of rights. The contribution of Giordano et al. offers a synthesis of intent and outcome that is still relatively rare in the profession. The full Giordano et al. document can be seen in the Supervisor's Toolbox.

Professional Disclosure Statements

While statements about the supervisor's credentials, supervision approach, experience, and the like, are often included in supervision contracts (e.g., Giordano et al., 2000: Osborn & Davis, 1996), some supervisors develop separate statements that specifically outline their credentials, their approach to supervision, and additional information to educate the supervisee about them and about their supervision. This practice of preparing professional disclosure statements has become more common as states have increasingly required them for mental health practitioners. Because therapists have experienced the advantage of preparing such statements for their clients, they began preparing statements specific to supervision for their supervisees.

Professional disclosure statements provide a slightly different slant than the supervision contract. Because they tend not to be individualized for each supervisee, they provide a look at the constants that a particular supervisor offers. If they go beyond the nuts and bolts type of statements, they can also be used as a "handout" to help to orient the supervisee to a particular process with a particular supervisor. We have found that putting one's beliefs, policies, and approaches on paper is good grounding for both supervisor and supervisee and is much more productive than attempting to convey an equal amount of information verbally.

A professional disclosure statement is required as part of the application process for the Approved Clinical Supervisor (ACS) credential (Center for Credentialing and Education, 2000). CCE, an affiliate of the National Board for Certified Counselors, Inc., requires that applicants for the ACS submit a professional disclosure statement that addresses the following:

1. Name, title, business address, and business telephone number
2. A listing of degrees, credentials, and licenses
3. General areas of competence in mental health practice in which the applicant can supervise
4. A statement documenting training in supervision and experience in providing supervision
5. A general statement addressing model(s) of or approach to supervision, including the role of the supervisor, objectives and goals of supervision, and modalities
6. A description of the evaluation procedures to be used in the supervisory relationship
7. A statement indicating the limits and score of confidentiality and privileged communication within the supervisory relationship
8. A statement, when applicable, indicating that the applicant is under supervision and that the supervisee's actions may be discussed with the applicant's supervisor
9. A fee schedule (when applicable)
10. A way to reach the applicant in an emergency situation
11. A statement indicating that the applicant follows a relevant credentialing body's Code of Ethics and CCE's Standards for the Ethical Practice of Clinical Supervision.

See the Supervisor's Toolbox for a sample of a professional disclosure statement created by a faculty supervisor for distribution to master's level practicum supervisees, and Fall and Sutton (2004) for additional examples of professional disclosure statements.

As we stated at the beginning of this section, the organizational suggestions described above are foundational; that is, they provide the framework for supervision and continue to reap benefits for supervisor and supervisee throughout the time they work together. In fact, it is very difficult later in a supervisory relationship to recover from a disorganized beginning. The few tasks that follow fall in the category of maintenance and are much less onerous when foundational tasks have received adequate attention.

ONGOING ORGANIZATIONAL TASKS

Communication, Communication, Communication

We have already discussed the importance of initial communication among all parties in establishing field placements. And supervision contracts and professional disclosure statements certainly are organized around the value of clear and open communication. The balance of supervision must reflect adequate communication as well. "Communication is the heart and soul of the counseling profession, yet, too often, communications among site supervisor, the intern, and the [training] program get garbled" (Roberts et al., 2001). The need for increased communication between the field and graduate programs has been echoed by others as well (Kahn, 1999; Lee & Cashwell, 2001).

While communication among several parties once meant a number of phone calls, site visits, or clearly crafted memos, the Internet significantly reduces the effort that must be expended to keep everyone abreast of changes. An email address book of site supervisors would allow the training program to communicate efficiently regarding program developments (an area that almost always gets neglected, at least in the short run). Chat rooms could invite site supervisor input to campus supervisory discussions. With very little technological expertise or effort required, the communication between training program and site could be vastly improved.

While technology serves an important purpose in communication, it cannot replace site visits or contacts by phone. Meetings on campus for site supervisors are also essential in allowing a forum for discussion and professional development. Training programs should attempt to communicate new developments in the area of supervision to their site supervisors. Although site supervisors have a wealth of practical knowledge, traditionally they have not stayed as current as university types in terms of the research on supervision, new models and techniques, and the supervision literature in general. Therefore, in-service training for site supervisors or seminars in which both campus and site supervisors share their ideas and experiences comprise a special kind of communication activity (Beck, Yager, Williams, Williams, & Morris, 1989; Brown & Otto, 1986; Roberts et al., 2001).

Just as it is critical for the university supervisor to keep the site supervisor abreast of pro-

grammatic developments, it is equally important for the site supervisor to keep the university current. Political, organizational, and fiscal developments may affect trainees both in their field experiences and employment search. When campus supervisors are kept current about what is going on in their sites, they are better able to advise students about the professions that they are entering.

An invaluable contribution that site supervisors can make to training programs is to communicate their opinion of the training that the students have received prior to their field placement. Once a site supervisor has overseen several trainees from the same program, the supervisor is in a position to see thematic strengths and weaknesses. To do this, however, site supervisors must have a template that allows them to view the trainee in a variety of ways so that this type of appraisal can be accomplished in a valid and consistent manner. This template can emerge from either the site or the training program, though it is more likely to come from the latter.

Perhaps the most important time for prompt and thoughtful communication between program and site is when there is conflict between the supervisee and the site or if the site supervisor is concerned about the performance of the supervisee (Elman et al., 1999; Igartua, 2000; Leonardelli & Gratz, 1985). It is important that training programs encourage sites to contact the training program if a supervisee shows any signs of unprofessional behavior, impairment, or developmental stagnation. Occasionally, it is the supervisee who raises issues of concern. Although it is important for students to have experience in resolving conflict, the power differential between them and their site supervisors may make this difficult in some cases. In such instances, the program supervisor has a legitimate role to play. Leonardelli and Gratz (1985) outlined three sources of conflict for which it is appropriate for the campus supervisor to become involved:

1. *Inconsistency in performance expectations.* An example of this type of conflict is if the student understood that he or she would be spending the majority of time at the site in direct service and finds, instead, that the site supervisor expects a sizable amount of time to be spent in meetings, outreach activities, written work, and the like.

2. *Incompatibility between expectations and reality of the facility.* Recently, one of our students experienced this kind of conflict. She was placed in a community center that offered a program for high-risk children. She was advised that she would be working with the parents while the children were in group therapy. Parent involvement, however, was very low and the student spent the majority of her time assisting in play therapy, not one of her career goals. In a review of unsuccessful field placements, Holtzman and Raskin (1988) found that a major contributing factor to their failure was "limited exploration and monitoring by the school of the learning opportunities in different agencies" (p. 131). Obviously, the faculty supervisor cannot be held accountable if an agency misrepresents itself, but it is probably more common that the faculty's investigation prior to the placement of the student is incomplete.

3. *Inconsistency between expectations of the educational facility and the field site.* A prime example of this would be when the educational facility expected that clinical supervision would occur primarily on the site, but the site expected the reverse.

In conflict situations, Leonardelli and Gratz (1985) asserted that the campus supervisor should attempt to mediate and find the best compromise between the site and the trainee, with either party potentially being asked to adjust to the other.

Finally, as specified by Hardcastle (1991), the site supervisor must organize communication within the agency to benefit the trainee. It happens occasionally that a trainee has contact only with the supervisor and feels isolated from the rest of the agency. In some instances, trainees are made to feel disloyal if they happen to ask some advice from another employee other than their supervisors. This always leads to a negative outcome. The supervisor should have a plan as to how the trainee will be integrated into the agency, including attendance at staff meetings and joint projects with other staff members.

Communication and Evaluation. Finally, it is the prerogative and responsibility of the university supervisor to develop an evaluation plan and to conduct all summative evaluations. The extent to which the site is being asked to evaluate the supervisee must be clearly communicated (Olsen & Stern, 1990). As Rosenblum and Raphael (1987) noted, however, site supervisors typically dread evaluating university students. Kadushin (1992c) offered empirical support that evaluation was among supervisors' least favorite responsibilities. When the site supervisor's experience with a trainee has been positive, evaluation tends to be glowing; when the trainee has not met expectations, the evaluation is sometimes avoided. It is our belief that site supervisors, because their relationships with trainees are short term and because their relationships with the universities are rarely mandated, should not be asked to carry out discriminating summative evaluations. For example, the site supervisor should not be asked to grade the student except to give a pass or fail recommendation. On the other hand, it is important for site supervisors to give feedback, both to the trainee and to the university supervisor. But the task of translating feedback into a final grade is clearly the charge of the program faculty. (Evaluation procedures were delineated in Chapter 2.)

Supervisor as Agency Representative. Another communication function, but one that the site supervisor is less likely to perceive as such, is to serve as a liaison or advocate between supervisees and agency administration. (Even if the supervisor wears two hats, when in the role of clinical supervisor, the supervisor must communicate administrative issues to supervisees.) This function is unique enough to be addressed separately and is critical to the supervisee's professional development. Often, the site supervisor fulfills this role in an informal manner, sharing bits and pieces of both spoken and unspoken rules, agency politics, and the like. When done in an informal fashion, however, the trainee is more likely to get incomplete information and/or become triangulated in organizational power struggles. It is far better for the interface between service delivery and organizational realities to be covered in supervision in a deliberate way. Perhaps part of each supervision session could be reserved for organizational issues, not as a gripe session but as a learning process. Munson (1993) stated that interns may avoid certain interventions because they perceive them as being contrary to organizational policy. Whether or not the trainee is correct, this is an important area of discussion for the trainee and supervisor.

It is far more likely, however, that trainees will be naive about organizations (Munson, 1993). Every person who has worked in an organization knows that there are unspoken rules that must be understood in order to succeed in the environment. Some of these must be learned through experience. But how the ecology of an agency affects each branch of its operation is something that can be addressed during the field experience. In summary, the trainee should leave the field experience with some systemic understanding of the site and how this affected the trainee's particular role in that site. While many supervisees figure out some of this on their own, site supervisors can assist them in this task and help them to frame their experience positively.

Another liaison function of the site supervisor is to structure some way that other agency personnel can give input about the performance of the trainee. Again, it is too common for this to occur informally and therefore inconsistently. The site supervisor can devise a short form and ask colleagues to complete it once or twice during the field placement. This kind of overture can have several positive effects.

1. It lessens the trainee's isolation by involving additional personnel in the trainee's experience.
2. It can provide the trainee with additional feedback from different perspectives or role positions.
3. It can confirm or confront the supervisor's own evaluation of the trainee.

Managing Time

Time management has become a cliché, even as the challenge to "find time" seems to increase. Supervisors are busy people. Whether at the university or in the human service agency, many obligations compete with supervision. Because supervision is an enjoyable role for many professionals, they often take it on when they really have little extra time. Time management, therefore, becomes a crucial skill; one that needs to be exercised and modeled for trainees who themselves are juggling several roles. Falvey (1987) listed several simple time-management strategies for administrative supervisors, which include coordinating activities to maximize one's productivity (e.g., tackling difficult tasks when one's energy is high), avoiding escapists behaviors (e.g., doing an unpleasant task first thing in the morning, rather than allowing it to bear on one's mind all day), and dividing difficult tasks so that they do not appear overwhelming.

Perhaps the most central time-management skill is the ability to set priorities and keep to them. It is virtually impossible to end one's work day with absolutely no work left over for the following day. Rather, supervisors who can manage time have addressed the most important concerns immediately and have learned to pace themselves in accomplishing less pressing tasks. For some supervisors, it is a seemingly natural ability to take control of one's schedule; for others, it is a constant struggle that can be supplemented by time-management strategies suggested in the literature. Covey et al. (1994) warned against falling into an urgency mentality; that is, what is immediate is always treated as urgent, even when it is not. They also cautioned against using time-management strategies to fit an unreasonable amount of activity into one's schedule, a sentiment echoed by Osborn (in press). In other words, time management can become part of the problem, not the solution. Regardless of how the supervisor accomplishes the goal of finding and protecting time for supervision, the supervisor must realize that making time must be a deliberate choice and is not something that will take care of itself.

Assuming that one has found an adequate amount of time to dedicate to supervision, the issue of timing emerges. When is it best to supervise? How often should supervisees be monitored? Does it matter? We will discuss the supervision issues imbedded in the timing of supervision in Chapter 9. Based on these, the supervisor should attempt to devise the most productive supervision schedule for the supervisee.

Time Management and Burnout. The site supervisor has considerable control over the atmosphere within which the trainee (and all supervisees) work. The trainee is not likely to refer to an initial experience as one of burnout, but trainees have often referred to being overwhelmed and too busy to be able to integrate the experience (Kaslow & Rice, 1985). Supervisors who work with trainees often realize that all employees need to have their work environment managed. All mental health practitioners need time to regroup and consult if they are to remain vital in their direct service responsibilities. Structuring time so that supervisees have a variety of activities and the opportunity for collegial support in their day will raise not only the quality of the work environment, but also the quality of service delivery (Falvey, 1987; Osborn, in press). Protecting supervisees from overload communicates a respect for the practitioner and also respect for the work that needs to be done, work that should be done by persons who can perform at their optimal level.

The issue of supervisor burnout is relevant to this discussion. Managing from a perspective that protects supervisees must encompass a respect for the supervisor's multiple responsibilities as well. In their survey of clinical supervisors, Nichols, Nichols, and Hardy (1990) found that supervisors were less invested in doing supervision than supervisors were a decade earlier. Though the reasons for this decline in interest were not reported, the demands of supervision in organizations that do not provide adequate resources for this demanding role must be considered as a reasonable hypothesis. It seems imperative, therefore, that supervisors take themselves into consideration when developing a plan for supervision, a plan that allows them the time and support that they need to conduct clinical supervision in a manner that adds to the quality of their work environment.

Time Management and Choosing Supervision Methods. Chapters 9, 10, and 11 outline a variety of ways in which the process of supervision can be conducted. Deciding on the form that supervision will take and implementing the desired process can be an organizational task of significant proportion. For example, the supervisor might decide that using Interpersonal Process Recall (Kagan, 1976; Kagan & Kagan, 1997) would be desirable with a particular supervisee because of difficulties the supervisee is having with one of her clients. Using the technique, however, will require that videotape equipment be made available and that arrangements be made for videotaping the next therapy session. It is understandable, though regrettable, that supervisors often default on their supervision plans because the method that supervision *should* take becomes logistically too complicated. If the supervisor is convinced that a particular process (e.g., IPR or live supervision) is essential for the supervisee's learning, it is incumbent on the supervisor to work out the logistical details. When supervisors continue to put aside their teaching instincts because of the time and care required, the quality of supervision eventually deteriorates. Perhaps there is no organizational responsibility so essential to clinical supervision as the choreography required to ensure that the method of supervision match the learning needs of supervisees.

Record Keeping

In a litigious era the process of record keeping has gained in importance for helping professionals of all disciplines. Falvey and Cohen (2003) asserted that from a legal perspective "if it isn't documented, it didn't occur." Others have concurred that good clinical records serve as a desirable defense against litigation (Brantley, 2000; Snider, 1987; Soisson, Vandecreek, & Knapp, 1987; Swenson, 1997).

Whether supervising from campus or on site, it is the supervisor's responsibility to be sure that client records are complete. Most agencies and university professors have established record-keeping procedures that have evolved over time. But with an ever changing professional and legal climate, the wise supervisor reviews the record-keeping system occasionally to be sure that it is current with national trends. Among the items that should be considered for inclusion in client records are the following (Mitchell, 1991; Munson, 2002; Schultz, 1982):

1. Written and signed informed consents for all treatment, as well as signed informed consent for all transmissions of confidential information
2. Treatment contracts, if used
3. Notes on all treatment contacts made, either in person or by telephone, including descriptions of significant events and interventions made
4. Notes on all contacts or consultation with significant others, including correspondence
5. A complete history and symptom picture leading to diagnosis, with regular review (every 90 days) and revision of the diagnosis, as well as treatment direction based on diagnosis
6. A record of all prescriptions and current drug use profile
7. Any instructions, suggestions, or directives made to the client that he or she failed to follow through on
8. Records relevant to supervision, including permission to tape sessions, and consultations sought by either supervisee or supervisor regarding a case
9. A record of termination and an aftercare plan (Beis, 1984)

Recent research conducted by Worthington, Tan, and Poulin (2002) underscored the wisdom of supervisor vigilance regarding supervisee documentation of work with clients. Of the behaviors viewed by supervisees and supervisors as unethical, one of the most frequently committed (as reported by supervisees about their own behavior) was failure "to complete documentation of client records within the required time frame" (p. 335). Additionally, while both supervisors and super-

visees found this behavior to be problematic, supervisees found it less so than supervisors. The authors concluded that:

> . . . documentation is one of the most important protections against legal liability because of its importance in establishing whether a given liability claim meets the criteria for malpractice, and failure to complete documentation may increase exposure to liability if harm comes to a client—a set of circumstances that may be more salient to supervisors than it is to supervisees. (p. 345)

Most supervisors are far more careful about client records than about supervision records. Yet, as the Tarasoff case pointed out (*Tarasoff v. Regents of the University of California*, 1976), supervision records can be equally important in a liability suit. On a more optimistic note, supervision records discipline supervisors to pause and consider their supervision with each supervisee, offering moments of insight that would not otherwise occur. Therefore, for legal and instructional reasons, supervisors must keep accurate and complete supervision records.

Munson's (2002) suggested outline for supervision records is as follows:

1. the supervisory contract, if used or required by the agency;
2. a brief statement of supervisee experience, training, and learning needs;
3. a summary of all performance evaluations;
4. notation of all supervisory sessions;
5. cancelled or missed sessions;
6. notation of cases discussed and significant decisions; and
7. significant problems encountered in the supervision and how they were resolved, or whether they remain unresolved and why. (p. 256)

We offer the Supervision Record Form (SRF) which asks the supervisor to focus on goals for supervision and subsequent supervision interventions (including a rationale for each). While the primary purpose of the SRF is the assist the supervisor in reflecting upon his/her supervision, the form also includes a section directed at supervision risk management (see Figure 8.2).

FIGURE 8.2 Supervision Record Form

Date: _____

Supervisor: _____ Therapist: _____

First name(s) of client(s) discussed: _____

For the names of clients listed, indicate whether you heard/saw a portion of the counseling session:

_____

Pre-session goals for the supervision session:

_____

_____

_____

_____

Extent to which pre-session goals were met: (Comment)

_____

_____

_____

_____

Major topics that emerged during the supervision session (either supervisor-initiated or supervisee-initiated):

_____

_____

_____

_____

List client(s)-focused supervision interventions (including a rationale for each):

_____

_____

_____

_____

List supervisee-focused supervision interventions (including a rationale for each):

_____

_____

_____

_____

Goals for next supervision session:

_____

_____

_____

_____

Risk management review. Note any concerns based on review of supervisee's entire caseload. Include (a) 1st name [or case number] of client, (b) nature of the concern, and (c) supervision intervention at this time.

_____

_____

_____

_____

_____

Signature

Elaborating on the risk management theme, Falvey, Caldwell, and Cohen (2002) developed the Focused Risk Management Supervisory System (FoRMSS). The system addresses more directly the legal liability of supervisors for the well-being of their supervisees' clients, as well as the challenge of offering ethical and comprehensive supervision in light of the trend toward brief managed care. Although FoRMSS is a complete documentation system, only the Supervisory Record Form is reprinted here (see Figure 8.3) and is the central method for tracking supervision, as well as monitoring client well-being. Not only does the form require an updated case review, but it also requires the supervisor to record recommendations in several categories, including training recommendations for the supervisee. Finally, and most critical for risk management, the supervisor is alerted to review several ethical, clinical, and supervisory topics to ensure that these complicating issues are not neglected in supervision. If the supervisor is concerned about any issues listed in the shaded area, he or she documents whatever action is taken and this becomes part of the supervision record. FoRMSS represents a new standard for supervision record keeping and benefits the entire therapy system by keeping supervision focused on its multiple levels from a variety of angles.

Planning for the Exceptions

While most of supervision is organized to address the norm, the best supervisors have planned ahead for situations that may or may not occur (Rinas & Clyne-Jackson, 1988). It is frustrating, if not frightening, for a trainee to face an emergency with a client, for example, the need to hospitalize, and have no idea how the situation is to be handled. While it may be the supervisor's intention or assumption that a supervisee will never handle an emergency alone, the unexpected happens, and emergency procedures should be in written form, given to the trainee during orientation, and placed in a convenient place for reference should an emergency occur.

Another time when planning ahead is crucial is when the supervisor will be away. For example, it is not unusual for all clinical supervisors in a training program to attend the same conference, leaving a university-based clinic either in the hands of doctoral students or fill-in supervisors. With the rush to prepare the paper that will be presented at the conference or the arrangements that

FIGURE 8.3 FoRMSS Supervision Record

Date: _____ Supervisee: _____ Client ID: _____ Review Method: _____

Updated Case Review: _____

_____

_____

Interventions and Client Progress: _____

_____

_____

Supervisee Concerns: _____

_____

_____

SUPERVISION SESSION SUMMARY

Discussion (theoretical bases, case conceptualization, clinical judgment, etc.): _____

_____

_____

_____

Treatment Recommendations: _____

_____

_____

Referrals (also record on FoRMSS Case Overview): _____

_____

Observations and Training Recommendations: _____

_____

_____

CURRENT RISK MANAGEMENT ISSUES

☐ Informed Consent	☐ Child Abuse/Neglect	☐ Supervisee Expertise	☐ Releases Needed
☐ Parental Consent	☐ Risk of Significant Harm	☐ Supervisor Expertise	☐ Vol./Invol. Hospitalization
☐ Confidentiality	☐ Duty to Warn	☐ Institutional Conflict	☐ 3rd Party/UR Review
☐ Recordkeeping	☐ Substance Abuse	☐ Dual Relationship	☐ Discharge/Termination
☐ Records Security	☐ Medical Exam Needed	☐ Sexual Misconduct	☐ _____

Action Taken: _____

_____

_____

From *Documentation in Supervision: Focused Risk Management Supervision System (FoRMSS), 1st edition* by Falvey/Caldwell/Cohen. Copyright © 2002. Reprinted with permission of Wadsworth, a division of Thomson Learning: www.thomsonrights.com. FAX 800 730-2215.

must be made to cover one's classes, it often happens that a colleague from the field or another department is asked to cover supervision with little or no information about the operations of the clinic, the status of any worrisome clients, or the student staff. This could easily be a case for which the lack of managerial foresight takes on the characteristics of questionable ethical practice.

By planning ahead we do not mean to suggest that the supervisor compulsively worry about every possible way that things may go wrong. "The sky is falling" is not a productive supervisory posture. Rather, we urge supervisors to take reasonable care regarding their responsibilities and, especially, to give themselves the time to plan well and to put their plans into action.

EVALUATION AND DEBRIEFING

The many dimensions of evaluation were covered in Chapter 2; therefore, at this point, we only remind the supervisor that evaluation is both a maintenance task and a final activity for the supervisor. Chapter 2 offered many ways to organize the evaluative aspect of supervision, and these should be reflected in the supervision contract and the record-keeping system.

While most supervisees receive some sort of final evaluation, many do not experience a quality debriefing of their time under supervision. This is unfortunate, because many worthwhile insights could be offered by both supervisor and supervisee during a debriefing session. In fact, debriefing is a perfect context for the supervisor to receive feedback about the supervision package that was offered to the supervisee, including how well supervision was organized. A debriefing can also include comments about how the supervisee might approach future supervision experiences in ways that build on the experience just ended.

SOME FINAL THOUGHTS

Short of receiving training in time management or developing training manuals, what can the clinical supervisor do to achieve organizational com-

petence (not that the former wouldn't be a good idea)? This chapter has presented many of the goals that the clinical supervisor might set for himself or herself. The following are five additional guidelines that can be of use as one sets out to achieve these goals.

Get Support. Before clinical supervisors commit themselves to the substantial task of supervising either on or off a university campus, they should be sure that they have administrative support for their activity (Copeland, 1998). Beck, Yager, Williams, Williams, and Morris (1989) found that clinical supervision was compromised if the agency director did not support having trainees on site. This position was reiterated by Holloway and Roehlke (1987) regarding APA-accredited internship sites. Likewise, an academic program director must appreciate the time it takes to develop good field sites, to organize the operation of practicum and internship, and to serve as an ongoing liaison with sites. If, as most accrediting bodies suggest, the faculty supervisor also offers to train site supervisors, the responsibilities can begin to grow exponentially. The greater the support offered by superiors, the more that can be accomplished and the better the quality of the supervision. If support is limited, the clinical supervisor must decide if minimal standards can be met. If they cannot, the supervisor must decline an offer to supervise on ethical grounds.

Know Yourself. As simple as it sounds, there seems to be a relatively high degree of unawareness among clinical supervisors about their ability to organize themselves and those under their supervision. Perhaps supervisors assume that they should already have the organizational skills to manage the supervisory process and therefore resist admitting that this is an area in which they need to grow. Perhaps the expectation that they already have all the skills they need to do the job comes from others around them, leaving them little room to be tentative. Regardless of the source, a cycle of false assumptions, followed by denial, can keep a clinical supervisor operating at a less than satisfactory level regarding the managerial responsibilities of the supervisor's position.

Organization comes far more naturally to some than to others. When supervisors believe that they fall in the latter category, they should find a member of their staff or a professional colleague who they believe can help to develop a plan or, more likely, help to implement a plan. (For example, a highly intuitive thinker on the Myers–Briggs Type Indicator would benefit from consultation with a more sensing type.) The beginning of implementation is a critical juncture that calls for different abilities than those required for arriving at the original plan. This is the point at which many clinical supervisors could use assistance.

Gather Data.   There is nothing particularly virtuous about reinventing the wheel. As supervisors approach the task of organizing a training program or the clinical operation of an agency, they might contact other training programs or agencies and ask for samples of policy statements, supervision forms, and other materials relevant to their tasks. When a specific issue arises, consulting with colleagues and determining how they have managed a similar issue is a sound strategy. Isolating oneself is a common supervisor flaw, both in terms of clinical work and organizational tasks. Supervisors have a tremendous amount to learn from each other, and they need to model for their supervisees the ability to consult with others as part of good clinical practice.

The professional literature is another source for data collection. There is less about the management of clinical supervision in the literature than there might be, but the careful reader will gather important information from the research on supervision and from others' investigations and descriptions of the process of supervision that should then influence organizational decisions. For those receiving training in supervision, the development of a supervision portfolio of criteria for evaluation, templates for supervision contracts and record keeping, and the like, will serve well in the future.

Get Feedback.   Any new procedure should be considered a pilot study of sorts. An organizational strategy may work well from the supervisor's vantage point, but be untenable for supervisees. The competent supervisor knows how to manipulate procedures to work for people and the program or agency, not the other way around. Part of this competence is demonstrated by seeking the opinions of others. The result is an organizational style that is always being fine-tuned without continually starting over from scratch.

Be Intentional.   One way to avoid having to scrap one plan for another (and thereby keeping those under supervision in a state of turmoil) is for supervisors to give themselves permission to build their organizational plan slowly, but deliberately. No one who is supervising for the first time will be totally organized in the first year. Rather, one should begin with those aspects of supervision that are most critical for ethical and safe practice and eventually pay heed to items that add to convenience and expediency of communication, a variety of training goals, among other things. In addition to being practical, being intentional encourages the supervisor to immediately home in on those things that are absolutely essential to any supervisory operation. Discriminating between issues that are essential and those that are desirable is the beginning and the core of organizational competence.

CONCLUSION

Although organizational issues tend to fall to the bottom of the list of driving forces for clinical supervisors, the manner in which they are handled may be more predictive of long-term success as a supervisor than clinical expertise. Organizational tasks are tedious only when they are viewed as distractors. When viewed as building blocks for the essential work of supervision, organizational challenges can tap the energy typically reserved for activities such as establishing a working relationship with a supervisee. Paradoxically, the energy invested in the organization of clinical supervision may produce the greatest payoff in terms of protecting time and providing a context for exemplary supervisory practice. Fall and Sutton (2004) offer additional resources to arrive at this outcome.

CHAPTER 9

SUPERVISION INTERVENTIONS
INDIVIDUAL SUPERVISION

Having described the major parameters of supervision and the supervisory relationship, we are finally prepared to consider more specifically the delivery of a variety of supervision interventions. This chapter on individual supervision is only one of three chapters that will look at methods of supervision. It will be followed by chapters on group supervision and live supervision. It should also be noted that, in a way, most of the chapters in this text have supervision intervention implications. Individual differences, interpersonal issues, ethical dilemmas, delivering evaluative feedback—all require specific supervision interventions. This chapter serves a more general purpose, a template so to speak, for how supervision takes place in a one-on-one context.

Individual supervision is still considered the cornerstone of professional development. Although most supervisees will experience some form of group supervision in their training and some may have an opportunity to work within a live supervision paradigm, virtually all supervisees will experience individual supervision sessions. Whether these individual conferences will produce memories and insights that will linger long into the supervisee's career or will frustrate or perhaps even bore the supervisee has something to do with the supervisor's skill in choosing and using a variety of supervision methods. At this point in the history of the helping professions, there are many different approaches and techniques from which the supervisor can choose to conduct an individual case conference. This chapter will outline the most common of these assorted approaches and discuss their advantages and occasional disadvantages. Although all the supervision interventions described in this chapter are appropriate for individual conferences, many also could be applied within a group supervision context. Chapter 10 on group supervision, however, focuses on strategies that rely on group dynamics for their implementation.

Finally, we return to our previous comment about the connectedness between this chapter (as well as the two following) and the rest of the book. When writing a textbook of this sort, each chapter becomes an artificial compartmentalization of one aspect of the whole. The gestalt, so to speak, is violated. Although this cannot be avoided, it seems particularly problematic as we consider methods and techniques of supervision. Of all the many aspects of clinical supervision, methods of supervision perhaps are the most vulnerable to abuse. That is, it is possible to conduct supervision using a great many different formats without stepping back to consider the bigger picture—a conceptual base, an evaluation plan, ethical constraints, cultural differences, and so on. We urge the reader, therefore, to view this chapter not in isolation, but in the context of other concepts presented in this book.

INITIAL CRITERIA FOR CHOOSING SUPERVISION INTERVENTIONS

A supervisor's initial choice of method is influenced by a number of factors, both rational and irrational in nature. The supervisor might believe that without an audiotape or videotape of counseling or therapy there is no real way to know what has transpired between supervisees and their clients. Or the supervisor might be adamant that self-report is the only form of supervision that provides a glimpse at the supervisee's internal reasoning. The list can, and indeed does, go on. To help ensure more rational choices Borders and Leddick (1987) listed six reasons for choosing specific supervision methods: "The supervisee's learning goals, the supervisee's experience level and developmental issues, the supervisee's learning style, the supervisor's goals for the supervisee, the supervisor's theoretical orientation, and the supervisor's own learning goals for the supervisory experience" (p. 28).

Chapter 5 addressed many of the issues of individual differences among supervisees, including developmental level and learning style. Authors have often implied that developmental constraints and learning style dictate the amount of structure that is called for in working with specific supervisees. This chapter will offer some thoughts about the issue of structure in supervision. Beyond and in addition to such considerations are the supervisee's goals and the supervisor's goals for the process and outcome of supervision.

Supervision is best placed somewhere on the continuum between training and consultation. In other words, the supervisee should come to supervision with some ability to articulate learning goals based on initial experiences in training, but cannot be expected to function autonomously with only occasional needs for consultation. Supervision methods, therefore, will need to take into account the supervisee's stated goals and known supervision needs, as well as how far down the training–supervision–consultation axis the supervisee has traveled. By and large, however, supervision methods will reflect the supervisor's vision of supervision more than the supervisee's, with the exception perhaps of the more advanced supervisee. The issue of vision, therefore, deserves attention before describing unique supervision modalities.

By supervisor vision we mean the convictions held by the supervisor about how supervisees become competent practitioners. Whether this vision is derived from the professional literature, personal experience, or some other cluster of factors is irrelevant to our discussion. Regardless of its origin or validity, the supervisor's vision will inspire the process of supervision. The supervisor may or may not be aware of having a vision of supervision, but the vision will influence greatly the supervisor's selection of models and the methods that derive from them.

As described earlier in Chapter 4, supervision has grown significantly in terms of options available to the supervisor. While increased attention has been given in the recent past to more interactive forms of supervision (e.g., live supervision, teleconferencing), there is a new emergence of authors calling for supervision methods that will increase supervisees' thoughtfulness and ability to reflect on their work as they increase in skill (Carroll, 2001; Koch, Arhar, & Wells, 2000; Nelson & Neufeldt, 1998; Neufeldt, 1997; Skovholt & Rønnestad, 1992, 1995). Neufeldt (1997) argued that the supervisor may choose to deliberately ignore empirical findings that indicate that novice trainees prefer structured supervision interventions in order to encourage reflectivity in the supervisee. But if the supervisee is not only a novice but concrete in conceptual style, some structured intervention may be necessary to usher the supervisee into a process that may lead to reflectivity.

Methods and techniques, therefore, must be malleable and conducive to reaching a variety of supervision goals. Technical eclecticism may be as important to supervisors as it has been argued to be for therapists. Our point is that within the supervisor's vision there may be a variety of methods from which to choose. The supervisor's vision need not be compromised, but creative alternatives may be needed to accomplish immediate goals, as well as goals that are more long range.

Finally and most specifically, an additional aid for the supervisor in determining what method to use in a given situation is to pinpoint the immediate function of supervision. There are three general functions of supervision interventions (Borders et al., 1991): (1) assessing the learning needs of the supervisee, (2) changing, shaping, or supporting the supervisee's behavior, and (3) evaluating the performance of the supervisee. Although the majority of supervision falls within the second function, supervisors are continually reassessing their supervisee's learning needs and evaluating their progress. As these separate functions are being addressed, the supervisor might find that different methods serve one function better than others. For example, a supervisor might choose to watch a videotape of a supervisee to assess that person's skills, but rely on process notes to accomplish the second function of attempting to change, support, or redirect the supervisee's work.

STRUCTURED VERSUS UNSTRUCTURED INTERVENTIONS

Much of the literature addressing developmental issues, cognitive style of the supervisee, and numerous other topics refers to the relative need of structure in supervision. Rarely, however, do authors describe specifically what is meant by structure or the lack of it. Highly structured supervision can be viewed as an extension of training, while unstructured supervision can be viewed as approaching consultation. Although methods of supervision are often associated with a particular degree of structure, it is the supervisor's use of the method that will determine the level of structure. For example, Rigazio-DiGilio and Anderson (1994) noted that a structured use of live supervision might entail the use of the bug-in-the-ear, thus coaching the supervisee through a therapy session, while a less structured form might rely on presession planning, midsession coaching, and postsession debriefing. (See Chapter 11 for a complete description of these options.) Similarly, individual supervision based on audiotape may be directed by the supervisor and follow the supervisor's instructional agenda, or the use of audiotape may be requested by the supervisee to reflect on a moment in a counseling session that had special meaning for the supervisee.

In short, structure or the lack of structure is not dictated by the modality used. Rather, structured interventions are supervisor directed and involve a reasonably high amount of supervision control; unstructured interventions may be supervisor or supervisee directed and require more discipline on the part of the supervisor to allow learning to take place without directing it. For the supervisor who is impatient or who dislikes ambiguity, unstructured interventions will be more challenging; for the supervisor who has difficulty planning ahead and organizing learning, structured interventions will be more challenging. The great majority of supervisees will benefit from both types of interventions at different junctures in their professional development.

METHODS, FORMS, AND TECHNIQUES OF SUPERVISION

With technology and computer capabilities becoming more sophisticated every day and with the helping professions exhibiting a heightened interest in supervision, different techniques, methods, and paradigms for conducting supervision continue to evolve at a rapid pace. Because of the dynamic nature of the field, therefore, we do not presume to present an inclusive list of supervision interventions. Rather, we hope to reflect the diversity of choices that has been spawned as clinical supervision continues to evolve, to give some rationale for using different methods, and to report the findings on their frequency of use and relative strengths and weaknesses as reported in the literature.

The remainder of this chapter has been designed to review some of the supervision methods that accomplish that work, advancing from those methods that allow the least direct observation by the supervisor to those that allow the most. Therefore, self-report begins our list as a supervision format that relies on the supervisee's recollections of counseling or therapy as the source of information to be used for supervision.

Self-report

Although it is a simple form of supervision in one sense, we consider self-report to be a difficult method to perform well. In fact, some of the best and the worst supervision can be found within the domain of self-report. Under the best of conditions, supervisees will be challenged conceptually and personally and will learn a great deal. Many supervisors relying on self-report, however, have fallen into stagnation; supervision becomes pro forma, with little difference evident from session to session or from supervisee to supervisee.

The professional literature has given relatively little attention to self-report in the recent past, focusing much more in earnest on forms of supervision that include direct samples of the supervisee's work. Self-report, however, continues to be a commonly used form of supervision, especially for postgraduate supervision (e.g., Goodyear & Nelson, 1997; Magnuson, 1995). At its best, self-report is an intense tutorial relationship in which the supervisee fine-tunes both case conceptualization ability and personal knowledge as each relates to therapist–client relationships. At its worst, self-report becomes a perfect modality when the supervisee is experiencing the pressure to distort (rather than report) his or her work, whether or not this is conscious (Noelle, 2002). Self-report is generally viewed as far less appropriate for novice supervisees for reasons delineated by Holloway (1988), who doubted the wisdom of a supervision model that excludes direct observation, including the use of audio- or videotape. Hollway stated that supervision without direct observation forfeits "the opportunity for (a) independent judgment regarding the client's problem, and (b) illustrating directly with the case in question how to draw inferences from client information" (p. 256). Holloway's point is well taken and underscores one of the key vulnerabilities of the self-report method: As a supervision strategy, it is only as good as the observational and conceptual abilities of the supervisee and the seasoned insightfulness of the supervisor. It seems, therefore, that self-report offers too many opportunities for failure if it represents the complete supervision plan.

Campbell (1994) supported this contention on ethical and legal grounds. He referred to the study conducted by Muslin, Thurnblad, and Meschel (1981) in which more than 50% of the important issues evident in videotapes of therapy sessions of psychiatric trainees were not reported in supervision; furthermore, some degree of distortion characterized more than 50% of supervisees' reports. Campbell described such supervision as supervision in absentia and stated that

As a result of their inexperience, trainees find it difficult to comprehend the problems of their clients. Because they do not observe trainees, supervisors find it difficult to correct their errors. Thus, trainees struggle with what they do not understand; and supervisors labor with what they cannot see. (p. 11)

A more recent study further indicted the memories of therapists when a group of licensed psychologists was asked to recall the molar (main) and molecular (supporting) ideas from specific segments of actual therapy sessions. Wynne, Susman, Ries, Birringer, and Katz (1994) reported only a 42% recall rate for molar ideas and 30% recall for molecular ideas. It seems reasonable to ask whether such a rate is adequate for the purposes of supervision, especially when the supervisee is relatively inexperienced.

Because self-report is the grandfather of supervision forms, there also is a tendency to return to it when other supervisory processes become tiring or tiresome. In fact, studies that investigated the frequency of methods used in supervision continue to find self-report as a relatively dominant method and often the most frequently used method (Anderson, Schlossberg, & Rigazio-DiGilio, 2000; Borders, Cashwell, & Rotter, 1995; Coll, 1995; Romans, Boswell, Carlozzi, & Ferguson, 1995; Wetchler, Piercy, & Sprenkle, 1989). When these same supervisees (and sometimes supervisors) were asked to identify the most valuable form of supervision, self-report dropped in its primacy (e.g., Wetchler et al.). In a study that compared perceptions of best and worst supervision, Anderson et al. (2000) found that their subjects were far more likely to consider self-report as representing their worst supervision experiences than their best supervision experiences. Supporting a cautious stance toward self-report as the supervision modality of choice, Rogers and McDonald (1995) found that when supervisors used more direct methods of supervision they evaluated their supervisees as less prepared for the job than when they used self-report. Such results reinforce the argument that self-report is weakest when used with supervisees who have not reached a minimally acceptable level of professional competence.

Finally, an interesting investigation conducted by Wetchler and Vaughn (1992) homed in on the supervision method used during what, in retrospect, was identified as a critical supervisory incident that had a positive developmental impact on the supervisee. For both supervisors and supervisees, the method most frequently noted was an individual conference without reference to the use of any technology. Although this study may seem to contradict other findings, it may be viewed as underscoring our earlier statement that self-report includes some of the best as well as some of the weakest supervision experiences. When a situation is highly charged for the supervisee, it may take the more open-ended context of a conference based on self-report to help the supervisee to process the meaning of what is occurring. At times, information does not enlighten but rather detracts from the issues. (Our discussion of encouraging reflective practice later in this chapter will pick up on this theme.) Knowing when to limit the information flow in order to take a more introspective approach to supervision requires both experience and a posture of keen attentiveness.

Process Notes and Case Notes

Process notes are the supervisee's written explanation of the content of the therapy session, the interactional processes that occurred between therapist and client, the therapist's feelings about the client, and the rationale and manner of intervention (Goldberg, 1985). As such, process notes can be very extensive and therefore time consuming. It is unlikely that a supervisor would require complete process notes for each session that a supervisee conducts. They may, however, be a worthwhile endeavor on occasion, especially if the supervisor believes that the supervisee would benefit from a more intensive review of supervisee–client interactions and the outcomes of these.

Case notes, on the other hand, are a normative aspect of counseling and supervision (see Chapter 8). Case notes should include all pertinent information from a counseling session, including the interventions used. As such, case notes are the therapeutic, institutional, and legal record of counseling. This being said, case notes can also be used deliberately as part of the supervision conference. While some information should be apparent in all therapy case notes, a supervisor may ask the supervisee to reflect and write on specific questions that meet supervision goals. For example, questions could be posed to assist the supervisee in a reflective process (discussed later in this chapter), to assist the supervisee in linking conceptualization to intervention, or to be vigilant regarding cultural dynamics. When used in this way, case notes become a supervision intervention that can direct the conference. Case notes can and perhaps should be used in conjunction with any other supervision modality. (See Table 9.1 for sample leads that may be helpful to supervisees in preparing for supervision.)

Audiotape

Although live observation and videotape have led to some of the more dramatic breakthroughs in the supervision process, the audiotape was the first to revolutionize our perceptions of what could be accomplished in supervision, and Rogers (1942) and Covner (1942a, b) are attributed with this development (Goodyear & Nelson, 1997). Without the facilities of a laboratory and without the funds, technological expertise, or necessary space to utilize videotape, the audiotape allowed supervisees to transport an accurate (albeit partial) recording of counseling or therapy to a supervisor who was not present at the time that the session occurred. The audiotape is still one of the most widely used sources of information for supervisors who expect to have some sort of direct access to the work of

TABLE 9.1 Leads to Assist the Supervisee in Preparing for the Supervision Case Conference

1. A. Briefly describe the client's presenting problem.
   B. What were your objectives for this session?
2. Describe the dynamics in the session (your own reactions to the client and the interactions between you and the client).
3. A. Describe other important information that was learned during the session, including contextual information.
   B. Summarize key issues discussed during the session.
4. Describe relevant cultural or developmental information as it relates to the presenting problem(s).
5. A. What is your initial conceptualization of the client's issue(s)? (Be sure that your comments are theoretically sound.)
   B. Explain changes (or expansions) of your conceptualizations of the presenting problem(s).
6. List relevant diagnostic impressions, including DSM code and axis.
7. A. To the extent possible, describe initial treatment plan for this client.
   B. Explain changes (or expansions) of your treatment plan for this client.
8. Based on your treatment plan, what are your objectives for the next session?
9. To what extent were your objectives for this session met?
10. Does any aspect of this case raise ethical concerns for you?
11. Share any personal reflections on the session.
12. What specific questions do you have for your supervisor?

Leads relevant to (A) initial counseling session and (B) subsequent counseling sessions.

their supervisees (e.g., Borders et al., 1995; Coll, 1995; Olsen & Stern, 1990). Furthermore, this supervision method continues to find support among those who investigate its effectiveness. As one example, when Magnuson, Wilcoxon, and Norem (2000) asked experienced counselors to reflect on exemplary supervision that they had received, the review of audio- or videotapes with their supervisors surfaced as examples of supervision that led to strong positive recollections.

When audiotape is first required of supervisees (especially if they have been relying on self-report or process notes), there is often some resistance that takes the form of "My clients won't be comfortable." This reaction is occasionally echoed at practicum or internship sites when a training institution asks for audiotapes of the supervisee's clinical work. Although client resistance to taping may be real and must be addressed in a sensitive and ethical manner, it is often not the client but the trainee who is experiencing the greatest amount of discomfort at the prospect of being scrutinized. In fact, the majority of clients are open to having their sessions audiotaped as long as they have an assurance that confidentiality will not be compromised and the supervisee's demeanor is professional when presenting the topic of audiotaping. Additionally, once over their initial reactions, Ellis et al., (2002) found that taping (audio or video) did not cause significant anxiety in supervisees. In fact, any aversive reactions to taping as a supervision method were negligible.

Planning Supervision. The least productive way to use an audiotape in supervision may be that which is depicted in the following vignette: The supervisee arrives with two or three audiotapes of recent counseling sessions, without having reviewed any of them privately. Because the supervisee has made no decision about which session to discuss during supervision, the supervisee spends several minutes telling the supervisor about the cases that are on tape. The supervisor eventually picks one tape, which the trainee must then rewind. The counseling session is played from the beginning until something strikes the supervisor as important.

Our point is simple: The process of supervision must be based on a plan, and it is the supervisor's responsibility to outline that plan. We do believe that spontaneity is important, but it is unlikely to emerge when the supervision process has no vitality. Listening to an audiotape for 20 minutes with a supervisee saying, "Gee, I guess the part I was talking about was further into the session than I realized" is one sure way to kill supervision vitality.

Audiotaped segments can be used in several ways. West, Bubenzer, Pinsoneault, and Holeman (1993) noted that delayed review of audiotapes (and videotapes) is best used to facilitate the supervisee's perceptual–conceptual skills. Goldberg (1985) identified several teaching goals that can be accomplished using audiotape, including focusing on specific therapy techniques, helping the supervisee see the relationship between process and content, focusing on how things are said (paralanguage), and helping the supervisee differentiate between a conversational tone and a therapeutic one. Audiotape can also be used to provide an experiential moment for the supervisee if a segment of tape is chosen where it is obvious that the supervisee is struggling personally or interpersonally in the taped session.

During the initial phase of a supervision relationship, it may be advisable for the supervisor to listen to an entire counseling session prior to supervision in order to get an overview of the supervisee's ability and have control over what segment of tape will be chosen for supervision. It is important also to help the supervisee understand the rationale behind the choice of a taped segment if this is not apparent. Preselected segments can be chosen for a variety of reasons:

1. To highlight the most productive part of the session

2. To highlight the most important part of the session
3. To highlight the part of the session where the supervisee is struggling the most
4. To underscore any number of content issues, including metaphors and recurring themes
5. To ask about a confusing part of the session, perhaps because paralanguage contradicts content
6. To focus attention on the point in the session where interpersonal or cross-cultural dynamics were either particularly therapeutic or particularly strained or where cultural encapsulation is evident (Cashwell, Looby, & Housley, 1997).

In other words, supervisors will almost always have in mind a teaching function when they preselect a section of audiotape for supervision.

This process should evolve, however, as the supervisee develops in conceptual ability and experience. Relatively quickly the supervisee can be preselecting the section of tape that will determine the direction of supervision. Often supervisees are just asked to choose a part of the session where they felt confused, lost, overwhelmed, or frustrated. The supervisor will then listen to the segment with them and proceed from there. If this format is used, the supervisee should be prepared to

- State the reason for selecting this part of the session for discussion in supervision
- Briefly state what transpired up to that point
- Explain what he or she was trying to accomplish at that point in the session
- Clearly state the specific help desired from the supervisor

Although a valid supervision format, the same format used repeatedly may make supervision become stagnant. When the supervisee is repeatedly asked to select a troublesome tape segment, for example, the supervision may become skewed toward problems in counseling sessions, with little opportunity for the supervisee to enjoy successes.

As an alternative method of using audiotapes, the supervisor might assign a theme for the next session and have the supervisee be responsible for producing the segment of tape. For example, the supervisor might suggest that reframing would be of great help for a particular client or family and that the supervisee should try to reframe as often as possible in the next session and choose the most successful of these attempts to present in the next supervision session. In addition to using supervision to sharpen a skill, this strategy also allows the supervisor to connect technique to a counseling situation and to get data on the supervisee's self-evaluation ability. The types of assignments that can direct the use of audiotape are potentially limitless and can focus on the process of therapy, the conceptual issues in therapy, personal or interpersonal issues, and ethical dilemmas, among others; it can also reflect different supervisee developmental levels. In summary, careful preselection of an audiotape segment is perhaps most crucial in making the audiotape a powerful supervision tool.

Although the use of direct supervision methods is not usually associated with psychodynamic approaches to therapy, Aveline (1992) and Brandell (1992) have addressed the unique advantages of using audiotaped segments in supervision. In a particularly adroit description of the benefit of hearing a supervisee's session, Aveline stated

> *I am stimulated by the way in which words are used, the metaphors deployed and the images evoked. Snatches of interaction often vividly illustrate the central dilemmas of a person's life. . . . The medium is particularly well placed to identify such phenomena as the patient filling all the space of [the] session with words so as to leave no room for the therapist to say anything for fear that what might be said will disrupt the inner equilibrium; the nervous laugh that as surely indicates that there is an issue of importance at hand as does the bird with trailing wing that the nest is nearby; the therapist whose words of encouragement are belied by his impatient tone or gesture; and the patient whose placatory dependence is shot through with hostility.* (p. 350)

Despite his convincing arguments in favor of the use of audiotaping for supervision, Aveline also cautioned that there are significant disadvantages. Primarily, Aveline argued that a tape recorder *always* has an effect on therapy, and its meaning to the client (and the therapist) must be explored. He cautioned that taping might even be abusive to a client who is in too weak a position to refute its use. Similarly, Aveline saw the possibility that taping could hurt the supervisory relationship if the exposure that the tape allowed led to humiliation for the therapist. In all cases, Aveline stressed that the supervisor must be willing to address the consequences that the audiotape has produced. "Taping is a supervisory aid; it is servant, not master" (Aveline, 1992, p. 351).

Written Critique of Audiotapes.   For those who are more visual than auditory, the supervisor can combine a written analysis of an audiotape with individual supervision. Many supervisors choose to listen to tapes between supervision sessions rather than during them. This is especially so during the beginning stages of supervision. Rather than taking notes to use in a subsequent supervision session, the supervisor writes an analysis of the session that can be given to the student. Word processors make this chore somewhat more palatable, and the exercise forces the supervisor to conceptualize the feedback before the supervision session. Additionally, the critiques automatically become a record of supervision; they allow the supervisee to review comments made by the supervisor, and they can become a way of coordinating supervision if other supervisors are involved (e.g., a site supervisor could be sent a copy of the critique prepared by the university supervisor). In fact, the critiques serve as excellent instructional material for the training of supervisors in the planning and giving of feedback. It must be noted, however, that such written feedback does not replace either individual or group supervision.

Transcripts.   Finally, supervisors occasionally ask supervisees to transcribe their audiotapes (or, more infrequently, their videotapes) and submit these for supervision. Brandell (1992) used transcripts to assist the supervisee in understanding the process of psychoanalytic psychotherapy. He described a format where a 5- to 10-minute excerpt from a therapy session is transcribed, and both supervisor and supervisee complete a checklist about the client's focal conflict. The checklist requires that decisions be made about the client's wishes, reactions, maladaptive solutions, and adaptive solutions. The completed checklists become the source for the instructional learning that will take place in supervision.

Arthur and Gfoerer (2002) argued that transcripts were especially helpful for supervisees in early stages of training (e.g., a first practicum). They proposed that basing supervision on transcripts of sessions facilitates a collaborative style of feedback and becomes a building block for supervision that is more helpful for an intermediate or advanced intern. In other words, because the sessions are in print form, it is more likely that supervisees will be able to notice faulty interventions, such as multiple questions or a run of incomplete statements, than might be possible using audiotape alone. This, then, allows the student greater opportunity to critique their own work (at this early stage) than taping alone might afford. Additionally, because transcripts utilize a more familiar educational modality (a paper document), it may be helpful for students who seem to be having a particularly difficult time making the transition from classroom to clinical supervision.

Arthur and Gfoerer (2002) gathered survey data from 30 graduates of a training program, all of whom had been supervised by the same supervisor using transcription as the focus of supervision. For 11 of 12 questions regarding the value of the transcripts, 11 were answered positively by the vast majority of the respondents. Only the item "The use of transcripts made me anxious" caused mixed results. While 16 of the 30 disagreed with this statement, 13 agreed (and 1 gave no response). It is unknown, however, if those who found this form of supervision anxiety provoking would have found another form to be less so.

Arthur and Gfoerer (2002) also asked their respondents to identify positive and negative attributes that they associated with transcript use in supervision. Positive attributes included the fact that the supervisor saw the whole session, and that transcripts gave supervisees a visual reminder of the session, and that transcripts were concrete and allowed for equally concrete examples of what the intern needed to work on and made it easier for the intern to critique his or her own work. Negative attributes associated with the transcripts was the fact that they were so time consuming for both intern and supervisor, that nonverbal cues and all paralanguage were not included in supervision, that mistakes were even more visible than they may have been through other supervision modalities, and that they were too focused on the content of a session, rather than the overall development of the supervisee.

Transcripts of counseling sessions provide an enormous amount of material for a subsequent supervision session that seem to result in several positive outcomes, at least for novice interns. In light of the time-consuming nature of this form of supervision, however, as well as its other limitations, perhaps an intermittent or abbreviated (i.e., transcription of a certain number of minutes of a session) use of this supervision method represents its optimal use.

Videotape

Although the audiotape is still our backup, the videotape has certainly taken center stage as the technology of choice in supervision (e.g., Carlozzi, Romans, Boswell, Ferguson, & Whisenhunt, 1997; Romans, Boswell, Carlozzi, & Ferguson, 1995; Wetchler et al., 1989). Those who use videotape are firm about its superiority over audiotape (e.g., Broder & Sloman, 1982; Stoltenberg & Delworth, 1987). We want to emphasize, however, that many of the process variables that we mentioned for using audiotape could be used with videotape, as well as the reverse.

With no intention of insulting our readers, we will point out that the videotape has one major advantage, the addition of the picture, and two major disadvantages, its expense and its bulk (though costs are reasonable and better equipment continues to reduce the latter issue). To say that a picture is worth a thousand words is less trite when one sees a client that one has heard but not seen up to that time. A voice that is gruff matched with a persona that is gentle, a precise presentation of plot when the physical presentation is disorganization, the smiles, the nods, the looking away, the hand gestures—all comprise a wealth of information. When the client is a family, the phenomenon grows exponentially. In fact, experiencing an overload of data is one of the reasons that Goldberg (1985) suggested using videotape at later stages of supervision. Or, as Rubinstein and Hammond (1982) aptly put it, "[p]aradoxically, the greatest limitation of videotape may result from what it best provides the supervisor—a wealth of material about the recorded session" (p. 161).

The bulk of the videotape (camera, recorder, and monitor) makes it more likely to be used in group supervision, but there are notable exceptions to this (e.g., interpersonal process recall). Regardless of the numbers involved, videotape supervision will take more room than working with audiotape. If one does supervision within the confines of a small private office, feedback based on videotape may have to be foregone. Another drawback of using videotape is a slightly higher level of comfort with technology that is required for its use. If someone throws the wrong switch in a clinical facility, the supervisor who does not like to tinker may be unduly frustrated by using videotape.

According to Munson (1983), the associations that trainees may make between videotaped supervision and commercial television can present yet another problem. Because television connotes entertainment, Munson saw the dual problem of observers not finding others' sessions entertaining enough and trainees feeling they must "perform" on videotape, thereby suffering from excessive "performance anxiety." The supervisor's role, according to Munson, includes structuring supervision so that observers are stimulated cognitively (usually by means of a specific task related to the videotaped segment), while at the same time attempting to safeguard the integrity of the trainee on tape. Munson's admonition has been supported by more recent empirical findings that videotape review of counseling sessions caused a shift from

positive mood at the end of a counseling session to a lowered mood after videotape review for therapists and therapists-in-training (Hill et al., 1994). It seems, therefore, that the obvious advantage of videotape can become a liability and must be monitored carefully by the supervisor. As one supervisee put it, "[v]ideotape is a little like some hotel room mirrors; the reflection is *too* accurate."

Despite all these valid cautions regarding the use of videotape in supervision, there is no question that our knowledge base and experiential alternatives have increased greatly as a result of this technology. With videotape, supervisees can literally see themselves in the role of helper, thus allowing them to be an observer of their work, which is not possible with audiotape (Sternitzke et al., 1988; Whiffen, 1982).

In an excellent discussion of the use of videotape in the supervision of marriage and family therapy, Breunlin, Karrer, McGuire, & Cimmarusti (1988) argued that videotape supervision should be focused on the interaction between trainee and clients, as well as on the far more subtle internal processes experienced by the trainee during both the therapy session and the supervision session. To focus on one to the exclusion of the other would be an error, according to Breunlin et al. Furthermore, they stated that therapists can never be objective observers of their own roles separate from the family (or individual) client, as this is an interactional impossibility. Breunlin et al., therefore, recommended six guidelines for working with both the cold accuracy of the videotape and the dynamic reality experienced by the supervisee (pp. 199–204). These guidelines, when followed, help to alleviate some of the dangers noted by Munson (1983) and Hill et al. (1994). (We should note that the guidelines outlined by Breunlin et al. also apply to other methods of supervision.)

1. *Focus videotape supervision by setting realistic goals for the supervised therapy session.* This has two advantages: It reduces the sense of information overload by narrowing down the field to those interventions that are connected to goals, and it increases the possibility that the supervisee will emerge from the session moderately satisfied because realistic goals are attainable.

2. *Relate internal process across contexts.* The point here is that what the therapist experiences in the session is important to discuss in supervision. Furthermore, Breunlin et al. (1988) emphasized that supervisors should allow supervisees to disclose their perceptions first, rather than supervisors offering their observations. Most important, however, is the issue of validating the internal processes of the supervisee, rather than forfeiting such a discussion in favor of "strategy review." Interpersonal process recall (Kagan, 1976, 1980; Kagan & Kagan, 1997), as described later in this chapter, is an excellent model for meeting this guideline.

3. *Select tape segments that focus on remedial performance.* By this, the authors mean that the focus of corrective feedback should be on performance that the supervisee has the ability to change. In other words, focusing on aspects of the supervisee's personal style or on skills that are too complex for immediate attainment will be nonproductive.

4. *Use supervisor comments to create a moderate evaluation of performance.* The authors relied on the research of Fuller and Manning (1973) to arrive at this guideline. The latter found that a moderate discrepancy between performance and the target goal is optimal for learning. Therefore, the supervisor must find videotape segments that are neither exemplary nor too far from the stated goal. We can begin to appreciate the kind of supervisor commitment that is required to use the suggestions of Breunlin et al. (1988).

5. *Refine goals moderately.* This guideline underscores the fact that videotape review must be seen in the larger context of supervisee development. Sometimes the multitude of possibilities that a review can generate are irrespective of the skill level of the supervisee. Additionally, Breunlin et al. (1988) remind us that what appears easy when viewing a session can be far more difficult

to pull off in therapy. Moderation, therefore, must remain the constant focus for the supervisor.

6. *Maintain a moderate level of arousal.* The authors posited that attending to the first five guidelines will take care of the sixth. The supervisor, however, must always be cautious that the supervisee is stimulated to grow without becoming overly threatened. Therefore, the supervisor, as always, must be alert to multiple levels of experience.

Also addressing supervisee internal processes, Rubinstein and Hammond (1982) maintained that the supervisor who uses videotape must have a healthy respect for its power. There is no hiding from the stark reality of one's picture and voice being projected into the supervision room. Therefore, Rubinstein and Hammond cautioned that videotape should not be used unless there is a relatively good relationship between supervisor and supervisee. We would concur up to a point, but also postulate that a good relationship can be formed in the process of using videotape sensitively. In addition, the supervisee will be far less camera shy if videotape was used in training prior to supervision. Rubinstein and Hammond made one fine suggestion that supervisors appear on videotape prior to having their supervisees do the same. More recently, Kaplan, Rothrock, & Culkin (1999) also suggested this kind of modeling. Providing samples of one's own counseling can serve many purposes, but especially attractive is dispelling the myth that supervisors conduct perfect therapy sessions. As all supervisors know, the insight and cleverness that are evidenced in supervision are rarely matched in one's own therapy.

Finally, Rubinstein and Hammond (1982) suggested that the use of the videotape remain technologically simple. They are not in favor of split screens, superimposed images, or other such equipment capabilities, believing that it detracts from the lifelike experience of watching the taped session. Of course, decisions about using videotape reflect the supervisor's comfort, or lack thereof, with this type of technology, as well as the supervision goals. And yet, as we stated earlier, supervisor comfort and technological expertise may need to increase as the present technological revolution continues (Casey, Bloom, and Moan, 1994). Each supervisor ultimately will find a viable comfort level with technological advances, but the supervisor would still be wise to remember Rubinstein and Hammond's caution lest technology and its multiple uses become the center of supervision.

Interpersonal Process Recall. Perhaps the most widely known supervision method using videotape is interpersonal process recall (IPR) (Kagan, 1976, 1980; Kagan & Kagan, 1997; Kagan & Kratwohl, 1967; Kagan et al., 1965; Kagan et al., 1963). As a result of a national survey of counselor education programs, Borders and Leddick (1988) found that, at that time, IPR was one of only two clearly delineated methods of supervision taught in supervision courses, the other being live supervision. IPR began as a therapy model and occasionally is still used as such; for our purposes here, however, we will confine ourselves to the use of IPR in supervision. Kagan (1980) asserted that there are many psychological barriers to open, honest communication and that these operate in counseling and therapy as they do in other daily interactions. Primary among these is the strongly socialized habit of behaving diplomatically. As a result, much of what a supervisee thinks, intuits, and feels during counseling and therapy is disregarded almost automatically, because allowing such perceptions to surface would confront the predisposition to be diplomatic.

The purpose of IPR, then, is to give the supervisee a safe haven for these internal reactions. Kagan (1980) strongly maintained that all persons are "the best authority of their own dynamics and the best interpreter of their own experience" (pp. 279–280). Starting with this assumption, therefore, the supervisor's role becomes that of a facilitator to stimulate the awareness of the supervisee beyond the point at which it operated during the counseling session.

The process of IPR is relatively simple. The supervisor and trainee view a prerecorded videotape of a counseling session together. At any point at which either person believes that something of importance is happening on tape, especially something that is not being addressed in the counseling session, the videotape is stopped (dual controls are helpful, but it is easy enough to signal the person holding the controls to stop the tape). If the trainee stops the tape, the trainee will speak first, saying, for example "I was getting really frustrated here. I didn't know what she wanted. We had been over all of this before. I thought it was resolved last week but here it is again." At this point, it is essential that the supervisor not adopt a teaching role and instruct the trainee about what might have been done. Rather, the supervisor needs to allow the trainee the psychological space to investigate internal processes to some resolution. At the same time, the good facilitator, or "inquirer," as Kagan preferred to call it, can ask direct questions that are challenging to the supervisee. Some possibilities for the above example are these: What do you wish you had said to her? How do you think she might have reacted if you said those things to her? What kept you from saying what you wanted to say? If you had the opportunity now, how might you tell her what you are thinking and feeling? Once it is felt that the dynamics for the chosen segment of tape have been sufficiently reexamined, the tape is allowed to continue. Table 9.2 lists a variety of lead statements that reflect different supervision goals. Specifically, leads are listed that inspire affective exploration, check out unstated agendas, encourage cognitive examination, get at images, or help to search out expectations. As one can certainly discern, this process is slow. Only a portion of a therapy session can be reviewed in this manner unless supervision is extended significantly. Therefore, choosing the most interpersonally weighted or most metaphorically meaningful segment of videotape will be most productive for supervision purposes.

One caution is advisable: Because IPR often puts interpersonal dynamics under a microscope,

TABLE 9.2   Supervisor Leads for Use with Interpersonal Process Recall

LEADS THAT INSPIRE AFFECTIVE EXPLORATION
- How did that make you feel?
- How did that make you feel about him or her?
- Do you remember what you were feeling?
- Were you aware of any feelings?
- What do those feelings mean to you?
- Does that feeling have any special meaning to you?
- Is it a familiar feeling?
- What did you do (or decide to do) about that feeling you had?
- Did you want to express that feeling at any time?
- Did you have any fantasies of taking any risk?

LEADS THAT CHECK OUT UNSTATED AGENDAS
- What would you have liked to have said to her or him at this point?
- What's happening here?
- What did you feel like doing?
- How were you feeling about your role as counseling at this point?
- What had that meant to you?
- If you had more time, where would you have liked to have gone?

LEADS THAT ENCOURAGE COGNITIVE EXAMINATION
- What were you thinking at that time?
- What thoughts were you having about the other person at that time?
- Something going on there?
- Anything going on there?
- Had you any ideas about what you wanted to do with that?
- Did you fantasize taking any risks?
- Were you able to say it the way you wanted to?
- Did you want to say anything else then?
- Did you have any plan of where you wanted the session to go next?
- Did you think that the other person knew what you wanted?
- What kind of image were you aware of projecting?
- Is that the image you wanted to project?
- Can you recall what effect the setting had on you or the interaction?
- Can you recall what effect you thought that the setting had on the other person?
- Did the equipment affect you in any way?
- (If reaction to the recorder) What did you want, or not want, the recorder to hear from you?

LEADS THAT GET AT IMAGES
- Were you having any fantasies at that moment?
- Were any pictures, images, or memories flashing through your mind then?
- What was going on in your mind at that time?
- Did it remind you of anything?
- Did you think that you had "been there before"? Is that familiar to you?
- Where had that put you in the past?

(continued)

TABLE 9.2 Continued

LEADS THAT EXPLORE MUTUAL PERCEPTIONS BETWEEN CLIENT AND COUNSELOR
- What did you think that she or he was feeling about you?
- How do you think that she or he was seeing you at that point?
- Do you think that she or he was aware of your feelings? Your thoughts?
- What message do you think that she or he was trying to give you?
- Did you feel that he or she had any expectations of you at that point?
- What did you think that she or he wanted you to think or feel or do?
- Do you think that your description of the interaction would coincide with her or his description?
- Was she or he giving you any cues as to how she or he was feeling?
- How do you think that she or he felt about talking about this problem?
- How do you think that she or he felt about continuing to talk with you at this point?

LEADS THAT HELP SEARCH OUT EXPECTATIONS
- What did you want her or him to tell you?
- What did you want to hear?
- What would you have liked from her or him?
- Were you expecting anything of her or him at that point?
- Did you want her or him to see you in some particular way? How?
- What do you think that her or his perceptions were of you?
- What message did you want to give to her or him?
- Was there anything in particular that you wanted her or him to say or do or think?
- Was she or he "with you"? How did her or his responses hit you?
- What did you really want to tell her or him at this moment? What prevented you from doing so?
- What did you want her or him to do?
- Did you want her or him to do something that would have made it easier for you?
- What would that have been?

it is possible that they will be magnified to the extent of distortion (Bernard, 1981). In other words, what is a perfectly functional helping relationship can come to look somehow dysfunctional when overexposed, and as all persons in the helping professions know, some relationship dynamics are best left underexposed. We need not be in perfect sync with all our clients to be of help to them. The clinical skill comes in determining which interactions are important and which are not. IPR is not a method to guide *what* is to be examined. Therefore, it is up to the supervisor and supervisee to decide which interactions warrant explo-

ration and which do not. Because the supervisee is usually more reticent than the supervisor, the supervisor will most often be left to make such decisions. Answering the following two questions may be useful in selecting segments for IPR: From what I can observe, does this interaction seem to be interrupting the flow of counseling? From what I know of the trainee, would focusing on this interaction aid in his or her development as a mental health professional? Finally, it is important that the supervisor refrain from asking questions to make statements. Loaded questions will very quickly be discerned by the supervisee and will most assuredly shut down the process as it was intended.

The Reflective Process

Goodyear and Nelson (1997) described efforts to develop reflectivity in supervisees as an elaboration on some of the tenets of IPR. Neufeldt, Karno, and Nelson (1996) provided the following description of the reflective process:

> The reflective process itself is a search for understanding of the phenomena of the counseling session, with attention to therapist actions, emotions, and thoughts, as well as to the interaction between the therapist and the client. The intent to understand what has occurred, active inquiry, openness to that understanding, and vulnerability and risk-taking, rather than defensive self-protection, characterize the stance of the reflective supervisee. Supervisees use theory, their prior personal and professional experience, and their experience of themselves in the counseling session as sources of understanding. If they are to contribute to future development, reflections must be profound rather than superficial and must be meaningful to the supervisees. To complete the sequence, reflectivity in supervision leads to changes in perception, changes in counseling practice, and an increased capacity to make meaning of experiences. (p. 8)

As was discussed in Chapter 5, Neufeldt et al. (1996) noted that supervisee personality and cognitive capacities, as well as the supervision environment, must be considered when attempting to move the supervisee toward reflectivity. As might be surmised by the reader, producing a reflective practitioner may be the most challenging task of the clinical supervisor.

Prior to discussing ways of encouraging reflectivity, we should note that the focus on reflectivity is paired with the knowledge that expertise in counseling or psychotherapy is not a brief process. Skovholt, Rønnestad, and Jennings (1997) concluded that it takes a minimum of 10 years to move from novice to expert in any specific area of therapy practice. Referring to this conclusion, Nelson

and Neufeldt (1998) emphasized the short amount of time that supervisors typically have with supervisees and the importance, therefore, that reflective tools be established in order for supervisees to be able to assist in their own subsequent development. Nelson and Neufeldt also specified what needs to occur in order for reflection to occur:

> there must be a problem, a dilemma—something about which the learner feels confusion or dissonance and intends to search for a solution. The problem should revolve around an issue of consequence, one that is important to good practice. Reflection occurs in a context of the learner's capacity to tolerate the ambiguity of not knowing and an educational setting in which the learner has space to struggle with ideas as well as the safety to experience not knowing as acceptable. (pp. 81–82)

Therefore, the first task of the supervisor is to establish a context for reflection. To do this, they must at the very least provide time, encouragement, and psychological space for this activity, as well as a supervisory relationship that is built on trust (Nelson & Neufeldt, 1998; Ward & House, 1998). Additionally, supervisors need to choose techniques and interventions that will provide reflective possibilities in supervision. In recent years, several authors have offered such tools (Griffith & Frieden, 2000; Koch, Arhar, & Wells, 2000; Neufeldt, 1999).

Griffith and Frieden (2000) argued the usefulness of four supervision interventions to facilitate reflective thinking among supervisees. The first of these is Socratic questioning, emphasizing the role of the supervisor as the source of important questions, rather than the source of all the answers. This age-old method of stimulating reflection is highly relevant to clinical contexts. Griffith and Frieden encourage primarily "how" and "what" questions to help dualistic thinkers to broaden their horizons. While Socratic questioning may be best used in group supervision contexts, it certainly has a place in individual supervision as well.

Griffith and Frieden (2000) also suggested that supervisors require supervisees to engage in journal writing. While journals are often used earlier in the training programs, they are less likely to be used as part of supervision. Griffith and Frieden recommended that journals be used by supervisees to critically evaluate their counseling and to focus not only on external events, but also on their internal reality, including painful emotional experiences that are stimulated by either the therapeutic or supervisory context. Finally, these authors argued that, similar to the effects of Socratic questions, journal writing can be used to assist students to move beyond a description of events in counseling to identifying themes and patterns, thus assisting them in the necessary cognitive development from concrete thinking to that which is more complex and abstract (Rigazio-DiGilio, Daniels, & Ivey, 1997).

The third strategy suggested by Griffith and Frieden (2000) is IPR, which has already been described in this chapter. Griffith and Frieden agreed with Kagan that well-constructed reflective probes could stimulate new insight for the supervisee regarding internal processes that may have been outside one's consciousness, but nevertheless influenced the direction of counseling. Griffith and Frieden's last strategy is the use of a reflective team (Anderson, 1987). The reflective team technique is used during live supervision (though Griffith and Frieden described a process for its use in group supervision) and clearly exists outside the purview of individual supervision. The reflective team approach to live supervision is described in Chapter 11.

While presented for implementation as a group counseling activity, Koch et al. (2000) described an approach to engaging students in reflective practice that spans an entire semester of supervision. Each supervisee is first invited to reflect on a dilemma that resonates for them, consistent with Nelson and Neufeldt's (1998) conditions for reflectivity. Typical examples would include these: How can I prevent clients from manipulating me? How do I keep focused on client's concerns and keep my personal issues from clouding my judgment? Once they have been challenged to do this, supervisees are asked to spend a couple of weeks identifying their own dilemma while the supervisor stays alert to the

same for them during supervision. After several weeks of the semester, supervisees are asked to present their dilemma to their peers. The other students in the supervision group are advised to ask open-ended questions to gain clarity (and are discouraged from giving advice). Following this session, which includes debriefing for the intern involved, supervisees are asked to develop an action plan to help them to address their dilemma. Koch et al. cautioned that supervision after this point must continue to encourage reflectivity through assignments such as a reflection journal. They also emphasized the importance for the supervisee to follow contemplation with "making informed decisions and taking action in a way that addresses the dilemmas in a socially and ethically responsible manner" (pp. 263–264). In this way the supervisee experiences a complete process from problem identification through reflection and growth to some resolution. It also important for supervisees to be aware that this process can and should be revisited at more profound levels.

Inspired by the work of Skovholt and Rønnestad (1995), who determined the importance of continuous professional reflection, Neufeldt (1999) advanced the importance of helping supervisees learn to self-reflect. Supervisees are directed to respond to a number of questions (see Table 9.3) immediately after a session in which they encountered a puzzle or dilemma. While time consuming, challenging supervisees to complete such an assessment independently is essential for helping them to claim ownership of reflective skills. Of course, this exercise can become the subject of a subsequent supervision session.

We conclude this section by referring to Carroll's (2001) use of the concept of the "philosophy of supervision." Carroll drew a distinction between "functional" supervision (supervision as technology) and a philosophy of supervision that focused on the "being" of people and the meaning supervision has for the supervisor. That is, supervision is not something someone *does,* but something that someone *is.* In short, supervisors who have a philosophy of supervision reflect on their supervision; they view reflective behavior as

TABLE 9.3   Self-reflection Activity: Questions to Answer Regarding a Therapy
Session Dilemma

1. Describe the therapy events that precipitated your puzzlement.
2. State your question about these events as clearly as you can.
3. What were you thinking during this portion of the session?
4. What were you feeling? How do you understand those feelings now?
5. Consider your own actions during this portion of the session. What did you intend?
6. Now look at the interaction between you and the client. What were the results of your interventions?
7. What was the feel, the emotional flavor, of the interaction between you? Was it similar to or different from your usual experience with this client?
8. To what degree do you understand this interaction as similar to the client's interactions in other relationships? How does this inform your experience of the interaction in session?
9. What theories do you use to understand what is going on in session?
10. What past professional or personal experiences affect your understanding?
11. How else might you interpret the event and interaction in the session?
12. How might you test out the various alternatives in your next counseling session? (Be sure to look for what confirms and what disconfirms your interpretations.)
13. How will the clients' responses inform what you do next?

From "Training in Reflective Processes in Supervision," by S. A. Neufeldt, 1999. In E. Holloway and M. Carroll (Eds.), *Training Counselling Supervisors* (p. 101). London: Sage Publications.

something to engage, not something to teach. Only through their own reflection can the supervisor continue to pair functional supervision with a maturing philosophy of supervision. Clearly, Carroll implied that a nonreflective supervisor would be hard pressed to create a reflective context for others. Perhaps concerning this issue, more than around many other activities, "do as I do" is the only credible posture.

Live Observation

Live observation is a frequent form of supervision in many training programs; it is used less frequently in the field because of scheduling difficulties and structural constraints. We differentiate between live observation and live supervision, the former being a method of observing the supervisee, but not interacting with the supervisee during the session (except in case of emergency) and the latter being a combination of observation and active supervision during the session. Because the involvement of the supervisor in live supervision rep-

resents a paradigm shift from all other supervisory methods, we treat it separately in Chapter 11.

Live observation offers several advantages over all other forms of supervision, with the exception of live supervision. First, there is a high safeguard for client welfare when live observation is employed because the supervisor is immediately available to intervene in case of emergency. A second advantage of live observation is that it affords the supervisor a more complete picture of clients and supervisees than is attainable through the use of audiotape or videotape. When using the latter, for example, the camera position is often fixed throughout a session, giving only side views of both client and supervisee or focusing on one or the other exclusively. Supervisors who have used both live observation and taping can certainly attest to the more firsthand experience that live observation provides.

A third, and perhaps most utilized, advantage of live observation is that it offers the utmost flexibility regarding the timing of the case conference. Should the supervisor choose to conduct supervision immediately after the counseling session, the supervisee has the maximum amount of time available to use supervision in preparing for the next counseling session. Certainly, the use of live observation will reduce the chances of a most frustrating situation when the supervisor is watching a videotape of a session only to be told that the supervisee has seen the client again since the video was made. It is difficult to make supervision fresh when the therapy session is stale. Because the timing of a supervision session affects all individual supervision, we will address this topic separately.

One advantage of live observation must be monitored carefully. When other trainees are present in the observation room, there is an opportunity to offer instruction based on the session that is transpiring. This instruction can become very objective and candid, and the supervisor might point out dynamics that he or she might not consider helpful to mention to the counselor. This, of course, will affect the level of trust among all the members of the supervisory group. Whenever other supervisees are present during an observation, a protocol must be established, such as that all comments will be shared with the counselor either in individual or group supervision.

Technology and Supervision

The advances made in technology over the past two decades are astounding. In the early 1990s, there were only a handful of Web sites. Now it is surprising if a product or resource that one is seeking is not easily located on the Web (recognizing this, we now maintain a Web site devoted to supervision practice, teaching, and research issues; see the Supervisor's Toolbox). We have all gone beyond the fascination and delight of email and now wonder what we used to do with all those hours spent catching up (or not) on our email. It is unlikely that anyone reading this book is not on at least one listserv. Distance learning seems as common a term as syllabus. Acronyms like IATV (real-time video conferencing) may still be foreign to some, but will most likely be fully integrated into our repertoire of technological lingo in the foreseeable future. (We should note that even the

term foreseeable future has a different meaning when we think of technology. Fast track seems to be the only track.)

To date, technological advancements have been modest in the normative practice of psychotherapy or clinical supervision. McMinn, Buchanan, Ellens, and Ryan (1999) surveyed psychologists to determine their use of technology in their practice. Of the over 400 who responded, the only technologies used frequently were the telephone, the copier, and the fax machine. The only exceptions to this were the use of software programs for test scoring or interpretation, electronic filing with insurance companies, and using a computer to generate client bills. McMinn et al. observed that their results differed little from data collected by Farrell (1989) a decade earlier.

VandenBos and Williams (2000) found similar results when they surveyed nearly 500 psychologists and compared their use of the telephone with their use of Internet or satellite technology in the delivery of services. While virtually all respondents reported using the telephone, only 2% used the more sophisticated technology.

Three of the items on the McMinn et al. (1999) survey related to supervision specifically. Of these, only slightly less that 2.5% of respondents reported that they used the telephone or teleconferencing for clinical supervision fairly often or very often. None of the respondents reported using email in their supervision.

Despite the present sluggishness among mental health providers in the use of the Internet or satellite transmissions for therapy or supervision, the topic is gaining steam in the professional literature (e.g., Bloom, 2000; Graf & Stebnicki, 2002; Jerome et al., 2000; Kanz, 2001; Maheu & Gordon, 2000; McMinn et al., 1999; Nickelson, 1998; Olson, Russell, & White, 2001; Sampson & Bloom, 2001; Sampson, Kolodinsky, & Greeno, 1997; Stebnicki & Glover, 2001; VandenBos & Williams, 2000). Barriers to using technology most often cited include cost for real-time technologies (though these are steadily decreasing), unequal availability of technology, the loss of all nonverbal cues for technologies such as email, the essentiality of the relationship to both counseling and supervision, fears regarding informed consent and breaches of confidentiality, lack of training in the use of technology, the ramifications of technological failure, and issues having to do with state-bound licensure laws (Bloom, 2000; Jerome et al., 2000; Kanz, 2001; Maheu & Gordon, 2000; Nickelson, 1998; Olson et al., 2001; Sampson et al., 1997).

Despite these very real and important issues, the advantages to using technology will no doubt move us forward. The most obvious advantage of technology is that it makes geography moot. Good supervision is not always accessible to rural mental health providers (Kanz, 2001) or for persons with disabilities. Even when supervision is generally accessible in person, Kanz noted that situations that are clinically or culturally unfamiliar to the practitioner and local supervisor may call for long-distance supervision or consultation. Although we are focusing on individual supervision in this chapter, technology allows for groups of supervisees to interact frequently through listservs. Furthermore, the simple use of email can enhance communication between supervisors who may be working with the same supervisee. If videoconferencing is not feasible on a regular basis, it could be a highly worthwhile venue for special case conferences addressing tough supervision cases (similar to what is often done in workshop format).

Because of the very limited use of technology in the mental health professions, research regarding the effects of supervision delivered by the Internet is equally limited. One qualitative study has been reported (Graf [Glover] & Stebnicki, 2002; Stebnicki & Glover, 2001) that analyzed results of using email as a vehicle for supervision (e-supervision) of rehabilitation counselors as a supplement to more traditional individual and group supervision. Practicum students were required to stay in touch with the instructor by email throughout the semester and were required to email a minimum of once per week. While the analyzed data were produced by three students only, results indicated that the content and quality of email messages from students progressed over the semester. Graf and

Stebnicki (2002) found that conceptual messages from students fell into three categories: messages about consumers (clients), messages about the onsite supervisors, and messages about themselves. While messages about clients stayed positive throughout the practicum (though increasing in complexity), messages about the site supervisors seemed to follow a more predictable developmental path, moving from highly positive to becoming more critical and ending with a more balanced view of their supervisors. The students' messages about themselves reflected the following pattern: an initial sense of anticipation and lack of confidence, a period of boredom when responsibility was withheld from them, increased confidence paired with increased responsibility, a sense of frustration over inability to make sufficient changes, and, finally, a more reflective place of increased awareness and more realistic goals.

Although these data were not compared to interactions using another form of supervision, they seem to support developmental models of supervision and, for our purposes here, seem to indicate that e-supervision can at least document, if not stimulate, development for a supervisee. (It is, of course, impossible to know the relative role that individual and group supervision played for these supervisees.) Additionally, supervisees reported that they found the e-supervision to be beneficial. Specifically, supervisees reported that they benefited from the ongoing access to their supervisor, from the more relaxed and informal style of communication that email afforded, and from the time to process and clarify thoughts during the formation of their emails while at the same time receiving immediate supervisor input at critical times (Stebnicki & Glover, 2001).

Stebnicki and Glover cautioned that e-supervision has certain limitations that must be addressed. They suggested that supervisors develop clear guidelines about the use of email for supervision, including methods to protect client confidentiality, a schedule for email communications, and attention to documenting e-supervision. Stebnicki and Glover also addressed the time-management issue that plagues all distance education. They emphasized the need to develop a comprehensive supervision plan that clearly indicates the place that e-supervision will hold in the overall plan. Finally, Stebnicki and Glover cautioned that supervisees are different, and supervisors must be sensitive to the fact that some may not benefit by e-supervision and may need more face-to-face contact. While it is very unlikely that e-supervision will eradicate the need for face-to-face individual or group supervision, it may prove to be an excellent adjunct to these more traditional formats and, as demonstrated by Stebnicki and Glover, may allow us a relatively efficient means for tracking supervisee cognitive development.

Timing of Supervision

Regardless of the methods used to produce the material for the case conference, an additional matter, the timing of the conference, must be considered. Little has been said in the professional literature about the timing of supervision except to warn that supervision that is scheduled for convenience only (e.g., every Tuesday at 10:00 for 1 hour) may invite legal liability if there are no provisions for the occasion when the supervisee experiences a more pressing need for supervision (Cohen, 1979; Disney & Stephens, 1994).

Couchon and Bernard (1984) conducted a study that examined how several variables were influenced by the timing of supervision. Among the variables that were considered were supervisor and counselor behavior in supervision, follow-through from supervision to counseling, client and counselor satisfaction with counseling, and counselor satisfaction with supervision. Three treatments were introduced: supervision within 4 hours prior to an upcoming counseling session, supervision the day before a specified counseling session, and supervision occurring more than 2 days before a specified counseling session.

Some provocative results emerged from this study. Perhaps the most surprising result was that the timing of supervision seemed to affect supervisor behavior in the supervision session more so than counselor behavior. Supervision the day be-

fore a specified counseling session was very content oriented. Perhaps because the counseling session was still 1 day away, supervisors felt the permission to offer several alternative strategies for counselors to consider. The supervisor was more likely to adopt an instructional mode and therefore was doing more of the work in the supervision session. We do not know how much the supervisee actually learned in these supervision sessions, but follow-through to the subsequent counseling session was low. In other words, strategies discussed and approved by the supervisor in the supervision session were not acted on in counseling to any significant degree. We can hypothesize that because information was so voluminous in supervision the counselor was not able to prioritize or translate supervisory information into counseling strategies.

Supervision conducted within 4 hours of a subsequent session was very different. With the press of the upcoming session, the supervisor was far less likely to offer content and, instead, adopted a more consultative role. Fewer strategies were discussed, more of the strategies were offered by the counselor than by the supervisor, and those that were suggested met with more supervisor approval. Furthermore, there was far more follow-through from supervision to counseling for this treatment condition. Therefore, we can view supervision immediately before counseling to be more of a work session for the counselor with support from the supervisor as needed.

The third timing of supervision, more or less midway between counseling sessions, had no strong effects. Because other counseling sessions with other clients intervened and there was no immediate pressure to prepare for an upcoming session, the supervision conference was simply more diffuse in its content and follow-through.

The Couchon and Bernard (1984) study highlighted the importance of timing as a process variable in supervision. Depending on the developmental and learning needs of the supervisee, different timing of supervision might be appropriate. For example, "a counselor who conceptualizes well but who implements ideas poorly might benefit more from supervision immediately before counseling. On the other hand, a counselor who performs well but who lacks conceptual ability might benefit from supervision conducted the day before counseling" (p. 18).

Contrary to the assumptions of many supervisors, the counselors in the Couchon and Bernard (1984) study were equally satisfied with supervision regardless of when supervision was offered. (Timing also did not affect client or counselor satisfaction with counseling.) It should be noted, however, that an important time for supervision, immediately after counseling, was not studied. We hypothesize that if there is a time that would get an elevated satisfaction rating it would be immediately after counseling when the supervisee might benefit from support and reinforcement. This hypothesis was supported in part by Smith (1984), who found that practicum students evaluated post-session supervisor feedback as most effective among several choices. The same preference for immediate individual feedback was reported by Ray and Altekruse (2000). Though we know that supervisee satisfaction is high when feedback is delivered immediately, the amount and kind of learning resulting from this timing of supervision are still unknown.

Supervision Formats: Frequency of Use

Several investigators in the fields of counseling, psychology, and marriage and family therapy have sought to establish the types of supervision formats that are used in a variety of contexts (Anderson et al., 2000; Borders et al., 1995; Carlozzi et al., 1997; Coll, 1995; Freeman & McHenry, 1996; Nichols et al., 1990; Romans et al., 1995; Wetchler et al., 1989). It must be noted that the parameters of each study are distinct; thus, comparing the results across studies cannot be done in any definitive manner. Yet the variety of studies across several disciplines, describing methods used both within and beyond training, established the leading supervision formats. Within individual supervision, self-report was the most common in the field, while supervision using videotape re-

play was the strongest within training programs. Live supervision and audiotape replay also were found to rate highly in particular studies and to rank third and fourth overall. In all the studies that included cotherapy as a form of supervision, this format ranked last with the exception of Freeman and McHenry (1996), where one form of live supervision (bug-in-the-ear) ranked lowest (while other forms of live supervision ranked second in frequency). Finally, it was difficult to discern when studies collapsed the use of process notes with self-report; therefore, the former is not considered separately. It would seem that if one goal of supervision is to prepare the supervisee to successfully use supervision in the future (certainly a goal of training programs) exposure to several different supervision formats would expedite that goal.

Supervisor Use of Data

For the most part, our discussion thus far has focused on the methods used by the supervisor to obtain the data that will be used in supervision, as well as the timing of the supervision conference. Although important, these issues do not automatically translate into a productive supervision session. The supervisor also must produce behaviors that will match supervisory intentions (Strozier, Kivlighan, & Thoreson, 1993). Interpersonal process recall, for example, uses videotape as the method for obtaining supervision data, but the technique is intended to increase supervisee reflectivity regarding the interpersonal dynamics that were present during the session. If the supervisor had concerns about the supervisee's ability to be reflective at the level that IPR requires, this technique should be avoided and a less challenging form of stimulating reflectivity (e.g., journal writing) should be considered.

As part of their developmental model (described in Chapter 4), Loganbill et al. (1982) described five supervisor techniques–strategies that would assist supervisees to get beyond stagnation or confusion and move toward integration for any of Chickering's (1969) eight vectors addressed by Loganbill et al. in their model. These interventions are not limited to a specific format for supervision (e.g., the use of audiotape).

1. *Facilitative interventions* are as much a set of assumptions and attitudes as direct interventions (similar to Carroll's philosophy of supervision). They are supervisee centered and help to promote the natural developmental process. Inherent in this category is the belief that with support and reflective activity the supervisee can learn and change.

2. *Confrontive interventions* are a type of intervention that "brings together two things for examination and comparison" (Longbill et al., 1982, p. 33). The discrepancy can be internal to the supervisee, for example, a conflict between feelings and behavior, or it can be a discrepancy between the supervisee and an external actuality, for example, the supervisor seeing client dynamics in a way very different from how they have been perceived by the supervisee. When the discrepancy is internal, it provides the dissonance necessary for reflective activity (Nelson & Neufeldt, 1998).

3. *Conceptual interventions* occur whenever the supervisor is asking the supervisee to think analytically or theoretically. Loganbill et al. (1982) cautioned the supervisor to take learning styles into consideration because some supervisees grasp theory through experience, whereas others need a theoretical grounding prior to experience.

4. *Prescriptive interventions* take the form of coaching the supervisee to either perform certain behaviors or to delete certain behaviors. This is the most direct intervention category described by Loganbill et al. (1982). Therefore, they warned that prescriptive interventions could thwart supervisee development if used too liberally or when a more conservative approach might be substituted. (We will find a similar caution in our discussion of live supervision in Chapter 11.) Client welfare is a frequent rationale for using prescriptive interventions.

5. *Catalytic interventions* include those supervisor statements that are "designed to get things moving" (Longbill et al., p. 35). Although the authors noted that in one sense all supervision interventions are catalytic, they also argued that catalytic interventions are qualitatively different from each of the other four. When a supervisor uses a catalytic intervention, the supervisor is seizing the moment to bring additional meaning to the supervisory process. Loganbill et al. (1982) offered two examples of catalytic interventions: helping the supervisee to appreciate realistic client potential for change and thereby setting appropriate goals (a buffer, the authors asserted, from burnout) and encouraging the supervisee to experiment with new roles in the therapeutic relationship. Both examples given by Loganbill et al. should also stimulate introspection within the supervisee as part of reflective practice.

To summarize, the process of developmental supervision using the Loganbill et al. (1982) model begins by assessing the supervisee on eight dimensions as either stagnant, confused, or integrated. The supervisor then relies on combinations of the five supervisor intervention categories to bring the supervisee to integration on as many dimensions as possible. The source of supervision information on which the supervisor relies would depend on the issue, some needing direct observation, others being more contemplative in nature.

Johnson and Moses (1988) followed Loganbill et al. (1982) by also relying on Chickering's (1969) vectors as the criteria for supervisee development. Rather than the five interventions proposed by Loganbill et al., however, Johnson and Moses reduced supervisor input to either *challenge* or *support*. If the supervisor offers too little challenge, the supervisee might slip into stagnation (borrowing from the Loganbill et al. model); with too much challenge and too little support, the supervisee may get discouraged or defensive. The choice between challenge and support was seen by Johnson and Moses as the most critical decision that the supervisor makes. Once this decision is made, Johnson and Moses referred to the Bernard (1979, 1997) schema of roles (teacher, consultant, counselor) as being the primary choices for the supervisor to help the supervisee to attain the desired growth. Although Johnson and Moses did not imply that either support or challenge interventions should constitute the majority of supervisor interventions, McCarthy et al. (1994) found that the most frequent supervisor technique was the offering of support and encouragement, while confrontation and the assignment of homework were rarely used. Between these two extremes were techniques such as interpretation, self-disclosure, and reflection of content and feelings.

In summary, then, supervision techniques are much the same as those used in counseling or therapy. The goals of the supervisor, however, are more complex, because techniques must not only serve the developmental needs of the supervisee, but indirectly must assure that the therapeutic needs of the client are met as well. Finally, approaches used by supervisors must allow them adequate data for the central task of supervisee evaluation, while simultaneously allowing for a productive relationship between supervisor and supervisee.

PUTTING IT ALL TOGETHER

Reviewing each supervision method is a bit like reviewing theories of psychotherapy. While in the process of considering a particular method, it may seem attractive and worthwhile; but, like psychotherapy, the use of supervision formats and techniques requires an acceptable level of expertise and a sound rationale that is compatible with the supervisor's vision. In general, technical eclecticism among supervisors is desirable because it allows the supervisor to help a variety of supervisees to attain a variety of supervision goals.

At the beginning of the chapter, we discussed initial criteria for choosing an intervention. Here we will attempt to draw on the information in this chapter, as well as broader topics, to form a list of questions to ask when selecting format and technique within individual supervision.

1. *How will this method of supervision be received?* No method is appropriate if the supervisee cannot become more expert as a result of the method. At times this may be a developmental issue only. For example, a supervisee may be too novice and/or too concrete to be able to benefit from the advantages of self-report. Occasionally, a particular method of supervision may simply be a bad fit for the supervisee as an individual. For example, is e-supervision a perfect fit for an introvert supervisee or a method that will retard growth? Not only developmental level and learning styles, but also temperament and cultural norms will determine the receptivity to particular supervision delivery systems.

2. *Am I being true to my beliefs about how one learns to be a mental health practitioner?* As stated earlier, if the supervisor believes that reflectivity is the cornerstone of becoming an expert therapist, then the supervision modality must achieve reflectivity. In such cases, supervisee behaviors will be viewed in the context of the larger dynamics of interpersonal or intrapersonal processes and meaning, not the other way around. Other supervisors will assume that supervisees will become more competent with a series of successes and will therefore focus more on therapeutic interventions. The larger point is that, if the supervisor doesn't accept the outcome of a supervision method as crucial to the supervisee's development, the method will most likely be used in a perfunctory manner.

3. *Am I considering the three functions of supervision?* Using a different format to evaluate clinical competence from one used to promote supervisee development may make the supervision process clearer to the supervisee. Furthermore, a change of format can help the supervisor to maintain boundaries between different supervisor roles.

4. *Am I considering the timing and/or relative structure of my supervision?* Busy professional schedules often dictate the timing of supervision. But for the supervisee who is floundering, timing may be a relatively easy and potentially important variable to manipulate to assist a breakthrough in learning. Similarly, the relative use of structure may be manipulated to allow a different and potentially potent learning opportunity for the supervisee.

5. *Are administrative constraints real or am I not advocating with a strong enough voice?* It is not uncommon to hear that a piece of media equipment is too expensive or that a method of supervision is too time consuming for a particular setting. Yet a strong supervision program can energize a setting so that what is accomplished is more efficient and of higher quality. Supervisors must advocate for the kind and level of supervision that they believe must be present. As models to supervisees, it is imperative that supervisors work in ways that are productive and credible.

6. *What does this particular supervisee need to learn next? Am I using the best method for this purpose?* There are times when the supervisor must realize that the method being used is simply not accomplishing the desired outcome. One supervisor reported that, after spending several frustrating weeks in supervision with the supervisee making little progress conceptualizing client issues, the supervisor began to assign homework that required the supervisee to come to the conference with three different avenues to take with each client to be discussed, one of which had to be unconventional. This assignment seemed to energize the counselor and she started to make significant gains in her area of weakness.

What the supervisee needs may also challenge the comfort level of the supervisor. It may be more comfortable to remain supportive when the supervisee needs to be challenged. It may be more natural to continue a highly structured approach to supervision when the supervisee is ready for the supervisor to be more of a consultant in approach. If supervision is fairly standard from supervisee to supervisee, the supervisor should question whether it is the supervisor that needs to be stretched.

7. *Am I skilled in the use of this particular method or technique?* Ultimately, supervision will fall flat if the method is used poorly. IPR is a good example of a technique that can easily deteriorate if the supervisor is not skilled at asking probing questions without loading them with the supervisor's opinion. As we stated earlier, self-report can be a highly charged method of supervision, but only when the supervisor is expert and

knows how to use the method to challenge the supervisee. Teleconferencing may be attempted before the supervisor is adequately tooled, leading to frustration and failure.

8. *Have I considered ethical safeguards?* Supervision is based on the premise that the supervisee is not yet expert enough to handle a wide range of clients autonomously. An important criterion for choosing a method of supervision, therefore, must be some judgment about the level of competence of the supervisee. This is one reason why self-report is considered foolhardy for novice counselors. The ethics of supervision include the supervisor's responsibility to the supervisee. Supervision that does not assist the supervisee in learning the helping process could be considered unethical. As was stated earlier, technology introduces a whole new array of ethical concerns.

9. *Is it time to try something new?* Even if the supervisor is adamant about the centrality of one aspect of therapeutic practice (e.g., establishing an empathic relationship with the client), there are different ways to help the supervisee to reach the goal. For example, Sterling and Bugental (1993) suggested using role play to help the supervisee to make phenomenological gains, Stone and Amundson (1989) suggested the technique of metaphoric case drawing to assist in conceptualization, and Deacon (2000) advocated for the use of visualization to help supervisees to think more creatively. The training literature is replete with examples of specific techniques to arrive at a variety of areas of competence. Trying something new is as important for the supervisor as the supervisee. The goal is to stay fresh or to use a new method or technique to stimulate new and sometimes unexpected learning.

10. *Can I document the success of my method?* It would be nice if supervisors had hard data to support their work with each supervisee. (Some methods, e.g., transcription, taping, e-supervision, lend themselves to the possibility of data collection.) In the absence of data, it is still important that the supervisor glean a sense of accomplishment from the method or techniques being used. Each method chosen translates to alternative methods rejected. Therefore, supervisors must seek some justification for the continuation of a particular approach to supervision. At the very least, supervisors should seek feedback from supervisees about what they experienced as most helpful to their learning.

11. *Am I willing to confront my own assumptions?* Good supervisors can revisit familiar tenets with new scrutiny. No vision is complete. No supervision method has been found to be indispensable. Supervision at its best is a healthy balance of authority and humility. Supervisors who opt for confusion over stagnation model the essence of professional growth for their supervisees.

CONCLUSION

As the supervisor conducts individual supervision, many options are available regarding the form that supervision will take. Much of this will be determined by prior experience, interest in experimenting with different methods, and perceived supervisee need. All methods carry with them opportunities and opportunities bypassed. The quality of supervision we offer is intimately related to the decisions we make about methods. But, presently, there is insufficient empirical evidence to either encourage or reject the use of any of the available methods. Clearly, supervisors need not only to expand their repertoire, but also to systematically study their methods and techniques, to examine both the process and the meaning of what they do (Carroll, 2001; Holloway & Carroll, 1996). In this way they can best serve both their supervisees and their profession. Fall and Sutton (2004) offer additional assistance to the supervisor looking to expand his or her repertoire of supervision techniques.

CHAPTER 10

SUPERVISION INTERVENTIONS
GROUP SUPERVISION

It is reasonable to assert that individual supervision is the cornerstone for professional training. Yet supervisors also provide a great deal of supervision in a group format. It is our impression, for example, that virtually all university training programs employ group supervision at one point or another in their clinical courses. CACREP standards (Council, 2001), in fact, require group supervision. Group supervision is also central in internship and other training settings, as several studies have indicated. Riva and Cornish (1995) found that 65% of predoctoral psychology internship sites reported using group supervision. And supervisors in two studies reported that, whereas they used individual supervision most frequently, group supervision was a close second. Supervisors surveyed in one of the studies (Goodyear & Nelson, 1997) were based in university counseling centers; those surveyed in the other were family therapy supervisors (Wetchler et al., 1989). That such similar findings were obtained across both supervisory orientation and setting indicates the general validity of the belief that group supervision is, indeed, widely practiced.

The purpose of this chapter is to provide an overview of group supervision. In so doing, we hope to dispel the myth that individual supervision is inherently superior (cf. McCarthy, DeBell, Kanuha, & McLeod, 1988). In fact, none of the few studies comparing individual and group supervision (Averitt, 1989; Lanning, 1971; Ray & Altekruse, 2000) has found training outcomes of one modality to exceed those of the other, though Ray and Altekruse (2000) did find that supervisees indicated a stronger preference for individual over group supervision.

For this chapter we will draw from the limited empirical literature that exists and supplement it liberally with available conceptual and practice-based writings. The assumptions that guide this chapter are aptly summarized by Cartwright and Zander's (1968) following three propositions about groups in general:

1. *groups mobilize powerful forces that produce effects of utmost importance to individuals;*
2. *groups may produce both good and bad consequences;*
3. *a correct understanding of group dynamics . . . permits the possibility that desirable consequences from groups can be deliberately enhanced.* (Cartwright & Zander, 1968, p. 23)

GROUP SUPERVISION: DEFINITION AND CONCEPTUALIZATION

Holloway and Johnston (1985) defined group supervision as a process "in which supervisors oversee a supervisee's professional development in a group of peers" (p. 333). We present our own more extended definition in Box 10.1. This definition of group supervision is consistent with Cartwright and Zander's (1968) definition of a group as "a collection of individuals who have relations to one another that make them interdependent to some significant degree" (p. 46). The one possible caveat is that our definition might seem to exclude meetings of postlicensure peers to consult with one another. But, whereas we will employ the term *peer group supervision* later in the chapter, this practice technically is consultation rather than supervision and so does not contradict our proposed definition.

Box 10.1 _____

Group Supervision Defined

Group supervision is the regular meeting of a group of supervisees

- with a designated supervisor or supervisors
- to monitor the quality of their work and to
- further their understanding of themselves as clinicians, of the clients with whom they work, and of service delivery in general.

These supervisees are aided in achieving these goals by their supervisor(s) and by their feedback from and interactions with each other.

Our definition does not speak to the issue of group size. The single available study of the differential training effects of supervision group size (Ray & Altekruse, 2000) was inconclusive. Several authors, though, have offered their opinions regarding group size. Aronson (1990) suggested "the optimal size seems to be 5 or 6 if one is to devote sufficient attention to each person, especially if each participant is treating a sizable caseload" (p. 91). Chaiklin and Munson (1983) recommended 6 to 12 members, whereas Schreiber and Frank (1983) suggested at least 7. Both sets of authors suggested that to involve fewer supervisees is to risk disruption because of absences and dropouts.

These optimal sizes are often difficult to achieve in practice. Riva and Comish (1995) found in their survey of psychology internship sites that the typical supervision group consisted of between three and five supervisees, a number typically dictated by the number of interns on site. In university training programs, on the other hand, practicum groups typically range in size up to 10 members, the maximum the Council for Accreditation of Counseling and Related Educational Programs (2001) permits in programs it accredits. The actual number often is guided by course enrollment constraints of the particular university in which the given practicum is offered.

Types of Supervision Groups

Wilbur, Roberts-Wilbur, Morris, Betz, & Hart (1991) and Wilbur, Roberts-Wilbur, Hart, Morris,

& Betz (1994) identified three modalities of supervision groups: the task process group modality, which seems to be a combination of didactic and case conceptualization material; the psychoprocess modality, which seems to parallel the intrapsychic growth expected in the interpersonal process group; and the socioprocess modality, which parallels the interpersonal relationship growth expected in the interpersonal process group.

Shulman (1982) conceptualized the supervision of staff groups (in a work setting) as falling into four categories. The first two of the categories (staff meetings and in-service training) are marginally related to our conception of supervision. His last two categories, though, were case consultation and group supervision. He differentiated between the two by referring to the former as focusing on the client and the latter as focusing on supervisee growth.

Shulman saw these as discrete categories because the former may occur even for the seasoned professional who may need consultation for a particular client, whereas the latter assumes less experienced supervisees who are developing in their professional identity. Furthermore, whereas the case consultation group remains fairly faithful to the task of case analysis, the group supervision groups can focus on a variety of topics central to supervisee development, including "job management skills and professional practice skills, impact skills, and learning skills" (p. 224).

Research on group supervision structure is scant. In one study we found, Kruger, Cherniss, Maher, and Leichtman (1988) conducted a multiple-case study of four supervision groups of paraprofessionals at a residential treatment facility for emotionally disturbed children and adolescents. They found the meetings to be highly task oriented, with 69 percent of comments related to solving client problems.

Prieto (1998) described a specific context and type of group supervision, the practicum class as taught in primarily master's level counseling programs. Survey participants reported that, on average, more than half the group time (56%) was devoted to case presentations. The remainder of the time was apportioned for lectures and discussions on clinical topics (15%), trainees' professional or personal issues (11%), administrative or practicum site issues (9%), and dynamics in the supervision group (8%). Interestingly, 62% of the supervisors required trainees to read a textbook and 69% required them to read scientific journal articles.

Table 10.1 depicts several authors' conceptualizations of group supervision. We have identified five discrete categories (didactic presentations, case conceptualization, supervisee individual development, group development, and organization issues) and one less discrete category (supervisee–supervisor issues), which legitimately might be subsumed under group development.

THE UTILITY OF GROUP SUPERVISION

Advantages of Group Supervision. Holloway and Johnston (1985) criticized the fact that the practice of group supervision so far outstrips the research available to support it. Their concern had merit then, a decade later (Prieto, 1996), and apparently even yet (Goodyear & Guzzard, 2000). But, despite the dearth of hard evidence concerning group supervision, its practitioners offer compelling reasons for using this format. It would seem ill advised to forego the use of group supervision while we await data concerning its processes and outcomes.

Following are 10 frequently suggested advantages of group supervision. For related discussions of the advantages of group supervision, the reader might consult Carroll (1996), Hawkins and

TABLE 10.1   Group Supervision Activities

	DIDACTIC PRESENTATIONS	CASE CONFERENCE	INDIVIDUAL DEVELOPMENT	GROUP DEVELOPMENT	ORGANIZATIONAL ISSUE	SUPERVISOR–SUPERVISEE ISSUES
Sansbury (1982)	✕	✕	✕	✕		
Getzel & Salmon (1985)			✕	✕	✕	✕
Holloway & Johnston (1985)	✕	✕	✕	✕		
Wilbur et al. (1994)	✕	✕	✕	✕		
Kruger et al. (1988)		✕	✕	✕		
Shulman (1982)	✕	✕	✕	✕		

Shohet (1989) or Hayes (1989); also Riva and Cornish (1995).

1. *Economies of time, money, and expertise.* Group supervision offers many of the same economies that group counseling or therapy affords, particularly those of time, money, and expertise (Hawkins & Shohet, 1989). Because this is perhaps the most obvious advantage of group supervision, we want to emphasize that these economies are being obtained even as other important advantages are obtained as well.

2. *Minimized supervisee dependence.* Advocates for group supervision often argue that its use can help to avoid or at least to minimize supervisee dependence (Getzel & Salmon, 1985; Parihar, 1983). In addition, group supervision can diminish the hierarchical issues between supervisor and supervisee by encouraging more input from other supervisees in case analysis (Allen, 1976; Cohen, Gross, & Turner, 1976).

3. *Opportunities for vicarious learning.* To observe peers' successes and failures as they conceptualize and intervene in particular ways can provide important vicarious learning. Significantly, Hillerbrand (1989) cited data that suggest that novices who observe peers performing a skill are more likely to exhibit skill improvement and increased self-efficacy than those who instead viewed an expert. Moreover, what is learned from peers typically will include the personal as well: To observe and then discuss other group members' experiences and feelings can serve as a valuable means to normalize them (Hawkins & Shohet, 1989) for all members of the group.

4. *Supervisee exposure to a broader range of clients.* During group supervision, supervisees are exposed to and learn about the clients with whom the other group members are working. This enables them to learn about a broader range of clients than if each were working only in dyadic supervision.

5. *Feedback for the supervisee: greater quantity and diversity.* Another justification for using group supervision is that the other supervisees can offer perspectives that are broader and more diverse than what a single supervisor could pro-

vide. Hawkins and Shohet (1989) suggested that a group enhances the range of life experiences and other individual differences available to those who give feedback to the supervisee. Such individual differences include age, gender, sexual orientation, race, and culture. This, in turn, increases the likelihood that at least one person will have empathy for the supervisee, the client, or both.

This diversity expands the range of within-group expertise. For example, in our group supervision we often have encouraged a supervisee of a particular background to serve as consultant to the group when the discussion concerns treatment of a client of that background (e.g., a Korean American supervisee who provided the group with information about Korean cultural norms when the focus had been on one supervisee's work with a Korean American client).

Supervisors must, of course, remain vigilant against putting one person in the position of representing an entire cultural group. Yet some recognition of group identity can encourage a discussion of the importance of culture for both therapy and supervision. Therefore, the supervisor must be skilled in using peer consultants to open the group to new considerations, but not close down the group in deference to an "expert."

6. *Feedback for the supervisee: greater quality.* Hillerbrand (1989) drew from the cognitive science literature on the development of expertise (see, e.g., Ericcson & Lehmann, 1996) to discuss unique strengths of group supervision. The expertise literature suggests that as people become expert in any domain their knowledge becomes more "proceduralized." That is, problem solving will occur at an increasingly automatic level and with less conscious awareness. Therefore, "although experts are able to perform cognitive skills, they . . . are generally poor at post hoc descriptions of their actual cognitive processes" (p. 294). By contrast, novices (i.e., fellow supervisees) are more likely to employ language that is more understandable to other novices than that of the supervisor–expert. Moreover, they may be better able to decode nonverbal cues that other novices use to indicate confusion.

7. *A more comprehensive picture of the supervisee.* The group supervision format enriches the ways that the supervisor perceives and ultimately evaluates the supervisee. A particular supervisee might, for example, seem blocked when discussing his or her own work and yet still be an intelligent and insightful contributor to group discussions. The opportunity to see this can allow the supervisor to view the supervisee's difficulties in a different way (e.g., as a function of fear, isomorphism, etc.) than might be the case if the supervisee were seen only in individual supervision. Relatedly, this feature of the group context can help to moderate potentially deleterious countertransference reactions the supervisor might develop (Aronson, 1990).

Hawkins and Shohet (1989) suggested that the supervisor is able to gain important information by observing reactions that the supervisees are having to material being discussed, to one another, and to the supervisor. Expanding on this point, Counselman and Gumpert (1993) argued that parallel processes can be especially transparent in groups: "Group member reactions such as boredom, anger, anxiety, and excessive helpfulness can serve as important clues to the case dynamics" (p. 26). Moreover, they suggested that to receive feedback about these processes from a number of peers often has more impact than similar feedback delivered by a single supervisor.

8. *Greater opportunity to use action techniques.* Supervisors who employ action techniques will find the group especially useful (Hawkins & Shohet, 2000; Williams, 1995). Williams, whose particular emphasis has been on the use of psychodrama, provided an illustration of how he has used an action approach:

> [I]f one is going to conduct a supervision group using action, it is desirable to establish an "action culture" as soon as possible . . . to take the awe out of the method, to make it seem ordinary. [For example, in an initial session, the supervisor might] ask the supervisee [Tina] to imagine a line in the room, one end of which represents 0 and the other 10. Let us suppose that one of Tina's selected training needs is "more strength in hypothesizing about

cases," and she stands at a "3" on her present strength. The supervisor interviews her as she stands on that spot to find out what "3" means in terms of hypothesizing strength. She then is asked where she will be (rather than "would like to be") at the end of the year . . . let us say that she goes to a "7," wavers, and ends up at "6". Again, the supervisor interviews her as if she is that "6 person". . . . After a couple of demonstrations, the supervisor might ask those who have already been interviewed to interview the remainder of the group using [this] physical scaling. This brings into operation one of the most important guidelines for group supervision: Use the group. (Williams, 1995, pp. 215–216)

9. *Mirroring the supervisees' intervention (specific to the supervision of group therapists).* A final advantage of group supervision pertains specifically to the supervision of one treatment modality: that of group counseling or therapy. By having a supervision format that mirrors that of the treatment being supervised, supervisees and the supervisor alike have the opportunity to benefit (Hart, 1982; Hawkins & Shohet, 1989). For example, parallel processes and isomorphism are more likely to be observed, and supervisees can apply group process learnings from their supervision group to their counseling groups.

Limitations of Group Supervision. Despite these important advantages of group supervision, few authors actually have suggested that it *replace* individual supervision. Working with supervisees in a group consistently has been viewed as a complement to individual supervision or as a format to follow individual supervision in the course of training and, most often, beyond training (e.g., through peer consultation groups). Moreover, some drawbacks to group supervision warrant consideration. The following list is adapted from suggestions made by Carroll (1996), supplemented by other sources and our own observations.

1. *The group format may not permit individuals to get what they need.* This can occur for several reasons.

   a. Supervisees with heavy caseloads may not get all the supervision time that they need.

b. In groups that are heterogeneous with respect to group members' skill levels, the more skilled members may not get what they need.

c. The learning available to each group supervisee may be too diffuse to be worthwhile (Hamlin & Timberlake, 1982).

d. An overpowering group member might rob others of their instructional needs, or the structure itself might fit the majority of members, but offer virtually nothing to a distinct minority of the members (Parihar, 1983).

2. *Confidentiality concerns.* In group supervision, there are issues concerning the confidentiality of both (a) the clients who are the focus of attention and (b) the supervisees in the group. In both cases, confidentiality is less secure in groups. Group supervisors, therefore, have a specific obligation to minimize breaches of confidentiality by addressing this issue explicitly with the group.

3. *The group format is not isomorphic with that of individual counseling.* Most group supervision focuses on counseling occurring in an individual format. Consequently, the group is less likely to mirror some of the individual processes that occur in that counseling format. This limits opportunities to observe isomorphic and parallel processes.

4. *Certain group phenomena can impede learning.* Between-member competition and scapegoating, in particular, are among the phenomena that, if unchecked, can interfere with learning. In some cases, these even can result in deleterious effects to one or more of the supervisees.

5. *The group may devote too much time to issues of limited relevance to or interest for the other group members.* As Aronson (1990) pointed out, though, it is the supervisor's responsibility to ensure that all members perceive that they are getting something from the group.

SUPERVISOR ROLES, TASKS, AND STRATEGIES: GENERAL

Blocher (1983) argued that an effective supervisor would offer a balance of challenge and support.

Challenge can have several forms, including supervisor confrontation and persuading the supervisee to stretch to try out new behaviors. Support, too, can have multiple forms, including encouragement and positive feedback. The supervisor is to offer enough challenge to help to propel supervisees forward to try new behaviors, but not so much that they feel overwhelmed. At the same time, the supervisor is to provide support while the supervisees attempt to meet the challenges with which they have been presented, but not so much support that the supervisor infantilizes the supervisees or conveys the belief that they are too fragile or inept to handle honest feedback or work tasks.

To offer this balance of challenge and support is an ongoing supervisory responsibility. Its particular form and salience to supervisees, though, will likely change during group supervision according to the stage of the group's development. For example, one important earlier challenge is aimed at the group itself. This is for the supervisor to have group members assume shared responsibility for the group by, for example, only "filling in the gaps," rather than being the sole feedback provider. To the extent that the supervisor successfully models a balanced delivery of challenge and support, the group will adopt and begin responding to effective norms.

Some practitioners employ the intrapsychic concept that group members, individually and collectively, reenact earlier relationships with their primary group, the family (Bion, 1961). This suggests particular ways to understand group behavior. Cooper and Gustafson (1985) have asserted, for example, that "When adults' group behavior unfolds, it is all too apparent that a group character is emerging which dramatizes (in the here and now) patterned roles, sets of expectations, and tests all deriving from family group experiences" (p. 7).

Because of these patterns that supervisees have adopted from their earlier family interactions, the quality and form of at least some of their within-group behavior might be understood as responses that occur outside their awareness. These include difficulties of handing over inordinate authority over oneself to the supervisor out of unconscious respect for one's parents. This speaks to old family loyalties. Old family sacrifices also color interactions. These might, for example, cause a supervisee to react negatively to any feedback of a personal nature that comes from an authority figure because the supervisee suffered an excessive amount of humiliation within his or her family of origin. Each of these factors will shape the manner in which challenge and support are offered and received by supervisees.

Supervisors using any group format are responsible for optimizing the balance between challenge and support. Format, though, does affect the manifestations of these supervisor conditions. For example, group supervisors can capitalize on the support available through a cohesive work group; their challenges might include the demands, implicit or otherwise, for supervisees to face the group the following week by having accomplished some particular task.

But at least two other factors affect the forms of challenge and support available to the group supervisor. One is the conceptual model of the supervisor, which is illustrated by the discussion in the paragraphs immediately above. The other is the developmental stage of the particular supervision group. For example, the supervisor's responsibility for providing support and ensuring safety is very different in the earliest weeks of a supervision group than in the middle stages.

Sansbury (1982) suggested the following four group supervision tasks:

1. *teaching interventions directed at the entire group;*
2. *presenting specific case-oriented information, suggestions or feedback;*
3. *focusing on affective responses of a particular supervisee as the feelings pertain to the client;*
4. *processing the group's interaction and development, which can be used to facilitate supervisee exploration, openness and responses.* (p. 54)

Getzel and Salmon (1985) differed from Sansbury in that they suggested that the focus should be on the relationship between the supervisee and client. In addition, they included as legitimate foci (1) the supervision group's interpersonal relationships, (2) supervisor–supervisee relationships, and (3) supervisee relationships to the organizations (either training programs or mental health settings) in which they practiced.

Maximizing Helpful Phenomena and Minimizing Those That Are Hindering.   An effective supervisor should be sensitive to what supervisees themselves report to help or hinder their learning. Two related studies by the same research team have investigated this (Enyedy et al., 2003; Goodyear et al., in review). Both studies started with the same large national sample of group supervisees, who were asked to describe phenomena in group supervision that they had found to be (1) helpful or (2) hindering to their learning (hindering *"in the sense that your functioning was somehow negatively affected by this event or process"*). For each study, a separate subset of supervisees then clustered these helpful and hindering events according to their degree of similarity. Table 10.2 depicts the results.

As is clear from the table, a few categories of phenomena might affect the supervisee in *either* a helpful or a hindering way, depending on how they are manifest. For example, supervisees indicated that the supervisor could either help or hinder their learning, as could other group members. Also, at the affective level, the supervision group itself could be a source of either anxiety or other negative affects (hindering) or of support and safety (helpful).

Interestingly, other phenomena tended not to demonstrate this characteristic of occurring on a continuum of helpful–hindering impact. For example, with respect to hindering phenomena, supervisees indicated that logistical constraints such as room size or time of day negatively affected learning. As well, supervisees gave several examples of poor time management. The first of these often is outside supervisor control. However, time management is a supervisor skill, and therefore responsibility for poor use of it belongs to the supervisor.

With respect to helpful phenomena that did not have a parallel in the hindering phenomena, supervisees suggested one (specific instruction) that could be considered a type of supervisor intervention. They also noted two personal effects on them (self-understanding and validation of experience) that were in the service of helping their learning.

SUPERVISOR ROLES, TASKS, AND STRATEGIES: SPECIFIC TO GROUP STAGE

Stages of Group Supervision

Supervision groups, like groups of most other types, typically move through relatively predictable stages. Based on a review of the literature, Tuckman (1965) proposed and then later refined (Tuckman & Jensen, 1977) what has become one of the best recognized models of group development. This model suggests that groups proceed through five stages, each with characteristic goals for the members:

1. *Forming.* Members work to become comfortable with one another.
2. *Storming.* Members work to resolve issues of power; in a supervisory context, this is the stage at which between-member competitiveness is likely to be in its most direct and obvious form.
3. *Norming.* Members work to set norms for appropriate within-group behavior. Norms concern what is expected of those who are participating in the group (Hayes, 1989). Although these may develop and function outside group members' conscious awareness, they still exert powerful influences on behavior. Sanctions for their violation can be strong. Supervisors have a particular responsibility both (a) to be aware of emerging norms and (b) to shape them by, for example, modeling behaviors that should become normative (e.g., starting the group on time) and helping the members to identify the norms that are developing. In the next section

our discussion of establishing ground rules and structure addresses this stage.
4. *Performing.* This is the stage at which members tackle work-related tasks. It is the group's most productive stage.
5. *Adjourning:* Members work on saying goodbye to one another.

Although the stages through which a supervision group typically will move (i.e., *forming, storming, norming, performing,* and *adjourning*) are characteristic of groups of all types, different types of groups will move through them differently and with varying levels of intensity. Therefore, whereas it is important that group supervisors be sensitive to these stages, they should also keep in mind that supervision is a task oriented rather than a therapy experience and that movement through the stages will reflect this difference.

The Tuckman (1965; Tuckman & Jensen, 1977) stages provide a useful, albeit imperfect organizer for discussing the supervisors' roles, tasks, and strategies. In the section that follows, we address these, with particular emphasis on the forming, performing, and adjourning stages. We begin, though, with attention to the work of the supervisor before the group ever is convened. We refer to this as the pregroup stage.

Pregroup

Even though pregroup is not one of the Tuckman stages, at least two specific tasks precede the development of the supervision group. There are the screening of group members and the determination of where to hold the group meetings.

Screening Group Members. One of the supervisor's very early responsibilities is to screen the members who will comprise the group. In many cases, the supervisor will have relatively little discretion in this matter (e.g., in the case of teaching a university-based practicum or field placement). Nevertheless, some issues concerning screening merit attention. Perhaps the most important of

TABLE 10.2   Helpful and Hindering Phenomena in Group Supervision

HELPFUL PHENOMENA	HINDERING PHENOMENA
Supervisor impact: supervisor openness, sense of humor, competence, making the group feel comfortable, sharing past experiences, feedback	**Problems with Supervisors** Subcluster a **Negative supervisor behaviors:** lack of focus, dominating the group, either not listening or misunderstanding material presented, being overly critical, bragging about knowledge in nonhelpful ways, going on tangents Subcluster b **Supervisor's lack of experience or clinical focus:** insufficient expertise, lacked a theoretical focus, more wrapped up in administrative processes than clinical issues Subcluster c **Problems in co supervision:** cosupervisors had conflicting theoretical orientations or did not in their interactions "practice what they preached"
Peer impact: getting peer feedback; hearing feedback given to others; critiquing other's audio- or videotapes; observing differences in presentation styles	**Between-member problems** Subcluster a **Negative supervisee behaviors:** within-group competition; between-supervisee conflict; bossy and controlling group members; members who did not engage or participate Subcluster b **Personal reaction to negative behaviors:** compared to the first subcluster, this concerned the participants' personal reactions, including "the group criticized me for not doing it their way"
Support and safety: the group was a safe place to ask questions and to vent about site concerns; there were camaraderie and mutual support; it felt safe to share fears, successes, and questions	**Supervisee anxiety and other negative affects:** feeling unsafe, alienated, unsupported, or anxious; pressured to self-disclose; being the only male or female, African-American, etc.
Specific instruction: being given reading assignments; going over legal and ethical issues; lectures on clinical issues; watching videos that showed client and counselor interactions	**Logistical constraints:** lack of variety in cases; room size; group scheduled too late in the day; main supervisor out ill
Self-understanding: learning from my own mistakes in counseling; being able to process my own countertransference; self-reflection in preparation for the group; the opportunity to explore differences and difficulties	**Poor group time management:** not enough time to discuss cases or to get questions and issues addressed; one person dominated the group's time; some cases were lengthy and time was not allotted to other cases; too many people needing time; too much time spent on things other than supervisees' cases
Validation of experience: therapeutic interventions and skills were validated; the supervisee felt affirmed; experiences were normalized	

The list of helpful phenomena is from Goodyear et al.; the list of hindering phenomena is from Enyedy et al. (2003). This table reorganizes the order in which phenomena were presented in those studies.

these concerns the extent to which a group could or should be homogeneous or heterogeneous with respect to such matters as supervisee ability, experience level, theoretical orientation, and characteristics of field site.

For novices, there seems to be a case for relative homogeneity among the group members. When supervisees are at more or less the same experience level, they are likely to have greater empathy for one another and to more easily accomplish trust building. Furthermore, in a homogeneous group, one's relative strength can be more readily appreciated because experience level does not cloud perceptions of individual talent. It may be the case, for example, that one supervisee is more likely to take a risk by using a novel intervention, whereas another will lead the group in conceptualization ability. Although an awareness of the relative strengths of the group members can feed between-member competitiveness, it also can enhance supervisees' self-awareness. The supervisor's responsibility is to have supervisees identify their baseline strengths and build from there.

Supervisees are more likely to find themselves in heterogeneous supervision groups in field training sites. Chaiklin and Munson (1983) noted that it is the more experienced supervisees who lose when the group is mixed. Parihar (1983) also found heterogeneity to be a disadvantage in that different experience levels meant that supervisees brought very different expectations to supervision. Therefore, the group supervisor would be bound to make compromises in a mixed group, leading to some level of dissatisfaction with the experience. Allen (1976) echoed these concerns and suggested that heterogeneity is a major drawback for supervision groups in mental health settings.

Wendorf, Wendorf, and Bond (1985) were more positive about the heterogeneous group, arguing that it is more realistic and allows different group members to adopt more responsible roles, as they are ready. In the meantime, more experienced clinicians can be taking appropriate leadership positions and modeling higher-level functioning for those who are less experienced. Getzel and Salmon (1985) also asserted that too much homogeneity would stifle the exact benefits hoped for in group supervision, including spontaneity. Furthermore, they pointed out that homogeneity of cultural background could produce an undesirable situation, especially if the clientele being served is culturally diverse. Finally, Schreiber and Frank (1983) recommended a heterogeneity perspective for experienced clinicians in private practice pursuing peer supervision: "Our sense was that at a more advanced state in career development these differences (in perspective and expertise) are welcomed and perceived as edifying. By this time each of us was secure enough about our skills to feel comfortable with a peer having another approach in which she was expert" (p. 31).

Because there seems no simple resolution to the homogeneity versus heterogeneity issue, the supervisor must consider the makeup of the group carefully and attempt to compensate for the disadvantages of either situation through group structure and ground rules.

Meeting Place(s). Whether the group meets on common ground (e.g., the work site) or rotates meeting place (e.g., one meeting at each member's home) will affect the feelings that group members have about each other and accelerate or delay cohesion. Because of the value of mirroring the structure of therapy, it probably is important as much as possible when establishing meeting places to maintain appropriate boundaries with respect to such matters as meeting time, professionalism of the setting and members' demeanor.

Forming Stage

For the supervisor to establish ground rules and structure is a particular focus of the forming stage of the group. In fact, if the supervisor does not exert leadership in setting these rules, the group members will.

The following sections on frequency of meetings, attendance, and manner of case presentation all are matters of ground rules and structure. We will discuss each in turn. Although we are attempting to convey what we understand to be conventional clinical wisdom with respect to these matters, we realize that not all supervisors would agree on these points. What is important, though, is that supervisors be clear about how they intend to handle these several matters and then to convey that clearly to group members.

Frequency of Meetings.   How often the group meets will affect group process: meeting once a month, for instance, might make it difficult to develop a viable atmosphere, whereas, on the other extreme, to meet twice a week might be untenable for some members. Marks and Hixon (1986) found that groups that met weekly (as opposed to biweekly) provided their members with the most growth, including "an increased willingness to deal with feelings associated with the treatment process, and a marked decrease in anxiety due to an increase in trust" (p. 422). By contrast, groups that met biweekly remained more cognitive and formal.

Attendance.   Regular attendance is an especially important ground rule to adopt and enforce. Absences affect the group in multiple ways, including the sense of cohesion that members feel, as well as the energy and vitality experienced during the meeting. Moreover, group members essentially are committing to be there for one another. As well, members will attach meaning to absences of other supervisees. For example, the supervisee who does not come the week after she presents a difficult case will cause others to worry that their feedback might have been too confrontive. This will not only affect the group session with the missing member, but, if not addressed in the group, will affect the quality of feedback given to this member when she returns.

Manner of Case Presentation.   Another matter involving structure is the means by which cases will be presented. Ground rules concerning case presentations are essential if the group is to serve any consistent purpose. A ground rule of openness and respect can be achieved at the outset if the supervisor states his or her expectations regarding

confidentiality, responsibility of each member, and level of participation of each group member and protects members from undue peer pressure or intimidation. Many of the ground rules for group supervision have to do with how clinical material will be presented and processed. For example, Munson (1983) offered the following guidelines for case presentations:

1. *The supervisor should present a case first.*
2. *The supervisee should be granted time to prepare the case for presentation.*
3. *The presentation should be based on written or audiovisual material.*
4. *The presentation should be built around questions to be answered.*
5. *The presentation should be organized and focused.*
6. *The presentation should progress from client dynamics to supervisee dynamics.* (p. 104)

Munson also outlined ground rules for supervisors, suggesting that they avoid

(1) presentation of several cases in a short session, (2) presentation of a specific problem rather than the case in context, (3) presentation of additional problems in a single case, (4) therapist dynamics preceding case dynamics during discussion, and (5) intervention expectations beyond the capabilities of [the] therapist (p. 104).

Perhaps the most common ground rules for group supervision have to do with the offering of feedback to each other as a result of case presentation. The supervisor can suggest these ground rules, but they also should receive some level of group consensus. Table 10.3 is one such set of guidelines that helps the group members to organize their thoughts and provide feedback in a focused way. Note that it is organized so that the supervisee presenting a case will speak first, using the first five items to guide that presentation. Subsequent items are to guide group members' observations and comments.

Wilbur and Wilbur (1983; also, Wilbur et al., 1994) have devised a structure that distracts supervisees from some of their more personal issues and seems, in our experience, to work very well with groups that approach the task of case con-

TABLE 10.3 Guidelines for Using a Case Conference Format

THE SUPERVISEE: PRESENTING TO GROUP

---

1. Of what content, events, and processes were you most aware in today's session (perhaps playing selected tape segments to illustrate)?   [description]
2. What do you believe is the most likely explanation for the content (events or processes)?   [inference]
3. What feelings were you experiencing toward the client during the session? Also, were you aware of any thoughts or fantasies about the client during the session?
4. What feelings and thoughts do you believe that the client was having with you during the session?
5. State the specific feedback that you particularly want from the group.

GROUP MEMBERS

---

1. Note what the counselor did.
    a. What were things you liked about the counselor's approach? (No one likes to hear criticism right off the bat.)
    b. What seemed to be the client's reaction to the counselor's behavior?
    c. What would you have added to the session?
    d. What things did the counselor do that might have been done in a different way?
    e. Were there any things in the session done by the counselor that you think were unhelpful? If so, what were they? What do you believe should have been done instead?
2. Note what the client did.
    a. What do you think of this client's concerns?
    b. What feelings did this client elicit in you?
    c. What themes were evident?
    d. Were you confused by any inconsistencies?
    e. Did the client's input seem to make things clearer?
3. Note what the session accomplished.
    a. Given what you know about this client, were appropriate process or outcome goals accomplished during this session?
    b. What would you say was the major accomplishment of this session?
    c. What would you say was the major flaw of this session?
4. If this were your client, what would be reasonable and productive goals for the next session? How would you accomplish these goals?

---

ferences in an overly cautious fashion. Their structured group supervision model (SGS) is presented in Table 10.4.

Storming

In Chapter 7 we discussed supervisees' needs both to feel and to seem competent. This supervisee need is present in all supervision formats. In group

supervision, though, it can help to fuel between-supervisee competition, especially over which particular supervisee will be perceived as the best or perhaps the supervisor's favorite. This likely will be a continuing, latent issue throughout the group experience. However, it is most prominent during the storming phase.

Some level of between-supervisee competition is inevitable. In fact, when it is appropriately

TABLE 10.4 Steps of the Structured Group Supervision Model

Step 1: Plea for Help. The supervisee states what assistance is being requested from the supervision group. The supervisee provides the group with summary information relating to the request for assistance. Information may be in the form of audio- or videotaped material, a written summary, or verbal communication. Following the presentation of the summary information, supervisee makes Plea for Help statement, e.g., "I need your help with . . . ."

Step 2: Question Period. The supervision group members ask the supervisee questions about the information presented in step 1. This step allows group members to obtain additional information or clarify any misperceptions concerning the summary information. One at a time, in an orderly manner, group members ask one question at a time of the supervisee. The process is repeated until there are no more questions.

Step 3: Feedback or Consultation. Group supervision members respond to the information provided in steps 1 and 2 by stating how they would handle the supervisee's issue, problem, client, etc. During this step, the supervisee remains silent but may take notes regarding the comments or suggestions. When giving feedback, group members again proceed one at a time, stating how they would handle the supervisee's dilemma. First person is used, e.g., "If this were my client, I would." The process is repeated until there is no additional feedback.

Pause or Break. There is a 10- to 15-minute break between steps 3 and 4. Group members should not converse with the supervisee during this break. This is time for the supervisee to reflect on the group's feedback and to prepare for step 4.

Step 4: Response Statement. The group members remain silent and the supervisee, in round-robin fashion, responds to each group member's feedback. The supervisee tells group members which of their statements were helpful, which were not helpful, and why they were beneficial or not.

Step 5: Discussion (optional). The supervisor may conduct a discussion of the four-step process, summarize, re-act feedback offered, process group dynamics, etc.

From M. P. Wilbur, J. Roberts-Wilbur, C. M. Hart, I. R. Morris, and R. L. Betz (1994). Structured group supervision (SGS): A pilot study. *Counselor Education and Supervision, 33,* 262–279. Copyright © 1994 ACA. Reprinted by permission. No further reproduction authorized without written permission of the American Counseling Association.

channeled, competition can be useful in stimulating group members to stretch to be the best that they can. The supervisor, though, has an important role in containing and channeling it.

In some educational contexts, educators actually encourage an openly competitive atmosphere. Aronson (1990) pointed out that one of the clearest examples occurs in some law schools: Because legal practice is adversarial, to encourage the development of combative skills is to prepare the students for practice. Aronson, though, was blunt when he asserted that "this model is totally inappropriate for the training of psychotherapists" (p. 89).

Competition must be acknowledged in order for group members to put it into proper perspective. The following is one supervisor's attempt to make between-supervisee competition an open issue and to diffuse its negative effects:

Could it be that the seminar is skirting around the question of who is the best therapist here? That is no doubt a hot potato, and what is even hotter is the question of who is the worst therapist. The issue of competition can contribute to the work of the group (everyone tries to do the best he [sic] can . . . it may also interfere (people become too afraid of being rejected or envied). (Rioch et al., 1976, p. 24)

Norming

Helping the group to establish effective norms can minimize the risk of having some supervisees establish counterproductive norms. For example, the wrong norms might allow the group to become a place for some supervisees to ventilate their miseries, expressing sensitive material in order to keep sympathies of the other members high, but their feedback low. This norm can be readily adopted in supervision groups, for the members are helping professionals who have a vocation or calling to take care of others.

This illustrates only one of a number of possibly counterproductive norms that might be established if the supervisor does not take an active role in influencing norm development. In fact, by imposing an optimal level of structure, the supervisor not only influences the development of norms, but also helps to provide group members with the sense of safety that is needed to risk exposing their clinical work—and themselves—to their peers. Yet the key word here is optimal, for if structure is too rigid, it can create its own tension by stifling spontaneity and fitting some members far better than others. The supervisor, therefore, needs not only to create an initial structure, but also to monitor its effect on the group and be prepared to alter or abandon part of the group's structure based on group feedback (in fact, to request feedback is itself a structural matter).

Although norming is an evolving process that occurs most heavily during one period of the group, supervisors will have laid essential groundwork for the group's norming when they established structure and ground rules during the forming stage.

Performing Stage

Keith, Connell, and Whitaker (1992) suggested that therapy groups begin with the therapist adopting a *maternal* role. That is, the therapist invites the group members to be comfortable, is nurturing, and is solicitous of their feelings. The leader gradually shifts to a *paternal* role as she or he begins setting limits on topics and making demands on group members. Then, as the members' emotional investment in the group increases, the therapist gradually turns more and more of the leadership over to them. Supervision groups, though, are different. Keith et al. noted that the supervision group

> *passes through similar stages, but the maternal and paternal periods are usually brief. And to the extent the supervisor is either maternal or paternal, the parenting model is that of parent and older teenager; that is, it is very limited, acknowledging the freedom and maturity of the second generation. . . . The early 4 to 6 sessions require guidance; like learning to drive a car. Then the teacher becomes less active . . . (the driving instructor chooses to move to the back seat).* (p. 98)

This observation would suggest, then, that the supervision group should be into the performing stage by the fourth to the sixth session.

By the time the group reaches the performing stage, much important work already will have occurred. If this work has been effective, group members will have assumed appropriate levels of shared responsibility for the group and for one another. Individually, they will have begun to trust and will have become energized by a commitment to explore and examine their own therapeutic efforts. Supervisees will present cases that show them stretching the upper limits of their skill, rather than cases that either are too clear or are to impossible to elicit critical comments.

One supervisory behavior that might be expected to change as a function of group stage is the proportion of speech activity exhibited by the supervisor versus the group members. That is, it is reasonable to assume that, with increased cohesion and the movement into a performing mode, the supervisees will speak a greater proportion of the time (and the supervisor, consequently, will speak less) than earlier in the group. Unfortunately, we are aware of only two studies that concern this.

Kruger et al. (1988) conducted a multiple-case study of four supervision groups with paraprofessional counselors. Two were led by more experienced supervisors; two, by novices. They found that the more experienced supervisors were less active than the less experienced supervisors (mean proportion of supervisor speech acts across sessions: 50.6% versus 55.96%, respectively). Unfortunately, they did not report data in such a way to allow inferences about trends of speech activity across sessions.

Ravets, Goodyear, and Halon (1994) conducted an intensive case study of two supervision groups: one, for practicum students, was co-led by a faculty supervisor and a teaching assistant; the other, for more advanced supervisees, was run by a single supervisor in an agency setting. In the first group the two supervisors together accounted for an average of 21% of the speech acts across 10 sessions (range from 12% to 31%). In the other group, the supervisor's average proportion of speech activity was 33.6% (range from 18% to 55%). There were no apparent trends in speech activity as a function of group stage. However, because this has such clear practice implications, it is one area of group supervision that merits more research attention.

But having helped the group to arrive at this performing stage, the supervisor will continue to have issues and tasks to address, albeit of a somewhat different form than in the earlier stages. The sensitive supervisor will be watching for signs of "nonwork" occurring and will change direction, ask the group for feedback, or offer the group some process feedback if this occurs. On the other hand, the supervisor must understand the importance of recycling some issues in order to permit them to be understood and confronted at new levels. What might feel like an old theme revisited might be a theme that finally is understood.

Borders (1989c) proposed a model in which the supervisor employs the roles of both *moderator* and *process commentator.* As moderator, the supervisor keeps the group on task, choreographs the experience, and summarizes feedback. As process commentator, the supervisor attends to immediate group dynamics. For both roles, Borders empha-

sized the need for the supervisor to be cognizant of the developmental level of supervisees (e.g., novice counselors needing more direction and structure and more advanced supervisees being able to take on more responsibility). The model, therefore, requires a good deal of supervisor flexibility. "Indeed, the success of this approach depends on the supervisor's artistry in recognizing a needed and appropriate intervention, assigning tasks to particular peer group members, and orchestrating the feedback. Often working at several levels, the supervisor helps a productive learning experience to unfold" (pp. 5–6).

Borders (1989c) suggested a structured group exercise that can breathe life into group processes when they become stagnant. She relies on videotape for the presentation of cases and requires supervisees to present specific questions about the client or the session and to ask for specific feedback. Other group members are then assigned one of four tasks to direct their observation of the videotape segment, depending on the issues raised by the supervisee.

The first task is to engage in focused observation. A peer might be asked to focus on the use of one type of skill (e.g., confrontation) or one aspect of the session, such as the relationship between the counselor and client. Borders pointed out that a particular observation task could be used to develop specific skills of the observer. For example, the observer who has a tendency to quicken the pace of his or her sessions might be asked to observe the pace of the videotaped session.

The second task is role taking. An observer might be asked, for example, to take the role of the counselor, of the client, or even of some significant person in the client's life (e.g., a parent or a spouse). For family sessions, the assignment could be to represent the family member who refuses to come to therapy. After the videotape has been shown, the observer gives feedback from the perspective of the person that he or she represents.

The third task is to observe the session from a particular theoretical orientation. One observer could be assigned this task, or several observers could be looking at a session from different theoretical perspectives. For example, one supervisee could be asked to observe another supervisee's counseling session from a systemic perspective; another, from a cognitive–behavioral perspective. Not only does this exercise help supervisees to apply theory to practice, but it also helps to elicit underlying assumptions about problem formation and resolution.

The fourth task is for an observer to watch the session with the assignment of developing a descriptive metaphor. Borders reported that this approach has been particularly helpful when the issue is the interpersonal dynamics between the client and counselor or the counselor feeling "stuck." For example, an observer might be asked to think of a road map and describe the direction that counseling is taking or to view the counselor–client relationship within the context of a movie and describe each person's part in the drama.

Final Observations about the Performing Stage

We have two additional observations about the performing stage in group supervision. The first of these is that individual differences should be more salient at this stage. Because there is more group cohesion, there is less need for group conformity. For example, each person's style of humor should be more evident at this stage, as should personal philosophies of life and of helping. When a supervision group is working well, there are no stars (including the supervisor) and no dunces. Rather, each supervisee is known for his or her particular talents, idiosyncratic way of viewing clients, and personal supervision goals. Everyone has something to gain from and to offer the group.

Some groups may never get fully to this performing stage, and probably all groups have some periods of "nonwork" throughout their life span. Shulman (1982) argued that the supervision group's "culture" is an important phenomenon to keep in mind. The culture is the gestalt that makes the group feel different from all other groups; these are the norms and rules that the group has adopted. Many of these are outside members' conscious awareness, but powerful nevertheless. One

such rule might be "Give feedback, but don't make anyone angry." Although such a rule might be benign enough in the initial stages of group supervision, it would adversely affect the work of the group if it were to persevere as more powerful than the injunction to be honest.

It is rewarding when nonproductive aspects of the supervision group's culture are called into question by supervisees. But if this does not occur, it is ultimately up to the supervisor to be aware of and to confront the limitations brought about by certain aspects of the group's culture.

The second of our concluding observations about the performing stage is that optimal group functioning at this stage depends on mutual trust and support among group members. Reed (1990) suggested that many students anticipate the group supervision that occurs as part of practicum as "a boot camp for counselors" and that when they complete it "they would know they were no longer students; they were beginning counselors" (p. 3). This acknowledges group supervision's importance. But in invoking a military metaphor, Reed implicitly suggests that the experience may be harrowing and perhaps even abusive. Perhaps this is true in some few instances. We believe, however, that many, or even most supervisees actually find group supervision to offer a greater amount of support than does individual supervision.

Nicholas (1989) suggested that in the early stages of the supervision group the supervisor must provide "nurturant" energy. But as group members begin to invest emotionally in the group and in each other, primary responsibility for this nurturant energy shifts from the supervisor to the group members. This process corresponds with the development of group cohesiveness, which Yalom (1985) asserted is the group equivalent of empathy.

These processes, then, lead to an atmosphere of support between and among group members. And as support levels increase, so too do levels of between-member trust and therefore the extent to which supervisees are willing to become vulnerable with one another and to reveal their mistakes and weaknesses. All this contributes to the increasing value of the supervisory group to members.

Support might be understood to counterbalance between-member competitiveness. In fact, competition typically is more manifest in the early stages of the group but then becomes moderated as group cohesiveness and mutual support develop.

One interesting supportive phenomenon that we have observed concerns the situation in which a particular member of the supervision group clearly is faltering badly and the group rallies to protect that person. This protectiveness takes the form of giving softened and nurturing feedback and often even worrying that the supervisor may be behaving in an unduly harsh manner with this group member (despite objective evidence to the contrary).

Adjourning Stage

Most supervision groups probably are time limited. Some, however, are ongoing. Therefore, it is appropriate to discuss each type of group separately in terms of their termination processes.

The Time-limited Group.   The time frames for many supervisory relationships are determined by a training calendar. Often this corresponds to a semester or to an internship cycle or rotation.

For practicum and internship groups, the supervision experience can be one of weeks, rather than months or years. Especially when the life of the supervision group is across a single semester, the ending of the group may feel premature to almost everyone. In addition, toward the conclusion of the semester, the urgency that supervisees may experience in managing the termination of their clients might override any consideration of the closure issues in the group itself.

It would be a mistake, though, to end a supervision group without allowing the group to process this phase. Moreover, because the ending of the supervisees' therapeutic relationships usually coincide with the ending of the supervisory group, the parallels become a useful tool and provide important material to process.

Virtually all brief therapy models have a particular structure, an emphasis on a treatment plan, and a particular emphasis on the process of termination. In a sense, this is a model that applies to supervision, whether in dyadic or group formats. The goals of the supervision group should be specific enough to be noticed when they have been achieved so that supervisees can feel a sense of accomplishment upon ending. At the same time, the supervisor needs to help supervisees to put their learning into context to alleviate any panic at ending the supervision experience and finding that they still are not the totally competent practitioners that they imagined they might or should be. Of course, training is only the beginning of the practitioner's learning of his or her trade (in fact, supervision among experienced practitioners is becoming more and more prevalent). It is important to discuss this reality when concluding group supervision. It is equally important to give each supervisee some direction regarding the learning to be accomplished in the immediate future. This may need to be done individually, although certainly some supervision groups will have developed sufficiently to handle this task within the group.

The point is that a time-limited experience inherently limits what supervisees have the opportunity to learn. Therefore, it is essential that they leave the supervision experience with a plan for self-improvement. One part of this plan for each supervisee most likely will be the securing of additional supervision. An important culminating experience, therefore, would be to crystallize what can be learned from supervision and how one goes about securing this type of supervision for oneself.

One aspect of time-limited supervision that can be frustrating for the supervisor is the nearly universal tendency of supervisees to begin withdrawing from the group when the end is in sight. Supervisees who are simultaneously approaching closure with their clients will complain that their clients have stopped "working." Often these same supervisees will be unaware that they are working less with each other in the supervision group. The need for psychological distance in order to cope with the loss both of people and of a valuable process is important to address in the group as supervisees handle multiple closure experiences.

The Ongoing Supervision Group.   A danger of the ongoing supervision group is that it might fizzle out, rather than end in a clear fashion. Like a relationship that fizzles out, the group that terminates in this manner is left with more unfinished business and perhaps an inadequate understanding of what caused the ending to occur. To avoid this, it is advisable to schedule an ending from the outset of the group. Like all social systems, groups need markers in order to appreciate their development. An ending can provide this kind of marker, even if the group should reconstitute itself immediately with no change of membership.

The kind of ending that we suggesting may be an appointed time when the group reviews the assumptions and decisions that were made in the pregroup phase. It is a time when as many things as possible become negotiable, including ground rules and the process of supervision itself. It is a time for supervisees to evaluate their individual development and their level of commitment and contribution to the goals of the group. Also, it is a time for the supervisor to evaluate the amount of responsibility that has been shared with group members, the process that has been in place, and the feasibility of continuance.

Endings can be added to the life of a group in several ways. One way is to freeze membership for a certain amount of time, say one year, at which time some members might leave and others might enter. In a sense, the change of membership gives the group a chance to start over. Another way is for the process of the group itself to change. For example, a supervisor might decide that it is time for the group to change from a supervisor-led group to a peer supervision group. This juncture could be planned as an ending. Time can also be manipulated to produce a marker. A break of 4 to 6 weeks could be planned to occur every 6 months to encourage an evaluation and renegotiation period prior to or immediately after the break. Each group will find its own way to end once it appreciates the importance of ending.

A Procedure for Supervisee Assessment and Feedback

Advances in computer and software technology have made sophisticated statistical procedures user friendly and accessible to many clinical supervisors who previously have perceived them as too daunting to use. The Windows-based versions of the more popular statistical packages such as SPSS (Statistical Package for the Social Sciences) have made it relatively easy to understand and use statistical procedures. The user does not have to write programming commands, but only to "point and click." Such advances have the potential to affect supervisory practices in important ways.

One statistical procedure that many supervisors may find valuable is multidimensional scaling (MDS). MDS provides a means for obtaining a picture of how the supervisees in a supervision group perceive one another. Such a picture can be an important form of feedback for the supervisees; it also can provide valuable additional data to the supervisor who is attempting to develop evaluative (formative or summative) impressions of the supervisee.

MDS is "designed to detect the hidden structure of similarity judgments" (Stalans, 1995, p. 138). This structure then is plotted in two- (or more) dimensional space. It is analogous to creating the group's map of the location of the various members in relationship to one another.

MDS is based on a series of comparisons of the perceived relatedness or proximities between pairs of concepts. For our purposes, the supervisees in the supervision group are the concepts on which we are focusing. For the purpose of simplicity and brevity, let us assume that a particular supervision group had five students: Joe, Sally, Celeste, Alicia, and Will. Each group member rates the degree of similarity (e.g., on a 7-point scale) for each possible between-member comparison (e.g., Joe-Sally Joe-Celeste, etc.). Data are entered in a similarity matrix. When MDS is run, the number of dimensions is constrained to two. As Figure 10.1 indicates, whereas the group members perceived Joe, Sally, and Alicia as relatively similar to one another, they perceived Celeste and Will as different both from the larger group and from each other.

The usefulness of this is that the supervisor gets the group's mental map of the members in relationship to one another without necessarily

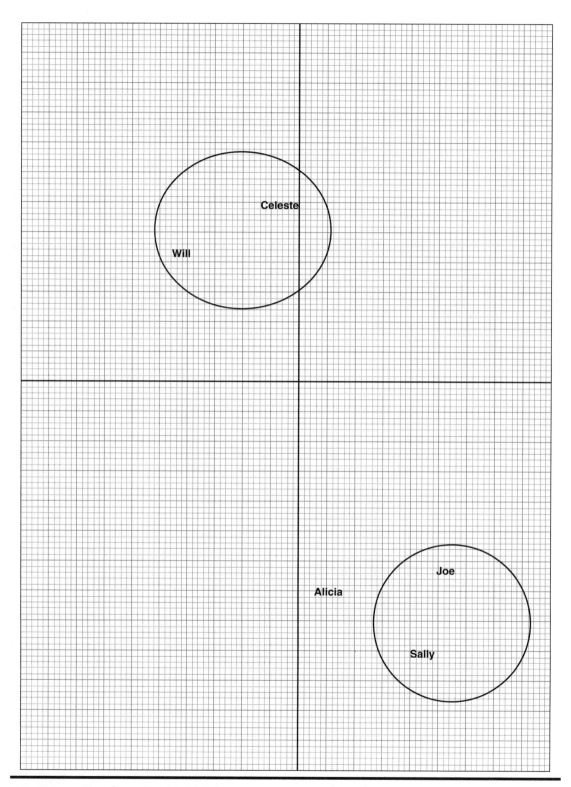

FIGURE 10.1 Two-dimensional MDS Solution Depicting Members of a Supervision Group

involving a good–bad dimension. In fact, the understanding of the dimensions is done after the fact. It could be that the vertical dimension of Figure 10.1 is one of activity versus passivity, whereas the horizontal dimension is one of task oriented versus relationship oriented. In this case, characterizing group members is simply descriptive of style.

Evaluation and Feedback of the Supervisor

The ending of the group also presents the supervisor with an opportunity to obtain feedback about the quality of his or her work. If the group is offered as a practicum class, most universities will ensure that students complete end-of-term course evaluations. But these typically indicate more global information, such as how much the students learned and how prepared they believed the instructor to have been. Course evaluations typically do not provide information specific to effectiveness in supervising a group.

Researchers are beginning to recognize the need for instruments that will help to provide group supervisors with more specific feedback than has been available to date. There now are three of which we know. White and Rudolph (2000) developed the Group Supervisory Behavior Scale, which has six subscales developed by rational means (*Facilitation of an Open Climate; Demonstration of Professional Understanding; Clear Communication; Encouragement of Self-Evaluation; Efficiency and Clarity of Evaluation; Overall Quality of Behavior*). Arcinue (2002) developed the Group Supervision Scale (available in the Supervisor's Toolbox). Its three factor-analytically derived scales are *Group Safety, Skill Development and Case Conceptualization,* and *Group Management.* And Getzelmon (2003) developed the Group Supervision Impact Scale, which measures impact of (a) the supervisor, (b) peers, and (c) the group environment. To have group members use instruments with established psychometric qualities to provide their supervisor with feedback about his or her performance can be very useful, not only during the adjourning stage of the group, but at other points as well.

GROUP SUPERVISION VARIANTS

Balint Groups

Balint groups (Balint, 1985; Norell, 1991) are employed worldwide in the training of novice physicians. Balint groups were developed from a psychodynamic model and initially had the primary purpose of teaching novice physicians to respond empathically to their patients. In this country, though, they have become more didactic in their format, have broader goals, and most frequently are found in family practice residencies. Brock and Stock (1990) found in their survey of family practice residencies that most such groups meet weekly for 2 to 3 years and follow a format of having the novice physicians spontaneously present cases from memory. As a group, the surveyed supervisors indicated that their two primary objectives for Balint groups were (1) to provide support for the residents and (2) to help residents to resolve professional role conflicts.

It is interesting that professionals in different domains may engage in very similar work, yet have no substantial commerce with one another. This is the case with respect to Balint groups, for many mental health professionals are unfamiliar with them. It is possible, though, that there may be aspects of this supervision tradition from which we in mental health might draw.

Peer Group Supervision

In Chapter 1 we differentiated supervision from consultation, noting that the former included evaluation and was an ongoing, hierarchical relationship. The practice of peer supervision, though, is not hierarchical and does not include formal evaluation. In this sense, it is more like consultation than supervision. But, at the same time, it is ongoing, and group members feel more accountable to each other than they might in a consulting relationship. It is difficult, therefore, to properly categorize it as being either supervision or consultation. But, however categorized, peer supervision seems to be a growing phenomenon and an important ingredient to the vitality of the mental health professions. Therefore, it is an important topic to address.

Anyone who has been in the helping professions for a while has heard colleagues talk about the problem of isolation and the fear of practitioner burnout, along with the fear of becoming stale. Also, professional organizations have begun highlighting the need for continuing supervision, often incorporating the expectation for posttraining supervision into certification requirements. An increasing number of post licensure professionals, therefore, are turning to peer group supervision to meet these needs.

Although peer supervision has received only modest coverage in the professional literature, Lewis, Greenburg, & Hatch (1988) found, at least among psychologists in private practice, that 23% of a national sample were currently members of peer supervision groups, 24% had belonged to such a group in the past, and 61% expressed a desire to belong to a group if one were available. Among the reasons for joining peer groups (in rank order by importance) were (1) suggestions for problem cases, (2) discussing ethical professional issues, (3) countering isolation, (4) sharing information, (5) exploring problematic feelings and attitudes toward clients, (6) learning and mastering therapeutic techniques, (7) support for stress in private practice, (8) countering burnout, and (9) exposure to other theoretical approaches.

Wiley (1994) reported a survey of members of the American Psychological Association's Division of Counseling Psychology who were in private practice. She found that the proportion of those who reported participating either weekly or biweekly in peer supervision groups were as follows:

- Those who were 3 to 7 years postdoctorate, 25%
- Those who were 8 to 15 years postdoctorate, 38%
- Those 16 or more years postdoctorate, 32%

The sizes of her samples were small, but the findings were generally consistent with the Lewis et al. (1988) findings. Moreover, they were relatively consistent over time, even for very experienced practitioners.

Peer supervision groups can either develop from supervisor-led groups to peer groups or can be conceived as peer supervision groups from the outset. In either case, at the point that peers attempt to offer each other supervision (or consultation, as some authors prefer to designate it), certain conditions must exist if the process is to be successful. Chaiklin and Munson (1983) noted that a sincere desire to improve one's clinical skills is, of course, the primary condition for peer supervision. They also favored the model of a peer group beginning with a supervisor whose role is to work him or her out of a job. For practitioners working in mental health settings, the second major condition is administrative backing (Chaiklin & Munson, 1983; Marks & Hixon, 1986). If administrators do not view peer supervision as valuable and cost effective and if this is not communicated by the provision of space and time to conduct supervision meetings, the within-agency peer group will certainly falter.

The independent peer group (i.e., outside any employment setting) has probably the greatest potential for compatibility among its members because such a group tends to be formed by professionals who already know and respect each other. For the peer group formed within an institution, there may be some history to overcome among some of the members, such as political entanglements, competitiveness, or personality issues (Hamlin & Timberlake, 1982). In addition, lack of homogeneity of experience is far more likely for the within-agency group, which means that the group will most likely veer toward either the more experienced or least experienced members, to the potential frustration of the other members of the group. Regardless of the initial compatibility of the peer group, however, the group stages outlined by Tuckman and Jensen (1977) will still occur and need attention. It is a common error of professionals who are already comfortable with one another to forego the planning stage for the group until issues begin to arise. Another potential for all supervision groups, but more so with peer groups, is differential contact among its members outside supervision. Ground rules may need to be outlined regarding any processing of supervision outside the group so as not to drain off energy that legitimately belongs within the group.

The Process of Peer Supervision Groups.

Peer supervision groups tend to be more informal than other types of supervision groups (Lewis et al., 1988). This might be considered an error, at least in the beginning. Without the direction of a designated leader, structure can give the group some measure of stability while it is finding its particular rhythm.

Part of the structure must be, in fact, a plan for handling the leadership of the group. Although leaderless by definition, peer groups have realized that ignoring the issue of leadership gives rise to competitiveness (Schreiber & Frank, 1983). Therefore, many groups rotate the leadership role, with one person directing each meeting. The leader may concern himself or herself with group leadership issues only or may also be asked to take responsibility for secretarial issues arising as a result of the meeting, including communicating with absent members about the next meeting, keeping records of supervision meetings and actions taken, and the like.

The process also includes a plan for case presentation. Typically, one or two cases are the maximum that can be reasonably discussed at one meeting. Marks and Hixon (1986) suggested that the presenter come prepared with two or three questions about the case to direct the group's discussion. They also suggested that a process observer be appointed (different from either the presenter or the designated leader). This person would give feedback at the end of the supervision meeting about the group process that he or she observed, including "a statement regarding the group's ability to stay task-oriented, its adherence to ground rules, what group building may have occurred and the participation level of the group members" (p. 421).

Advantages and Disadvantages of Peer Supervision Groups.

Those practitioners who participate in peer supervision groups tend to be very favorable about them. There is every reason to assume, therefore, that the numbers of peer supervision groups will grow. Among the advantages ascribed to peer supervision groups are the following (Hamlin & Timberlake, 1982; Lewis et al., 1988; Marks & Hixon, 1986; Schreiber & Frank, 1983; Wendorf et al., 1985):

1. They help clinicians to remain reflective about their work and offer clinicians options beyond their individual frameworks. Skovholt and Rønnestad (1992b) found in their qualitative study of therapists across the life span that one theme that predicted therapists' ongoing professional development was their willingness to engage in reflective activity. Peer supervision groups serve this purpose.
2. They offer the type of environment that is especially attractive to adult learners.
3. They provide a forum for the reexamination of familiar experiences (e.g., early terminations or working with one particular ethnic group).
4. They provide a peer review process that maintains high standards for practice, thus reducing the risk of ethical violations.
5. They provide a forum for transmitting new information, thus providing continuing education for members.
6. They provide the continuity necessary for serious consultation.
7. They can provide some of the therapeutic factors often attributed to group process, including reassurance, validation, and a sense of belonging. As a result, they can reduce the potential for burnout.
8. They enable clinicians to become more aware of countertransference issues and parallel process.
9. Because peers, rather than experts, offer feedback, supervision is less likely to be compromised by conflicts with authority figures.

The major limitation reported by members of peer supervision groups came from within-agency groups (Marks & Hixon, 1986). Because group members might form their own coalitions, interagency communication might not be facilitated. Also, when group members must work with each other outside the group, they may be reticent to self-disclose and are less trustful in the group. Finally, the structure of the group may be inflexible in dealing with crisis situations that are bound occasionally to occur in agencies. Allen (1976) mentioned one additional disadvantage of peer groups: they may limit the amount of individual supervision sought by the group members. However, Marks and Hixon (1986) found that peer group supervision strengthened individual supervision by "pointing out its gaps" (p. 423).

CONCLUSION

Group supervision is a cost-effective form of supervision that offers the supervisee the benefits of peer relationships, exposure to a greater number of cases, and vicarious as well as direct learning. There is little doubt that group supervision will continue to be an important supplement to individual supervision. Therefore, supervision practitioners would be well advised to give this vital form of supervision more empirical attention as practitioners develop and test group supervision models. Fall and Sutton (2004) include exercises relevant to group supervision in their handbook.

CHAPTER 11

SUPERVISION INTERVENTIONS
LIVE SUPERVISION

In Chapters 9 and 10 we reviewed the supervision interventions that typically transpire in individual case conferences and in the context of group supervision. That material addressed supervision as it is practiced by the majority of mental health professionals. A significant number of supervisors, however, rely on and often prefer the use of live supervision interventions. For obvious reasons, live supervision is especially popular in training programs where facilities are more conducive to its application (Carlozzi, Romans, Boswell, Ferguson, & Whisenhunt, 1997).

Live supervision represents a paradigmatic shift from either individual supervision or group supervision; therefore, it cannot be considered a subgroup of either. This shift essentially consists of two components: (1) The distinction between counseling or therapy and supervision is less pronounced than in traditional supervision, and (2) the role of the supervisor is significantly changed to include both coaching and cotherapist dimensions. As a result of these essential differences, the process of live supervision and its advantages and drawbacks are different from other forms of supervision. This chapter will address the evolution of live supervision, describe its process both with and without a supervision team, note the advantages and disadvantages for both forms of live supervision, and address the available empirical findings about its effectiveness.

Until recently, live supervision was considered the "hallmark of family therapy" (Nichols, 1984, p. 89). Marriage and family therapy training programs still rely heavily on live supervision (Nichols et al., 1990), but its popularity has grown among the other mental health professions

(Bubenzer, West, & Gold, 1991; Carlozzi et al., 1997; Kivlighan, Angelone, & Swafford, 1991), and Saba (1999) reported the use of live supervision in medical training. Live supervision began as an intensive method for working with an individual trainee (or perhaps two trainees working as cotherapists). In more recent years, the team form of live supervision has gained in momentum. The team is a group of therapists or trainees, with or without a supervisor, who work together on their cases. Because of the significantly different dynamics between live supervision without a team and team supervision, we will begin with the former and address team supervision later in the chapter. Furthermore, because "the literature suggests that the one-way mirror may be as basic to family therapy as the couch was to psychoanalysis" (Lewis & Rohrbaugh, 1989, p. 323), our discussion will follow suit and assume, in most cases, that the client is a family. Finally, we will not attempt to make clear distinctions between training or supervision (with the supervisee as the focus) and intervention (with the family system as the focus), even though we are aware that such distinctions sometimes are made in the literature on live supervision.

Live supervision was initiated by Jay Haley and Salvadore Minuchin (Simon, 1982) in the late 1960s as a result of a rather singular project. At the time, both were invested in treating poor families, but were not enamored with the idea of trying to teach middle-class therapists what it was like to be poor. Therefore, they decided to recruit people from poor communities with no more than a high school education and train them to work with other poor families. Because of the real need to protect the families being treated, Haley and Minuchin devised a live supervision model in which they could guide these inexperienced and untrained therapists as they worked. The result? In Haley's words: "Actually they did very well. We worked with them in live supervision, 40 hours a week for two years. Nobody has ever been trained that intensely" (Simon, 1982, p. 29).

Live supervision combines direct observation of the therapy session with some method that enables the supervisor to communicate with and thereby influence the work of the supervisee during the session. Therefore, the supervisor is simultaneously in charge of both training the therapist and controlling the course and ultimately the outcome of therapy (Lewis, 1988). Because of the dual agenda of both observing and interacting with the supervisee, much has been written about the technology of live supervision, especially about different methods for communicating with the supervisee. We begin, therefore, by reviewing the different technologies used to communicate with the supervisee(s); we also consider the messages that are given by the supervisor during live supervision, as well as the function of presession and postsession deliberations. Once we have explored how live supervision is conducted, we will back up to consider some of the guidelines for the use of live supervision.

METHODS OF LIVE SUPERVISION

Bubenzer, Mahrle, and West (1987) listed six methods used to conduct live supervision: *bug-in-the-ear, monitoring, in vivo, walk-in, phone-in,* and *consultation.* We will explain each of these briefly, as well as *using computer and interactive television technology* to communicate with the therapist (Johnson & Combs, 1997; Kinsella, 2000; Klitzke & Lombardo, 1991; Neukrug, 1991; Smith, Mead, & Kinsella, 1998).

Bug-in-the-Ear

The bug-in-the-ear (BITE) consists of a wireless earphone that is worn by the supervisee through

which the supervisor can coach the supervisee during the therapy session. It has three major advantages: First, it allows the supervisor to make minor adjustments (e.g., "Get them to talk to each other") or to briefly reinforce the therapist (e.g., "Excellent") without interrupting the flow of the therapy session. In fact, much of what can be communicated through BITE might not warrant a more formal interruption of the session. Second, it has been established that BITE works as a behavioral strategy on the part of the supervisor to increase trainee behaviors through such reinforcement (Gallant, Thyer, & Bailey, 1991). Third, BITE protects the therapy relationship more fully than other live supervision technologies because clients are unaware which comments are the direct suggestions of the supervisor (Alderfer, 1983, as cited in Gallant & Thyer, 1989).

The disadvantages of BITE emerge from its advantages: Because BITE is seemingly so nonintrusive, it can be overused by the supervisor and can be a distraction to the supervisee who is trying to track the family, as well as take in advice from the supervisor (Smith et al., 1998). Similarly, there is a danger of "echo therapy" (Byng-Hall, 1982, as cited in Adamek, 1994): the trainee simply parrots the words of the supervisor with little or no assimilation of the therapeutic implications of what is being said, thus encouraging trainee dependence. Finally, because it is a less visible form of live supervision, it can produce awkward moments. For example, the trainee who is attempting to listen to a supervisor comment might need to interrupt the family in order to focus on the supervisory input. Furthermore, because family members do not know when the supervisee is receiving input, the device itself can produce ambivalent feelings because of the secrecy it symbolizes.

Monitoring

The second form of live supervision, monitoring, is used minimally. Monitoring is the process whereby the supervisor observes the session and intervenes directly into the session if the therapist is in difficulty (Minuchin & Fishman, 1981). By implication, therefore, monitoring can be either a way to safeguard client welfare (in which case it is really not live supervision per se, but something that many supervisors might do if they felt a sense of urgency) or a form of live supervision that is less sensitive to the dynamics between therapist and clients. Conversely, an advantage of monitoring, assuming that the supervisor takes over when entering the room, is that it allows the supervisor to directly experience the family dynamics. A final advantage of monitoring is that it allows the trainee to benefit from the modeling provided by the supervisor working with the family.

For more experienced therapists, supervisors can be called into an ongoing case as a consultant–supervisor (Richman, Aitken, & Prather, 1990). The supervisor is briefed ahead of time about the case and the difficulties that the therapist is having. The supervisor then conducts a session with the therapist present, typically referring particularly to the impasse that is being faced in therapy. Richman et al. remarked that using supervision in this way models and normalizes appropriate help-seeking behavior for the clients, as well as providing a helpful alteration to the therapy system that has been established.

In Vivo

In vivo has some similarity to monitoring in that it allows clients to see the supervisor in operation. Rather than taking over for the therapist, however, the supervisor consults with the therapist in view of the clients. With in vivo supervision, there is an assumption that the family deserves to have access to all information, including a discussion of interventions. Seen from a different angle, the conversation between supervisor and therapist can itself constitute an intervention by heightening the family's awareness of particular dynamics, especially when dynamics are therapeutically reframed for the benefit of the family. In vivo supervision has some similarity to some forms of team supervision that will be discussed later in the chapter.

The Walk-in

A final intervention that has similar characteristics to the two previous ones is the walk-in. The supervisor enters the room at some deliberate moment, interacts with both the therapist and the clients, and then leaves. The walk-in does not imply an emergency, nor does it imply the kind of collegiality that is evident with in vivo supervision. A walk-in, therefore, can be used to redirect therapy and to establish certain dynamics between the supervisor and the family or the therapist and the family. As a result, it can be viewed as more of a therapy intervention than either monitoring or in-vivo supervision. All three methods of supervision that involve having the supervisor enter the therapy room are more intrusive in the therapy relationship than the methods that follow.

Phone-ins and Consultation Breaks

The most common forms of live supervision are phone-ins or consultation breaks. These methods are similar in that both interrupt therapy for the therapist to receive input from the supervisor. There is little opportunity for the therapist to react to the intervention, however, when it is phoned in using an intercom system. In the consultation break, the therapist leaves the therapy room to consult with the supervisor (when the supervisor alerts the therapist by, for example, knocking on the door, when the therapist feels the need to consult, or at a predetermined point in the therapy hour). The therapist then has an opportunity to clarify what the supervisor is suggesting prior to returning to the therapy room. While both of these methods have documented training and supervision advantages, they have the disadvantage of intruding into the therapy system by virtue of the interruption.

Using Computers and Interactive Television for Live Supervision

Referred to as "a bug-in-the-eye" by Klitzke and Lombardo (1991), this alternative to BITE uses a monitor in the therapy room in a fashion similar to how teleprompters are used in broadcast journalism. Rather than speaking into the ear of the supervisee, supervisors can unobtrusively make suggestions by typing them from a keyboard in the observation room to be read on the monitor placed behind the client.

Proponents of this method argue that it retains all the advantages while eliminating the disadvantages of BITE. Because the supervisee controls when it is an opportune time to read the supervisor's message, the supervisee feels less distracted by the method. Supposedly, this translates to a smooth session from the client's perspective. Neukrug (1991) added that the ability to save supervisor feedback on a disk in order to print it out for the supervisee is an additional advantage that allows the supervisee to review the feedback (along with an audiotape or videotape of the session) or the supervisor and supervisee to discuss the feedback at length in supervision.

Despite the arguments for using a monitor for supervision comments, this method also has been criticized for potentially overwhelming the supervisee with input. Follette and Callaghan (1995) proposed a significantly simpler cue of a graph line, heading up or down, to alert the therapist about his or her progress in the session. Tracy et al. (1995, as cited in Smith, Mead, & Kinsella, 1998) used a monitor and a 14-icon system to offer the supervisee live feedback. In an attempt to find a "happy medium" between the minimal feedback offered by a graph line and the monitor methods that potentially deliver more information than the therapist can use during a session, Smith et al. (1998) developed a method that they have labeled Direct Supervision. Direct Supervision uses software developed by Smith and Mead (1996) to give supervisees feedback about the supervisor's perceptions about the clients' and therapist's behavior, the expected therapeutic behaviors, and the therapist's "on target" behaviors. Direct Supervision uses a numbering system (1 to 4) in each of four quadrants on the monitor to alert the therapist during the session. Like the system proposed by Neukrug (1991), a permanent record of super-

vision input is kept and can be used to enhance postsession supervision. Smith et al. claimed that trainees find the method to be nonintrusive and helpful.

Finally, Johnson and Combs (1997) advocated for two-way video transmission in order to conduct live supervision from campus to off-campus sites. Because live supervision tends to be more popular in training settings than clinical settings, the authors argued that this would allow trainees to benefit from live supervision while also benefiting from "real life" clinical settings. The disadvantages of the model delineated by Johnson and Combs include its cost, the time and training required to use the model, and potential trust, safety, and ethical issues. Because these disadvantages will be viewed as daunting by most clinical settings, it is unlikely that this model will be widely used in the field.

Some supervisors are firmly committed to one method of live supervision. For example, Todtman, Bobele, and Strano (1988) suggested that the phone is the most desirable method because it is culturally familiar to the client system. They also commented that it is less intrusive than a supervisor walking into the therapy room, but stops therapy nonetheless, avoiding the confusion that can occur when using the bug-in-the-ear or other more subtle forms of live supervision. Others feel equally strongly about the advantages of consultation breaks during the session. Most of the literature on live supervision, however, underplays the method used for live supervision, focusing instead on guidelines for the intervention or directive, parameters that must be respected when using live supervision, the acculturation of supervisees and clients to live supervision, and supervisee issues while working within the live supervision framework.

THE LIVE SUPERVISION INTERVENTION

Supervisor to supervisee communications during live supervision are typically referred to as the *supervisory intervention* or *supervisor directives*. For our purposes here, the terms are interchangeable. We will discuss interventions delivered by means of the bug-in-the-ear, phone-ins, and consultation breaks, as these are the most commonly used methods of live supervision. Consultation breaks also are a commonly used intervention when a team is involved in live supervision. Consultation within the context of team supervision will be discussed later in the chapter.

Prior to implementing a live supervision intervention, the supervisor should ask (1) Is redirection necessarily called for in the session? (2) Might the therapist redirect the session without an intervention? (3) Will the therapist be able to carry out the intervention successfully? (4) Is the driving force of the intervention to attend to the needs of the therapist and the client or on the supervisor's desire to do cotherapy? (Frankel & Piercy, 1990; Heath, 1982; Liddle & Schwartz, 1983). Additionally, the supervisor must consider the strengths and limitations of the intervention modality to be used.

Bug-in-the-Ear Interventions

There is no question that this form of sending a supervision directive is the most limited for the reasons already discussed. In particular situations and for specific reasons, however, BITE may still be the intervention method of choice. BITE is especially recommended for novice supervisees (Adamek, 1994) when relatively frequent, yet brief, suggestions are warranted. The new supervisee would also benefit from the reinforcing potential of BITE (e.g., "Nice question") that might be lost using other methods of supervision. It stands to reason that the use of BITE implies that the supervisor will not be attempting to focus on other than the most basic executive skills during the therapy session. Additionally, it follows that if BITE is the method of delivering interventions the major part of supervision must occur either before or after the session. Finally, because BITE is inherently distracting, the supervisor must be sensitive to its effect for each supervisee. There may be instances, for example, when the use of BITE has no benefits at all because of the reactivity of

the supervisor and the supervisee's inability to conduct a coherent session while receiving information through BITE.

It might be appropriate to use BITE for a more advanced supervisee if the supervisee has a specific goal for a particular session. For example, if a supervisee has been consistently sidetracked by a particular client, the supervisor could alert the supervisee when this was occurring in the session using BITE. As this example demonstrates, BITE interventions take the form of *coaching,* whether they are delivered to novice supervisees or more experienced therapists.

Telephone Interventions

Unlike BITE, telephone interventions have the advantage of stopping the therapy session. This allows the supervisee to listen to the directive without having to attempt to pay attention to the client at the same time. The phone-in has another advantage in that the client is alerted simultaneously that the therapist is being advised and will be prepared for a change in direction in the session. Furthermore, because the client knows that the therapist is receiving feedback, the directive can be the intervention itself. For example, if the supervisor believes that a member of the family is getting lost, the therapist might be advised to continue the session with "My supervisor thinks that we women (referring to herself and the mother) have been doing all the talking and we're not letting John (the father) have a say. My supervisor would like to hear what you think is going on between your wife and your son."

As is the case for all live supervision interventions, telephone directives should be used conservatively; furthermore, they should be brief, concise, and generally action oriented (Haley, 1987; Lewis & Rohrbaugh, 1989; Mauzey & Erdman, 1997; Rickert & Turner, 1978; Wright, 1986). Depending on the developmental level of the supervisee, a verbatim directive might be given (e.g., "Ask the mother 'What is your worst fear about Thomas if he continues with his present crowd?' "), or, for the more advanced trainee, a more flexible directive might be given (e.g., "Reframe Mom's behavior as concern") (Rickert & Turner, 1978; Wright, 1986). Other generally accepted guidelines when phoning in interventions include avoiding process statements (or keeping them very brief) and refraining from complex directives, not exceeding two instructions per phone-in, being sensitive to the timing of the intervention and avoiding interventions during the first 10 minutes of the therapy session, limiting phone-ins to a maximum of five per therapy session, and communicating that it is the supervisee's decision when a suggestion can be worked into the session (unless the supervisor has clearly stipulated a time for the intervention) (Frankel & Piercy, 1990; Lewis & Rohrbaugh, 1989; Wright, 1986).

Wright asserted additionally that it is sometimes strategically wise to begin an intervention with positive reinforcement of what has transpired in the session up to the present. In other words, taking the time to say "You're really doing a terrific job keeping Dad from taking over" might be worth the time and increase the supervisee's investment in carrying out future interventions. This advice was supported by research that found that supervisees experienced phone-ins that included support components as "most effective"; conversely, supervisees were twice as likely as their supervisors to judge phone-in interventions without support as "least effective" (Frankel, 1990). Unfortunately, Frankel found that supervisors using phone-ins employed supportive interventions only about one-third as often as they used directive behaviors.

Mauzey and Erdman (1997) conducted a phenomenological study of the effect of phone-in interventions on trainees that confirmed these earlier suggestions as valid. In addition, they found that well-received phone-ins focused on the welfare of the client more than on training, were "on track" rather than suggesting that therapy go in a new direction, flowed from a trusting relationship with the supervisor, and considered both the anxiety level and developmental level of the trainee.

In summary, the phone-in is the optimal live supervision method when the message is relatively brief, uncomplicated, and action oriented. It is less effective for more complicated process issues. When the supervisee needs more clarification than can be provided with a phone directive, the supervisee should leave the room for a consultation break (Haley, 1987).

Consultation Break Interventions

Even if a phone system is available to the supervisor, a consultation break may be the method of choice. In addition to the supervisee's need for clarification, consultation will be preferred if it is the opinion of the supervisor that

1. the intervention will be lengthy and the supervisee will need some extra time to absorb it (Rickert & Turner, 1978);
2. the supervisee will need a rationale for the intervention, which is not accomplished well using the phone-in (Rickert & Turner, 1978);
3. the supervisee will profit from the opportunity to react to the intervention, perhaps to be sure that it is understood or compatible with how the supervisee is experiencing the family; and
4. it will be important to check out some impressions with the supervisee as part of forming the intervention.

When consultation is used, it is essential that the supervisor be attentive to the amount of time that the conference takes away from therapy. There is a momentum to the therapy session that is diluted by a live supervision conference. This momentum must be considered as part of the formula for successful live supervision. If the therapist remains out of the therapy room too long, the intervention that is carried back to the client might be moot. A partial exception to this admonition is if the client system has been forewarned that a lengthy consultation is part of the therapy hour. In fact, when strategic family therapy is being implemented, the consultation may take place somewhere near the halfway mark of the therapy hour and the supervisee might return to the session only to deliver the final directive, usually in the form of a homework assignment. That being said, Locke and McCollum's (2001) findings that clients were satisfied with live supervision as long as its perceived helpfulness outweighed its perceived intrusiveness remains important guidance.

We end with a study that provided some insight into the breadth of interventions delivered during individual therapy sessions (Heppner et al., 1994). Using a walk-in mode, supervisors were instructed to intervene when the therapy session seemed to lack direction, when the therapist seemed stuck, or when the supervisors were concerned for the client's welfare. Supervisors intervened between one and three times a session. An analysis of the interventions found that six dimensions were identifiable, each being bidirectional (pp. 230–232):

1. *Directing–instructing versus deepening.* At one end of this dimension, the supervisor offered the supervisee explicit suggestions or direction. The opposite pole of this dimension found the supervisor offering minor adjustment to deepen an already well moving emotional process occurring in the session.

2. *Cognitive clarification versus emotional encouragement.* On one side, the supervisor focused on the content of the session or a task and attempted to help the therapist come to a better understanding of what was transpiring. The opposite side for this dimension was described as supervisors attempting to get supervisees to express the feelings that they were having in the session, especially as they related to the client.

3. *Confronting versus encouraging the client.* At one end, the supervisor was identifying how the client was impeding the supervisee and how this could be altered; on the opposite end of this dimension, the supervisor engaged in attempting to make the client more comfortable and willing to take risks.

4. *Didactic–distant versus emotionally involved.* At one end of this dimension, the supervisor seemed to be taking a detached, expert stance, while at the other end the supervisor seemed emotionally involved with both supervisee and client and appeared highly invested in the outcome of therapy.

5. *Joining versus challenging the trainee.* For this dimension, it was the relationship between supervisor and trainee that seemed to vary from reinforcing the trainee and attempting to help the client understand what the trainee was trying to accomplish to the supervisor challenging the trainee to examine his or her approach and perhaps consider a different approach.

6. *Providing direction versus resignation.* On one end of the continuum, the supervisor was highly invested in the session and worked hard to get the process to move forward, while on the other end the supervisor communicated that there was little that could be done from the supervisor's standpoint to move the session forward.

The Heppner et al. (1994) study can be used to evaluate live supervision after the fact, especially if the supervisor is dissatisfied with the outcome of a live supervision session. If, for example, most interventions challenged the supervisee (dimension 5), admonitions from other authors would suggest that leaning toward challenge rather than support may indeed be the problem (Frankel 1990; Mauzey & Erdman, 1997).

In summary, during-session interventions are far more complex than they may appear. A good directive must be succinct and add clarity, not confusion, to the supervisee's deliberations. Even consultation breaks must be efficient in their use of therapy time and should focus primarily on the supervisee's executive skills (West et al., 1993). For the supervisee to have an opportunity to develop perceptual and cognitive skills, presession and postsession conferences are requisite.

PRESESSION PLANNING AND POSTSESSION DEBRIEFING

Although the interaction between the supervisor and the therapy system is the crux of live supervision, what comes before and after are the foundation for the successful implementation of the model. Especially because of the level of activity involved in live supervision, there is a necessity for groundwork to be done in order for the activity during the session to remain meaningful.

As one might suppose, the goal of the presession is to prepare the trainee for the upcoming therapy session. There will be some speculation about what the family might bring to this session. The supervisor will have two goals in the presession: to prepare the trainee for the upcoming session and to focus on the trainee's own learning goals as they pertain to the upcoming session. Piercy stated that he wants his trainees to show evidence of having a "theoretical map" and then to be able to "tie it to a practical understanding of how to bring about change" (West, Bubenzer, & Zarski, 1989, p. 27). Additionally, trainees are often asked to attempt a particular technique (e.g., to raise the intensity of the interactions between family members), or they may be asked if they have something particular that they would like the supervisor to observe. In other words, it is important that both the supervisee and supervisor complete the presession with some clarity about their roles for the therapy session.

On the other hand, Okun argued that family therapy "cannot be organized like a lesson plan" (West et al., 1989, p. 27). Families will force both trainees and supervisors to be spontaneous even if they are adequately prepared for the session. The developmental level of the trainee must be reflected in presession planning just as it is in the therapy session. The supervisor will be more active with the novice trainee in terms of both helping to provide a conceptual overview and planning for immediate interventions. Once the trainee has gained in experience, it is expected that the supervisor will take a more consultative position (West et al., 1989; West et al., 1993).

The postsession debriefing allows the trainee and the supervisor to discuss what transpired in the session. Because they were both involved in the therapy but held different vantage points, this is an important time to share perceptions, review the effectiveness of interventions, offer feedback, and address any unfinished business from the session as a precursor to planning the next session.

If homework has been assigned to the family, this is also a time to consider ways in which the family might respond to the assignment and to begin to consider future interventions based on the family's response. In other words, the successful postsession will leave the trainee with some food for thought to consider prior to the next presession (West et al., 1989).

Although the presession conference is an important coaching session, the postsession debriefing is the optimal time for the conceptual growth of the supervisee. This conference, therefore, should not be rushed. If there is no opportunity to meet immediately after the therapy session, it should be scheduled at another time, but far enough prior to the next therapy session so it does not feel like another presession conference. Couchon and Bernard (1984) found that supervisor behaviors are significantly influenced by the timing of a supervision session in relation to the next counseling session for the supervisee. Specifically, when a supervisee is facing an upcoming session, the supervisor will become far more directive in order to help the supervisee to prepare, even if the last session has not been previously critiqued with the supervisee. Therefore, the postsession must occur at a time when the next session with the same client is not imminent and when there is ample time to move beyond intervention issues to larger conceptual and relationship issues.

Now that the overall process of live supervision has been described, we turn our attention to conditions for the effective use of live supervision.

IMPLEMENTING LIVE SUPERVISION

In his seminal article, Montalvo (1973) listed six guidelines for live supervision that continue to be relevant today.

1. *Supervisor and supervisee agree that a supervisor can either call the supervisee out, or that the latter can come out for feedback when he* [sic] *wishes.*
2. *Supervisor and supervisee, before settling down to work, agree on defined limits within which both will operate.* [For example, the supervisor outlines under what condition, if any, the supervisee can reject the supervisor's intervention.]

3. *The supervisor endeavors not to inhibit the supervisee's freedom of exploration and operation too much, but, if he does so, the supervisee is expected to tell him.*
4. *The mechanism for establishing direction is routine talks before and after the session.* [Montalvo felt strongly that the family should not be privy to these discussions and that efforts to "democratize" the therapy process have not proved useful. To date, there is no uniform opinion among family therapy theorists about this issue.]
5. *The supervisor tries to find procedures that best fit the supervisee's style and preferred way of working.*
6. *The beginner should understand that at the start he may feel as if he is under remote control.* (pp. 343–345)

These guidelines reflect Montalvo's structural family therapy bias. The wisdom of the guidelines, however, lies in both their clarity regarding the supervision hierarchy and their respect for the integrity, if not the ego, of the supervisee. Insufficient attention to one of these issues can result in an unsatisfactory experience with live supervision.

Elizur (1990) later revisited baseline conditions for live supervision. Because Elizur perceived live supervision to be an inherently anxiety provoking model, his first admonition was that the use of live supervision should be agreed to by each supervisee within an explicit supervision contract. Elizur also emphasized that the supervisee must trust that the supervisor has the welfare of the clients at heart and will not let harm come to the clients. Additionally, supervisors must be supportive of trainees as they struggle to enlarge their intervention repertoire by gauging their level of expertise and allowing them to attempt new interventions, while appreciating the stress inherent in such a process. McCollum (1995) addressed the supervisor's own stress in these moments by posing a question: "How do I keep my own anxiety under control and curb my own oldest-brother wish to take over and make things 'right' versus letting the [supervisee] and clients stew with their troubles?" (p. 4).

Bubenzer et al. (1987) made four suggestions to help desensitize supervisees to live supervision.

Using phone-ins as their method, they suggested that supervisors first show new supervisees videotapes of family sessions during which the phone rings and the session is interrupted. By doing this, trainees are able to observe how clients react when the phone rings and how things proceed afterward. This is often one of the first concerns for new trainees. Second, new supervisees are allowed to be observers while live supervision is being conducted with other counselors. They are encouraged to ask the supervisor any questions as things proceed. Third, hypothetical cases are presented to the trainees for them to practice the consecutive stages of pretreatment (or presession planning), counseling during session, and posttreatment (or postsession debriefing). At this time the possible use of phone-ins is discussed. Finally, again through role play of hypothetical cases, the supervisees conduct sessions, following through on their plans and experiencing phone-ins during the session as previously discussed. With the amount of anxiety that can surround supervision of any type, the idea of allowing a trial run as described by Bubenzer et al. makes intuitive sense and has been implemented elsewhere (e.g., Neukrug, 1991). It should also be noted that this type of careful and caring orientation to the use of live supervision is consistent with the comments made by trainees in the Mauzey and Erdman (1997) study when describing positive experiences with live supervision.

Once the therapist becomes used to the idea of the inevitability of being interrupted during therapy and knows what form this will take, the pressure is on the supervisor to be concise and helpful. Berger and Dammann (1982) offered two astute observations about the supervisor's reality versus the supervisee's reality during live supervision. Because of the one-way mirror separating them, the supervisor "will see patterns more quickly and will be better able to think about them—to think meta to them—than the therapist will" (p. 338). Second, "the supervisor will lack accurate information as to the intensity of the family affect. This becomes readily apparent if the supervisor enters the room to talk with the family" (pp. 338–339).

There are outgrowths to each of these perceptual differences. Because of the advantage that the supervisor enjoys by being behind the one-way mirror, a common reaction for the therapist, according to Berger and Dammann (1982), is to "feel stupid" (p. 338) once something is called to the therapist's attention. The reason, of course, that the trainee feels stupid is because what is pointed out seems painfully obvious, but is something that eluded the trainee during the therapy session. The wise supervisor will prepare supervisees for this reaction and allow them opportunities to experience firsthand the cleverness that comes from being at a safe distance from the therapy interaction.

Regarding the intensity issue, the supervisee might rightfully feel that the supervisor does not understand the family if the supervisor is underestimating the intensity of family affect. It is for this reason, that is, the direct contact with the family experienced primarily by the supervisee, that Berger and Dammann (1982) supported others who believed that, except for an emergency, "the supervisor proposes and the therapist disposes" (p. 339).

Gershenson and Cohen (1978) also noted that the relationship between trainee and supervisor can begin on rocky ground because of the vulnerability felt by the trainee. This vulnerability can be experienced as anxiety and resistance, persecutory fantasies, and anger. It could be conjectured that at this stage the trainee is reacting to the unfair advantage of the supervisor (behind the one-way mirror), along with extreme embarrassment at the mediocrity of his or her own performance. Fortunately, this initial stage seems to be short-lived for most trainees and, indeed, Mauzey, Harris, and Trusty (2000) found that both anger and anxiety diminished with more exposure to live supervision. According to Gershenson and Cohen, a second stage follows characterized by having high emotional investment in the process and perceiving the supervisor as a supporter rather than as critic. We can assume that this stage also represents a heightened dependence on the supervisor. Finally, a third stage emerges in which "the directions of our supervisor became less important as techniques to be implemented and instead served as a stimulus to our own thinking . . . [we] reached a point at which we were able to initiate our own therapeutic strategies" (p. 229).

ADVANTAGES AND DISADVANTAGES

Advantages

The advocates of live supervision have been ardent (Bubenzer et al., 1991). The well-documented advantage of live supervision is that through this form of coaching by a more experienced clinician there is a much greater likelihood that counseling and therapy will go well. There is also an assumption and some empirical evidence (Kivlighan, Angelone, & Swafford, 1991; Landis & Young, 1994; Storm, 1994) that the supervisee will learn more efficiently and, perhaps, more profoundly as a result of these successful therapy sessions. To return to our coaching metaphor, it is better to be coached and to win the game than to be playing independently and suffer defeat.

In addition to the training function of live supervision, there is a built-in safeguard for client welfare. Because the supervisor is immediately accessible, clients are protected more directly. This also allows trainees to work with more challenging cases, which might be too difficult for them if another form of supervision were being used (Cormier & Bernard, 1982; Jordan, 1999). Of course, the difficulty of the case must be considered carefully. Too difficult a therapy case will mean that the trainee is simply the voice of the supervisor and little more. The supervisor must be astute regarding the developmental level of the trainee and determine which cases are within the trainee's grasp. A similar advantage to live supervision is that the trainee is more likely to risk more in conducting therapy because of the knowledge that the supervisor is there to help with interventions (Berger & Dammann, 1982). Furthermore, because of the direct involvement of the highly skilled supervisor, clients assigned to trainees will receive better treatment (Rickert & Turner, 1978).

Another set of advantages related to live supervision has to do with the trainee's relationship with the supervisor. Because the supervisor often will share responsibility for interventions, the supervisor is far more vulnerable than in other forms of supervision. Especially if a verbatim directive is given, the supervisor cannot come back later and say, "You misunderstood the intent of my comment." This kind of sharing of responsibility, when it occurs, will reduce the distance between supervisor and trainee. Not all supervisors, however, value an egalitarian relationship with their supervisees (e.g., Montalvo, 1973); this is a topic that has particular relevance for team supervision and will be considered later in the chapter.

The use of live supervision also affords supervisees the opportunity to appreciate the extent to which therapists become entrenched in the family system, because they experience a jarring removal from the family system when called for a consultation break. Proponents of live supervision believe that such entrenchment is inevitable (if not desirable if therapists are to understand the parameters of the family), but only live supervision offers an opportunity for the trainee to understand the power of this dynamic by moving in and out of the family system.

Finally, the trainee's view of the process of therapy will also be affected by live supervision, because it should unfold more systematically due to the input from the supervisor. When the supervisor gives a rationale for an intervention, predicts reactions, and proves to be right, the therapist experiences firsthand the predictability of some client patterns. This is an exciting moment for the therapist; fortunately, it is balanced by those moments when clients react unpredictably, thus ensuring a sense of our fallibility as helpers.

Disadvantages

The most noted disadvantages of live supervision are the time it demands of supervisors (Bubenzer et al., 1991) (although the efficiency with which supervisees are trained has been reported to offset this initial time commitment), the cost of facilities, the problem of scheduling cases to accommodate all those who are to be involved, and the potential reactions of clients and trainees to this unorthodox form of supervising (e.g., Anonymous, 1995). Additionally, Schwartz, Liddle, and Breunlin (1988) returned to one of Montalvo's (1973) initial concerns and alerted supervisors to the tendency of "robotization" in using live supervision. Unless the supervisor is highly systematic in giving the trainee more and more autonomy, live supervision can produce clinicians who show little initiative or creativity during therapy and who conceptualize inadequately. This potential disadvantage of live supervision has been echoed by others (e.g., Adamek, 1994; Kaplan, 1987; Montalvo, 1973; Rickert & Turner, 1978; Storm, 1997; Wright, 1986). Schwartz et al. (1988) noted that both critics and proponents of live supervision are concerned about how live supervision potentially undercuts the therapist's own observations and intuitions in favor of the supervisor's. More recently, Liddle et al. (1997) have asserted that research does not support major concerns about harmful effects stemming from live supervision.

Whether or not there is a danger of the supervisor dominating therapy through live supervision, there is some danger that the supervisor will suggest "dramatic, yet inappropriate, interventions" (Goodman, 1985, p. 48). In other words, Goodman acknowledged the very human possibility of the supervisor being tempted to show off in front of trainees. Even if an intervention is appropriate, the supervisor must determine whether it is one that the trainee can carry off successfully. If not, the supervisor is trying to do therapy through the supervisee, rather than conducting live supervision. Viewed somewhat differently, Moorhouse and Carr (2001) found that isomorphism between supervisor and therapist was met with resistance more often than cooperation from the client. These authors hypothesized that if therapist and supervisor were highly attuned to one another they may generate more creative, novel interventions, thus stimulating resistance in their clients. Therefore, Moorhouse and Carr seemed to be suggesting that, while the professionals are taking pleasure in their ingenuity, they may be losing sight of the immediate needs of the clients or their readiness to experiment with unorthodox strategies.

Finally, there is virtually no evidence in the professional literature that skills learned within a live supervision context generalize to other counseling situations (Gallant et al., 1991; Kivlighan, Angelone, & Swafford, 1991). This is a serious gap in our knowledge for both trainee and client welfare, especially in cases for which supervision is limited to the live supervision modality.

TEAM SUPERVISION

To this point we have focused on the supervisor–therapist relationship in live supervision. More and more, however, live supervision has become synonymous with team supervision, that is, live supervision with other supervisees (in addition to the supervisor) behind the one-way mirror. Although team therapy was originally developed by seasoned practitioners (peers) as a means to study and improve their trade, it has become increasingly popular as a method of training even novice practitioners (e.g., Haley, 1987; Heppner et al., 1994; Landis & Young, 1994). Team supervision can also take on a variety of forms. Defining the two most common forms, Roberts (1983) differentiated between supervisor-guided live supervision, in which the supervisor is the only or primary person from the team who offers direction to the trainee, and the collaborative team model (also described by Sperling et al., 1986), in which, although the supervisor offers initial direction, team members are encouraged to take more and more responsibility for the direction of therapy as time goes on. For our purposes here, we believe that supervisor-guided live supervision, as described by Roberts, differs very little from live supervision as it has been presented thus far in this chapter, the only difference being that observers have an opportunity to learn vicariously while the supervisor is working with the supervisee. Therefore, we will focus our attention on the collaborative team model, where team members are actively involved in the progress of therapy and in the development of the supervisee.

Briefly described, the process of team supervision involves a group of trainees present with the

supervisor behind the one-way mirror during the therapy session while another trainee serves as the therapist with the clients. As with supervisor-only live supervision, the technology most frequently used in team supervision is the phone. The other common method of communication is consultation in the observation room.

Therefore, while the therapist is working with the family, the team is observing family interactions, metacommunication, and so on, to arrive at some sort of decision regarding the direction that therapy should go. The observation room is as busy, if not busier, than the therapy room. The team members have the luxury of being one step removed, allowing them to see the entire therapeutic system, including the therapist. The assumption is that this more objective posture will aid the conceptualization process, as will the synergy of ideas as the family is discussed. Team supervision also allows the supervisor to do a great deal of teaching while therapy is being conducted and to culminate an important clinical lesson with a timely intervention sent to the family through the therapist. Team supervision, therefore, becomes therapy, supervision, and classroom all in one.

To facilitate the activity and efficiency of the team, it is sometimes helpful to assign specific tasks to different team members (West et al., 1989). These tasks can be assigned by the supervisor or, if the therapist is looking for specific feedback, by the therapist. For example, the therapist trainee who is concerned about her ability to maintain appropriate boundaries within the session might ask one team member to observe only this aspect of the session.

Bernstein, Brown, and Ferrier (1984) presented a model describing what they considered essential roles in team supervision: the *therapist,* the person who will sit with the family during the session and will remain attuned to the mechanics of running the session; the *taskmaster,* the member of the team assigned to direct the conference and keep the team from deviating from the previously agreed on structure for analyzing the information being produced by the family, while ensuring an atmosphere conducive to creativity and spontaneity; and the *historian,* the person responsible for maintaining the threads of continuity across and within treatment sessions.

The supervisor can organize the team to accomplish any number of goals. One member could be asked to observe one member of the family or one relationship (e.g., father–child) or to track one theme, such as what happens in the family when feelings are introduced. Such assignments allow the supervisor to teach the importance of particular dynamics for progress in therapy. Furthermore, the supervisor can assign tasks to specific team members that represent their unique training goals. For instance, the team member who has a difficult time joining with children in counseling sessions can be asked to observe another trainee's joining style with children. The team, therefore, offers not only the advantage of in-session assistance but also numerous and rich possibilities for learning and postsession feedback.

The Reflecting Team

In his seminal work, Anderson (1987) described a novel team approach to working with families. His *reflecting team* represented a way to demystify the team approach to therapy for the family. Rather than leaving the family to their conjectures when the therapist joined the team for consultation, Anderson proposed that light and sound be switched from the therapy room to the observation room and that the family and therapist listen to the team reflect on what they have heard during the session to that point. Anderson suggested that the team's reflections could either be sought by the therapist (e.g., "I wonder if the team has any ideas that might be helpful at this point") or could be offered by the team (e.g., "We have some ideas that might be useful to your conversation"). As a therapy model, the reflecting team approach is embedded in the work of Bateson (1972) and others, and the team's deliberations are carefully formed to reflect communication patterns within the family's repertoire. Because our interest in the reflecting team is as a supervision model, we will not focus on this aspect of the model.

By having the team's deliberations observed by the family, a certain egalitarianism was added to the live supervision model that seemed to be an advantage in accomplishing therapeutic goals. Rather than receiving one central message delivered by a spokesperson for the team, the family was able to hear the deliberations themselves and draw from them as they might. Reflections could represent competing, yet equally sound, alternatives that allowed the family to reflect on others' impressions of their options. The input from the team, therefore, was far richer from the family's perspective.

For the team, the reflecting team model made all deliberations public. Because there could be no throwaway comments within this model, team members were more attentive as observers and more disciplined in their reflections. Guidelines for framing comments became more important than they were with confidential consultation breaks.

Anderson suggested that there be three team members who would participate in the model (not counting the therapist who stayed with the family). This way a third person could react to the deliberations of the other two. If the team was larger than this, Anderson advised that additional members be observers, participating only if called on by the team. Additionally, Anderson noted that persons could change rooms if it was not possible to reverse lights and sound within a facility. In the original discussion of reflecting teams, trainees were mentioned only tangentially. Anderson stated that trainees were invited to participate as reflecting team members as they felt ready, and most became increasingly active with experience.

Since Anderson's introduction of the reflecting team approach, the model has received attention as a supervision model (e.g., Roberts, 1997; Shilts, Rudes, & Madigan, 1993; Young et al., 1989). Young et al. offered a strong rationale for the reflecting team based on the disadvantages of the more standard live supervision team. The disadvantages of nonreflecting teams, according to Young et al., were at least four in number: First, regardless of the espoused support of the team, the trainee in the room filling the role of therapist felt anxious and on the spot, not only with the family, but also in relation to the observing team. By contrast, the reflecting team spreads out the spotlight. The therapist is no longer the sole representative of the team of experts. The experts can speak for themselves and may look no more impressive than the therapist. Second, trainees found it very difficult to disengage from the family, join the team in any meaningful way, and reengage with the family in the short times available for consultations. With the reflecting team, the therapist stays with the family, both physically and systemically. The therapist hears the team's thoughts as the family does and is in a position to facilitate the family's response to the team's comments from the vantage point of a neutral position. Third, the message delivered back to the family in traditional team approaches was often construed under time pressures and with uneven contributions from team members. With the reflecting team, the reflections themselves become the intervention and therefore need only develop as far as they can logically in the time allotted. The value is in the musings themselves as team members attempt to view the family's situation from different angles. Also, because of the structure of the team, the likelihood that one member will dominate is greatly diminished. Finally, Young et al. cited the relationship between clients and the team as a problem that the reflecting team addresses. In the more traditional model, the team becomes a cause for suspicion, "spies" from on high, persons of dubious motives. This apprehension is erased when clients hear the team members firsthand, not with slick interventions to transmit, but with their spontaneous interactions on the family's behalf.

Because the contributions of all members are part of the process, Young et al. (1989) suggested guidelines for all deliberations:

1. *All remarks or comments are made in terms of positive connotations and genuine respect for family members.*
2. *Ideas and speculations are put in terms of the family's beliefs, not the team member's beliefs.*
3. *The team's beliefs about the family's beliefs are couched in "possibilities" or "maybes."*

4. *As a result, as many sides as can be seen of a situation are argued, by different team members.*
5. *Team members should enjoy trust and respect for each other.* (p. 70)

Young et al. (1989) sought feedback from supervisors, trainees, and clients about the use of the reflecting team. Supervisors expressed initial nervousness that team members would say negative, unhelpful things (as they had done in confidential team meetings). When this did not occur, they found themselves trusting the process more and ultimately feeling liberated. Trainees felt rudderless at the thought of the process, but found the experience itself to be affirming. Of 20 responses received from clients, 18 found the reflecting team to be either extremely helpful or moderately helpful; the remaining 2 were unsure of their reactions. In a separate study of clients' reaction to the reflecting team, Smith, Yoshioka, and Winton (1993) found that clients also reacted positively to the reflecting team's ability to offer them multiple perspectives. They determined that these multiple perspectives were most helpful "when they contained dialectic tensions. Clients who are confronted with two or more credible explanations of the same event benefited from teams able to articulate the differences between positions and hence their dialectic" (p. 40).

In spite of the many strengths claimed about reflecting teams as a therapy model and a method of supervision, some reasonable questions may be posed. Is the egalitarianism it espouses an evolution of training and supervision (Hardy, 1993) or is it a model that fuses therapy and supervision to a point that supervision is compromised? Does the model diffuse individual contributions in its focus on the collective? Does the therapist lose the feeling of control over the outcome of therapy (Young et al., 1989)? In spite of these concerns, it seems that the reflecting team will continue to contribute to our understanding of live supervision.

Other Novel Forms of Team Supervision

As many practitioners have discovered, once the traditional mold of therapy has been broken, the possibilities for reconstructing both therapy and supervision, and a combination of the two, are innumerable. There have been several variations on the theme of the therapeutic team, each carrying with it new assumptions and parameters for both therapy and supervision.

For example, Olson and Pegg (1979) described what they referred to as direct open supervision (DOS). In their model the team is present in the therapy room and is used in therapy as needed. For example, Olson and Pegg described one case in which the husband and wife would do battle whenever they tried to negotiate. Two team members were asked to role play one of their arguments and to then model some negotiating behaviors. Following this, the couple gave feedback about what they thought that they could use from the role play and what would not work for them. At the end of the session, the team processes what transpired in the therapy session with the family present. Like the reflecting team, no private deliberations are allowed in this model. Whatever team members and the supervisor have to say to each other is heard by the family.

An even busier model than DOS is the "Pick-a-Dali Circus (PDC) (Landau & Stanton, 1983; Stanton & Stanton, 1986) in which all team members (including the therapist) are asked to play a variety of roles in order to highlight family dynamics and push the family toward resolution.

> *In many ways, PDC is like theater of the absurd. Team members respond singularly, in couples or small groups, or in unison in an ongoing, flowing way during the session. They may physically situate themselves at different places in the room, change their position, leave the room alone or in groups to observe through a one-way mirror, and so on, in accordance with the therapeutic stratagem of the moment.* (Stanton & Stanton, 1986, p. 171)

We assume that careful preparation and a highly regarded supervisor are necessary elements for the successful implementation of PDC, lest therapy does become theater of the absurd.

Finally, Brodsky and Myers (1986) presented a model similar to those that have already been described, but designed for individual clients.

Again, the entire team is present in the room for what the authors described as in vivo rotation. A client contracts for 13 weekly sessions. For the first four to six sessions, the supervisor conducts counseling with the trainees observing, followed by each trainee taking a turn in the therapist role for the next several weeks. The supervisor again assumes the role of therapist for the final session.

Each session follows three phases. During the first, the therapist works with the client for 45 minutes. Next, the therapist joins the observers (in view of the client) for a 30-minute discussion of what has transpired in counseling, including client dynamics and therapist technique. The therapist then rejoins the client for 15 minutes, and they process the issues raised by the observation group. At no time are observers allowed to intervene directly with the client. Although the authors reported substantial benefits from the use of the in vivo rotation, they admitted that it is not for everyone.

Because it is not possible to cover adequately all the dynamics to be considered for these various team models, we will use as our reference for the rest of the chapter the standard model in which the team and supervisor are positioned behind the one-way mirror, with the therapist and client group in the therapy room.

Team Dynamics

With the variety of opportunities offered by team supervision, it is perhaps not surprising that a team approach involves some initial issues and complications not typically associated with other forms of supervision. The most central of these is the cohesion of the group that will form the team. Wendorf (1984) suggested that, before the team attempts to work as a unit in offering therapy, they come together as a group through a careful examination of group process. To help the team understand each member's needs and agendas, Wendorf recommended that the group alternate between meetings with a supervisor and meetings with peers only. His experience has been that team members will relate to each other differently depending on whether the supervisor is present and that prior to doing therapy the team needs to know as much as possible about each member.

As might be expected, Wendorf's recommendations are not universally accepted. Theoretical compatibility among team members has been viewed as another essential ingredient for success (Cade, Speed, & Seligman, 1986). Although another type of supervision group might be enhanced by participants coming from widely varying assumptions about therapy, this would be far less so with a therapeutic team. Because there is a limited amount of time within a session for the team to confer and recommend an intervention, there needs to be enough theoretical compatibility to allow the team to work efficiently. Furthermore, the supervisee cannot be expected to integrate different theoretical assumptions within such a complex supervision process. (Later in this chapter we will present an opposing view as argued by Markowski & Cain, 1983.)

In-session (Midsession) Dynamics.   The therapist's right to accept or reject the intervention (i.e., supervision) is a chronic supervisory issue and one that is exacerbated with a team. Unlike the situation with a solitary supervisor, for which a trainee might be asked to carry out an intervention even though not totally committed to it, the dynamic is more complicated when a group of peers is primarily responsible for the intervention. Even if the supervisor is supportive of the team's direction, it is more important for the trainee to be in agreement with the directive than it is when no team exists. If not, the therapist will eventually feel manipulated by his or her peers, and team dynamics might eventually override the goal of providing sound therapy. This concern is supported by the research of Mauzey and Erdman (1997), who found that directives initiated by the supervisor were received more favorably by trainees than directives coming from team members.

Heath (1982) asserted that it is the supervisor's responsibility to choreograph the input from the team to the therapist and to be sure that the intervention is compatible with the therapist's style "unless the style has become part of the problem"

(p. 192). Heath also acknowledged that prior to the in-session conference, the supervisor may be confronted with competitiveness among team members, an understandable phenomenon when the role of therapist is curtailed in favor of the team approach to therapy and training.

A final issue that should receive attention prior to the actual therapy session is which and how many team members will be allowed to formulate interventions for the therapist. When consultation is the method used, this is less of an issue, especially if there is a designated taskmaster to translate the group discussion into an intervention. However, when directives are phoned in or the therapist is called into the consultation room to receive the directive, rather than to confer with the team, will several members of the team be allowed to be involved in the interchange or just one? This may seem like a minor issue, but it is probably one of the most critical process issues for a team if relations between the therapist and the team are to remain intact. Once again, it is up to the supervisor to monitor the activity level of the observation room and the readiness of individual team members to participate in a more direct fashion.

Pre- and Postsession Dynamics.   Because of the complexity and intensity of team supervision during the therapy session, it is vital for planning sessions and debriefing sessions to occur. Liddle and Schwartz (1983) maintained that the presession conference should address family, trainee, relationship, and teaching considerations. If the team goes into the session knowing pretty well what is to be accomplished with the family and what the trainee will be working on personally, the during-session consultations should serve the function of "mid-course corrections to the general session plan" (p. 478). Additionally, giving time in the presession to team dynamics, taking time to convey a respect for the position and perspective of the therapist, and addressing how this particular session reflects overall training goals will prepare the team for the intensity and activity of team supervision.

The postsession conference is equally important. Regardless of the amount of planning that has occurred, team members, especially the therapist, will have a need to debrief. Furthermore, Adams (1995) reported that trainees ask their best questions during the postsession. Heath (1982) suggested that the supervisor allow the therapist to suggest a format for the discussion. In addition to a general discussion of the session, including a discussion of hypotheses and goals, the postsession should include some feedback to the therapist and to the team (Heath, 1982). Heath also maintained that emotional reactions on the part of different team members can be appropriate to address if they enhance the process, but that criticism be offered only if paired with alternative action. In a similar vein, Cade et al. (1986) stated that

> [t]he therapist will often need time to "disengage" mentally and emotionally from the family before feeling able to consider what the team has to offer. The advantages of multiple perspectives can become a disadvantage if the therapist becomes swamped with ideas, particularly where these are conflicting ideas arising out of conflicting frameworks. (pp. 112–113).

Once more immediate session issues have been processed, the supervisor should help the team to address the session that just occurred as it fits in the larger context of training (Adams, 1995; Liddle & Schwartz, 1983) and direct team members' thinking for the next scheduled presession.

Advantages and Disadvantages of Team Supervision

Advantages. We stated earlier that advocates of live supervision tend to be enthusiastic in their support. This is true of working with the team model of live supervision as well. Among the advantages enumerated are the following (Cade et al., 1986; Elizur, 1990; Hardy, 1993; Landis & Young, 1994; Quinn, Atkinson, & Hood, 1985; Speed, Seligman, Kingston, & Cade, 1982; Sperling et al., 1986):

1. Team work appears to be highly satisfying. "Family therapy is always difficult, sometimes nerve-wracking and sometimes depressing; working in teams can be creative, highly supportive, challenging and very often fun" (Speed et al., 1982, p. 283).
2. When a crisis occurs within a case, the therapist can attend to the immediate needs of the client, while the team wrestles with conceptualizing the case.
3. As with other forms of group supervision, the therapeutic team reinforces the value of case consultation. Because the team must brainstorm during the session, the criticism that live supervision is primarily a model for executive skill development is canceled.
4. The model requires that team members work on their feet, thus training them to arrive at therapeutic interventions more quickly.
5. The team model automatically multiplies the numbers of interesting cases with which each team member has the opportunity to work.
6. The team itself can be used to enhance therapeutic goals. For example, a team split can be used as the intervention (Sperling et al., 1986); for example, the team is said to be in disagreement behind the mirror and sends in two opposing courses of action. This allows the therapist to stay in a neutral position and help the family to look at alternatives while acknowledging that there is more than one valid way to proceed.
7. A group of therapists is more likely to take greater risks and operate at a more creative level than an individual therapist. For highly intransigent cases, creative approaches to intervention are called for if the client system is to improve.
8. When the supervisor is clearly directing the team and the team is stuck, the supervisor must assess whether he or she is part of the problem (Elizur, 1990). As a result, supervisors are less insulated from their own blind spots, and team members benefit from realizing that challenge is part of therapy regardless of the expertness of the therapist.
9. Because the team will present different cultural backgrounds, the therapy process is more likely to reflect a sensitivity to culture, as will training (Hardy, 1993).

Disadvantages.   Although the team model is intriguing and dynamic, certain disadvantages and pitfalls must be considered and avoided (Cade et al., 1986; Smith et al., 1998; Todd, 1997; Wendorf et al., 1985):

1. Because of the intensity of the team's efforts, the group can find itself engaged in unproductive interactions with members unable to extricate themselves.
2. It is very difficult for competitive team members to resist using the therapy sessions to prove their conceptual superiority. This not only means that team members are competing with each other instead of supporting each other, but also that sometimes interventions sent in to families are unduly complicated or clever and not necessarily the most productive for accomplishing therapeutic goals.
3. Team supervision may not prepare therapists adequately for solo practice (i.e., using delayed supervision models), still the most common situation for most therapists. Therefore, team supervision may inadvertently contribute to a difficult transition from training to a practice setting.
4. Because of the high level of group cohesiveness that typically is associated with therapeutic teams, members can become overprotective and fail to challenge each other. For peer team groups, members might drop from the team, rather than pursue a different line of thinking.
5. If a team is a subunit of an agency or a training program, the members of the team can pose a threat to other staff members. "A mystique can develop around what a particular team is 'up to.' Other staff feel 'put down' or patronized when in discussion with team members who can somehow convey that they are in possession of 'the truth'" (Cade et al., 1986, pp. 114–115). At the very least, team members will share a common experience not available to others, thus promoting an atmosphere of an in group and an out group.
6. For a team that has a long span of time to work together, there is a danger of becoming the "other family." We believe, as did Cade et al., that every group has a limited creative life-span, at least without the impetus of new members or a change of context. Supervisors need to be sensitive to systemic and developmental dynamics within teams as well as within client groups.
7. For some cases, the team approach is more intensive than is needed and may distort client dynamics through unnecessary scrutiny. One way to compensate for this pitfall is to vary one's approaches to supervision. We think the Quinn et al. (1985) "stuck-case clinic" is an excellent approach to team supervision. Rather than having the team consider all cases (and thereby running the risk of overkill for some cases), each team member is charged with bringing his or her most difficult case to the team. As a result, the team's time is spent efficiently, and the risk of client distortion is diminished.
8. Finally, it seems to us that team supervision is as much a closed system as some other forms of supervision. By this we mean that there is definitely some self-selection among those supervisors who choose team supervision as their method of choice. They might, for example, be somewhat more theatrical than other supervisors, or perhaps they enjoy therapy more than supervision. Whatever the reasons, training programs that wed themselves entirely to team supervision might be discriminating against some of their trainees unknowingly—trainees who are equally talented but more traditional in their approach to therapy. Supervisors should be challenged to vary their approaches to supervision, just as trainees are challenged to vary their approaches to therapy.

RESEARCH RESULTS AND QUESTIONS

Live supervision has been found to be effective in training supervisees in initial counseling techniques (Gallant et al., 1991; Heppner et al., 1994; Kivlighan et al., 1991; Klitzke & Lombardo, 1991) and marriage and family therapy skills (e.g., Fennell, Hovestadt, & Harvey, 1986). To date, however, in spite of the ardor of those supervisors who prefer a live supervision model, there is no evidence that live supervision is better than, or weaker than, any other method of supervision.

Because live supervision breaks many normative canons of psychotherapy having to do with privacy and the centrality of relationship to therapy, there has been a good deal of interest in the reaction of clients and trainees to the model. Piercy, Sprenkle, and Constantine (1986) conducted a follow-up study of both groups and found that almost one-third (32%) of trainees would have preferred no observers to their therapy, and family members reported discomfort with the model in certain situations. Although comfort level was impeded, it is important to note that for these therapists and families the outcome of therapy did not seem to be affected by their negative feelings. Liddle, Davidson, and Barrett (1988) found that novice supervisees were most sensitive to evaluation issues during live supervision, while more experienced therapists focused on power and control issues. Reactions of both groups, however, minimized with continued use of live supervision, a result supported by Wong's (1997) subsequent research. In a study focusing on client reactions only, Locke and McCollum (2001) found that clients were satisfied with live supervision as long as perceived helpfulness outweighed perceived intrusiveness. Finally, Smith, Yoshioka, and Winton (1993) conducted a qualitative study to determine client reactions to reflective teams. Clients were asked about their reactions at three different times during therapy (fourth week, seventh week, and eighth week), and the questions became more sophisticated as the clients gained more experience with the model. The results indicated that clients had a reasonable grasp of the process, found much of the process to be beneficial, and were able to articulate some limitations (e.g., feeling overwhelmed by the additional team members, the team going off on its on tangent, and the abruptness experienced when a session had some emotional content and the team interrupted).

Another issue that has received empirical attention is the relative frequency of use of live supervision. Earlier studies (Lewis & Rohrbaugh, 1989; McKenzie, Atkinson, Quinn, & Heath 1986; Nichols, Nichols, & Hardy, 1990) asked marriage and family therapy supervisors to disclose the frequency with which they used live supervision. Although live supervision was considered the most productive form of supervision by many of these supervisors, it was not used as frequently as reviewing audiotapes or relying on process notes. A more recent study (Carlozzi et al., 1997) tracked methods of supervision in CACREP-accredited counseling programs and COAMFTE-accredited marriage and family therapy programs. Programs with either accreditation relied most heavily on videotape review for supervision. Live supervision was the second most frequent supervision modality for marriage and family therapy programs and the third most frequent for CACREP programs.

It is possible that live supervision has grown in popularity in the last decade or so. It is equally possible, and perhaps more likely, that the discrepancy between the Carlozzi et al. (1997) study and former studies has to do with context. Only the Carlozzi et al. study focused on training programs exclusively. As we have already implied, live supervision is a more realistic supervision modality for training programs than for clinical settings because of the presence of adequate facilities.

Taking a slightly different slant, Anderson et al. (2000) surveyed marriage and family therapists regarding the modality used for their "best" supervision experiences and their "worst" supervision experiences. Similar to the frequency studies, videotape and live supervision were most often referenced for best supervision experiences. Because of their frequency, they were also frequently referenced as the modality for worst supervision, although self-report led in this category. Therefore, it would seem that modality per se is independent from the factors that determine whether supervision will be viewed as exemplary or deficient.

As live supervision has become less novel to the mental health professions and as its overall tenability as a supervision modality has been established, there has been more interest in understanding the discrete contributions of different aspects of this supervision approach. Mauzey et al. (2000) investigated the power of delayed supervision, phone-ins, or the bug-in-the-ear to increase trainee anxiety and anger. Their results indicated that modality was not correlated with these affective states; rather, having a predisposition to anxiety and/or anger was predictive of having these states increase during the initial stages of supervision.

We have already reported the work of Frankel (1990) and Frankel and Piercy (1990) that investigated types of supervisor directives and their different effects. Kivlighan et al. (1991) conducted a similar study that focused on supervisee intentions, rather than supervisor intentions. Supervisees in this study were learning an interpersonal–dynamic approach to individual psychotherapy. Kivlighan et al. were interested in the difference between supervisees exposed to live supervision versus those using videotaped supervision. The dependent variable was the intention motivating each therapist response. Overall, the intentions for those in the live supervision treatment were consistent with the interpersonal approach to therapy (i.e., more support and relationship intentions). Therefore, the authors concluded that the live supervision approach allowed supervisees to learn more quickly. In addition to types of intentions, the authors hypothesized that live supervision would lead to stronger working alliances with clients and to therapy sessions that were *deeper* and *rougher* (Stiles, Shapiro, & Firth-Cozens, 1988). The working alliance was considered stronger by clients for the live supervision condition than for the videotape condition, and sessions were viewed as rougher. Sessions were not experienced as deeper, however, a characteristic typically associated with interpersonal–dynamic therapy.

Although Lee (1997) found that therapist cooperation increased when phone-ins were longer than 30 seconds, Moorhouse and Carr (1999) found that frequency of phone-ins seemed to be more important than length in relation to particular supervisor and therapist behaviors. Fewer

phone-ins led to more collaboration between supervisor and therapist and more cooperation (less resistance) from clients. (One would assume that a collaboration posture would take more than 30 seconds to establish, thus supporting Lee's earlier findings.) Moorhouse and Carr also found that fewer phone-ins led to a less collaborative interaction between therapist and client. Therefore, although clients cooperated with therapy goals, therapists did not engage them as often in collaborative discourse. A separate analysis of these same interactions (Moorhouse & Carr, 2001) found that no particular supervisor style (i.e., support, teaching, or collaboration) was associated with increased client cooperation. What their results did determine was that isomorphism between supervisor and therapist (i.e., therapist using the same style with the client as had been used by the supervisor with the therapist) led to decreased client cooperation. The Moorhouse and Carr results raise interesting questions about the supervisory system and the relationships within it (i.e., therapist and supervisor, therapist and client, supervisor and client). Their results also differ from earlier research conducted by Wark (1995), who found that supervisees receiving live supervision using a combination of a nonegalitarian supervisory hierarchy (involving instruction and support) paired with adequate autonomy to be the most helpful to them. Obviously, more research is required before we can come to any definitive conclusions concerning these important relationship matters.

Though the research base regarding live supervision is growing, it is still relatively small. There are many questions to be asked; among them are the following:

1. Thus far, most live supervision experience and observation have been done with supervisees conducting family therapy. Although live supervision has become popular outside of family therapy, we know very little about its utility across theoretical approaches (Bubenzer et al., 1991). The requisite interruptions of therapy when conducting live supervision may dis-

courage levels of the interpersonal depth required of some therapies.

2. As more authors argue for an increased egalitarianism within live supervision (e.g., Hardy, 1993; Moorhouse & Carr, 1999; Woodside, 1994), the relationship between such a movement and the ability of the supervisor to evaluate supervisees must be measured.

3. There has been virtually no study of the generalizability or continuity of the therapist behaviors exhibited as a result of live supervision (Gallant et al., 1991; Kivlighan et al., 1991).

4. Hardy (1993) proposed that live supervision may change dramatically to reflect changes in our understanding of cultural variables, especially as they relate to power. To date, these variables have not been isolated within live supervision research.

5. Finally, with the exception that BITE is best used with more novice trainees, the developmental level of the trainee has received little empirical attention within live supervision research. Especially in terms of team activity, the developmental needs and abilities of supervisees are unknown.

LIVE SUPERVISION IN DIFFERENT CONTEXTS

As we have already noted, live supervision is more prevalent in training settings than in work settings. In part, this reflects both the facilities requirements and the break with tradition that live supervision represents. For professionals trained within a live supervision model, one consequence might be a disenchantment in the supervision offered beyond training. Conversely, if live supervision remains only realistic within a training context, academic programs might eventually be criticized for not providing their students with supervision that will translate to future work sites.

Although live supervision has been a topic in the professional literature for over 30 years, there are still very few references in the literature to this type of activity other than to those settings that were developed as specialized marriage and family therapy clinics, such as the Ackerman Institute or the Philadelphia Guidance Clinic. We will report the experiences of two public agencies that introduced live supervision to their operation, one agency subscribing to a systemic framework and one committed to diverse conceptual frameworks.

We might assume that live supervision is easier to implement if the staff already operates within a systemic framework. Based on Lewis's (1988) discussion, it seems that this assumption is valid. Lewis described the infusion of live supervision into a rural public mental health and substance abuse agency. Although the problems of the clients varied greatly, the staff and agency had adopted a systemic orientation. It is possible, therefore, that several staff members had experienced live supervision prior to their employment. Lewis reported no resistance to the live supervision paradigm, either from clinical staff, administration, or clients. He does, however, make a distinction between live supervision and live consultation, the latter being the use of a team, but with no evaluative responsibility.

Markowski and Cain (1983), on the other hand, reported the introduction of live supervision to a community mental health center staffed by clinicians of various theoretical persuasions. The goal of the mental health center was to increase the skill of a group of core staff in marriage and family therapy. Therefore, an outside consultant was hired to conduct live (team) supervision one-half day per week for the purpose of helping this core staff acquire sufficient competence to function without the consultant. An additional incentive for the staff was meeting the criteria for state certification as marriage and family therapists. For this eclectic staff, it was critical that the consultant be supportive of different clinical orientations so that the integrity of the staff members involved was protected.

Markowski and Cain (1983) reported that the bug-in-the-ear was an unsatisfactory method for their teams (two were formed) and that consultation breaks became the method of choice. We assume that the range of theoretical positions of the team required the kind of give and take that is possible during consultations, but not using BITE.

The fact that BITE proved unsatisfactory is also consistent with more recent research affirming the importance of consultation between supervisor–team and therapist. In time Markowski and Cain also found that team members became more sensitive to their differences and were better able to suggest interventions that fit the therapist's own style and therapeutic assumptions. Therefore, it might be argued that, in this case, live supervision made the members of a diverse staff more respectful of their individual contributions, rather than clones of the supervisor, as some authors have feared.

Although a positive experience, Markowski and Cain (1983) recounted difficulties, too, especially as they related to record keeping, the necessity of separation of services, and the reliance on the individual illness model by third-party insurers. The authors concluded that if there is respect and administrative support for such a program "both the individual and the systems models can co-exist in productive harmony" (p. 44).

CONCLUSION

The introduction of live supervision to the mental health professions represents a blending of skills training and the more contemplative forms of clinical supervision. Its primary advantage is the closing of the gap between the supervisee's experience and the supervisor's review of that experience; the assumed outcome of this advantage is accelerated learning and improved service to clients. The disadvantages of the model revolve around the time commitment required of the supervisor, the need for specific facilities, and the intrusion into the therapy relationship. Team approaches to live supervision offer additional training possibilities, as well as additional challenges and potential disadvantages. The reflecting team moves live supervision to a point that it may as likely be called live consultation (Lewis, 1988).

In recent years, live supervision has moved from its identity as a family therapy training model exclusively to increased use within the other mental health professions (Carlozzi et al., 1997; Schroll & Walton, 1991). Empirical investigation of live supervision has commenced and shows promise of ultimately assisting clinical supervisors in determining the optimal conditions for the use of live supervision, as well as its most necessary components.

CHAPTER 12

TEACHING AND
RESEARCHING SUPERVISION

In the previous 11 chapters, we have employed the conceptual model presented in Chapter 1 to organize and present a broad review of supervision theory, research, and practice. This, our culminating chapter, is intended to depart from that conceptual model to build on what we have presented to this point. It addresses the development and teaching of supervisors, as well as research on supervision processes and outcomes. We cover each in turn.

BECOMING SUPERVISORS: DEVELOPMENTAL AND TEACHING PROCESSES

Hoffman (1994) characterized the traditional lack of formal training for supervisors as the mental health professions' "dirty little secret" (p. 25). Like others (e.g., Pope & Vasquez, 1991; Stoltenberg & Delworth, 1987), she suggested that supervisors who practice without having been trained as supervisors are doing so unethically. For example, the American Psychological Association's (2002) ethical code is very explicit about the importance of providing only services for which the person has been trained. Pope and Vasquez (1991) asserted that "[I]t would be no more ethical to 'improvise' supervision if one lacked education, training, and supervised experience than if one were to improvise hypnotherapy, systematic desensitization, or administration of a Hallstead–Retan Neuropsychological Test Battery without adequate preparation" (p. 171).

Fortunately, practitioners in the several mental health professions now increasingly acknowledge how important it is for supervisors to receive for-

mal training. This is encouraged also by the increasing emphasis that accreditation and regulatory bodies now give to supervision training. For these and other reasons, then, it is reasonable to conclude that there is growing momentum for training programs to include and enhance formal supervisor training.

We have organized this section of this chapter so that the first portion addresses developmental processes of supervisors and the second discusses training and supervising supervisors. Following the convention suggested by Hoffman (1990, 1994), we will use the acronym SIT to refer to the "supervisor in training."

Supervisor Development Models

Shechter (1990) noted that to become a supervisor is one additional step in professional development. It is, though, a step that involves shifts in identity that in many ways are as substantial as those experienced by the person who moves into the professional world of the counselor or therapist for the first time. Moreover, this shift in perceptions of self and role is not a one-time, single event, but a process that unfolds as new supervisors gain experience.

Several theorists have described these relatively normative changes that supervisors experience in terms of developmental stages, similar in type to the counselor developmental models we discussed in Chapter 4. Conceptions of supervisor development are relatively recent. We suspect this is a function of two trends: (1) interest in supervision as a distinct intervention meriting its own research and practice has been relatively recent, and (2) supervisor development models have largely been adaptations of counselor development models, most of which have a only a two-decade history.

So far, only a few models of supervisor development have been proposed. Table 12.1 telegraphically summarizes the stages of five models that we discuss in the sections that follow.

Alonso's Model. Alonso (1983) proposed one of the earliest supervisor development models. It was influenced both by (1) psychodynamic and (2) life-span developmental perspectives. Because of the latter perspective, her model encompasses the person's entire professional life as a supervisor. This is in contrast to the several other supervisor development models, which each suggest three or four stages that might *all* be traversed in a matter of only a few years, perhaps a decade or less. Each of Alonso's supervisor developmental stages can be characterized in terms of three themes: (1) self and identity, (2) relationship between supervisor and therapist, and (3) relationship between the supervisor and the administrative structure within which the supervisor works.

During the *novice* stage, supervisors are nurturing a dream about what they might become, but also are confronted with developing a sense of self-as-supervisor. They also must cope with the anxiety that comes from needing to deal with narcissistic developmental needs (e.g., for validation, for approval, and for role models) that emerge in response to the need to defend themselves as novices once again after already having achieved some sense of mastery as therapists. These issues are exacerbated by the fact that their trainees typically are about the same age and are themselves career novices who are taking on new levels of responsibility.

In the *midcareer* stage, supervisors generally conform to Levinson's (1978) description of the ideal mentor. That is, they are moving from a focus on self to more of a focus on others.

Late career supervisors are often faced with the need to maintain self-esteem in the face of our culture's tendency to devalue older people. But, at the same time, they are in a position to enjoy the sta-

TABLE 12.1 Summary of Supervisor Development Stages Suggested by Developmental Theorists

ALONSO	HESS	RODENHAUSER	STOLTENBERG, McNEILL, & DELWORTH	WATKINS
Novice	Beginning	Emulation	Level 1	Role shock
		Conceptualization		Role recovery and transition
	Exploration		Level 2	
		Incorporation		Role consolidation
Midcareer	Confirmation of supervisor identity	Consolidation	Level 3	Role mastery
Late career			Level 3 integrated	

From Alonso (1983), Hess (1986, 1987), Rodenhauser (1994; 1997), Stoltenberg et al. (1998), Watkins (1990; 1993).

tus of village elder, using the supervisory role as a medium to exhibit their wisdom and expertise. This role provides an opportunity to work through conflicts regarding integrity versus despair. This stage seems very similar to the last phase Rønnestad and Skovholt (2003) discuss (see Chapter 4).

Alonso may be unique among the supervisor developmental theorists in the attention she gave the role of institutional context. Supervision usually takes place in the context of an institution, and this inevitably will affect the supervisor. For example, novice supervisors are likely to feel a greater need to be recognized by the institution and therefore may respond to trainees more harshly and critically than their more advanced colleagues. Conversely, because of their own still unresolved issues as former trainees, they might overidentify with their own trainees when they struggle with institutional rules and procedures.

Hess's Model. Hess (1986, 1987) suggested that supervisor development occurs across three stages. In the *beginning* stage, the person changes roles (e.g., from trainee to supervisor) and reference groups (i.e., from novices to more experienced clinicians). This shift into new terrain with all its attendant ambiguity about roles and technique renders the supervisors vulnerable to self-consciousness and sensitivity to peer and trainee criticism. They compensate by (1) employing a concrete structure in supervision and (2) focusing on the client and the teaching of technique.

As supervisors gain experience, they develop both competence and confidence, along with a corresponding internalized belief in the professional value of supervision as an intervention. This characterizes the second or *exploration* stage. Hess suggested, though, that supervisors at this stage are prone to two potentially problematic response sets. One is to be too restrictive in their supervisory roles; the other is to become too intrusive with the trainee, addressing issues that are unrelated to the trainee's work as a therapist. The trainee is likely to respond to either with resistance.

When supervisors reach the third stage, *confirmation of supervisor identity,* they find more of

their gratification and professional pride in their trainees' successes and, consequently, feel less dependent on receiving validation from others that they are "good supervisors." They are able to respond more to the trainee's learning agenda and actually to *be* in the relationship with the trainee, rather than dealing with the relationship at a cognitive level. Their sense of professional identity is strong and established.

Rodenhauser's Model. Rodenhauser (1994, 1997) observed that the newest supervisors will emulate their previous role models (*emulation stage*). This identification establishes an essential foundation on which to begin developing competence and identity as a supervisor. Gradually, though, new supervisors will encounter the limits of emulation and begin to search for their own methods and guidelines (*conceptualization stage*). Much of this search typically will occur in discussions with peers. This process of interacting with peers has the additional advantage of establishing alliances that reduce supervisors' likelihood of overidentifying with their supervisees.

The *incorporation stage* occurs as supervisors begin to develop an increasing awareness of the importance of the supervisory relationship. This awareness comes with increased sensitivity to the impact of their personal style on supervisees and, ultimately, on the supervisee–client relationship. Concomitant to this is supervisors' heightened awareness of individual differences (gender, race, culture, etc.) that affect the supervisory triad.

Finally, in the *consolidation stage,* supervisors consolidate their learning and experience. One aspect of this stage is an increasing ability to use the supervisee's countertransference reactions in supervision, but also to balance this against the supervisees' need for privacy. Without deliberate effort, the supervisor at this stage is able to continually monitor parallel processes for instructional cues.

The IDM Model. Stoltenberg et al. (1998) suggested that supervisors move through a series of stages analogous to those suggested in their counselor development model. In fact, they assume a sort of interlocking of counselor development and supervisor development stages. That is, Stoltenberg et al. assert that the level 1 supervisor first should have reached the stage of at least a late level 2 counselor (see Chapter 4 for our summary and discussion of these counselor stages).

Level 1 supervisors, like level 1 counselor trainees, feel characteristically anxious and are eager to "do the right thing." They frequently have a mechanistic and structured way with trainees, are likely to assume an "expert" stance, and often are eager to push their own theoretical orientation and techniques on trainees. In turn, they are relatively dependent on their own supervisors for support.

SITs at level 1 are often very effective when they are responsible for supervising beginning counselor trainees—who *want* the structure and "expertness" the beginning supervisor will tend to offer. Stoltenberg et al. (1998), in fact, noted that level 1 supervisors who also are at level 2 in terms of their development as counselors frequently will be "far better" (p. 161) as supervisors than as counselors.

Level 2 is characterized by confusion and conflict. Fortunately, this tends to be a short-lived stage. SITs now understand supervision to be more complex and difficult than they originally had thought it would be. They may tend to focus heavily on the trainee, with a consequent risk of losing objectivity and, with it, the ability to guide and confront. But, at the same time, SITs at this level may vary in their motivation to be supervisors, with the consequence that they may then blame trainees for their own problems as supervisor and become angry and withdraw. Stoltenberg et al. (1998) noted that level 2 SITs need their own supervisors to be expert and consistent with them.

Level 3 is characterized by a consistent motivation toward the supervisor role, which they approach as but one of the many that they have as professionals. Supervisors at this level function with relative autonomy, though they may seek consultation or even regular supervision as needed. They are able to engage in honest and relatively accurate self-appraisals. Level 3 integrated super-

visors might be called master supervisors. They can work well with trainees at any level of development and are unlikely to have strong preferences about trainee level. In their agencies, they often are in the role of supervising less advanced supervisors.

Watkins's Model.   In a series of articles, Watkins (Watkins, 1993, 1994, 1995b, 1995c, 1995d, 1995e; Watkins, Schneider, Haynes, & Nieberding, 1995) reviewed the several conceptions of developmental stages through which supervisors progress. Watkins (1993) suggested a model of supervisor development that is based on counselor development models originated by Hogan (1964) and enhanced by Stoltenberg (1981). Because of this very direct lineage, Watkins called his the *supervision complexity model* (SCM; Watkins, 1990a; Watkins, 1993).

Watkins's (1994) basic concept is that development occurs as a response to increased challenge along several dimensions as the supervisor gains experience. Although there are many potential developmental issues across the stages, Watkins suggested four as being "central to much developmental thought." These principal developmental issues are: (1) *competency versus incompetency,* (2) *autonomy versus dependency,* (3) *identity versus identity diffusion,* and (4) *self-awareness versus unawareness.*

Stage 1, *role shock,* is marked by the feeling of being an imposter. Watkins (1990) described the supervisor at this stage as "playing the role of supervisor." Supervisors are more likely to experience general, unresolved conflict at this stage than at any other time. They typically employ a concrete, rules-oriented approach, with little attention to the processes occurring between them and their supervisees. Novice supervisors are likely either to withdraw from trainees or to impose a too rigid structure.

Supervisors at stage 2, that of *role recovery and transition,* are beginning to develop a supervisory identity, along with self-confidence and a more realistic perception of strengths and weaknesses. Nevertheless, supervisors at this level are prone to wide fluctuations in self-appraisals, vacillating rapidly from feeling good about their performance to feeling bad. Their tolerance of ambiguity is greater, as is their ability to recognize supervisory processes such as transference and countertransference (though their ability to address them is not yet at a commensurate level).

Supervisors at stage 3, *role consolidation,* are increasingly consistent in their thinking and acting as supervisors and in both self-confidence and accuracy of self-appraisal. They have begun to feel generally qualified for their role and, in fact, have begun to solidify a consistent and definably supervisory role. They are less controlling and leading with trainees and instead are more encouraging and supportive. Transference and countertransference issues no longer pose a significant threat. These and similar process issues become considerations during supervision.

Supervisors at stage 4, *role mastery,* have developed a consistent, solid sense of confidence as well as an integrated and well-elaborated sense of identity. Their supervisory style is well integrated, theoretically consistent, and personalized.

Conclusions Regarding Supervisory Development Models. Fifteen years ago, Worthington (1987) concluded from his review of the literature that empirical research on ways that supervisors change with experience was "at a rudimentary level" (p. 206) and that relatively few researchers had yet made this a focus of their research. As a consequence, there was little understanding of how supervisors' conceptual abilities or cognitive styles might change as they gain experience.

Most of the supervisor development models summarized in this chapter have been published since Worthington's article appeared. But as Russell and Petrie (1994) reminded us, they are in their formative stages and consequently are not yet supported by empirical data. Their conclusions about these models, as apt today as they were a decade ago, were as follows:

1. *There is considerable similarity among the theories of supervisor development. The theoretical models presented offer slightly different perspectives; however, all appear to describe a general process through which supervisors move from a new role in which they are overwhelmed, self-conscious, anxious, and insecure to an integrated identity where they feel comfortable, secure, and competent. Given these similar descriptions, there appears to be at least clinical, if not empirical support. What currently is needed, however, is model testing and not further model building.*

2. *The models of supervisor development provide preliminary guidelines for creating effective supervisory dyads in training environments. To develop the most effective training environments (i.e., supervisory dyads) for supervisees, training directors should pay attention to not only the developmental level of the supervisee, but also the level of the supervisor.*

3. *These models provide guidelines for developing training environments for supervisors. Awareness of the supervisor's developmental level may be helpful in guiding supervisor trainers in their interactions with their student supervisors.*

4. *These models provide directions and hypotheses for research on supervisor development. Although research examining supervisor developmental models has been virtually nonexistent, these models allow for specific hypotheses concerning supervisors' behaviors, thinking styles, emotions, and perceptions to be proposed and tested.* (pp. 34–35)

Training and Supervising Supervisors

Supervisor training can be offered in a number of formats and for audiences of different types. It might be provided, for example, as a workshop or series of workshops for practitioners who already are working as supervisors. Alternatively, it might be provided as one or more formal university courses for graduate students.

We recognize that these training formats and target audiences inevitably will affect what is taught and how. Nevertheless, we believe that all effective supervision training should have both *didactic* and *experiential* training components. Also, just as is the case of training in counseling or therapy, it should be designed as a series of graded experiences across time so that learners can have the opportunity to get consistent feedback based on practice.

Our discussion of supervisor training is written with university-based supervision courses specifically in mind. We believe, however, that the concepts pertain much more broadly and that they therefore generalize readily to other supervision training formats as well. In line with this goal of offering more generalizable principles, we do not intend here to provide a detailed syllabus for a supervision course (though syllabi are available through our Web site, listed in the Supervisor's Toolbox).

Minimum Qualifications for SITs.   State licensing boards typically stipulate the minimum amounts of experience required for someone to assume the legally sanctioned role of supervisor. Usually, this is stated in terms of the number of postlicensure years of experience. Some professional associations and accrediting bodies also speak to the matter of necessary background. For example, the Association for Counselor Education and Supervision (ACES) has developed standards for counselor supervisors that suggest that the supervisor should have postgraduate credentialing and licensure as a counselor, along with graduate courses and continuing education workshops in supervision. It certainly makes sense that those who are to function autonomously as supervisors should be licensed in their own discipline. After all, supervision involves not only the professional development of the trainee, but *also* the protection of the client's well-being. For this latter role, a professional license would seem the minimal professional credential.

On the other hand, it makes sense to begin training supervisors while they still are in graduate programs. This, for example, was the recommendation of the APPIC supervision competency group (Falender et al., in press). Within this context, it is possible for a particular supervisor to have more limited responsibilities with respect to helping trainees develop as therapists. There are three frequent circumstances in which this might occur:

1. The supervisor is university based and supervising a trainee who is working in a field setting where his or her work is monitored by an on-site supervisor who will take responsibility for client welfare.

2. The supervisor is working as part of a vertical supervision team and has the relatively circumscribed role of helping the trainee to develop as a therapist. The supervisor's own supervisor would offer the necessary monitoring of client welfare. This occurs, for example, in situations where the person, in the practicum component of a graduate-level supervision course, supervises a beginning practicum student; it also occurs during internship when an intern supervises practicum students.

3. The supervisor might be a fellow student (or perhaps a fellow counselor) who is functioning as a peer supervisor (see, e.g., Benshoff, 1993). Bernard (1992), in fact, described one university's training program for master's-level students to serve as peer supervisors. Although this practice is useful both to the peer supervisor and to the person receiving that supervision, she did note that (in contrast to the training of doctoral students as supervisors) this practice posed several dual relationship dilemmas that require particular attention by the faculty supervisor. These included (a) being careful about how the peer supervisor is involved in the summative evaluation process, (b) being more guarded during supervision-of-supervision in commenting on the performance of practicum students than might be acceptable if the supervision-of-supervision was with doctoral student SITs, and (c) difficulties of the peer supervisors and trainees sharing the same off-campus placements.

Any one of these three circumstances would allow nonlicensed professionals, including graduate students, to serve as supervisors. Common sense would dictate, however, that SITs would have at least *some* experience as counselors or therapists and that the level of this experience would exceed that of trainees they are to supervise. Ellis and

Douce (1994) suggested that the SIT have 1 to 2 years of supervised practicum training as a counselor; Russell and Petrie (1994) suggested at least 1 year of practicum. To have at least this level of supervised experience is not only a matter of having the requisite skills, but also of having reached an appropriate level of professional identity, experience, and professional maturity (see, e.g., our discussion above of the Stoltenberg et al. supervisory development model).

SIT Assessment: The First Step in Training.   As with *any* intervention, SIT training should begin with some form of assessment. In this case, it would be of SIT (1) competencies and (2) training needs. This helps the trainers. But such an assessment also may usefully stimulate SITs' reflections about their own experiences, thereby constituting an important initial aspect of their training (cf. Bonney, 1994; Borders & Leddick, 1988; Hawkins & Shohet, 1989; Hoffman, 1990, 1994). Figure 12.1 depicts a flow chart of the steps Hawkins and Shohet (1989) suggested were necessary in becoming supervisor. Notably, the beginning point is that of self-assessment.

Bonney reported asking SITs to remember and discuss their own first clinical experiences with clients and then to consider ways in which these feelings might resemble their current feelings

about beginning to supervise. Borders and Leddick (1987) had new supervisors begin by constructing a "résumé" of past supervision-relevant experiences. Their purpose was to stimulate a systematic review of the multiple relevant experiences that the SIT will have had as counselor, teacher, consultant, researcher, and peer supervisor. They reason that each contributes to the SIT's new role of supervisor. They often enter supervisor training with substantial life and professional experiences that can be generalized to their work as supervisors.

Hoffman (1990) described a procedure that encourages SITs to reflect on their prior experiences as supervisees. She asked them to complete a Supervision Life Line (SLL), which lists past experiences of being supervised. For this task, they draw a vertical line down which they arrange their previous supervised experience in chronological order.

The SITs are directed to list each of their experiences as a supervisee, with the first one at the top, the next directly below it, and so on. For *each* experience, the SIT is directed to jot down on the left side of the vertical line demographic information about the former supervisor. This includes the supervisor's professional discipline, gender, age, and years of experience. On the right side of the line, directly opposite to this listing of supervisor

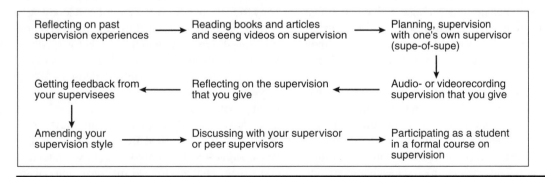

FIGURE 12.1 Supervision Learning Cycle

From P. Hawkins and R. Shohet (2000). *Supervision in the helping professions, Second edition.* Buckingham, UK: Open University Press. Copyright © (2000) by Open University Press. Reprinted by permission.

demographics, SITs are to note the year of the particular supervision and its duration (e.g., "1995, 6 months") and to rate the value of this experience to their professional development (using a scale of 1 to 10, where 1 = *worst* and 10 = *best*).

Once SITs have done this, Hoffman suggested assigning two follow-up tasks:

1. *Fleshing out the various supervisory experiences in narrative form.* For example, SITs might be asked to describe for each listed experience the client population that was served, the theoretical orientation that seemed to influence the supervisor's approach to supervision, the supervisor's approach to supervising, the most salient learnings from this supervisory experience, the aspects of the experience that were particularly easy and particularly difficult, and, finally, anything that was felt to be missing from the supervisory experience.

2. *Writing a discussion of what they have learned from both the SLL and the narrative material that they wrote about it.* This discussion would include such observations as their conclusions regarding their preferred styles of learning, differences in how they appreciated didactic versus experiential learning at various stages in their development, lessons from the way(s) conflict was handled during supervision, the various barriers to learning that they encountered, and their preferences with respect to such supervisor attributes as age, gender, and discipline. Hoffman reported that she concludes this exercise with a discussion among group members about what they had learned from it and how this might be useful to them as they begin adopting the role of supervisor themselves.

The Didactic Component of Supervisor Training.
The specifics of what is offered in the didactic portion of supervisory training are dictated by a number of factors, including instructors' characteristics (especially their professional discipline and theoretical orientation) and the characteristics of the particular institution or context in which training is offered. Nevertheless, those who train supervisors will be guided by a desire to cover essential areas.

Borders et al. (1991) suggested that supervisor training should address the following seven core areas:

1. Models of supervision
2. Counselor development
3. Supervision methods and techniques
4. Supervisory relationship
5. Evaluation
6. Executive skills
7. Ethical, legal, and professional regulatory issues

Borders et al. (1991) also suggested three sets of learning objectives for each of these seven areas: (1) *self-awareness,* (2) *theoretical and conceptual knowledge,* and (3) *skills and techniques.* The result is therefore a 7 by 3 matrix with 21 types of learning objectives, which the authors then supplement with a list of more than 200 specific learning objectives. Russell and Petrie (1994) characterized this as the "most extensive set of recommendations for supervisor training" (p. 38), but then also suggested that the model "falls victim to its own complexity" (p. 38). Russell and Petrie responded to the Borders et al. (1991) proposal by suggesting three essential areas for supervision training:

1. *Theoretical models of supervision.* They suggested that these be covered both with available books on supervision and with videotapes demonstrating supervision from several approaches. They recommend, for example, Goodyear's (1982) videotape series that illustrates supervision from five different theoretical perspectives: Albert Ellis (rational–emotive), Carl Rogers (client centered), Erving Polster (gestalt), Rudolph Ekstein (psychodynamic), and Norman Kagan (interpersonal process recall).

2. *Supervision research.* To familiarize students with the empirical literature, Russell and Petrie suggested two complementary strategies: (a) to assign students to read specific empirical articles that examine research issues in supervision; among these are selected research reviews and critiques (e.g. Avis & Sprenkle, 1990; Ellis, 1991b; Ellis & Ladany, 1997; Ellis et al., 1996; Holloway,

1984; Holloway & Neufeldt, 1995; Lambert & Ogles, 1997); and (b) to develop a research proposal as their primary written product for the course. In doctoral programs and those master's degree programs that require a thesis, this paper might prove a springboard for some students' dissertation or thesis.

3. *Ethical and professional issues.* A review of ethical and legal issues that affect their work is important, especially as this is the first time that students have been responsible for both the client *and* the trainee. Moreover, Russell and Petrie pointed out that there is a broader training opportunity in reviewing ethical and legal issues at this level. That is, it is a chance to revisit the issues at a time when the trainees are developmentally ready to consider them in a less rule bound and more critical manner than when they were first exposed to those issues earlier in training.

More recently, Falender et al. (in press) have listed minimal knowledge and skills that a supervisor should acquire. Their lists overlap considerably with that of Borders et al. (1991). One important addition is that this offers the reminder that a supervisor should have basic knowledge of the area being supervised. Like Russell and Petrie (1994), Falender et al. considered knowledge of supervision research to be a core competency.

Because the number of supervision texts and books is growing at an accelerating rate, the supervision trainer now has available a substantial literature from which to draw. Our own bias is that to assign one or more texts for a supervision course provides important but insufficient coverage of the material. Students should read not only research articles (studies, critiques, articles on methodology) such as Falender et al., as Russell and Petrie recommend, but they should also be exposed to original work, including articles that are in some way "supervision classics" (such as, for example, Searles, 1955, and Stoltenberg, 1981).

Laboratory Skills Training for SITs. Virtually all graduate students in the mental health professions participate early on in a *laboratory skills* or

prepracticum experience to learn basic counseling or therapeutic techniques. This equips them to see real clients in an actual treatment setting. Analogously, SITs should be provided with some basic supervision skills training prior to their actual work with supervisees.

In our own supervision training, we prefer to begin skills training by having SITs work in groups of about three to develop skits in which they depict "absolutely awful" supervision. This and the discussions that follow can have an ice-breaking role for a new group (and usually it is fun, for the nature of the task is really nonthreatening). But in addition, it begins to define for the group what supervision *should not be.* To define what something is *not* is a developmental step for beginning to define what it should or might be.

To begin developing skills that the SITs will use in work with trainees, we provide them with early exposure to Kagan's IPR technique (see Chapter 9 for a description). In his workshops, Kagan often would discuss the "inquirer" role as one that would enable someone to function even as a "supervisor paraprofessional." That is, like the supervisor role that Williams (1995) advocates, the supervisor is to ask simple questions from a position of naive curiosity.

Early training in IPR techniques empowers the SIT, who is now equipped with some skills on which to fall back. Moreover, it helps the trainee to screen out the teacher role, which often is difficult for beginning SITs to do.

Drawing from the microcounseling model that Allen (1967) originally had developed, Richardson and Bradley (1984) suggested a "microsupervision" model for the training of supervisors. In its emphasis on a teaching role, it seems to provide an excellent complement to the IPR model.

It is useful to think in terms of the three stages that Richardson and Bradley (1984) suggested were operative in microsupervision training: (1) *assessment* (to assess the SIT's skills and skill deficits and then to rank the deficits in a hierarchy), (2) *modeling* (to use videotape for modeling of each supervisory skill to be taught by microsupervision), and (3) *transfer* (to transfer the skill to real practice settings through supervision role plays and self-evaluations of performance).

These supervisory skills, though, should be accompanied by shifts in the ways the SITs think of themselves. Specifically, they need eventually to make the cognitive shift from thinking like a counselor to thinking like a supervisor [one simple indicator is when SITs no longer inadvertently refer to their trainees as "my client(s)"]. This shift often will occur simply as SITs gain experience and training in supervision. Borders (1992), though, has suggested some strategies to help this occur.

One simple strategy is to have SITs review and take notes on a trainee tape as if they were going to meet with that counselor for supervision during the following hour. After watching (or listening to) 10 to 15 minutes of the tape, SITs are stopped and asked to review their notes. They are to count the number of statements about the *client* versus those about the *supervisee*.

> *Typically, participants report few if any statements about the counselor. This has been especially true of experienced clinicians in inservice workshops. Then they are reminded that they will be meeting with the counselor, not the client, during the next hour. What are they going to do during the supervision session to help the counselor? They are to keep this question utmost in their minds as they review the remainder of the session.* (Borders, 1992, p. 139)

A second strategy that Borders suggests is to encourage SITs to employ deliberate educational planning for their supervision sessions. This is guided by two types of data: (1) SITs' own assessment of trainees' strengths and weaknesses, based on a review of one or more of the trainees' counseling tapes and (2) the three to five learning goals for the supervisory experience that SITs have trainees develop during the initial supervisory session. SITs are then to use both trainees' learning goals and their own assessment of the trainees' work to guide the feedback that they give the trainee.

Supervision-of-Supervision. When Hansen and Stevic (1967) argued 35 years ago for the devel-

opment of practica in supervision, virtually none were offered. Fortunately, this has been changing. In the section that follows we will discuss the practicum component of supervision training. A key aspect of this practicum experience is the supervision that the SIT receives for his or her work. This supervision-of-supervision sometimes is referred to informally as "supe-of-supe."

The institutional context will determine the point at which SITs actually begin their practicum experience. For example, if their training is occurring in a university that offers a sequence of two or more supervision courses, the practicum component usually will begin after at least a term of didactic and laboratory skills preparation. On the other hand, if there is only a single course, the practicum might begin much earlier and coincide with the didactic portion. Still another scenario is practicum at an internship training site where it might begin very early, perhaps after an orienting workshop or two.

The techniques and format for supe-of-supe could reasonably be any that are used in the supervision of counseling or therapy. Moreover, there have been discussions of some very innovative techniques and formats for supe-of-supe, including videotape review of the supe-of-supe (Wilcoxon, 1992), live supe-of-supe (Constantine, Piercy, & Sprenkle, 1984), and even role reversals in which the SIT then supervises his or her own supervisor.

We speculate, however, that group may be the most frequent modality, for supe-of-supe is often a component of a graduate-level course in which there also is simultaneous seminar-type didactic coverage of supervision-relevant material. Group also has other learning advantages, as Frayn (1991) makes clear in his discussion of the 13-year history of a supe-of-supe group for psychiatrists.

Ellis and Douce (1994) summarized one model of group supe-of-supe based on 13 years of experience with approximately 35 groups and 175 SITs. In their model, the supe-of-supe group meets 2 hours weekly and typically consists of five to eight SITs and two trainers. During each session

(1) the first 30 to 60 minutes is spent monitoring the supervisory work of the various group members and then (2) one SIT presents a supervisory case, supplementing that presentation with the playing of audio and/or videotapes. Each SIT presents in this manner at least twice during the term.

The developmental models that we discussed earlier should provide some guidance for the structuring of these supervisory experiences. In fact, there seems to be some general agreement among the several models about the needs of the beginning level SIT (i.e., the one most typically to be seen in a supervisor training course or workshop). That is, very much like the novice counselor, the novice supervisor will want direction and structure.

Watkins (1994) made several suggestions for meeting the needs of novice supervisors, including

(1) very closely monitoring the cases the trainee works with (which can . . . contribute to a feeling of being held, secured, and stabilized in the supervision relationship; "I am not alone in this"); (2) having a "setness" about the supervision of the supervisor trainee (i.e., having regularly scheduled meeting times that are clearly set as to place, time, frequency, and duration, which further grounds and stabilizes the supervision context); and (3) having a policy established about supervisory crises (i.e., if something comes up that the supervisor trainee feels unable to handle and which seemingly demands immediate attention, how can he/she then go about talking with the supervisor?), with which both the supervisor trainee and his/her supervisor feel comfortable. (p. 422)

Another step in providing structure and prescriptions for the beginning SIT should concern what to do during the first session(s) with a newly assigned trainee. Both Bonney (1994) and Borders and Leddick (1987) suggested that this first session be scheduled, if possible, before the trainee actually begins to see clients (if this is not possible, the session should address clients only in general terms).

The primary foci of this session should be at least a beginning of a mutual understanding of the nature and process of supervision, immediate and long range goals of each, their theoretical or philosophical orientations and the supervisee's relevant past experiences. A discussion of role expectations and a beginning of mutual role definitions would also be helpful. If all this proves to be overwhelming for one interview some of it may be delayed until a later time. (Bonney, 1994, p. 32)

Hoffman (1994) suggested that supervision might be thought of as having three phases: (1) beginning, (2) middle, and (3) end. This is a useful way to think not only about supervision itself, but also about the supe-of-supe. Each stage suggests certain natural tasks. We already have discussed some of the tasks of the beginning stage and therefore now will address the latter two.

Middle Phase.   This is the longest of the stages and the one during which most of the work of both supervision and supe-of-supe will occur. Ellis and Douce (1994) suggested eight issues that commonly occur during supe-of-supe, especially at this phase. We summarize five of them in Box 12.1

End Phase.   Two primary issues confront the SIT during the end phase of supervision. One is dealing with termination issues (certainly, dealing with the termination of the SIT–trainee relationship, but often also helping the trainee to deal with termination issues as they are occurring with clients); the other is to address the matter of providing a summative evaluation of the trainee (Chapter 2).

The one addition we would make to those earlier discussions is our assertion that it is important for the SIT to have had *some* role in evaluating the supervisee and for the supervisee to be fully apprised of this SIT role and its nature from the very beginning. This gives ecological validity to the supervisory experience. That is, supervision occurs in an evaluative context; without having had evaluative responsibilities, the SIT will have missed a crucial aspect of the supervisory experience.

Of course, the SIT is also terminating supe-of-supe at this stage, while also dealing with his or her own evaluation issues. These processes then provide an opportunity for the SIT to reflect on and integrate the experiences that she or he has had as

Box 12.1

Five SIT Issues That Ellis and Douce (1994) Found to Arise during Supe-of-Supe

1. Balancing responsibility: As SITs move into the role of supervisor, their responsibility for the client continues. But they now face the sometimes frustrating fact that they do not have the same direct access to the client that they are used to having. Moreover, as supervisors they now have the additional responsibility of facilitating the counselor trainee's development. Attaining a balance between these responsibilities is often difficult for the new supervisor. And sometimes these responsibilities can be at odds, or at least seem to be. Ellis and Douce (1994) suggested two interventions to address this: to assign and then discuss relevant literature (ethical, legal, and professional role related) and to suggest that SITs use an IPR technique with their supervisees.

2. Parallel process: SITs will most likely encounter and find themselves responding to parallel processes (e.g., Ekstein & Wallerstein, 1972; Mueller & Kell, 1972) during this, the middle phase. What we would add to our discussion in Chapter 6 is that supe-of-supe adds yet *another* level through which parallel processes may reverberate: Whereas in supervision the supervisor must be aware of reverberations of processes between the client–counselor and the supervisor–trainee relationships, in supe-of-supe these processes might find expression at the additional level of the SIT and his or her supervisor. As Ellis and Douce (1994) pointed out, it is during supe-of-supe that parallel processes are most likely to be noticed. Noticing the patterns at this level gives a unique opportunity not only for teaching, but also for modification of that pattern.

3. Power struggles: A basic rule for counselors is to avoid overtly asserting their wills against those of the client. Yet there are characteristics of supervision that make power struggles more likely to occur here than in therapy. Therefore, it is important that SITs learn to handle power struggles. These characteristics include the fact that the relationship is evaluative, that it has a teaching function, and that supervisors ultimately are responsible for ensuring that the client's welfare is protected (and therefore

are likely occasionally to adopt a directive stance when they believe that they know what is best for the client). Compounding these already present characteristics is that beginning SITs are more likely than their more advanced colleagues to behave in a structured, controlling manner, while also remaining especially sensitive to any perceived threats to their authority.

4. Individual differences: Ellis and Douce (1994) suggested that attention to individual differences (especially race, culture, gender, sexual orientation, and religion) is important during supe-of-supe. There are opportunities for SITs to help their supervisees to address these issues in counseling; there are also opportunities to address them as they are salient in the supervisory relationship itself. Ellis and Douce suggested that supervision trainers have particular responsibility for ensuring that individual differences are addressed during supe-of-supe.

5. Sexual attraction: Sexual attraction, either between counselor and client or between supervisor and supervisee, is likely to be an issue during supe-of-supe. Such attraction can pose particular challenges for the SIT and/or the supervisor trainer. This problem is compounded by the fact that sexual attraction remains somewhat taboo, and therefore the involved professionals may feel uncomfortable addressing it openly when it occurs.

Ellis and Douce (1994) suggested that the supervisor trainer has a particular obligation to watch for instances of sexual attraction and then to address them openly. That is, sexual attraction is natural: In surveys, Pope, Spiegel, and Tabachnik (1986) found 95% of men and 76% of women psychologists reported having felt sexually attracted to a client. In another study, Pope, Tabachnik, and Spiegel (1987) found that 91% of psychologists reported this experience. However, although SITs generally are clear that sexual contact between either counselor and client or supervisor and trainee is unethical, they often are given too little training in the management of these naturally occurring feelings.

a novice supervisor. One way we have fostered this process has been to require that SITs end the term by making a formal presentation that summarizes their work across the term with at least one trainee. This is a chance, then, to review the course of their work together, including (1) interventions that worked and did not, (2) the nature of any conflicts that occurred and how they were resolved, (3) transference and countertransferences that seemed to have affected their work, and (4) any parallel processes that might have affected the work.

In so doing, SITs have the chance to get summative feedback from the trainer, as well as from other group members. But, in addition, they can reflect on feedback that their supervisees have given them. This feedback should have been available in several forms.

1. During the summative evaluation of the supervisee, the SIT should have solicited feedback from him or her about aspects of the supervision experience that were especially useful or not.
2. The SIT should have looked for informal ways to obtain feedback during the course of the relationship. For example, the regular use of an IPR technique is one means by which the SIT might get ongoing feedback.
3. We also believe it is important for the SIT to have used paper and pencil measures to obtain from the trainee regular and systematic feedback (after every session if possible). This is consistent with a scientist–practitioner orientation and has at least the following benefits:
   a. Obtaining repeated measures from supervisees by using one or more specific questionnaires allows SITs to obtain feedback that is systematic and that can be compared across sessions. They can look back over the supervisory experience and regard it essentially as $n = 1$ research. For example, which session(s) was rated especially high and what was occurring during that session? Which session(s) was rated low and why?

(In fact, we encourage this process by asking that the SIT, during the end-of-term summary presentations, provide session evaluation data, plotted across sessions if possible, with discussions of possible supervisory processes that might explain these data trends.)
   b. It may be more comfortable for both trainee and SIT to have the trainee give constructive feedback in written form, rather than in a face-to-face meeting.
   c. By making the solicitation of feedback a regular expectation, it can diffuse potential conflicts that otherwise might arise as the trainee "sits on" grievances or other bad feelings.
   d. As SITs might receive negative feedback, it allows them the opportunity to reflect on it in private (as well as in supe-of-supe) and to consider what they will do with constructive feedback (e.g., Williams, 1994). There are a number of possible measures that SITs might use to obtain feedback from trainees. Some of them, like the Supervisory Styles Inventory (Friedlander & Ward, 1984) and other measures are included in the Supervisor's Toolbox.

Research on Supervision Training Outcomes. Recognition that supervision training is necessary has been growing, but still is not universal. As a consequence, research on the effectiveness of such training remains virtually nonexistent. Milne and James (2002) and Milne and Westerman (2001) have conducted small-n, multiple case studies in which they demonstrated that "consultancy" (what we would call supe-of-supe) is effective in shaping these supervisor's (coded) behaviors. This is a beginning. More such research is needed.

Conclusions. Hawkins and Shohet (1989) pointed out that the psychoanalyst Ronald Winnicott's concept of the "good-enough mother" provides a useful analogy for supervisors: that they should aspire to be "good-enough supervisors." By this, Hawkins and Shohet meant that the supervisor should be able to meet the trainee's needs, even in those times when the trainee is responding with wariness, avoidance, or even anger. Certainly, this concept of the "good-enough supervisor" logically extends the developmental metaphors that we have used in this chapter and throughout the book. However, it also suggests that the supervisor will have received adequate preparation for this role.

A final point is that to learn to be a supervisor can be very empowering to the person taking on this role. This is especially true of advanced students. They are affirmed that they really *do* have professional wisdom to pass on. Moreover, the very act of supervising can help SITs gain new perspectives on their work as therapists.

SUPERVISION PROCESS AND OUTCOME RESEARCH

We often hear of the singular breakthrough in science. But science more often is incremental and relies on the gradual accretion of new findings that will supplement and extend older ones. Paradigm shifts (cf. Kuhn, 1970) may refocus researchers' emphases and the concepts that they use, but do not alter the sometimes tedious, step-by-step process of science that occurs through ongoing research programs. When this characteristic of science is considered in the context of the brief history of supervision research, it really is remarkable that such a solid empirical foundation for supervision practice has already begun to develop.

Counseling and psychotherapy research have a relatively short history, dating only from approximately the end of World War II (Garfield, 1983). Supervision research has an even shorter history. It was only a couple of decades ago that Kell, Morse, and Grater (undated) asserted that "[t]he training of counselors and psychotherapists can perhaps be described by the old epigram, 'the blind leading the blind.' It is an attempt to teach, using methods about which we know practically nothing,

a process about which we know far too little." Harkness and Poertner (1989) reported that the first published study of social work supervision appeared in 1958. At about that time also, *Counselor Education and Supervision* was founded (1961) to provide a journal outlet for articles on counselor training and supervision (this journal, along with the *Journal of Counseling Psychology* and *Professional Psychology: Research and Practice,* is consistently among the several journals where supervision research is most likely to be found).

Many researchers have conducted an occasional study of supervision during the past several decades. A number have been doctoral students who focus their dissertations on a topic very central to their academic lives at the time that they are choosing a research topic. Perhaps only a score of researchers, though, are engaged in programmatic investigations of supervision. This seems generally consistent with Price's (1963) law, which is that

> If k is the number of persons active in a discipline, then the square root of this number approximates the size of that subset who produced half of the contributions. Thus, about 250 composers are responsible for the music played in the classical repertoire. The square root of this number is 15.8. It turns out that a mere 16 composers put their names on half of all the pieces performed and recorded. (Simonton, 1994)

But the cumulative effort both of this core group of supervision researchers and of those more occasional researchers has resulted in a healthy forward momentum to the science of supervision that Holloway and Hosford (1983) called for two decades ago. Moreover, as researchers develop instrumentation (e.g., Ellis et al., 1994; Ellis & Ladany, 1997; Friedlander & Ward, 1984; McNeill, Stoltenberg, & Romans, 1992; Watkins et al., 1995) and models (see Chapter 4) unique to supervision, this science increasingly is becoming independent of psychotherapy theory and research.

Some of this growing volume of research on supervision has been summarized in critiques and reviews. Ellis, Ladany, Krengel, and Schult (1996) noted that there had been at least 32 reviews of empirically based studies of supervision. Anyone seriously interested in conducting supervision research should begin by reading some of these available commentaries (e.g., Borders, 1989b; Ellis et al., 1996; Goodyear & Guzzard, 2000; Holloway, 1984, 1992; Holloway & Hosford, 1983; Lambert, 1980; Lambert & Arnold, 1987; Lambert & Ogles, 1997; Russell et al., 1984; Wampold & Holloway, 1997; Worthington, 1987).

In Chapter 1, we cited Schön's (1983) belief that professional training is a process of inculcating in trainees two distinct realms of knowledge: formal theories and observations that have been confirmed, or are confirmable, by research; and knowledge that has been accrued from the professional experience of practitioners. Because of our scientist–practitioner orientation, we have drawn from both realms in writing this book. We hope, then, that readers will have found at least some research questions to intrigue them as they read the first 11 chapters. In fact, our coverage of research at the end of this book reflects our hope that at this point readers will have been stimulated to think about which supervision-related questions still seem in need of empirical answers.

Research Strategies for a Science of Supervision

We anticipate that readers of this book will vary widely in their sophistication about research in general and supervision research specifically. Many will be graduate students who may be considering supervision as a thesis or dissertation topic. Others will be supervision practitioners whose interest is more focused on the implications of the research for their work as supervisors. We have written the following comments on supervision research methodology in a way that we hope is simultaneously accessible and useful to readers across a spectrum of research sophistication.

Perhaps we should begin this section, though, by asserting that all studies in the behavioral sciences have limitations. Gelso (1979) vividly captured this issue in his discussion of the "bubble hypothesis":

> *A few years ago, a graduate student in a seminar I teach on counseling and psychotherapy research . . . proposed that the conduct of science was analogous to the placement of a sticker on a car windshield. During the placement, a bubble would appear. The owner presses the bubble in an attempt to eliminate it, but it reappears in another place. The only way to get rid of it is to eliminate the entire sticker. The student termed this phenomenon the "bubble hypothesis" . . . the idea behind it is obvious, ubiquitous—and all too infrequently in the awareness of students and researchers.* (p. 12)

Thus, a researcher might employ a very rigorous design to achieve high internal validity, but at the expense of external validity (generalizability). To redesign the study to have greater external validity, the researcher likely would have to sacrifice internal validity. Gelso (1979) discussed this tension as one between *rigor* and *relevance*. There is no perfect study, though obviously studies can be characterized in terms of level of quality.

Two decades ago, Holloway and Hosford (1983) provided a useful conceptual model for understanding supervision research. It remains helpful. They asserted that, in accordance with the progressive nature of science, supervision research should proceed through three stages: (1) one of descriptive observation in which a phenomenon is observed in its natural environment, (2) one in which important, specific variables are identified and relationships between and among them are clarified, and (3) one in which a theory is developed based on the empirically derived evidence about variables and their interrelationships. This stage model provides a convenient framework for organizing the next two sections of the chapter.

Stage 1: Descriptive Research. No one methodological approach is uniquely suited for providing the descriptive data that characterize this stage of research. We believe, in fact, that it is essential to encourage methodological diversity. Invoking a metaphor to comment on this issue, Harmon

(1989) noted that when a car does not run the problem can be explained "by either a mechanic or a physicist without either of them necessarily understanding what the other was talking about. The point to be made here is that neither level of abstraction is wrong, it just depends on what your needs are" (p. 87).

With this metaphor in mind, we offer summaries of four research strategies that seem to have particular utility for describing supervision processes. Although all would be consistent with what Mahrer (1988) called a "discovery oriented" approach, they each give a somewhat different perspective of supervision. Each has potential to offer hypotheses to drive later research that is of a more experimental or quasi-experimental nature.

Qualitative Research.   Although qualitative research is regarded by many as unacceptably "soft," it has an increasing presence in the supervision literature. Goodyear and Guzzard (2000) noted that, whereas there had been virtually no qualitative research just a decade before, they had identified at least 10 studies that had some qualitative features (e.g., Caldwell, Becvar, Bertolino, & Diamond, 1997; Fukuyama, 1994; Mauzey & Erdman, 1997; Kleintjes & Swartz, 1996; Neufeldt et al., 1996; Skovholt & Rønnestad, 1992; Smith, Winton, & Yoshioka, 1992; Smith, Yoshioka, & Winton, 1993; Williams et al., 1997; Worthen & McNeill, 1996). Others have been published since the Goodyear and Guzzardo review, including those of Gray, Ladany, Walker, & Ancis (2001), Ladany et al., (2000), and Nelson & Friedlander (2001). Moreover, a quick review of PsychLit reveals that a number of recent, unpublished dissertation studies of supervision have employed a qualitative design.

Qualitative studies can provide a rich source of information about the subjective experiences of supervisors and supervisees. It usually is inappropriate to generalize from qualitative studies (because of nonrandom sampling and small numbers of participants). However, they can be important in suggesting hypotheses to be followed up in subsequent research. For example, Nelson and Friedlander's (2001) finding that supervisees who experienced conflictual supervision also experienced higher-than-usual levels of role conflict is one that easily can be followed up on in quantitative research.

Several computer programs have been developed to assist qualitative researchers to identify structure and meaning in text and narrative. One of the better known of these has the intriguing acronym NUDIST (Nonnumerical Unstructured Data Indexing Searching and Theorizing; e.g., see Gorely, Gordon, & Ford, 1994). New tools such as these seem to have much to offer supervision researchers, both to make their work easier and to demonstrate intercoder reliabilities in ways that previously were not possible. No supervision studies using this type of software have yet been reported.

Another prominent trend in counseling research is the standardization of qualitative methods in a way that reduces concerns about reliability. To this end, the consensual qualitative method of Hill, Thompson, and Williams (1997) seems to be gaining wide acceptance.

Case Study Research.   A case study is a useful vehicle to address the first, descriptive stage of science, for it provides "a holistic methodology for studying how multiple variables interact to affect the process and outcome of psychotherapy for an individual" (Hill, 1989, p. 17). Early case studies (e.g., Freud's cases of Dora and of Ratman), although perhaps clinically useful, were retrospective accounts by the therapist. For this reason and because there was no corroborating evidence, they inevitably were limited by the subjectivity and omissions of the person who recounted the case.

Doehrman's (1976) multiple-case study of parallel processes constituted a methodological improvement in supervision research. She employed structured interviews and an observer's perspective to gather and interpret data. Further rigor has been possible through innovations that Hill and her colleagues have made to case studies in counseling research (e.g., Hill, Carter, & O'Farrell, 1981). By employing multiple measures that include psychometric data, the evaluations of trained raters, and the observations of the involved parties, she brought rigor to the case study. This approach to case studies has much to offer supervision researchers and has been employed in several studies (e.g., Alpher, 1991; Friedlander et al., 1989; Martin et al., 1987; Strozier et al., 1993).

The videotape series that Goodyear (1982) developed has allowed for between-supervisor comparisons that actually are multiple-case studies (e.g., Abadie, 1985; Friedlander & Ward, 1984; Harris & Goodyear, 1990; Holloway et al., 1989). These have in common a focus on supervisor–supervisee interactions and also employ the interactional research strategy covered in the next section.

Interactional Research. Because supervision is largely a verbal endeavor, the verbal discourse between the supervisor and supervisee (and, perhaps, between the supervisee and client) is an important source of information. Studies of this nature have been conducted for some time (e.g., Dodenhoff, 1981; Lambert, 1974; Pierce & Schauble, 1970). The sophistication with which supervisor–supervisee interactions have been analyzed, however, has increased considerably during the past decade, largely through the research program of Holloway and her colleagues (e.g., Holloway, 1982; Nelson & Holloway, 1990). Tracey and Sherry (1993) are among others who have conducted interactional research in supervision.

Interactional research can provide important information about patterns of interaction that occur between supervisors and supervisees. One limitation, though, is that they are concerned with moment-to-moment interactions, and these patterns cannot easily be linked to other behaviors that occur at later points. Moreover, the use of interactional analyses in naturalistic settings results in correlational data that preclude the making of causal inferences. Despite these and other limitations, however, interactional research is a very promising way to begin addressing the descriptive stage of science. A useful overview of interactional research methods can be found in Lichtenberg and Heck (1986), Wampold (1986), and Claiborn and Lichtenberg (1989).

An Events Paradigm. Stiles, Shapiro, and Elliott (1986) suggested another research approach, the "events paradigm." Heppner and Claiborn (1989) summarize it as having three components:

> *first, the identification of a specific context for examining the process of interest . . . second, the manipulation of specific interventions to set the process in motion (such as different interpretation styles or levels of discrepancy); and, third, the measurement of effects (that is, attitude change in the direction of the interpretation). All of this can be done in a single session or series of sessions in ongoing counseling. The approach is based on the ideas that sessions themselves have outcomes and that the processes leading to them ought to be the focus of process research.* (p. 375)

In short, then, a specific behavior occurs within the session and it elicits a particular kind of response from the other person. Such a bracketed sequence of behavior constitutes an event. To the extent that predictability in this sequence can be observed across different sessions and across different participants, we have learned something new about supervision processes.

These, then, are four of the possible methods for conducting the descriptive research called for by Holloway and Hosford (1983) as stage 1 of their model. Methods used in their second stage are designed to examine relationships between and among supervision-related variables.

Stages 2 and 3: Hypothesis and Theory Building.
Descriptive research provides an important source of hypotheses that then might be tested. Particular methodological challenges must be met by supervision researchers who wish to undertake studies of the next type, that is, studies consistent with stages 2 or 3 of the Holloway and Hosford model. Eight of these challenges seem especially important.

Sample Sizes. The first issue is the practical one of obtaining a sufficient number of subjects to conduct supervision research. This is a greater difficulty in supervision research than it is in research on counseling or psychotherapy. Whereas clients, or at least people who might be reasonably construed as potential clients, are readily accessible, the same typically is not true of supervisors and/or supervisees. There are, though, several strategies that researchers might employ to address this problem.

First, researchers can extend the time of their project (e.g., in universities, data can be gathered across two or more semesters). This, of course, can be a substantial hurdle for the doctoral student who is eager to complete dissertation research and does not have the luxury of time.

Second, researchers can employ mailed surveys or questionnaires. The advent of the Internet and the availability of Web-distributed questionnaires have made it even easier to obtain national or even international samples with relatively little effort.

Although such studies have been the source of much of our empirical knowledge of supervision, they do not allow observation of actual supervision events. Also, return rates in typical studies of this sort pose interpretive problems. For example, if 40% of a sample does not respond to a survey, the investigator is left to speculate about the representativeness of the 60% who did return their materials. Did they, for example, return their materials because of a special investment in the issue being addressed (a type of investment that might bias results in particular ways)?

A third strategy is to design the study so that it is an analogue that does not employ actual supervisors or supervisees. An example of this is the study by Stone (1980), who used introductory psychology students as "inexperienced supervisors." Another is that of Hilton et al., (1995), who also used undergraduates as supervisees in their study of the effects of race on supervision. Studies of this sort may be of special value in the preliminary stages of investigations of previously unexamined phenomena. But they do have substantial limitations, as we discuss in a later section.

Cross-sectional versus Other Designs. Researchers, especially those interested in investigations of developmental models, should consider alternatives to cross-sectional designs (see Holloway, 1987). The use of the (too infrequent) longitudinal study (e.g., Hill, Charles, & Reed, 1981) adds an important dimension, though it too has its limitations, such as those associated with cohort effects. Ellis et al. (1988) recommended instead a sequential design that combines aspects of both cross-sectional and longitudinal designs.

Information about Raters. "When using raters and rating procedures, provide sufficient information about the raters and their training for the reader to evaluate the raters' qualifications, potential for biases (e.g., whether they are blind to experimental conditions), standardization of ratings, and how rating materials were assigned to raters" (Ellis, Ladang, Krengel, & Schult, 1988, p. 9). In fact, in their review of published studies, Goodyear, Ettelson, O'Neil, Sakai, and Smart (1996) found considerable variability in the extent and type of information that researchers provide about their coding procedures.

Demographics Report. "In case of nonrandomized studies, full reporting of participant demographics (e.g., age, sex, degree program) and other data germane to the study (e.g., amount of supervised counseling experience, theoretical orientation, types of clients seen) are needed to assess for differences among groups" (Ellis et al., 1988, p. 10).

Multiple Roles for Participants. "Avoid using participants in multiple roles (e.g., as both supervisor in one group and supervisee in another). If this is unavoidable, control for this confound methodologically and statistically" (Ellis et al., 1988, p. 11).

Clear Working Definitions. Basic to social science is that phenomena being investigated have well-accepted and clear operational definitions. However, a number of important concepts in supervision have proved difficult to operationalize, at least in a consistent way. The concept of parallel processes, for example, is intuitively compelling to practitioners, but has proved difficult to define clearly for research purposes.

Many possible examples of such supervision concepts have been difficult to operationalize. Two examples will suffice. The first of these is the notion of developmental level, which has been challenged on conceptual grounds (Holloway, 1987) and too often has been defined only in terms of the trainee's amount of experience or practicum level. Also, the concept of level of structure, which is central to many discussions of supervisory relationships and interventions, is another that is difficult to operationalize.

But, if a field is to advance, it is not sufficient that a researcher develop a clear working definition of a concept that only he or she uses. Other researchers must use the definition as well if we are to make sense of the aggregated findings from multiple studies that purport to measure the concept. One example of this issue is with the definition of interpersonal power, or relational control, which Lichtenberg and Wettersten (1996) showed to have been operationalized in multiple ways in counseling and supervision research. An inextricably related matter is that of the instruments used in supervision research. The particular measure used automatically becomes the de facto operational definition of the particular variable. Fortunately, as we discuss later in this chapter, supervision researchers have been giving increasing attention to instrument development.

Self-reports of Satisfaction. In her discussion of the future research agenda in supervision, Borders (1989a) called for a moratorium on the use of self-reports of supervisee satisfaction as an outcome measure. Satisfaction is imperfectly correlated with effectiveness. For example, during periods of confrontation by and conflict with the supervisor, the supervisee may find himself or herself very dissatisfied and even angry, even though the effects on his or her functioning as a therapist or practitioner may eventually be very positive.

We recently heard an analogy to illustrate the imperfect link between satisfaction and actual outcome. Consider persons who are just leaving a doughnut shop: If they were asked whether they liked the product and would return for more, they very likely would affirm that they would. This is very different, though, from evaluating the nutritional value of the doughnuts consumed. Yet, information about supervisee satisfaction does have value. Worthington (personal communication, 1990) made the point that satisfied supervisees might be expected to learn better than those who are dissatisfied. He argued that, as an alternative to imposing a moratorium on the use of satisfaction data, supervision researchers give more empirical attention to determining the actual link between supervisees' satisfaction and supervision outcome.

One alternative to satisfaction measures is to have the supervisee rate the quality of the supervision and the extent to which it met his or her expectations and needs. An example of this is the Supervision Questionnaire that Ladany et al. (1996) developed (see the Supervisor's Toolbox).

Analogue versus Real-life Studies. Analogue studies can provide high internal validity ("rigor" in Gelso's, 1979, discussion of rigor–relevance tensions). They can be of particular value in the first stages of attempting to extrapolate the implications of a particular theory (cf. Stone, 1984). Analogue designs can also be useful to safeguard clients or trainees when researchers are investigating phenomena that have the potential for harm. For example, one reasonable research question concerns the potential effects on clients of therapists' erotic disclosures to them (Goodyear & Shumate, 1996); whereas it might be possible to have potential clients give their perceptions of a tape depicting a therapist's erotic disclosure to a client, no responsible researcher actually would expose a real client to this as an experimental manipulation.

But useful as analogue studies can be, there comes a point in a program of counseling and supervision research when real-life situations must be employed. For example, the research on the social influence model (for recent discussions of its applications to supervision, see Dixon & Claiborn, 1987; Stoltenberg et al., 1995) has been based primarily on analogue research. In their review of this model, Heppner and Claiborn (1989) urged "researchers to move away from analogue methodologies . . . [it] seems absolutely essential that the social influence process be examined in realistic counseling situations" (p. 383).

We do not intend to suggest, though, an either–or, all-or-nothing situation with respect to analogue versus real-life studies. It is possible, in fact, to think of studies as varying in their degrees of "analogueness" or artificiality (Munley, 1974; Strong, 1971). Strong (1971) proposed useful criteria for gauging the degree of artificiality of a particular analogue study. Specifically, he suggested that researchers meet as many of five "boundary conditions" as possible in designing analogue research. These are that (1) counseling (and supervision) is a conversation between two or more people, (2) the interactants (supervisor and supervisee or supervisee and client) have clearly defined roles that constrain conversation, (3) supervision exists in varying (though usually extended) durations, (4) clients (and supervisees) are motivated to change, and (5) many clients are psychologically distressed and heavily invested in the behaviors that they wish to change (the parallel here to supervisees should be obvious).

Significantly, though, there has been an increasing recent focus on realistic field studies in supervision (cf., Ellis et al., 1996). The extra effort required to conduct experimental and quasi-experimental field research is well worth it in terms of its value to the field.

Efficacy Studies.   A great deal of attention currently is being given to evidence-based practice, both in medicine and psychotherapy. Efficacy studies are only one way to establish that a treatment has been empirically supported (see the excellent discussion and alternative suggestions of Wampold (2001) and of Wampold, Lichtenberg, & Waehler, 2002). Nevertheless, efficacy studies currently have broad acceptance as the standard for evidence-based practice, at least for psychological interventions. They stand in distinction from effectiveness studies, which are studies conducted in real-life settings of psychotherapy.

Psychotherapy efficacy studies are conducted with a treatment manual and "consist of a brief and

fixed duration of treatment, manualized treatment, a single simple disorder, and random assignment of clinic volunteers to type of treatment" (Seligman, 1998, p. 2). However, these several criteria have been difficult for supervision researchers to meet.

In Chapter 1, we distinguished between supervision and training. In the latter domain, a number of studies might be considered to have concerned efficacy (see, e.g., the studies reviewed by Baker, Daniels, & Greeley, 1990). That is, these studies test a particular training model (for example, IPR versus microcounselor skills training), are of a fixed duration, and employ a training protocol (i.e., a "manual"). But virtually no such studies exist in supervision. We believe there are several reasons for this.

1. Existing supervision models are limited in the extent to which they can be prescriptive. They tend, instead, to be based on relatively broad principles (e.g., developmental models specify that beginning supervisees will need more structure than their more advanced colleagues).

2. Supervision researchers have not had available manuals to guide their work. They have had only the Neufeldt, Iverson, and Juntunen (1995) manual, and even it was developed for training purposes, rather than to explicate a particular supervisory model (see Neufeldt, 1994). It is possible that supervision never will be manualized to any significant extent (Holloway, 1992).

3. Goodyear and Bernard (1998) also pointed out that it is difficult to design a supervision efficacy study that provides sufficient protection to clients. These studies require that a particular approach to supervision be compared to a no-treatment control group. In psychotherapy research, this means that clients assigned to a control group receive no active treatment. In most cases, this does not put clients at risk. But a no-treatment control group in supervision research would involve supervisees being unmonitored, which ultimately exposes their clients to unacceptable risk.

One reasonable alternative to using no-treatment control groups is to compare a new treatment with one that is known to be effective (see, e.g., Rothman & Michels, 1994). So far, however, there are no supervision models of established effectiveness that might be employed in such a manner.

Mediators and Moderators. Supervision can be conceptualized as having particular direct effects on supervisees. But supervision also can work through mediation or moderation of other factors (for excellent discussions of the distinctions between mediation and moderation, see Baron & Kenny, 1986, and Holmbeck, 1997).

Moderation is probably the more familiar concept to most researchers, even if the term itself is unfamiliar. "A moderator variable is one that affects the relationship between two variables, so that the nature of the impact of the predictor on the criterion varies according to the level or value of the moderator" (Holmbeck, 1997, p. 599). It speaks to interaction effects. Therefore, if a researcher were examining a particular impact of supervision and believed that it was moderated by supervisor sex, he or she would look for gender-by-intervention (supervision) interaction effects on outcomes (i.e., whether men and women differentially responded to supervision).

Mediators, though, are mechanisms through which an independent variable influences a particular dependent variable. For example, it might be possible to hypothesize that supervisees' level of anxiety mediates supervision's effects on supervisees' self-efficacy. This would mean that supervision could be understood to affect supervisee anxiety levels and that anxiety levels in turn affect self-efficacy.

Although they may not have used the term, supervision researchers have been conducting research with moderators for some time. But research on mediation of supervision-related variables upon one another has been virtually nonexistent. Noting this, both Goodyear and Guzzard (2000) and Wampold and Holloway (1997) have suggested its use in supervision research. A drawback, though, is that it often requires relatively large samples, especially if structural equation modeling (Hoyle, 1995) is employed for the analyses.

Mediational research has the potential to add substantially to our knowledge of supervision impacts. For example, we earlier noted that the effects of supervision on client outcomes have been poorly established. But one reasonable hypothesis is the mediational one suggested in Figure 12.2. The relationship between the first two variables is suggested by research of Patton and Kivlighan (1997), demonstrating that supervisory alliances affect the supervisees' working alliances with their clients. The relationship between the latter two variables is suggested by research (e.g., Horvath & Symonds, 1991; Orlinsky, Grawe, & Parks, 1994) demonstrating that client–therapist working alliances are associated with therapeutic outcomes. When these two strands of research are considered together, it therefore is very reasonable to hypothesize that trainees' working alliances mediate the relationship between supervision and client outcomes. This is but one example of mediational research. Studies of this type have the potential to substantially enrich our understanding of supervision's mechanisms of impact.

Criteria and Measures in Supervision Research

The previous section concerned some methodological issues in conducting supervision research. Two additional issues are essential to consider as well. The first concerns the criteria to employ in assessing supervision processes and, especially, outcomes. The second revisits the discussion we already have had about the need to operationalize variables in a satisfactory manner. In this case, though, our interest specifically is on the instruments available to supervision researchers.

FIGURE 12.2 One Illustrative Mediational Model of Supervision Effects

Choice of Variables and Criteria.   Gelso (1979) noted that the selection of appropriate criteria has been a problem for researchers since the beginning of psychology and especially so for counseling and psychotherapy researchers. Because of supervision's greater complexity, this problem becomes even more pronounced in that domain.

Gelso found promise in Strupp and Hadley's (1977) tripartite model of mental health whereby any assessment of therapy outcomes would include the perspectives of the *therapist, client,* and *society* (including people significant in the life of the client). Strupp and Hadley suggested eight different outcome combinations that might be judged from the three vantage points. "The critical point for the present discussion is these researchers' demonstration of a variety of ways in which outcome criteria can be conflicting when the three vantage points are combined (as they need to be)" (Gelso, 1979, p. 19). There are even more vantage points in supervision, though, for there are both more people involved and more contexts in which the evaluations might be conducted.

It is useful, then, to consider Holloway's (1984) suggested framework. Analogous to Strupp and Hadley (1977), she recommended that researchers employ multiple criteria that evolve from the perspectives of the supervisor, supervisee, client (or client system), and an external observer. Each of these might evaluate the supervisor, the supervisee, and the client in the contexts of either counseling or supervision. Table 12.2 depicts the 24 possible data points this would yield. As can be seen, six (shaded cells) make no conceptual sense to employ. Her suggested framework is of potential usefulness to researchers planning investigations of supervision and to those who attempt to make sense of this research.

In short, it is useful to obtain more than one perspective when assessing supervisors' effectiveness. For example, supervisors have an investment in perceiving positive change in their trainees. Supervisees, on the other hand, may make judgments of their satisfaction with supervision that are unrelated to their actual gains (e.g., a supervisor might have given feedback that was jarring to the supervisee, thereby causing a sense of dissatisfaction, but which resulted in substantial, positive change in the supervisee's functioning). To use both these perspectives, as well as others, yields richer possible understanding of the experience. Contradictions that emerge between and among various perspectives (e.g., supervisees' perceptions of support versus what actually seems to be offered) are important to know of and can suggest directions for additional, second-generation research.

TABLE 12.2   Summary of Holloway's (1984) Conceptual Model of Possible Measures of Supervision Outcome

Evaluator	EVALUATION CONTEXT: SUPERVISION INTERVIEW			EVALUATION CONTEXT: COUNSELING INTERVIEW		
	Person Evaluated			*Person Evaluated*		
	Supervisor	Supervisee	Client	Supervisor	Supervisee	Client
Supervisor	X	X		X	X	X
Supervisee	X	X		X	X	X
Client				X	X	X
Observer	X	X		X	X	X

Shaded areas indicate that these combinations would not be sensible to use in outcome research.

Client Outcome as a Criterion. As the foregoing has made clear, a number of criteria might be used to assess the success of supervision (Holloway, 1984; Lambert & Ogles, 1997; Russell et al., 1984). But the most rigorous and important of these reasonably is client outcome (Holloway & Neufeldt, 1995). Ellis and Ladany (1997) considered client outcome to be "the acid test of supervision" (p. 485).

Yet almost no such studies exist, and those that do do not permit definitive conclusions. Ellis and Ladany (1997) identified nine such studies published since 1981. However, they primarily focused on session impact, rather than on client symptom reduction or other treatment outcomes. Moreover, Ellis and Ladany (1997) concluded that methodological and other problems made it possible to draw "few justifiable conclusions" (p. 488).

It may be that mediational studies such as we discussed earlier will be the way to tackle this problem. In the meantime, studies establishing a causal link between supervision and client outcomes remain a challenge to supervision researchers.

Measures of Supervision Process and Outcome. Ellis et al. (1988) made a number of recommendations based on their review of 7 years (1981–1987) of published supervision research. One of these was "for psychometrically sound measures for supervision" (p. 9). Almost all instruments that have been used to assess supervision process and outcomes variables were originally developed for other purposes, such as psychotherapy or (occasionally) classroom instructional research. Lambert and Ogle's (1997) review of 50 different instruments that have been used in supervision research vividly illustrates the extent to which this is true.

When measures designed for counseling or instructional research have been used in supervision research, they have often been modified with minimal attention to possible changes in their meanings. One example of this has been the use of the Counselor Rating Form (CRF) in supervision research. Barak and LaCrosse (1975) designed the CRF to measure perceptions of counselors' expertness, attractiveness, and trustworthiness, but it has been used in supervision studies after simply substituting the word *supervision* or *supervisor* for *counseling* or *counselor* and retitling it the Supervision Rating Form.

There are at least two problems with this practice of adapting instruments from other domains for supervision research by simply changing some of the words. First, to tinker with an instrument through word changes, and so on, without then checking its psychometric properties results in an instrument that has been changed in unknown ways. Second, using such instruments can perpetuate the use of roles and metaphors from interventions *other* than supervision (e.g., therapy or teaching). Ellis et al. (1988) recommended that when using such measures the researcher should, at minimum, conduct a pilot study to examine the psychometric properties of the measure in the new setting and report internal consistency (e.g., Cronbach's alpha) based on the entire sample.

Importantly, though, there is a clear trend toward the development of instruments that are specifically for supervision and that have some established psychometric properties. We provide some of these with the authors' permission in the Supervisor's Toolbox at the end of this book.

We should note that we are not including here measures of the level and/or type of trainee performance, though some number are available to supervision researchers and practitioners. Some of these scales require third-party observers to rate individual trainee responses with respect to certain qualities such as empathy or other "facilitative conditions" (e.g., Carkhuff, 1969) or to categorize them as being of certain types (e.g., Hill, 1986). Still others have the supervisor rate the trainee's level of functioning (e.g., Jones, Krasner, & Howard, 1992; Robiner, Fuhrman, Ristvedt, Bobbi, & Schirvar, 1994). And some have been developed to assess very specific proficiencies. An example is LaFromboise, Coleman, and Hernandez's (1991) scale to assess trainees' cross-cultural competence.

We conclude this portion of the chapter with the following statement by Russell et al. (1984):

> [A]*s we see it, there have been four primary obstacles to progress in supervision research: (1) the failure of theory in most cases to offer clear-cut directions/or supervisory research, (2) the small sample sizes of trainees and supervisors available at most training sites, (3) the difficulty, in both pragmatic and ethical terms, of manipulating independent variables in real-life training settings, and (4) the "criterion problem," which includes such issues as how best to measure change, from whose perspective, and on what dimensions.* (pp. 667–668)

These observations remain relevant today. And equally relevant is their subsequent observation that these obstacles are not insurmountable.

CONCLUSION

Raimy (1950) once stated with some irony that "[p]sychotherapy is an undefined technique applied to unspecified problems with unpredictable outcomes. For this technique we recommend rigorous training" (p. 93). Fortunately, though, circumstances now are much different. We have a substantial empirical literature to undergird the practice of counseling and therapy, and the literature to undergird the "rigorous training" of which Raimy spoke is also evolving at a healthy rate.

The recent growth in the quantity and quality of supervision research is heartening to those concerned with improving the practice of supervision. But, though growing, the empirical foundation for supervisory practice is still relatively small. Moreover, it is also not uniform across the various supervision modalities and models. The body of research on family therapy training and supervision, for example, remains especially small. But this very unevenness in the literature is an opportunity for those interested in conducting supervision research. Because supervision is a young field, practitioners and researchers alike have much yet to learn. It is our hope that this book will play a small role in contributing to this discovery process.

In concluding this chapter, we also conclude the book. In doing this, we want to borrow from Keith et al., (1992), who ended their article by expressing the worry that they had not accomplished exactly what they set out to do. But they then invited readers to think of them as cooks who were offering elements of a recipe that other cooks might follow to produce a "uniquely flavored result" (p. 109). This useful metaphor characterizes our intentions as well. In this book, we have tried as best we could within space and other constraints to characterize the existing practical, theoretical, and empirical literature concerning supervision. Moreover, we have attempted to do so by drawing from the literature of the various mental health professions. We conclude, then, by expressing our hope that in reading this book you have found some essential recipe(s) that can help you to concoct your own, unique perspectives on the nature and practice of supervision.

THE SUPERVISOR'S TOOLBOX

This toolbox offers resources to support the research, practice, and teaching of supervision. Because space limits what we can offer here, we also are maintaining a related *Fundamentals of Clinical Supervision* Web site. It will complement this printed version of the Supervisor's Toolbox, links to supervision-related material from professional associations, and links to course syllabi and to sites devoted to supervision, as well as our updates and material. Please visit it at URL www.ablongman.com/bernard3e.

SUPERVISION TOOLBOX CONTENTS

Following are the contents of the Toolbox, listed in the order in which they appear.

Documents for Use in Supervision

- **Sample Counseling Supervision Contract.** Adapted from Osborn and Davis (1996).
- **Professional Disclosure Statement.**
- **Supervisee's Bill of Rights.** Giordano et al. (2000).
- **Supervision Agreement Based on the Supervisee's Bill of Rights.** Giordano et al. (2000).

Measures for Supervision Research and Practice

Measures of supervision impacts
- **Supervision Questionnaire.** A supervision outcome measure. From Ladany et al. (1996).
- **Group Supervision Scale.** A measure of group supervision effects, with three subscales: Group Safety, Skill Development and Case Conceptualization, and Group Management. From Arcinue (2002).

Measures of supervisee attributes and experiences
- **Supervisee Levels Questionnaire, Revised.** Based on the IDM model (Stoltenberg et al., 1998), this measures three supervisee attributes: Self and Other Awareness, Motivation, and Dependency–Autonomy. From McNeill et al. (1992).

Process measures
- **Supervisee Perceptions of Supervision.** Measures (1) Role ambiguity and (2) Role conflict. From Olk and Friedlander (1992).
- **Evaluation Process within Supervision Inventory.** Measures (1) Goal-setting and (2) Feedback. From Lehrman-Waterman and Ladany (2001).
- **Supervisory Working Alliance—Supervisor Form.** Measures (1) Rapport, (2) Client Focus, and (3) Identification. From Efstation et al. (1990).
- **Supervisory Working Alliance—Trainee Form.** Measures (1) Rapport and (2) Client Focus. From Efstation et al. (1990).
- **Working Alliance Inventory—Supervisor Form.** Measures (1) Tasks, (2) Goals, and (3) Bonds. Adapted from Horvath and Greenburg (1989).
- **Working Alliance Inventory—Supervisee Form.** Measures (1) Tasks, (2) Goals, and (3) Bonds. Adapted from Horvath and Greenburg (1989).

Measures of supervisor styles, efficacy, and competencies

- **Supervisory Styles Inventory.** Has one scale for each of three supervision styles: (1) Attractive, (2) Interpersonally Sensitive, and (3) Task Oriented. From Friedlander & Ward (1984).
- **Counselor Supervisor Self-efficacy Scale.** Assesses supervisors' self-efficacy in six domains: (1) Theories and Techniques, (2) Group Supervision, (3) Supervisory Ethics, (4) Self in Supervision, (5) Multicultural Competence, and (6) Knowledge of Legal Issues. From Barnes (2002).
- **Multicultural Supervision Competencies Questionnaire.** Assesses (1) Attitude and Beliefs, (2) Knowledge and Understanding, (3) Skills and Practices, and (4) Relationship. From Wong and Wong (1999).

Supervision Ethics Codes

- **The Approved Clinical Supervisor Code of Ethics, Center for Credentialing and Education, an affiliate of the National Board for Certified Counselors**
- **Ethical Guidelines for Counseling Supervisors, Association for Counselor Education and Supervision**

SAMPLE COUNSELING SUPERVISION CONTRACT*

This contract serves as verification and a description of the counseling supervision provided by Jane Doe, Ph.D., LMHC ("Supervisor"), to _____ ("Supervisee"), Counselor Trainee enrolled in Practicum in the Community Counseling Program at Exemplar University for _____ semester 20__. (For doctoral student supervisors, need to identify self as such, and need to mention name of practicum instructor as "Faculty Supervisor.")

I. *Purpose, Goals, and Objectives*
    a. Monitor and ensure welfare of clients seen by supervisee
    b. Promote development of supervisee's professional counselor identity and competence
    c. Fulfill academic requirement for supervisee's practicum
    d. Fulfill requirements in preparation for supervisee's pursuit of counselor licensure (when applicable)

II. *Context of Services*
    a. One (1) clock hour of individual supervision weekly
    b. Supervision will revolve around counseling conducted with _____ (population[s] to be served)
    c. Individual supervision will be conducted in Humdrum Hall, Exemplar University on _____ (day of week), from _____ to _____(time), where monitor/ VCR is available to review videotape
    d. The Discrimination Model, interpersonal process recall, progress notes, and tape review will be used in supervision

III. *Method of Evaluation*
    a. Feedback will be provided by the supervisor during each session, and a formal evaluation, using the program's standard evaluation of student clinical skills, will be conducted at mid-term and at the conclusion of the semester. A narrative evaluation will also be provided at mid-semester and at the conclusion of the semester as an addendum to the objective evaluations completed.
    b. Specific feedback provided by supervisor will focus on supervisee's demonstrated counseling skills and clinical documentation.
    c. Supervisee will evaluate supervisor at mid-semester and at the close of _____ semester, using the program's standard evaluation form for evaluating supervisors. A narrative evaluation will also accompany the objective evaluations.
    d. Supervision notes will be shared with supervisee at supervisor's discretion and at the request of the supervisee.

---

*Adapted from C. J. Osborn and T. E. Davis (1996). The supervision contract: Making it perfectly clear. *Clinical Supervisor, 14*(2), 121–134.

IV. *Duties and Responsibilities of Supervisor and Supervisee*
a. Supervisor
   a. Examine client presenting complaints and treatment plans
   b. View videotapes of supervisee's counseling sessions outside of regularly scheduled supervision sessions
   c. Sign off on all client documentation
   d. Challenge supervisee to justify approach and techniques used
   e. Monitor supervisee's basic attending skills
   f. Support supervisee's development as a counselor
   g. Present and model appropriate directives
   h. Intervene when client welfare is at risk
   i. Ensure that ethical guidelines are upheld
   j. Maintain weekly supervision case notes

b. Supervisee
   a. Uphold ethical guidelines
   b. View counseling session videotapes in preparation for weekly supervision
   c. Be prepared to discuss all client cases; have client files, current and completed client case notes, and counseling session videotapes ready to review in weekly supervision sessions
   d. Justify client case conceptualizations made and approach and techniques used
   e. Complete case notes and place in appropriate client files
   f. Consult with field placement staff and supervisor in cases of emergency
   g. Implement supervisory directives in subsequent sessions

V. *Procedural Considerations*
   a. Supervisee's written case notes, treatment plans, and videotapes will be reviewed and evaluated in each session.
   b. Issues related to supervisee's professional development will be discussed.
   c. Sessions will be used to discuss issues of conflict and failure of either party to abide by directives outlined here in contract. If concerns of either party are not resolved in supervision, _____ (practicum instructor of supervisee's practicum section), will be consulted.
   d. In event of emergency, Supervisee is to contact Supervisor at the office at (   ) _____ or at home, (   ) _____.

VI. *Supervisor's Scope of Competence*
Dr. Doe received her Ph.D. in counselor education, is a National Certified Counselor and is licensed in ___ as a Mental Health Counselor and Marriage and Family Therapist. She is a CCE Approved Clinical Supervisor and AAMFT Approved Supervisor. Dr. Doe is a Professor at Exemplar University and teaches clinical courses on a regular basis, as well as the doctoral level supervision course. She has written several articles in the areas of clinical supervision, children's adjustment to divorce, and eating disorders. Dr. Doe presently sits on the mental health counselor licensure board for the state of _____.

VII. *Terms of the Contract*

This contract is subject to revision at any time, upon the request of either the supervisor or supervisee. A formal review of the contract will be made at the mid-term of _____Semester 20__, and revisions will be made only with consent of supervisee and approval of the supervisor.

We agree, to the best of our ability, to uphold the directives specified in this supervision contract and to conduct our professional behavior according to the ethical principles of our professional association.

Supervisor: _____/ Date: _____

Supervisee: _____/ Date: _____

Community Counseling Program

522 Humdrum Hall

Exemplar University

This contract is effective from _____ (start date)

to _____ (finish date).

(Date of revision or termination)

_____

EXAMPLE
PROFESSIONAL DISCLOSURE STATEMENT
Prepared by Course Instructor for Practicum Supervision

As your Practicum instructor, I am responsible for the individual and group supervision you receive this semester. This statement is to be used in conjunction with your syllabus, which spells out all the requirements of Practicum. My purpose in presenting this to you is to acquaint you with some of my goals for supervision, to provide you with an overview of the supervision process, and to outline some of the conditions under which we both must operate.

Prior to addressing the points listed above, I'd like to review my qualifications for conducting supervision. (Includes degrees in counseling, licenses, and certifications.)

I have been engaged in clinical supervision for over (number) years, mostly through my department responsibilities at (name of university[ies]). (List areas of specialization that will inform and/or limit one's supervision. List other activity that qualifies one to supervise, e.g., publications in supervision, workshops conducted) I adhere to the (identify professional ethics adhered to) Code of Ethics (attach for supervisee) and to the (name relevant supervisor code of ethics and attach for supervisee).

Clinical supervision has two goals: the development of the counseling skills of the supervisee (counselor-in-training) and the protection of the client. These are always operating simultaneously when supervision is occurring. Most of the time, it will seem that primary attention is being paid to your developing skills. When this is so, it is because a judgment has been made that your client(s) is receiving adequate counseling services. When there is any question about the adequacy of the counseling that your client(s) is receiving, supervision will become more active and, perhaps, more intrusive.

You will work with two supervisors this semester. You will have weekly hour-long individual sessions with a doctoral student supervisor. This weekly session will occur at your mutual convenience. The individual supervisors receive weekly supervision-of-supervision by me. On occasion, I will observe your individual supervision sessions. All supervision sessions will be audiotapted or videotaped. The Practicum class (or group supervision) will be conducted by me and will be a weekly three-hour session. Group supervision allows you to learn from your peers as well as from your supervisors. Both individual and group supervision are explained in greater detail in your syllabus.

You are required to submit a *minimum* of one audiotaped counseling session per week to your individual supervisor. Additionally, you will be required to submit audiotapes as part of group supervision (on average, one every three weeks). You will also be required to submit case notes on all individual, family, and group counseling sessions that you conduct each week. It is your responsibility to turn in the required tapes and paperwork. It is my responsibility to coordinate your supervision from me, your individual supervisor, and, in some cases, your site supervisor. Your case notes and records of all individual supervision sessions will be maintained by the Department for seven years.

Your supervisors may draw from different supervision models. You can count on the following, however: You will be encouraged to consider your thoughts, your behaviors, and your feelings as you conduct counseling sessions. Your supervisors will draw from the roles of teacher, consultant, and counselor to assist you in doing this. The supervision you will be offered will be developmentally appropriate (that is, the supervision will be matched to your level of experience and your relative ability). The supervision you receive will include discussions about cultural context, your own, the supervisor's, and the client's, and how these affect the counseling and supervision relationships of which you are a part. The supervision you receive will be sensitive to your personal goals for yourself as a counselor and will be consistent with how you conceptualize client issues theoretically. You will be challenged and supported throughout supervision. You will be treated with respect.

Although one of your supervisors may draw on a counselor role, it is important for you to understand that this is only to help you understand any personal reactions you may be having that are diminishing your positive effect as a counselor. The resolution of personal difficulties cannot be attained through supervision. A referral list of counseling services is available in campus publications and can also be obtained through any Department faculty member. It is not unusual for a student to seek personal counseling while working toward a counseling degree.

You will receive a copy of the Evaluation of Counselor Behaviors form on the first day of class. This will be used by me and by your individual supervisor throughout the semester to track your progress and to give you specific, formative feedback. You will receive two formal feedback sessions, one slightly before the mid-point of the semester and one at the end. At this time, you will receive written feedback. If I have any serious concerns about your progress in practicum, I will inform you of these concerns as soon as possible, preferably at the first formal feedback session.

Because you are a student in a counselor training program, I cannot guarantee confidentiality of information gained in supervision **if** it is relevant to your overall progress in the program. I can, however, commit to honoring and respecting all information I receive in supervision about you and/or your clients and keeping all such information confidential to the degree possible. Occasionally, there are situations that occur that make confidentiality impossible. These include: 1. Threats to harm self or others; 2. Reasonable suspicion of abuse of a child or other vulnerable person; 3. When ordered by the court. Confidentiality may also be broken in one's defense against a legal action before a court.

Please feel free to call me at home **whenever you have any concern about a client** for the duration of the practicum. My home number is _____. For regular communications, please call me at the office (_____) or e-mail me at _____. In case of emergency when I am out of town, you will be advised regarding who is the most appropriate contact person in my absence.

Although it is rare, occasionally a student does not feel that he or she has received adequate supervision or a fair evaluation. If this should occur, your first step is to attempt to resolve the issue with me. If you remain dissatisfied, this course is protected by the same appeal procedure as any other course as is outlined in Department materials and the SOE catalogue. If you believe I have acted unethically in any way, you may report your complaint to:

(National certifying body, state regulatory board or professional association with phone number of ethics officer)

Although the many parameters of the Practicum course listed in this document may make the experience sound tedious or intimidating, I assure you that on the contrary this is a most exciting time in your development as a professional counselor. I look forward to working with you and to celebrating your progress as your take the next step in your goal of entering a noble profession.

Please sign, date, and return one copy of this form.

_____   _____
Supervisor Signature   Student Signature

DATE: _____   DATE: _____

SUPERVISEE'S BILL OF RIGHTS*

Introduction

The purpose of the Bill of Rights is to inform supervisees of their rights and responsibilities in the supervisory process.

Nature of the Supervisory Relationship

The supervisory relationship is an experiential learning process that assists the supervisee in developing therapeutic and professional competence. A professional counselor supervisor who has received specific training in supervision facilitates professional growth of the supervisee through:

Monitoring client welfare
Encouraging compliance with legal, ethical, and professional standards
Teaching therapeutic skills
Providing regular feedback and evaluation
Providing professional experiences and opportunities

Expectations of the Initial Supervisory Session

The supervisee has the right to be informed of the supervisor's expectations of the supervisory relationship. The supervisor shall clearly state expectations of the supervisory relationship that may include:

Supervisee identification of supervision goals for oneself
Supervisee preparedness for supervisory meetings
Supervisee determination of areas for professional growth and development
Supervisor's expectations regarding formal and informal evaluations
Supervisor's expectations of the supervisee's need to provide formal and informal self-evaluations
Supervisor's expectations regarding the structure and/or the nature of the supervisory sessions
Weekly review of case notes until supervisee demonstrates competency in case conceptualization

The supervisee shall provide input to the supervisor regarding the supervisee's expectations of the relationship.

Expectations of the Supervisory Relationship

A supervisor is a professional counselor with appropriate credentials. The supervisee can expect the supervisor to serve as a mentor and a positive role model who assists the supervisee in developing a professional identity.

The supervisee has the right to work with a supervisor who is culturally sensitive and is able to openly discuss the influence of race, ethnicity, gender, sexual orientation, religion,

*Maria A. Giordano, Michael K. Altekruse, & Carolyn W. Kern (2000). Reprinted by permission of authors.

and class on the counseling and the supervision process. The supervisor is aware of personal cultural assumptions and constructs and is able to assist the supervisee in developing additional knowledge and skills in working with clients from diverse cultures.

Since a positive rapport between the supervisor and supervisee is critical for successful supervision to occur, the relationship is a priority for both the supervisor and supervisee. In the event that relationship concerns exist, the supervisor or supervisee will discuss concerns with one another and work toward resolving differences.

Therapeutic interventions initiated by the supervisor or solicited by the supervisee shall be implemented only in the service of helping the supervisee increase effectiveness with clients. A proper referral for counseling shall be made if appropriate.

The supervisor shall inform the supervisee of an alternative supervisor who will be available in case of crisis situations or known absences.

Ethics and Issues in the Supervisory Relationship

1. **Code of Ethics and Standards of Practice:** The supervisor will ensure the supervisee understands the *American Counseling Association Code of Ethics and Standards of Practice* and legal responsibilities. The supervisor and supervisee will discuss sections applicable to the beginning counselor.
2. **Dual Relationships:** Since a power differential exists in the supervisory relationship, the supervisor shall not utilize this differential to her or his gain. Since dual relationships may affect the objectivity of the supervisor, the supervisee shall not be asked to engage in social interaction that would compromise the professional nature of the supervisory relationship.
3. **Due Process:** During the initial meeting, supervisors provide the supervisee information regarding expectations, goals and roles of the supervisory process. The supervisee has the right to regular verbal feedback and periodic formal written feedback signed by both individuals.
4. **Evaluation:** During the initial supervisory session, the supervisor provides the supervisee a copy of the evaluation instrument used to assess the counselor's progress.
5. **Informed Consent:** The supervisee informs the client that she is in training and is being supervised, and she receives written permission from the client to audiotape or videotape.
6. **Confidentiality:** The counseling relationship, assessments, records, and correspondences remain confidential. Failure to keep information confidential is a violation of the ethical code and the counselor is subject to a malpractice suit. The client must sign a written consent prior to counselor's consultation.
7. **Vicarious Liability:** The supervisor is ultimately liable for the welfare of the supervisee's clients. The supervisee is expected to discuss with the supervisor the counseling process and individual concerns of each client.
8. **Isolation:** The supervisor consults with peers regarding supervisory concerns and issues.
9. **Termination of Supervision:** The supervisor discusses termination of the supervisory relationship and helps the supervisee identify areas for continued growth and explore professional goals.

Expectations of the Supervisory Process

The supervisee shall be encouraged to determine a theoretical orientation that can be used for conceptualizing and guiding work with clients.

The supervisee has the right to work with a supervisor who is responsive to the supervisee's theoretical orientation, learning style, and developmental needs.

Since it is probable that the supervisor's theory of counseling will influence the supervision process, the supervisee needs to be informed of the supervisor's counseling theory and how the supervisor's theoretical orientation may influence the supervision process.

Expectations of Supervisory Sessions

The weekly supervisory session shall include a review of all cases, audiotapes, and videotapes and may include live supervision.

The supervisee is expected to meet with the supervisor face-to-face in a professional environment that ensures confidentiality.

Expectations of the Evaluation Process

During the initial meeting, the supervisee shall be provided with a copy of the formal evaluation tool(s) that will be used by the supervisor.

The supervisee shall receive verbal feedback and/or informal evaluation during each supervisory session.

The supervisee shall receive written feedback or written evaluation on a regular basis during beginning phases of counselor development. Written feedback may be requested by the supervisee during intermediate and advanced phases of counselor development.

The supervisee should be recommended for remedial assistance in a timely manner if the supervisor becomes aware of personal or professional limitations that may impede future professional performance.

Beginning counselors receive written and verbal summative evaluation during the last supervisory meeting. Intermediate and advanced counselors may receive a recommendation for licensure and/or certification.

References

American Association for Counselor Education & Supervision. (1995). Ethical guidelines for counseling supervisors. *Counselor Education & Supervision, 34,* 270–276.

American Counseling Association. (1997). *Code of Ethics and Standards of Practice.* American Counseling Association: Alexandria, VA.

Bernard, J. M., & Goodyear, R. K. (1998). *Fundamentals of clinical supervision.* (2nd ed.). Boston: Allyn and Bacon.

Borders, L. D., & Leddick, G. R. (1987). *Handbook of counseling supervision.* Alexandria, VA: Association for Counselor Education and Supervision.

Rønnestad, M. H., & Skovholt, T. M. (1993). Supervision of beginning and advanced graduate students of counseling and psychotherapy. *Journal of Counseling and Development, 71,* 396–405.

Supervision Interest Network, Association for Counselor Education and Supervision (Summer, 1993). ACES ethical guidelines for counseling supervisors. *ACES Spectrum, 5*(4), 5–8.

SUPERVISION AGREEMENT:
Based on the Supervisee's Bill of Rights

The supervisory relationship is an experiential learning process that assists the supervisee in developing therapeutic and professional competence. This contract is designed to assist the supervisor and supervisee in establishing clear expectations about the supervisory process.

Supervisee

Read the *Supervisee's Bill of Rights* and this agreement. Complete the sections on skills, goals, and professional opportunities and bring this agreement to the initial supervisory session.

Prior to the first supervisory session, read the American Counseling Association *Code of Ethics and Standards of Practice.*

Introduction and Expectations of the Supervisory Experience

Supervisor

1. Introduce yourself; discuss your credentials, licenses, academic background, counseling experience, and your supervisory style.
2. Describe your role as a supervisor: teacher, consultant, counselor, evaluator.
3. Discuss your responsibilities: monitoring client welfare, teaching therapeutic skills, providing regular verbal and written feedback and evaluation, and ensuring compliance with legal, ethical, and professional standards.
4. Ask the supervisee about his or her learning style and developmental needs.

Supervisee

1. Introduce yourself and describe your academic background, clinical experience, and training.
2. Briefly discuss information you want to address during the supervisory meetings.
3. Describe the therapeutic skills you want to enhance and professional development opportunities you want to experience during the next three months.

List three therapeutic skills you would like to further develop.

1. _____
2. _____
3. _____

List three general goals you would like to attain during the supervisory process.

1. _____
2. _____
3. _____

List three specific counseling or professional development experiences you would like to have during the next three months. (Attending a conference, facilitating a group, presentation, etc.)

1. _____
2. _____
3. _____

Expectations of the Supervisory Relationship

Supervisor and Supervisee

1. Discuss your expectations of the supervisory relationship.
2. Discuss how you will work toward establishing a positive and productive supervisory relationship. Also, discuss how you will address and resolve conflicts.
3. The supervisory experience will increase the supervisee's awareness of feelings, thoughts, behavior, and aspects of self that are stimulated by the client. Discuss the role of the supervisor in assisting with this process.
4. Share your thoughts with one another about the influence of race, ethnicity, gender, sexual orientation, religion, and class on the counseling and the supervision process.

Supervisee

1. Describe how you would like to increase your awareness of personal cultural assumptions, constructs, and ability to work with clients from diverse cultures.

Supervisor

1. If the supervisee needs to consult with you prior to the next supervision session, discuss how you would like to be contacted. Also, if you are unavailable during a period of time, inform the supervisee of an alternate supervisor who will be available in your absence.

ETHICS AND ISSUES IN THE SUPERVISORY RELATIONSHIP

1. Discuss the *Code of Ethics and Standards of Practice*. Review key issues not listed in this section.
2. A professional relationship is maintained between the supervisor and supervisee. The supervisor and supervisee do not engage in social interaction that interferes with objectivity and professional judgment of the supervisor.
3. After the initial supervisory meeting, the supervisee and supervisor can reestablish goals and expectations and discuss roles of the supervisory process. The supervisor and supervisee provide one another with regular feedback.
4. During the initial counseling session, the supervisee will inform the client that she or he is in training and is being supervised. If the supervisee wishes to audiotape or videotape, the client needs to give written consent.
5. Discuss confidentiality and the importance of obtaining a written release from the client prior to consultation with other professionals who are serving the client.
6. The supervisor is ultimately responsible for the welfare of the supervisee's clients. During each supervisory session, the supervisee will review each client's progress and relate specific concerns to the supervisor in a timely manner.

Expectations of the Supervisory Process

Supervisor

1. Describe your theory of counseling and how it influences your counseling and supervision style.
2. Discuss your theory or model of supervision.

Supervisee

1. Discuss your learning style and your developmental needs.
2. Discuss your current ideas about your theoretical orientation.

Expectations of Supervisory Sessions

Supervisee

Discuss your expectations about the learning process and interest in reviewing audiotapes, videotapes, and case notes.

Supervisor

Describe the structure and content of the weekly supervisory sessions.

Discuss your expectations regarding supervisee preparedness for supervisory sessions (audiotapes, videotapes, case notes).

CACREP standards require students in their internship experience to receive a minimum one hour of individual supervision per week and ninety minutes of group supervision each week.

The weekly supervisory session will take place face to face in a professional environment that ensures confidentiality. Decide on the location, day, and time.

Location _____ Day _____ Time _____

Expectations Regarding Evaluation

Supervisee: Discuss your interest in receiving weekly feedback in areas such as relationship building, counseling techniques, client conceptualization, and assessment.

Supervisor: Discuss your style of providing verbal feedback and evaluation.

Provide the supervisee with a copy of the formal evaluation you will use; discuss the evaluation tools and clarify specific items that need additional explanation.

Discuss the benefit of self-evaluation; provide a copy of self-evaluation forms, and clarify specific items that need additional explanation.

_____   _____
Supervisor's Signature   Date

_____   _____
Supervisor's Signature   Date

SUPERVISION QUESTIONNAIRE*

1. How would you rate the quality of the supervision you have received?

1	2	3	4
Excellent	Good	Fair	Poor

2. Did you get the kind of supervision you wanted?

1	2	3	4
No, definitely not	No, not really	Yes, generally	Yes, definitely

3. To what extent has this supervision fit your needs?

4	3	2	1
Almost all my needs have been met	Most of my needs have been met	Only a few of my needs have been met	None of my needs have been met

4. If a friend were in need of supervision, would you recommend this supervisor to him or her?

1	2	3	4
No, definitely not	No, I don't think so	Yes, I think so	Yes, definitely

5. How satisfied are you with the amount of supervision you have received?

1	2	3	4
Quite satisfied	Indifferent or mildly dissatisfied	Mostly satisfied	Very satisfied

6. Has the supervision you received helped you to deal more effectively in your role as a counselor or therapist?

4	3	2	1
Yes, definitely	Yes, generally	No, not really	No, definitely

7. In an overall, general sense, how satisfied are you with the supervision you have received?

4	3	2	1
Very satisfied	Mostly satisfied	Indifferent or mildly dissatisfied	Quite dissatisfied

8. If you were to seek supervision again, would you come back to this supervisor?

1	2	3	4
No, definitely not	No, I don't think so	Yes, I think so	Yes, definitely

*The score is the sum of the items.

Developed by N. Ladany, C. E. Hill, & E. A. Nutt (1996). Unpublished instrument. Reprinted by permission of authors.

GROUP SUPERVISION SCALE

For each of the following items, circle the number that best describes your experience with your group supervisor. Use a five-point scale where 1 = *strongly disagree* and 5 = *strongly agree.*

1. The supervisor provides useful feedback regarding my skills and interventions.   1 2 3 4 5

2. The supervisor provides helpful suggestions and information related to client treatment.   1 2 3 4 5

3. The supervisor facilitates constructive exploration of ideas and techniques for working with clients.   1 2 3 4 5

4. The supervisor provides helpful information regarding case conceptualization and diagnosis.   1 2 3 4 5

5. The supervisor helps me to comprehend and formulate clients' central issues.   1 2 3 4 5

6. The supervisor helps me to understand the thoughts, feelings, and behaviors of my clients.   1 2 3 4 5

7. The supervisor encourages trainee self-exploration appropriately.   1 2 3 4 5

8. The supervisor enables me to express opinions, questions, and concerns about my counseling.   1 2 3 4 5

9. The supervisor created a safe environment for group supervision.   1 2 3 4 5

10. The supervisor is attentive to group dynamics.   1 2 3 4 5

11. The supervisor effectively sets limits and establishes norms and boundaries for the group.   1 2 3 4 5

12. The supervisor provides helpful leadership for the group.   1 2 3 4 5

13. The supervisor encourages supervisees to provide each other feedback.   1 2 3 4 5

14. The supervisor redirects the discussion when appropriate.   1 2 3 4 5

15. The supervisor manages time well among all the group members.   1 2 3 4 5

16. The supervisor provides enough structure in the group supervision.   1 2 3 4 5

Scoring: *Group Safety Scale:*   Sum items 7 through 10 and 13; divide by 5.

Skill Development and Case Conceptualization Scale: Sum items 1 through 6; divide by 6.

Group Management Scale: Sum items 11, 12, 15, and 16; divide by 4.

Developed by F. Arcinue (2002). Unpublished instrument. Reprinted by permission of author.

SUPERVISEE LEVELS QUESTIONNAIRE—REVISED

Answer the items that follow in terms of your own *current* behavior. In responding to these items, use the following scale:

			Half		Most of	
Never	Rarely	Sometimes	the Time	Often	the Time	Always
1	2	3	4	5	6	7

1. I feel genuinely relaxed and comfortable in my counseling/therapy sessions.

   1   2   3   4   5   6   7

2. I am able to critique counseling tapes and gain insights with minimum help from my supervisor.

   1   2   3   4   5   6   7

3. I am able to be spontaneous in counseling/therapy, yet my behavior is relevant.

   1   2   3   4   5   6   7

4. I lack self-confidence in establishing counseling relationships with diverse client types.

   1   2   3   4   5   6   7

5. I am able to apply a consistent personalized rationale of human behavior in working with my clients.

   1   2   3   4   5   6   7

6. I tend to get confused when things don't go according to plan and lack confidence in the ability to handle the unexpected.

   1   2   3   4   5   6   7

7. The overall quality of my work fluctuates; on some days I do well, on other days I do poorly.

   1   2   3   4   5   6   7

8. I depend on my supervision considerably in figuring out how to deal with my clients.

   1   2   3   4   5   6   7

9. I feel comfortable confronting my clients.

   1   2   3   4   5   6   7

10. Much of the time in counseling/therapy I find myself thinking about my next response instead of fitting my intervention into the overall picture.

    1   2   3   4   5   6   7

11. My motivation fluctuates from day to day.

    1   2   3   4   5   6   7

12. At times, I wish my supervisor could be in the counseling/therapy session to lend a hand.

    1   2   3   4   5   6   7

13. During counseling/therapy sessions, I find it difficult to concentrate because of my concern about my own performance.

    1   2   3   4   5   6   7

14. Although at times I really want advice/feedback from my supervisor, at *other* times I really want to do things my own way.

    1   2   3   4   5   6   7

15. Sometimes the client's situation seems so hopeless. I just don't know what to do.

    1   2   3   4   5   6   7

16. It is important that my supervisor allow me to make my own mistakes.

    1   2   3   4   5   6   7

17. Given my current state of professional development, I believe I know when I need consultation from my supervisor and when I don't.

    1   2   3   4   5   6   7

18. Sometimes I question how suited I am to be a counselor/therapist.

    1   2   3   4   5   6   7

19. Regarding counseling/therapy, I view my supervisor as a teacher/mentor.

    1   2   3   4   5   6   7

20. Sometimes I feel that counseling/therapy is so complex that I never will be able to learn it all.

    1   2   3   4   5   6   7

21. I believe I know my strengths and weaknesses as a counselor sufficiently well to understand my professional potential and limitations.

    1   2   3   4   5   6   7

22. Regarding my counseling/therapy, I view my supervisor as a peer/colleague.

    1   2   3   4   5   6   7

23. I think I know myself well and am able to integrate that into my therapeutic style.

    1   2   3   4   5   6   7

24. I find I am able to understand my clients' view of the world, yet help them to objectively evaluate alternatives.

    1   2   3   4   5   6   7

25. At my current level of professional development, my confidence in my abilities is such that my desire to do counseling/therapy doesn't change much from day to day.

    1   2   3   4   5   6   7

26. I find I am able to empathize with my clients feeling states, but still help them focus on problem resolution.

    1   2   3   4   5   6   7

27. I am able to adequately assess my interpersonal impact on clients and use that knowledge therapeutically.

    1   2   3   4   5   6   7

28. I am adequately able to assess the client's interpersonal impact on me and use that therapeutically.

    1   2   3   4   5   6   7

29. I believe I exhibit a consistent professional objectivity and ability to work within my role as a counselor without *undue overinvolvement* with my clients.

    1   2   3   4   5   6   7

30. I believe I exhibit a consistent professional objectivity and ability to work within my role as a counselor without *excessive distance* from my clients.

    1   2   3   4   5   6   7

Scoring key: *Self and Other Awareness Items:*
              1, 3, 5, 9, 10*, 13*, 24, 26, 27, 28, 29, 30

Motivation Items: 7, 11*, 15*, 18*, 20*, 21, 23, 25

Dependency–Autonomy Items: 2, 4*, 6*, 8, 12*, 14, 16, 17, 19*, 22

*Indicates reverse scoring. To score, sum the items in the scale and then divide by the number of items.

Developed by C. Stoltenberg. Unpublished version of Supervisee Levels Questionnaire—Revised. Reprinted by permission of author.

SUPERVISEE PERCEPTIONS OF SUPERVISION

Instructions: The following statements describe some problems that therapists-in-training may experience during the course of clinical supervision. Read each statement and then rate the extent to which you have experienced difficulty in supervision in your most recent clinical training.

For each of the following, circle the most appropriate number, where 1 = *not at all* and 5 = *very much so.*

I HAVE EXPERIENCED DIFFICULTY IN MY CURRENT OR
MOST RECENT SUPERVISION BECAUSE:

1. I was not certain about what material to present to my supervisor.   1 2 3 4 5

2. I have felt that my supervisor was incompetent or less competent than I. I often felt as though I was supervising him/her.   1 2 3 4 5

3. I have wanted to challenge the appropriateness of my supervisor's recommendations for using a technique with one of my clients, but I have thought it better to keep my opinions to myself.   1 2 3 4 5

4. I wasn't sure how best to use supervision as I became more experienced, although I was aware that I was undecided about whether to confront her/him.   1 2 3 4 5

5. I have believed that my supervisor's behavior in one or more situations was unethical or illegal and I was undecided about whether to confront him/her.   1 2 3 4 5

6. My orientation to therapy was different from that of my supervisor. She or he wanted me to work with clients using her or his framework, and I felt that I should be allowed to use my own approach.   1 2 3 4 5

7. I have wanted to intervene with one of my clients in a particular way and my supervisor has wanted me to approach the client in a very different way. I am expected both to judge what is appropriate for myself and also to do what I am told.   1 2 3 4 5

8. My supervisor expected me to come prepared for supervision, but I had no idea what or how to prepare.   1 2 3 4 5

9. I wasn't sure how autonomous I should be in my work with clients.   1 2 3 4 5

10. My supervisor told me to do something I perceived to be illegal or unethical and I was expected to comply.   1 2 3 4 5

11. My supervisor's criteria for evaluating my work were not specific.   1 2 3 4 5

12. I was not sure that I had done what the supervisor expected me to do in a session with a client.   1 2 3 4 5

13. The criteria for evaluating my performance in supervision were not clear.   1   2   3   4   5

14. I got mixed signals from my supervisor and I was unsure of which signals to attend to.   1   2   3   4   5

15. When using a new technique, I was unclear about the specific steps involved. As a result, I wasn't sure how my supervisor would evaluate my work.   1   2   3   4   5

16. I disagreed with my supervisor about how to introduce a specific issue to a client, but I also wanted to do what the supervisor recommended.   1   2   3   4   5

17. Part of me wanted to rely on my own instincts with clients, but I always knew that my supervisor would have the last word.   1   2   3   4   5

18. The feedback I got from my supervisor did not help me to know what was expected of me in my day-to-day work with clients.   1   2   3   4   5

19. I was not comfortable using a technique recommended by my supervisor; however, I felt that I should do what my supervisor recommended.   1   2   3   4   5

20. Everything was new and I wasn't sure what would be expected of me.   1   2   3   4   5

21. I was not sure if I should discuss my professional weaknesses in supervision because I was not sure how I would be evaluated.   1   2   3   4   5

22. I disagreed with my supervisor about implementing a specific technique, but I also wanted to do what the supervisor thought best.   1   2   3   4   5

23. My supervisor gave me no feedback and I felt lost.   1   2   3   4   5

24. My supervisor told me what to do with a client, but didn't give me very specific ideas about how to do it.   1   2   3   4   5

25. My supervisor wanted me to use an assessment technique that I considered inappropriate for a particular client.   1   2   3   4   5

26. There were no clear guidelines for my behavior in supervision.   1   2   3   4   5

27. The supervisor gave no constructive or negative feedback and, as a result, I did not know how to address my weaknesses.   1   2   3   4   5

28. I didn't know how I was doing as a therapist, and as a result, I didn't know how my supervisor would evaluate me.   1   2   3   4   5

29. I was unsure of what to expect from my supervisor.   1   2   3   4   5

Scoring key: *Role Ambiguity Items:*
1, 4, 8, 9, 11, 12, 13, 18, 20, 21, 23, 24, 26, 27, 28, 29

Role Conflict Items: 2, 3, 5, 6, 7, 10, 14, 15, 16, 17, 19, 22, 25

From M. Olk & M. L. Friedlander (1992). Trainees' experiences of role conflict and role ambiguity in supervisory relationships. *Journal of Counseling Psychology, 39,* 389–397. Copyright © 1992 by the American Psychological Association. Reprinted with permission.

EVALUATION PROCESS WITHIN SUPERVISION INVENTORY

Indicate the extent to which you agree or disagree with each of the following statements. For each, circle the appropriate number on a 7-point scale, where 1 = *strongly disagree* and 7 = *strongly agree.*

1. The goals that my supervisor and I generated generated for my training seem important. 1 2 3 4 5 6 7

2. My supervisor and I created goals that were easy for me to understand. 1 2 3 4 5 6 7

3. The objectives that my supervisor and I created were specific. 1 2 3 4 5 6 7

4. My supervisor and I created goals that were realistic. 1 2 3 4 5 6 7

5. I think my supervisor would have been against my reshaping/changing my learning objectives over the course of our work together. 1 2 3 4 5 6 7

6. My supervisor and I created goals that seemed too easy for me. 1 2 3 4 5 6 7

7. My supervisor and I created objectives which were measurable. 1 2 3 4 5 6 7

8. I felt uncertain as to what my most important goals were for this training experience. 1 2 3 4 5 6 7

9. My training objectives were established early in our relationship. 1 2 3 4 5 6 7

10. My supervisor and I never had a discussion about my objectives for my training experience. 1 2 3 4 5 6 7

11. My supervisor told me what he/she wanted me to learn from the experience without inquiring about what I hoped to learn. 1 2 3 4 5 6 7

12. Some of the goals that my supervisor and I established were not practical in light of the resources available at my site (e.g., requiring videotaping and not providing equipment). 1 2 3 4 5 6 7

13. My supervisor and I set objectives that seemed practical given the opportunities available at my site (e.g., if career counseling skills was a goal, I was able to work with people with career concerns). 1 2 3 4 5 6 7

14. My supervisor welcomed comments about his or her style as a supervisor. 1 2 3 4 5 6 7

15. The appraisal I received from my supervisor seemed impartial. 1 2 3 4 5 6 7

16. My supervisor's comments about my work were understandable. 1 2 3 4 5 6 7

17. I didn't receive information about how I was doing as a counselor until late in the semester. 1 2 3 4 5 · 6 7

18. I had a summative, formal evaluation of my work at the end of the semester. 1 2 3 4 5 6 7

19. My supervisor balanced his or her feedback between positive and negative statements. 1 2 3 4 5 6 7

20. The feedback that I received from my supervisor was based on his or her direct observation of my work. 1 2 3 4 5 6 7

21. The feedback that I received was directly related to the goals we established. 1 2 3 4 5 6 7

Scoring: First, reverse score the following items: 5, 6, 8, 10, 11, 12, and 17.

Goal Setting: Sum of items 1 through 13.

Feedback: Sum of items 14 through 21.

From D. Lehrman-Waterman, & N. Ladany (2001). Development and validation of the evaluation process within supervision inventory. *Journal of Counseling Psychology, 48,* 168–177. Copyright © 2001 by the American Psychological Association. Reprinted with permission.

SUPERVISORY WORKING ALLIANCE INVENTORY: SUPERVISOR FORM INSTRUCTIONS

Indicate the frequency with which the behavior described in each of the following items seems characteristic of your work with your supervisee. After each item, check the space over the number corresponding to the appropriate point on the following 7-point scale:

	1	2	3	4	5	6	7
	Almost never						Almost always

1. I help my trainee work within a specific treatment plan with his/her client.
1 2 3 4 5 6 7

2. I help my trainee stay on track during our meetings.
1 2 3 4 5 6 7

3. My style is to carefully and systematically consider the material that my trainee brings to supervision.
1 2 3 4 5 6 7

4. My trainee works with me on specific goals in the supervisory session.
1 2 3 4 5 6 7

5. In supervision, I expect my trainee to think about or reflect on my comments to him or her.
1 2 3 4 5 6 7

6. I teach my trainee through direct suggestion.
1 2 3 4 5 6 7

7. In supervision, I place a high priority on our understanding the client's perspective.
1 2 3 4 5 6 7

8. I encourage my trainee to take time to understand what the client is saying and doing.
1 2 3 4 5 6 7

9. When correcting my trainee's errors with a client, I offer alternative ways of intervening.
1 2 3 4 5 6 7

10. I encourage my trainee to formulate his/her own interventions with his/her clients.
1 2 3 4 5 6 7

11. I encourage my trainee to talk about the work in ways that are comfortable for him/her.
1 2 3 4 5 6 7

12. I welcome my trainee's explanations about his/her client's behavior.
1 2 3 4 5 6 7

13. During supervision, my trainee talks more than I do.
1 2 3 4 5 6 7

14. I make an effort to understand my trainee.
1 2 3 4 5 6 7

15. I am tactful when commenting about my trainee's performance.
1 2 3 4 5 6 7

16. I facilitate my trainee's talking in our sessions.

    1   2   3   4   5   6   7

17. In supervision, my trainee is more curious than anxious when discussing his/her difficulties with me.

    1   2   3   4   5   6   7

18. My trainee appears to be comfortable working with me.

    1   2   3   4   5   6   7

19. My trainee understands client behavior and treatment techniques similar to the way I do.

    1   2   3   4   5   6   7

20. During supervision, my trainee seems able to stand back and reflect on what I am saying to him/her.

    1   2   3   4   5   6   7

21. I stay in tune with my trainee during supervision.

    1   2   3   4   5   6   7

22. My trainee identifies with me in the way he/she thinks and talks about his/her clients.

    1   2   3   4   5   6   7

23. My trainee consistently implements suggestions made in supervision.

    1   2   3   4   5   6   7

The Supervisor Form of the SWA has three scales, scored as follows:

Rapport: Sum items 10 through 16, then divide by 7.

Client Focus: Sum items 1 through 9, then divide by 9.

Identification: Sum items 17 through 23, then divide by 7.

From J. F. Efstation, M. J. Patton, and C. M. Kardash (1990). Measuring the working alliance in counselor supervision. *Journal of Counseling Psychology, 37,* 322–329. Copyright © 1990 by the American Psychological Association. Reprinted with permission.

SUPERVISORY WORKING ALLIANCE INVENTORY:
TRAINEE FORM INSTRUCTIONS

Indicate the frequency with which the behavior described in each of the following items seems characteristic of your work with your supervisee. After each item, check the space over the number corresponding to the appropriate point on the following 7-point scale:

	1	2	3	4	5	6	7
	Almost never						Almost always

1. I feel comfortable working with my supervisor.

   1   2   3   4   5   6   7

2. My supervisor welcomes my explanations about the client's behavior.

   1   2   3   4   5   6   7

3. My supervisor makes the effort to understand me.

   1   2   3   4   5   6   7

4. My supervisor encourages me to talk about my work with clients in ways that are comfortable for me.

   1   2   3   4   5   6   7

5. My supervisor is tactful when commenting about my performance.

   1   2   3   4   5   6   7

6. My supervisor encourages me to formulate my own interventions with the client.

   1   2   3   4   5   6   7

7. My supervisor helps me to talk freely in our sessions.

   1   2   3   4   5   6   7

8. My supervisor stays in tune with me during supervision.

   1   2   3   4   5   6   7

9. I understand client behavior and treatment technique similarly to the way my supervisor does.

   1   2   3   4   5   6   7

10. I feel free to mention to my supervisor any troublesome feelings I might have about him/her.

    1   2   3   4   5   6   7

11. My supervisor treats me like a colleague in our supervisory sessions.

    1   2   3   4   5   6   7

12. In supervision, I am more curious than anxious when discussing my difficulties with clients.

    1   2   3   4   5   6   7

13. In supervision, my supervisor places a high priority on our understanding the client's perspective.

    1   2   3   4   5   6   7

14. My supervisor encourages me to take time to understand what the client is saying and doing.

    —   —   —   —   —   —   —
    1   2   3   4   5   6   7

15. My supervisor's style is to carefully and systematically consider the material I bring to supervision.

    —   —   —   —   —   —   —
    1   2   3   4   5   6   7

16. When correcting my errors with a client, my supervisor offers alternative ways of intervening with that client.

    —   —   —   —   —   —   —
    1   2   3   4   5   6   7

17. My supervisor helps me to work within a specific treatment plan with my clients.

    —   —   —   —   —   —   —
    1   2   3   4   5   6   7

18. My supervisor helps me to stay on track during our meetings.

    —   —   —   —   —   —   —
    1   2   3   4   5   6   7

19. I work with my supervisor on specific goals in the supervisory session.

    —   —   —   —   —   —   —
    1   2   3   4   5   6   7

The trainee form of the SWAI has two scales, scored as follows:

Rapport: Sum items 1 through 12, then divide by 12.

Client Focus: Sum items 13 through 19, then divide by 6.

From J. F. Efstation, M. J. Patton, and C. M. Kardash (1990). Measuring the working alliance in counselor supervision. *Journal of Counseling Psychology, 37,* 322–329. Copyright © 1990 by the American Psychological Association. Reprinted with permission.

WORKING ALLIANCE INVENTORY
Supervisor's Form

The following sentences describe some of the different ways a person might think or feel about his or her supervisee. As you read the sentences, mentally insert the name of your supervisee in place of _____ in the text.

For each statement, there is a 7-point scale.

1	2	3	4	5	6	7
Never	Rarely	Occasionally	Sometimes	Often	Very often	Always

If the statement describes the way you *always* feel (or think), circle the number 7; if it *never* applies to you, circle the number 1. Use the numbers in between to describe the variations between these extremes.

Please work fast: Your first impressions are the ones we would like to have. PLEASE DO NOT FAIL TO RESPOND TO *EVERY* ITEM.

Thank you for your cooperation.

1. I feel uncomfortable with _____. 1 2 3 4 5 6 7

2. _____ and I agree about the steps to be taken to improve his/her work as a therapist. 1 2 3 4 5 6 7

3. I have some concerns about the outcome of these sessions. 1 2 3 4 5 6 7

4. _____ and I both feel confident about the usefulness of our current activity in supervision. 1 2 3 4 5 6 7

5. _____ and I have a common perception of her/his goals. 1 2 3 4 5 6 7

6. I feel I really understand _____. 1 2 3 4 5 6 7

7. _____ finds what we are doing in supervision confusing. 1 2 3 4 5 6 7

8. I believe _____ likes me. 1 2 3 4 5 6 7

9. I sense a need to clarify the purpose of our sessions for _____. 1 2 3 4 5 6 7

10. I have some disagreements with _____ about the goals of these sessions. 1 2 3 4 5 6 7

11. I believe that the time _____ and I are spending together is not spent efficiently. 1 2 3 4 5 6 7

12. I have doubts about what we are trying to accomplish in supervision. 1 2 3 4 5 6 7

13. I am clear and explicit about what _____'s responsibilities are in supervision. 1 2 3 4 5 6 7

14. The current goals of these sessions are important for _____. 1 2 3 4 5 6 7

15. I find that what _____ and I are doing in supervision is unrelated to his/her current concerns. 1 2 3 4 5 6 7

16. I feel confident that the things we do in supervision will help _____ to accomplish the changes he/she desires. 1 2 3 4 5 6 7

17. I am genuinely concerned for _____'s welfare. 1 2 3 4 5 6 7

18. I am clear as to what I expect _____ to do in these sessions. 1 2 3 4 5 6 7

19. _____ and I respect each other. 1 2 3 4 5 6 7

20. I feel that I am not totally honest about my feelings toward _____. 1 2 3 4 5 6 7

21. I am confident in my ability to help _____. 1 2 3 4 5 6 7

22. We are working toward mutually agreed upon goals. 1 2 3 4 5 6 7

23. I appreciate _____ as a person. 1 2 3 4 5 6 7

24. We agree on what is important for _____ to work on. 1 2 3 4 5 6 7

25. As a result of these sessions, _____ is clearer as to how he/she might able to improve his/her work as a therapist. 1 2 3 4 5 6 7

26. _____ and I have built a mutual trust. 1 2 3 4 5 6 7

27. _____ and I have different ideas on what his/her learning needs are. 1 2 3 4 5 6 7

28. Our relationship is important to _____. 1 2 3 4 5 6 7

29. _____ has some fears that if she/he says or does the wrong things I will stop working with him/her. 1 2 3 4 5 6 7

30. _____ and I have collaborated in setting goals for these sessions. 1 2 3 4 5 6 7

31. _____ is frustrated by what I am asking him/her to do in supervision. 1 2 3 4 5 6 7

32. We have established a good understanding between us of the kind of changes that would be good for _____. 1 2 3 4 5 6 7

33. The things that we are doing in supervision don't make much sense to _____. 1 2 3 4 5 6 7

34. _____ doesn't know what to expect as the result of supervision. 1 2 3 4 5 6 7

35. _____ believes the way we are working with his/her issues is correct. 1 2 3 4 5 6 7

36. I respect _____ even when she/he does things I do not approve of. 1 2 3 4 5 6 7

A. O. Horvath (1982). *Working Alliance Inventory (Revised edition).* Vancouver, BC: Simon Fraser University. Reprinted with permission.

WORKING ALLIANCE INVENTORY
Supervisee's Form

The following sentences describe some of the different ways a person might think or feel about his or her supervisee. As you read the sentences, mentally instert the name of your supervisor in place of _____ in the text.

For each statement, there is a 7-point scale.

1	2	3	4	5	6	7
Never	Rarely	Occasionally	Sometimes	Often	Very often	Always

If the statement describes the way you *always* feel (or think), circle the number 7; if it *never* applies to you, circle the number 1. Use the numbers in between to describe the variations between these extremes.

Please work fast: Your first impressions are the ones we would like to have. PLEASE DO NOT FAIL TO RESPOND TO *EVERY* ITEM.

Thank you for your cooperation.

1. I feel uncomfortable with _____. 1 2 3 4 5 6 7
2. _____ and I agree about the things I will need to do to improve my abilities as a therapist. 1 2 3 4 5 6 7
3. I am worried about the outcome of these sessions. 1 2 3 4 5 6 7
4. What I am doing in supervision gives me new ways of looking at how I approach my work as a therapist. 1 2 3 4 5 6 7
5. _____ and I understand each other. 1 2 3 4 5 6 7
6. _____ perceives accurately what my goals are. 1 2 3 4 5 6 7
7. I find what I am doing in supervision confusing. 1 2 3 4 5 6 7
8. I believe _____ likes me. 1 2 3 4 5 6 7
9. I wish _____ and I could clarify the purpose of our sessions. 1 2 3 4 5 6 7
10. I disagree with _____ about what I ought to get out of supervision. 1 2 3 4 5 6 7
11. I believe that the time _____ and I are spending together is not spent efficiently. 1 2 3 4 5 6 7
12. _____ doesn't understand what I am trying to accomplish in supervision. 1 2 3 4 5 6 7
13. I am clear on what my responsibilities are in supervision. 1 2 3 4 5 6 7
14. The goals of these sessions are important to me. 1 2 3 4 5 6 7
15. I find that what _____ and I are doing in supervision is unrelated to my concerns. 1 2 3 4 5 6 7
16. I feel the things I do in supervision will help me to improve as a therapist. 1 2 3 4 5 6 7
17. I believe _____ is genuinely concerned for my welfare. 1 2 3 4 5 6 7

18. I am clear as to what _____ wants me to do in these sessions.   1   2   3   4   5   6   7

19. _____ and I respect each other.   1   2   3   4   5   6   7

20. I feel that _____ is not totally honest about his/her feelings toward me.   1   2   3   4   5   6   7

21. I am confident in _____'s ability to help me.   1   2   3   4   5   6   7

22. _____ and I are working toward mutually agreed upon goals.   1   2   3   4   5   6   7

23. I feel that _____ appreciates me.   1   2   3   4   5   6   7

24. We agree on what is important for me to work on.   1   2   3   4   5   6   7

25. As a result of these sessions, I am clearer as to how I might be able to improve my work as a therapist.   1   2   3   4   5   6   7

26. _____ and I trust one another.   1   2   3   4   5   6   7

27. _____ and I have different ideas on what my difficulties are.   1   2   3   4   5   6   7

28. My relationship with _____ is very important to me.   1   2   3   4   5   6   7

29. I have the feeling that if I say or do the wrong things, _____ will stop supervising me.   1   2   3   4   5   6   7

30. _____ and I collaborate on setting goals for supervision.   1   2   3   4   5   6   7

31. I am frustrated by the things I am doing in supervision.   1   2   3   4   5   6   7

32. We have established a good understanding of the kind of changes that would be good for my work as a therapist.   1   2   3   4   5   6   7

33. The things that _____ is asking me to do don't make sense to me.   1   2   3   4   5   6   7

34. I don't know what to expect as the result of my supervision.   1   2   3   4   5   6   7

35. I believe the way we are working in supervision is correct.   1   2   3   4   5   6   7

36. I feel _____ cares about me even when I do things that he/she does not approve of.   1   2   3   4   5   6   7

Scoring key (both supervisor and supervisee forms):

     Task: 2, 4, 7*, 11*, 13, 15*, 16, 18, 24, 31*, 33*,35

     Bond: 1*, 5, 8, 17, 19, 20*, 21, 23, 26, 28, 29*, 36

     Goal: 3*, 6, 9*, 10*, 12*, 14, 22, 25, 27*, 30, 32, 34*

         Note: Items marked with asterisk (*) are scored in reverse direction.

From A. O. Horvath (1982). *Working Alliance Inventory (Revised Edition).* Vancouver, BC: Simon Fraser University. Reprinted with permission. Additional psychometric information on the WAI can be found in Horvath and Greenburg (1989).

Note that item stems for both the supervisor and supervisee forms were modified by Baker (1990) for use in supervision research.

SUPERVISORY STYLES INVENTORY

For trainees' form: Indicate your perception of the style of your current or most recent supervisor of psychotherapy/counseling on each of the following descriptors. Circle the number on the scale, from 1 to 7, that best reflects your view of him or her.

For supervisors' form: Indicate your perceptions of your style as a supervisor of psychotherapy/counseling on each of the following descriptors. Circle the number on the scale, from 1 to 7, that best reflects your view of yourself.

	1	2	3	4	5	6	7
	Not very						Very
1. goal-oriented	1	2	3	4	5	6	7
2. perceptive	1	2	3	4	5	6	7
3. concrete	1	2	3	4	5	6	7
4. explicit	1	2	3	4	5	6	7
5. committed	1	2	3	4	5	6	7
6. affirming	1	2	3	4	5	6	7
7. practical	1	2	3	4	5	6	7
8. sensitive	1	2	3	4	5	6	7
9. collaborative	1	2	3	4	5	6	7
10. intuitive	1	2	3	4	5	6	7
11. reflective	1	2	3	4	5	6	7
12. responsive	1	2	3	4	5	6	7
13. structured	1	2	3	4	5	6	7
14. evaluative	1	2	3	4	5	6	7
15. friendly	1	2	3	4	5	6	7
16. flexible	1	2	3	4	5	6	7
17. prescriptive	1	2	3	4	5	6	7
18. didactic	1	2	3	4	5	6	7
19. thorough	1	2	3	4	5	6	7
20. focused	1	2	3	4	5	6	7
21. creative	1	2	3	4	5	6	7
22. supportive	1	2	3	4	5	6	7
23. open	1	2	3	4	5	6	7
24. realistic	1	2	3	4	5	6	7
25. resourceful	1	2	3	4	5	6	7
26. invested	1	2	3	4	5	6	7
27. facilitative	1	2	3	4	5	6	7
28. therapeutic	1	2	3	4	5	6	7
29. positive	1	2	3	4	5	6	7
30. trusting	1	2	3	4	5	6	7
31. informative	1	2	3	4	5	6	7
32. humorous	1	2	3	4	5	6	7
33. warm	1	2	3	4	5	6	7

Scoring key: *Attractive:* Sum items 15, 16, 22, 23, 29, 30, 33; divide by 7.

Interpersonally sensitive: Sum items 2, 5, 10, 11, 21, 25, 26, 28; divide by 8.

Task oriented: Sum items 1, 3, 4, 7, 13, 14, 17, 18, 19, 20; divide by 10.
Filler items: 6, 8, 9, 12, 24, 27, 31, 32.

Developed by M. L. Friedlander and L. G. Ward (1984). Unpublished instrument. Reprinted by permission of authors.

Bernard J. M. & Goodyear R. K.(2004). *Fundamentals of Clinical Supervision.* 3rd ed. Boston, MA: Pearson Education, Inc.

COUNSELOR SUPERVISOR SELF-EFFICACY SCALE

Directions: Each item listed below is related to a task performed in counselor supervision. Rate your level of confidence for completing each task *right now.* Circle the number that reflects your confidence level. Please answer every question, regardless of whether you have actually performed the corresponding activity.

1	2	3	4	5	6	7	8	9	10
Not confident at all				Somewhat confident					Completely confident

1. Select supervision interventions congruent with the model/theory being used

    1   2   3   4   5   6   7   8   9   10

2. Articulate to a supervisee the ethical standards regarding client welfare

    1   2   3   4   5   6   7   8   9   10

3. Present procedures for assessing and reporting an occurrence of child abuse

    1   2   3   4   5   6   7   8   9   10

4. Describe the strengths and limitations of the various supervision modalities (e.g., self-report, live observation, audiotape review)

    1   2   3   4   5   6   7   8   9   10

5. Assist a supervisee to deal with termination issues

    1   2   3   4   5   6   7   8   9   10

6. Assist a supervisee to include relevant cultural variables in case conceptualization

    1   2   3   4   5   6   7   8   9   10

7. Model effective decision making when faced with ethical and legal dilemmas

    1   2   3   4   5   6   7   8   9   10

8. Demonstrate knowledge of various counseling theories, systems, and their related methods

    1   2   3   4   5   6   7   8   9   10

9. Structure supervision around a supervisee's learning goals

    1   2   3   4   5   6   7   8   9   10

10. Assist a supervisee to develop working hypotheses about her/his clients

    1   2   3   4   5   6   7   8   9   10

11. Solicit critical feedback on my work as a supervisor from either my peers or an evaluator

    1   2   3   4   5   6   7   8   9   10

12. Understand key research on counselor development and developmental models as they pertain to supervision

    1   2   3   4   5   6   7   8   9   10

13. Assist a supervisee to develop a strategy to address client resistance

    1   2   3   4   5   6   7   8   9   10

14. Encourage a supervisee to share his/her negative feelings about supervision without becoming defensive

    1   2   3   4   5   6   7   8   9   10

15. Listen carefully to concerns presented by a supervisee

    1   2   3   4   5   6   7   8   9   10

16. Identify key ethical and legal issues surrounding client confidentiality
    1   2   3   4   5   6   7   8   9   10
17. Address a supervisee's race or ethnic identity as a counseling process variable
    1   2   3   4   5   6   7   8   9   10
18. Understand appropriate supervisor functions of teacher, counselor, and consultant
    1   2   3   4   5   6   7   8   9   10
19. Employ interventions appropriate to a supervisee's learning needs
    1   2   3   4   5   6   7   8   9   10
20. Describe the legal liabilities involved in counseling minors
    1   2   3   4   5   6   7   8   9   10
21. Establish a plan to safeguard a supervisee's due process within supervision
    1   2   3   4   5   6   7   8   9   10
22. Help a supervisee assess the compatibility between his/her in-session behaviors
    and espoused theoretical orientation
    1   2   3   4   5   6   7   8   9   10
23. Model strategies that may enhance a supervisee's case conceptualization skills
    1   2   3   4   5   6   7   8   9   10
24. Conduct supervision in strict accordance to the ethical standards governing my
    profession
    1   2   3   4   5   6   7   8   9   10
25. Facilitate a supervisee's cultural awareness
    1   2   3   4   5   6   7   8   9   10
26. Appear competent in interactions with a supervisee
    1   2   3   4   5   6   7   8   9   10
27. Receive critical feedback from a supervisee on my performance as a
    supervisor without becoming defensive or angry
    1   2   3   4   5   6   7   8   9   10
28. State a rationale for choosing a supervision intervention based on theory,
    client/counselor dynamics, and/or setting
    1   2   3   4   5   6   7   8   9   10
29. Recognize possible dual relationship issues that may arise within supervision
    1   2   3   4   5   6   7   8   9   10
30. Demonstrate respect for a supervisee who has a different worldview from myself
    1   2   3   4   5   6   7   8   9   10
31. Assess a supervisee's multicultural competencies
    1   2   3   4   5   6   7   8   9   10
32. Address parallel processes as they arise within the supervisory relationship
    1   2   3   4   5   6   7   8   9   10
33. Communicate due process procedures to a supervisee if he/she is unhappy
    with the supervision I have provided
    1   2   3   4   5   6   7   8   9   10
34. Demonstrate respect for various learning styles and personal characteristics
    within supervision
    1   2   3   4   5   6   7   8   9   10
35. Facilitate case discussion during group supervision
    1   2   3   4   5   6   7   8   9   10

36. Balance the needs of the group with the individual needs of each supervisee during group supervision
    1   2   3   4   5   6   7   8   9   10
37. Model appropriate responses to affect presented in group supervision
    1   2   3   4   5   6   7   8   9   10
38. Offer adequate support to all members of a group during group supervision
    1   2   3   4   5   6   7   8   9   10
39. Integrate an understanding of supervisees' learning styles into the group supervision process
    1   2   3   4   5   6   7   8   9   10

Scoring key:

Theories and Techniques: 1, 4, 8, 9, 10, 12, 13, 18, 19, 21, 22, 23, 28, 32

Group Supervision: 35 through 39

Supervisory Ethics: 2, 5, 7, 15, 24, 26, 29, 33

Self in Supervision: 11, 14, 27, 30, 34

Multicultural Competence: 6, 17, 25, 31

Knowledge of Legal Issues: 3, 16, 20

Developed by K. L. Barnes. Unpublished instrument. Reprinted by permission of author.

MULTICULTURAL SUPERVISION COMPETENCIES QUESTIONNAIRE (MSCQ)

This questionnaire is intended to evaluate the quality of multicultural supervision. If you have had a supervisor that is culturally or racially different from you, I would like you to complete this questionnaire with respect to this particular supervisor.

Your ethnic/racial identity

_____

Your supervisor's ethnic/racial background

_____

Your gender _____ Your supervisor's gender _____

How long ago? _____ How long did you have him/her as supervisor? _____

What was the level of your clinical training during this supervision?

_____

What was the nature of the clinical site where this supervision took place?

_____

Based on your experiences and observation, rate the following statements according to the following scale:

1	2	3	4	5
Strongly disagree	Disagree	Undecided	Agree	Strongly agree

Circle the response code (e.g., 4 for Agree, or 2 for Disagree) at the end of each statement that most clearly reflects your opinion about this supervisor. Try to use 3 sparingly.

1. Understands my culture and value systems	1	2	3	4	5
2. Shows openness and respect for culturally different supervisees	1	2	3	4	5
3. Actively avoids cultural biases and discriminatory practices in working with minority students	1	2	3	4	5
4. Understands the worldviews of supervisees and clients from other cultures	1	2	3	4	5
5. Understands the tendency and the problem of racial stereotyping	1	2	3	4	5
6. Makes an effort to understand and accommodate culturally different supervisees	1	2	3	4	5
7. Is able to avoid racial stereotypes by taking into account both the uniqueness of individuals as well as the known characteristics of the culture	1	2	3	4	5
8. Makes use of every opportunity to increase supervisees' multicultural competence in counseling	1	2	3	4	5

9. Is able to clarify presenting problems and arrives at culturally relevant case conceptualization with clients from different cultural backgrounds   1   2   3   4   5

10. Shows an understanding of how culture, ethnicity, and race influence supervision and counseling   1   2   3   4   5

11. Is able to overcome cultural and language barriers in relating to minority students and clients   1   2   3   4   5

12. Has never mentioned that race is an important consideration in supervision and counseling   1   2   3   4   5

13. Demonstrates skills to balance between the generic characteristics of counseling and the unique values of different cultural groups   1   2   3   4   5

14. Shows sensitivity and skills in supervising culturally different trainees   1   2   3   4   5

15. Shows unconditional acceptance of all supervisees, regardless of their race, ethnicity, and culture   1   2   3   4   5

16. Recognizes the limitations of models and approaches based on Western assumptions in working with culturally different individuals   1   2   3   4   5

17. Knows how to encourage discussion of cultural and racial issues in counseling and supervision   1   2   3   4   5

18. Shows interest in learning new skills and enhancing own multicultural competence in supervision and counseling   1   2   3   4   5

19. Recognizes that what is inappropriate from the standpoint of the majority culture may be appropriate for some minority cultures   1   2   3   4   5

20. Takes into account cultural biases in assessing supervisees and forming clinical judgments   1   2   3   4   5

21. Exhibits respect for other cultures without overly identifying self with minority culture or becoming paternalistic   1   2   3   4   5

22. Is willing to advocate for minorities who experience institutional discrimination   1   2   3   4   5

23. Understands the cultural reasons why minority students and clients tend to defer to authority figures   1   2   3   4   5

24. Communicates effectively with culturally different supervisees at both the verbal and nonverbal levels   1   2   3   4   5

25. Understands cultural differences in help-giving and help-seeking   1   2   3   4   5

26. Believes that Western models and approaches of counseling are equally generalizable to ethnic minorities   1   2   3   4   5

27. Gives emotional support and encouragement to minority students   1   2   3   4   5

28. Is very rigid and dogmatic regarding what constitutes the proper approach of counseling   1   2   3   4   5

29. Shows an interest in helping minority students to overcome systemic and institutional barriers   1   2   3   4   5

30. Welcomes my input even when I express different views   1 2 3 4 5
    and values
31. Knows how to consult or refer to resources available in   1 2 3 4 5
    ethnocultural communities
32. Takes into account racial biases and sociopolitical   1 2 3 4 5
    implications in counseling and supervision
33. Considers supervisees' cultural and linguistic   1 2 3 4 5
    backgrounds in giving them feedback and evaluation
34. Shows a genuine interest in learning about other cultures   1 2 3 4 5
35. Recognizes individual differences in ethnic/racial identity   1 2 3 4 5
36. Demonstrates a familiarity with the value systems of   1 2 3 4 5
    diverse cultural groups
37. Knows that biases and assumptions of Western   1 2 3 4 5
    counseling models can have a negative effect on
    culturally different supervisees and clients
38. Knows how to adapt knowledge of cultural differences to   1 2 3 4 5
    supervision and counseling
39. Does not seem to be aware of own limitations in working   1 2 3 4 5
    with culturally different supervisees or clients
40. Does not pay any attention to the demographics of   1 2 3 4 5
    supervisees
41. Is able to develop culturally appropriate treatment plans   1 2 3 4 5
    for clients from different cultural backgrounds
42. Makes an effort to establish a relationship of trust and   1 2 3 4 5
    acceptance with culturally different supervisees
43. Is flexible in adjusting his/her supervisory style to   1 2 3 4 5
    culturally different supervisees
44. Assists supervisees in formulating culturally appropriate   1 2 3 4 5
    assessment and treatment plans
45. Makes use of the support network of minorities   1 2 3 4 5
46. Does not seem to be aware of own implicit cultural   1 2 3 4 5
    biases in counseling and supervision
47. Acknowledges that his or her own life experiences,   1 2 3 4 5
    values, and biases may influence the supervision process
48. Actively interacts with minority students outside   1 2 3 4 5
    counseling and classroom settings
49. Knows something about how gender, socioeconomic   1 2 3 4 5
    status, and religious issues are related to minority status
50. Shows some knowledge about the cultural traditions of   1 2 3 4 5
    various ethnic groups
51. Is able to integrate own beliefs, knowledge, and skills in   1 2 3 4 5
    forming relationships with culturally different supervisees
52. Is able to reduce my defensiveness, suspicions, and anxiety 1 2 3 4 5
    about having a supervisor from a different culture
53. Shows no interest in understanding my cultural   1 2 3 4 5
    background and ethnic/racial heritage

54. Negatively evaluates supervisees who do not conform to   1   2   3   4   5
    supervisor's own theoretical orientation and approach to
    counseling

55. Has a tendency to abuse supervisory power (e.g., imposes   1   2   3   4   5
    view on supervisees)

56. Respects the worldview, religious beliefs, and values of   1   2   3   4   5
    culturally different supervisees

57. Demonstrates competence in a wide variety of methods of   1   2   3   4   5
    assessment and interventions, including nontraditional ones

58. Provides guidance to international students and new   1   2   3   4   5
    immigrants to facilitate their acculturation

59. Makes minority supervisees feel safe to share their   1   2   3   4   5
    difficulties and concerns

60. Is able to relate to culturally different supervisees while   1   2   3   4   5
    maintaining own cultural values

Scoring: Before scoring, reverse the scoring of the following items: 12, 26, 28, 39, 40, 46, 53, 54, 55.

Attitude and beliefs (how the supervisor feels about multicultural issues and culturally different supervisees): 2, 12, 16, 19, 21, 26, 34, 39, 40, 46, 47, 56

Knowledge and understanding (what the supervisor knows about multicultural supervision): 1, 4, 5, 10, 23, 25, 36, 37, 49, 50

Skills and practices (how the supervisor demonstrates multicultural competencies in actual practices of supervision): 7, 8, 9, 13, 14, 17, 18, 20, 24, 28, 31, 32, 33, 35, 38, 41, 43, 44, 45, 52, 54, 57

Relationship (how the supervisor relates to culturally different supervisees): 3, 6, 11, 15, 22, 27, 29, 30, 42, 48, 51, 53, 55, 58, 59, 60

© 2003 Paul T. P. Wong and Lilian C. J. Wong. Unpublished instrument. Reprinted by permission of authors.

SUPERVISION ETHICS CODES
The Approved Clinical Supervisor Code of Ethics

In addition to following your profession's Code of Ethics, clinical supervisors shall:

1. Ensure that supervisees inform clients of their professional status (e.g., intern) and of all conditions of supervision. Supervisors need to ensure that supervisees inform their clients of any status other than being fully qualified for independent practice or licensed. For example, supervisees need to inform their clients if they are a student, intern, or trainee or, if licensed with restrictions, the nature of these restrictions, e.g., associate or conditional. In addition, clients must be informed of the requirements of supervision, e.g., the audiotaping of all counseling sessions for purposes of supervision.

2. Ensure that clients have been informed of their rights to confidentiality and privileged communication when applicable. Clients also should be informed of the limits of confidentiality and privileged communication. The general limits of confidentiality are when harm to self or others is threatened; when the abuse of children, elders, or disabled persons is suspected; and in cases when the court compels the counselor to testify and break confidentiality. These are generally accepted limits to confidentiality and privileged communication, but they may be modified by state or federal statute.

3. Inform supervisees about the process of supervision, including supervision goals, case management procedures, and the supervisor's preferred supervision model(s).

4. Keep and secure supervision records and consider all information gained in supervision as confidential.

5. Avoid all dual relationships with supervisees that may interfere with the supervisor's professional judgment or exploit the supervisee. Although all dual relationships are not in and of themselves inappropriate, any sexual relationship is considered to be a violation. Sexual relationship means sexual contact, sexual harassment, or sexual bias toward a supervisee by a supervisor.

6. Establish procedures with their supervisees for handling crisis situations.

7. Provide supervisees with adequate and timely feedback as part of an established evaluation plan.

8. Render assistance to any supervisee who is unable to provide competent counseling services to clients.

9. Intervene in any situation where the supervisee is impaired and the client is at risk.

10. Refrain from endorsing an impaired supervisee when such impairment deems it unlikely that the supervisee can provide adequate counseling services.

11. Refrain from offering supervision outside their area(s) of competence.

12. Ensure that supervisees are aware of the current ethical standards related to their professional practice, as well as legal standards that regulate the practice of counseling. Current ethical standards would mean standards published by the National Board for

Certified Counselors and other appropriate entities such as the American Counseling Association. In addition, it is the supervisor's responsibility to ensure that the supervisee is aware that state and federal laws might regulate the practice of counseling and to inform the supervisee of key laws that affect counseling in the supervisee's jurisdiction.

13. Engage supervisees in an examination of cultural issues that might affect supervision and/or counseling.

14. Ensure that both supervisees and clients are aware of their rights and of due process procedures.

Reprinted with permission of the Center for Credentialing and Education, an affiliate of the National Board for Certified Counselors, 3 Terrace Way, Suite D., Greensboro, NC 27403-3660.

ETHICAL GUIDELINES FOR COUNSELING SUPERVISORS
Association for Counselor Education and Supervision

Adopted by ACES Executive Counsel and Delegate Assembly, March 1993

Preamble

The Association for Counselor Education and Supervision (ACES) is composed of people engaged in the professional preparation of counselors and people responsible for the ongoing supervision of counselors. ACES is a founding division of the American Counseling Association (ACA) and as such adheres to ACA's current ethical standards and to general codes of competence adopted throughout the mental health community.

ACES believes that counselor educators and counseling supervisors in universities and applied counseling settings, including the range of education and mental health delivery systems, carry responsibilities unique to their job roles. Such responsibilities may include administrative supervision, clinical supervision, or both. Administrative supervision refers to those supervisory activities that increase the efficiency of the delivery of counseling services, whereas clinical supervision includes the supportive and educative activities of the supervisor designed to improve the application of counseling theory and technique directly to clients.

Counselor educators and counseling supervisors encounter situations that challenge the help given by general ethical standards of the profession at large. These situations require more specific guidelines that provide appropriate guidance in everyday practice.

The Ethical Guidelines for Counseling Supervisors are intended to assist professionals by helping them to:

1. Observe ethical and legal protection of clients' and supervisees' rights;
2. Meet the training and professional development needs of supervisees in ways consistent with clients' welfare and programmatic requirements; and
3. Establish policies, procedures, and standards for implementing programs.

The specification of ethical guidelines enables ACES members to focus on and to clarify the ethical nature of responsibilities held in common. Such guidelines should be reviewed formally every five years, or more often if needed, to meet the needs of ACES members for guidance.

The Ethical Guidelines for Counselor Educators and Counseling Supervisors are meant to help ACES members in conducting supervision. ACES is not currently in a position to hear complaints about alleged noncompliance with these guidelines. Any complaints about the ethical behavior of any ACA member should be measured against the ACA Ethical Standards and a complaint lodged with ACA in accordance with its *procedures* for doing so.

One overriding assumption underlying this document is that supervision should be ongoing throughout a counselor's career and not stop when a particular level of education, certification, or membership in a professional organization is attained.

Definitions Of Terms

Applied counseling settings   Public or private organizations of counselors such as community mental health centers, hospitals, schools, and group or individual private practice settings.

Supervisees Counselors-in-training in university programs at any level who work with clients in applied settings as part of their university training program, and counselors who have completed their formal education and are employed in an applied counseling setting.

Supervisors Counselors who have been designated within their university or agency to directly oversee the professional clinical work of counselors. Supervisors also may be persons who offer supervision to counselors seeking state licensure and so provide supervision outside the administrative aegis of an applied counseling setting.

1. Client Welfare and Rights

1.01 The primary obligation of supervisors is to train counselors so that they respect the integrity and promote the welfare of their clients. Supervisors should have supervisees inform clients that they are being supervised and that observation and/or recordings of the session may be reviewed by the supervisor.

1.02 Supervisors who are licensed counselors and are conducting supervision to aid a supervisee to become licensed should instruct the supervisee not to communicate or in any way convey to the supervisee's clients or to other parties that the supervisee is himself/herself licensed.

1.03 Supervisors should make supervisees aware of clients' rights, including protecting clients' right to privacy and confidentiality in the counseling relationship and the information resulting from it. Clients also should be informed that their right to privacy and confidentiality will not be violated by the supervisory relationship.

1.04 Records of the counseling relationship, including interview notes, test data, correspondence, the electronic storage of these documents, and audio- and videotape recordings, are considered to be confidential professional information. Supervisors should see that these materials are used in counseling, research, and training and supervision of counselors with the full knowledge of the clients and that permission to use these materials is granted by the applied counseling setting offering service to the client. This professional information is to be used for full protection of the client. Written consent from the client (or legal guardian, if a minor) should be secured prior to the use of such information for instructional, supervisory, and/or research purposes. Policies of the applied counseling setting regarding client records also should be followed.

1.05 Supervisors shall adhere to current professional and legal guidelines when conducting research with human participants such as Section D-1 of the ACA Ethical Standards.

1.06 Counseling supervisors are responsible for making every effort to monitor both the professional actions, and failures to take action, of their supervisees.

2. Supervisory Role

Inherent and integral to the role of supervisor are responsibilities for:
   a. Monitoring client welfare;
   b. Encouraging compliance with relevant legal, ethical, and professional standards for clinical practice;
   c. Monitoring clinical performance and professional development of supervisees; and
   d. Evaluating and certifying current performance and potential of supervisees for academic, screening, selection, placement, employment, and credentialing purposes.

2.01   Supervisors should have had training in supervision prior to initiating their role as supervisors.

2.02   Supervisors should pursue professional and personal continuing education activities such as advanced courses, seminars, and professional conferences on a regular and ongoing basis. These activities should include both counseling and supervision topics and skills.

2.03   Supervisors should make their supervisees aware of professional and ethical standards and legal responsibilities of the counseling profession.

2.04   Supervisors of postdegree counselors who are seeking state licensure should encourage these counselors to adhere to the standards for practice established by the state licensure board of the state in which they practice.

2.05   Procedures for contacting the supervisor, or an alternative supervisor, to assist in handling crisis situations should be established and communicated to supervisees.

2.06   Actual work samples via audio- and/or videotape or live observation in addition to case notes should be reviewed by the supervisor as a regular part of the ongoing supervisory process.

2.07   Supervisors of counselors should meeting regularly in face-to-face sessions with their supervisees.

2.08   Supervisors should provide supervisees with ongoing feedback on their performance. This feedback should take a variety of forms, both formal and informal, and should include verbal and written evaluations. It should be formative during the supervisory experience and summative at the conclusion of the experience.

2.09   Supervisors who have multiple roles (e.g., teacher, clinical supervisor, administrative supervisor) with supervisees should minimize potential conflicts. Where possible, the roles should be divided among several supervisors. Where this is not possible, careful explanation should be conveyed to the supervisee as to the expectations and responsibilities associated with each supervisory role.

2.10   Supervisors should not participate in any form of sexual contact with supervisees. Supervisors should not engage in any form of social contact or interaction that would compromise the supervisor–supervisee relationship. Dual relationships with supervisees that might impair the supervisor's objectivity and professional judgment should be avoided and/or the supervisory relationship terminated.

2.11   Supervisors should not establish a psychotherapeutic relationship as a substitute for supervision. Personal issues should be addressed in supervision only in terms of the impact of these issues on clients and on professional functioning.

2.12   Supervisors, through ongoing supervisee assessment and evaluation, should be aware of any personal or professional limitations of supervisees that are likely to impede future professional performance. Supervisors have the responsibility of recommending remedial assistance to the supervisee and of screening from the training program, applied counseling setting, or state licensure those supervisees who are unable to provide competent professional services. These recommendations should be clearly and professionally explained in writing to the supervisees who are so evaluated.

2.13   Supervisors should not endorse a supervisee for certification, licensure, completion of an academic training program, or continued employment if the supervisor believes the supervisee is impaired in any way that would interfere with the performance of counseling duties. The presence of any such impairment should begin a process of feedback and remediation wherever possible so that the supervisee understands the nature of the impairment and has the opportunity to remedy the problem and continue with his/her professional development.

2.14 Supervisors should incorporate the principles of informed consent and participation; clarity of requirements, expectations, roles and rules; and due process and appeal into the establishment of policies and procedures of their institutions, program, courses, and individual supervisory relationships. Mechanisms for due process appeal of individual supervisory actions should be established and made available to all supervisees.

3. Program Administration Role

3.01 Supervisors should ensure that the programs conducted and experiences provided are in keeping with current guidelines and standards of ACA and its divisions.

3.02 Supervisors should teach courses and/or supervise clinical work only in areas where they are fully competent and experienced.

3.03 To achieve the highest quality of training and supervision, supervisors should be active participants in peer review and peer supervision procedures.

3.04 Supervisors should provide experiences that integrate theoretical knowledge and practical application. Supervisors also should provide opportunities in which supervisees are able to apply the knowledge they have learned and understand the rationale for the skills they have acquired. The knowledge and skills conveyed should reflect current practice, research findings, and available resources.

3.05 Professional competencies, specific courses, and/or required experiences expected of supervisees should be communicated to them in writing prior to admission to the training program or placement/employment by the applied counseling setting and, in case of continued employment, in a timely manner.

3.06 Supervisors should accept only those persons as supervisees who meet identified entry level requirements for admission to a program of counselor training or for placement in an applied counseling setting. In the case of private supervision in search of state licensure, supervisees should have completed all necessary prerequisites as determined by the state licensure board.

3.07 Supervisors should inform supervisees of the goals, policies, theoretical orientations toward counseling, training, and supervision model or approach on which the supervision is based.

3.08 Supervisees should be encouraged and assisted to define their own theoretical orientation toward counseling, to establish supervision goals for themselves, and to monitor and evaluate their progress toward meeting these goals.

3.09 Supervisors should assess supervisees' skills and experience in order to establish standards for competent professional behavior. Supervisors should restrict supervisees' activities to those that are commensurate with their current level of skills and experiences.

3.10 Supervisors should obtain practicum and fieldwork sites that meet minimum standards for preparing students to become effective counselors. No practicum or fieldwork setting should be approved unless it truly replicates a counseling work setting.

3.11 Practicum and fieldwork classes would be limited in size according to established professional standards to ensure that each student has ample opportunity for individual supervision and feedback. Supervisors in applied counseling settings should have a limited number of supervisees.

3.12 Supervisors in university settings should establish and communicate specific policies and procedures regarding field placement of students. The respective roles of the student counselor, the university supervisor, and the field supervisor should be clearly differentiated in areas such as evaluation, requirements, and confidentiality.

3.13 Supervisors in training programs should communicate regularly with supervisors in agencies used as practicum and/or fieldwork sites regarding current professional practices, expectations of students, and preferred models and modalities of supervision.

3.14 Supervisors at the university should establish clear lines of communication among themselves, the field supervisors, and the students/supervisees.

3.15 Supervisors should establish and communicate to supervisees and to field supervisors specific procedures regarding consultation, performance review, and evaluation of supervisees.

3.16 Evaluations of supervisee performance in universities and in applied counseling settings should be available to supervisees in ways consistent with the Family Rights and Privacy Act and the Buckley Amendment.

3.17 Forms of training that focus primarily on self-understanding and problem resolution (e.g., personal growth groups or individual counseling) should be voluntary. Those who conduct these forms of training should not serve simultaneously as supervisors of the supervisees involved in the training.

3.18 A supervisor may recommend participation in activities such as personal growth groups or personal counseling when it has been determined that a supervisee has deficits in the areas of self-understanding and problem resolution that impede his/her professional functioning. The supervisors should not be the direct provider of these activities for the supervisee.

3.19 When a training program conducts a personal growth or counseling experience involving relatively intimate self-disclosure, care should be taken to eliminate or minimize potential role conflicts for faculty and/or agency supervisors who may conduct these experiences and who also serve as teachers, group leaders, and clinical directors.

3.20 Supervisors should use the following prioritized sequence in resolving conflicts among the needs of the client, the needs of the supervisee, and the needs of the program or agency. Insofar as the client must be protected, it should be understood that client welfare is usually subsumed in federal and state laws such that these statutes should be the first point of reference. Where laws and ethical standards are not present or are unclear, the good judgment of the supervisor should be guided by the following list.

a. Relevant legal and ethical standards (e.g., duty to warn, state child abuse laws);
b. Client welfare;
c. Supervisee welfare;
d. Supervisor welfare; and
e. Program and/or agency service and administrative needs.

From Supervision Interest Network, Association for Counselor Education and Supervision (1993, Summer). ACES ethical guidelines for counseling supervisors. *ACES Spectrum, 53*(4), 5–8. Copyright © 1993 by the Association for Counselor Education and Supervision. Reprinted by permission.

Abadie, P. D. (1985). *A study of interpersonal communication processes in the supervision of counseling.* Unpublished doctoral dissertation, Kansas State University.

Abbott, A. A., & Lyter, S. C. (1998). The use of constructive criticism in field supervision. *Clinical Supervisor, 17*(2), 43–57.

Abreu, J. M. (1999). Conscious and nonconscious African American stereotypes: Impact on first impression and diagnostic ratings by therapists. *Journal of Consulting and Clinical Psychology, 67,* 387–393.

Abroms, G. M. (1977). Supervision as metatherapy. In F. W. Kaslow (Ed.). *Supervision, consultation, and staff training in the helping professions.* San Francisco: Jossey-Bass, 81–99.

Acker, M. (July 1992). *The relationship in clinical supervision.* Paper presented at the B.A.S.P.R. International Conference on Supervision, London, England.

Acuff, C., Bennett, B. E., Bricklin, P. M., Canter, M. B., Knapp, S. J., Moldawsky, S., et al. (1999). Considerations for ethical practice in managed care. *Professional Psychology: Research and Practice, 30,* 563–575.

Adamek, M. S. (1994). Audio-cueing and immediate feedback to improve group leadership skills: A live supervision model. *Journal of Music Therapy, 31,* 135–164.

Adams, J. (1995). Perspectives on live supervision: Working live. *The Supervision Bulletin, 8*(2), 4.

Ahia, C. E., & Martin, D. (1993). The danger-to-self-or-others exception to confidentiality. In T. P. Remley (Series Ed.). *The ACA legal series: Vol. 8.* Alexandria, VA: American Counseling Association.

Aiello, J. R., & Douthitt, E. A. (2001). Social facilitation from Triplett to electronic performance monitoring. *Group Dynamics: Theory, Research, and Practice, 5,* 163–180.

Albee, G. W. (1970). The uncertain future of clinical psychology. *American Psychologist, 25,* 1071–1080.

Alderfer, C. (1983). *The supervision of the therapeutic system in family therapy.* Unpublished manuscript.

Allen, D. W. (Ed.). (1967). *Mictroteaching: A description.* Stanford, CA: Stanford Teacher Education Program.

Allen, J. (1976). Peer group supervision in family therapy. *Child Welfare, 55,* 183–189.

Allphin, C. (1987). Perplexing or distressing episodes in supervision: How they can help in the teaching and learning of psychotherapy. *Clinical Social Work Journal, 15,* 236–245.

Alonso, A. (1983). A developmental theory of psychodynamic supervision. *Clinical Supervisor, 1*(3), 23–26.

Alonso, A., & Rutan, J. S. (1988). Shame and guilt in supervision. *Psychotherapy, 25,* 576–581.

Alpher, V. S. (1991). Interdependence and parallel processes: A case study of structural analysis of social behavior in supervision and short-term dynamic psychotherapy. *Psychotherapy, 28,* 218–231.

American Association for Marriage and Family Therapy. (1991). *Code of ethics* (rev. ed.). Washington, DC: Author.

American Association for Marriage and Family Therapy. (2002). Standards of Accreditation, Version 10.1. Alexandria, VA: Author.

American Counseling Association. (1995). *Code of ethics* (rev. ed.). Alexandria, VA: Author.

American Psychological Association. (1996). *Guidelines and principles for accreditation of programs in professional psychology.* Washington, DC: Author.

American Psychological Association (2002). *Ethical principles of psychologists and code of conduct: 2002.* Washington, DC: Author.

American Psychological Association Ethics Committee. (1992). Ethical principles of psychologists and code of conduct. *American Psychologist, 47,* 1597–1611.

Anderson, J. R. (1996). ACT: A simple theory of complex cognition. *American Psychologist, 51,* 355–365.

Anderson, S. A., Schlossberg, M., & Rigazio-DiGilio, S. (2000). Family therapy trainees' evaluations of their best and worst supervision experiences. *Journal of Marital and Family Therapy, 26*(1), 79–91.

Anderson, T. (1987). The reflecting team: Dialogue and meta-dialogue in clinical work. *Family Process, 26,* 415–428.

Andrews, J. D. W. (1989). Integrating visions of reality: Interpersonal diagnosis and the existential vision. *American Psychologist, 44,* 803–817.

Anonymous. (1991). Sexual harassment: A female counseling student's experience. *Journal of Counseling and Development, 69,* 502–506.

Anonymous. (1995). Perspectives on live supervision: A client's voice. *Supervision Bulletin, 8*(2), 5.

Ansbacher, H., & Ansbacher, R. (1956). *The individual psychology of Alfred Adler.* New York: Basic Books.

Aponte, H. J. (1994). How personal can training get? *Journal of Marital and Family Therapy, 20,* 3–15.

Appelbaum, P. S. (1993). Legal liability and managed care. *American Psychologist, 48,* 251–257.

Arcinue, F. (2002). *The development and validation of the Group Supervision Scale.* Unpublished doctoral dissertation, University of Southern California.

Arkowitz, S. W. (2001). Perfectionism in the supervisee. In S. Gill (Ed.). *The supervisory alliance: Facilitating the psychotherapist's learning experience* (pp. 33–66). Northvale, NJ: Jason Aronson, Inc.

Aronson, M. L. (1990). A group therapist's perspectives on the use of supervisory groups in the training of psychotherapists. *Psychoanalysis and psychotherapy, 8,* 88–94.

Arthur, G. L., & Gfoerer, K. P. (2002). Training and supervision through the written word: A description and intern feedback. *Family Journal: Counseling and Therapy for Couples and Families, 10,* 213–219.

Atwood, J. D. (1986). Self-awareness in supervision. *Clinical Supervisor, 4*(3), 79–96.

Ault-Riche, M. (1988). Teaching an integrated model of family therapy: Women as students, women as supervisors. *Journal of Psychotherapy and the Family, 3,* 175–192. Available online at http://www.aamft.org/about/COAMFTE/standards_of_accreditation.htm.

Aveline, M. (1992). The use of audio and videotape recordings of therapy sessions in the supervision and practice of dynamic psychotherapy. *British Journal of Psychotherapy, 8,* 347–358.

Averitt, J. (1989). *Individual versus group supervision of counselor trainees.* Doctoral dissertation, University of Tennessee, 1988). *Dissertation Abstracts International, 50,* 624.

Avis, J. M., & Sprenkle, D. H. (1990). Outcome research on family therapy training: A substantive and methodological review. *Journal of Marital and Family Therapy, 16,* 241–264.

Bahrick, A. S. (1989). Role induction for counselor trainees: Effects on the supervisory working alliance. *Dissertation Abstracts International, 51*(3-B), 1484.

Bahrick, A. S. (1990). Role induction for counselor trainees: Effects on the supervisory working alliance. *Dissertation Abstracts International, 51*(3-B), 1484 (Abstract No. 1991-51645).

Bahrick, A. S., Russell, R. K., & Salmi, S. W. (1991). The effects of role induction on trainees' perceptions of supervision. *Journal of Counseling and Development, 69,* 434–438.

Baker, D. B., & Benjamin, L. T. (2000). The affirmation of the scientist–practitioner: A look back at Boulder. *American Psychologist, 55,* 241–247.

Baker, D. E. (1990). The relationship of the supervisory working alliance to supervisor and supervisee narcissism, gender, and theoretical orientation. *Dissertation Abstracts International, 51*(7-B), 3602–3603 (Abstract No. 1991-54991).

Baker, S. D., Daniels, T. G., & Greeley, A. T. (1990). Systematic training of graduate-level counselors: Narrative and meta-analytic reviews of three major programs. *Counseling Psychologist, 18,* 355–321.

Balint, E. (1985). The history of training and research in Balint groups. *Psychoanalytic Psychotherapy, 1,* 1–9.

Balint, M. (1948). On the psychoanalytic training system. *International Journal of Psychoanalysis, 29,* 163–173.

Barak, A., & LaCrosse, M. B. (1975). Multidimensional perception of counselor behavior. *Journal of Counseling Psychology, 22,* 471–476.

Bargh, J. A., & Chartrand, T. L. (2001). The unbearable automaticity of being. *American Psychologist, 54,* 462–479.

Barlow, D. H. (Ed.).(2001). *Clinical handbook of psychological disorders: A step-by-step treatment manual* (3rd ed.). New York: Guilford Press.

Barnes, K. L. (2002). *Development and initial validation of a measure of counselor supervisor self-efficacy.* Unpublished dissertation, Syracuse University.

Barnes, K. L., & Bernard, J. M. (2003). Women in counseling and psychotherapy supervision. In M. Kopala, & M. Keitel (Eds.). *The handbook of counseling women.* Thousand Oaks, CA: Sage Publications, pp. 535–545.

Baron, R. M., & Kenny, D. A. (1986). The moderator–mediator variable distinction in social psychological research: Conceptual, strategic, and statistical considerations. *Journal of Personality and Social Psychology, 51*(60), 1173–1182.

Bartell, P. A., & Rubin, L. J. (1990). Dangerous liaisons: Sexual intimacies in supervision. *Professional Psychology: Research and Practice, 21,* 442–450.

Bartlett, F. C. (1932). Remembering: An experimental and social study. New York: Cambridge University Press.

Bartlett, F. C. (1958). *Thinking.* New York: Basic Books.

Bateson, G. (1936/1958). *Naven.* New York: Cambridge University Press.

Bateson, G. (1972). *Steps to an ecology of mind.* New York: Ballantine Books.

Bauman, W. F. (1972). Games counselor trainees play: Dealing with trainee resistance. *Counselor Education and Supervision, 11,* 251–256.

Baumeister, R. F., & Leary, M. R. (1995). The need to belong: Desire for interpersonal attachments as a fundamental human motivation. *Psychological Bulletin, 117,* 497–529.

Bear, T. M., & Kivlighan, D. M., Jr. (1994). Single-subject examination of the process of supervision of beginning and advanced supervisees. *Professional Psychology: Research and Practice, 25,* 450–457.

Beavers, W. R. (1986). Family therapy supervision: An introduction and consumer's guide. *Family Therapy Education and Supervision, 1*(4), 15–24.

Beck, T. D., Yager, G. G., Williams, G. T., Williams, B. R., & Morris, J. R. (March 1989). *Training field supervisors for adult counseling situations.* A paper presented at the annual meeting of the American Association for Counseling and Development, Boston.

Behling, J., Curtis, C., & Foster, S. A. (1988). Impact of sex-role combinations on student performance in field instruction. *Clinical Supervisor, 6*(3), 161–168.

Beis, E. (1984). *Mental health and the law.* Rockville, MD: Aspen.

Belar, C. D., Bieliauskas, L. A., Klepac, R. K., Larsen, K. G., Stigall, T. T., & Zimet, C. N. (1993). National conference on postdoctural training in professional psychology. *American Psychologist, 48,* 1284–1289.

Benedek, T. (1954). Countertransference in the training analyst. *Bulletin of the Menninger Clinic, 18,* 12–16.

Benjamin, L. S. (1974). Structural analysis of social behavior. *Psychological Review, 81,* 392–425.

Benshoff, J. M. (1993). Peer supervision in counselor training. *Clinical Supervisor, 11*(2), 89–102.

Bent, R., Carlson, C., Eisman, E., Hammeke, T., James, L., King, C., et al. (November 9, 2002). Specialties and proficiencies of professional psychology. Work group product at the Association of Psychology Postdoctoral and Internship Centers 2002 Competencies Conference, Scottsdale, AZ.

Berger, M., & Dammann, C. (1982). Live supervision as context, treatment, and training. *Family Process, 21,* 337–344.

Bernard, J. L. (1975). Due process in dropping the unsuitable clinical student. *Professional Psychology, 6,* 275–278.

Bernard, J. L., & Jara, C. S. (1986). The failure of clinical psychology graduate students to apply understood ethical principles. *Professional Psychology: Research and Practice, 17,* 313–315.

Bernard, J. M. (1979). Supervisor training: A discrimination model. *Counselor Education and Supervision, 19,* 60–68.

Bernard, J. M. (1981). Inservice training for clinical supervisors. *Professional Psychology, 12,* 740–748.

Bernard, J. M. (1982). *Laboratory training for clinical supervisors: An update.* Paper presented at the annual meeting of the American Psychological Association, Washington, DC.

Bernard, J. M. (1989). Training supervisors to examine relationship variables using IPR. *Clinical Supervisor, 7*(1), 103–112.

Bernard, J. M. (1992). The challenge of psychotherapy-based supervision: Making the pieces fit. *Counselor Education and Supervision, 31,* 232–237.

Bernard, J. M. (1994a). Multicultural supervision: A reaction to Leong and Wagner, Cook, Priest, and Fukuyama. *Counselor Education and Supervision, 34,* 159–171.

Bernard, J. M. (1994b). Reaction: On-campus training of doctoral-level supervisors. In J. E.

Myers (Ed.). *Developing and directing counselor education laboratories* (pp. 141–144). Alexandria, VA: American Counseling Association.

Bernard, J. M. (1997). The Discrimination Model. In C. E. Watkins, *Handbook of psychotherapy supervision* (pp. 310–327). New York: Wiley.

Bernard, J. M. (1997). Evaluation of Counselor Behaviors—Revised. In J. M. Bernard and R. K. Goodyear (1998). *Fundamentals of Clinical Supervision* (pp. 335–33, 2nd ed). Boston: Allyn and Bacon.

Berne, E. (1964). *Games people play.* New York: Grove Press.

Berne, E. (1972). *What do you say after you say hello? The psychology of human destiny.* New York: Grove Press.

Bernstein, B. L. (1993). Promoting gender equity in counselor supervision: Challenges and opportunities. *Counselor Education and Supervision, 32,* 198–202.

Bernstein, B. L., & Lecomte, C. (1979). Self-critique technique training in a competency-based practicum. *Counselor Education and Supervision, 19,* 69–76.

Bernstein, R. M., Brown, E. M., & Ferrier, M. J. (1984). A model for collaborative team processing in brief systemic family therapy. *Journal of Marital and Family Therapy, 10,* 151–156.

Betan, E. J., & Stanton, A. L. (1999). Fostering ethical willingness integrating emotional and contextual awareness with rational analysis. *Professional Psychology: Research and Practice, 30,* 295–301.

Betcher, R. W., & Zinberg, N. E. (1988). Supervision and privacy in psychotherapy training. *American Journal of Psychiatry, 145,* 796–803.

Beutler, L. E. (1988). Introduction: Training to competency in psychotherapy. *Journal of Consulting and Clinical Psychology, 56,* 651–652.

Beutler, L. E., Moleiro, C., & Talebi, H. (2002a). Resistance in psychotherapy: What conclusions are supported by research. *Journal of*

Clinical Psychology/In Session: Psychotherapy in Practice, 58, 207–217.

Beutler, L. E., Moleiro, C., & Talebi, H. (2002b). Resistance. In J. C. Norcross (Ed.). *Psychotherapy relationships that work: Therapist contributions and responsiveness to patients* (pp. 129–144). New York: Oxford University Press.

Bion, W. (1961). *Experience in groups.* New York: Basic Books.

Birk, J. M., & Mahalik, J. R. (1996). The influence of trainee conceptual level, trainee anxiety, and supervision evaluation on counselor developmental level. *Clinical Supervisor, 14*(1), 123–137.

Blackwell, T. L., Strohmer, D. C., Belcas, E. M., & Burton, K. A. (2002). Ethics in rehabilitation counselor supervision. *Rehabilitation Counseling Bulletin, 45,* 240–247.

Blocher, D. (1983). Toward a cognitive developmental approach to counseling supervision. *Counseling Psychologist, 11,* 27–34.

Blocher, D. H. (1987). On the uses and misuses of the term theory. *Journal of Counseling and Development, 66,* 67–68.

Blodgett, E. G., Schmidt, J. F., & Scudder, R. R. (1987). Clinical session evaluation: The effect of familiarity with the supervisee. *Clinical Supervisor, 5*(1), 33–43.

Bloom, B. S., Engelhart, M. D., Furst, F. J., Hill, W. H., & Krathwohl, D. R. (1956). *Taxonomy of educational objectives: Cognitive domain.* New York: McKay.

Bloom, J. W. (2000). Technology and web counseling. In H. Hackney (Ed.). *Practice issues for the beginning counselor* (pp. 183–202). Boston: Allyn and Bacon.

Bob, S. (1999). Narrative approaches to supervision and case formulation. *Psychotherapy: Theory/research/practice/training, 36,* 146–153.

Bonney, W. (1994). Teaching supervision: Some practical issues for beginning supervisors.

Bonosky, N. (1995). Boundary violations in social work supervision: Clinical, educational and legal implications. *Clinical Supervisor, 13*(2), 79–95.

Borders, L. D. (1989a). A pragmatic agenda for developmental supervision research.

Borders, L. D. (1989b). Developmental cognitions of first practicum supervisees. *Journal of*

Borders, L. D. (1990). Developmental changes during supervisees' first practicum. *Clinical Supervisor, 8*(2), 157–167.

Borders, L. D. (1992). Learning to think like a supervisor. *Clinical Supervisor, 10*(2), 135–148.

Borders, L. D. (2001). Counseling supervision: A deliberate educational process. In D. Locke, J. Myers, & E. Herr (Eds.). *Handbook of counseling* (pp. 417–432). Thousand Oaks, CA: Sage.

Borders, L. D., Bernard, J. M., Dye, H. A., Fong, M. L., Henderson, P., & Nance, D. W. (1991). Curriculum guide for training counseling supervisors: Rationale, development, and implementation. *Counselor Education and Supervision, 31,* 58–82.

Borders, L. D., & Cashwell, C. S. (1992). Supervision regulations in counselor licensure legislation. *Counselor Education and Supervision, 31,* 209–218.

Borders, L. D., Cashwell, C. S., & Rotter, J. C. (1995). Supervision of counselor licensure applicants: A comparative study. *Counselor Education and Supervision, 35,* 54–69.

Borders, L. D., & Fong, M. L. (1991). Evaluations of supervisees: Brief commentary and research report. *Clinical Supervisor, 9*(2), 43–51.

Borders, L. D., Fong, M. L., & Neimeyer, C. J. (1986). Counseling students' level of ego development and perceptions of clients. *Counselor Education and Supervision, 26,* 36–49.

Borders, L. D., & Leddick, G. R. (1987). *Handbook of Counseling Supervision.* Alexandria, VA: Association for Counselor Education and Supervision.

Borders, L. D., & Leddick, G. R. (1988). A nationwide survey of supervision training. *Counselor Education and Supervision, 27*(3), 271–283.

Borders, L. D., & Usher, C. H. (1992). Postdegree supervision: Existing and preferred practices. *Journal of Counseling and Development, 70,* 594–599.

Bordin, E. S. (1979). The generalizability of the psychodynamic concept of the working alliance. *Psychotherapy: Theory, research, and practice, 16,* 252–260.

Bordin, E. S. (1983). A working alliance model of supervision. *Counseling Psychologist, 11,* 35–42.

Bowen, M. (1978). *Family therapy in clinical practice.* New York: Aronson.

Bowlby, J. (1969). *Attachment and loss: Attachment* (Vol. 1). New York: Basic Books.

Bowlby, J. (1977). The making and breaking of affectional bonds. I. Aetiology and psychopathology in the light of attachment theory. *British Journal of Psychiatry, 130,* 201–210.

Bowlby, J. (1978). Attachment theory and its therapeutic implications. In S. C. Feinstein & P. C. Giovacchini (Eds.). *Adolescent psychiatry* (Vol. VI: Development and clinical studies, pp. 5–33). Chicago: University of Chicago Press.

Bownan, V. E., Hatley, L. D., & Bownan, R. L. (1995). Faculty–student relationships: The dual role controversy. *Counselor Education and Supervision, 34,* 232–242.

Boxley, R., Drew, C., & Rangel, D. (1986). Clinical trainee impairment in APA approved internship programs. *Clinical Psychologist, 39,* 49–52.

Boyd, J. (1978). *Counselor supervision: Approaches, preparation, practices.* Muncie, IN: Accelerated Development, Inc.

Bradey, J., & Post, P. (1991). Impaired students: Do we eliminate them from counselor education programs? *Counselor Education and Supervision, 31,* 100–108.

Bradley, C., & Fiorini, J. (1999). Evaluation of counseling practicum: National study of programs accredited by CACREP. *Counselor Education & Supervision, 30*(2), 110–119.

Bradley, J. R., & Olson, J. K. (1980). Training factors influencing felt psychotherapeutic competence of psychology trainees. *Professional Psychology, 11,* 930–934.

Bradley, L. J., & Gould, L. J. (1994). Supervisee resistance. *ERIC Digest.* ERIC Identifier: ED372344. Greensboro, NC: ERIC Clearinghouse on Counseling and Student Services.

Bradshaw, W. H., Jr. (1982). Supervision in black and white: Race as a factor in supervision. In M. Blumenfield (Ed.). *Applied supervision in psychotherapy* (pp. 199–220). New York: Grune & Stratton.

Brandell, J. R. (1992). Focal conflict analysis: A method of supervision in psychoanalytic psychotherapy. *Clinical Supervisor, 10*(1), 51–69.

Brantley, A. P. (2000). A clinical supervision documentation form. In L. VandeCreek and T. L. Jackson (Eds.). *Innovations in clinical practice: A sourcebook* (Vol. 18, pp. 301–307). Sarasota, FL: Professional Resource Press.

Brashears, F. (1995). Supervision as social work practice: A reconceptualization. *Social Work, 40,* 692–699.

Brehm, J. (1966). *A theory of psychological reactance.* New York: Academic Press.

Brehm, S. S., & Brehm, J. W. (1981). *Psychological reactance: A theory of freedom and control.* New York: Wiley.

Breunlin, D., Karrer, B., McGuire, D., & Cimmarusti, R. (1988). Cybernetics of videotape supervision. In H. Liddle, D. Breunlin, & R. Schwartz, (Eds.). *Handbook of family therapy training and supervision* (pp. 194–206). New York: Guilford.

Bridges, N. A. (1999). The role of supervision in managing intense affect and constructing boundaries in therapeutic relationships. *Journal of Sex Education and Therapy, 24*(4), 218–225.

Bridges, N. A., & Wohlberg, J. W. (1999). Sexual excitement in therapeutic relationships: Clinical and supervisory management. *Clinical Supervisor, 18*(2), 123–141.

Brill, R., Wolkin, J., & McKeel, N. (1987). Strategies for selecting and securing the predoctoral clinical internship of choice. In R. H. Dana & W. T. May (Eds.). *Internship training in professions psychology* (pp. 220–226). New York: Hemisphere.

Brock, C. D., & Stock, R. D. (1990). A survey of Balint group activities in U.S. family practice residency programs. *Family Medicine, 22,* 33–37.

Broder, E., & Sloman, L. (1982). A contextual comparison of three training programmes. In R. Whiffen & F. Byng-Hall (Eds.). *Family therapy supervision: Recent developments in practice* (229–242). London: Academic Press.

Brodsky, A. (1980). Sex role issues in the supervision of therapy. In A. K. Hess (Ed.). *Psychotherapy supervision: Theory, research and practice* (pp. 509–524). New York: John Wiley.

Brodsky, S., & Myers, H. H. (1986). In vivo rotation: An alternative model for psychotherapy supervision. *Clinical Supervisor, 4*(1), 95–104.

Brown, L. M., & Gilligan, C. (1990, August). *Listening for self and relational voices: A responsive/resisting reader's guide.* Paper presented at the annual meeting of the American Psychological Association, Boston.

Brown, R. W., & Otto, M. L. (1986). Field supervision: A collaborative model. *Michigan Journal of Counseling and Development, 17*(2), 48–51.

Bruce, M. A. (1995). Mentoring women doctoral students: What counselor educators and supervisors can do. *Counselor Education and Supervision, 35,* 139–149.

Bruss, K. V., Brack, C. J., Brack, G., Glickauf-Hughes, C., & O'Leary, M. (1997). A developmental model for supervising therapists treating gay, lesbian, and bisexual clients. *Clinical Supervisor, 15*(1), 61–73.

Bubenzer, D. L., Mahrle, C., & West, J. D. (1987). *Live counselor supervision: Trainee acculturation and supervisor interventions.* Paper presented at the American Association for Counseling and Development Annual Convention, New Orleans, LA.

Bubenzer, D. L., West, J. D., & Gold, J. M. (1991). Use of live supervision in counselor preparation. *Counselor Education and Supervision, 30,* 301–308.

Buhrke, R. A. (1989). Incorporating lesbian and gay issues into counselor training: A resource guide. *Journal of Counseling and Development, 68,* 77–80.

Buhrke, R. A., & Douce, L. A. (1991). Training issues for counseling psychologists in working with lesbian women and gay men. *Counseling Psychologist, 19,* 216–234.

Burian, B. K., & Slimp, A. O. (2000). Social dual-role relationships during internship: A decision-making model [Special issue]. *Professional Psychology: Research and Practice, 31*(3), 332–338.

Burke, W., Goodyear, R. K., & Guzzard, C. (1998). A multiple-case study of weakenings and repairs in supervisory alliances. *American Journal of Psychotherapy, 52,* 450–462.

Burns, C. I., & Holloway, E. L. (1989). Therapy in supervision: An unresolved issue. *Clinical Supervisor, 7*(4), 47–60.

Byng-Hall, J. (1982). The use of the earphone in supervision. In R. Whiffen & J. Byng-Hall (Eds.). *Family therapy supervision: Recent developments in practice* (pp. 47–56). London: Academic Press.

Cade, B. W., Speed, B., & Seligman, P. (1986). Working in teams: The pros and cons. *Clinical Supervisor, 4,* 105–117.

Caldwell, K., Becvar, D. S., Bertolino, R., & Diamond, D. (1997). A postmodern analysis of a course on clinical supervision. *Contemporary Family Therapy, 19,* 269–287.

Caligor, L. (1984). Parallel and reciprocal processes in psychoanalytic supervision. In L. Caligor, P. M. Bromberg, & J. D. Meltzer (Eds.). *Clinical perspectives on the supervision of psychoanalysis and psychotherapy.* New York: Plenum.

Campbell, T. W. (1994). Psychotherapy and malpractice exposure. *American Journal of Forensic Psychology, 12,* 5–41.

Campione, K. M. (1993). Pretraining by role induction: A test of effect on supervision (counselor education). *Dissertation Abstracts International, 54*(7-A), 2511.

Caplan, G. (1970). *The theory and practice of mental health consultation.* New York: Basic Books.

Caplow, T. (1968). *Two against one: Coalitions in triads.* Upper Saddle River, NJ: Prentice Hall.

Capraro, R. M., & Capraro, M. M. (2002). Myers-Briggs Type Indicator score reliability across studies: a meta-analytic reliability generalization study. *Educational and Psychological Measurement, 62,* 590–602.

Carey, J. C. & Lanning, W. L. (1993). Supervisors emphases in the master's practicum. *Clinical Supervisor, 11*(1), 203–215.

Carey, J. C., & Williams, K. S. (1986). Cognitive style in counselor education: A comparison of practicum supervisors and counselors in training. *Counselor Education and Supervision, 26,* 128–136.

Carkhuff, R. R. (1969). *Helping and human relations* (Vol. 2). New York: Holt, Rinehart and Winston.

Carkhuff, R. R., & Truax, C. B. (1965). Training in counseling and psychotherapy: An evaluation of an integrated didactic and experiential approach. *Journal of Consulting Psychology, 29,* 333–336.

Carlozzi, A. F., Romans, J. S. C., Boswell, D. L., Ferguson, D. B., & Whisenhunt, B. J. (1997). Training and supervision practices in counseling and marriage and family therapy programs. *Clinical Supervisor, 15*(1), 51–60.

Carroll, M. (1996). *Counseling supervision: Theory, skills, and practice.* London: Cassell.

Carroll, M. (2001). The spirituality of supervision. In M. Carroll & M. Tholstrup (Eds.). *Integrative approaches to supervision.* London: Jessica Kingsley Publishers, pp. 76–89.

Carson, R. C. (1969). *Interaction concepts of personality.* Chicago: Aldine.

Carter, R. T., & Qureshi, A. (1995). A typology of philosophical assumptions in multicultural counseling and training. In P. Ponterotto, J. M. Casas, L. A. Suzuki, & C. M. Alexander (Eds.). *Handbook of multicultural counseling* (pp. 239–262). Thousand Oaks, CA: Sage.

Cartwright, D., & Zander, A. (1968). *Group dynamics: Research and theory* (3rd ed.). New York: Harper & Row.

Casey, J. A., Bloom, J. W., & Moan, E. R. (1994). Use of technology in counselor supervision. In L. D. Borders (Ed.). *Supervision: Exploring the effective components.* Greensboro, NC: ERIC/CASS, EDO-CG-94-25.

Cashwell, C. S., Looby, E. J., & Housley, W. F. (1997). Appreciating cultural diversity through clinical supervision. *Clinical Supervision, 15*(1), 75–85.

Celenza, A. (1998). Prescursors to the therapist sexual misconduct: Preliminary findings. *Psychoanalytic Psychology, 15,* 378–395.

Center for Credentialing and Education (2001). *Approved Clinical Supervisor.* Greensboro, NC: Author.

Chagnon, J., & Russell, R. K. (1995). Assessment of supervisee developmental level and supervision environment across supervisor experience. *Journal of Counseling and Development, 73,* 553–558.

Chaiklin, H., & Munson, C. E. (1983). Peer consultation in social work. *Clinical Supervisor, 1,* 21–34.

Chaimowitz, G. A., Glancy, G. D., & Blackburn, J. (2000). The duty to warn and protect: Impact on practice. *Canadian Journal of Psychiatry, 45,* 899–904.

Chambless, D. L., Baker, M. J., Baucom, D. H., Beutler, L. E., Calhoun, K. S., Crits-Christoph, P., Williams, D. A. & Woody, S. R. (1998). Update on empirically validated therapies, II. *Clinical Psychologist, 51,* 3–16.

Chapin, J., & Ellis, M. V. (2002). Effects of role induction workshops on supervisee anxiety. Paper presented at the annual meeting of the American Psychological Association, Chicago.

Chen, E. C., & Bernstein, B. L. (2000). Relations of Complementarity and supervisory issues to supervisory working alliance: A comparative analysis of two cases. *Journal of Counseling Psychology, 47,* 485–497.

Chickering, A. W. (1969). *Education and identity.* San Francisco: Jossey-Bass.

Chung, Y. B., Marshall, J. A., & Gordon, L. L. (2001). Racial and gender biases in supervisory evaluation and feedback [Special issue]. *Clinical Supervisor, 20*(1), 99–111.

Claiborn, C. D., Etringer, B. D., & Hillerbrand, E. T. (1995). Influence processes in supervision. *Counselor Education and Supervision, 35,* 43–53.

Claiborn, C. D., Goodyear, R. K., & Horner, P. A. (2002). Feedback. In J. C. Norcross (Ed.). *Psychotherapy relationships that work: Therapist contributions and responsiveness to patients* (pp. 217–234). New York: Oxford University Press.

Claiborn, C. D., & Lichtenberg, J. W. (1989). Interactional counseling. *Counseling Psychologist, 17,* 355–453.

Clarkson, P. (1994). In recognition of dual relationships. *Transactional Analysis Journal, 24,* 32–38.

Clifton, D., Doan, R., & Mitchell, D. (1990). The reauthoring of therapist's stories: Taking doses of our own medicine. *Journal of Strategic and Systemic Therapies, 9*(4), 61–66.

Cobia, D. C., & Boes, S. R. (2000). Professional disclosure statements and formal plans for supervision: Two strategies for minimizing the risk of ethical conflicts in post-master's supervision. *Journal of Counseling and Development, 78*(3), 293–296.

Cobia, D. C., & Pipes, R. B. (2002). Mandated supervision: An intervention for disciplined professionals. *Journal of Counseling and Development, 80,* 140–144.

Coffey, D. (2002). *Receiving corrective feedback: A special set of skills.* Presentation at the Association for Counselor Education and Supervision Convention. Park City, UT.

Cohen, B. Z. (1987). The ethics of social work supervision revisited. *Social Work, 32,* 194–196.

Cohen, M., Gross, S., & Turner, M. (1976). A note on a developmental model for training family therapists through group supervision. *Journal of Marriage and Family Counseling, 2,* 48–56.

Cohen, R. J. (1979). *Malpractice: A guide for mental health professionals.* New York: Free Press.

Coll, K. M. (1995). Clinical supervision of community college counselors: Current and preferred practices. *Counselor Education and Supervision, 35,* 111–117.

Collins, D., & Bogo, M. (1986). Competency-based field instruction: Bridging the gap between laboratory and field learning. *Clinical Supervisor, 4*(3), 39–52.

Congress, E. P. (1992). Ethical decision making of social work supervisors. *Clinical Supervisor, 10*(1), 157–169.

Constantine, J. A., Piercy, F. P., & Sprenkle, D. H. (1984). Live supervision-of-supervision in family therapy. *Journal of Marital and Family Therapy, 10,* 95–97.

Constantine, M. G. (1997). Facilitating multicultural competency in counseling supervision: Operationalizing a practical framework. In D. B. Pope-Davis and H. L. K. Coleman (Eds.). *Multicultural counseling competencies: Assessment, education and training, and supervision* (pp. 310–324). Thousand Oaks, CA: Sage.

Constantine, M. G. (2001). Multiculturally-focused counseling supervision: Its relationship to trainees' multicultural self-efficacy. *Clinical Supervisor, 20*(1), 87–98.

Cook, D. A. (1994). Racial identity in supervision. *Counselor Education and Supervision, 34,* 132–141.

Cook, D. A., & Helms, J. E. (1988). Visible racial/ethnic group supervisees' satisfaction with cross-cultural supervision as predicted by relationship characteristics. *Journal of Counseling Psychology, 35,* 268–274.

Cooper, L., & Gustafson, J. P. (1985). Supervision in a group: An application of group theory. *Clinical Supervisor, 3,* 7–25.

Copeland, S. (1998). Counselling supervision in organizational contexts: New challenges and perspectives [Special issue]. *British Journal of Guidance and Counselling, 26*(3), 377–386.

Corey, G., Corey, M. S., & Callanan, P. (1993). *Issues and ethics in the helping professions* (4th ed.). Pacific Grove, CA: Brooks/Cole.

Cormier, L. S., & Bernard, J. M. (1982). Ethical and legal responsibilities of clinical supervisors. *Personnel and Guidance Journal, 60,* 486–491.

Cornell, W. F. (1994). Dual relationships in transactional analysis: Training, supervision, and therapy. *Transactional Analysis Journal, 24,* 21–30.

Corrigan, J. D., Dell, D. M., Lewis, K. N., & Schmidt, L. D. (1980). Counseling as a social influence process: A review [Monograph]. *Journal of Counseling Psychology 27,* 395–441.

Costa, L. (1994). Reducing anxiety in live supervision. *Counselor Education and Supervision, 34,* 30–40.

Couchon, W. D., & Bernard, J. M. (1984). Effects of timing of supervision on supervisor and counselor performance. *Clinical Supervisor, 2*(3), 3–20.

Council for the Accreditation of Counseling and Related Educational Programs (1994). *CACREP Accreditation Standards and Procedures Manual.* Alexandria, VA: Author.

Council for Accreditation of Counseling and Related Educational Programs (CACREP). (2001). *The 2001 Standards.* Author. http://www.counseling.org/cacrep/2001standards700.htm.

Counselman, E. F., & Gumpert, P. (1993). Psychotherapy supervision in small leader-led groups. *Group, 17,* 25–32.

Covey, S. R., Merrill, A. R., & Merrill, R. R. (1994). *First things first.* New York: Simon & Schuster.

Covner, B. J. (1942a). Studies in phonographic recordings of verbal material: I. The use of phonographic recordings in counseling practice and research. *Journal of Consulting Psychology, 6,* 105–113.

Covner, B. J. (1942b). Studies in phonographic recordings of verbal material: II. A device for transcribing phonographic recordings of verbal material. *Journal of Consulting Psychology, 6,* 149–151.

Craig, C. H., & Sleight, C. C. (1990). Personality relationships between supervisors and students in communication disorders as determined by the Myers–Briggs Type Indicator. *Clinical Supervisor, 8*(1), 41–51.

Cummings, A. L., Hallberg, E. T., Martin, J., Slemon, A., & Hiebert, B. (1990). Implications of counselor conceptualizations for counselor education. *Counselor Education and Supervision, 30,* 120–134.

Daniels, J., D'Andrea, M., & Kim, B. S. K. (1999). Assessing the barriers and changes of cross-cultural supervision: A case study. *Counselor Education and Supervision, 38*(3), 191–204.

Daniels, J. A., & Larson, L. M. (2001). The impact of performance feedback on counseling self-efficacy and counselor anxiety. *Counselor Education and Supervision, 41*(2), 120–130.

Dawes, R. M. (1994). *House of cards: Psychology and psychotherapy built on myth.* New York: The Free Press.

Deacon, S. A. (2000). Using divergent thinking exercises within supervision to enhance therapist creativity. *Journal of Family Psychotherapy, 11*(2), 67–73.

Delaney, D. J. (1972). A behavioral model for the practicum supervision of counselor candidates. *Counselor Education and Supervision, 12,* 46–50.

deMayo, R. A. (2000). Patients' sexual behavior and sexual harassment: A survey of clinical supervisors. *Professional Psychology: Research and Practice, 31*(6), 706–709.

Dennin, M. K., & Ellis, M. V. (2003). Effects of a method of self-supervision for counselor trainees. *Journal of Counseling Psychology, 50,* 69–83. *Development, 66,* 67–68.

Dickey, K. D., Housley, W. F., & Guest, C. (1993). Ethics in supervision of rehabilitation counselor trainees: A survey. *Rehabilitation Education, 7,* 195–201.

Disney, M. J. & Stephens, A. M. (1994). Legal issues in clinical supervision. Alexandria, VA: ACA Press.

Division 44/Committee on Lesbian, Gay, and Bisexual Concerns Joint Task Force on Guidelines for Psychotherapy with Lesbian, Gay, and Bisexual Clients. (2000). Guidelines for psychotherapy with lesbian, gay, and bisexual clients. *American Psychologist, 55,* 1440–1451.

Dixon, D. N., & Claiborn, C. D. (1987). A social influence approach to counselor supervision. In J. E. Maddux, C. D. Stoltenberg, & R.

Rosenwein (Eds.). *Social processes in clinical and counseling psychology* (pp. 83–93). New York: Springer-Verlag.

Dodds, J. B. (1986). Supervision of psychology trainees in field placements. *Professional Psychology: Research and Practice, 17,* 296–300.

Dodenhoff, J. T. (1981). Interpersonal attraction and direct–indirect supervisor influence as predictors of counselor trainee effectiveness. *Journal of Counseling Psychology, 28,* 47–52.

Doehrman, M. (1976). Parallel processes in supervision and psychotherapy. *Bulletin of the Menninger Clinic, 40,* 3–104.

Dombeck, M. T., & Brody, S. L. (1995). Clinical supervision: A three-way mirror. *Archives of psychiatric nursing, 9,* 3–10.

Douce, L. (1989, August). *Classroom and experiential training in supervision.* Paper presented at the annual meeting of the American Psychological Association, New Orleans, LA.

Dowd, E. T. (1989). Stasis and change in cognitive psychotherapy: Client resistance and reactance as mediating variables. In W. Dryden & P. Trower (Eds.). *Cognitive psychotherapy: Stasis and change* (pp. 139–158). New York: Springer-Verlag.

Dowling, S. (1984). Clinical evaluation: A comparison of self, self with videotape, peers, and supervisors. *Clinical Supervisor, 2*(3), 71–78.

Duan, C., & Roehlke, H. (2001). A descriptive "snapshot" of cross-racial supervision in university counseling center internships [Special issue]. *Journal of Multicultural Counseling and Development, 29*(2), 131–146.

Duys, D. K., & Hedstrom, S. M. (2000). Basic counselor skills training and counselor cognitive complexity. *Counselor Education and Supervision, 40,* 8–18.

Dye, A. (1994). Training doctoral student supervisors at Purdue University. In J. E. Myers (Ed.). *Developing and directing counselor education laboratories* (pp. 121–130). Alexandria, VA: American Counseling Association.

Edwards, J. K., and Chen, M. W. (1999). Strength-based supervision: Frameworks, current prac-

tice, and future directions: A Wu Wei method. *Family Journal, 7,* 349–357.

Efstation, J. F., Patton, M. J., & Kardash, C. M. (1990). Measuring the working alliance in counselor supervision. *Journal of Counseling Psychology, 37,* 322–329.

Eisenberg, S. (1956). *Supervision in the changing field of social work.* Philadelphia: Jewish Family Service of Philadelphia.

Ekstein, R. (1964). Supervision of psychotherapy: Is it teaching? Is it administration? Or is it therapy? *Psychotherapy, Research, and Practice, 1,* 137–138.

Ekstein, R., & Wallerstein, R. S. (1972). *The teaching and learning of psychotherapy* (2nd ed.). New York: International Universities Press.

Elizur, J. (1990). "Stuckness" in live supervision: Expanding the therapist's style. *Journal of Family Therapy, 12,* 267–280.

Elks, M. A., & Kirkhart, K. E. (1993). Evaluating effectiveness from the practitioner perspective. *Social Work, 38,* 554–563.

Ellis, A. (1974). *The techniques of Disputing Irrational Beliefs (DIBS).* New York: Institute for Rational Living.

Ellis, A. (1989). Thoughts on supervising counselors and therapists. *Psychology: A Journal of Human Behavior, 26,* 3–5.

Ellis, M. V. (1991). Critical incidents in clinical supervision and in supervisor supervision: Assessing supervisory issues. *Journal of Counseling Psychology,* 342–349.

Ellis, M. V., Anderson-Hanley, C. M., Dennin, M. K., Anderson, J. J., Chapin, J. L., & Polstri, S. M. (August, 1994). *Congruence of expectation in clinical supervision: Scale development and validity data.* Paper presented at the American Psychological Association, Los Angeles.

Ellis, M. V., Chapin, J. L., Dennin, M. K., & Anderson-Hanley, C. (August 1996). *Role induction for clinical supervision: Impact on neophyte supervisees.* Paper presented at the American Psychological Association, Toronto, ON.

Ellis, M. V., & Dell, D. M. (1986). Dimensionality of supervisor roles: Supervisors' perceptions of supervision. *Journal of Counseling Psychology, 33,* 282–291.

Ellis, M. V., Dell, D. M., & Good, G. E. (1988). Counselor trainees' perceptions of supervisor roles: Two studies testing the dimensionality of supervision. *Journal of Counseling Psychology, 35,* 315–322.

Ellis, M. V., Dennin, M. K., Anderson-Hanley, C., Chapin, J. L., Swagler, M. A., & DelGenio, J. (August 1993). *Performance anxiety in clinical supervision: Scale construction and validation.* Paper presented at the meeting of the American Psychological Association, Toronto, ON.

Ellis, M. V., & Douce, L. A. (1994). Group supervision of novice clinical supervisors: Eight recurring issues. *Journal of Counseling and Development, 72,* 520–525.

Ellis, M. V., Krengel, M., & Beck, M. (2002). Testing self-focused attention theory in clinical supervision: Effects of supervisee anxiety and performance. *Journal of Counseling Psychology, 49,* 101–116.

Ellis, M. V., & Ladany, N. (1997). Inferences concerning supervisees and clients in clinical supervision: An integrative review. In C. E. Watkins, Jr. (Ed.). *Handbook of psychotherapy supervision* (pp. 467–507). New York: Wiley.

Ellis, M. V., Ladany, N., Krengel, V., & Schult, D. (August 1988). *An investigation of supervision research methodology: Where have we gone wrong?* Paper presented at the annual meeting of the American Psychological Association, Atlanta, GA.

Ellis, M. V., Ladany, N., Krengel, M., & Schult, D. (1996). Clinical supervision research from 1981 to 1993: A methodological critique. *Journal of Counseling Psychology, 43,* 35–50.

Ellis, M. V., & Robbins, E. S. (1993). Voices of care and justice in clinical supervision: Issues and interventions. *Counselor Education & Supervision, 32,* 203–212.

Enyedy, K. C., Arcinue, F., Puri, N. N., Carter, J. W., Goodyear, R. K., & Getzelman. M. (2003). Hindering phenomena in group supervision: Implications for Practice. *Profes-sional Psychology: Research and Practice, 34,* 312–317.

Epstein, L. (2001). Collusive selection inattention to the negative impact of the supervisory interaction. In S. Grill (Ed.). *The supervisory alliance: Facilitating the psychotherapist's learning experience* (pp. 139–163). Northvale, NJ: Jason Aronson, Inc.

Erera, I. P., & Lazar, A. (1994). The adminstrative and educational functions in supervision: Indications of incompatibility. *Clinical Supervisor, 12*(2), 39–55.

Ericcson, K. A., & Lehmann, A. C. (1996). Expert and exceptional performance: Evidence of maximal adaptation to task constraints. *Annual Review of Psychology, 47,* 273–305.

Erwin, W. J. (2000). Supervisor moral sensitivity. *Counseling Education and Supervision, 40,* 115–127.

Falender, C., Cornish, J. A. E., Goodyear, R. K., Hatcher, R., Kaslow, N. J., Leventhal, G., et al. (in press). Defining competencies in psychology supervision: A consensus statement. *Journal of Clinical Psychology.*

Fall, M., & Sutton, J. M. Jr. (2004). *Clinical Supervision: A handbook for practitioners.* Boston: Allyn and Bacon.

Falvey, J. E. (1987). *Handbook of administrative supervision.* Alexandria, VA: Association for Counselor Education and Supervision.

Falvey, J. E. (2002). *Managing clinical supervision: Ethical practice and legal risk management.* Pacific Grove, CA: Brooks/Cole.

Falvey, J. E., Caldwell, C. F., & Cohen, C. R. (2002). *Documentation in supervision: The focused risk management supervision system.* Pacific Grove, CA: Brooks/Cole.

Falvey, J. E., & Cohen, C. R. (2003). The buck stops here: Documenting clinical supervision. Unpublished manuscript.

Farrell, A. D. (1989). Impact of computers on professional practice: A survey of current practices and attitudes. *Professional Psychology: Research and Practice, 20,* 172–178.

Feiner, A. H. (1994). Comments on contradictions in the supervisory process. *Contemporary Psychoanalysis, 30,* 57–75.

Fennell, D. L., Hovestadt, A. J., & Harvey, S. J. (1986). A comparison of delayed feedback and live supervision models of marriage and family therapist clinical training. *Journal of Marital and Family Therapy, 12,* 181–186.

Fiscalini, J. (1985). On supervisory parataxis and dialogue. In M. H. Rock (Ed.). *Psychodynamic supervision: Perspectives of the supervisor and supervisee* (pp. 29–51). Northvale, NJ: Jason Aronson, Inc.

Fisher, B. (1989). Differences between supervision of beginning and advanced therapists: Hogan's hypothesis empirically revisited. *Clinical Supervisor, 7*(1), 57–74.

Fitzgerald, L. E., & Osipow, S. H. (1986). An occupational analysis of counseling psychology: How special is the specialty? *American Psychologist, 41,* 535–544.

Fleming, J. (1953). The role of supervision in psychiatric training. *Bulletin of the Menninger Clinic, 17,* 157–159.

Fleming, J., & Benedek, T. (1966). *Psychoanalytic supervision.* New York: Grune and Stratton.

Fly, B. J., van Bark, W. P., Weinman, L., Kitchener, K. S., & Lang, P. R. (1997). Ethical transgressions of psychology graduate students: Critical incidents with implications for training. *Professional Psychology: Research and Practice, 28,* 492–495.

Follette, W. C., & Callaghan, G. M. (1995). Do as I do, not as I say: A behavior–analytic approach to supervision. *Professional Psychology: Research and Practice, 26,* 413–421.

Fong, M. L., Borders, L. D., Ethington, C. A., & Pitts, J. H. (1997). Becoming a counselor: A longitudinal study of student cognitive development. *Counselor Education and Supervision, 37*(2), 100–114.

Fong, M. L., Borders, L. D., & Neimeyer, G. J. (1986). Sex role orientation and self-disclosure flexibility in counselor training. *Counselor Education and Supervision, 25*(3), 210–221.

Fong, M. L., & Lease, S. H. (1997). Cross-cultural supervision: Issues for the white supervisor. In D. B. Pope-Davis and H. L. K. Coleman (Eds.). *Multicultural counseling competencies: Assessment, education and training, and supervision* (pp. 387–405). Thousand Oaks, CA: Sage.

Ford, S. J. W., & Britton, P. J. (2002). *Multicultural supervision: What's really going on?* Presentation at the American Counselor Education and Supervision Conference. Park City, UT.

Forrest, L., Elman, N., Gizara, S., & Vacha-Haase, T. (1999). Trainee impairment: A review of identification, remediation, dismissal, and legal issues. *Counseling Psychologist, 27*(5), 627–686.

Foster, J. T. (2002). *Attachment behavior and psychotherapy supervision.* Unpublished dissertation, Department of Psychological Research in Education, University of Kansas, Lawrence, KS.

Fox, R. (1983). Contracting in supervision: A goal oriented process. *Clinical Supervisor, 1*(1), 37–49.

Frame, M. W. (2001). The spiritual genogram in training and supervision. *Family Journal—Counseling and Therapy for Couples and Families, 9*(2), 109–115.

Frame, M. W., & Stevens-Smith, P. (1995). Out of harm's way: Enhancing monitoring and dismissal processes in counselor education programs. *Counselor Education and Supervision, 35,* 118–129.

Frank, A. D. (1961). *Persuasion and healing.* Baltimore: Johns Hopkins University Press.

Frankel, B. R. (1990). Process of family therapy live supervision: A brief report. *Commission on Supervision Bulletin, 3*(1), 5–6.

Frankel, B. R., & Piercy, F. P. (1990). The relationship among selected supervisor, therapist, and client behaviors. *Journal of Marital and Family Therapy, 16,* 407–421.

Frawley-O'Dea, M. G., & Sarnat, J. E. (2001). *The supervisory relationship: A contemporary psychodynamic approach.* New York: Guilford Press.

Frayn, D. H. (1991). Supervising the supervisors: The evolution of a psychotherapy supervisors' group. *American Journal of Psychotherapy, 45,* 31–42.

Freeman, B., & McHenry, S. (1996). Clinical supervision of counselors-in-training: A nationwide survey of ideal delivery, goals, and theoretical influences. *Counselor Education and Supervision, 36,* 144–158.

Freeman, S. C. (1993). Reiterations on client-centered supervision. *Counselor Education and Supervision, 32,* 213–215.

French, J. R. P., Jr., & Raven, B. (1959). The bases of social power. In D. Cartwright (Ed.), *Studies in social power.* Ann Arbor, MI: Institute for Social Research.

Freud, S. (1909). Analysis of a phobia in a five-year-old boy. In Standard edition of the complete psychological works. Volume X. London: Hogarth, 1973.

Freud, S. (1986). On the history of the psychoanalytic movement (first published in 1914) in *Historical and Expository Works on Psychoanalysis.* Harmondsworth, England: Penguin.

Frick, D. E., McCartney, C. I., Lazarus, J. A. (1995). Supervision of sexually exploitive psychiatrists: APA district branch experience. *Psychiatric Annals, 25,* 113–117.

Fried, L. (1991). Becoming a psychotherapist. *Journal of College Student Psychotherapy, 5,* 71–79.

Fried, Y., Tiegs, R. B., & Bellamy, A. R. (1992). Personal and interpersonal predictors of supervisors' avoidance of evaluating subordinates. *Journal of Applied Psychology, 77,* 462–468.

Friedberg, R. D., & Taylor, L. A. (1994). Perspectives on supervision in cognitive therapy. *Journal of Rational–Emotive & Cognitive Behavior Therapy, 12*(3), 147–161.

Friedlander, M. L. (1980). The effects of delayed role induction on counseling process and outcome. *Dissertation Abstracts International, 41*(10-B), 3887.

Friedlander, M. L., Keller, K. E., Peca-Baker, T. A., & Olk, M. E. (1986). Effects of role conflict on counselor trainees' self-statements, anxiety level, and performance. *Journal of Counseling Psychology, 33,* 73–77.

Friedlander, M. L., & Schwartz, G. S. (1985). Toward a theory of strategic self-presentation in counseling and psychotherapy. *Journal of Counseling Psychology, 32,* 483–501.

Friedlander, M. L., Siegel, S. M., & Brenock, K. (1989). Parallel process in counseling and supervision: A case study. *Journal of Counseling Psychology, 36,* 149–157.

Friedlander, M. L., & Snyder, J. (1983). Trainees' expectations for the supervisory process: Testing a developmental model. *Counselor Education and Supervision, 22,* 342–348.

Friedlander, M. L., & Ward, L. G. (1984). Development and validation of the Supervisory Styles Inventory. *Journal of Counseling Psychology, 31,* 542–558.

Friedman, D., & Kaslow, N. J. (1986). The development of professional identity in psychotherapists: Six stages in the supervision process. *Clinical Supervisor, 4*(1–2), 29–49.

Friedman, R. (1983). Aspects of the parallel process and counter-transference issues in student supervision. *School Social Work Journal, 8*(1), 3–15.

Frohman, A. L. (1998). Building a culture for innovation. *Research Technology Management, 41,* 9–12.

Fukuyama, M. A. (1994). Critical incidents in multicultural counseling supervision: A phenomenological approach to supervision. *Counselor Education and Supervision, 34,* 142–151.

Fulero, S. M. (1988). Tarasoff: 10 years later. *Professional Psychology: Research and Practice, 19,* 184–190.

Fuller, F. F., & Manning, B. A. (1973). Self-confrontation reviewed: A conceptualization for video playback in teacher education. *Review of Educational Research, 43,* 469–528.

Galassi, J. P., & Brooks, L. (1992). Integrating scientist and practitioner training in counseling psychology: Practicum is the key. *Counselling Psychology Quarterly, 5,* 57–65.

Gallant, J. P., & Thyer, B. A. (1989). The "bug-in-the-ear" in clinical supervision: A review. *Clinical Supervisor, 7*(2), 43–58.

Gallant, J. P., Thyer, B. A., & Bailey, J. S. (1991). Using bug-in-the-ear feedback in clinical supervision. *Research on Social Work Practice, 1,* 175–187.

Garfield, S. L. (1983). Effectiveness of psychotherapy: The perennial controversy. *Professional Psychology: Theory, Research, and Practice, 14,* 35–43.

Garfield, S. L. (1986). Research on client variables in psychotherapy. In S. L. Garfield & A. E. Bergin (Eds.). *Handbook of psychotherapy and behavior change* (3rd ed.). New York: John Wiley and Sons.

Garfield, S. L., & Kurtz, R. M. (1976). Clinical psychologists in the 1970s. *American Psychologist, 31,* 1–9.

Gatmon, D., Jackson, D., Koshkarian, L., Koshkarian, L., Martos-Perry, N., Molina, A., et al. (2001). Exploring ethnic, gender, and sexual orientation variables in supervision: Do they really matter? *Journal of Multicultural Counseling and Development, 29*(2), 102–113.

Gautney, K. (1994). What if they ask me if I am married? *Supervisor Bulletin, 7*(1), 3, 7.

Gelso, C. A., & Carter, A. (1985). The relationship in counseling and psychotherapy. *Counseling Psychologist, 13,* 155–243.

Gelso, C. J. (1979). Research in counseling: Methodological and professional issues. *Counseling Psychologist, 8*(3), 7–36.

Gershenson, J., & Cohen, M. (1978). Through the looking glass: The experiences of two family therapy trainees with live supervision. *Family Process, 17,* 225–230.

Getzel, G. S., & Salmon, R. (1985). Group supervision: An organizational approach. *Clinical Supervisor, 3*(1), 27–43.

Getzelman, M. (2003). Development and Validation of the Group Supervision Impact Scale. Unpublished dissertation, University of Southern California.

Gilbert, L. A., & Rossman, K. M. (1992). Gender and the mentoring process for women: Implications for professional development. *Professional Psychology: Research and Practice, 23,* 233–238.

Gilbert, P. (1998). What is shame: Some core issues and controversies. In P. Gilbert & B. Andrews (Eds.). *Shame: Interpersonal behavior, psychopathology, and culture* (pp. 3–38). New York: Oxford University Press.

Gill, S. (Ed.). (2001). *The supervisory alliance: Facilitating the psychotherapist's learning experience.* Northvale, NJ: Jason Aronson.

Gilligan, C. (1982). *In a different voice.* Cambridge, MA: Harvard University Press.

Giordano, M. A., Altekruse, M. K., & Kern, C. W. (2000). *Supervisee's bill of rights.* Unpublished manuscript.

Glaser, R. D., & Thorpe, J. S. (1986). Unethical intimacy. *American Psychologist, 41,* 43–51.

Glenn, E., & Serovich, J. M. (1994). Documentation of family therapy supervision: A rationale and method. *American Journal of Family Therapy, 22,* 345–355.

Glidden, C. E., & Tracey, T. J. (1992). A multidimensional scaling analysis of supervisory dimensions and their perceived relevance across trainee experience levels. *Professional Psychology: Research and Practice, 23,* 151–157.

Gloria, A. M., & Robinson, S. E. (1994). The internship application process: A survey of program training directors and intern candidates. *Counseling Psychologist, 22,* 474–488.

Goldberg, D. A. (1985). Process notes, audio, and videotape: Modes of presentation in psychotherapy training. *Clinical Supervisor, 3,* 3–13.

Goldstein, A. P., Heller, K., & Sechrest, L. B. (1966). *Psychotherapy and the psychology of behavior change.* New York: John Wiley.

Gonccalves, O. F. (1994). Cognitive narrative psychotherapy: The hermeneutic construction of alternative meanings. *Journal of Cognitive Psychotherapy, 8,* 105–125.

Gonzalez, R. C. (1997). Postmodern supervision: A multicultural perspective. In D. B. Pope-Davis and H. L. K. Coleman (Eds.). *Multicultural counseling competencies: Assessment, education and training, and supervision* (pp. 350–386). Thousand Oaks, CA: Sage.

Good, G. E., & Mintz, L. B. (1990). Gender role conflict and depression in college men: Evidence for compounded risk. *Journal of Counseling and Development, 69,* 17–21.

Goodman, R. W. (1985). The live supervision model in clinical training. *Clinical Supervisor, 3*(2), 43–49.

Goodyear, R. K. (1982). *Psychotherapy supervision by major theorists* [Videotape series]. Manhattan, KS: Kansas State University Instructional Media Center (for further information, contact the author at the University of Southern California).

Goodyear, R. K. (1990). Gender configurations in supervisory dyads: Their relation to supervisee influence strategies and to skill evaluations of the supervisee. *Clinical Supervisor, 8*(2), 67–79.

Goodyear, R. K. (1997). Psychological expertise and the role of individual differences: An exploration of issues. *Educational Psychology Review, 9,* 251–265.

Goodyear, R. K., Abadie, P. D., & Efros, F. (1984). Supervisory theory into practice: Differential perceptions of supervision by Ekstein, Ellis, Polster, and Rogers. *Journal of Counseling Psychology, 31,* 228–237.

Goodyear, R. K., & Bernard, J. M. (1998). Clinical supervision: Lessons from the literature. *Counselor Education and Supervision, 38,* 6–22.

Goodyear, R. K., Cortese, J., Guzzardo, C. R., Allison, R. D., Claiborn, C. D., & Packard, R. (2000). Factors, trends and topics in the evolution of counseling psychology training. *Counseling Psychologist, 28,* 603–621.

Goodyear, R. K., Enyedy, K. C., Arcinue, F., Puri, N. N., Carter, J. W., & Getzelman. M. (under review). Helpful phenomena in group supervision: A concept map.

Goodyear, R. K., Ettelson, D. M., O'Neil, S. H., Sakai, P., & Smart, R. (August 1996). *Training and deploying process research coders: A review of practices.* Paper presented at the American Psychological Association, Toronto, ON.

Goodyear, R. K., & Guzzard, C. R. (2000). Psychotherapy supervision and training. In S. D. Brown & R. W. Lent (Eds.). *Handbook of counseling psychology* (3rd ed., pp. 83–108). New York: John Wiley.

Goodyear, R. K., & Nelson, M. L. (1997). The major supervision formats. In C. E. Watkins, *Handbook of psychotherapy supervision.* New York: John Wiley.

Goodyear, R. K., & Robyak, J. E. (1982). Supervisors theory and experience in supervisory focus. *Psychological Reports, 51,* 978.

Goodyear, R. K., & Shumate, J. (1996). Perceived effects of therapist self-disclosure of attraction to clients. *Professional Psychology: Research and Practice, 27,* 613–616.

Goodyear, R. K., & Sinnett, E. D. (1984). Current and emerging ethical issues for counseling psychologists. *Counseling Psychologist, 12*(3), 87–98.

Goodyear, R. K., Wertheimer, A., Cypers, S., & Rosemond, M. (in press). Refining the map of the counselor's developmental journey: Response to Rønnestad and Skovholt. *Journal of Career Development.*

Gordon, S. P. (1990). Developmental supervision: An exploratory study of a promising model. *Journal of Curriculum and Supervision, 5,* 293–307.

Gorely, T., Gordon, S., & Ford, I. (1994). NUD·IST: A qualitative data analysis system for sport psychology research. *Sport Psychologist, 8,* 319–320.

Graf, N. M., & Stebnicki, M. A. (2002). Using e-mail for clinical supervision in practicum: A qualitative analysis. *Journal of Rehabilitation, 68*(3), 41–49.

Granello, D. H. (1996). Gender and power in the supervisory dyad. *Clinical Supervisor, 14*(2), 53–67.

Granello, D. H. (2000). Encouraging the cognitive development of supervisees: Using Bloom's taxonomy in supervision. *Counselor Education and Supervision, 40*(1), 31–46.

Granello, D. H. (2002). Assessing the cognitive development of counseling students: Changes in epistemological assumptions. *Counselor Education and Supervision, 41,* 279–293.

Granello, D. H. (2003). Influence strategies in the supervisory dyad: An investigation into the effects of gender and age. *Counselor Education and Supervision, 42,* 189–202.

Granello, D. H., Beamish, P. M., & Davis, T. E. (1997). Supervisee empowerment: Does gender make a difference? *Counselor Education and Supervision, 36,* 305–317.

Gray, L. A., Ladany, N., Walker, J. A., & Ancis, J. R. (2001). Psychotherapy trainees' experience of counterproductive events in supervision. *Journal of Counseling Psychology, 48,* 371–383.

Green, S. L., & Hansen, J. C. (1986). Ethical dilemmas in family therapy. *Journal of Marital and Family Therapy, 12,* 225–230.

Grey, A. L., & Fiscalini, J. (1987). Parallel process as transference–countertransference interaction. *Psychoanalytic Psychology, 4,* 131–144.

Griffith, B. A., & Frieden, G. (2000). Facilitating reflective thinking in counselor education. *Counselor Education and Supervision, 40,* 82–93.

Guest, C. L., Jr., & Dooley, K. (1999). Supervisor malpractice: Liability to the supervisee in clinical supervision. *Counselor Education and Supervision, 38*(4), 269–279.

Guest, P. D., & Beutler, L. E. (1988). Impact of psychotherapy supervision on therapist orientation and values. *Journal of Consulting and Clinical Psychology, 56,* 653–658.

Gurk, M. D., & Wicas, E. A. (1979). Generic models of counselor supervision: Counseling/instruction dichotomy and consultation meta-model. *Personnel and Guidance Journal, 57,* 402–407.

Haas, L. J. (1991). Hide-and-seek or show-and-tell? Emerging issues of informed consent. *Ethics and Behavior, 1,* 175–189.

Haas, L. J., & Cummings, N. A. (1991). Managed outpatient mental health plans: Clinical, ethical and practical guidelines for participation. *Professional Psychology: Research and Practice, 22,* 45–51.

Haas, L. J., Malouf, J. L., & Mayerson, N. H. (1986). Ethical dilemmas in psychological practice: Results of a national survey. *Professional Psychology: Research and Practice, 17,* 316–321.

Hackney, H. L., & Goodyear, R. K. (1984). Carl Rogers' client-centered supervision. In R. F. Levant and J. M. Schlien (Eds.). *Client-centered therapy and the person-centered approach.* New York: Praeger.

Hahn, W. K. (2002). The experience of shame in psychotherapy supervision. *Psychotherapy, 38,* 272–284.

Hahn, W. K., & Molnar, S. (1991). Intern evaluation in university counseling centers: Process, problems, and recommendations. *Counseling Psychologist, 19,* 414–430.

Haj-Yahia, M. M., & Roer-Strier, D. (1999). On the encounter between Jewish supervisors and Arab supervisees in Israel. *Clinical Supervisor, 18*(2), 17–37.

Haley, J. (1976). *Problem solving therapy.* San Francisco: Jossey-Bass.

Haley, J. (1987). *Problem solving therapy* (2nd ed.). San Francisco: Jossey-Bass.

Hall, J. E. (1988a). Protection in supervision. *Register Report, 14*(4), 3–4.

Hall, J. E. (1988b). Dual relationships in supervision. *Register Report, 15*(1), 5–6.

Halpert, S. C., & Pfaller, J. (2001). Sexual orientation and supervision: Theory and practice. *Journal of Gay and Lesbian Social Services: Issues in Practice, Policy and Research, 13*(3), 23–40.

Hamilton, J. C., & Spruill, J. (1999). Identifying and reducing risk factors related to trainee–client sexual misconduct. *Professional Psychology: Research and Practice, 30,* 318–327.

Hamilton, N., & Else, J. F. (1983). *Designing field education: Philosophy, structure and process.* Springfield, IL: Charles C Thomas.

Hamlin, E. R., II, & Timberlake, E. M. (1982). Peer group supervision for supervisors. *Social Casework, 67,* 82–87.

Handley, P. (1982). Relationship between supervisors' and trainees' cognitive styles and the supervision process. *Journal of Counseling Psychology, 25,* 508–515.

Hanna, M. A., & Smith, J. (1998). Using rubrics for documentation of clinical work supervision. *Counselor Education and Supervision, 37,* 269–278.

Hansen, J., & Stevic, R. (1967). Practicum in supervision: A proposal. *Counselor Education and Supervision, 7,* 205–206.

Hansen, N. D., & Goldberg, S. G. (1999). Navigating the nuances: A matrix of considerations for ethical–legal dilemmas. *Professional Psychology: Research and Practice, 30,* 495–503.

Hardcastle, D. A. (1991). Toward a model for supervision: A peer supervision pilot project. *Clinical Supervisor, 9*(2), 63–76.

Hardy, K. V. (1989). The theoretical myth of sameness: A critical issue in family therapy training and treatment. *Journal of Psychotherapy and the Family, 6*(1–2), 17–33.

Hardy, K. V. (1993). Live supervision in the postmodern era of family therapy: Issues, reflections, and questions. *Contemporary Family Therapy: An International Journal, 15,* 9–20.

Harkness, D., & Poertner, A. (1989). Research and social work supervision: A conceptual review. *Social Work, 34,* 115–119.

Harmon, L. W. (1989). The scientist/practitioner model and choice of research paradigm. *Counseling Psychologist, 17*(1), 86–89.

Harrar, W. R., VandeCreek, L., & Knapp, S. (1990). Ethical and legal aspects of clinical supervision. *Professional Psychology: Research and Practice, 21,* 37–41.

Harris, M. B. C. (1994). Supervisory evaluation and feedback. In L. D. Broders (Ed.). *Supervision: Exploring the effective components.* Greensboro, NC: ERIC/CASS.

Harris, S., & Goodyear, R. K. (April 1990). *The circumplex model in four supervisory dyads: A study of interaction.* Paper presented at the annual meeting of the American Educational Research Association, Boston.

Hart, G. (1982). *The process of clinical supervision.* Baltimore, MD: University Park Press.

Harvey, C., & Katz, C. (1985). *If I'm so successful, why do I feel like a fake? The impostor phenomenon.* New York: St. Martin's Press.

Harvey, O. J., Hunt, D. E., & Schroeder, H. M. (1961). *Conceptual systems and personality organization.* New York: Holt, Rinehart and Winston.

Hawkins, P., & Shohet, R. (1989). *Supervision in the helping professions.* Milton Keynes, UK: Open University Press.

Hawkins, P., & Shohet, R. (2000). *Supervision in the helping professions: An individual, group and organizational approach* (2nd ed.). Philadelphia: Open University Press.

Hayes, J. R. (1981). *The complete problem solver.* Philadelphia: Franklin Institute Press.

Hayes, R. L. (1989). Group supervision. In L. J. Bradley & J. D. Boyd (Eds.). *Counselor supervision* (2nd ed., pp. 399–421). Muncie, IN: Accelerated Development.

Hayes, R. L., Blackman, L. S., & Brennan, C. (2001). Group supervision. In L. Bradley & N. Ladany (Eds.). *Counselor supervision: Principles, process, and practice* (3rd ed., 183–206). Philadelphia: Brunner-Routledge.

Hayes, S. C., Follette, V. M., Dawes, R. M., & Grady, K. E. (Eds). (1995). *Scientific standards of practice: Issues and recommendations.* Reno, NV: Context Press.

Heath, A. (1982). Team family therapy training: Conceptual and pragmatic considerations. *Family Process, 21,* 187–194.

Heesacker, M., Wester, S. R., Vogel, D. L., Wentzel, J. T., Mejia-Millan, C. M., & Goodholm, C. R. (1999). Gender-based emotional stereotyping. *Journal of Counseling Psychology, 46,* 483–495.

Helms, J. E. (1990). *Black and white racial identity: Theory, research and practice.* New York: England Greenwood Press.

Helms, J. E. (1994). Racial identity and career assessment. *Journal of Career Assessment, 2,* 199–209.

Helms, J. E., & Cook, D. A. (1999). *Using race and culture in counseling and psychotherapy: Theory and process.* Boston: Allyn and Bacon.

Helms, J. E., & Piper, R. E. (1994). Implications of racial identity theory for vocational psychology. *Journal of Vocational Behavior, 44,* 124–138.

Hemlick, L. M. (1998). The role of shame in clinical supervision: Development of the Shame in Supervision Instrument. *Dissertation Abstracts International: Section B: The Sciences & Engineering Vol. 58(7-B),* January 1998, 3924.

Henderson, P. (1994). Administrative skills in counseling supervision. In L. D. Borders (Ed). *Supervision: Exploring the effective components.* Greensboro, NC: ERIC/CASS, EDO—CG-94-25.

Heppner, P. P., & Claiborn, C. D. (1989). Social influence research in counseling: A review and critique [Monograph]. *Journal of Counseling Psychology, 36,* 365–387.

Heppner, P. P., & Dixon, D. N. (1981). A review of the interpersonal influence process in counseling. *Personnel and Guidance Journal, 59,* 542–550.

Heppner, P. P., & Handley, P. G. (1982). A study of the interpersonal influence process in supervision. *Journal of Counseling Psychologist, 28,* 437–444.

Heppner, P. P., Kivlighan, D. M., Burnett, J. W., Berry, T. R., Goedinhaus, M., Doxsee, D. J., et al. (1994). Dimensions that characterize supervisor interventions delivered in the context of live supervision of practicum counselors. *Journal of Counseling Psychology, 41,* 227–235.

Heppner, P. P., & Roehlke, H. J. (1984). Differences among supervisees at different levels of training: Implications for a developmental model of supervision. *Journal of Counseling Psychology, 31,* 76–90.

Herman, K. C. (1993). Reassessing predictors of therapist competence. *Journal of Counseling and Development, 72,* 29–32.

Hess, A. K. (1980). Training models and the nature of psychotherapy supervision. In A. K. Hess (Ed.). *Psychotherapy supervision: Theory, research, and practice* (pp. 15–28). New York: John Wiley and Sons.

Hess, A. K. (Ed.).(1981). *Psychotherapy supervision: Theory, research, and practice.* New York.

Hess, A. K. (1986). Growth in supervision: Stages of supervisee and supervisor development. *Clinical Supervisor, 4*(1–2), 51–67.

Hess, A. K. (1987). Psychotherapy supervision: Stages, Buber, and a theory of relationship. *Professional Psychology: Research and Practice, 18,* 251–259.

Hess, A. K., & Hess, K. A. Psychotherapy supervision: A survey of internship training practices. *Professional Psychology: Research and Practice, 14,* 504–513.

Hewson, J. (1999). Training supervisors to contract in supervision. In E. Holloway & M. Carroll (Eds.). *Training counselling supervisors* (pp. 67–91). London: Sage.

Hill, C. E. (1986). An overview of the Hill counselor and client verbal response category systems. In L. Greenberg & W. Pinsof (Eds.). *The psychotherapeutic process: A research handbook* (pp. 131–160). New York: Guilford.

Hill, C. E. (1989). *Therapist techniques and client outcomes: Eight cases of psychotherapy.* Newbury Park, CA: Sage.

Hill, C. E., Carter, J. A., & O'Farrell, M. K. (1981). A case-study of the process and outcome of time-limited counseling. *Journal of Counseling Psychology, 30,* 428–436.

Hill, C. E., Charles, D., & Reed, K. G. (1981). A longitudinal analysis of changes in counseling skills during doctoral training in counseling psychology. *Journal of Counseling Psychology, 28,* 428–436.

Hill, C. E., & Knox, S. (2002). Self-disclosure. In J. C. Norcross (Ed.). *Psychotherapy relationships that work: Therapist contributions and responsiveness to patients* (pp. 255–266). New York: Oxford University Press.

Hill, C. E., O'Grady, K. E., Balenger, V., Busse, W., Falk, D. R., Hill, M., et al. (1994). Methodological examination of videotape-assisted reviews in brief therapy: Helpfulness ratings, therapist intentions, client reactions, mood, and session evaluation. *Journal of Counseling Psychology, 41,* 236–247.

Hill, C. E., Thompson, B. J., & Williams, E. N. (1997). A guide to conducting consensual qualitative research. *Counseling Psychologist, 25,* 517–572.

Hillerbrand, E. T. (1989). Cognitive differences between experts and novices: Implications for group supervision. *Journal of Counseling and Development, 67,* 293–296.

Hillerbrand, E. T., & Claiborn, C. D. (1990). Examining reasoning skill differences between expert and novice counselors. *Journal of Counseling and Development, 68,* 684–691.

Hilton, D. B., Russell, R. K., & Salmi, S. W. (1995). The effects of supervisor's race and level of support on perceptions of supervision. *Journal of Counseling and Development, 73,* 559–563.

Hipp, J. L., & Munson, C. E. (1995). The partnership model: A feminist supervision/consultation perspective. *Clinical Supervisor, 13*(1), 23–38.

Hird, J. S., Cavalieri, C. E., Dulko, J. P., Felice, A. A., & Ho, T. A. (2001). Visions and realities: Supervisee perspective of multicultural supervision. *Journal of Multicultural Counseling and Development, 29,* 114–130.

Hoffman, L. W. (1990). *Old scapes, new maps: A training program for psychotherapy supervisors.* Cambridge, MA: Milusik Press.

Hoffman, L. W. (1994). The training of psychotherapy supervisors: A barren scape. *Psychotherapy in Private Practice, 13,* 23–42.

Hogan, R. (1964). Issues and approaches in supervision. *Psychotherapy: Theory, Research, and Practice, 1,* 139–141.

Holiman, M., & Lauver, P. J. (1987). The counselor culture and client-centered practice. *Counselor Education and Supervision, 26,* 184–191.

Holloway, E. L. (1982). Interactional structure of the supervision interview. *Journal of Counseling Psychology, 29,* 309–317.

Holloway, E. L. (1984). Outcome evaluation in supervision research. *Counseling Psychologist, 12,* 167–174.

Holloway, E. L. (1987). Developmental models of supervision: Is it supervision? *Professional Psychology: Research and Practice, 18,* 209–216.

Holloway, E. L. (1988). Instruction beyond the facilitative conditions: A response to Biggs. *Counselor Education and Supervision, 27,* 252–258.

Holloway, E. L. (1992). Supervision: A way of teaching and learning. In S. D. Brown & R. W. Lent (Eds.). *Handbook of Counseling Psychology* (pp. 177–214). New York: John Wiley.

Holloway, E. L. (1995). *Clinical supervision: A systems approach.* Thousand Oaks, CA: Sage.

Holloway, E. L. (1997). Structures for the analysis and teaching of psychotherapy. In C. E. Watkins, Jr. (Ed.). *Handbook of psychotherapy supervision* (pp. 249–276). New York: John Wiley.

Holloway, E. L., & Carroll, M. (1996). Reaction to the special section on supervision research: Comment on Ellis et al. (1996), Ladany et al. (1996), Neufeldt et al. (1996), & Worthen & McNeill (1996). *Journal of Counseling Psychology, 43,* 51–55.

Holloway, E. L., Freund, R. D., Gardner, S. L., Nelson, M. L., & Walker, B. R. (1989). Relation of power and involvement to theoretical orientation in supervision: An analysis of discourse. *Journal of Counseling Psychology, 36,* 88–102.

Holloway, E. L., & Hosford, R. E. (1983). Toward developing a prescriptive technology of counselor supervision. *Counseling Psychologist, 11,* 73–77.

Holloway, E. L., & Johnston, R. (1985). Group supervision: Widely practiced but poorly understood. *Counselor Education and Supervision, 24,* 332–340.

Holloway, E. L., & Neufeldt, S. A. (1995). Supervision: Its contributions to treatment efficacy. *Journal of Consulting and Clinical Psychology, 63,* 207–213.

Holloway, E. L., & Roehlke, H. J. (1987). Internship: The applied training of a counseling psychologist. *Counseling Psychologist, 15,* 205–260.

Holloway, E. L., & Wampold, B. E. (1983). Patterns of verbal behavior and judgments of satisfaction in the supervision interview. *Journal of Counseling Psychology, 30,* 227–234.

Holloway, E. L., & Wampold, B. E. (1986). Relationship between conceptual level and counseling-related tasks: A meta-analysis. *Journal of Counseling Psychology, 33,* 310–319.

Holloway, E. L., & Wolleat, P. (1994). Supervision: The pragmatics of empowerment. *Journal of Educational and Psychological Consultation, 5,* 23–43.

Holmbeck, G. N. (1997). Toward terminological, conceptual, and statistical clarity in the study of mediators and moderators: Examples from the child-clinical and pediatric psychology literatures. *Journal of Consulting and Clinical Psychology, 65,* 599–610.

Holmes, G. R., Stader, S. R., Swaim, K. F., Haigler, E. D., & Myers, D. (1998). Adolescent group psychotherapy supervision in a group format: An emerging model. *Journal of Child and Adolescent Group Therapy, 8,* 197–206.

Holtzman, R. F., & Raskin, M. S. (1988). Why field placements fail: Study results. *Clinical Supervisor, 6*(3), 123–136.

Horvath, A. O., & Greenberg, L. S. (1989). Development and validation of the working alliance inventory. *Journal of Counseling Psychology, 36,* 223–233.

Horvath, A. O., & Luborsky, L. (1993). The role of the therapeutic alliance in psychotherapy. *Journal of Consulting and Clinical Psychology, 61,* 561–573.

Horvath, A. O., & Symonds, B. D. (1991). Relation between working alliance and outcome in psychotherapy: A meta-analysis. *Journal of Counseling Psychology, 38,* 139–149.

Hotelling, K., & Forrest, L. (1985). Gilligan's theory of sex-role development: A perspective for counseling. *Journal of Counseling and Development, 64,* 183–186.

Hoyle, R. H. (Ed.). (1995). *Structural equation modeling: Concepts, issues, and applications.* Thousand Oaks, CA: Sage.

Hoyt, M. F., & Goulding, R. (1989). Resolution of a transference–countertransference impasse: Using Gestalt techniques in supervision. *Transactional Analysis Journal, 19,* 201–211. http://

www.wvu.edu/~lawfac/jelkins/lp-2001/saxe. html.

Hutto, B. (2001). Some lessons best learned from psychotherapy supervision. *Psychiatric Times,* 18(7). On-line journal. http://www. psychiatrictimes.com/P017553.html.

Igartua, K. J. (2000). The impact of impaired supervisors on residents. *Academic Psychiatry,* 24(4), 188–194.

Itzhaky, H., & Sztern, L. (1999). The take over of parent-child dynamics in a supervisory relationship: Identifying the role transformation. *Clinical Social Work Journal, 27,* 247–258.

Ivery, A. (1986). *Developmental therapy: Theory into practice.* San Francisco: Jossey-Bass.

Jackson, H., & Nuttall, R. L. (2001). A relationship between childhood sexual abuse and professional sexual misconduct. *Professional Psychology: Research and Practice, 32,* 200–204.

Jacobs, D., David, P., & Meyer, D. J. (1995). *The supervisory encounter: A guide for teachers of psychodynamic psychotherapy and analysis.* New Haven, CT: Yale University Press.

Jakubowski-Spector, P., Dustin, R., & George, R. L. (1971). Toward developing a behavioral counselor education model. *Counselor Education and Supervision, 11,* 242–250.

Jerome, L. W., DeLeon, P. H., James, L. C., Folen, R., Earles, J., & Gedney, J. J. (2000). The coming age of telecommunications in psychological research and practice. *American Psychologist, 55,* 407–421.

Johnson, E., & Moses, N. C. (August 1988). *The dynamic developmental model of supervision.* Paper presented at the annual convention of the American Psychological Association, Atlanta, GA.

Johnson, E. A., & Stewart, D. W. (2000). Clinical supervision in Canadian academic and service settings: The importance of education, training, and workplace support for supervisor development. *Canadian Psychology, 41,* 124–130.

Johnson, S. W., & Combs, D. C. (1997). The use of interactive television in live supervision. *TCA Journal, 25*(1), 10–18.

Johnson, W. B., & Campbell, C. D. (2002). Character and fitness requirements for professional psychologists: Are there any? *Professional Psychology: Research and Practice, 33,* 46–53.

Jones, S. H., Krasner, R. F., & Howard, K. I. (1992). Components of supervisors' ratings of therapists' skillfulness. *Academic Psychiatry, 16,* 29–36.

Jordan, K. (1999). Live supervision for beginning therapists in practicum: Crucial for quality counseling and avoiding litigation. *Family Therapy, 26*(2), 81–86.

Juhnke, G. A. (1996). Solution-focused supervision: Promoting supervisee skills and confidence through successful solutions. *Counselor Education and Supervision, 36,* 48–57.

Kadushin, A. (1968). Games people play in supervision. *Social Work, 13,* 23–32.

Kadushin, A. (1976). *Supervision in social work.* New York: Columbia University Press.

Kadushin, A. (1992a). *Supervision in social work* (3rd ed.). New York: Columbia University Press.

Kadushin, A. (1992b). What's wrong, what's right with social work supervision. *Clinical Supervisor, 10*(1), 3–19.

Kadushin, A. (1992c). Social work supervision: An updated survey. *Clinical Supervisor, 10*(2), 9–27.

Kadushin, A., & Harkness, D. (2002). *Supervision in social work* (4th ed.). New York: Columbia University Press.

Kagan, H. K., & Kagan, N. I. (1997). Interpersonal process recall: Influencing human interaction. In C. E. Watkins, Jr. (Ed.). *Handbook of Psychotherapy Supervision* (pp. 296–309). New York: John Wiley.

Kagan, N. (1976). *Influencing human interaction.* Mason, MI: Mason Media; or Washington, DC: American Association for Counseling and Development.

Kagan, N. (1980). Influencing human interaction—eighteen years with IPR. In A. K. Hess (Ed.). *Psychotherapy supervision: Theory, research and practice* (pp. 262–286). New York: John Wiley.

Kagan, N., & Krathwohl, D. R. (1967). *Studies in human interaction: Interpersonal process recall stimulated by videotape.* East Lansing, MI: Michigan State University.

Kagan, N., Krathwohl, D. R., & Farquahar, W. W. (1965). *IPR—Interpersonal process recall by videotape: Stimulated recall by videotape.* East Lansing, MI: Michigan State University.

Kagan, N., Krathwohl, D. R., & Miller, R. (1963). Stimulated recall in therapy using videotape—a case study. *Journal of Counseling Psychology, 10,* 237–243.

Kahn, B. (1999). Priorities and practices in field supervision of school counseling students. *Professional School Counseling, 3*(2), 128–136.

Kanz, J. E. (2001). Clinical-supervision.com: Issues in the provision of online supervision. *Professional Psychology: Research and Practice, 32*(4), 415–420.

Kaplan, D. M., Rothrock, D., & Culkin, M. (1999). The infusion of counseling observations into a graduate counseling program. *Counselor Education and Supervision, 39*(1), 66–75.

Kaplan, M. (1983). A woman's view of DSM-III. *American Psychologist, 38,* 786–792.

Kaplan, R. (1987). The current use of live supervision within marriage and family therapy training programs. *Clinical Supervisor, 5*(3), 43–52.

Karger, H. J. (1989). The common and conflicting goals of labor and social work. *Administration in Social Work, 13,* 1–17.

Kaslow, N. J., & Rice, D. G. (1985). Developmental stresses of psychology internship training: What training staff can do to help. *Professional Psychology: Research and Practice, 16,* 253–261.

Katz, J. H. (1985). The sociopolitical nature of counseling. *Counseling Psychologist, 13,* 615–624.

Kaul, T. J., & Bednar, R. L. (1986). Research on group and related therapies. In S. L. Garfield & A. E. Bergin (Eds.), *Handbook of psychotherapy and behavior change* (3rd ed., pp. 671–714). New York: John Wiley and Sons.

Keith, D. V., Connell, G., & Whitaker, C. A. (1992). Group supervision in symbolic experiential family therapy. *Journal of Family Psychotherapy, 3*(1), 93–109.

Kell, B. L., & Burow, J. M. (1970). *Developmental counseling and therapy.* Boston: Houghton Mifflin.

Kell, B. L., Morse, J., & Grater, H. (undated). The supervision and training of counselors and psychotherapists: An instance of ego-evaluation, support, and development. Unpublished paper.

Kell, B. L., & Mueller, W. J. (1966). *Impact and change: A study of counseling relationships.* New York: Appleton-Century-Crofts.

Kelly, G. A. (1955). *The psychology of personal constructs* (2 vols). New York: Norton, 1955.

Kennard, B. D., Stewart, S. M., & Gluck, M. R. (1987). The supervision relationship: Variables contributing to positive versus negative experiences. *Professional Psychology: Research and Practice, 18,* 172–175.

Kerl, S. B., Garcia, J. L., McCullough, C. S., & Maxwell, M. E. (2002). Systematic evaluation of professional performance: Legally supported procedure and process. *Counselor Education and Supervision, 41,* 321–334.

Kerr, B. A., Claiborn, C. D., & Dixon, D. N. (1982). Training counselors in persuasion. *Counselor Education and Supervision, 22,* 138–148.

Kiesler, D. J. (1983). The 1982 Interpersonal Circle: A taxonomy for complementarity in human transactions. *Psychological Review, 90,* 185–214.

Killian, K. D. (2001). Differences making a difference: Cross-cultural interactions in supervisory relationships. *Journal of Feminist Family Therapy, 12*(2–3), 61–103.

King, D., & Wheeler, S. (1999). The responsibilities of counsellor supervisors: A qualitative study. *British Journal of Guidance and Counselling, 27*(2), 215–229.

Kinsella, J. A. (2000). Direct supervision: A computer feedback method used in the live supervision of first practicum marriage and family therapy students. *Dissertation Abstracts International: Section B: The Sciences & Engineering, 60*(9-B), 4870.

Kitchener, K. S. (1984). Intuition, critical evaluation and ethical principles: The foundation for ethical decisions in counseling psychology. *Counseling Psychologist, 12,* 43–55.

Kitchener, K. S. (1988). Dual role relationships: What makes them so problematic? *Journal of Counseling and Development, 67,* 217–221.

Kitzrow, M. A. (2001). Application of psychological type in clinical supervision. *Clinical Supervisor, 20*(2), 133–146.

Kivlighan, D. M., Angelone, E. O., & Swafford, K. G. (1991). Live supervision in individual psychotherapy: Effects on therapist's intention use and client's evaluation of session effect and working alliance. *Journal of Counseling Psychology, 22,* 489–495.

Kleintjes, S., & Swartz, L. (1996). Black clinical psychology trainees at a "white" South African University: Issues for clinical supervision. *Clinical Supervisor, 14*(1), 87–109.

Klitzke, M. J., & Lombardo, T. W. (1991). A "bug-in-the-eye" can be better than a "bug-in-the-ear": A teleprompter technique for on-line therapy skills training. *Behavior Modification, 15,* 113–117.

Knapp, S., & VandeCreek, L. (1997). Ethical and legal aspects of clinical supervision. In C. E. Watkins, Jr. (Ed.). *Handbook of Psychotherapy Supervision* (pp. 589–602). New York: John Wiley.

Knoff, H. M., & Prout, H. T. (1985). Terminating students from professional psychology programs: Criteria, procedures and legal issues. *Professional Psychology: Research and Practice, 16,* 789–797.

Koch, L. C., Arhar, J. M., & Wells, L. M. (2000). Educating rehabilitation counseling students in reflective practice. *Rehabilitation Education, 14,* 255–268.

Koerin, B., & Miller, J. (1995). Gate-keeping policies: Terminating students for nonacademic reasons. *Journal of Social Work Education, 31,* 247–260.

Kollock, P., Blumstein, P., & Schwartz, P. (1985). Sex and power in interaction: Conversational privileges and duties. *American Sociological Review, 50,* 34–46.

Kopp, R. R., & Robles, L. (1989). A single-session, therapist-focused model of supervision of resistance based on Adlerian Psychology. *Individual Psychology, 45,* 212–219.

Kozlowska, K., Nunn, K., & Cousins, P. (1997). Adverse experiences in psychiatric training. Part 2. *Australian and New Zealand Journal of Psychiatry, 31,* 641–652.

Krause, A. A., & Allen, G. J. (1988). Perceptions of counselor supervision: An examination of Stoltenberg's model from the perspectives of supervisor and supervisee. *Journal of Counseling Psychology, 35,* 77–80.

Kruger, L. J., Cherniss, C., Maher, C. A., & Leichtman, H. M. (1988). A behavioral observation system for group supervision. *Counselor Education and Supervision, 27,* 331–343.

Kugler, P. (1995). *Jungian perspectives on clinical supervision.* Einsiedeln, Switzerland: Daimon.

Kuhn, T. S. (1970). *The structure of scientific revolutions* (2nd ed.). Chicago: University of Chicago Press.

Ladany, N., Brittan-Powell, C. S., & Pannu, R. K. (1997). The influence of supervisory racial identity interaction and racial matching on the supervisory working alliance and supervisee multicultural competence. *Counselor Education and Supervision, 36*(4), 284–304.

Ladany, N., Constantine, M. G., Miller, K., Erickson, C. D., & Muse-Burke, J. L. (2000). Supervisor countertransference: A qualitative investigation into its identification and description. *Journal of Counseling Psychology, 47,* 102–115.

Ladany, N., Ellis, M. V., & Friedlander, M. L. (1999). The supervisory working alliance, trainee self-efficacy, and satisfaction. *Journal of Counseling and Development, 77,* 447–455.

Ladany, N., & Friedlander, M. L. (1995). The relationship between the supervisory working alliance and trainees' experience of role conflict and role ambiguity. *Counselor Education and Supervision, 34,* 220–231.

Ladany, N., Hill, C. E., Corbett, M. M., & Nutt, E. A. (1996). Nature, extent, and importance of what psychotherapy trainees do not disclose to their supervisors. *Journal of Counseling Psychology, 43,* 10–24.

Ladany, N., Inman, A. G., Constantine, M. G., & Hofheinz, E. W. (1997). Supervisee multicultural case conceptualization ability and self-reported multicultural competence as functions of supervisee racial identity and supervisor focus. *Journal of Counseling Psychology, 44*(3), 284–293.

Ladany, N., & Lehrman-Waterman, D. E. (1999). The content and frequency of supervisor self-disclosures and their relationship to supervisor style and the supervisory working alliance. *Counselor Education and Supervision, 38,* 143–160.

Ladany, N., Lehrman-Waterman, D., Molinaro, M., Wolgast, B., & Laney, N. (August 1996). *Supervisor ethical practices as perceived by the supervisees they train.* Poster session presented at the American Psychological Association annual meeting, Toronto, ON.

Ladany, N., Lehrman-Waterman, D., Molinaro, M., & Wolgast, B. (1999). Psychotherapy supervisor ethical practices: Adherence to guidelines, the supervisory working alliance, and supervisee satisfaction. *Counseling Psychologist, 27,* 443–475.

Ladany, N., Marotta, S., & Muse-Burke, J. L. (2001). Counselor experience related to complexity of case conceptualization and supervision preference [Special issue]. *Counselor Education and Supervision, 40*(3), 203–219.

Ladany, N., & Melincoff, D. S. (1999). The nature of counselor supervisor nondisclosure. *Counselor Education and Supervision, 38,* 161–176.

Ladany, N., O'Brien, K. M., Hill, C. E., Melincoff, D. S., Knox, S., & Petersen, D. A. (1997). Sexual attraction toward clients, use of supervision, and prior training: A qualitative study of predoctoral psychology interns. *Journal of Counseling Psychology, 44,* 413–424.

Ladany, N., Walker, J. A., & Melincoff, D. S. (2001). Supervisory style: Its relation to the supervisory working-alliance and supervisor self-disclosure. *Counselor Education and Supervision, 40,* 263–275.

Ladmila, A. (1997). Shame, knowledge, and modes of inquiry in supervision. In G. Shipton (Ed.), *Supervision of psychotherapy and counseling: Making a place to think* (pp. 35–46). Philadelphia: Open University Press.

LaFromboise, T. D., Coleman, H. L., & Hernandez, A. (1991). Development and factor structure of the Cross-Cultural Counseling Inventory—Revised. *Professional Psychology: Research and Practice, 22,* 380–388.

Lamb, D. H., & Catanzaro, S. J. (1998). Sexual and nonsexual boundary violations involving psychologists, clients, supervisees, and students: Implications for professional practice. *Professional Psychology: Research and Practice, 29,* 498–503.

Lamb, D. H., Cochran, D. J., & Jackson, V. R. (1991). Training and organizational issues associated with identifying and responding to intern impairment.

Lamb, D., Presser, N., Pfost, K., Baum, M., Jackson, R., & Jarvis, P. (1987). Confronting professional impairment during the internship: Identification, due process, and remediation. *Professional Psychology: Research and Practice, 18,* 597–603.

Lambert, M. E., & Meier, S. T. (1992). Utility of computerized case simulations in therapist training and evaluation. *Journal of Behavioral Education, 2,* 73–84.

Lambert, M. J. (1974). Supervisory and counseling process: A comparative study. *Counselor Education and Supervision, 14,* 54–60.

Lambert, M. J. (1980). Research and the supervisory process. In A. K. Hess (Ed.). *Psychotherapy supervision: Theory, research, and practice* (pp. 423–450). New York: John Wiley.

Lambert, M. J., & Arnold, R. C. (1987). Research and the supervision process. *Professional Psychology: Research and Practice, 18,* 217–224.

Lambert, M. J., Hansen, N. B., Umpress, V., Lunnen, K., Okiishi, J., & Burlingame, G. M. (1998). *Administration and scoring manual for the OQ-45.2.* American Professional Credentialing Service (e-mail: apcs@erols.com).

Lambert, M. J., & Ogles, B. M. (1997). The effectiveness of psychotherapy supervision. In C. E. Watkins, Jr. (Ed.). *Handbook of psychotherapy supervision* (pp. 421–446). New York: John Wiley.

Lambert, M. J., Whipple, J. L., Smart, D. W., Vermeersch, D. A., Nielson, S. L., & Hawkins, E. J. (2001). The effects of providing therapists with feedback on patient progress during psychotherapy: Are outcomes enhanced? *Psychotherapy Research, 11,* 49–68.

Landau, J., & Stanton, M. D. (1983). Aspects of supervision with the "Pick-a-Dali-Circus" model. *Journal of Strategic and Systemic Therapies, 2,* 31–89.

Landis, L. L., & Young, M. E. (1994). The reflecting team in counselor education. Special section: Marriage and family training methods. *Counselor Education and Supervision, 33,* 210–218.

Lane, R. C. (1986). The recalcitrant supervisee: The negative supervisory reaction. *Current Issues in Psychoanalytic Practice, 2,* 65–81.

Lanning, W. (1971). A study of the relation between group and individual counseling supervision and three relationship measures. *Journal of Counseling Psychology, 18,* 401–406.

Lanning, W., & Freeman, B. (1994). The Supervisor Emphasis Rating Form—Revised. *Counselor Education and Supervision, 33,* 294–304.

Larrabee, M. J., & Miller, G. M. (1993). An examination of sexual intimacy in supervision. *Clinical Supervisor, 11*(2), 103–126.

Lazar, A., & Mosek, A. (1993). The influence of the field instructor–student relationship on evaluation of students' practice. *Clinical Supervisor, 11*(1), 111–120.

Lazarus, J. A. (1995). Ethical issues in doctor–patient sexual relationships. Special issue: Clinical sexuality. *Psychiatric Clinics of North America, 18,* 55–70.

Leary, M. R., & Kowalski, R. M. (1990). Impression management: A literature review and two-component model. *Psychological Bulletin, 107,* 34–47.

Leary, T. (1957). Interpersonal diagnosis of personality: A theory and a methodology for personality evaluation. New York: Ronald Press.

Leddick, G. R. (1994). Counselor education clinics as community resources. In J. E. Myers (Ed.). *Developing and directing counselor education laboratories* (pp. 147–152). Alexandria, VA: ACA Press.

Leddick, G. R., & Bernard, J. M. (1980). The history of supervision: A critical review. *Counselor Education and Supervision, 19*(3), 186–196.

Leddick, G. R., & Dye, H. A. (1987). Effective supervision as portrayed by trainee expectations and preferences. *Counselor Education and Supervision, 27,* 139–154.

Lee, R. W., & Cashwell, C. S. (2001). Ethical issues in counseling supervision: A comparison of university and site supervisors. *Clinical Supervisor, 20*(2), 91–100.

Lee, R. W., & Gillam, S. L. (2000). Legal and ethic issues involving the duty to warn: Implications for supervisors. *Clinical Supervisor, 19*(1), 123–136.

Lee, S. R. (1997). A process study of student supervisory phone interventions in live supervision of marital therapy. *Dissertation Abstracts International: Section B: The Sciences and Engineering, 57*(8-B), 5332.

Lehrman-Waterman, D., & Ladany, N. (2001). Development and validation of the Evaluation Process within Supervision Inventory [Special issue]. *Journal of Counseling Psychology, 48*(2), 168–177.

Leonardelli, C. A., & Gratz, R. R. (1985). Roles and responsibilities in fieldwork experience: A social systems approach. *Clinical Supervisor, 3*(3), 15–24.

Leong, F. T. L., & Wagner, N. S. (1994). Cross-cultural counseling supervision: What do we know? What do we need to know? *Counselor Education and Supervision, 34,* 117–131.

Lesser, R. M. (1983). Supervision: Illusions, anxieties, and questions. *Contemporary Psychoanalysis, 19,* 120–129.

Levenson, E. A. (1984). Follow the fox. In L. Caligor, P. M. Bromberg, & J. D. Meltzer (Eds.). *Clinical perspectives on the supervision of psychoanalysis and psychotherapy* (pp. 153–167). New York: Plenum Press.

Levine, F. M., & Tilker, H. A. (1974). A behavior modification approach to supervision and psychotherapy. *Psychotherapy: Theory, Research and Practice, 11,* 182–188.

Levinson, D. J. (1978). *The seasons of a man's life.* New York: Alfred A. Knopf.

Levy, L. H. (1983). Evaluation of students in clinical psychology programs: A program evaluation perspective. *Professional Practice: Research and Practice, 14,* 497–503.

Lewis, G. J., Greenburg, S. L., & Hatch, D. B. (1988). Peer consultation groups for psychologists in private practice: A national survey. *Professional Psychology: Research and Practice, 9,* 81–86.

Lewis, H. B. (1971). *Shame and guilt in neurosis.* New York: International University Press.

Lewis, M. (2000). Self-conscious emotions: Embarrassment, pride, shame, and guilt. In M. Lewis & J. M. Haviland-Jones (Eds.). *Handbook of emotions* (pp. 623–636). New York: Guilford Press.

Lewis, W. (1988). A supervision model for public agencies. *Clinical Supervisor, 6*(2), 85–91.

Lewis, W., & Rohrbaugh, M. (1989). Live supervision by family therapists: A Virginia survey. *Journal of Marital and Family Therapy, 15,* 323–326.

Lewis, W. C. (2001). Transference in analysis and in supervision. In S. Gill (Ed.). *The supervisory alliance: Facilitating the psychotherapist's learning experience* (pp. 75–80). Northvale, NJ: Jason Aronson.

Levy, L. H. (1983). Evaluation of students in clinical psychology programs: A program evaluation perspective. *Professional Practice: Research and Practice, 14,* 497–503.

Lichtenberg, J. W., & Goodyear, R. K. (2000). The structure of supervisor–supervisee interactions [Special issue]. *Clinical Supervisor, 19*(2), 1–24.

Lichtenberg, J. W., Goodyear, R. K., & McCormick, K. (2000). The structure of supervisor–supervisee interactions. *Clinical Supervisor, 19,* 1–24.

Lichtenberg, J. W., & Heck, E. J. (1986). Analysis of sequence and pattern in process research. *Journal of Counseling Psychology, 33,* 170–181.

Lichtenberg, J. W., & Wettersten, K. B. (August 1996). *Relational control: Historical perspective and current empirical status.* Paper presented at the American Psychological Association, Toronto, ON.

Liddle, B. (1986). Resistance in supervision: A response to perceived threat. *Counselor Education and Supervision, 26,* 117–127.

Liddle, H. A. (1988). Systemic supervision: Conceptual overlays and pragmatic guidelines. In H. A. Liddle, D. C. Breunlin, & R. C. Schwartz (Eds.). *Handbook of family therapy training and supervision* (pp. 153–171). New York: Guilford Press.

Liddle, H. A., Becker, D., & Diamond, G. M. (1997). Family therapy supervision. In C. E. Watkins, Jr. (Ed.). *Handbook of psychotherapy supervision* (pp. 400–421). New York: John Wiley.

Liddle, H. A., Breunlin, D. C., Schwartz, R. C., & Constantine, J. A. (1984). Training family therapy supervisors: Issues of content, form and context. *Journal of Marital and Family Therapy, 10,* 139–150.

Liddle, H. A., Davidson, G., & Barrett, J. (1988). Outcome in live supervision: Trainee perspectives. In H. Liddle, D. Breunlin, & R. Schwartz (Eds.). *Handbook of family therapy training and supervision* (pp. 183–193). New York: Guilford Press.

Liddle, H. A., & Saba, G. W. (1982). Teaching family therapy at the introductory level: A conceptual model emphasizing a pattern which connects training and therapy. *Journal of Marital and Family Therapy, 8,* 63–72.

Liddle, H. A., & Saba, G. W. (1983). On context replication: The isomorphic relationship of family therapy and family therapy training. *Journal of Strategic and Systemic Therapies, 2*(2), 3–11.

Liddle, H. A., & Schwartz, R. C. (1983). Live supervision/consultation: Conceptual and pragmatic guidelines for family therapy trainers. *Family Process, 22,* 477–490.

Liese, B. S., & Beck, J. S. (1997). Cognitive therapy supervision. In C. E. Watkins, Jr. (Ed.). *Handbook of psychotherapy supervision* (pp. 114–133). New York: John Wiley.

Linehan, M. M. (1980). Supervision of behavior therapy. In A. K. Hess (Ed.), *Psychotherapy supervision: Theory, research and practice.* New York: John Wiley.

Littrell, J. M., Lee-Borden, N., & Lorenz, J. A. (1979). A developmental framework for counseling supervision. *Counselor Education and Supervision, 19,* 119–136.

Lloyd, A. P. (1992). Dual relationship problems in counselor education. In B. Herlihy & G. Corey (Eds.). *Dual relationships in counseling* (pp. 59–64). Alexandria, VA: American Association for Counseling and Development.

Lochner, B. T., & Melchert, T. P. (1997). Relationship of cognitive style and theoretical orientation to psychology interns' preferences for supervision. *Journal of Counseling Psychology, 44*(2), 256–260.

Locke, L. D., & McCollum, E. E. (2001). Clients' views of live supervision and satisfaction with therapy. *Journal of Marital and Family Therapy, 27*(1), 129–133.

Loganbill, C., Hardy, E., & Delworth, U. (1982). Supervision: A conceptual model. *Counseling Psychologist, 10,* 3–42.

Lopez, S. R. (1997). Cultural competence in psychotherapy: A guide for clinicians and their supervisors. In C. E. Watkins, Jr. (Ed.). *Handbook of psychotherapy supervision* (pp. 570–588). New York: John Wiley.

Lovell, C. (1999). Supervisee cognitive complexity and the Integrated Developmental Model. *Clinical Supervisor, 18*(1), 191–201.

Lower, R. B. (1972). Countertransference resistances in the supervisory relationship. *American Journal of Psychiatry, 129,* 156–160.

Lowy, L. (1983). Social work supervision: From models to theory. *Journal of Education for Social Work, 19*(2), 55–62.

Lumadue, C. A., & Duffey, T. H. (1999). The role of graduate programs as gatekeepers: A model for evaluating student counselor competence. *Counselor Education and Supervision, 39*(2), 101–109.

Magnuson, S. (1995). *Supervision of prelicensed counselors: A study of educators, supervisors, and supervisees.* Unpublished doctoral dissertation. University of Alabama.

Magnuson, S., Norem, K., & Wilcoxon, A. (2000). Clinical supervision of prelicensed counselors: Recommendations for consideration and practice. *Journal of Mental Health Counseling, 22*(2), 176–188.

Magnuson, S., Wilcoxon, S. A., & Norem, K. (2000). A profile of lousy supervision: Experienced counselors' perspectives. *Counselor Education and Supervision, 39,* 189–202.

Maheu, M. M., & Gordon, B. L. (2000). Counseling and therapy on the Internet. *Professional Psychology: Research and Practice, 31,* 484–489.

Mahoney, M. (1974). *Cognition and behavior modification.* Cambridge, MA: Ballinger.

Mahoney, M. J. (1977). Reflections on the cognitive-learning trend in psychotherapy. *American Psychologist, 32,* 5–13.

Mahoney, M. J. (1991). *Human change processes: The scientific foundations of psychotherapy.* New York: Basic Books.

Mahrer, A. R. (1988). Discovery-oriented psychotherapy research: Rationale, aims, and methods. *American Psychologist, 43,* 694–702.

Maki, D. R., & Bernard, J. M. (2002). The ethics of clinical supervision. In R. R. Cottone & V. M. Tarvydas (Eds.). *Ethical and professional issues in counseling* (2nd ed., pp. 387–412). Upper Saddle River, NJ: Merrill-Prentice Hall.

Maki, D. R., & Delworth, U. (1995). Clinical supervision: A definition and model for the rehabilitation counseling profession. *Rehabilitation Counseling Bulletin, 38,* 282–292.

Mallinckrodt, B., & Nelson, M. L. (1991). Counselor training level and the formation of the psychotherapeutic working alliance. *Journal of Counseling Psychology, 38,* 133–138.

Malouf, J. L., Haas, L. J., & Farah, M. J. (1983). Issues in the preparation of interns: Views of trainers and trainees. *Professional Psychology: Research and Practice, 14,* 624–631.

Marek, L. I., Sandifer, D. M., Beach, A., Coward, R. L., & Protinsky, H. O. (1994). Supervision without the problem: A model of solution-focused supervision. *Journal of Family Psychotherapy, 5,* 57–64.

Markowski, E. M., & Cain, H. I. (1983). Live marital and family therapy supervision. *Clinical Supervisor, 1*(3), 37–46.

Marks, J. L., & Hixon, D. F. (1986). Training agency staff through peer group supervision. *Social Casework, 67,* 418–423.

Marrow, A. J. (1969). *The practical theorist: The life and work of Kurt Lewin.* New York: Basic Books.

Martin, J., Slemon, A., & Hiebert, B. (1990). Implications of counselor conceptualizations for counselor education. *Counselor Education and Supervision, 30,* 120–134.

Martin, J. M. (1988). A proposal for researching possible relationships between scientific theories and the personal theories of counselors and clients. *Journal of Counseling and Development, 66,* 261–265.

Martin, J. M. (1990). Confusions in psychological skills training. *Journal of Counseling and Development, 68,* 402–407.

Martin, J. M., Slemon, A. G., Hiebert, B., Hallberg, E. T., & Cummings, A. L. (1989). Conceptualizations of novice and experienced counselors. *Journal of Counseling Psychology, 36,* 395–400.

Martin, J. S., Goodyear, R. K., & Newton, F. B. (1987). Clinical supervision: An intensive case study. *Professional Psychology: Research and Practice, 18,* 225–235.

Matarazzo, R. G., & Patterson, D. R. (1986). Methods of teaching therapeutic skill. In S. L. Garfield & A. E. Bergin (Eds.). *Handbook of psychotherapy and behavior change* (3rd ed., pp. 821–843). New York: John Wiley.

Matthews, G. (1986). Performance appraisal in the human services: A survey. *Clinical Supervisor, 3*(4), 47–61.

Matthews, G., Davies, D. R., & Lees, J. L. (1990). Arousal, extraversion, and individual differences in resource availability. *Journal of Personality and Social Psychology, 59,* 150–168.

Mauzey, E., & Erdman, P. (1997). Trainee perceptions of live supervision phone-ins: A phenomenological inquiry. *Clinical Supervisor, 15*(2), 115–128.

Mauzey, E., Harris, M. B. C., & Trusty, J. (2000). Comparing the effects of live supervision interventions on novice trainee anxiety and anger [Special issue]. *Clinical Supervisor, 19*(2), 109–122.

McCarthy, P., DeBell, C., Kanuha, V., & McLeod, J. (1988). Myths of supervision: Identifying the gaps between theory and practice. *Counselor Education and Supervision, 28,* 22–28.

McCarthy, P., Kulakowski, D., & Kenfield, J. A. (1994). Clinical supervision practices of licensed psychologists. *Professional Psychology: Research and Practice, 25,* 177–181.

McCarthy, P., Sugden, S., Koker, M., Lamendola, F., Maurer, S., & Renninger, S. (1995). A practical guide to informed consent in clinical supervision. *Counselor Education and Supervision, 35,* 130–138.

McColley, S. H., & Baker, E. L. (1982). Training activities and styles of beginning supervisors: A survey. *Professional Psychology, 13,* 283–292.

McCollum, E. (1995). Perspectives on live supervision: The supervisor's view. *Supervision Bulletin, 8(2),* 4.

McDaniel, S., Weber, T., & McKeever, J. (1983). Multiple theoretical approaches to supervision: Choices in family therapy training. *Family Process, 22,* 491–500.

McKenzie, P. N., Atkinson, B. J., Quinn, W. H., & Heath, A. W. (1986). Training and supervision in marriage and family therapy: A national survey. *American Journal of Family Therapy, 14,* 293–303.

McMinn, M. R., Buchanan, T., Ellens, B. M., & Ryan, M. K. (1999). Technology, professional practice, and ethics: Survey findings and implications. *Professional Psychology: Research and Practice, 30,* 165–172.

McNeill, B. W., Hom, K. L., & Perez, J. A. (1995). The training and supervisory needs of racial and ethnic minority students. *Journal of Multicultural Counseling and Development, 23,* 246–258.

McNeill, B. W., Stoltenberg, C. D., & Pierce, R. A. (1985). Supervisee's perceptions of their development: A test of the counselor complexity model. *Journal of Counseling Psychology, 32,* 630–633.

McNeill, B. W., Stoltenberg, C. D., & Romans, J. S. (1992). The Integrated Developmental Model of supervison: Scale development and validation procedures. *Professional Psychology: Research and Practice, 23,* 504–508.

McNeill, B. W., & Worthen, V. (1989). The parallel process in psychotherapy supervision. *Professional Psychology: Research and Practice, 20,* 329–333.

McRoy, R. G., Freeman, E. M., Logan, S. L., & Blackmon, B. (1986). Cross cultural field supervision: Implications for social work education. *Journal of Social Work Education, 22,* 50–56.

McWilliams, N. (1994). *Psychoanalytic diagnosis: Understanding personality structure in the clinical process.* New York: Guilford Press.

Mead, D. E. (1990). *Effective supervision: A task-oriented model for the mental health professions.* New York: Brunner/Mazel.

Meichenbaum, D. (1977). *Cognitive-behavior modification.* New York: Plenum Press.

Meyer, R. G. (1980). Legal and procedural issues in the evaluation of clinical graduate students. *Clinical Psychologist, 33,* 15–17.

Meyer, R. G., Landis, E. R., & Hays, J. R. (1988). *Law for the psychotherapist.* New York: Norton.

Miars, R. D. Tracey, T. J., Ray, P. B., Cornfield, L., O'Farrell, M., & Gelso, C. J. (1983). Variation in supervision process across trainee experience levels. *Journal of Counseling Psychology, 30,* 403–412.

Middleman, R. R., & Rhodes, G. B. (1985). *Competent supervision: Making imaginative judgments.* Upper Saddle River, NJ: Prentice Hall.

Miller, G. M., & Larrabee, M. J. (1995). Sexual intimacy in counselor education and supervision: A national survey. *Counselor Education and Supervision, 34,* 332–343.

Miller, H. L., & Rickard, H. C. (1983). Procedures and students' rights in the evaluation process. *Professional Psychology: Research and Practice, 14,* 830–836.

Miller, S. B. (1996). Shame in context. Hillsdale, NJ: Analytic Press.

Milne, D., & James, I. (2000). A systematic review of effective cognitive–behavioral supervision. *British Journal of Clinical Psychology, 39,* 111–127.

Milne, D., & James, I. (2002). The observed impact of training on competence in clinical supervision. *British Journal of Clinical Psychology, 41,* 55–72.

Milne, D., & Westerman, C. (2001). Evidence-based clinical supervision: Rationale and illustration. *Clinical Psychology and Psychotherapy, 8,* 444–457.

Minuchin, S., & Fishman, C. (1981). *Family therapy techniques.* Cambridge, MA: Harvard Press.

Mitchell, R. W. (1991). *Documentation in counseling records.* Alexandria, VA: American Counseling Association Press.

Mohl, P. C., Sadler, J. Z., & Miller, D. A. (1994). What components should be evaluated in a psychiatric residency. *Academic Psychiatry, 18,* 22–29.

Molnar, A., & de Shazer, S. (1987). Solution-focused therapy: Toward the identification of therapeutic tasks. *Journal of Marital and Family Therapy, 13,* 349–358.

Monks, G. M. (1996). *A meta-analysis of role induction studies. Dissertation Abstracts International: Section B: The Sciences & Engineering* (US: University Microfilms International), *56*(12-B), June 1996, 7051.

Montalvo, B. (1973). Aspects of live supervision. *Family Process, 12,* 343–359.

Montgomery, L. M., Cupit, B. E., & Wimberley, T. K. (1999). Complaints, malpractice, and risk management: Professional issues and personal experiences. *Professional Psychology: Research and Practice, 30,* 402–410.

Montgomery, M. L., Hendricks, C. B., & Bradley, L. J. (2001). Using systems perspectives in supervision. *Family Journal: Counseling and Therapy for Couples and Families, 9,* 305–313.

Moorhouse, A., & Carr, A. (1999). The correlates of phone-in frequency, duration and the number of suggestions made in live supervision. *Journal of Family Therapy, 21*(4), 407–418.

Moorhouse, A., & Carr, A. (2001). A study of live supervisory phone-ins in collaborative family therapy: Correlates of client cooperation [Special issue]. *Journal of Marital and Family Therapy, 27*(2), 241–249.

Moorhouse, A., & Carr, A. (2002). Gender and conversational behavior in family therapy and life supervision. *Journal of Family Therapy, 24,* 46–56.

Mothersole, G. (1999). Parallel process: A review. *Clinical Supervisor, 18,* 107–122.

Moy, C. T., & Goodman, E. O. (1984). A model for evaluating supervisory interactions in family therapy training. *Clinical Supervisor, 2*(3), 21–29.

Mueller, W. J. (1982). Issues in the application of "Supervision: A conceptual model" to dynamically oriented supervision: A reaction paper. *Counseling Psychologist, 10,* 43–46.

Mueller, W. J., & Kell, B. L. (1972). *Coping with conflict: Supervising counselors and therapists.* New York: Appleton-Century-Crofts.

Munley, P. H. (1974). A review of counseling analogue research methods. *Journal of Counseling Psychology, 21,* 320–330.

Munson, C. E. (1983). *An introduction to clinical social work supervision.* New York: Haworth Press.

Munson, C. E. (1993). *Clinical social work supervision* (2nd ed.). New York: Haworth Press.

Munson, C. E. (2002). *Handbook of clinical social work supervision* (3rd ed.). New York: Haworth Press.

Muratori, M. C. (2001). Examining supervisor impairment from the counselor trainee's perspective. *Counselor Education and Supervision, 41,* 41–56.

Murphy, J. A., Rawlings, E. I., & Howe, S. R. (2002). A survey of clinical psychologists on treating lesbian, gay, and bisexual clients. *Professional Psychology: Research and Practice, 33,* 183–189.

Murphy, J. W., & Pardeck, J. T. (1986). The "burnout syndrome" and management style. *Clinical Supervisor, 4,* 35–44.

Murray, G. C., Portman, T. A. A., & Maki, D. R. (2003). Clinical supervision: Developmental differences during preservice training. *Rehabilitation Education, 17,* 19–32.

Muslin, H. L., Thurnblad, R. J., & Meschel, G. (1981). The fate of the clinical interview: An observational study. *American Journal of Psychiatry, 138,* 822–825.

Myers, I. B. (1962). *The Myers–Briggs Type Indicator.* Palo Alto, CA: Consulting Psychologist Press.

Myers, I. B., & McCaulley, M. H. (1985). *Manual: A guide to the development and use of the Myers–Briggs Type Indicator.* Palo Alto, CA: Consulting Psychologists Press.

Myers, J. E. (Ed.). (1994). *Developing and directing counselor education laboratories.* Alexandria, VA: ACA Press.

Myers, J. E., & Hutchinson, G. H. (1994). Dual role or conflict of interest? Clinics as mental health providers. In J. E. Myers (Ed.). *Developing and directing counselor education laboratories.* Alexandria, VA: ACA Press.

Nathanson, D. L. (1992). *Shame and pride: Affect, sex, and the birth of the self.* New York: Norton.

National Association of Social Workers. (1990). *Code of ethics* (rev. ed.). Washington, DC: Author.

National Board for Certified Counselors. (1993). *A work behavior analysis of professional counselors.* Greensboro, NC: Author.

National Board for Certified Counselors. (1998). ACS Standards for the Ethical Practice of Clinical Supervision. Greensboro, NC: Author. (Adopted by the Center for Credentialing & Education, Inc., 2001.)

Navin, S., Beamish, P., & Johanson, G. (1995). Ethical practices of field-based mental health counselor supervisors. *Journal of Mental Health Counseling, 17,* 243–253.

Neimeyer, R. A. (1995). An invitation to constructivist psychotherapies. In R. A. Neimeyer & M. J. Mahoney (Eds.). *Constructivism in psychotherapy.* Washington, DC: American Psychological Association.

Neiss, R. (1988). Reconceptualizing arousal: Psychobiological states in motor performance. *Psychological Bulletin, 103,* 345–366.

Nelson, M. L. (October 2002). *How to be a lousy supervisor: Lessons from the research.* Paper presented at the annual meeting of the Association for Counselor Education and Supervision, Park City, UT.

Nelson, M. L., & Friedlander, M. L. (2001). A close look at conflictual supervisory relationships: The trainee's perspective. *Journal of Counseling Psychology, 48,* 384–395.

Nelson, M. L., Gray, L. A., Friedlander, M. L., Ladany, N., & Walker, J. A. (2001). Toward relationship-centered supervision: Reply to Veach (2001) and Ellis (2001). *Journal of Counseling Psychology, 48,* 407–409.

Nelson, M. L., & Holloway, E. L. (1990). Relation of gender to power and involvement in supervision. *Journal of Counseling Psychology, 37,* 473–481.

Nelson, M. L., & Neufeldt, S. A. (1998). The pedagogy of counseling: A critical examination.

Counselor Education and Supervision, 38, 70–88.

Nelson, T. S. (1991). Gender in family therapy supervision. *Contemporary Family Therapy: An International Journal, 13,* 357–369.

Neufeldt, S. A. (1994). Use of a manual to train supervisors. *Counselor Education and Supervision, 33,* 327–336.

Neufeldt, S. A. (1997). A social constructivist approach to counseling supervision. In T. E. Sexton & B. Griffin (Eds.). *Constructivist thinking in counseling research, practice, and supervision.* New York: Teacher's College Press.

Neufeldt, S. A. (1999). Training in reflective processes in supervision. In E. Holloway and M. Carroll (Eds.), *Training in counselling supervisors* (pp. 92–105). London, Sage Publications, Inc.

Neufeldt, S. A., Iverson, J. N., & Juntunen, C. L. (1995). *Supervision strategies for the first practicum.* Alexandria, VA: American Counseling Association.

Neufeldt, S. A., Karno, M. P., & Nelson, M. L. (1996). A qualitative analysis of experts' conceptualization of supervisee reflectivity. *Journal of Counseling Psychology, 43,* 3–9.

Neufeldt, S. A., & Nelson, M. L. (1999). When is counseling an appropriate and ethical supervision function? *Clinical Supervisor, 18,* 125–135.

Neukrug, E., Milliken, T., & Walden, S. (2001). Ethical complaints made against credentialed counselors: An updated survey of state licensing boards. *Counselor Education and Supervision, 41,* 57–70.

Neukrug, E. S. (1991). Computer-assisted live supervision in counselor skills training. *Counselor Education and Supervision, 31,* 132–138.

Nicholas, M. W. (1989). A systemic perspective of group therapy supervision: Use of energy in the supervisor–therapist–group system. *Journal of Independent Social Work, 3*(4), 27–39.

Nichols, M. (1984). *Family therapy: Concepts and methods.* New York: Gardner Press.

Nichols, W. C., Nichols, D. P., & Hardy, K. V. (1990). Supervision in family therapy: A decade restudy. *Journal of Marital and Family Therapy, 16,* 275–285.

Nickelson, D. W. (1998). Telehealth and the evolving health care system: Strategic opportunities for professional psychology. *Professional Psychology: Research and Practice, 29,* 527–535.

Nigam, T., Cameron, P. M., & Leverette, J. S. (1997). Impasses in the supervisory process: A resident's perspective. *American Journal of Psychotherapy, 51,* 252–272.

Noelle, M. (2002). Self-report in supervision: Positive and negative slants. *Clinical Supervisor, 21,* 125–134.

Norcross, J. C., & Halgin, R. P. (1997). Integrative approaches to psychotherapy supervision. In J. C. E. Watkins (Ed.). *Handbook of psychotherapy supervision.* New York: John Wiley.

Norcross, J. C., & Napolitano, G. (1986). Defining our journal and ourselves. *International Journal of Eclectic Psychotherapy, 5,* 249–255.

Norcross, J. C., Prochaska, J. O., & Farber, J. A. (1993). Psychologists conducting psychotherapy: New findings and historical comparisons on the psychotherapy division membership. *Psychotherapy, 30,* 692–697.

Norell, J. (1991). The International Balint Federation: Past, present, and future. *Family Practice, 8,* 378–381.

O'Byrne, K., & Rosenberg, J. I. (1998). The practice of supervision: A sociocultural perspective. *Counselor Education and Supervision, 38,* 34–42.

Ogloff, J. R. P., & Olley, M. C. (1998). The interaction between ethics and the law. The ongoing refinement of ethical standards for psychologists in Canada. *Professional Psychology: Research and Practice, 39,* 221–230.

Olk, M., & Friedlander, M. L. (1992). Trainees' experiences of role conflict and role ambiguity in supervisory relationships. *Journal of Counseling Psychology, 39,* 389–397.

Olsen, D. C., & Stern, S. B. (1990). Issues in the development of a family therapy supervision model. *Clinical Supervisor, 8*(2), 49–65.

Olson, M. M., Russell, C. R., & White, M. B. (2001). Technological implications for clinical supervision and practice. *Clinical Supervisor, 20*(2), 201–215.

Olson, U. J., & Pegg, P. F. (1979). Direct open supervision: A team approach. *Family Process, 18,* 463–470. Online at http://psychclassics.asu.edu/Mead/socialself.htm.

O'Neil, J. M. (1981). Male sex-role conflicts, sexism, and masculinity: Implications for men, women, and the counseling psychologist. *Counseling Psychologist, 9,* 61–80.

O'Neil, J. M., Good, G. E., & Holmes, S. (1995). Fifteen years of theory and research on men's gender role conflict. In R. F. Levant & W. S. Pollack (Eds.). *The new psychology of men* (pp. 164–206). New York: Basic Books.

O'Neil, J. M., Helms, B., Gable, R., David, L., & Wrightsman, L. (1986). Gender Role Conflict Scale: College men's fear of femininity. *Sex Roles, 14,* 335–350.

Orlinsky, D. E., Grawe, K., & Parks, B. K. (1994). Process and outcome in psychotherapy: noch einmal. In A. E. Bergin & S. L. Garfield (Eds.). *Handbook of psychotherapy and behavior change* (3rd ed., pp. 270–376). New York: John Wiley.

Osborn, C. J. (in press). Seven salutary suggestions for counselor stamina. *Journal of Counseling and Development.*

Osborn, C. J., & Davis, T. E. (1996). The supervision contract: Making it perfectly clear. *Clinical Supervisor, 14*(2), 121–134.

Osterberg, M. J. (1996). Gender in supervision: Exaggerating the differences between men and women. *Clinical Supervisor, 14*(2), 69–83.

Overholser, J. C. (1991). The Socratic method as a technique in psychotherapy supervision. *Professional Psychology: Research and Practice, 22,* 68–74.

Overholser, J. C., & Fine, M. A. (1990). Defining the boundaries of professional competence: Managing subtle cases of clinical incompetence. *Professional Psychology: Research and Practice, 21,* 462–469.

Page, S., & Wosket, V. (1994). *Supervising the counsellor: a cyclical model.* London: Routledge, 1994.

Papadopoulos, R. K. (2001). Refugee families: Issues of systemic supervision. *Journal of Family Therapy, 23,* 405–422.

Parihar, B. (1983). Group supervision: A naturalistic field study in a specialty unit. *Clinical Supervisor, 1*(4), 3–14.

Parry, A. (1991). A universe of stories. *Family Process, 30,* 37–50.

Parry, A., & Doan, R. E. (1994). *Story re-visions: Narrative therapy in the postmodern world.* New York: Guilford Press.

Patrick, K. D. (1989). Unique ethical dilemmas in counselor training. *Counselor Education and Supervision, 28,* 337–341.

Patterson, C. H. (1964). Supervising students in the counseling practicum. *Journal of Counseling Psychology, 11,* 47–53.

Patterson, C. H. (1983). Supervision in counseling: II. Contemporary models of supervision: A client-centered approach to supervision. *Counseling Psychologist, 11*(1), 21–25.

Patterson, C. H. (1986). *Theories of counseling and psychotherapy* (4th ed.). New York: Harper & Row.

Patterson, C. H. (1997). Client-centered supervision. In C. E. Watkins, Jr. (Ed.). *Handbook of psychotherapy supervision* (pp. 134–146). New York: John Wiley.

Patton, M. J., & Kivlighan, D. M., Jr. (1997). Relevance of the supervisory alliance to the counseling alliance and to treatment adherence in counselor training. *Journal of Counseling Psychology, 44,* 108–115.

Patton, M. J., Kivlighan, D. M., Jr., & Multon, K. D. (1997). The Missouri psychoanalytic counseling research project: Relation of changes in counseling process to client outcomes. *Journal of Counseling Psychology, 44,* 189–208.

Peace, S. D., & Sprinthall, N. A. (1998). Training school counselors to supervise beginning counselors: Theory, research, and practice. *Professional School Counseling, 1*(5), 2–8.

Pearson, B., & Piazza, N. (1997). Classification of dual relationships in the helping professions. *Counselor Education and Supervision, 37*(2), 89–99.

Pearson, Q. M. (2000). Opportunities and challenges in the supervisory relationship: Implications for counselor supervision. *Journal of Mental Health Counseling, 22,* 283–294.

Pedersen, P. B. (1991). Multiculturalism as a generic approach to counseling. *Journal of Counseling and Development, 70,* 6–12.

Penman, R. (1980). *Communication processes and relationships.* London: Academic Press.

Perlesz, A. J., Stolk, Y., & Firestone, A. F. (1990). Patterns of learning in family therapy training. *Family Process, 29,* 29–44.

Perris, C. (1994). Supervising cognitive psychotherapy and training supervisors. *Journal of Cognitive Psychotherapy, 8,* 83–103.

Perry, W. G., Jr. (1970). *Forms of intellectual and ethical development in the college years.* New York: Holt, Rinehart and Winston.

Perry, W. G., Jr. (1981). Cognitive and ethical growth: The making of meaning. In A. W. Chickering (Ed.). *The modern American college* (pp. 76–116). New York: Jossey-Bass.

Peterson, M. (1993). Covert agendas in supervision. *Supervision Bulletin, 6*(1), 1, 7–8.

Peterson, R. (November 7, 2002). Discussant. Panel discussion: Landscapes. (M. Willmuth, Chair). APPIC Competencies Conference. Scottsdale, AZ.

Peterson, R. L., Peterson, D. R., Abrams, J. C., & Stricker, G. (1997). The National Council of Schools and Programs of Professional Psychology Educational Model. *Professional Psychology: Research and Practice, 28,* 373–386. Available on-line at http://www.am.org/ncspp/peterson.html.

Petty, R. E., & Cacioppo, J. T. (1986). *Communication and persuasion: Central and peripheral routes to attitude change.* New York: Springer-Verlag.

Pierce, R. M., & Schauble, P. G. (1970). Graduate training of facilitative counselors: The effects of individual supervision. *Journal of Counseling Psychology, 17,* 210–215.

Pierce, R. M., & Schauble, P. G. (1971). Toward the development of facilitative counselors: The effects of practicum instruction and individual supervision. *Journal of Counseling Psychology, 17,* 210–215.

Piercy, F. P., Sprenkle, D. H., & Constantine, J. A. (1986). Family members' perceptions of live, observation/supervision: An exploratory study. *Contemporary Family Therapy, 8,* 171–187.

Pilkington, N. W., & Cantor, J. M. (1996). Perceptions of heterosexual bias in professional psychology programs. *Professional Psychology: Research and Practice, 27,* 604–612.

Pinsof, W. M., & Wynne, L. C. (1995). The efficacy of marital and family therapy: An empirical overview, conclusions, and recommendations. *Journal of Marital and Family Therapy, 21,* 585–613.

Pistole, M. C., & Watkins, C. E. (1995). Attachment theory, counseling process, and supervision. *Counseling Psychologist, 23,* 457–478.

Poertner, J. (1986). The use of client feedback to improve practice: Defining the supervisor's role. *Clinical Supervisor, 4*(4), 57–67.

Polanski, P. J. (2003). Spirituality in supervision. *Counseling and Values, 47,* 131–141.

Polkinghorne, D. (1988). *Narrative knowing and the human sciences.* Albany, NY: State University of New York Press.

Ponterotto, J. G. (1987). Client hospitalization: Issues and considerations for the counselor. *Journal of Counseling and Development, 65,* 542–546.

Pope, K. S., & Bajt, T. R. (1988). When laws and values conflict: A dilemma for psychologists. *American Psychologist, 45,* 1066–1070.

Pope, K. S., Levenson, H., & Schover, L. R. (1979). Sexual intimacy in psychology training: Results and implications of a national survey. *American Psychologist, 34,* 682–689.

Pope, K. S., Spiegel, K. P., & Tabachnik, B. G. (1986). Sexual attraction to clients: The human therapist and the sometimes inhuman training system. *American Psychologist, 41,* 147–158.

Pope, K. S., Tabachnik, B. G., & Spiegel, P. K. (1987). Ethics of practice: The beliefs and behaviors of psychologists and therapists. *American Psychologist, 42,* 993–1006.

Pope, K. S., & Vasquez, M. J. T. (1991). *Ethics in psychotherapy and counseling: A practical guide for psychologists.* San Francisco: Jossey-Bass.

Pope, K. S., & Vetter, V. A. (1992). Ethical dilemmas encountered by members of the American Psychological Association. *American Psychologist, 47,* 397–411.

Popper, K. (1968). Predicting overt behavior versus predicting hidden states. *Behavioral and Brain Sciences, 9,* 254.

Porter, N. (1994). Empowering supervisees to empower others: A culturally responsive supervision model. *Hispanic Journal of Behavioral Sciences, 16,* 43–56.

Porter, N., & Vasquez, M. (1997). Covision: Feminist supervision, process, and collaboration. In J. Worell & N. G. Johnson (Eds.). *Shaping the future of feminist psychology: Education, research, and practice.* American Psychological Association: Washington, DC.

Preli, R., & Bernard, J. M. (1993). Making multiculturalism relevant for majority culture graduate students. *Journal of Marital and Family Therapy, 19,* 5–16.

Presbury, J., Echterling, L. G., & McKee, J. E. (1999). Supervision for inner-vision: Solution-focused strategies. *Counselor Education and Supervision, 39,* 146–155.

Prest, L. A., Darden, E. C., & Keller, J. F. (1990). "The fly on the wall" reflecting team supervision. *Journal of Marital and Family Therapy, 16,* 265–273.

Price, D. (1963). *Little Science, Big Science.* New York: Columbia University Press.

Priest, R. (1994). Minority supervisor and majority supervisee: Another perspective of reality. *Counselor Education and Supervision, 34,* 152–158.

Prieto, L. R. (1996). Group supervision: Still widely practiced but poorly understood. *Counselor Education and Supervision, 35,* 295–307.

Prieto, L. R. (1998). Practicum class supervision in CACREP-accredited counselor training programs: A national survey. *Counselor Education and Supervision, 38,* 113–123.

Proctor, B. (1991). On being a trainer. In W. Dryden & B. Thorne (Eds.). *Training and supervision for counselling in action* (pp. 49–73). London: Sage.

Proctor, B., & Inskipp, F. (1988). *Skills for supervising and being supervised.* St. Leonards on Sea, Sussex, England: Alexia Publications.

Protinsky, H., & Preli, R. (1987). Interventions in strategic supervision. *Journal of Strategic and Systemic Therapies, 6*(3), 18–23.

Prouty, A. (2001). Experiencing feminist family therapy supervision. *Journal of Feminist Family Therapy, 12,* 171–203.

Prouty, A. M., Thomas, V., Johnson, S., & Long, J. K. (2001). Methods of feminist family therapy supervision. *Journal of Marital and Family Therapy, 27,* 85–97.

Putney, M. W., Worthington, E. L., & McCullough, M. E. (1992). Effects of supervisor and supervisee theoretical orientation and supervisor–supervisee matching on interns' perceptions of supervision. *Journal of Counseling Psychology, 39,* 258–265.

Quarto, C. J., & Tracey, T. J. (August 1989). *Factor structure of the supervision level scale.* Paper presented at the annual meeting of the American Psychological Association, New Orleans, LA.

Quinn, W. H., Atkinson, B. J., & Hood, C. J. (1985). The stuck-case clinic as a group supervision model. *Journal of Marital and Family Therapy, 11,* 67–73.

Rabinowitz, F. E., Heppner, P. P., & Roehlke, H. J. (1986). Descriptive study of process and outcome variables of supervision over time. *Journal of Counseling Psychology, 33,* 292–300.

Raichelson, S. H., Herron, W. G., Primavera, L. H., & Ramirez, S. M. Incidence and effects of parallel processes in psychotherapy supervision. *Clinical Supervisor, 15,* 37–48.

Raimy, V. C. (Ed.). (1950). *Training in clinical psychology.* Upper Saddle River, NJ: Prentice Hall.

Ramos-Sánchez, L., Esnil, E., Goodwin, A., Riggs, S., Touster, L. O., Wright, L. K., et al. (2002). Negative supervisory events: Effects on supervision satisfaction and supervisory alliance. *Professional Psychology: Research and Practice, 33,* 197–202.

Raskin, M. S. (1985). Field placement decisions: Art, science or guesswork? *Clinical Supervisor, 3*(3), 55–67.

Ratliff, D. A., Wampler, K. S., & Morris, G. H. B. (2000). Lack of consensus in supervision. *Journal of Marital and Family Therapy, 26*(3), 373–384.

Ravets, P., Goodyear, R. K., & Halon, A. M. (August 1994). *Group supervision: An intensive, multiple case study.* Paper presented at the annual meeting of the American Psychological Association, Los Angeles.

Ray, D., & Altekruse, M. (2000). Effectiveness of group supervision versus combined group and individual supervision. *Counselor Education and Supervision, 40,* 19–30.

Reed, J. R. (1990). *What group practicum events do students relate to their development as counselors?* Paper presented at the American Educational Research Association, Boston.

Reid, E., McDaniel, S., Donaldson, C., & Tollers, M. (1987). Taking it personally: Issues of personal authority and competence for the female in family therapy training. *Journal of Marital and Family Therapy, 13,* 157–165.

Reising, G. N., & Daniels, M. H. (1983). A study of Hogan's model of counselor development and supervision. *Journal of Counseling Psychology, 30,* 235–244.

Remington, G., & DaCosta, G. (1989). Ethnocultural factors in resident supervision: Black supervisor and White supervisees. *American Journal of Psychotherapy, 43,* 398–404.

Remley, T. R., Jr., & Herlihy, B. (2001). *Ethical, legal, and professional issues in counseling.* Upper Saddle River, NJ: Prentice Hall.

Resnick, R. F., & Estrup, L. (2000). *Supervision: A collaborative endeavor. Gestalt Review, 4,* 121–137.

Retzinger, S. M. (1998). Shame in the therapeutic relationship. In P. Gilbert & B. Andrews (Eds.). *Shame: Interpersonal behavior, psychopathology, and culture.* New York: Oxford University Press.

Rice, L. N. (1980). A client-centered approach to the supervision of psychotherapy. In A. K. Hess (Ed.). *Psychotherapy supervision: Theory, research and practice.* New York: John Wiley.

Richardson, B. K., & Bradley, L. J. (1984). Microsupervision: A skill development model for training clinical supervisors. *Clinical Supervisor, 2*(3), 43–54.

Richman, J. M., Aitken, D., & Prather, D. L. (1990). In-therapy consultation: A supervisory and therapeutic experience from practice. *Clinical Supervisor, 8*(2), 81–89.

Rickert, V. L., & Turner, J. E. (1978). Through the looking glass: Supervision in family therapy. *Social Casework, 59,* 131–137.

Rigazio-DiGilio, S. A. (1995). *The four SCDS cognitive–developmental orientations.* Unpublished document.

Rigazio-DiGilio, S. A. (1998). Toward a reconstructed view of counselor supervision. *Counselor Education and Supervision, 38,* 43–51.

Rigazio-DiGilio, S. A., & Anderson, S. A. (1994). A cognitive–developmental model for marital and family therapy supervision. *Clinical Supervisor, 12*(2), 93–118.

Rigazio-DiGilio, S. A., Anderson, S. A., & Kunkler, K. P. (1995). Gender-aware supervision in marriage and family counseling and therapy: How far have we actually come? *Counselor Education and Supervision, 34,* 344–355.

Rigazio-DiGilio, S. A., Daniels, T. G., Ivey, A. E. (1997). Systemic cognitive-developmental supervision: A developmental-integrative approach to psychotherapy supervision. In C. E.

Watkins, Jr. (Ed.). *Handbook of psychotherapy supervision.* New York: John Wiley & Sons.

Rinas, J., & Clyne-Jackson, S. (1988). *Professional conduct and legal concerns in mental health practice.* Norwalk, CT: Appleton & Lange.

Rioch, M. J., Coulter, W. R., & Weinberger, D. M. (1976). *Dialogues for therapists: Dynamics of learning and supervision.* San Francisco: Jossey-Bass.

Rita, E. S. (1998). Solution-focused supervision. *Clinical Supervisor, 17*(2), 127–139.

Riva, M. T., & Cornish, J. A. E. (1995). Group supervision practices at psychology predoctoral internship programs: A national survey. *Professional Psychology: Research and Practice, 26,* 523–525.

Roberts, J. (1983). Two models of live supervision: Collaborative team and supervisor guided. *Journal of Strategic and Systemic Therapies, 2,* 68–78.

Roberts, J. (1997). Reflecting processes and "supervision": Looking at ourselves as we work with others. In T. C. Todd and C. L. Storm (Eds.). *The complete systemic supervisor: Context, philosophy, and pragmatics* (pp. 334–348). Boston: Allyn and Bacon.

Roberts, W. B., Morotti, A. A., Herrick, C., & Tilbury, R. (2001). Site supervisors of professional school counseling interns: Suggested guidelines. *Professional School Counseling, 4,* 208–215.

Robiner, W. N., Fuhrman, M., & Ristvedt, S. (1993). Evaluation difficulties in supervising psychology interns. *Clinical Psychologist, 46,* 3–13.

Robiner, W. N., Fuhrman, M., Ristvedt, S. L., Bobbit, B., & Schirvar, J. (1994). The Minnesota Supervisory Inventory (MSI): Development, psychometric characteristics, and supervisory evaluation issues. *Clinical Psychologist, 47,* 4–17.

Robiner, W. N., Saltzman, S. R., Hoberman, H. M., Semrud-Clikeman, M., & Schirvar, J. A. (1997). Psychology supervisors' bias in evaluations and letters of recommendation. *Clinical Supervisor, 16*(2), 49–72.

Robinson, W. L., & Reid, P. T. (1985). Sexual intimacies in psychology revisited. *Professional Psychology: Reseach and Practice, 16,* 512–520.

Robyak, J. E., Goodyear, R. K., & Prange, M. (1987). Effects of supervisors sex, focus, and experience on preferences for interpersonal power bases. *Counselor Education and Supervision, 26,* 299–309.

Rock, M. L. (1997). Effective supervision. In M. R. Rock (Ed.), *Psychodynamic supervision: Perspectives of the supervisor and supervisee* (pp. 107–132). Northvale, NJ: Jason Aronson, Inc.

Rodenhauser, P. (1994). Toward a multidimensional model for psychotherapy supervision based on developmental stages. *Journal of Psychotherapy Practice and Research, 3,* 1–15.

Rodenhauser, P. (1997). Psychotherapy supervision: Prerequisites and problems in the process. In C. E. Watkins (Ed.), *Handbook of psychotherapy supervision* (pp. 527–548). New York: John Wiley.

Rodenhauser, P., Rudisill, J. R., & Painter, A. F. (1989). Attributes conducive to learning in psychotherapy supervision. *American Journal of Psychotherapy, 43,* 368–377.

Rodolfa, E., Rowen, H., Steier, D., Nicassio, T., & Gordon, J. (1994). Sexual dilemmas in internship training: What's a good training director to do? *APPIC Newsletter, 19*(2), 1, 22–24.

Rodway, M. R. (1991). Motivation and team building of supervisors in a multi-service setting. *Clinical Supervisor, 9*(2), 161–169.

Rogers, C. R. (1942). The use of electrically recorded interviews in improving psychotherapeutic techniques. *American Journal of Orthopsychiatry, 12,* 429–434.

Rogers, C. R. (1951). *Client-centered therapy.* Boston: Houghton-Mifflin.

Rogers, C. R. (1957). The necessary and sufficient conditions of therapeutic personality change. *Journal of Consulting Psychology, 21,* 95–103.

Rogers, C. R., Gendlin, E. T., Kiesler, D. J., & Truax, C. B. (Eds.). (1967). *The therapeutic relationship and its impact: A study of psychotherapy with schizophrenics.* Madison: University of Wisconsin Press.

Rogers, G., & McDonald, P. L. (1995). Expedience over education: Teaching methods used by field instructors. *Clinical Supervisor, 13*(2), 41–65.

Romans, J. S. C., Boswell, D. L., Carlozzi, A. F., & Ferguson, D. B. (1995). Training and supervision practices in clinical, counseling, and school psychology programs. *Professional Psychology: Research and Practice, 26,* 407–412.

Rønnestad, M. H., Orlinsky, D. E., Parks, B. K., & Davis, J. D. (1997). Supervisors of psychotherapy: Mapping experience level and supervisory confidence. *European Psychologist, 2,* 191–201.

Rønnestad, M. H., & Skovholt, T. M. (1993). Supervision of beginning and advanced graduate students of counseling and psychotherapy. *Journal of Counseling and Development, 71,* 396–405.

Rønnestad, M. H., & Skovholt, T. M. (2003). The journey of the counselor and therapist: Research findings and perspectives on professional development. *Journal of Career Development, 30,* 5–44.

Rosenbaum, M., & Ronen, T. (1998). Clinical supervision from the standpoint of cognitive-behavior therapy. *Psychotherapy, 35,* 220–230.

Rosenblum, A. F., & Raphael, F. B. (1987). Students at risk in the field practicum and implications for field teaching. *Clinical Supervisor, 5*(3), 53–63.

Ross, L. (1977). The intuitive psychologist and his shortcomings: Distortions in the attribution process. In L. Berkowitz (Ed.). *Advances in experimental social psychology, 10,* 174–220.

Ross, R. P., & Goh, D. S. (1993). Participating in supervision in school psychology: A national survey of practices and training. *School Psychology Review, 22,* 63–80.

Rothman, K. F., & Michels, K. D. (1994). The continuing unethical use of placebo controls. *New England Journal of Medicine, 331,* 394–398.

Royal, E., & Golden, S. (1981). Attitude similarity and attraction to an employee group. *Psychological Reports, 48,* 251–254.

Rubinstein, M., & Hammond, D. (1982). The use of videotape in psychotherapy supervision. In M. Blumenfield (Ed.). *Applied supervision in psychotherapy* (pp. 143–164). New York: Grune & Stratton.

Rudolph, B., Craig, R., Leifer, M., & Rubin, N. (1998). Evaluating competency in the diagnostic interview among graduate psychology students: Development of generic scales. *Professional Psychology: Research and Practice, 29,* 488–491.

Russell, G. M., & Greenhouse, E. M. (1997). Homophobia in the supervisory relationship: An invisible intruder. *Psychoanalytic Review, 84*(1), 27–42.

Russell, P. A., Lankford, M. W., & Grinnell, R. M., Jr. (1983). Attitudes toward supervisors in a human service agency. *Clinical Supervisor, 1*(3), 57–71.

Russell, R. K., Crimmings, A. M., & Lent, R. W. (1984). Counselor training and supervision: Theory and research. In S. D. Brown & R. W. Lent (Eds.). *Handbook of counseling psychology* (pp. 625–681). New York: John Wiley.

Russell, R. K., & Petrie, T. (1994). Issues in training effective supervisors. *Applied and Preventive Psychology, 3,* 27–42.

Ryde, J. (2000). Supervising across difference. *International Journal of Psychotherapy, 5*(1), 37–48.

Ryder, R., & Hepworth, J. (1990). AAMFT ethical code: "Dual relationships." *Journal of Marital and Family Therapy, 16,* 127–132.

Saba, G. W. (1999). Live supervision: Lessons learned from behind the mirror. *Academic Medicine: Journal of the Association of American Medical Colleges, 74,* 856–858.

Sabini, J., Garvey, B., & Hall, A. L. (2001). Shame and embarrassment revisited. *Personality and Social Psychology Bulletin, 27,* 104–117.

Safran, J. D., & Muran, J. C. (1996). The resolution of ruptures in the therapeutic alliance. *Journal of Consulting and Clinical Psychology, 64,* 447–458.

Safran, J. D., & Muran, J. C. (2000). Resolving therapeutic alliance ruptures: Diversity and integration. *Journal of Clinical Psychol-*

ogy: In Session: Psychotherapy in Practice, 56, 233–243.

Safran, J. D., & Muran, J. C. (2001). A relational approach to training and supervision in cognitive psychotherapy. *Journal of Cognitive Psychotherapy: An International Quarterly, 15,* 3–15.

Sagrestano, L. M. (1992). Power strategies in interpersonal relationships. *Psychology of Women Quarterly, 16,* 439–447.

Sakinofsky, I. (1979). Evaluating the competence of psychotherapists. *Canadian Journal of Psychiatry, 24,* 193–205.

Sampson, J. P., & Bloom, J. W. (2001). The potential for success and failure of computer applications in counseling and guidance. In D. Locke, J. Myers, & E. Herr (Eds.), *Handbook of counseling* (pp. 613–627). Thousand Oaks, CA: Sage.

Sampson, J. P., Kolodinsky, R. W., & Greeno, B. P. (1997). Counseling on the information highway: Future possibilities and potential problems. *Journal of Counseling and Development, 75,* 203–212.

Samuel, S. E., & Gorton, G. E. (1998). National survey of psychology internship directors regarding education for prevention of psychologist-patient sexual exploitation. *Professional Psychology: Research and Practice, 29,* 86–90.

Sansbury, D. L. (1982). Developmental supervision from a skill perspective. *Counseling Psychologist, 10*(1), 53–57.

Sanville, J. (1989). The play in supervision. *Smith College Studies in Social Work, 59,* 157–159.

Sarnat, J. E., & Frawley-O'Dea, M. G. (April 2001). *Supervisory relationship: Contemporary psychodynamic approach.* Discussion hour (S. A. Pizer, moderator) at the 21st Annual Spring meeting of the APA Division of Psychoanalysis, Sante Fe, NM.

Saxe, J. D. (1865). The blind men and the elephant. In *Clever Stories of Many Nations.* Boston: Ticknor and Fields. Available on-line at http://www.wordfocus.com/word-act-blindmen.html.

Scanlon, C. R., & Gold, J. M. (1996). The balance between the missions of training and service at a university counseling center. *Clinical Supervisor, 14*(1), 163–173.

Schacht, A. J., Howe, H. E., & Berman, J. J. (1989). Supervisor facilitative conditions and effectiveness as perceived by thinking- and feeling-type supervisees. *Psychotherapy, 26,* 475–483.

Schein, E. (1973). *Professional education.* New York: McGraw-Hill.

Schimel, J. L. (1984). In pursuit of truth: An essay on an epistemological approach to psychoanalytic supervision. In L. Caligor, P. M. Bromberg, & J. D. Meltzer (Eds.). *Clinical perspectives on the supervision of psychoanlysis and psychotherapy* (pp. 231–241). New York: Plenum Press.

Schlenker, B. R., & Leary, M. R. (1982). Social anxiety and self-presentation: A conceptualization and model. *Psychological Bulletin, 92,* 641–669.

Schmidt, J. P. (1979). Psychotherapy supervision: A cognitive–behavioral model. *Professional Psychology, 10,* 278–284.

Schneider, S. (1992). Transference, countertransference, projective identification and role responsiveness in the supervisory process. *Clinical Supervisor, 10*(2), 71–84.

Schön, D. A. (1983). *The reflective practitioner: How professionals think in action.* New York: Basic Books.

Schrag, K. (1994). Disclosing homosexuality. *Supervisor Bulletin, 7*(1), 3, 7.

Schreiber, P., & Frank, E. (1983). The use of a peer supervision group by social work clinicians. *Clinical Supervisor, 1*(1), 29–36.

Schroll, J. T., & Walton, R. N. (1991). The interaction of supervision needs with technique and context in the practice of live supervision. *Clinical Supervisor, 9*(1), 1–14.

Schultz, J. C., Ososkie, J. N., Fried, J. H., Nelson, R. E., & Bardos, A. N. (2002). Clinical supervision in public rehabilitation counseling settings. *Rehabilitation Counseling Bulletin, 45,* 213–222.

Schultz, B. M. (1982). *Legal liability in psychotherapy.* San Francisco: Jossey-Bass.

Schwartz, R. C., Liddle, H. A., & Breunlin, D. C. (1988). Muddles in live supervision. In A. A. Liddle, D. C. Breunlin, & R. C. Schwartz (Eds.). *Handbook of family therapy training and supervision* (pp. 183–193). New York: Guilford Press.

Scott, K. J., Ingram, K. M., Vitanza, S. A., & Smith, N. G. (2000). Training in supervision: A survey of current practices. *Counseling Psychologist, 28,* 403–422.

Searles, H. (1955). The informational value of the supervisor's emotional experiences. *Psychiatry, 18,* 135–146.

Sechrest, L., Brewer, M. B., Garfield, S. L., Jackson, J. S., Kurz, R. B., Messick, S. J., et al. (1982). *Report of the task force on the evaluation of education, training, and service in psychology.* Washington, DC: American Psychological Association.

Seligman, M. E. P. (1998). The effectiveness of therapy. *American Psychological Association Monitor, 29*(5), 2.

Sells, J. N., Goodyear, R. K., Lichtenberg, J. W., & Polkinghorne, D. E. (1997). Relationship of supervisor and trainee gender to in-session verbal behavior and ratings of trainee skills. *Journal of Counseling Psychology, 44,* 406–412.

Shanklin, A. (1994). The development of a role-induction procedure for novice supervisees. *Dissertation Abstracts International, 55*(12-A), 3792.

Shapiro, C. H. (1988). Burnout in social work field instructors. *Clinical Supervisor, 6*(4), 237–248.

Shapiro, F. (2001). *Eye movement desensitization and reprocessing: Basic principles, protocols, and procedures* (2nd ed.). New York: Guilford Press.

Shaw, B. F., & Dobson, K. S. (1988). Competency judgements in the training and evaluation of psychotherapists. *Journal of Consulting and Clinical Psychology, 56,* 666–672.

Shechter, R. A. (1990). Becoming a supervisor: A phase in professional development. *Psychoanalysis and Psychotherapy, 8,* 23–28.

Shechtman, Z., & Wirzberger, A. (1999). Need and preferred style of supervision among Israeli school counselors at different stages of professional development. *Journal of Counseling and Development, 77,* 456–464.

Sherry, P. (1991). Ethical issues in the conduct of supervision. *Counseling Psychologist, 19,* 566–584.

Shilts, L., Rudes, J., & Madigan, S. (1993). The use of a solution-focused interview with a reflecting team format: Evolving thoughts from clinical practice. *Journal of Systemic Therapies, 12*(1), 1–10.

Shoben, E. J. (1962). The counselor's theory as personal trait. *Personnel and Guidance Journal, 40,* 617–621.

Shulman, L. (1982). *Skills of supervision and staff management.* Itasca, IL: F. E. Peacock.

Siegel, M. (1979). Privacy, ethics and confidentiality. *Professional Psychology, 10,* 249–258.

Simon, R. (1982). Beyond the one-way mirror. *Family Therapy Networker, 26*(5), 19, 28–29, 58–59.

Simonton, D. K. (1994). *Greatness: Who makes history and why.* New York: Guilford Press.

Skolnik, L. (1988). Field instruction in the 1980s—Realities, issues, and problem-solving strategies. *Clinical Supervisor, 6*(3), 47–75.

Skovholt, T. M., & Rønnestad, M. H. (1992). Themes in therapist and counselor development. *Journal of Counseling and Development, 70,* 505–515.

Skovholt, T. M., & Rønnestad, M. H. (1995). *The evolving professional self: Stages and themes in therapist and counselor development.* Chichester, England: Wiley.

Skovholt, T. M., Rønnestad, M. H., & Jennings, L. (1997). Searching for expertise in counseling, psychotherapy, and professional psychology. *Educational Psychology Review, 9,* 169–361.

Slater, L. (January 26, 2003). Full disclosure. *New York Times.* http://www.nytimes.com/2003/01/26/magazine/26WWLN.html.

Slavkin, J. H. (1994). On making rules: Toward a reformulation of the dynamics of transference in psychoanalytic treatment. *Psychoanalytic Dialogues, 4,* 253–274.

Slimp, P. A. O., & Burian, B. K. (1994). Multiple role relationships during internship: Consequences and recommendations. *Professional Psychology: Research and Practice, 25,* 39–45.

Sluzki, C. E., Beavin, J., Tarnopolski, A., & Vernon, E. (1967). Transactional disqualifications: Research on the double-bind. *Archives of General Psychiatry, 16,* 494–504.

Smadi, A. A., & Landreth, G. G. (1988). Reality therapy supervision with a counselor from a different theoretical orientation. *Journal of Reality Therapy, 7*(2), 18–26.

Smith, H. D. (1984). Moment-to-moment counseling process feedback using a dual-channel audiotape recording. *Counselor Education and Supervision, 23,* 346–349.

Smith, J., Staudinger, U. M., & Baltes, P. B. (1994). Occupational settings facilitating wisdom-related knowledge: The sample case of clinical psychologists. *Journal of Consulting and Clinical Psychology, 62,* 989–999.

Smith, L. W. (1994). The effects of role induction on counselor trainees' experiences of the supervisory working alliance and evaluations of supervision. *Dissertation Abstracts International, 55*(6-A), 1477.

Smith, M. L., & Glass, G. V. (1977). Meta-analysis of psychotherapy outcome studies. *American Psychologist, 32,* 752–760.

Smith, R. C., & Mead, D. E. (1996). *CRB Tracker.* Unpublished software program. St. Louis, MO, and Provo, UT.

Smith, R. C., Mead, D. E., & Kinsella, J. A. (1998). Direct supervision: Adding computer-assisted feedback and data capture to live supervision. *Journal of Marital and Family Therapy, 24*(1), 113–125.

Smith, T. E., Winton, M., & Yoshioka, M. (1992). A qualitative understanding of reflective-teams: II. Therapists' perspectives. *Contemporary Family Therapy: An International Journal, 14,* 419–432.

Smith, T. E., Yoshioka, M., & Winton, M. (1993). A qualitative understanding of reflecting teams: I. Client perspectives. *Journal of Systemic Therapies, 12,* 28–43.

Snider, P. D. (1985). The duty to warn: A potential issue of litigation for the counseling supervisor. *Counselor Education and Supervision, 25,* 66–73.

Snider, P. D. (1987). Client records: Inexpensive liability protection for mental health counselors. *Journal of Mental Health Counseling, 9,* 134–141.

Soisson, E. L., Vandecreek, L., & Knapp, S. (1987). Thorough record keeping: A good defense in a litigious era. *Professional Psychology: Research and Practice, 18,* 498–502.

Somer, E., & Saadon, M. (1999). Therapist–client sex: Clients' retrospective reports. *Professional Psychology: Research and Practice, 30,* 504–509.

Sonne, J. L. (1994). Multiple relationships: Does the new ethics code answer the right questions? *Professional Psychology: Research and Practice, 25,* 336–343.

Sparks, D., & Loucks-Horsley, S. (1989). Five models of staff development for teachers. *Journal of Staff Development, 10*(4), 40–57.

Speed, B., Seligman, P. M., Kingston, P., & Cade, B. W. (1982). A team approach to therapy. *Journal of Family Therapy, 4,* 271–284.

Sperling, M. B., Pirrotta, S., Handen, B. L., Simons, L. A., Miller, D., Lysiak, G., et al. (1986). The collaborative team as a training and therapeutic tool. *Counselor Education and Supervision, 25,* 183–190.

Spotnitz, H. (1969). *Modern psychoanalysis of the schizophrenic patient.* New York: Grune and Stratton.

Stalans, L. J. (1995). Multidimensional scaling. In L. G. Grimm & P. R. Yarnold (Eds.). *Reading and understanding multivariate statistics* (pp. 137–168). American Psychological Association: Washington, DC.

Stanton, J. L., & Stanton, M. D. (1986). Family therapy and systems supervision with the "Pick-a-Dali Circus" model. *Clinical Supervisor, 4,* 169–182.

Staudinger, U. M., Smith, J., & Baltes, P. B. (1992). Wisdom-related knowledge in a life review task: Age differences and the role of professional specialization. *Psychology and Aging, 7,* 271–281.

Stebnicki, M. A., & Glover, N. M. (2001). E-supervision as a complementary approach to traditional face-to-face clinical supervision in rehabilitation counseling: Problems and solutions. *Rehabilitation Education, 15,* 283–293.

Stein, D. M., & Lambert, M. J. (1995). Graduate training in psychotherapy: Are therapy outcomes enhanced? *Journal of Consulting and Clinical Psychology, 63,* 182–196.

Stenack, R. J., & Dye, H. A. (1982). Behavioral descriptions of counseling supervision roles. *Counselor Education and Supervision, 22,* 295–304.

Sterling, M. M., & Bugental, J. F. (1993). The meld experience in psychotherapy supervision. *Journal of Humanistic Psychology, 33,* 38–48.

Sternberg, R. J. (Ed.). (1990). *Wisdom: Its nature, origins, and development.* New York: Cambridge University Press.

Sternitzke, M. E., Dixon, D. N., & Ponterotto, J. G. (1988). An attributional approach to counselor supervision. *Counselor Education and Supervision, 28,* 5–14.

Stevens-Smith, P. (1995). Gender issues in counselor education: Current status and challenges. *Counselor Education and Supervision, 34*(4), 283–293.

Steward, R. J. (1998). Connecting counselor self-efficacy and supervisor self-efficacy: The continued search for counseling competence. *Counseling Psychologist, 26*(2), 285–294.

Steward, R. J., Breland, A., & Neil, D. M. (2001). Novice supervisees' self-evaluations and their perceptions of supervisor style. *Counselor Education and Supervision, 41*(2), 131–141.

Stewart, A. E., & Stewart, E. A. (1996). Personal and practical considerations in selecting a psychology internship. *Professional Psychology: Research and Practice, 27,* 295–303.

Stigall, T. T., Bourg, E. F., Bricklin, P. M., Kovacs, A. L., Larsen, K. G., Lorion, R. P., et al. (Eds.). (1990). *Report of the Joint Council on Professional Education in Psychology.* Baton Rouge, LA: Joint Council on Professional Education in Psychology.

Stiles, W. B., Shapiro, D. A., & Elliott, R. (1986). "Are all psychotherapies equivalent?" *American Psychologist, 41,* 165–180.

Stiles, W. B., & Snow, J. S. (1984). Counseling session impact as viewed by novice counselors and their clients. *Journal of Counseling Psychology, 31,* 3–12.

Stoltenberg, C. (1981). Approaching supervision from a developmental perspective: The counselor-complexity model. *Journal of Counseling Psychologists, 28,* 59–65.

Stoltenberg, C., & Delworth, U. (1987). *Supervising counselors and therapists.* San Francisco: Jossey-Bass.

Stoltenberg, C. D., & Delworth, U. (1988). Developmental models of supervision: It is development—Response to Holloway. *Professional Psychology: Research and Practice, 19,* 134–137.

Stoltenberg, C. D., McNeill, B. W., & Crethar, H. C. (1994). Changes in supervision as counselors and therapists gain experience: A review. *Professional Psychology: Research and Practice, 25,* 416–449.

Stoltenberg, C. D., McNeill, B. W., & Crethar, H. C. (1995). Persuasion and development in counselor supervision. *Counseling Psychologist, 23,* 633–648.

Stoltenberg, C. D., McNeill, B. W., & Delworth, U. (1998). *IDM: An integrated developmental model for supervising counselors and therapists.* San Francisco: Jossey-Bass.

Stoltenberg, C. D., Pierce, R. A., & McNeill, B. W. (1987). Effects of experience on counselors needs. *Clinical Supervisor, 5,* 23–32.

Stone, D., & Amundson, N. (1989). Counselor supervision: An exploratory study of the metaphoric case drawing method of case presentation in a clinical setting. *Canadian Journal of Counseling, 23,* 360–371.

Stone, G. L. (1980). Effects of experience on supervision planning. *Journal of Counseling Psychology, 27,* 84–88.

Stone, G. L. (1984). Reaction: In defense of the "artificial." *Journal of Counseling Psychology, 31,* 108–110.

Stone, G. L. (1997). Multiculturalism as a context for supervision: Perspectives, limitations, and implications. In D. B. Pope-Davis & H. L. K. Coleman (Eds.). *Multicultural counseling competencies: Assessment, education, training, and supervision.* Thousand Oaks, CA: Sage.

Stoppard, J. M., & Miller, A. (1985). Conceptual level matching in therapy: A review. *Current Psychological Research and Reviews, 4,* 47–68.

Storm, C., & Heath, A. W. (1982). Strategic supervision: The danger lies in discovery. *Journal of Strategic and Systemic Therapies, 1,* 71–72.

Storm, C. L. (1997). Back to the future: A review through time. In T. C. Todd and C. L. Storm (Eds.). *The complete systemic supervisor: Context, philosophy, and pragmatics* (pp. 283–287). Boston: Allyn and Bacon.

Storm, C. L., & Haug, I. E. (1997). Ethical issues: Where do you draw the line? In T. C. Todd & C. L. Storm (Eds.). *The complete systemic supervisor: Context, philosophy, and pragmatics* (pp. 26–40). Boston: Allyn and Bacon.

Storm, H. A. (1994). *Enhancing the acquisition of psychotherapy skills through live supervision.* Paper presented at the annual meeting of the American Psychological Association, Los Angeles.

Stout, C. E. (1987). The role of ethical standards in the supervision of psychotherapy. *Clinical Supervisor, 5*(1), 89–97.

Strassle, C. G. (2001). Role induction, perseverance in therapy and psychotherapy outcome. *Dissertation Abstracts International, 62*(8-B), 3816.

Strean, H. S. (2000). Resolving therapeutic impasses by using the supervisor's countertransference. *Clinical Social Work Journal, 28,* 263–279.

Strein, W., & Hershenson, D. B. (1991). Confidentiality in nondyadic counseling situations. *Journal of Counseling and Development, 69,* 312–316.

Strong, S. R. (1968). Counseling: An interpersonal influence process. *Journal of Counseling Psychology, 15,* 215–224.

Strong, S. R. (1971). Experimental laboratory research in counseling. *Journal of Counseling Psychology, 18,* 106–110.

Strong, S. R., & Hills, H. (1986). *Interpersonal Communication Rating Scale.* Richmond, VA: Virginia Commonwealth University.

Strozier, A. L., Kivlighan, D. M., & Thoreson, R. W. (1993). Supervisor intentions, supervisee reactions, and helpfulness: A case study of the process of supervision. *Professional Psychology: Research and Practice, 24,* 13–19.

Strupp, H. H., & Binder, J. (1984). *Psychotherapy in a new key: A guide to time-limited dynamic psychotherapy.* New York: Basic Books.

Strupp, H. H., & Hadley, S. W. (1977). A tripartite model of mental health and therapeutic outcomes. *American Psychologist, 32,* 187–196.

Strupp, H. H., & Hadley, S. W. (1979). Specific versus nonspecific factors in psychotherapy. *Archives of General Psychiatry, 36,* 1125–1136.

Stryker, S., & Statham, A. (1985). Symbolic interactionism and role theory. In G. Lindzey and E. Aronson (Eds.). *The handbook of social psychology* (3rd ed., Vol. 1, pp. 311–378). New York: Random House.

Sullivan, H. S. (1953). *The interpersonal theory of psychiatry.* New York: Norton.

Sumerel, M. B., & Borders, L. D. (1996). Addressing personal issues in supervision: Impact of counselor's experience level on various aspects of the supervisory relationship. *Counselor Education and Supervision, 35*(4), 268–286.

Supervision Interest Network, Association for Counselor Education and Supervision (1990). Standards for counseling supervisors. *Journal of Counseling and Development, 69,* 30–32.

Supervision Interest Network, Association for Counselor Education and Supervision. (Summer 1993). ACES ethical guidelines for counseling supervisors. *ACES Spectrum, 53*(4), 5–8.

Sutter, E., McPherson, R. H., & Geeseman, R. (2002). Contracting for supervision. *Profes-*

sional Psychology: Research and Practice, 33, 495–498.

Sutton, J. M., Jr. (2000). Counselor licensure. In H. Hackney (Ed.). *Practice issues for the beginning counselor* (pp. 55–78). Boston: Allyn and Bacon.

Sutton, J. M., Jr., Nielson, R., & Essex, M. (1998). *A descriptive study of the ethical standards related to supervisory behavior employed by counselor licensing boards.* Paper presented at the annual conference of the American Association of State Counseling Boards, Tucson, AZ.

Sutton, J. R. (1998). Fostering client engagement in counseling through the use of videotaped role induction (anxiety, intake session). *Dissertation Abstracts International, 59*(4-A), 1082.

Swanson, J. L., & O'Saben, C. L. (1993). Differences in supervisory needs and expectations by trainee experience, cognitive style, and program membership. *Journal of Counseling and Development, 71,* 457–464.

Swenson, L. S. (1997). *Psychology and law for the helping professions* (2nd ed.). Pacific Grove, CA: Brooks/Cole.

Tabachnick, B. G., Keith-Spiegel, P., & Pope, K. S. (1991). Ethics of teaching beliefs and behaviors of psychologists as educators. *American Psychologist, 46,* 506–515.

Talen, M. R., & Schindler, N. (1993). Goal-directed supervision plans: A model for trainee supervision and evaluation. *Clinical Supervisor, 11*(2), 77–88.

Tangney, J. P., Wagner, P., Fletcher, C., & Gramzow, R. (1992). Shamed into anger? The relation of shame and guilt to anger and self-reported aggression. *Journal of Personality and Social Psychology, 62,* 669–675.

Tarasoff v. *Regents of the University of California.* 118 Cal. Rptr. 129, 529 P 2d 533 (1976).

Tarvydas, V. M. (1995). Ethics and the practice of rehabilitation counselor supervision. *Rehabilitation Counseling Bulletin, 38,* 294–306.

Teitelbaum, S. H. (1990). Supertransference: The role of the supervisor's blind spots. *Psychoanalytic Psychology, 7,* 243–258.

Tennen, H. (1988). Supervision of integrative psychotherapy: A critique. *Journal of Integrative and Eclectic Psychotherapy, 7,* 167–175.

Tetlock, P. E., & Tyler, A. (1996). Churchill's cognitive and rhetorical style: The debates over Nazi intentions and self-government for India. *Political Psychology, 17,* 149–170.

Thomas, F. N. (1996). Solution-focused supervision: The coaxing of expertise. In S. D. Miller, M. A. Hubble, & B. L. Duncan (Eds.). *Handbook of solution-focused therapy* (pp. 128–151). San Francisco: Jossey-Bass.

Thoreson, R. W., Shaughnessy, P., Heppner, P. P., & Cook, S. W. (1993). Sexual contact during and after the professional relationship: Attitudes and practices of male counselors. *Journal of Counseling and Development, 71,* 429–434.

Thyer, B. A., Sowers-Hoag, K., & Love, J. P. (1988). The influence of field instructor–student gender combinations on student perceptions of field instruction quality. *Clinical Supervisor, 6*(3), 169–179.

Tinsley, H. E. A., Bowman, S. L., & Ray, S. B. (1988). Manipulation of expectancies about counseling and psychotherapy: A review and analysis of expectancy manipulation strategies and results. *Journal of Counseling Psychology, 35,* 99–108.

Tinsley, H. E. A., Workman, K. R., & Kass, R. A. (1980). Factor analysis of the domain of client expectancies about counseling. *Journal of Counseling Psychology, 27,* 561–570.

Todd, T. C. (1997). Purposive systemic supervision models. In T. C. Todd & C. L. Storm (Eds.). *The complete systemic supervisor: Context, philosophy and pragmatics* (pp. 173–194). Boston: Allyn and Bacon.

Todtman, D. A., Bobele, M., & Strano, J. D. (1988). An inexpensive system for communication across the one-way mirror. *Journal of Marital and Family Therapy, 14,* 201–203.

Tracey, M., Froehle, T., Kelbley, T., Chilton, T., Sandhofer, R., Woodward, D., et al. (April 1995). *Data centric counseling: The development of a computer-assisted observation system* for use in process studies in counseling, supervision, and counselor training. Paper presented at the annual meeting of the American Educational Reseach Association, San Francisco.

Tracey, T. J. G. (1993). An interpersonal stage model of the therapeutic process. *Journal of Counseling Psychology, 40,* 1–14.

Tracey, T. J. G. (2002). Stages of counseling and therapy: An examination of complementarity and the working alliance. In G. S. Tryon (Ed.). *Counseling based on process research: Applying what we know.* Boston: Allyn and Bacon.

Tracey, T. J. G., Ellickson, J. L., & Sherry, P. (1989). Reactance in relation to different supervisory environments and counselor development. *Journal of Counseling Psychology, 36,* 336–344.

Tracey, T. J. G., Hays, K. A., Malone, J., & Herman, B. (1988). Changes in counselor response as a function of experience. *Journal of Counseling Psychology, 35,* 119–126.

Tracey, T. J. G., & Sherry, P. (1993). Complementary interaction over time in successful and less successful supervision. *Professional Psychology: Research and Practice, 24,* 304–311.

Tracey, T. J. G., Sherry, P., & Albright, J. M. (1999). The interpersonal process of cognitive-behavioral therapy: An examination of complementarity over the course of treatment. *Journal of Counseling Psychology, 46,* 80–91.

Triantafillou, N. (1997). A solution-focused approach to mental health supervision. *Journal of Systemic Therapies, 16,* 305–328.

Tuckman, B. W. (1965). Developmental sequence in small groups. *Psychological Bulletin, 63,* 384–399.

Tuckman, B. W., & Jensen, M. A. C. (1977). Stages of small group development revisited. *Group and Organizational Studies, 2,* 419–427.

Turban, D. B., & Jones, A. P. (1988). Supervisor-subordinate similarity: Types, effects, and mechanisms. *Journal of Applied Psychology, 73,* 228–234.

Turban, D. B., Jones, A. P., & Rozelle, R. M. (1990). Influences of supervisor liking of a subordinate and the reward context on the treatment and evaluation of that subordinate. *Motivation and Emotion, 14,* 215–233.

Turner, J. (1993). Males supervising females: The risk of gender-power blindness. *Supervisor Bulletin, 6,* 4, 6.

Twohey, D., & Volker, J. (1993). Listening for the voices of care and justice in counselor supervision. *Counselor Education and Supervision, 32,* 189–197.

Upchurch, D. W. (1985). Ethical standards and the supervisory process. *Counselor Education and Supervision, 25,* 90–98.

Usher, C. H., & Borders, L. D. (1993). Practicing counselors' preferences for supervisory style and supervisory emphasis. *Counselor Education and Supervision, 33,* 66–79.

VandenBos, G. R., & Williams, S. (2000). The Internet versus the telephone: What is telehealth, anyway? *Professional Psychology: Research and Practice, 31,* 490–492.

VanderKolk, C. (1974). The relationship of personality, values, and race to anticipation of the supervisory relationship. *Rehabilitation Counseling Bulletin, 18,* 41–46.

Vargas, L. A. (August 1989). *Training psychologists to be culturally responsive: Issues in supervision.* Paper presented at the Annual Convention of the American Psychological Association, New Orleans, LA.

Vasquez, M. J. (1999). Trainee impairment: A response from a feminist/multicultural retired trainer. *Counseling Psychologist, 27,* 687–692.

Vasquez, M. J. T. (1988). Counselor–client sexual contact: Implications for ethics training. *Journal of Counseling and Development, 67,* 238–241.

Vasquez, M. J. T. (1992). Psychologist as clinical supervisor: Promoting ethical practice. *Professional Psychology: Research and Practice, 23,* 196–202.

Vogel, D. (1994). Narrative perspectives in theory and therapy. *Journal of Constructivist Psychology,* 243–261.

Vygotsky, L. S. (1978). *Mind in society: The development of higher psychological processes.* (M. Cole, V. John-Steiner, S. Scribner, & E.

Souberman, Eds. and Trans.). Cambridge, MA: Harvard University Press.

Walker, J. A., & Gray, L. A. (June 2002). *Categorizing supervisor countertransference.* Paper presented at the annual meeting of the Society for Psychotherapy Research International Conference, Santa Barbara, CA.

Walter, C. A., & Young, T. M. (1999). Combining individual and group supervision in educating for the social work profession. *Clinical Supervisor, 18*(2), 73–89.

Walzer, R. S., & Miltimore, S. (1993). Mandated supervision: Monitoring, and therapy of disciplined health care professionals. *Journal of Legal Medicine, 14,* 565–596.

Wampold, B. E. (1986). State of the art in sequential analysis: Comment on Lichtenberg and Heck. *Journal of Counseling Psychology, 33,* 182–185.

Wampold, B. E. (2001). *The great psychotherapy debate: Models, methods, and findings.* Mahwah, NJ: Lawrence Erlbaum.

Wampold, B. E., & Holloway, E. L. (1997). Methodology, design, and evaluation in psychotherapy supervision research. In C. E. Watkins (Ed.). *Handbook of psychotherapy supervision.* New York: John Wiley.

Wampold, B. E., Lichtenberg, J. W., & Waehler, C. A. (2002). Principles of empirically supported interventions in counseling psychology. *Counseling Psychologist, 30,* 197–217.

Warburton, J. R., Newberry, A., & Alexander, J. (1989). Women as therapists, trainees, and supervisors. In M. McGoldrick, C. Anderson, & F. Walsh (Eds.). *Women in families: A framework for family therapy* (pp. 152–165). New York: Norton.

Ward, L. G., Friedlander, M. L., Schoen, L. G., & Klein, J. G. (1985). Strategic self-presentation in supervision. *Journal of Counseling Psychology, 32,* 111–118.

Wark, L. (1995). Defining the territory of live supervision in family therapy training: A qualitative study and theoretical discussion. *Clinical Supervisor, 13*(1), 145–162.

Watkins, C. E., Jr. (1990a). Development of the psychotherapy supervisor. *Psychotherapy, 27,* 553–560.

Watkins, C. E., Jr. (1990b). The separation–individuation process in psychotherapy supervision. *Psychotherapy, 27,* 202–209.

Watkins, C. E., Jr. (1993). Development of the psychotherapy supervisor: Concepts, assumptions, and hypotheses of the supervisor complexity model. *American Journal of Psychotherapy, 47,* 58–74.

Watkins, C. E., Jr. (1994). The supervision of psychotherapy supervisor trainees. *American Journal of Psychotherapy, 48,* 417–431.

Watkins, C. E., Jr. (1995b). Considering psychotherapy supervisor development: A status report. *Psychotherapy Bulletin, 29*(4), 32–34.

Watkins, C. E., Jr. (1995c). Psychotherapy supervisor and supervisee: Developmental models and research nine years later. *Clinical Psychology Review, 15,* 647–680.

Watkins, C. E., Jr. (1995d). Psychotherapy supervisor development: On musings, models, and metaphor. *Journal of Psychotherapy Practice and Research, 4,* 150–158.

Watkins, C. E., Jr. (1995e). Researching psychotherapy supervisor development: Four key considerations. *Clinical Supervisor, 13*(2), 111–118.

Watkins, C. E., Jr. (1999). The beginning psychotherapy supervisor: How can we help? *Clinical Supervisor, 18,* 63–72.

Watkins, C. E., Jr., Lopez, F. G., Campbell, V. L., & Himmell, C. D. (1986). Contemporary counseling psychology: Results of a national survey. *Journal of Counseling Psychology, 33,* 301–309.

Watkins, C. E., Jr., Schneider, L. J., Haynes, J., & Nieberding, R. (1995). Measuring psychotherapy supervisor development: An initial effort at scale development and validation. *Clinical Supervisor, 13*(1), 77–90.

Watson, M. F. (1993). Supervising the person of the therapist: Issues, challenges and dilemmas. Special Issue: Critical issues in marital and family therapy education. *Contemporary Family Therapy an International Journal, 15,* 21–31.

Watzlawick, P., & Beavin, J. (1976). Some formal aspects of communication. In P. Watzlawick & J. H. Weakland (Eds.). *The interactional view* (pp. 56–67). New York: Norton.

Watzlawick, P., Beavin, J. H., & Jackson, D. D. (1967). *Pragmatics of human communication: A study of interactional patterns, pathologies, and paradoxes.* New York: Norton.

Webb, A., & Wheeler, S. (1998). How honest do counsellors dare to be in the supervisory relationship?: An exploratory study. *British Journal of Guidance and Counselling, 26,* 509–524.

Webster's New World Dictionary of the American Language. (1966). New York: World Publishing.

Weisinger, H., & Lobsenz, N. M. (1981). *Nobody's perfect: How to give criticism and get results.* Los Angeles: Stratford.

Wendorf, D. J. (1984). A model for training practicing professionals in family therapy. *Journal of Marital and Family Therapy, 10,* 31–41.

Wendorf, D. J., Wendorf, R. J., & Bond, O. (1985). Growth behind the mirror: The family therapy consortiums' group process. *Journal of Marriage and Family Therapy, 11,* 245–255.

Wessler, R. L., & Ellis, A. (1983). Supervision in counseling: Rational–emotive therapy. *Counseling Psychologist, 11*(1), 43–49.

West, J. D., Bubenzer, D. L., & Delmonico, D. L. (1994). Preparation of doctoral-level supervisors. In J. E. Myers (Ed.). *Developing and directing counselor education laboratories.* Alexandria, VA: ACA Press.

West, J. D., Bubenzer, D. L., Pinsoneault, T., & Holeman, V. (1993). Three supervision modalities for training marital and family counselors. Special section: Marriage and family counselor training. *Counselor Education and Supervision, 33,* 127–138.

West, J. D., Bubenzer, D. L., & Zarski, J. J. (1989). Live supervision in family therapy: An interview with Barbara Oken and Fred Piercy. *Counselor Education and Supervision, 29,* 25–34.

Wester, S. R. (2002). *Male restricted emotionality and counseling supervision.* Paper presented at the annual meeting of the American Psychological Association, Chicago.

Wester, S. R. & Vogel, D. L. (2002). Working with the masculine mystique: Male gender role conflict, counseling self-efficacy, and the training of male psychologists. *Professional Psychology: Research and Practice, 33,* 370–376.

Wetchler, J. L. (1989). Supervisors' and supervisees' perceptions of the effectiveness of family therapy supervisor interpersonal skills. *American Journal of Family Therapy, 17,* 244–256.

Wetchler, J. L., & Vaughn, K. A. (1992). Perceptions of primary family therapy supervisory techniques: A critical incident analysis. *Contemporary Family Therapy: An International Journal, 14,* 127–136.

Wetchler, J. L., Piercy, F. P., & Sprenkle, D. H. (1989). Supervisors' and supervisees' perceptions of the effectiveness of family therapy supervisory techniques. *American Journal of Family Therapy, 17,* 35–47.

Wheeler, S., & King, D. (2000). Do counselling supervisors want or need to have their supervision supervised? An exploratory study. *British Journal of Guidance and Counselling, 28*(2), 279–290.

Whiffen, R. (1982). The use of videotape in supervision. In R. Whiffen and J. Byng-Hall (Eds.). *Family therapy supervision: Recent developments in practice.* New York: Academic Press.

Whiston, S. C., & Emerson, S. (1989). Ethical implications for supervisors in counseling of trainees. *Counselor Education and Supervision, 28,* 318–325.

White, H. D., & Rudolph, B. A. (2000). A pilot investigation of the reliability and validity of the Group Supervisory Behavior Scale (GBS). *Clinical Supervisor, 19,* 161–171.

White, L. J., Rosenthal, D. M., & Fleuridas, C. L. (1993). Accountable supervision through systematic data collection: Using single-case designs. *Counselor Education and Supervision, 33,* 32–46.

White, M. B., & Russell, C. S. (1997). Examining the multifaceted notion of isomorphism in marriage and family therapy supervision: A quest for conceptual clarity. *Journal of Marital and Family Therapy, 23,* 315–333.

White, R. W. (1959). Motivation reconsidered: The concept of competence. *Psychological Review, 66,* 297–323.

White, V. E., & Queener, J. (2000). Supervisor and supervisee attachments and social provisions related to the supervisory working alliance. *Counselor Education & Supervision.*

Wiggins, J. S. (1985). Interpersonal circumplex models: 1948–1983. *Journal of Personality Assessment, 49,* 626–631.

Wilbur, M. P., & Roberts-Wilbur, J. (1983). Schemata of the steps of the SGS model. Unpublished table.

Wilbur, M. P., Roberts-Wilbur, J. M., Hart, G., Morris, J. R., & Betz, R. L. (1994). Structured Group Supervision (SGS): A pilot study. *Counselor Education & Supervision, 33,* 262–279.

Wilcoxon, S. A. (1992). Videotape review of supervision-of-supervision in concurrent training: Allowing trainees to peer through the door. *Family Therapy, 19,* 143–153.

Wiley, M., & Ray, P. (1986). Counseling supervision by developmental level. *Journal of Counseling Psychology, 33,* 439–445.

Wiley, M. O. (August 1994). *Supervising oneself in independent practice: From student to solo practitioner.* Paper presented at the American Pscyhological Association, Los Angeles.

Williams, A. (1995). *Visual and active supervision: Roles, focus, technique.* New York: Norton.

Williams, A. B. (2000). Contribution of supervisors' covert communication to the parallel process. *Dissertation Abstracts International Section A: Humanities & Social Sciences, Vol. 61(3-A),* 1165.

Williams, E. N., Judge, A. B., Hill, C. E., & Hoffman, M. A. (1997). Experiences of novice therapists in prepracticum: Trainees', clients', and supervisors' perceptions of therapists' personal reactions and management strategies. *Journal of Counseling Psychology, 44*(4), 390–399.

Williams, L. (1994). A tool for training supervisors: Using the Supervision Feedback Form (SFF). *Journal of Marital and Family Therapy, 20,* 311–315.

Williams, M. H. (2000). Victimized by "victims": A taxonomy of antecedents of false complaints against psychotherapists. *Professional Psychology: Research and Practice, 31,* 75–81.

Williams, S., & Halgin, R. P. (1995). Issues in psychotherapy supervision between the Whites supervisor and the Black supervisee. *Clinical Supervisor, 13,* 39–61.

Winter, M., & Holloway, E. L. (1991). Relation of trainee experience, conceptual level, and supervisor approach to selection of audiotaped counseling passages. *Clinical Supervisor, 9*(2), 87–103.

Wise, P. S., Lowery, S., & Silverglade, L. (1989). Personal counseling for counselors in training: Guidelines for supervisors. *Counselor Education and Supervision, 28,* 326–336.

Wolpe, J., Knopp, W., & Garfield, Z. (1966). Postgraduate training in behavior therapy. *Exerta Medica International Congress Series, No. 150.* Proceedings of the IV World Congress of Psychiatry, Madrid, Spain.

Wong, P. T. P., & Wong, L. C. J. (1999). Assessing multicultural supervision competencies. In W. J. Lonner, D. L. Dinnel, D. K. Forgays, & S. A. Hayes (Eds.). *Merging past, present and future in cross-cultural psychology* (pp. 510–519). Lisse, The Netherlands: Swets & Zeitlinger.

Wong, Y.-L. S. (1997). Live supervision in family therapy: Trainee perspectives. *Clinical Supervisor, 15*(1), 145–157.

Wood, B., Klein, S., Cross, H., Lammers, C., & Elliot, J. (1985). Impaired practitioners: Psychologists' opinions about prevalence, and proposals for intervention. *Professional Psychology: Research and Practice, 16,* 843–850.

Woods, P. J., & Ellis, A. (1996). Supervision in rational emotive behavior therapy. *Journal of Rational–Emotive & Cognitive Behavior Therapy, 14,* 135–152.

Woodside, D. B. (1994). Reverse live supervision: Leveling the supervisory playing field. *Supervision Bulletin, 7*(2), 6.

Woodworth, C. B. (2000). Legal issues in counseling practice. In H. Hackney (Ed.). *Practice issues for the beginning counselor* (pp. 119–136). Boston: Allyn and Bacon.

Woody, R. H., and Associates. (1984). *The law and the practice of human services.* San Francisco: Jossey-Bass.

Woolley, G. (1991). Beware the well-intentioned therapist. *Family Therapy Networker, 30.*

Worthen, V., & McNeill, B. W. (1996). A phenomenological investigation of "good" supervision events. *Journal of Counseling Psychology, 43,* 25–34.

Worthington, E. L., Jr. (1987). Changes in supervision as counselors and supervisors gain experience: A review. *Professional Psychology: Research and Practice, 18,* 189–208.

Worthington, E. L., Jr., & Roehlke, H. J. (1979). Effective supervision as perceived by beginning counselors-in-training. *Journal of Counseling Psychology, 26,* 64–73.

Worthington, E. L., Jr., & Stern, A. (1985). Effects of supervisor and supervisee degree level and gender on the supervisory relationship. *Journal of Counseling Psychology, 32,* 252–262.

Worthington, R. L., Tan, J. A., & Poulin, K. (2002). Ethically questionable behaviors among supervisees: An exploratory investigation. *Ethics and Behavior, 12,* 323–351.

Wright, L. M. (1986). An analysis of live supervision "phone-ins" in family therapy. *Journal of Marital and Family Therapy, 12,* 187–191.

Wynne, M. E., Susman, M., Ries, S., Birringer, J., & Katz, L. (1994). A method for assessing therapists' recall of in-session events. *Journal of Counseling Psychology, 41,* 53–57.

Yalom, I. D. (1985). *The theory and practice of group psychotherapy* (3rd ed.). New York: Basic Books.

Yerkes, R. M., & Dodson, J. D. (1908). The relation of strength of stimulus to rapidity of habit formation. *Journal of Comparative Neurology and Psychology, 18,* 459–482.

Yerushalmi, H. (1999). The roles of group supervision of supervision. *Psychoanalytic Psychology, 16,* 426–447.

Yogev, S. (1982). An eclectic model of supervision: A developmental sequence for beginning psychotherapy students. *Professional Psychology, 13,* 236–243.

Young, J., Perlesz, A., Paterson, R., O'Hanlon, B., Newbold, A., Chaplin, R., et al. (1989). The reflecting team process in training. *Australia and New Zealand Journal of Family Therapy, 10,* 69–74.

Zajonc, R. B. (1965). Social facilitation. *Science, 149,* 269–274.

Zarski, J. J., Sand-Pringle, C., Pannell, L., & Lindon, C. (1995). Critical issues in supervision: Marital and family violence. *Family Journal: Counseling and Therapy for Couples and Families, 3*(1), 18–26.

Zuniga, M. E. (1987). Mexican-American clinical training: A pilot project. *Journal of Social Work Education, 23,* 11–20.

Author Index

Abadie, P. D., 76, 97, 175, 295
Abbott, A. A., 32
Abrams, J. C., 4
Abreu, J. M., 178
Abroms, G. M., 137
Acker, M., 172–173
Acuff, C., 53, 66
Adamek, M. S., 261, 267
Adams, J., 273
Ahia, C. E., 69
Aiello, J. R., 166
Aitken, D., 259
Albee, G. W., 11
Alderfer, C., 258
Alexander, J., 128
Allen, D. W., 287
Allen, G. J., 93, 112
Allen, J., 237, 243, 256
Allison, R. D., 23
Allphin, C., 170
Alonso, A., 86, 163, 164, 280
Alper, V. S., 140, 295
Altekruse, M. K., 146, 197, 198, 229,
    234, 235, 303
American Association for Marriage and
    Family Therapy, 2, 50
American Counseling Association,
    50, 312
American Psychological Association, 2,
    50, 58, 279
Amundson, N., 232
Anderson, J. J., 145, 146, 292
Anderson, J. R., 87
Anderson, S. A., 102, 104, 107, 125,
    128, 211, 212, 229, 275
Anderson, T., 224, 269
Anderson-Hanley, C. M., 145, 146, 169,
    196, 286, 292, 293, 298
Andrews, J. D. W., 107
Angelone, E. O., 257, 266, 268, 274,
    276, 277
Ansbacher, H., 83
Ansbacher, R., 83
Antis, J. R., 294
Aponte, H. J., 60
Appelbaum, P. S., 66
Arcinue, F., 241, 242, 253, 303, 317
Arhar, J. M., 210, 223, 224
Arkowitz, S. W., 138, 154
Arnold, R. C., 76, 144, 153, 293
Aronson, M. L., 235, 238, 239, 246
Arthur, G. L., 217
Atkinson, B. J., 273, 274, 275
Atwood, J. D., 44

Ault-Riche, M., 125, 127
Aveline, M., 216
Averitt, J., 234
Avis, J. M., 286

Bahrick, A. S., 145, 146, 147, 169, 196
Bailey, J. S., 258, 268, 274, 277
Bajt, T. R., 72
Baker, D. B., 4
Baker, D. E., 145, 147, 331
Baker, E. L., 6, 159
Baker, M. J., 81
Baker, S. D., 298
Balenger, V., 218
Balint, E., 253
Balint, M., 176
Baltes, P. B., 13
Barak, A., 301
Bardos, A. N., 147, 149
Bargh, J. A., 166, 178
Barlow, D. H., 80, 81
Barnes, K. L., 126, 130, 304
Baron, R. M., 299
Barrett, J., 275
Bartell, P. A., 58, 60
Bartlett, F. C., 14
Bateson, G., 174, 269
Baucom, D. H., 81
Baum, M., 39, 40
Bauman, W. F., 168
Baumeister, R. F., 162
Beach, A., 29
Beamish, P. M., 64, 129
Bear, T. M., 112
Beavers, W. R., 188, 192
Beavin, J. H., 31, 176
Bechtel, M. A., 21
Beck, J. S., 80, 81
Beck, M., 160, 166, 169, 214
Beck, T. D., 199, 207
Becker, D., 81, 267
Becvar, D. S., 294
Bednar, R. L., 146, 195
Behling, J., 130
Beis, E., 203
Belar, C. D., 36
Belcas, E. M., 57
Bellamy, A. R., 23, 44
Bellatin, A. M., 263, 268, 274
Benedek, T., 145, 176
Benjamin, L. S., 174
Benjamin, L. T., 4
Bennett, B. E., 53, 66
Benshoff, J. M., 284

Bent, R., 17
Berger, M., 265, 266
Berman, J. J., 107
Bernard, J. L., 42, 68, 70
Bernard, J. M., 21, 23, 31, 33, 36, 44,
    56, 67, 70, 71, 75, 80, 95, 96, 97,
    100, 101, 108, 116, 118, 120, 125,
    126, 130, 146, 149, 161, 169, 180,
    188, 210, 222, 228, 229, 230, 264,
    266, 284, 286, 287, 298, 312
Berne, E., 167
Bernstein, B. L., 33, 126, 127, 147, 149
Bernstein, R. M., 268
Berry, T. R., 263, 268, 274
Bertolino, R., 294
Betan, E. J., 72
Betcher, R. W., 154
Betz, R. L., 235, 236, 244, 246
Beutler, L. E., 5, 76, 81, 107, 112, 158,
    159, 161
Bieliauskas, L. A., 36
Binder, J., 153
Bion, W., 240
Birk, J. M., 108
Birringer, J., 212
Blackburn, J., 69
Blackmon, B., 123
Blackwell, T. L., 57
Blocher, D. H., 13, 86, 114, 168,
    174, 239
Blodgett, E. G., 33, 44
Bloom, B. S., 115
Bloom, J. W., 220, 226, 227
Blumstein, P., 128
Bob, S., 83
Bobbit, B., 19, 301
Bobele, M., 260
Boes, S. R., 57
Bogo, M., 27, 35
Bond, O., 243, 255, 274
Bonney, W., 285, 289
Bonosky, N., 60
Borders, L. D., 3, 16, 17, 23, 31, 33, 48,
    56, 63, 86, 101, 108, 109, 110, 111,
    112, 115, 125, 168, 180, 210, 212,
    214, 220, 229, 248, 285, 286, 287,
    288, 289, 293, 297, 312
Bordin, E. S., 78, 145, 146, 154, 169
Boswell, D. L., 212, 217, 229, 257,
    275, 278
Bourg, E. F., 22
Bowen, M., 142
Bowlby, J., 162
Bowman, S. L., 146

Bownan, R. L., 60
Bownan, V. E., 60
Boxley, R., 51
Boyd, J., 80
Brack, C. J., 131, 132
Brack, G., 131, 132
Bradey, J., 51
Bradley, 80
Bradley, C., 22
Bradley, J. R., 5
Bradley, L. J., 82, 159, 287
Bradshaw, W. H., Jr., 119
Brandell, J. R., 216
Brantley, A. P., 202
Brashears, F., 5, 183
Brehm, J. W., 113, 160, 161
Brehm, S. S., 160, 161
Breland, A., 34
Brenock, K., 30, 137, 140, 295
Breunlin, D.C., 141, 218, 219, 267
Brewer, M. B., 1, 97
Bricklin, P. M., 22, 53, 66
Bridges, N. A., 57, 61, 164
Brill, R., 191
Brittan-Powell, C. S., 120, 124,
    147, 150
Britton, P. J., 118, 123
Brock, C. D., 253
Broder, E., 217
Brodsky, A., 59
Brodsky, S., 271
Brody, S. L., 165
Brooks, L., 30
Brossart, D. F., 263, 268, 274
Brown, E. M., 268
Brown, L. M., 126
Brown, R. W., 199
Bruce, M. A., 130
Bruss, K. V., 131, 132
Bubenzer, D. L., 188, 215, 257, 258,
    263, 264, 265, 266, 267, 268, 276
Buchanan, T., 226
Bugental, J. F., 232
Buhrke, R. A., 131, 132
Burian, B. K., 60, 61
Burke, W., 47, 109, 110, 155
Burlingame, G. M., 30
Burnett, J. W., 263, 268, 274
Burns, C. I., 61
Burow, J. M., 18, 166
Burton, K. A., 57
Busse, W., 218
Byng-Hall, J., 258

Cacioppo, J. T., 173
Cade, B. W., 272, 273, 274
Cain, H. I., 272, 277–278
Caldwell, C. F., 70, 205, 206
Caldwell, K., 294
Calhoun, K. S., 81
Caligor, L., 77

Callaghan, G. M., 260
Callanan, P., 59
Cameron, P. M., 154
Campbell, C. D., 23
Campbell, T. W., 64, 212
Campbell, V. L., 4
Campione, K. M., 196
Canter, M. B., 53, 66
Cantor, J. M., 131
Caplan, G., 10
Caplow, T., 143
Capraro, M. M., 104
Capraro, R. M., 104
Carey, J. C., 22, 103
Carkhuff, R. R., 80, 144, 301
Carlozzi, A. F., 212, 217, 229, 257,
    275, 278
Carlson, C., 17
Carr, A., 130, 267, 276, 277
Carroll, M., 6, 95, 98, 139, 210, 224,
    233, 237, 239
Carson, R. C., 174
Carter, A., 79, 136, 144–145
Carter, J. A., 294
Carter, J. W., 241, 242
Carter, R. T., 119
Cartwright, D., 234
Casey, J. A., 220
Cashwell, C. S., 63, 199, 212, 214, 215,
    229
Catanzaro, S. J., 58, 60
Cavalieri, C. E., 116
Celenza, A., 57
Center for Credentialing and Education,
    49, 198
Chagnon, J., 85
Chaiklin, H., 235, 243, 254
Chaimowitz, G. A., 69
Chambless, D. L., 81
Chapin, J. L., 145, 146, 164, 169, 196,
    286, 292, 293, 298
Chaplin, R., 269–270
Charles, D., 5, 86, 88, 296
Chartrand, T. L., 166, 178
Chen, E. C., 147, 149
Chen, M. W., 12
Cherniss, C., 235, 236, 248
Chickering, A. W., 92, 229, 230
Chilton, T., 260
Chung, Y. B., 123, 128
Cimmarusti, R., 218, 219
Claiborn, C. D., 23, 31, 110, 149, 164,
    173, 174, 295, 297
Clarkson, P., 60
Clifton, D., 84
Clyne-Jackson, S., 64, 205
Cobia, D.C., 12, 57
Cochran, D. J., 39, 40, 41, 42, 51
Coffey, D., 23, 24
Cohen, B. Z., 19, 47, 55
Cohen, C. R., 70, 202, 205, 206

Cohen, M., 237, 266
Cohen, R. J., 68, 228
Coleman, H. L., 301
Coll, K. M., 212, 214, 229
Collins, D., 27, 35
Combs, D.C., 258, 260
Comish, J. A. E., 4, 33, 86, 284, 287
Congress, E. P., 186
Connell, G., 247, 302
Constantine, J. A., 141, 275, 288
Constantine, M. G., 118, 123, 124, 134,
    140, 176, 177, 294
Cook, D. A., 120, 121, 122, 123, 134
Cook, S. W., 58
Cooper, L., 240
Copeland, S., 185, 188, 196, 207
Corbett, M. M., 23, 26, 51, 147, 152,
    153, 166, 167, 297, 303, 316
Corey, G., 59
Corey, M. S., 59
Cormier, L. S., 266
Cornell, W. F., 60
Cornfield, L., 93, 112
Cornish, J. A. E., 234, 235, 237
Corrigan, J. D., 173
Cortese, J., 23
Costa, L., 24
Couchon, W. D., 228, 229, 264
Coulter, W. R., 165, 247
Council for the Accreditation of
    Counseling and Related Educational
    Programs, 2, 234, 235
Counselman, E. F., 238
Counselor Education and Supervision,
    312, 346
Cousins, P., 151, 182
Covey, S. R., 186, 201
Covner, B. J., 78, 213
Coward, R. L., 29
Craig, C. H., 103, 114
Craig, R., 22
Crethar, H. C., 86, 94, 109, 174, 297
Crimmings, A. M., 86, 93, 97, 138,
    293, 301, 302
Crits-Christoph, P., 81
Cross, H., 68
Culkin, M., 219
Cummings, A. L., 108, 109, 110,
    113, 115
Cummings, N. A., 53, 54
Cupit, B. E., 67, 69
Curtis, C., 130
Cypers, S., 90

DaCosta, G., 120
Dammann, C., 265, 266
D'Andrea, M., 116
Daniels, J. A., 34, 116
Daniels, M. H., 93, 112, 168
Daniels, T. G., 102, 104, 114, 224, 298
Darden, E. C., 84

David, L., 127
David, P., 77, 78
Davidson, G., 275
Davies, D. R., 165
Davis, J. D., 4
Davis, T. E., 129, 196, 198, 202, 303
Dawes, R. M., 5
Deacon, S. A., 232
DeBell, C., 234
Delaney, D. J., 80
DeLeon, P. H., 226, 227
Dell, D. M., 97, 173
Delmonico, D. L., 188
Delworth, U., 7, 13, 27, 75, 86, 87, 89, 90, 92, 93, 94, 100, 109, 112, 131, 161, 168, 169, 171, 183, 191, 217, 229, 230, 279, 280–282, 287, 303
DeMayo, R. A., 59
Dennin, M. K., 91, 145, 146, 169, 196, 286, 292, 293, 298
De Shazer, S., 84
Deuce, L. A., 131, 132
Diamond, D., 294
Diamond, G. M., 81, 267
Dickey, K. D., 61
Disney, M. J., 50, 51, 52, 53, 54, 64, 66, 68, 70, 228
Dixon, D. N., 44, 45, 173, 174, 218, 297
Doan, R. E., 83, 84
Dobson, K. S., 19
Dodds, J. B., 188, 189
Dodenhoff, J. T., 112, 295
Dodson, J. D., 165
Doehrman, M., 10, 11, 139, 140, 294
Dombeck, M. T., 165
Donaldson, C., 127
Dooley, K., 49, 64
Douce, L. A., 59, 94, 141, 146, 178, 284–285, 288, 289, 290
Douthitt, E. A., 166
Dowd, E. T., 161
Dowling, S., 33
Doxsee, D. J., 263, 268, 274
Drew, C., 51
Duan, C., 120, 123
Duffey, T. H., 40
Dulko, J. P., 116
Durham, R. J., 263, 268, 274
Dustin, R., 80
Duys, D. K., 109
Dye, A., 188
Dye, H. A., 23, 33, 97, 101, 180, 186, 210, 286, 287

Earles, J., 226, 227
Echterling, L. G., 84, 85
Edwards, J. K., 12
Efros, F., 76, 97
Efstation, J. F., 145, 148, 152–153, 172, 303, 325, 327
Eisenberg, S., 14

Eisikovits, 112
Eisman, E., 17
Eitington, M., 14, 77
Ekstein, R., 8, 11, 23, 34, 77, 78, 86, 94, 95, 137, 138, 160, 176, 286, 290
Elizur, J., 265, 273
Elks, M. A., 35
Ellens, B. M., 226
Ellickson, J. L., 109, 112, 114, 168
Elliot, J., 68
Elliott, R., 295
Ellis, A., 80, 81, 286
Ellis, M. V., 15, 59, 86, 91, 92, 93, 97, 99, 101, 109, 113, 114, 126, 127, 141, 145, 146, 148, 160, 164, 166, 169, 178, 196, 214, 284–285, 286, 288, 289, 290, 292, 293, 296, 298, 301
Elman, N., 20, 23, 39, 40, 50, 51, 54, 68, 188, 190, 199
Else, J. F., 192, 194
Emerson, S., 55, 61
Emery, 80
Engelhart, M. D., 115
Enyedy, K. C., 241, 242
Epstein, L., 137, 160, 161
Erdman, P., 261, 262, 263, 265, 266, 272, 294
Erera, I. P., 180, 181
Ericcson, K. A., 13, 238
Erickson, C. D., 140, 176, 177, 294
Erwin, W. J., 61
Esnil, E., 147, 150, 154
Essex, M., 64
Estrup, L., 76
Ethington, C. A., 109, 111, 115
Etringer, B. D., 174
Ettelson, D. M., 296

Falender, C., 4, 33, 86, 284, 287
Falk, D. R., 218
Fall, M., 48, 57, 72, 135, 198, 208, 233
Falvey, J. E., 66, 70, 180, 196, 201, 202, 205, 206
Farah, M. J., 183, 190
Farber, J. A., 4
Farquahar, W. W., 74, 220
Farrell, A. D., 226
Feiner, A. H., 12, 141
Felice, A. A., 116
Fennell, D. L., 275
Ferguson, D. B., 212, 217, 229, 257, 275, 278
Ferrier, M. J., 268
Fine, M. A., 21, 64
Fiorini, J., 22
Firestone, A. F., 21, 33
Firth-Cozens, 276
Fiscalini, J., 17, 136, 137, 170
Fisher, B., 93, 112
Fishman, C., 259

Fitzgerald, L. E., 4, 23
Fleming, J., 85, 145
Fletcher, C., 163
Fleuridas, C. L., 30
Fly, B. J., 56, 65
Folen, R., 226, 227
Follette, W. C., 260
Fong, M. L., 23, 33, 48, 101, 109, 111, 115, 118, 119, 120, 125, 180, 210, 286, 287
Ford, I., 294
Ford, S. J. W., 118, 123
Forrest, L., 20, 23, 39, 40, 50, 51, 54, 68, 128, 188, 190, 199
Foster, J. T., 163
Foster, S. A., 130
Fox, R., 23
Frame, M. W., 21, 51, 133
Frank, A. D., 173
Frank, E., 235, 243, 255
Frankel, B. R., 261, 262, 263, 276
Frawley-O'Dea, M. G., 9, 77, 78, 136, 137, 138, 139, 152, 170, 178
Frayn, D. H., 77, 288
Freeman, B., 22, 229
Freeman, E. M., 123
Freeman, S. C., 79, 168
French, J. R. P., Jr., 129, 149, 173
Freud, S., 77
Freund, R. D., 76, 107, 175, 295
Frick, D. E., 12
Fried, J. H., 147, 149
Fried, L., 13
Fried, Y., 23, 44
Friedberg, R. D., 80
Frieden, G., 223, 224–225
Friedlander, M. L., 24, 30, 45, 75, 76, 94, 97, 101, 107, 108, 109, 137, 140, 145, 146, 147, 148, 149, 151, 152, 154, 165, 167, 168, 182, 195, 291, 292, 294, 295, 303, 304, 321, 332
Friedman, D., 86
Friedman, R., 137
Froehle, T., 260
Frohman, A. L., 185
Fuhrman, M., 19, 20, 21, 22, 45, 46, 155, 301
Fukuyama, M. A., 123, 294
Fulero, S. M., 69
Fuller, F. F., 219
Furst, F. J., 115

Gable, R., 127
Galassi, J. P., 30
Gallant, J. P., 258, 268, 274, 277
Garcia, J. L., 40, 41
Gardner, S. L., 76, 107, 175, 295
Garfield, S. L., 1, 3, 146, 195, 292
Garfield, Z., 80
Gatmon, D., 118, 120, 123, 124, 147, 150

Gautney, K., 131, 132
Gedney, J. J., 226, 227
Geeseman, R., 196
Gelso, C. A., 79, 136, 144–145
Gelso, C. J., 93, 112, 293, 297, 300
Gendlin, E. T., 80
George, R. L., 80
Gershenson, J., 266
Getzel, G. S., 236, 237, 240, 243
Getzelman, M., 241, 242
Gfoerer, K. P., 217
Gilbert, L. A., 125
Gilbert, P., 163
Gill, S., 78, 136
Gillam, S. L., 69
Gillespie, K. N., 21
Gilligan, C., 126
Giordano, M. A., 146, 197, 198, 303
Gizara, S., 20, 23, 39, 40, 50, 51, 54, 68, 188, 190, 199
Glancy, G. D., 69
Glaser, R. D., 58
Glenn, E., 20
Glickauf-Hughes, C., 131, 132
Glidden, C. E., 97, 112
Gloria, A. M., 191
Glover, N. M., 226, 227
Gluck, M. R., 107
Goedinhaus, M., 263, 268, 274
Goh, D. S., 6
Gold, J. M., 188, 257, 266, 267, 276
Goldberg, D. A., 213, 215, 218
Goldberg, S. G., 71
Golden, S., 43
Goldstein, A. P., 173
Gonccalves, O. F., 84
Gonzalez, R. C., 131
Good, G. E., 97, 125, 127
Goodholm, C. R., 127
Goodman, E. O., 93
Goodman, R. W., 267
Goodwin, A., 147, 150, 154
Goodyear, R. K., 1, 4, 7, 17, 23, 33, 43, 47, 60, 76, 79, 86, 90, 97, 103, 109, 110, 128, 129, 130, 155, 164, 168, 171, 175, 212, 213, 223, 234, 237, 241, 242, 248, 284, 286, 287, 293, 294, 295, 296, 297, 298, 299, 312
Gordon, B. L., 66, 226, 227
Gordon, J., 59
Gordon, L. L., 123, 128
Gordon, S. P., 114, 294
Gorely, T., 294
Gorton, G. E., 57
Gould, L. J., 159
Goulding, R., 76
Graf, N. M., 226, 227
Gramzow, R., 163
Granello, D. H., 109, 111, 115, 117, 128, 129
Grater, H., 292

Gratz, R. R., 199, 200
Grawe, K., 19, 153, 299
Gray, L. A., 146, 176, 177, 294
Greeley, A. T., 298
Green, S. L., 61
Greenburg, L. S., 145, 147–148, 150, 152, 303, 331
Greenburg, S. L., 254, 255
Greenhouse, E. M., 131, 132, 133
Greeno, B. P., 226, 227
Grey, A. L., 137
Griffith, B. A., 223, 224–225
Grinnell, R. M., Jr., 183
Gross, S., 237
Grus, C., 4, 33, 86, 284, 287
Guest, C. L., Jr., 49, 61, 64
Guest, P. D., 76, 107, 112
Gumpert, P., 238
Gurk, M. D., 97
Gustafson, J. P., 240
Guzzard, C. R., 1, 23, 47, 86, 103, 109, 110, 155, 237, 248, 293, 294, 295, 299

Haas, L. J., 52, 53, 54, 68, 183, 190
Hackney, H. L., 17, 79, 171
Hadjistavropoulos, 72
Hadley, S. W., 73, 300
Hahn, W. K., 20, 22, 28, 29, 30, 163, 164
Haj-Yahia, M. M., 124
Haley, J., 137, 142, 257–258, 261, 262, 268
Halgin, R. P., 100, 120
Hall, J. E., 56, 63
Hallberg, E. T., 108, 109, 110, 113, 115
Halon, A. M., 248
Halpert, S. C., 131
Hamilton, J. C., 56, 57
Hamilton, N., 192, 194
Hamlin, E. R., II, 239, 254, 255
Hammeke, T., 17
Hammond, D., 218, 219
Handen, B. L., 268, 273–289
Handley, P., 103, 114
Handley, P. G., 112
Hanna, M. A., 28
Hansen, J., 288
Hansen, J. C., 61
Hansen, N. B., 30
Hansen, N. D., 71
Hardcastle, D. A., 181, 186, 187, 200
Hardy, E., 7, 13, 75, 86, 90, 92, 93, 169, 229, 230
Hardy, K. V., 83, 118, 202, 229, 257, 270, 273, 275, 277
Harkness, D., 14, 77, 181, 182, 184, 292
Harmon, L. W., 293–294
Harrar, W. R., 54
Harris, M. B. C., 28, 266, 276

Harris, S., 295
Hart, G., 7, 73, 235, 236, 239, 244, 246
Harvey, C., 170
Harvey, O. J., 87
Harvey, S. J., 275
Hatch, D. B., 254, 255
Hatcher, R., 4, 33, 86, 284, 287
Hatley, L. D., 60
Haug, I. E., 71
Hawkins, E. J., 30
Hawkins, P., 12, 32, 75, 98, 99, 185, 237, 238, 239, 285, 291
Hayes, J. R., 13
Hayes, R. L., 237
Haynes, J., 282, 292
Hays, J. R., 50, 68, 69
Hays, K. A., 109, 110, 115
Heath, A. W., 82, 261, 272, 273, 275
Heck, E. J., 295
Hedstrom, S. M., 109
Heesacker, M., 127
Heller, K., 173
Helm, J. E., 120
Helms, B., 127
Helms, J. E., 119, 120, 121, 122, 134, 150
Hemlick, L. M., 164
Henderson, P., 23, 33, 101, 180, 181, 210, 286, 287
Hendricks, C. B., 82
Hendricks, F. M., 263, 268, 274
Heppner, P. P., 58, 93, 112, 149, 168, 169, 173, 263, 268, 274, 295, 297
Hepworth, J., 60
Herlihy, B., 49, 68, 70
Herman, B., 109, 110, 115
Herman, K. C., 19, 20
Hernandez, A., 301
Herrick, C., 192, 199
Herron, W. G., 140
Hershenson, D. B., 65
Hertel, J. B., 263, 268, 274
Hess, A. K., 6, 86, 95, 280, 281
Hess, K. A., 6
Hewson, J., 196
Hiebert, B., 108, 109, 110, 113, 115
Hill, C. E., 5, 23, 26, 51, 57, 86, 88, 109, 110, 112, 135, 147, 149, 152, 153, 166, 167, 218, 294, 296, 297, 301, 303, 316
Hill, M., 218
Hill, W. H., 115
Hillerbrand, E. T., 16, 34, 110, 174, 237, 238
Hills, H., 174, 175
Hilton, D. B., 123, 296
Himmell, C. D., 4
Hipp, J. L., 130
Hird, J. S., 116
Hixon, D. E., 244, 254, 255, 256
Ho, T. A., 116

Hoberman, H. M., 43, 44, 45, 47
Hoffman, L. W., 279, 285–286, 289
Hoffman, M. A., 109, 110, 112, 294
Hofheinz, E. W., 124
Hogan, R., 85, 86, 87, 282
Holeman, V., 215, 263, 264
Holiman, M., 119
Holloway, E. L., 2, 18, 61, 74, 75, 76, 85, 86, 87, 90, 93, 94, 95, 99, 107, 109, 111, 112, 114, 129, 130, 153, 172, 175, 188, 207, 212, 233, 234, 236, 237, 285–286, 287, 292, 293, 295, 296, 297, 298, 299, 300, 301
Holmbeck, G. N., 299
Holmes, S., 127
Holtzman, R. F., 188, 200
Homer, P. A., 164
Hood, C. J., 273, 274
Horn, K. L., 124
Horvath, A. O., 145, 147–148, 150, 152, 153, 299, 303, 329, 331
Hosford, R. E., 292, 293, 295
Hotelling, K., 128
House, 223
Housley, W. F., 61, 215
Hovestadt, A. J., 275
Howard, K. I., 301
Howe, H. E., 107
Howe, S. R., 131
Hoyle, R. H., 299
Hoyt, M. F., 76
Hunt, D. E., 87
Hutchinson, G. H., 188
Hutto, B., 14

Igartua, K. I., 188, 199
Ingram, K. M., 6
Inman, A. G., 124
Inskipp, F., 160
Itzhaky, H., 15
Iverson, J. N., 139, 298
Ivey, A. E., 102, 104, 114, 224

Jackson, D., 31, 118, 120, 123, 124, 147, 150
Jackson, H., 56
Jackson, J. S., 1
Jackson, R., 39, 40
Jackson, V. R., 39, 40, 41, 42, 51
Jacobs, D., 77, 78
Jakubowski-Spector, P., 80
James, I., 80, 291
James, L., 17
James, L. C., 226, 227
Jara, C. S., 68, 70
Jarvis, P., 39, 40
Jennings, L., 223
Jensen, M. A. C., 236, 241, 254
Jerome, L. W., 226, 227
Johanson, G., 64
Johnson, E., 230

Johnson, E. A., 6
Johnson, S., 130
Johnson, S. W., 258, 260
Johnson, W. B., 23
Johnston, R., 234, 236, 237
Jones, A. P., 43, 44
Jones, S. H., 301
Jordan, K., 266
Judge, A. B., 109, 110, 112, 294
Juhnke, G. A., 84
Juntunen, C. L., 139, 298

Kadushin, A., 14, 23, 30, 34, 47, 167, 168, 181, 182, 183, 184, 200
Kagan, H. K., 74, 161, 202, 219, 220
Kagan, N. I., 74, 84, 161, 202, 219, 220, 286
Kahn, B., 188, 199
Kanuha, V., 234
Kanz, J. E., 66, 226, 227
Kaplan, D. M., 219
Kaplan, M., 43
Kaplan, K., 267
Kardash, C. M., 145, 148, 152–153, 172, 303, 325, 327
Karger, H. J., 183
Karno, M. P., 223, 294
Karrer, B., 218, 219
Kaslow, N.J., 4, 33, 86, 183, 202, 284, 287
Kass, R. A., 146
Katz, C., 170
Katz, J. H., 118
Katz, L., 212
Kaul, T. J., 146, 195
Keith, D. V., 247, 302
Keith-Spiegel, P., 58
Kelbley, T., 260
Kell, B. L., 18, 78, 86, 137, 138, 154, 166, 169, 170, 290, 292
Keller, J. F., 84
Keller, K. E., 165
Kelly, G. A., 83
Kenfield, J. A., 3, 130, 231
Kennard, B. D., 107
Kenny, D. A., 299
Kerl, S. B., 40, 41
Kern, C. W., 146, 197, 198, 303
Kerr, B. A., 174
Kiesler, D. J., 80, 174
Killian, K. D., 116, 118, 119, 122, 124
Kim, B. S. K., 116
Kim, H., 263, 268, 274
Kinder, M. H., 263, 268, 274
King, C., 17
King, D., 66, 68
Kingston, P., 273
Kinnetz, 97
Kinsella, J. A., 258, 260, 274
Kirkhart, K. E., 35
Kitchener, K. S., 56, 61, 65, 71

Kitzrow, M. A., 104, 106
Kivlighan, D. M., 229, 257, 263, 266, 268, 274, 276, 277, 295
Kivlighan, D. M., Jr., 112, 140, 147, 153, 162, 299
Klein, J. G., 45, 167
Klein, S., 68
Kleintjes, S., 120, 124, 294
Klepac, R. K., 36
Klitzke, M. J., 258, 259, 274
Knapp, S. J., 53, 54, 66, 202
Knoff, H. M., 51
Knopp, W., 80
Knox, S., 57, 135, 149
Koch, L. C., 210, 223, 224
Koerin, B., 51
Koffler, S., 17
Koker, M., 55
Kollock, P., 128
Kolodinsky, R. W., 226, 227
Kopp, R. R., 76
Koshkarian, L., 118, 120, 123, 124, 147, 150
Kovacs, A. L., 22
Kowalski, R. M., 167
Kozlowska, K., 151, 182
Krasner, R. F., 301
Kratwohl, D. R., 74, 115, 220
Krause, A. A., 93, 112
Krengel, M., 160, 166, 169, 214, 292
Krengel, V., 296, 301
Kruger, L. J., 235, 236, 248
Krull, L. A., 263, 268, 274
Kugler, P., 76
Kuhn, T. S., 292
Kulakowski, D., 3, 130, 231
Kunkler, K. P., 125
Kurtz, R. M., 3
Kurz, R. B., 1

LaCrosse, M. B., 301
Ladany, N., 9, 23, 24, 26, 27, 30, 32, 51, 57, 59, 86, 109, 110, 112, 113, 114, 120, 124, 135, 140, 146, 147, 148, 149, 150, 151, 152, 153, 155, 166, 167, 171, 176, 177, 286, 292, 294, 296, 297, 301, 303, 316, 323
Ladmila, A., 163
LaFromboise, T. D., 301
Lamb, D. H., 39, 40, 41, 42, 51, 58, 60
Lambert, M. E., 29, 30
Lambert, M. J., 30, 76, 109, 144, 153, 287, 293, 295, 301
Lamendola, F., 55
Lammers, C., 68
Landau, J., 271
Landis, E. R., 50, 68, 69
Landis, L. L., 84, 266, 268, 273
Landreth, G. G., 76
Lane, R. C., 170
Laney, N., 59

Lang, P. R., 56, 65
Lankford, M. W., 183
Lanning, W. L., 22, 234
Larrabee, M. J., 58, 60
Larsen, K. G., 22, 36
Larson, L. M., 21, 34
Lauver, P. J., 119
Lazar, A., 48, 112, 180, 181
Lazarus, J. A., 12, 60
Leary, M. R., 162, 167
Leary, T., 174
Lease, S. H., 118, 119, 120, 125
Lecomte, C., 33
Leddick, G. R., 31, 80, 186, 188, 210, 220, 285, 289, 293, 312
Lee, R. W., 69, 199
Lee, S. R., 276
Lee-Borden, N., 85, 86
Lees, J. L., 165
Lehmann, A. C., 13, 238
Lehrman-Waterman, D., 9, 24, 27, 30, 32, 59, 147, 148, 149, 150, 155, 171, 303, 323
Leichtman, H. M., 235, 236, 248
Leifer, M., 22
Lent, R. W., 86, 93, 97, 138, 293, 301, 302
Leonardelli, C. A., 199, 200
Leong, F. T. L., 119, 123
Lesser, R. M., 136, 154, 171
Levenson, E. A., 7, 73
Levenson, H., 58
Leventhal, G., 4, 33, 86, 284, 287
Leverette, J. S., 154
Levine, F. M., 80
Levinson, D. J., 280
Levy, L. H., 47
Lewin, K., 73
Lewis, G. J., 254, 255
Lewis, H. B., 163
Lewis, K. N., 173
Lewis, M., 163
Lewis, W., 170, 171, 257, 258, 261, 262, 275, 277, 278
Lichtenberg, J. W., 31, 128, 130, 168, 295, 297, 298
Liddle, B., 159
Liddle, H. A., 16, 81, 137, 141, 142, 261, 267, 272, 273, 275
Liese, B. S., 81
Lindon, C., 113, 114
Linehan, M. M., 80
Littrell, J. M., 85, 86
Lloyd, A. P., 60
Lobsenz, N. M., 32
Lochner, B. T., 103, 108, 114
Locke, L. D., 262–263, 275
Logan, S. L., 123
Loganbill, C., 7, 13, 75, 86, 90, 92, 93, 169, 229, 230
Lombardo, T. W., 258, 259, 274

Long, J. K., 130
Looby, E. J., 215
Lopez, F. G., 4
Lopez, S. R., 23, 63
Lorenz, J. A., 85, 86
Lotion, R. P., 22
Loucks-Horsley, S., 185
Love, J. P., 130
Lovell, C., 109
Lower, R. B., 15, 176, 177, 178
Lowery, S., 61
Lowy, L., 183
Luborsky, L., 145
Lumadue, C. A., 40
Lunnen, K., 30
Lysiak, G., 268, 273–289
Lyter, S. C., 32

McCarthy, P., 3, 55, 130, 231, 234
McCartney, C. I., 12
McCaulley, M. H., 102
McColley, K., 6, 159
McCollum, E. E., 262–263, 265, 275
McCormick, K., 168
McCullough, C. S., 40, 41
McCullough, M. E., 76, 107, 108, 114, 130
McDaniel, S., 81, 127
McDonald, P. L., 213
McGuire, D., 218, 219
McHenry, S., 229
McKee, J. E., 84, 85
McKeel, N., 191
McKeever, J., 81
McKenzie, P. N., 275
McLeod, J., 234
McMinn, M. R., 226
McNeill, B. W., 27, 75, 86, 87, 89, 94, 100, 101, 109, 110, 112, 115, 124, 139, 140, 150, 151, 161, 168, 171, 174, 182, 280–282, 292, 294, 297, 303
McPherson, R. H., 196
McRoy, R. G., 123
McWilliams, N., 140, 167
Madigan, S., 269
Magnuson, S., 22, 26, 30, 31, 60, 66, 150, 182, 212, 214
Mahalik, J. R., 108
Maher, C. A., 235, 236, 248
Maheu, M. M., 66, 226, 227
Mahoney, M., 80, 83
Mahrer, A. R., 294
Mahrle, C., 258, 265
Maki, D. R., 56, 67, 70, 71, 87, 112
Mallinckrodt, B., 109
Malloy, 72
Malone, J., 109, 110, 115
Malouf, J. L., 68, 183, 190
Manning, B. A., 219
Marek, L. I., 29

Markowski, E. M., 272, 277–278
Marks, J. L., 244, 254, 255, 256
Marotta, S., 109, 110, 149
Marrow, A. J., 73
Marshall, J. A., 123, 128
Martin, D., 69
Martin, J. M., 10, 108, 109, 110, 113, 115
Martin, J. S., 175, 295
Martos-Perry, N., 118, 120, 123, 124, 147, 150
Matarazzo, R. G., 8, 144
Matthews, G., 23, 165
Matthews, J., 17
Maurer, S., 55
Mauzey, E., 261, 262, 263, 265, 266, 272, 276, 294
Maxwell, M. E., 40, 41
Mayerson, N. H., 68
Mead, D. E., 27, 258, 260, 274
Mead, M., 136
Meichenbaum, D., 80
Meier, S. T., 29, 30
Mejia-Millan, C. M., 127
Melchert, T. P., 103, 108, 114
Melincoff, D. S., 32, 57, 59, 112, 135, 147, 149
Merrill, A. R., 186, 201
Merrill, R. R., 186, 201
Meschel, G., 212
Messick, S. J., 1
Meyer, D. J., 77, 78
Meyer, R. G., 42, 50, 51, 68, 69
Miars, R. D., 93, 112
Michels, K. D., 299
Middleman, R. R., 27
Miller, A., 108, 113
Miller, D., 268, 273–289
Miller, D. A., 22
Miller, G. M., 58, 60
Miller, H. L., 42
Miller, J., 51
Miller, K., 140, 176, 177, 294
Miller, R., 74, 220
Miller, S. B., 163
Milliken, T., 56, 63
Milne, D., 80, 291
Miltimore, S., 12
Mintz, L. B., 125, 127
Minuchin, S., 257–258, 259
Mitchell, D., 84
Mitchell, R. W., 203
Moan, E. R., 220
Mohl, P. C., 22
Moldawsky, S., 53, 66
Moleiro, C., 158, 159, 161
Molina, A., 118, 120, 123, 124, 147, 150
Molinaro, M., 9, 59, 147, 148, 150, 155, 171
Molnar, A., 84
Molnar, S., 20, 22, 28, 29, 30

Monks, G. M., 168, 195
Montalvo, B., 264, 265, 267
Montgomery, L. M., 67, 69
Montgomery, M. L., 82
Moorhouse, A., 130, 267, 276, 277
Morotti, A. A., 192, 199
Morris, G. H. B., 31
Morris, J. R., 199, 207, 235, 236, 244, 246
Morse, J., 292
Mosek, A., 48
Moses, N. C., 230
Mothersole, G., 139, 140
Moy, C. T., 93
Mueller, W. J., 78, 86, 137, 138, 154, 169, 170, 290
Multon, K. D., 162
Munley, P. H., 298
Munson, C. E., 32, 33, 130, 196, 197, 201, 203, 218, 235, 243, 244, 254
Muran, J. C., 80, 81, 155, 156, 157
Muratori, M. C., 39
Murphy, J. A., 131
Murphy, J. W., 183
Murray, G. C., 112
Muse-Burke, J. L., 109, 110, 140, 149, 176, 177, 294
Muslin, H. L., 212
Myers, H. H., 271
Myers, I. B., 102
Myers, J. E., 187, 188

Nance, D. W., 23, 33, 101, 180, 210, 286, 287
Napolitano, G., 100
Nathanson, D. L., 163
National Association of Social Workers, 50
National Board for Certified Counselors, 23, 49, 50
Navin, S., 64
Neil, D. M., 34
Neimeyer, C. J., 111
Neimeyer, G. J., 125
Neimeyer, R. A., 83
Neiss, R., 165
Nelson, M. L., 7, 9, 24, 76, 101, 107, 109, 129, 146, 150, 151, 152, 154, 171, 175, 182, 210, 212, 213, 223, 224, 230, 234, 248, 294, 295
Nelson, P., 17
Nelson, R. E., 147, 149
Nelson, T. S., 125, 130
Neufeldt, S. A., 2, 9, 139, 153, 171, 210, 212, 223, 224, 225, 230, 286, 287, 294, 298, 301
Newberry, A., 128
Newbold, A., 269–270
Newton, F. B., 175, 295
Nicassio, T., 59

Nicholas, M. W., 249
Nichols, D. P., 202, 229, 257, 275
Nichols, M., 257
Nichols, W. C., 202, 229, 257, 275
Nickelson, D. W., 226, 227
Nieberding, R., 282, 292
Nielson, R., 64
Nielson, S. I., 30
Nigam, T., 154
Noelle, M., 212
Norcross, J. C., 4, 100
Norell, J., 253
Norem, K., 26, 30, 31, 60, 66, 150, 182, 214
Nunn, K., 151, 182
Nutt, E. A., 23, 26, 51, 147, 152, 153, 166, 167, 297, 303, 316
Nuttall, R. L., 56

O'Brien, K. M., 57, 135
O'Byrne, K., 119
O'Farrell, M., 93, 112, 294
Ogles, B. M., 144, 287, 293, 301
Ogloff, J. R. P., 49, 68, 70
O'Grady, K. E., 218
O'Hanlon, B., 269–270
Okiishi, J., 30
O'Leary, M., 131, 132
Olk, M., 109, 145, 151, 152, 165, 303, 321
Olley, M. C., 49, 68, 70
Olsen, D.C., 23, 188, 194, 200, 214
Olson, J. K., 5
Olson, M. M., 226, 227
Olson, U. J., 271
O'Neil, J. M., 127
O'Neil, S. H., 296
Orlinsky, D. E., 4, 19, 153, 299
O'Saben, C. L., 103, 109, 111, 114
Osborn, C. J., 184, 185, 196, 198, 201, 202, 303
Osipow, S. H., 4, 23
Ososkie, J. N., 147, 149
Osterberg, M. J., 127
Otto, M. L., 199
Overholser, J. C., 21, 64

Packard, R., 23
Page, S., 15
Pannell, L., 113, 114
Pannu, R. K., 120, 124, 147, 150
Papadopoulos, R. K., 82
Pardeck, J. T., 183
Parihar, B., 237, 239, 243
Parks, B. K., 4, 19, 153, 299
Parry, A., 83, 84
Paterson, R., 269–270
Patrick, K. D., 55, 61
Patterson, C. H., 8, 73, 74, 79
Patterson, D. R., 8, 144

Patton, M. J., 140, 145, 147, 148, 152–153, 162, 172, 299, 303, 325, 327
Peace, S. D., 115
Pearson, B., 39, 56, 57, 58, 59, 60, 61
Pearson, Q. M., 159
Peca-Baker, T. A., 165
Pedersen, P. B., 116
Pegg, P. F., 271
Penman, R., 175
Perez, J. A., 124
Perlesz, A. J., 21, 33, 269–270
Perris, C., 80
Perry, W. G., Jr., 111
Petersen, D. A., 57, 135
Peterson, D. R., 4
Peterson, M., 59, 61
Peterson, R., 5
Peterson, R. L., 4
Petrie, T., 283, 285, 286, 287
Petty, R. E., 173
Pfaller, J., 131
Pfost, K., 39, 40
Piazza, N., 39, 56, 57, 58, 59, 60, 61
Pierce, R. A., 109, 110, 112, 168
Pierce, R. M., 144, 295
Piercy, F. P., 212, 217, 229, 234, 261, 262, 275, 276, 288
Pilkington, N. W., 131
Pinsof, W. M., 19
Pinsoneault, T., 215, 263, 264
Piper, R. E., 119
Pipes, R. B., 12
Pirrotta, S., 268, 273–289
Pistole, M. C., 162
Pitts, J. H., 109, 111, 115
Poertner, A., 14, 77, 292
Poertner, J., 32
Polanski, P. J., 133
Polkinghorne, D. E., 83, 128, 130
Polster, E., 286
Polstri, S. M., 145, 146, 292
Ponterotto, J. G., 44, 45, 50, 218
Pope, K. S., 49, 54, 55, 58, 59, 65, 72, 279, 290
Popper, K., 74
Porter, N., 12, 118, 125
Portman, T. A. A., 112
Post, P., 51
Potenza, M. T., 21
Poulin, K., 54, 67, 203
Prange, M., 129
Prather, D. L., 259
Preli, R., 82, 116
Presbury, J., 84, 85
Presser, N., 39, 40
Prest, L. A., 84
Price, D., 292
Priest, R., 118, 120
Prieto, L. R., 236, 237
Primavera, L. H., 140
Prochaska, J. O., 4

Proctor, B., 15, 160
Protinsky, H. O., 29, 82
Prout, H. T., 51
Prouty, A., 130, 131
Puri, N. N., 241, 242
Putney, M. W., 76, 107, 108, 114, 130

Queener, J., 172
Quinn, W. H., 273, 274, 275
Qureshi, A., 119

Rabinowitz, F. E., 93, 112, 169
Raichelson, S. H., 140
Raimy, V. C., 302
Ramirez, S. M., 140
Ramos-Sánchez, L., 147, 150, 154
Rangel, D., 51
Raphael, F. B., 200
Raskin, M. S., 188, 192, 200
Ratliff, D. A., 31
Raven, B., 129, 149, 173
Ravets, P., 248
Rawlings, E. I., 131
Ray, D., 229, 234, 235
Ray, P., 5, 93, 109, 112, 168
Ray, S. B., 146
Reed, J. R., 249
Reed, K. G., 5, 86, 88, 296
Reid, E., 127
Reid, P. T., 58
Reising, G. N., 93, 112, 168
Remington, G., 120
Remley, T. R., Jr., 49, 68, 70
Renninger, S., 55
Resnick, R. F., 76
Retzinger, S. M., 163
Rhodes, G. B., 27
Rice, D. G., 183, 202
Rice, L. N., 79
Richardson, B. K., 287
Richman, J. M., 259
Rickard, H. C., 42
Rickert, V. L., 261, 262, 266, 267
Ries, S., 212
Rigazio-DiGilio, S. A., 102, 104, 107, 114, 125, 128, 211, 212, 224, 229, 275
Riggs, S., 147, 150, 154
Rinas, J., 64, 205
Rioch, M. J., 165, 247
Ristvedt, S., 19, 20, 21, 22, 45, 46, 155, 301
Rita, E. S., 84
Ritchie, P., 17
Riva, M. T., 234, 235, 237
Robbins, E. S., 126, 127
Roberts, J., 268, 269
Roberts, W. B., 192, 199
Roberts-Wilbur, J. M., 235, 236, 244, 246

Robiner, W. N., 19, 20, 21, 22, 43, 44, 45, 46, 47, 155, 301
Robinson, S. E., 191
Robinson, W. L., 58
Robles, L., 76
Robyak, J. E., 76, 97, 129
Rock, M. L., 78
Rodenhauser, P., 280, 281
Rodolfa, E., 17, 59
Rodway, M. R., 182
Roehlke, H. J., 93, 112, 120, 123, 168, 169, 188, 207
Roer-Strier, D., 124
Rogers, C. R., 8, 17, 78, 79, 80, 171, 213, 286
Rogers, G., 213
Rohrbaugh, M., 257, 258, 261, 262, 275, 278
Romans, J. S., 87, 109, 115, 150, 212, 217, 229, 257, 275, 278, 292, 303
Ronen, T., 80, 81
Rønnestad, M. H., 4, 33, 75, 88, 89, 90, 91, 100, 101, 109, 115, 156, 161, 164, 166, 185, 210, 223, 224, 255, 281, 294, 312
Rosemond, M., 90
Rosenbaum, M., 80, 81
Rosenberg, J. I., 119
Rosenblum, A. F., 200
Rosenthal, D. M., 30
Ross, L., 45
Ross, R. P., 6
Rossman, K. M., 125
Rothman, K. F., 299
Rothrock, D., 219
Rotter, J. C., 212, 214, 229
Rowen, H., 59
Royal, E., 43
Rozelle, R. M., 44
Rubin, L. J., 58, 60
Rubin, N., 22
Rubinstein, M., 218, 219
Rudes, J., 269
Rudolph, B., 22, 253
Rush, 80
Russell, C. R., 226, 227
Russell, C. S., 141, 142
Russell, G. M., 131, 132, 133
Russell, P. A., 183
Russell, R. K., 85, 86, 93, 97, 123, 138, 145, 146, 169, 196, 283, 285, 286, 287, 293, 296, 301, 302
Rutan, J. S., 163, 164
Ryan, M. K., 226
Ryde, J., 134, 135
Ryder, R., 60

Saadon, M., 57
Saba, G. W., 137, 141, 142, 257
Sadler, J. Z., 22
Safran, J. D., 80, 81, 155, 156, 157

Sagrestano, L. M., 128
Sakai, P., 296
Sakinofsky, I., 20
Salmi, S. W., 123, 145, 146, 169, 196, 296
Salmon, R., 236, 237, 240, 243
Saltzman, S. R., 43, 44, 45, 47
Sampson, J. P., 226, 227
Samuel, S. E., 57
Sandhofer, R., 260
Sandifer, D. M., 29
Sand-Pringle, C., 113, 114
Sansbury, D. L., 92, 93, 168, 236, 240
Sanville, J., 26
Sarnat, J. E., 9, 77, 78, 136, 137, 138, 139, 152, 170, 178
Saxe, J. D., 74
Scanlon, C. R., 188
Schacht, A. J., 107
Schauble, P. G., 144, 295
Schein, E., 2
Schermer, 73
Schimel, J. L., 140
Schindler, N., 27, 33
Schirvar, J. A., 19, 43, 44, 45, 47, 301
Schlenker, B. R., 167
Schlossberg, M., 128, 212, 229, 275
Schmidt, J. F., 33, 44
Schmidt, J. P., 80
Schmidt, L. D., 173
Schneider, L. J., 282, 292
Schneider, S., 137
Schoen, L. G., 45, 167
Schön, D. A., 2, 4, 18, 293
Schover, L. R., 58
Schrag, K., 131, 132
Schreiber, P., 235, 243, 255
Schroeder, H. M., 87
Schroll, J. T., 278
Schult, D., 292, 296, 301
Schultz, B. M., 50, 69, 203
Schultz, J. C., 147, 149
Schwartz, G. S., 167
Schwartz, P., 128
Schwartz, R. C., 141, 261, 267, 272, 273
Scott, K. J., 6
Scudder, R. R., 33, 44
Searles, H., 10, 137, 287
Sechrest, L., 1, 173
Seligman, M. E. P., 298
Seligman, P., 272, 273, 274
Sells, J. N., 128, 130
Semrud-Clikeman, M., 43, 44, 45, 47
Serovich, J. M., 20
Shafranske, E., 4, 33, 86, 284, 287
Shanklin, A., 195
Shapiro, C. H., 188, 190
Shapiro, D. A., 276, 295
Shapiro, F., 73
Shaughnessy, P., 58
Shaw, B. F., 19, 80

Shechter, R. A., 279
Shechtman, Z., 109
Sherry, P., 63, 64, 65, 109, 112, 114, 168, 175, 295
Shilts, L., 269
Shoben, E. J., 76
Shohet, R., 12, 32, 75, 98, 99, 185, 237, 238, 239, 285, 291
Shulman, L., 235, 236, 249
Shumate, J., 297
Siegel, M., 65
Siegel, S. M., 30, 137, 140, 295
Sigmon, S., 4, 33, 86, 284, 287
Silverglade, L., 61
Simon, R., 257, 258
Simons, L. A., 268, 273–289
Simonton, D. K., 292
Sinnett, E. D., 60
Skolnik, L., 188
Skovholt, T. M., 4, 33, 75, 88, 89, 90, 91, 100, 101, 109, 115, 156, 161, 164, 166, 185, 210, 223, 224, 255, 281, 294, 312
Slater, L., 3
Slavkin, J. H., 152
Sleight, C. C., 103, 114
Slemon, A. G., 108, 109, 110, 113, 115
Slimp, A. O., 60, 61
Sloman, L., 217
Smadi, A. A., 76
Smart, D. W., 30
Smart, R., 296
Smith, H. D., 229
Smith, J., 13, 28
Smith, L. W., 195, 196
Smith, N. G., 6
Smith, R. C., 258, 260, 274
Smith, T. E., 270, 275, 294
Smith, Z., 14
Snider, P. D., 68, 70, 202
Snow, J. S., 30
Snyder, J., 109
Soisson, E. L., 202
Somer, E., 57
Sonne, J. L., 58
Sowers-Hoag, K., 130
Sparks, D., 185
Speed, B., 272, 273, 274
Sperling, M. B., 268, 273–289
Spiegel, K. P., 290
Spiegel, P. K., 290
Spotnitz, H., 161
Sprenkle, D. H., 212, 217, 229, 234, 275, 286, 288
Sprinthall, N. A., 115
Spruill, J., 56, 57
Stalans, L. J., 251
Stanton, A. L., 72
Stanton, J. L., 271
Stanton, M. D., 271
Staudinger, U. M., 13

Stebnicki, M. A., 226, 227
Steier, D., 59
Stein, D. M., 109
Stenack, R. J., 97
Stephens, A. M., 50, 51, 52, 53, 54, 64, 66, 68, 70, 228
Sterling, M. M., 232
Stern, A., 112, 114, 130
Stern, S. B., 23, 188, 194, 200, 214
Sternberg, R. J., 13
Sternitzke, M. E., 44, 45, 218
Stevens-Smith, P., 21, 51, 125
Stevic, R., 288
Steward, R. J., 34
Stewart, A. E., 191
Stewart, D. W., 6
Stewart, E. A., 191
Stewart, S. M., 107
Stigall, T. T., 22, 36
Stiles, W. B., 30, 276, 295
Stock, R. D., 253
Stolk, Y., 21, 33
Stoltenberg, C. D., 4, 27, 33, 75, 86, 87, 89, 94, 100, 109, 110, 112, 114, 115, 131, 150, 161, 168, 169, 171, 174, 183, 191, 217, 279, 280–282, 284, 286, 287, 292, 297, 303
Stone, D., 232
Stone, G. L., 8, 296, 297
Stoppard, J. M., 108, 113
Storm, C., 82
Storm, C. L., 71, 267
Storm, H. A., 266
Stout, C. E., 55, 61
Strano, J. D., 260
Strassle, C. G., 195
Strean, H. S., 176
Strein, W., 65
Stricker, G., 4
Strohmer, D.C., 57
Strong, S. R., 160, 173, 174, 175, 298
Strozier, A. L., 229, 295
Strupp, H. H., 73, 153, 300
Sugden, S., 55
Sullivan, H. S., 174
Sumerel, M. B., 112
Supervision Interest Network, Association for Counselor Education and Supervision, 49, 50, 63, 64, 101
Susman, M., 212
Sutter, E., 196
Sutton, J. M., Jr., 7, 48, 57, 64, 72, 135, 198, 208, 233
Sutton, J. R., 195
Suzuki, L. A., 21
Swafford, K. G., 257, 266, 268, 274, 276, 277
Swanson, J. L., 103, 109, 111, 114
Swartz, L., 120, 124, 294
Swenson, L. S., 67, 68, 202

Symonds, B. D., 153, 299
Sztern, L., 15

Tabachnick, B. G., 58, 290
Talebi, H., 158, 159, 161
Talen, M. R., 27, 33
Tan, J. A., 54, 67, 203
Tangney, J. P., 163
Tarvydas, V. M., 71
Taylor, L. A., 80
Teitelbaum, S. H., 176
Tennen, H., 76
Tharp, A., 263, 268, 274
Thomas, F. N., 84
Thomas, V., 130
Thompson, B. J., 294
Thoreson, R. W., 58, 229, 295
Thorpe, J. S., 58
Thurnblad, R. J., 212
Thyer, B. A., 130, 258, 268, 274, 277
Tiegs, R. B., 23, 44
Tilbury, R., 192, 199
Tilker, H. A., 80
Timberlake, E. M., 239, 254, 255
Tinsley, H. E. A., 146
Todd, T. C., 274
Todtman, D. A., 260
Tollers, M., 127
Toulouse, A., 21
Touster, L. O., 147, 150, 154
Tracey, J., 175, 295
Tracey, M., 260
Tracey, T. J., 93, 97, 109, 110, 112, 114, 115, 168, 174, 175
Triantafillou, N., 84
Truax, C. B., 80
Trusty, J., 266, 276
Tuckman, B. W., 236, 241, 254
Turban, D. B., 43, 44
Turner, J., 125, 128
Turner, J. E., 261, 262, 266, 267
Turner, M., 237
Twohey, D., 126

Umpress, V., 30
Upchurch, D. W., 64
Usher, C. H., 3, 112, 168

Vacha-Haase, T., 20, 23, 39, 40, 50, 51, 54, 68, 188, 190, 199
Van Bark, W. P., 56, 65
VandeCreek, L., 54, 202
VandenBos, G. R., 226
VanderKolk, C., 122
Vargas, L. A., 123, 138, 139, 178
Vasquez, M. J. T., 12, 21, 49, 54, 55, 59, 63, 279, 290
Vaughn, K. A., 113, 213
Vermeersch, D. A., 30
Vetter, V. A., 65
Vitanza, S. A., 6

Vogel, D. L., 84, 125, 127, 131
Volker, J., 126
Vygotsky, L. S., 16

Waehler, C. A., 298
Wagner, N. S., 119, 123
Wagner, P., 163
Walden, S., 56, 63
Walker, B. R., 76, 107, 175, 295
Walker, J. A., 112, 146, 147, 149, 176, 177, 294
Wallace, D. L., 263, 268, 274
Wallerstein, R. S., 8, 11, 23, 34, 77, 78, 86, 94, 137, 138, 160, 176, 290
Walton, R. N., 278
Walzer, R. S., 12
Wampler, K. S., 31
Wampold, B. E., 112, 114, 293, 295, 298, 299
Wang, L., 263, 268, 274
Warburton, J. R., 128
Ward, L. G., 45, 75, 76, 94, 97, 108, 149, 152, 154, 167, 168, 223, 291, 292, 295, 304, 332
Wark, L., 276
Watkins, C. E., Jr., 4, 85, 162, 163, 280, 282, 289, 292
Watson, M. F., 127, 128
Watzlawick, P., 31, 176
Webb, A., 9, 147, 152
Weber, T., 81
Weinberger, D. M., 165, 247
Weinman, L., 56, 65
Weisinger, H., 32
Wells, L. M., 210, 223, 224
Wendorf, D. J., 243, 255, 271, 274
Wendorf, R. J., 243, 255, 274
Wentzel, J. T., 127
Wertheimer, A., 90
Wessler, R. L., 80, 81
West, J. D., 188, 215, 257, 258, 263, 264, 265, 266, 267, 268, 276
Wester, S. R., 125, 127, 131
Westerman, C., 291
Wetchler, J. L., 107, 112, 113, 212, 213, 217, 229, 234

Wettersten, K. B., 297
Wheeler, S., 9, 66, 68, 147, 152
Whiffen, R., 218
Whipple, J. L., 30
Whisenhunt, B. J., 217, 229, 257, 275, 278
Whiston, S. C., 55, 61
Whitaker, C. A., 247, 302
White, H. D., 253
White, L. J., 30
White, M. B., 141, 142, 226, 227
White, R. W., 169
White, V. E., 172
Wicas, E. A., 97
Wiggins, J. S., 174
Wilbur, M. P., 235, 236, 244, 246
Wilcoxon, A., 60, 66
Wilcoxon, S. A., 26, 30, 31, 150, 182, 214, 288
Wiley, M., 3, 5, 109, 112, 168, 254
William of Occam, 73
Williams, A., 4, 13, 95, 98, 99, 238, 239, 287
Williams, A. B., 140
Williams, B. R., 199, 207
Williams, D. A., 81
Williams, E. N., 109, 110, 112, 294
Williams, G. T., 199, 207
Williams, K. S., 103
Williams, L., 291
Williams, M. H., 68
Williams, S., 120, 226
Wilson, 97
Wimberley, T. K., 67, 69
Winnicott, R., 291–292
Winter, M., 109, 111, 112
Winton, M., 270, 275, 294
Wirzberger, A., 109
Wise, P. S., 61
Witty, T. E., 263, 268, 274
Wohlberg, J. W., 57
Wolgast, B., 9, 59, 147, 148, 150, 155, 171
Wolkin, J., 191
Wolleat, P., 130
Wolpe, J., 80

Wong, L. C. J., 304, 336
Wong, P. T. P., 304, 336
Wong, Y.-L. S., 275
Wood, B., 68
Woods, P. J., 80, 81
Woodside, D. B., 277
Woodward, D., 260
Woodworth, C. B., 70
Woody, R. H., 52, 69
Woody, S. R., 81
Woolley, G., 131
Workman, K. R., 146
Worthen, V., 101, 139, 140, 151, 182, 294
Worthington, E. L., Jr., 76, 85, 86, 94, 107, 108, 112, 114, 130, 168, 283, 293, 297
Worthington, R. L., 54, 67, 203
Wosket, V., 15
Wright, G. E., 263, 268, 274
Wright, L. K., 147, 150, 154
Wright, L. M., 261, 262, 267
Wrightsman, L., 127
Wulf, 151
Wynne, L. C., 19
Wynne, M. E., 212

Yager, G. G., 97, 199, 207
Yalom, I. D., 249
Yeates, K., 17
Yerkes, R. M., 165
Yerushalmi, H., 164
Yogev, S., 34
Yoshioka, M., 270, 275, 294
Young, J., 269–270
Young, M. E., 84, 266, 268, 273

Zajonc, R. B., 166
Zander, A., 234
Zarski, J. J., 113, 114, 264, 268
Zimet, C. N., 36
Zinberg, N. E., 154
Zuniga, M. E., 120

SUBJECT INDEX

AAMFT, 2, 3, 4, 6
Academic dismissals, 40, 42
Academy of Certified Social Workers, 2
Accountability, 49, 185, 186
Accrediting bodies, 2, 3, 6, 22
ACES. *See* Association for Counselor
    Education and Supervision
    (ACES)
Action techniques in group supervision,
    238–239
Adherence to treatment protocols,
    working alliance and, 153
Adjourning group stage, 237, 250–251
Administrative structure
    burnout and, 182–183
    evaluation and, 24–25
Administrative supervision, clinical
    supervision vs., 181–182
Advanced student phase, 89
Advising trainees for clinical
    instruction, 190–191
Advocate, role as, 47, 232
Agency, 185–186
Agency, service delivery
    conflict with supervisee, 199–200
    field site supervisor as representative
      of, 200–201
    goals of, 188–190
    orientation, 195
    placement interview as metaphor
      for, 195
    role induction, 195–196
    supervision contracts with, 196–197
Agency supervision, functions of,
    186–187
Agreements of understanding
    (supervision contracts), 196–197
Ambiguity, role, 151–152
American Association for Marriage and
    Family Therapists (AAMFT), 2,
    3, 4, 6
American Board of Examiners in Social
    Work, 3
American Board of Professional
    Psychology, 2, 3
American Psychiatric Association, 60
American Psychological Association,
    2, 3
    ethical code, 279
    *Guidelines for Psychotherapy with
      Lesbian, Gay, and Bisexual
      Clients,* 133
Analogue vs. real-life studies, 297–298
Analysis competency in Bloom's
    Taxonomy, 117

Anchored evaluation rubrics, 28
Androgyny, 125, 130
Anxiety
    as arousal state, 165–166
    of supervisee, 164–169
      games response to, 167–168
      impression management of,
        166–168
      learning and, 165
      performance and, 165–166
      performance anxiety, 218
      sources of, 164
    of supervisor, 171–172
Anxious attachment, 162
APA Code of Ethics, 58, 279
APPIC Competencies Conference
    (2002), 4
    supervision competency group, 284
    Supervision Workgroup, 86
Application competency in Bloom's
    Taxonomy, 117
Approved Clinical Supervisor (ACS)
    credential, 198
Arab social workers, 124–125
Archetypes (root metaphors), 15, 94
Asian social workers, 122
Assessment. *See also* Evaluation; Self-
    assessment in evaluation
    in group supervision, 251–253
    quantified, 28
    of SITs, 285–286
    of supervision process and outcome,
      299–302
Association for Counselor Education
    and Supervision (ACES), 6, 284
    ethical guidelines, 64, 341–346
Assumptive world, 75, 108
Attachment style, 146
    supervisee, 162–163
    supervisor, 172
Attachment theory, 162
Attack on others, in reaction to
    shame, 164
Attack on self, in reaction to shame, 164
Attendance, group, 244
Attitude similarity, 43
Attraction
    romantic, 178
    sexual, 59, 178. *See also*
      Sexual relations
      as positive transference, 170
      during supe-of-supe, 290
Attribution theory, 45
Audiotape, 168–169, 213–217
    client resistance to, 214

preselecting segments of, 215–216
transcripts of, 216–217
use of, 215–216
written critique of, 216
Authority, nature of supervisor's, 78
Autonomy, 115
    in IDM, 87, 88
    live supervision and, 267
    principle of, 71
Autonomy-dependency conflict, 169
Avoidance reaction to shame, 163–164

Balint groups, 253
Beginning stage of supervisor
    development, 281
Beginning student phase, 89
Behavioral supervision. *See* Cognitive-
    behavioral supervision
Beneficence, principle of, 71
Bias(es)
    gender, 125–126, 128
    against management, 181
    of supervisor, 45, 47
Bill of Rights, Supervisee's, 197,
    310–312
    Supervision Agreement based on,
      313–315
Bisexual issues, 131–133, 134
Bloom's Taxonomy, application of,
    115–116, 117
Bonding, in working alliance, 145, 152
Bottom-up parallel processes, 138
"Bubble hypothesis," 293
Budapest School, 77
Bug-in-the-ear (BITE) intervention,
    258, 261, 277–278
Burnout
    administrative structure and, 182–183
    reduction by field site supervisor, 202

CACREP, 2, 3, 6, 234, 235
Can interventions, 160
Care, voice of, 126–127
Career counseling, 7
Caregiving, compulsive, 162
Case conceptualization, 235
Case conference
    format, 245
    leads to assist supervisee in preparing
      for, 214
    timing of, 228–229
Case consultation, 235–236
Case law, ethical decision making
    and, 72
Case notes, 213

Case presentation, 244–245, 255
Case study research, 294–295
Catalytic interventions, 230
Central information processes route, 173
Central-tendency bias, 45
Certification, 13
Challenge-support balance, 168, 230, 239–240
Circumplex model of interpersonal behavior, 174–175
Circumstantial multiple roles, 56
Clarity
  of evaluation, 23–24, 31–33
  experience level and, 110
  of theory, 73
CLEAR (Council on Licensure, Enforcement and Regulation), 3
Client(s)
  evaluation of supervisee and, 30
  group supervision and exposure to, 237
  informed consent with, 52–53
  legal privileges of, 69
  monitoring care of, 12, 13–14
  due process for, 50
  reaction to live supervision, 275
  resistance to audiotape, 214
  sexual relations with, 55
    client-supervisee relationship, 56–57
  welfare of
    ethical guidelines on, 343
    monitoring and, 259
Client conceptualization, 111
Client outcome as criterion, 301
Client problem type, supervisory relationship and, 137
Client records
  components of, 203
  confidentiality of, 64–66
Client-supervisee relationship, 56–57, 241
  working alliance, 153
Clinical competence, 19, 21–23
Clinical supervision, 1–18
  defining, 7–14
  experiential learning in, 5
  goals of, 12–14
  importance of, 1–4
  interdisciplinary approach to, 1
  as intervention, 1, 8–10
  metaphors for, 14–17
    master-apprentice, 16
    parent-child, 15–16
    sibling, 16
  in preparation of mental health professionals, 4–7
  realms of knowledge in, 4–5
  socialization function of, 10–11
Clinical wisdom, 13
Clinics, training, 187–188
  goals of, 188–190

Coercive power, 173
Cognitive-behavioral supervision, 76, 80–81
Cognitive complexity, 108–111, 115
  cognitive development and, 108–109
  experience level and, 110–111
  importance of, 113–114
Cognitive development
  cognitive complexity and, 108–109
  during formal training, 115
  as intentional process, 115–116
Cognitive styles, 102–108, 114, 115
  Myers-Briggs Type Indicator, 102–104, 111, 114
  Systemic Cognitive-Developmental Supervision, 104–107
  theoretical orientation and, 107–108
Collaborative team model, 268
Collegiality, 185
Commission on Accreditation for Marriage and Family Therapy Education, 3
Communication, 198–201
  conflicts due miscommunications or mismatched expectations, 155–156
  within cross-cultural supervision, 120
  of formative feedback, 30–33
  as function of supervision, 187
  nonverbal, 140
  privileged, 65–66
  professional disclosure statements, 57, 198, 308–309
  responsibilities for
    of field site supervisor, 199–201
    of university supervisor, 190, 192–194
  of summative evaluations, 35–39
  supervision contracts as, 196–197, 305–307
Community mental health center, live supervision in, 277
Competence, 62–64
  areas of, 22
  clinical, 19, 21–23
  core competencies, 4
  development of, 5
  evaluation for incompetence, 39–43
  felt, 169–170
  managerial/organizational, 182–184, 207–208
  monitoring, 63
  need for, 169–170
  retention of, 64
  in supervisory practice, 63–64
Competencies cube, 17
Competition
  between-supervisee, 239, 245–247, 250
  between supervisor and supervisee, 16
Complementarity in relationship, 174–175

Complexity, cognitive, 108–111, 113–114, 115
  cognitive development and, 108–109
  experience level and, 110–111
Complexity Model (Stoltenberg), 87
Comprehension competency in Bloom's Taxonomy, 117
Comprehensiveness of theory, 74
Compulsive caregiving, 162
Compulsive self-reliance, 162
Computer programs, 294
Computers, in live supervision, 259–260. *See also* Technology, use of
Conceptual interventions, 230
Conceptualization skills, 95
Conceptualization stage of supervisor development, 281
Conceptual level (CL) of functioning, 87, 111, 113–114. *See also* Cognitive complexity
Conceptual model
  of supervision, 17–18
  of supervisor, 240
Concrete cognitive style, 104
Conditioning models, 80–81
Conference, supervisory, 27
Confidence
  experience level and, 110
  as training goal, 5
Confidentiality
  ethics of, 64–66
  group supervision and, 239
  informed consent and, 53
Confirmation-of-supervisor-identity stage of supervisor development, 281
Conflict(s)
  between agency and supervisee, 199–200
  gender difference in style of, 129
  personality, 157
  reactivation of inner, 178
  role, 151–152
    gender, 127
    personal and professional, 56
  in supervisory relationship, 154–157
Confrontation rupture, 156
Confrontive interventions, 230
Confusion stage, 92
Consent, informed, 40, 42, 52–55
  with clients, 52–53
  supervision and, 53–54
  with trainees, 54–55
Consistency, 115, 141–142
Consolidation state of supervisor development, 281
Constructivist approaches, 83–85
  narrative approaches, 83–84
  solution-focused supervision, 84–85
Consultant role, 95, 96, 97
Consultant-supervisors, 259

Consultation
  case, 235–236
  as function of supervision, 186
  supervision vs., 9, 10
Consultation break intervention, 259,
    262–263
Contexts for supervision, 187–190. *See
    also* Field site supervisor;
    University supervisor
  field site, 188–190
  graduate programs, 187–188
Continuing education, 64
Contract(s)
  supervision (agreements of
    understanding), 196–197,
    305–307
  supervision-evaluation, 27
Conversational styles, 128
Coping with Conflict (Mueller &
    Kell), 154
CORBS, 32
Core competencies, supervision as one
    of, 4
"Costs" of evaluation, 47
Council for the Accreditation of
    Counseling and Related
    Educational Programs
    (CACREP), 2, 3, 6, 234, 235
Council on Licensure, Enforcement and
    Regulation (CLEAR), 3
Counseling
  career, 7
  conceptualizing process of, 115
  supervision vs., 9–10
Counseling centers, university, 187
*Counselor Education and
    Supervision*, 292
Counselor Rating Form (CRF), 301
Counselor supervisors, standards
    for, 284
*Counselor Supervisor Self-Efficacy
    Scale*, 333–335
Counselor-therapist role, 95, 96, 97
Countertransference
  supervisee, 161
  supervisor, 176–179
    categories of, 177–179
    parallel processes and, 139
    sources of, 177
Covision, 12
Credentialing groups, 2, 3
Credibility, institutional, 185
Criteria, choice of research, 300–302
Cross-sectional research, 296
Cultural countertransference, 178
Cultural differences, 101, 116–135
  competence in, 63
  experience level and, 111
  group supervision and, 238
  institutional culture, 184–186
  lesbian, gay, and bisexual issues,
    131–133, 134

political nature of helping
    professions and, 118–119
  psychotherapy culture, 119
  racial and ethnic issues, 119–125, 178
  supervision group culture, 249

Dangerousness, determination of, 69
Data, supervisor use of, 229–231
Data gathering, 208
Debriefing
  evaluation and, 207
  postsession, 264
Decision-making, ethical, 71–72, 186
Defensiveness of supervisee, 24
Definitions, working, 296–297
Demographics report, 296
Dependence of supervisee/trainee,
    169, 237
Dependency-autonomy conflict, 169
Descriptive research, 293–295
Development
  ethical, 71
  identity, 134–135
    lesbian, gay, and bisexual,
      131–132
    racial, 124
  supervisee developmental level,
    17–18
    experience as indicator of,
      109–111
    resistance and, 161
  of supervisor, 25
Developmental differences in
    supervisory relationship, 101,
    108–116
  cognitive, 108–109, 115–116
  conceptual level (CL) and, 111,
    113–114
  ego, 111
  experience level, 109–112, 114–115
  implications of, 113–116
  supervision environment and,
    112–113, 114, 115
Developmental model(s), 85–94,
    279–283
  of Alonso, 280–281
  conclusions about, 93–94, 283
  of Hess, 280, 281
  of individual supervision, 229–231
  Integrated Developmental Model
    (IDM), 87, 88, 281–282
  of Loganbill, Hardy, and Delworth,
    90–93
  organizing literature on, 86
  of Rodenhauser, 280, 281
  of Rønnestad and Skovholt, 87–90, 91
  of Stoltenberg, McNeil, and
    Delworth, 280, 281–282
  supe-of-supe and, 289
  supervisor, 279–283
  trends in, 279–280
  of Watkins, 280, 282–283

Dialectic orientation, 107
Didactic component of training, 283,
    286–287
Direct intervention in supervisory
    relationship conflicts, 156
Directiveness, supervisor, 160–161
Direct liability, 69–70
Direct open supervision (DOS), 271
Direct Supervision, 260
Disclosure
  professional disclosure statement
    (PDS), 57, 198, 308–309
  supervisees' willingness to disclose,
    152–153
  supervisor self-disclosure, 149
Discrimination model (Bernard), 45,
    95–98, 100
Disenfranchised groups, focus on, 116
Dismissals, academic, 40, 42
Dual relationships, 55–62
  categories of, 56
  non-sexual, 60–62
  sexual, 57–60
Due process, 50–52
  in evaluation, 40–42, 51
Duties, contractual agreement on, 197
Duty to protect, 69
Duty to warn, 68–69
Dyad, supervisory relationship as,
    144–157

Eclectic supervision, 100
Economies in group supervision, 237
Education, continuing, 64
Efficacy studies, 298–299
Egocentric bias, 45
Ego development, 111
Eitingon, Max, 14, 77
Elaboration likelihood model (ELM),
    173, 174
Email, 199
  supervision delivered by, 227–228
Emergency procedures, 53, 205
Emotions, ethical decision making
    and, 72
Emulation stage of supervisor
    development, 281
Energy, "nurturant," 249–250
Environment, supervision, 101, 102,
    112–113, 114, 115
E-supervision, 227–228
Ethical considerations, 49–67, 287
  in choosing supervision method, 232
  competence, 62–64
    monitoring supervisee, 63
    retention of, 64
    in supervisory practice, 63–64
  confidentiality, 64–66
  in decision making, 71–72, 186
  dual relationships, 55–62
    non-sexual, 60–62
    sexual, 57–60

informed consent, 40, 42, 52–55
  with clients, 52–53
  supervision and, 53–54
  with trainees, 54–55
management planning and foresight,
  206–207
marketplace issues, 66
organizational competence and, 183
due process, 40–42, 50–52
  Supervisee's Bill of Rights, 197,
    310–312
    Supervision Agreement based on,
      313–315
  supervisor's ethical behavior,
    working alliance and, 148
supervisor training, 5–7, 279
in supervisory relationship, 311
Ethical guidelines, 49, 72, 340–346
  APA Code of Ethics, 58, 279
  *Approved Clinical Supervisor Code
    of Ethics*, 340–341
  Association for Counselor Education
    and Supervision, 64, 341–346
  Supervision Interest Network, 50
Ethnic differences, working alliance
    and discussions of, 150. *See
    also* Racial and ethnic issues in
    multicultural supervision
Evaluation, 19–48
  chronic issues in, 47–48
  clinical competence and, 19
  competency in Bloom's Taxonomy,
    117
  conditions for, 23–26
  consequences of, 47
  contractual agreement on method
    of, 197
  "costs" of, 47
  criteria for, 19, 21–23
  debriefing and, 207
  dissonance surrounding, 20
  feedback in, 30–33
  formative, 20, 21, 27
  gender and, 128
  for impairment and incompetence,
    39–43
  instruments of, 28–30, 316–339
  methods of, 27–28
  negative, 47
  parent-child metaphor of supervision
    and, 15–16
  peer, 35, 48
  premature, 25
  due process in, 40–42, 51
  process of, 26–39
    expectations of, 312
  professional counseling performance,
    items included in, 41
  self-assessment in, 33–35
  subjective element in, 43–47
    rating idiosyncrasies, 45–47
    supervisee-supervisor familiarity, 44

supervisee-supervisor similarity,
    43–44
  supervisor priorities, 44–45
summative, 20–21, 35–39, 289, 291
  examples of, 36–38
  as learning experience for
    supervisor, 38–39
  nature of, 35–36
  by university supervisor, 200
supervision-evaluation contract, 27
of supervisor, 253
working alliance and supervisor's
    evaluation practices, 148–149
Evaluation of Counselor Behaviors-
    Revised form, 36
*Evaluation Process within Supervision
    Inventory* (EPSI), 148, 322–323
Evaluative nature of supervision, 11–12
Events paradigm, 295
Expectations
  congruence of, 145–146
  of educational facility and field site,
    inconsistency between, 200
  incompatibility between reality of
    facility and, 200
  mismatched, conflict due to, 155–156
  performance, conflict over
    inconsistency in, 199–200
  Supervisee's Bill of Rights on,
    310–311, 312
Experience, 109–112
  cognitive style and, 114
  as indicator of developmental level,
    109–111
  individual differences in, 114–115
  moderating variables and, 111–112
  prepracticum, 287–288
  prior, 284–285
  supervision structure and level of, 168
  unsupervised, 5
Experienced professional phase, 89–90
Experiential learning, 5
Experiential training, 283
Expertise, development of, 13
Expert power, 129, 131, 149
Exploration stage of supervisor
    development, 281
Extroversion (E) vs. Introversion (I),
    102, 105
Eye Movement Desensitization and
    Reprocessing (EMDR), 73

Facilitative interventions, 230
Failure to disclose, supervisees',
    152–153
Falsifiability of theory, 74
Familiarity, supervisee-supervisor, 44
Family(ies)
  live supervision and, 264, 266, 267
  monitoring and, 259
Family metaphors for supervision, 15–17
Family roles in group supervision, 240

Family therapists, systemic, 137
Family therapy, informed consent in, 53
Family therapy supervision, 81–83
Feedback
  on case presentation, 244
  definition of, 30
  in evaluation, 30–33
  in group supervision, 237–238, 248,
    251–253
  as interactional, 31–32
  on organizational strategy, 207
  on placement interview, 194–195
  saved to disk, 260
  summative, 291
  on supe-of-supe, 291
  for supervisor, 253
Feeling (F) vs. Thinking (T), 103,
    105–106
Felt competence, 169–170
Female supervisors, 127–128
Feminist supervision, 130–131
Fidelity, principle of, 71
Field instruction, 188–190
Field site supervisor, 194–202
  as agency representative, 200–201
  burnout reduction by, 202
  communication by, 199–201
  orientation by, 195
  placement interview by, 194–195
  supervision contracts with, 196–197
First impressions, perseverance of, 44
Flexibility in evaluation, 24
Foci of supervision, 95–96
  Hawkins-Shohet model of, 99
Focused observation, 248
Focused Risk Management Supervisory
    System (FoRMSS), 205, 206
Formal orientation, 104
Formative evaluation, 20, 21, 27
Formative feedback, communicating,
    30–33
Format (method), choice of, 75
Forming group stage, 237, 243–245
Frequency of group meetings, 244
Functions of supervision, 99

Games approach to anxiety
    management, 167–168
Gatekeeping model, 40
Gay issues, 131–133, 134
Gender bias, 125–126, 128
Gender issues within multicultural
    supervision, 125–131, 135
  empirical studies, 128–130
  feminist supervision, 130–131
  gender role conflict, 127
  male vs. female supervisors, 127–128
  power and, 128–130, 131, 134
  same-gender and cross-gender
    pairs, 130
  "voices," 126–127
Gender role conflict, 127

Generic supervisory role, 16
Goal-directed supervision, 27
Goals, 12–14
  contractual agreement on, 197
  focusing videotape supervision by
    setting realistic, 218–219
  for individual supervision, 231, 232
  resistance and disagreement about, 160
  of service delivery agency, 188–190
  shared, 145–146
  of supervisee, 210
  therapeutic, 142, 145
  of training institutions, 188–190
  in working alliance, 145–146
Good-enough supervisor, 292
Graduate program. *See also* University
    supervisor
  as context for supervision, 187–188
  inconsistency between expectations
    of field site and, 200
  initial communication between field
    site and, 192–194
  training supervisors while in, 284
Graf, Herbert (Little Hans), 77
Group counseling or therapy,
    supervision of, 239
Group supe-of-supe, 288–289
Group supervision, 7, 74, 234–256
  activities, 235, 236
  advantages of, 237–239
  assumptions informing, 234
  Balint groups, 253
  between-supervisee competition, 239,
    245–247, 250
  between-supervisee support, 240,
    249–250
  defined, 234–235
  evaluation and feedback of
    supervisor, 253
  family roles in, 240
  frequency of use, 234
  helpful and hindering phenomena in,
    241, 242
  limitations of, 239
  ongoing, 251
  parallel processes and, 238, 239
  peer group supervision, 253–256
  pregroup tasks, 241–243
    meeting place, 243
    screening, 241–243
  rules and structure, 243–245
  size of, 235
  stages of, 236–237, 243–251
    adjourning, 237, 250–251
    forming, 237, 243–245
    norming, 237, 247
    performing, 237, 247–250
    storming, 237, 245–247
  structured group supervision (SGS)
    model, 245, 246
  supervisee assessment, 251–253
    feedback, 237–238, 248, 251–253

tasks of supervisor in, 239–253
  general, 239–241
  specific, 241–253
  types of groups, 235–236
Group Supervision Scale, 253, 317
Group Supervisory Behavior Scale, 253
*Guidelines for Psychotherapy with
    Lesbian, Gay, and Bisexual
    Clients* (APA), 133
Guilt vs. shame, 163

*Handbook of Counseling
    Psychology,* 86
Harassment, sexual, 59
Helping professions, political nature of,
    118–119
Hippocratic oath, 2
Hispanic social workers, 120–122, 123
Historian role in team supervision, 269
Homophobia, 131, 132

Identity
  professional, 11
  racial, working alliance and, 150
Identity development, 134–135
  lesbian, gay, and bisexual, 131–132
  racial, 124
IDM, 87, 88, 281–282
Impairment
  definitions of, 21, 39–40
  evaluation for, 39–43
  of supervisee, 39–43
Impression management (strategic self-
    presentation), 166–168
Impression motivation, 167
Incompetence, evaluation for, 39–43.
    See also Competence
Incorporation stage of supervisor
    development, 281
Indirect intervention in supervisory
    relationship conflicts, 156
Individual differences, 101. *See also*
    Supervisory relationship
  evaluation and, 24
  in supe-of-supe, 290
Individual supervision, 209–233
  audiotape, 168–169, 213–217
    client resistance to, 214
    preselecting segments of, 215–216
    use of, 215–216
    written critique of, 216
  case notes, 213
  formats for, 229
    frequency of use, 229
    selecting, 231–233
  goals for, 231, 232
  live observation, 225–226
  process notes, 213
  self-report, 211–213
  structured vs. unstructured, 211
  timing of, 228–229
  videotape, 217–222

advantages and disadvantages of,
    217–218
  guidelines for working with,
    218–219
  interpersonal process recall (IRP),
    219, 220–222, 223, 229
  supervisory relationship and, 219
Influence
  interpersonal, supervisor's use
    of, 149–150
  power as, 149
  resistance of supervisor, 159
  social influence theory, 173–174
Information processes routes, 173–174
Informed consent, 40, 42, 52–55
  with clients, 52–53
  evaluation steps for, 42
  goals, in training program, 40
  supervision and, 53–54
  with trainees, 54–55
Inner conflicts, reactivation of, 178
Inquisitiveness, spirit of, 185
Institutional culture, 184–186
Instruments, supervision, 28–30,
    305–339
  adaptation from other domains, 301
  *Counselor Supervisor Self-Efficacy
    Scale,* 333–335
  *Evaluation Process within
    Supervision Inventory,* 148,
    322–323
  Group Supervision Scale, 253, 317
  *Multicultural Supervision
    Competencies Questionnaire*
    (MSCQ), 336–339
  Professional Disclosure Statement,
    57, 198, 308–309
  *Supervisee Levels Questionnaire-
    Revised,* 150, 318–319
  *Supervisee Perceptions of
    Supervision,* 320–321
  Supervisee's Bill of Rights, 197,
    310–312
    Supervision Agreement based on,
    313–315
  supervision contracts (agreements of
    understanding), 196–197,
    305–307
  Supervision Questionnaire, 316
  Supervisory Styles Inventory, 97–98,
    149, 291, 332
  *Supervisory Working Alliance
    Inventory,* 145, 324–327
  Working Alliance Inventory, 145,
    328–331
Integrated Developmental Model
    (IDM), 87, 88, 281–282
Integrationist supervision, 100
Integration stage, 92
Intentional, being, 208
Intentional tort, 67–68
Interactional research, 295

Interactive television, 259–260
Interdisciplinary approach, 1
International Psychoanalytic Society, 77
Internet, use of, 226. *See also*
   Technology, use of sites about
   licensure, credentialing, and
   accreditation, 2, 3
supervision delivered by, 227–228
Interpersonal dynamics, conflicts
   arising from participants',
   156–157
Interpersonal influence, supervisor's use
   of, 149–150
Interpersonal perspective, 174–175
Interpersonal power, 172–176
Interpersonal Process Recall (IPR), 74,
   202, 218, 219, 220–222, 223,
   229, 287
   supervisor leads for use with,
   221–222
Interpersonal triangles, 142–144
Intervention(s). *See also* Group
   supervision; Individual
   supervision; Live supervision
   clinical supervision as, 1, 8–10
   criteria for selecting, 209–211
   focus on, 95, 96
   functions of, 210–211
   by novice supervisees, 115
   paradoxical, 82
   strategic, 82–83
   supervision contract as, 196
   in supervisory relationship conflicts,
   156
Interview, placement, 194–195
Introversion (I) vs. Extroversion (E),
   102, 105
Intuiting (I) vs. Sensing (S), 103, 105
Intuitiveness of supervision, 43
Inverted-U hypothesis, 165, 166
In vivo rotation, 271
In vivo supervision, 259
Involvement, power and, 175
Iowa, University of, 86
IPR, 74, 202, 218, 219, 220–222, 223,
   229, 287
Isomorphism
   group supervision and, 239
   live supervision and client
   resistance, 267
   team supervision and, 276
   in supervisory relationship, 137,
   141–142

Jewish social workers, 124–125
Job analyses, 23
Joint Council on Professional Education
   in Psychology, 22
*Journal of Clinical Psychology: In
   Session: Psychotherapy in
   Practice,* 155, 158
Journal of Counseling Psychology, 292

Judging (J) vs. Perceiving (P), 103, 106
Justice
   principle of, 71
   voice of, 126–127

Knowledge
   competency in Bloom's
   Taxonomy, 117
   realms of, in clinical supervision, 4–5

Laboratory skills, training in, 287–288
Late career supervisors, 280–281
Lawsuits, malpractice, 67–70
   preventing, 70–71
Lay helper phase, 89
Leadership of peer supervision group,
   255
Learning
   experiential, 5
   group supervision and, 237, 239
   objectives for, 286
   supervisee anxiety and, 165
Learning alliance, 145
Learning styles, 102–108, 114
Legal considerations, 49–52, 67–71
   duty to warn, 68–69
   liability, 68, 69–70
   malpractice, 67–71
   due process, 40–42, 50–52
Legitimate power, 129
Leniency bias, 45, 46, 47
Lesbian issues, 131–133, 134
Lewin, Kurt, 73
Liability, 68, 69–70
Liaison function of site supervisor,
   200–201
Licensure, 2–3, 6–7, 13
Life-span approach, 280–281
Likert scales, 28
Linkage function of supervision, 187
Listservs, 227
Litigation, 49, 51. *See also* Legal
   considerations
   fear of, 21
   record keeping and, 202
Live observation, 225–226
Live supervision, 84, 257–278
   advantages of, 266–267
   computers in, 259–260
   in different contexts, 277–278
   disadvantages of, 267–268
   egalitarianism within, 277
   frequency of use of, 275
   implementation of, 264–266
   interventions, 260–263
   bug-in-the-ear (BITE), 258, 261,
   277–278
   consultation break, 259, 262–263
   telephone, 259, 261–262, 265
   methods of, 258–260
   postsession debriefing, 264
   presession planning, 263–264

research on, 274–277
team supervision, 74, 257, 268–274
   advantages of, 273
   direct open supervision (DOS), 271
   disadvantages of, 274
   dynamics of, 271–273
   forms of, 268–269
   Pick-a-Dali Circus (PDC), 271
   process of, 268
   reflecting team, 269–270
   roles in, 268–269
Longitudinal studies, 296
"Lousy" supervision
   characteristics of lousy
   supervisor, 151
   organizational-administrative
   incompetence and, 182

Male gender role conflict, 127
Male supervisors, 127–128
Malpractice suits, 67–70
   preventing, 70–71
Management, 180–208
   bias against, 181
   competence in, 182–184, 207–208
   contexts for supervision, 187–190
   field site supervisor, 194–202
   as agency representative, 200–201
   burnout reduction by, 202
   communication by, 199–201
   orientation by, 195
   placement interview by, 194–195
   supervision contracts with,
   196–197
institutional culture and, 184–186
ongoing tasks of, 198–207
   communication, 198–201
   method selection, 202
   record keeping, 202–205
   time management, 201–202
supervision plan and, 186–187
university supervisor, 190–194
   advising system for clinical
   instruction, 190–191
   agreements of understanding
   (supervision contracts) with,
   196–197
   evaluation by, 200
   site communication by, 192–194
   site selection by, 191–194
Manuals, 195, 298–299
Marketplace issues, 66
Marriage therapy, informed consent
   in, 53
Master-apprentice metaphor of
   supervision, 16
MBTI, 102–104, 111, 114
MDS, 251–253
Measurement and management, 185
Measures of supervision outcome,
   299–302
Mediational research, 299

Meeting places, for group supervision, 243
Mental health professionals, clinical supervision in preparation of, 4–7
Mental health professions, similarities in, 1
Mentoring, dual relationship vs., 61–62
Metacommunication, 156–157
Metaphor(s)
    for clinical supervision, 14–17
        master-apprentice, 16
        parent-child, 15–16
        sibling, 16
    root (archetypes), 15, 94
    voice, 126–127
Metatransference, 137–138
Methodological considerations, 293–299. *See also* Group supervision; Individual supervision; Live supervision
    choosing supervision method, time management and, 202
    criteria and measures, 299–302
    cross-sectional design, 296
    descriptive research, 293–295
    hypothesis and theory building, 295–299
        analogue vs. real-life studies, 297–298
        demographics report, 296
        efficacy studies, 298–299
        mediators and moderators, 299
        participant roles, 296
        rater information, 296
        self-reports of satisfaction, 297
        working definitions, 296–297
Mexican-American supervisees, 120–122
"Microsupervision" model, 287–288
Midcareer supervisors, 280
"Miracle question," 84
Mirrors, effect of one-way, 265
Model(s), 74, 83–100
    collaborative team, 268
    conceptual, 17–18
    conceptual map of, 75
    conditioning, 80–81
    developmental. *See* Developmental model(s)
    framework for describing supervisory, 78
    group development, 236–237
    "microsupervision," 287–288
    narrative, 83–84
    social role, 94–100
        discrimination model, 45, 95–98, 100
        of Hawkins and Shohet, 98–99
        Holloway Systems Model, 99–100
    solution-focused, 84–85
    theories and, 74–75
Moderator, supervisor as, 248, 299

Monitoring, 186, 258–259
Moral principles, 71–72. *See also* Ethical considerations
Motivation in IDM, 87, 88
Multiculturalism, training in, 118
Multicultural supervision, 119–135. *See also* Supervisory relationship
    gender issues within, 125–131, 135
        male vs. female supervisors, 127–128
        power and, 128–130, 131, 134
        same-gender and cross-gender pairs, 130
        "voices," 126–127
    lesbian, gay, and bisexual issues within, 131–133, 134
    racial and ethnic issues in, 119–125, 178
Multicultural Supervision Competencies Questionnaire (MSCQ), 336–339
Multidimensional scaling (MDS), 251–253
Must interventions, 160–161
Myers-Briggs Type Indicator (MBTI), 102–104, 111, 114

Narrative approaches to supervision, 83–84
National Board for Certified Counselors (NBCC), 2, 3, 4, 23
National Council of Schools and Programs of Professional Psychology, 4
Negative supervisory experiences, working alliance and, 150
Negative transference, 170
Negligence cases, 68
Negotiation, 185
Noncompliance, resistance as, 160
Nonlicensed professionals, 284–285
Nonmaleficence, principle of, 71
Nonverbal communication, 140
Normative conflicts, 156
Norming group stage, 237, 247
Notes, process and case, 213
Novice professional phase, 89
Novice supervisors, 280
    meeting needs of, 289
NUDIST (Nonnumerical Unstructured Data Indexing Searching and Theorizing), 294
"Nurturant" energy, 249–250

Observation
    focused, 248
    live, 225–226
Occam's razor, 73
One-way mirror, effect of, 265
Ongoing supervision groups, 251
Operationality of theory, 73–74
Organizing supervision experience, 180–208

additional guidelines, 207–208
competence in
    guidelines to achieve, 207–208
    importance of, 182–184
complicating factors in, 181–182
contexts for supervision, 187–190
evaluation and debriefing, 207
institutional culture, role of, 184–186
plan, 186–187
tasks, 190–207
    foundational, 190–198
    ongoing, 198–207
Orientation
    by field site supervisor, 195
    to use of live supervision, 265
Outcome Questionnaire-45, 30

Paradoxical interventions, 82
Paralanguage, 215
Parallel process(es)
    client issues transmitted by, 160
    group supervision and, 238, 239
    supe-of-supe and, 290
    supervisee transference originating in, 170–171
    in supervisory relationship, 137–141
    symmetrical, 139
Parameters of supervision, 17
Parent-child metaphor of supervision, 15–16
Parsimony of theory, 73
Participants, research, 296
Peer evaluation, 35, 48
Peer group supervision, 253–256
Perceiving (P) vs. Judging (J), 103, 106
Performance, supervisee anxiety and, 165–166
Performance anxiety, 218
Performing group stage, 237, 247–250
Peripheral information processes route, 173
Personal and professional role conflicts, 56
Personal characteristics
    countertransference of, 177–178
    of therapists, 20
Personal growth, 111
Personality conflicts, 157
Personalization skills, 95, 96
Person-centered supervision, 78–80
Persuasion and Healing (Frank), 173
Philosophy of supervision, 224–225
Phone interventions, 259, 261–262, 265
Pick-a-Dali circus (PDC), 271
Placement interview, 194–195
Planning
    for exceptional situations, 205–207
    in live supervision, 263–264
    for supervision, 186–187, 214–216
Playfulness in supervision, 26
Political nature of helping professions, 118–119

Popper, Karl, 74
Positive transference, 170
Postsession debriefing, 264
Power
coercive, 173
expert, 129, 131, 149
gender and, 128–130, 131, 134
interpersonal, 172–176
race and, 119–120
referent, 129, 149
in supervisory relationship, 128–130, 131, 134, 149, 172–176
Power struggles, 290
Practicality of theory, 74
Practicum component of training (supervision-of-supervision), 288–291
beginning phase of, 288–289
end phase of, 289–291
middle phase of, 289, 290
Preciseness of theory, 73
Predatory professional, 56
Pregroup tasks, 241–243
Preparation to supervise, necessary, 5–7, 279
Prepracticum experience, 287–288
Prescriptive interventions, 230
Presession planning, 263–264
Presuppositional language, 85
Priorities, evaluation and, 44–45
Privacy, 65
Privileged communication, 65–66
Probation, 41–42
Problem solving, in supervision groups, 235
Procedural due process, 50
Procedure, contractual agreement on, 197
Process commentator, supervisor as, 248
Process notes, 213
Professional counseling performance evaluation, items included in, 41
Professional disclosure statement (PDS), 57, 198
example of, 308–309
Professional functioning, enhancement of, 12, 13
Professional identity, 11
Professional issues, 287
Professional phases in Rønnestad and Skovholt model, 89–90
Professional Psychology: Research and Practice, 292
Professionals
attributes of, 1
nonlicensed, 284–285
self-regulation by, 2–3
Program administration role, ethical guidelines on, 345–346
Program concentration, as moderating variable to experience level, 111–112
Psychodynamic supervision, 76–78

Psycho education, 7
Psychological type, supervisory styles based on, 104, 105–106
Psychoprocess modality, 235
Psychotherapy-based theories, 76–85
cognitive-behavioral, 76, 80–81
constructivist, 83–86
narrative approaches, 83–84
solution-focused supervision, 84–85
person-centered, 78–80
psychodynamic, 76–78
systemic, 81–83
Psychotherapy culture, 119

Qualitative research, 294
Quantified assessment, 28
Questionnaires, 296

Racial and ethnic issues in multicultural supervision, 119–125
in countertransference, 178
empirical studies of, 122–125
power and, 119–120
statuses and approaches to, 121
Racial identity, working alliance and, 150
Racial identity development, 124
Rater information, 296
Rating idiosyncrasies, 45–47
Rating scale, intern, 28, 29
Reactance, supervisee trait, 161
Reactance potential, concept of, 113
Real-life vs. analogue studies, 297–298
Recall rate for therapy sessions, 212
Record keeping, 202–205
Referent power, 129, 149
Reflecting team, 269–270
"Reflection process," 137
Reflectivity in supervisees, 223–225
Report, demographics, 296
Research, 292–302
on cognitive complexity and development, 108–112
criteria and measures in, 299–302
history of, 292
on live supervision, 274–277
methodological considerations, 293–299
analogue vs. real-life studies, 297–298
cross-sectional design, 296
demographics report, 296
descriptive research, 293–295
hypothesis and theory building, 295–299
mediators and moderators, 299
participant roles, 296
rater information, 296
self-reports of satisfaction, 297
working definitions, 296–297
social influence theory, 173–174
stage model for, 293

on supervision, 286–287
on supervision training outcomes, 291
Resistance, supervisee, 158–162
circumstances eliciting, 160–161
interventions to address, 161
manifestations of, 159–160
Respondeat superior (vicarious liability), 68, 70
Responsibilities
balancing of, 290
contractual agreement on, 197
evaluation and, 19
Restrictive emotionality (RE), male gender role conflict and, 127
Rigor and relevance in research, tension between, 293
Risk management, 203, 205, 206
"Robotization" in live supervision, 267
Rogers, Carl, 17, 78–80, 171
Role(s), 94–95
choice of, 75
consultant, 95, 96, 97
counselor-therapist, 95, 96, 97
dual relationships and, 56
ethical guidelines on, 343–346
generic supervisory, 16
in group supervision, 240
in live supervision, 268–269
as program administrator, 345–346
of research participants, 296
of supervisor, 75, 95, 96–98
as teacher, 95, 96, 97
in team supervision, 268–269
Role ambiguity, 151–152
Role conflict, 151–152
gender, 127
personal and professional, 56
Role Conflict and Role Ambiguity Inventory (RCRAI), 152
Role consolidation stage of supervisor development, 283
Role induction, 146, 168–169, 195–196
Role mastery stage of supervisor development, 283
Role models, supervisors as, 11
Role recovery and transition stage of supervisor development, 282–283
Role shock, 282
Role taking, 248
Romantic relationships with supervisee, 60, 178
Root metaphors (archetypes), 15, 94
Rural public mental health, live supervision in, 277

Sample sizes in research, 295–296
SCDS, 104–107
Schema for supervision, 14–17
Science of supervision, research strategies for, 293–299
SCM, 282–283

Screening of group supervision
        members, 241–243
Selectivity, institutional, 184
Self-assessment in evaluation, 33–35
Self-attack, in reaction to shame, 164
Self-awareness, 115
Self-concept, racial identity and, 119
Self-disclosure, working alliance and
        supervisor, 149
Self-efficacy
    *Counselor Supervisor Self-Efficacy
        Scale,* 333–335
    multicultural counseling, 118
Self-knowledge, 207–208
Self-other awareness in IDM, 87, 88
Self-presentation, strategic (impression
        management), 166–168
Self-regulation, 2–3
Self-reliance, compulsive, 162
Self-report
    in individual supervision, 211–213
    of supervisee satisfaction, 297
Senior professional phase, 90
Sensing (S) vs. Intuiting (I), 103, 105
Sensitivity, temporal, 184
Sensorimotor orientation, 104
Sequential design, 296
Session Evaluation Questionnaire, 30
Sexual attraction, supervisor-supervisee,
        59, 178
    as positive transference, 170
    during supe-of-supe, 290
Sexual relations
    with client, 55
        client-supervisee relationship,
            56–57
    with supervisee, 57–60
Shame, supervisee, 163–164
Shifts in professional roles, 56
Shock, role, 282
Sibling metaphor of supervision, 16
"Signing off" for supervisees, 66
Similarity, supervisee-supervisor, 43–44
Simplicity of theory, 73
Site selection, 191–194
Site supervisor. *See* Field site
        supervisor
Six-focused model, 98
Skill mastery, 166
Skills. *See also* Competence
    conceptualization, 95, 96
    deterioration under observation, 166
    laboratory, 287–288
    personalization, 95, 96
SLL, 285–286
Social facilitation theory, 166
Social influence, power as, 149
Social influence theory, 173–174
Socialization function of clinical
        supervision, 10–11
Social role models, 94–100
    discrimination model, 45, 95–98, 100

of Hawkins and Shohet, 98–99
    Holloway Systems Model, 99–100
Social workers, ethnic, 120–122
Socioprocess modality, 235
Solution-focused supervision, 84–85
Speech activity of supervisees, 247–248
Stagnation stage, 92
STAMINA (organizational), 184–186
Standards, 22. *See also* Ethical
        considerations
    for counselor supervisors, 284
Standards for Counseling Supervisors,
        6, 63
State licensing boards, 6–7, 284
State regulatory boards, 2
Statistical Package for the Social
        Sciences (SPSS), 251
Stereotypes, 181
    avoiding, 135
Storming group stage, 237, 245–247
Strategic interventions, 82–83
Strategic self-presentation (impression
        management), 166–168
Strategy-focus, 75
Strictness bias, 45
Structure, supervisee anxiety
        management by supervision, 168
Structured group supervision (SGS)
        model, 245, 246
Structured multiple professional
        relationships, 60
Structured multiple professional roles, 56
Student phases in Rønnestad and
        Skovholt model, 89
Style(s)
    attachment, 146, 162–163, 172
    choice of, 75
    cognitive, 102–108, 114, 115
    of conflict, gender difference in, 129
    conversational, 128
    of learning, 102–108, 114
    supervisor
        supervisee resistance and, 161
        working alliance and, 149
Subjectivity, personal vs.
        professional, 43
Subjunctive language, 85
Substance abuse agency, live
        supervision in, 277
Substantive due process, 50
Summative evaluation, 20–21, 35–39,
        289, 291
    examples of, 36–38
    as learning experience for supervisor,
        38–39
    nature of, 35–36
    by university supervisor, 200
Summative feedback, 291
Supertransference, 176
Supervisee(s). *See also* Supervisory
        relationship; Trainee(s)
    adequacy feelings of, 170

adherence to treatment protocols, 153
amount of training and behavior
        of, 110
anxiety of, 164–169
    games response to, 167–168
    impression management of,
        166–168
    learning and, 165
    performance and, 165–166
    performance anxiety, 218
    sources of, 164
assessment of, 285–286. *See also*
        Evaluation; Self-assessment in
        evaluation
    in group supervision, 251–253
    quantified, 28
attachment style, 162–163
competence needs of, 169–170
competition between, 239,
        245–247, 250
conceptual level of, 87, 111, 113–114
conflict with agency, 199–200
countertransference by, 161
defensiveness of, 24
dependence of, 92, 237
deterioration of therapeutic skills
        under observation, 166
developmental level of, 17–18
ethnic, 120–122
goals of, 210
in group supervision, 238
impairment of, 39–43
informed consent for, 54–55
learning styles of, 102–108, 114
monitoring, 63
perspective on ethics, 66–67
reactions to, 178
reflectivity in, 223–225
relationship with client, 241
self-reports of satisfaction, 297
sexual attraction to, 178
    during supe-of-supe, 290
sexual relations with, 57–60
    between client and supervisee,
        56–57
    between supervisor and supervisee,
        57–60
shame, 163–164
"signing off" for, 66
speech activity of, 247–248
therapy with, 61
trainee distinguished from, 8
transference in, 170–171
    countertransference to, 178–179
vulnerability of, 161, 266
willingness to disclose, 152–153
*Supervisee Levels Questionnaire-
        Revised,* 150, 318–319
Supervisee Perceptions of Supervisees,
        320–321
Supervisee's Bill of Rights, 197,
        310–312

Supervision Agreement based on, 313–315

Supervision, 8–10

Supervision Agreement, based on Supervisee's Bill of Rights, 313–315

Supervision complexity model (SCM), 282–283

Supervision contracts (agreements of understanding), 196–197
sample, 305–307

Supervision environment, 101, 102, 112–113, 114, 115

Supervision-evaluation contract, 27

Supervision Interest Network, *Ethical Guidelines for Counseling Supervisors,* 50

Supervision Life Line (SLL), 285–286

Supervision-of-supervision, 288–291
beginning phase of, 288–289
end phase of, 289–291
middle phase of, 289, 290

Supervision processes, working alliance and, 150–152

Supervision Questionnaire, 316

Supervision Rating Form, 301

Supervision Record Form (SRF), 203, 204–205

Supervision records, outline of, 203

Supervision-therapy distinction, 257

Supervision-training distinction, 8

Supervisor(s)
anxiety of, 171–172
attachment style, 172
authority, nature of, 78
behavior, as alliance antecedent, 148–150
burnout of, 202
characteristics of lousy, 151
cognitive style of, 114
conceptual model of, 240
countertransference by, 176–179
categories of, 177–179
parallel processes and, 139
sources of, 177
development of, 25
evaluation and feedback of, 253
good-enough, 292
management of supervisee anxiety, 168–169
professional disclosure statements by, 57, 198, 308–309
role in addressing supervisee shame, 164
as role models, 11
supervisee transference and, 171
supervisory relationship and, 171–179
tasks, 17, 18
therapists as, 6
use of data, 229–231

Supervisor development models, 279–283

Supervisor directiveness, resistance and, 160–161

Supervisors in training (SITs). *See* Supervisee(s); Trainee(s); Training

Supervisor style
supervisee resistance and, 161
working alliance and, 149

Supervisor vision, 210

Supervisory conference, 27

Supervisory experience, resistance to, 160

Supervisory relationship, 101–135
client problem type and, 137
cultural differences and, 101, 116–135
gender issues, 125–131, 135
lesbian, gay, and bisexual issues, 131–133, 134
political nature of helping professions and, 118–119
psychotherapy culture, 119
racial and ethnic issues, 119–125, 178
definition of, 136
developmental differences in, 101, 108–116
cognitive, 108–109
conceptual level (CL) (cognitive level) and, 111, 113–114
ego, 111
experience level, 109–112, 114–115
implications of, 113–116
supervision environment and, 112–113, 114, 115
as dyad, 144–157
conflict in, 154–157
power in, 149
trust in, 160
working alliance in, 145–157
power in, 128–130, 131, 134, 149, 172–176
supervisee factors in, 158–171
anxiety and, 164–169
attachment, 162–163
competence needs and, 169–170
resistance, 158–162
shame, 163–164
transference and, 170–171
Supervisee's Bill of Rights on, 310–311
ethical considerations, 311
expectations, 310–311
supervisor factors in, 171–179
anxiety, 171–172
attachment style, 172
countertransference and, 176–179
interpersonal power, 172–176
trust, 171
as triadic system, 136–144
interpersonal triangles in, 143–144

isomorphism in, 137, 141–142
parallel processes in, 137–141
uniqueness of two individuals and, 101–102
in cognitive complexity and cognitive development, 108–112
in cognitive or learning styles, 102–108
experience level and, 108–112
supervision environment, 112–113
videotape and, 219

Supervisory role, generic, 16

Supervisory Styles Inventory (SSI), 97–98, 149, 291, 332

Supervisory Working Alliance Inventory, 145, 324–327
Supervisor Form Instructions, 324–325
Trainee Form Instructions, 326–327

Support
between-supervisee, 240, 249–250
for managerial competence, 207

Support-challenge balance, 168, 230, 239–240

Surveys, 296

Symmetrical parallel processes, 139

Synthesis competency in Bloom's Taxonomy, 117

Systemic Cognitive Developmental Supervision (SCDS), 104–107

Systemic family therapists, 137

Systemic supervision, 81–83

Tarasoff v. *Regents of the University of California,* 68–69, 203

Taskmaster role in team supervision, 268–269

Task process group modality, 235

Tasks
resistance and disagreement about, 160
of supervision, 99
supervisor, 17, 18
therapeutic, 145

Teaching, supervision vs., 8–9

Teaching and Learning of Psychotherapy, The (Ekstein & Wallerstein), 8

Teaching function of supervision, 4–5, 186

Team supervision, 74, 257, 268–274
advantages of, 273
direct open supervision (DOS), 271
disadvantages of, 274
dynamics of, 271–273
forms of, 268–269
Pick-a-Dali Circus (PDC), 271
process of, 268
reflecting team, 269–270
roles in, 268–269

Techniques of supervision. *See* Group supervision; Individual supervision; Live supervision

Technology, use of, 217, 218, 226–228, 259–260. *See also* Audiotape; Videotape
  advantages to, 227
  barriers to, 226–227
Telephone interventions, 259, 261–262, 265
Television, interactive, 259–260
Temporal sensitivity, 184
Termination of supe-of-supe, 289
Theoretical consistency, criteria for evaluation based on, 21–22
Theoretical models of supervision, 286
Theoretical orientation, 75
  cognitive style and, 107–108
  individual differences and, 114
  observing group supervision session from particular, 248–249
Theory(ies), 73–85. *See also* Model(s)
  cognitive-behavioral, 76, 80–81
  criteria for evaluating, 73–74
  narrative approaches, 83–84
  person-centered, 78–80
  psychodynamic, 76–78
  systemic, 81–83
Therapeutic alliances, working alliance and, 153
Therapeutic system, consistency in, 141–142
Therapist role in team supervision, 268
Therapists
  personal characteristics of, 20
  as supervisors, 6
Therapy-supervision distinction, 257
Thinking (T) vs. Feeling (F), 103, 105–106
Time-limited group, 250–251
Time management, 201–202
  group, 241, 242
Timing of supervision, 228–229, 264
Torts, 67–68
Trainee(s). *See also* Supervisee(s)
  advising, for clinical instruction, 190–191
  burnout of, 202
  developmental stages of, 90–92
  functions essential for success, 21
  impairment, 39–43
  incompetence, 39–43
  informed consent with, 54–55

manual for, 195
  reaction to live supervision, 275
  supervisee distinguished from, 8
Training, 283–292
  assessment, 285–286
  books on, 287
  didactic component of, 283, 286–287
  ethical necessity of, 5–7, 279
  experiential, 283
  as function of supervision, 186
  in laboratory skills, 287–288
  minimum qualifications, 284–285
  in multiculturalism, 118
  practicum component of (supervision-of-supervision), 288–291
    beginning phase of, 288–289
    end phase of, 289–291
    middle phase of, 289, 290
  supervisee behavior and, 110
  supervision distinguished from, 8
  traditional lack of formal, 279
Training clinics, 187–188
  goals of, 188–190
Transcripts of counseling sessions, 216–217
Transference, supervisee, 170–171
  countertransference to, 178–179
  parallel processes and, 139
Treatment protocols, working alliance and adherence to, 153
Triadic system, supervisory relationship as, 136–144
Triangles, interpersonal, 142–144
Trust
  between-group-member, 249–250
  within cross-cultural supervision, 120
  supervisor, 171
  in supervisory relationship, 160

Understanding, agreements of (supervision contracts), 196–197
Unintentional tort, 68
University supervisor, 190–194
  advising system for clinical instruction, 190–191
  agreements of understanding (supervision contracts) with, 196–197
  evaluation by, 200

site communication by, 192–194
  site selection by, 191–194

Variables, choice of research, 300–302
Vicarious learning, group supervision and, 237
Vicarious liability (*respondeat superior*), 68, 70
Videoconferencing, 227
Video recordings in supervision, 168–169
Videotape, 217–222
  advantages and disadvantages of, 217–218
  guidelines for working with, 218–219
  interpersonal process recall (IRP), 219, 220–222, 223, 229
  supervisory relationship and, 219
Viennese School, 77
Vision, supervisor, 210
Voice metaphor, 126–127
Vulnerability
  of supervisees, 161, 266

Walk-in supervision, 259, 263
Warn, duty to, 68–69
Wisdom, clinical, 13
Withdrawal, as response to shame, 163
Withdrawal ruptures, 156
Work design and coordination function of supervision, 186–187
Working alliance, 145–157
  antecedent and consequences of effective, 146–153
    dynamic process, 154–157
    outcomes, 152–153
    supervision processes, 150–152
    supervisor behavior, 148–150
  bonding aspect of, 145, 152
  experience effects on, 110
  goals of, 145–146
  mediational research on, 299
  model, 145
  racial identity similarity and, 124
Working Alliance Inventory, 145, 328–331
  Supervisee's Form, 330–331
  Supervisor's Form, 328–329
Working definitions, 296–297